iPhone®

ALL-IN-ONE

FOR

DUMMIES®

A Wiley Brand

3rd Edition

by Joe Hutsko
and
Barbara Boyd

iPhone® All-in-One For Dummies® 3rd Edition

Published by:
John Wiley & Sons, Inc.,
111 River Street,
Hoboken, NJ 07030-5774,
www.wiley.com

Contents at a Glance

Table of Contents

Book III: Communications Central: Calls, Messages, and the Web 195

Book IV: Making iPhone Your Personal Assistant 323

Chapter 1: Perfecting Your People Skills with Contacts 325

Chapter 2: Managing Your Time with Calendar, Reminders, and Clock 349

Introduction

*Y*ou hear a lot about tech taking over and smartphones — with iPhone at the lead — getting in the way of personal relationships. We won't lie to you, we love tech and telling people about it, but our goal is not for tech to take charge of your life: We want you to take charge of tech.

In this book, we tried to find the balance between simple, practical information for new users and new information for experienced users. Whatever your iPhone user level, we want this book to bring you to a point of using your iPhone at the maximum potential for you. For some that might mean using three or four apps such as Phone, Camera, and Messages, whereas for others, it may mean using most of the pre-loaded apps.

About This Book

To write this book, we looked into every nook and cranny of iPhone, and then we asked friends and family with iPhones to tell us their weirdest, most confusing and confounding iPhone circumstances, which we tried to solve. Armed with that information, we revised the previous edition of this book and believe we get pretty darn close to telling you all there is to know. That said, Apple releases iOS updates frequently — this book is based on iOS 7.0 — and we encourage you to keep your iPhone and app software up to date and stay informed as to how to use features that may be added with updates.

We're not perfect, so we undoubtedly missed something. Let us know. Your comments, questions, and compliments help us to improve future editions. Drop a note to us at `babsboyd@me.com`.

Conventions Used in This Book

To help you navigate this book efficiently, we use a few style conventions:

- Website addresses, or URLs, are shown in a special monofont typeface, `like this`.
- Numbered steps that you need to follow are set in **bold**.
- Sequential commands are shown as Settings⇨General⇨Network, which means tap Settings, tap General, and then tap Network on your iPhone. Store⇨View My Account means to click the Store menu and drag to click the View My Account option on your computer.

✔ The first time we mention a button or icon, we show you what it looks like in the margin or point it out in a figure so you can find it more easily on your iPhone. The same button may be used in different apps and tapping it elicits the same function regardless of the app it's in.

✔ Sidebars present technical information that you don't have to know but that might interest those of you who want to understand the technology behind the function.

What You're Not to Read

This book doesn't have to be read cover to cover — you can pick and choose the chapters that pertain to how you use your iPhone. For example, if you only want a broad overview of what your iPhone does and how to work with it, you can read Book I, which explains iPhone basics (what your iPhone can do, how your iPhone is organized, and how to use the multitouch screen and voice-recognition interface), and then just skim the other mini-books, which are divided by task, and explain each app in depth. If you're familiar with iPhone basics, jump ahead to Book V, which talks about the Camera and apps like iMovie.

You don't have to read sidebars. Reading the sidebars can increase your iPhone knowledge, but skipping them won't inhibit your iPhone use. Same goes for Technical Stuff blips: They contain fun information, but they're not life-threateningly necessary.

Foolish Assumptions

We made a few assumptions about you when writing this book. To make sure we're on the same page, we assume that

✔ You know something, but not necessarily a lot, about cellular phones and you want to learn the basics and more about iPhone.

✔ You have at least a general concept of how to use the web and e-mail.

✔ You'll read through the introductory chapters if you find yourself scratching your head when you see terms like *tap, swipe,* and *flick,* or anything else that we think you should know but you don't.

✔ You acknowledge that it's up to you to go on the web to find updated information about the products described throughout this book.

✔ You'll check with your cellular service provider to know how many minutes or megabytes are included in your monthly allotment and under what circumstances you might incur additional charges, although we do give you some warnings throughout the book when additional charges are more likely.

✔ You know that technology is changing faster than we can keep up and even geeks like us can't stay on top of everything. You will, therefore, let us know about cool stuff you find along the way of your iPhone journey so we can consider it for future editions of this book.

✔ You're not all work and no play. You want to have some fun with your iPhone and maybe even be entertained while you're learning how to use it.

How This Book Is Organized

This book is divided into mini-books, which are further divided into chapters. You can read it cover to cover, but we recommend you familiarize yourself with iPhone basics in Book I, and then skip to the book or chapters that talk about the functions or apps that you use most or are most interested in using. We think you should also take a look at functions you doubt you'll use because you might find you like those functions.

The mini-books are organized by topic, you find related apps together in the same chapters, or in some cases, such as Camera and Photos, references to them appear in both the Book V, Chapter 1, which discusses photos and Book V, Chapter 4 that talks about video.

The more you use your iPhone, the more you begin to understand the basic commands and techniques used across the iOS platform. We take you beyond the basics in the books and chapters that follow, giving you tips and showing you advanced settings throughout.

Book I: Meet iPhone

This minibook explains the functions you need to know to use your iPhone: basics like turning it on and off, adjusting the volume, charging the battery, and how to use the multitouch and voice-recognition (also known as Siri) interfaces. Buttons, icons, notifications, and badges that you might encounter are introduced. We give you an overview of the built-in apps and explain iPhone's settings in detail so you can customize them to your liking. This is also where you can find a troubleshooting question-and-answer guide and tips for avoiding problems.

Book II: Stocking iPhone with iTunes Apps and Add-ons

This minibook explains the concept of syncing (that is, having the same information in two or more devices and having changes made on one device appear automatically on the other device). Your iPhone uses iCloud to sync with your computers and any other iOS devices you have. Also in this minibook, you learn about the App Store and how to shop for other

Apple and third-party apps, as well as Newsstand, which manages your electronic periodical subscriptions, and Passbook, which stores your store cards, boarding passes, and event tickets. The last chapter discusses hardware accessories that enhance your iPhone, such as speakers and protective cases.

Book III: Communications Central: Calls, Messages, and the Web

This minibook gets to the core communications functions of your iPhone. It explains everything about making phone calls, checking voicemail, using iPhone's audio and video chat app FaceTime, sending text and e-mail messages, exchanging messages with Macs and other iOS devices with iMessage, and surfing the Internet with Safari, iPhone's web browser. For those of you who use social networks, we show you how Facebook, Twitter, and other social networks are integrated into various apps on your iPhone.

Book IV: Making iPhone Your Personal Assistant

Contact management, time management, getting directions, storing boarding passes and store cards, taking notes, and reminding you when to be somewhere to meet someone to do something — your iPhone can do it all and we explain it in this minibook. This minibook covers the unexpected iPhone apps like Maps and Compass, Weather, Stocks, and Calculator as well as the basic PDA (Personal Digital Assistant) apps: Contacts, Calendar, Reminders, Clock, Notes, and Voice Memos. We also introduce you to the iWork apps: Numbers, Pages, and Keynote.

Book V: Let iPhone Entertain You: Photos, Video, Music, and More

This minibook is about having fun with your iPhone. Amateur photographers and videographers like using iPhone as a still and video camera and for sharing images via Photo Stream as well as messages and e-mail. iPhone is also a pretty sophisticated editing tool for touching up photos in iPhoto or creating videos with iMovie. For those who never want to stop learning, there's an introductory course to iTunes U. This minibook also gives all the details for finding new media in the iTunes Store or Podcast catalog and then having the best experience when listening to music, watching movies and TV shows, reading books, and streaming podcasts.

Icons Used in This Book

To help emphasize certain information, this book displays different icons in the page margins.

The Tip icon points out bits of information that can help you do things better and more efficiently or tells you something useful that you might not know.

This icon highlights interesting information that isn't necessary to know, but can help explain why certain things work the way they do on your iPhone. Like sidebars, you can skip this information if you're in a hurry. On the other hand, you might find something helpful.

This icon gives you a heads-up about something that can go wrong if you're not careful. Be sure to read the warning fully before following related instructions.

This icon points out information that's been mentioned somewhere else in the book but is related to the topic nearby. If you ignore it, you won't cause problems, but you could miss something useful.

Beyond the Book

You can find additional features of this book online. Visit the web to find these extras:

- ✔ **Cheat Sheet:** Go to www.dummies.com/cheatsheet/iphoneaio to find this book's Cheat Sheet. Here, you can find references on the uses of the iPhone Home button, info on the functions of the icons and buttons of your iPhone, useful websites for iPhone owners, tips on using Siri, and info on Home screen apps.

- ✔ **Dummies.com online articles:** Go to www.dummies.com/extras/iphoneaio to find the Extras for this book. Four separate articles give you specific, task-oriented information — and ideas — for using your iPhone in ways you might not know about, such as creating an album with iPhoto, incorporating your iPhone into your home security system, and using your iPhone as a remote control when making a presentation.

✔ **Bonus chapters on the web:** The bonus chapters show you how to expand your iPhone beyond the standard Apple apps. Each chapter presents a selection of apps that add a feature or function to your iPhone, or enhance something it already does. For the business user or busy household manager, there are budgeting, task management, and faxing apps. For the social butterfly, there are communications and networking apps. Quiet types might enjoy e-reader and radio apps. There's something for everyone in the leisure, fitness, health, home, and travel apps. Access the online content at `www.dummies.com/extras/iphoneaio`.

✔ **Updates:** Our technology books sometimes have updates. To check for updates to this book, go to `www.dummies.com/extras/iphoneaio`.

Where to Go from Here

If you're new to iPhone, closely read the first few chapters to get an understanding of how your iPhone works, the command conventions it uses, and how to perform the basic functions. Then move on to chapters that interest you, perhaps starting with the phone and messaging functions before moving up to Internet access, and lastly looking at the multimedia apps like Music, Podcasts, and Camera.

If you're familiar with your iPhone already, skim through the opening chapters to learn about the recent iOS 7 changes, and then go where you wish; to a chapter on a function you haven't used before, which might be the video camera or Passbook, or to a function you use a lot but would like to know better, such as Messages.

No matter where you begin, our goal is to give you the tools to get the most out of your iPhone and encourage you to expand your knowledge and explore the many ways of iPhone.

Book I
Meet iPhone

getting started with iPhone

 web extras Visit www.dummies.com/extras/iphoneaio for great Dummies content online.

Contents at a Glance

Chapter 1: Exploring the Many Faces of iPhone

In This Chapter

✔ **Taking a look at the hardware**

✔ **Considering iPhone carriers**

✔ **Making phone calls**

✔ **Sending messages**

✔ **Surfing the web**

✔ **Taking photos and video**

✔ **Entertaining apps**

You probably already know a lot about what your iPhone can do but like any multifunction gadget — or new car for that matter — you bought it to do one thing and little by little discover how powerful it really is and lots of handy, helpful things it can do.

In this chapter, we try to pique your curiosity about things you may not have thought of doing with your iPhone by introducing you to all your iPhone can do. We talk about the hardware, review your cellular carrier options, and then we summarize the apps that come with your iPhone. You can then pick and choose the topics and tasks where you want to dive deeper and go to those chapters for the details. We'd like you to think about how you can incorporate your iPhone into your day-to-day activities but don't worry: We don't want technology to take charge of your life. We want you to take charge of the technology.

Looking at Your iPhone from Every Angle

With the latest release of iPhone 5c and iPhone 5s, Apple maintained the size, shape, and weight of the iPhone 5 but changed the casing material on the 5c and totally upgraded the internal processor, camera, and Home button on the 5s. Here we take a look at the hardware and a closer look at what's inside.

Front, back, top, bottom

The iPhone 4s has a glass body, front and back. iPhone 5s keeps the glass front (on the screen side), but replaces the back with an aluminum sheath bordered by inlaid glass at the top and bottom. iPhone 5c gives new, respectable meaning to plastic. Apple also introduced specific coordinated covers, which we talk about Book II, Chapter 3.

The metal band that you see on the 4s and 5s, and that's hidden under the plastic on the 5c, not only gives stability and structure to your iPhone, it also functions as two antennae. In addition to the antennae, the buttons and holes around the edges and on the front and back, which we explain in detail in Book I, Chapter 2, have the following functions:

- ✓ On/off sleep/wake button
- ✓ Microphones — two on the 4s, three on 5c and 5s
- ✓ Lightning port for connecting various cables and connectors
- ✓ Volume buttons
- ✓ Silent/ring switch
- ✓ Two video/still objective lenses
- ✓ LED light; dual LED True Tone flash on 5s
- ✓ SIM tray
- ✓ Speaker
- ✓ Headset jack
- ✓ Home button, with Touch ID fingerprint sensor on 5s

What you don't see can help you

Your iPhone has antennae and sensors to support the functions of the apps you use. One antenna is the metal band around the outside that connects to the cellular network. The iPhone actually switches between two antennae to receive and transmit, which increases data transfer speeds and call quality. Here's what those visible and not-so-visible parts do:

- ✓ **GPS and GLONASS:** Finds your location, gives you directions in Maps, and geo-tags your photos. In Book V, Chapter 1, we explain how geo-tagging identifies your location when you take a photo.
- ✓ **Wi-Fi:** Connects to available Wi-Fi networks.
- ✓ **Cellular antenna:** Connects you to a selection of the following networks: LTE, GSM/EDGE, CDMA EV-DO, UMTS/HSPA +/DC_HSDPA, 2G, 3G, or 4G networks. We explain the different types of cellular networks, and what all these nerdy terms and acronyms mean, in Book I, Chapter 2.

✔ **Three-axis Gyroscope:** Used to find your location when GPS or GLONASS aren't accessible.

✔ **Magnetic-field sensor:** Positions the Compass.

✔ **Proximity sensor:** Turns the touchscreen off when you hold the phone close to your ear, so you don't accidentally tap the mute button or call another number while you're in the middle of a conversation. As soon as you move iPhone a few 16ths of an inch from your head, the screen is activated.

✔ **Tilt sensor:** Senses motion, which is particularly useful when playing games that involve driving or flying.

✔ **Accelerometer:** Allows for landscape display.

✔ **Bluetooth:** Connects to other Bluetooth 4.0–enabled devices.

✔ **Ambientlight sensor:** Adjusts the screen when you're using your iPhone in low- or bright-light situations.

✔ **Fingerprint identity sensor (5s):** Recognizes authorized fingers pressed to the Home button to unlock iPhone and make purchases in the iTunes and Apps Stores, as well as iTunes U and Newsstand — for now, more services are likely to be added as this technology catches on.

✔ **Moisture sensor:** Lets Apple know if your iPhone has gone for a swim. If you purchased AppleCare+, Apple may replace or repair your phone for up to two accidents after you pay a deductible. Learn about AppleCare in Book I, Chapter 5.

Other stuff in the box

Your iPhone comes with a few nice accessories, too. Here's what you'll find when you open the box:

✔ **EarPods:** Stereo headphones with a built-in microphone and volume control buttons.

✔ **USB cable connector:** Connects your iPhone to a USB port on your computer, in your car, and on the USB power adapter. iPhone 5 and later models have the 9-pin reversible Lightning connector, whereas iPhone 4s and earlier has a 30-pin, one-way connector.

✔ **USB power adapter:** Connects to the USB cable connector and plugs into an outlet to charge your iPhone's battery.

✔ **Finger Tips guide:** Apple's quick guide to iPhone functions and features.

✔ **Product info:** Legal and technical information.

Considering iPhone Carriers and Configurations

In the United States, four national carriers support iPhone: AT&T, Sprint, T-Mobile, and Verizon, as well as smaller regional carriers. That's made a situation that is both competitive and confusing for the consumer. In Europe, Vodafone is popular, although many countries also have country-specific carriers with competitive pricing.

Unlocked iPhones, which are iPhones you purchase outright without a service contract, work with carriers who use the GSM standard (see the following paragraph). In the U.S., AT&T, T-Mobile, and 30 or so regional carriers use GSM, as do most of the carriers outside the U.S. A customer in good standing can request that his CDMA carrier unlock his iPhone so it can access the GSM networks overseas, but nonetheless remains tied to the national and roaming costs associated with the cellular service contract.

GSM (Global System for Mobile) and CDMA (Code Division Multiple Access) are the telecommunications standards used for cellular networks. GSM, as its name implies, is the worldwide standard, whereas CDMA is limited to America and parts of Asia. CDMA offers slightly better data transfer, although GSM is steadily improving. The GSM standard stores your phone number and account information on a SIM card, whereas in the CDMA standard, the phone number and account information is programmed in the phone itself. Some CDMA networks require a SIM in order to connect to a GSM network outside the U.S. Sprint offers one so you can access the GSM network used by Sprint's partners in Europe. iPhones come with either GSM (with an AT&T or T-Mobile contract or unlocked) or CDMA (Verizon or Sprint contracts).

You've probably heard a lot about LTE and have perhaps come to two conclusions: It's faster than other data transfer protocols and it's not available everywhere. You'd be right on both counts. LTE, which stands for Long Term Evolution and is sometimes referred to as 4G (for fourth-generation), is designed to use different radio frequencies at higher speeds. The iPhone 5c and 5s can access up to thirteen (depending on the carrier) LTE bands, giving greater possibility of finding LTE wherever you are. Without getting into a bunch of technical gobbledygook, LTE means your web page, e-mail, video streaming, and any other stuff you do online works faster. In Philadelphia, Joe found LTE to be up to two times faster than his Wi-Fi connection and depending on your location, you could find similar results. In North America as well as Europe, Japan, Russia, India, Australia, and Brazil, you find pretty good coverage in metropolitan areas, whereas in China, Mexico, and some emerging African and South American countries, 4G LTE support is in the works.

With so many different plans available from multiple national and regional carriers, we can't take responsibility for advising you on which to choose. We can, however, give you some things to think about — and questions to ask prospective providers — when choosing. Here are a few things to consider so you can compare plans from different carriers and make an informed decision:

✓ **How much time do you spend on the phone?** Do you make many calls or just check in now and then? Three hundred and sixty minutes for a month is 12 minutes a day, whereas 1,000 minutes is just over a half hour a day. If you're thinking about replacing your landline with a cell phone, an unlimited calling plan may be a better choice.

✔ **When do you use your phone?** Some plans offer lower nighttime and weekend rates. If you spend your weekdays at your office and make most of your calls on the company phone, this type of contract may work for you.

✔ **Who do you call?** Some plans offer a you-and-me or family discount for one number, or a group of numbers, that you call more than any other. Some offer unlimited mobile-to-mobile calls, even to other carriers.

✔ **Where do you use your phone?** If you travel around the country, you probably want a call plan with nationwide coverage. If you're a home-body, a regional plan is probably just fine.

✔ **Do you travel overseas?** If you do, shop around for the best roaming rate or, if you frequently go to the same country, consider getting a local, recharge-able SIM card and using that in your iPhone when you're out of the U.S.

✔ **Do you send text messages?** Text messages may be billed at a per-message rate or your plan may include a limited (or unlimited) number of messages or KBs and you pay a per-message or per KB rate if you exceed the limited number. iMessage lets you send text messages over the Wi-Fi or cellular data network to other iPhone, iPad, and iPod touch users (as well as users of Macs running OS X 10.8 or later).

✔ **How much cellular data usage do you need?** Wi-Fi is widespread in the U.S. and LTE is becoming more ubiquitous. Even the smallest one-café town seems to offer free Wi-Fi if you buy a cup of coffee, which makes cellular data less necessary. Most plans these days offer unlimited Internet access, although 50MB is the file size limit for downloading over a 3G or LTE cellular network.

When contracting with a cellular service provider, make sure to ask what charges you'll incur if you go over the minutes or data transfer limits — even going slightly over can cost a lot. Some carriers send an alert when you reach your limit, or while you can refer to the Cellular Data Usage section of Settings⇨Cellular, more often than not your carrier offers a free app that tracks your calling and data usage.

The Big Picture: It's All That and More!

Your iPhone is more than just a phone. It's your online communications tool, personal digital assistant, entertainment source, camera, and flashlight. With each new generation, iPhone has added more functions and features. iPhone itself is the hardware and the iOS and apps are the software that let you do so many things. In the next few sections, we take you for the proverbial spin around the block.

Phone

Clearly, iPhone is a cellular telephone (see Figure 1-1) that makes voice calls and offers text messaging. So what? All cell phones do that. Things get interesting when you send and receive multimedia messages with active links to web pages or a video of the pop fly your granddaughter just caught at the softball championship. Visual voicemail displays a list of messages so you can listen to the most important ones first rather than go through them in chronological order. Add to that three ways to communicate cost-free with other iOS device owners: FaceTime lets you make audio and video calls and iMessage, which is part of Messages, gives you multimedia message exchanges. We explain the ins and outs of phoning and messaging in Book III, Chapters 1 and 2. For those times you don't feel like talking to anyone, there's Do Not Disturb, which blocks incoming calls and alerts.

Figure 1-1: IPhone as phone.

Music and videos

With the iPhone 5 (and later)'s four-inch Retina display and excellent stereophonic output, your iPhone plays music, movies, podcasts, and more with crisp, clear sound and images. From the iTunes Store, you can download music, movies, TV shows, and audiobooks. iTunes Radio lets you create a personalized radio station. Download the iTunes Festival app to enjoy a month-long extravaganza of new and featured music, and the Trailers app shows you movies to anticipate in the coming months. Podcasts and iTunes U have their very own apps to download and enjoy podcasts and courseware. Connect your iPhone to a monitor or television with a cable or via AirPlay or Apple TV, watch everything on a big screen, and control the show with the free Remote app. All you have to do is pop the popcorn. Check out Book V, Chapters 2, 3, and 4 to learn all about the iPod, iTunes, and audio and video functions.

Camera and video camcorder

The eight megapixel iSight camera places the digital still camera on iPhone 4s and iPhone 5c in the same class as many digital cameras. The enhanced lens, ten frames per second burst mode for capturing action shots, and dual-color LED flash of the 5s may tempt even professional photographers to leave their DSLR home sometimes. What's more the rear-facing camera captures 240-degree panoramic photos and high-definition video in 1080 rows of pixels. Again, the 5s has evolved even further and offers improved video stabilization and slow motion capture. The LED flash next to the objective lens on the back of your iPhone illuminates both still photos and videos. The Photos app organizes your photos and videos after you capture them and gives you a few editing options. But if you purchased a new iPhone with iOS 7, you can download the iPhoto and iMovie apps and gain even more editing control over your images. Go to Book V, Chapters 1 and 4 for detailed information.

Personal digital assistant

With Siri, the voice-recognition interface that's available on an iPhone 4s or later, iPhone is your very personal personal digital assistant (PDA for short). Just speak your commands to Siri and she — or he, if you choose a male voice — does what you ask, such as reading your messages then typing and sending a dictated reply, finding a florist, or changing your dentist appointment. We explain how to use the Siri interface in Book I, Chapter 3.

Don't overlook your iPhone's other PDA features. The resident apps complete iPhone's PDA role. Contacts eliminates the need for a paper address book. Calendar replaces your time management system, and Notes makes all those scraps of ideas and grocery lists obsolete, while Reminders makes sure no task or appointment is forgotten. We show you how to use your iPhone's PDA apps along with Voice Memos, Clock, and Calculator in Book IV.

Passbook manages apps that track store cards, coupons, and boarding passes so you can (almost) leave your wallet at home and never miss out on a discount or point-accumulation opportunity. See Book II, Chapter 2 for how to use it.

If you purchased a new iPhone with iOS 7, you can download the iWork suite gratis, which includes the Pages word processing app and Keynote presentation creation app, which we explain in Book IV, Chapter 4, and the Numbers spreadsheet app that we talk about in Book IV, Chapter 3.

Internet communicator

The real power of your iPhone shows up when you go online. Able to access the Internet via either your cellular network or Wi-Fi, you never have to miss another time-sensitive e-mail or tweet. You can search the Internet with Safari as you would on any computer. For example, you can search for movie times, book airline tickets, settle bets with Wikipedia, and read the news from your favorite news outlets. Safari's Reading List function lets you store an article to read later, even when you're offline — you can catch up on your reading while flying. With iCloud, you can share tabs and bookmarks between all your devices. Book III, Chapter 3 explains Safari.

You access your e-mail accounts through Mail. If you have multiple accounts, you can sync them all with Mail and see them individually or all together. Learn all about Mail in Book III, Chapter 4.

Tap open the Share Sheet from apps like Photos, Maps, and Safari to send information via AirDrop (iPhone 5 or later) to other iOS devices, attached to a Mail or Messages message, or upload to Facebook or Twitter. From the Share Sheet, you can also copy or print a document or image. See Book I, Chapter 4 to learn more.

Your iPhone comes with some specific apps that gather information from the Internet, as shown in Figure 1-2. Stocks lets you follow international investment markets as well as your personal investments. Weather leans on Yahoo! to bring you the weather forecast for cities you want to know about. We take you through these apps in Book IV, Chapter 3.

Personal GPS navigator

Between the Compass and Maps apps and the GPS, Wi-Fi, and cellular sensors, 99 percent of the time, your iPhone can tell you where you are and tell you how to get where you want to go. What's more, in coordination with Yelp!, Maps and Siri can give you suggestions for vendors and services, like bookstores, museums, and restaurants, based on your location. The links in Maps are active — as they are in most iPhone apps — so you just click on the suggested vendor and the website for that vendor opens in Safari. We explain how to use Maps and Compass in Book IV, Chapter 3.

E-book and document reader

E-readers and tablets are all the rage and the iPhone 5 models' larger screens and document-reading capabilities makes reading on your iPhone easier than ever. We talk about Newsstand, which is preloaded on your iPhone, and organizes and updates your magazine and newspaper app subscriptions, in Book II, Chapter 2. For your reading pleasure, download iBooks, the free Apple app for electronic books, which we explain in Book V, Chapter 2.

You can read many types of documents on your iPhone. If a colleague sends you a PowerPoint presentation or a Pages document as an e-mail attachment, just tap on the attachment and your iPhone opens it so you can review it. With the iWork productivity apps, you can edit the document (without an additional app), and even without iWork, you can print the documents if there's an AirPrint-enabled printer on your wireless network.

Personal fitness trainer

In Book I, Chapter 4, we talk about the Nike+ iPod app, which tracks the distances and times of your runs or walks by receiving information from a sensor in certain models of Nike running shoes. That's not the only app that helps you stay fit. The App Store boasts dozens of apps that create workout routines or track your progress toward fitness goals. In Bonus Chapter 6, which you find online, we tell you about a few of our favorite fitness apps. For more on this book's online content, see the Introduction.

Book I
Chapter 1

Exploring the Many
Faces of iPhone

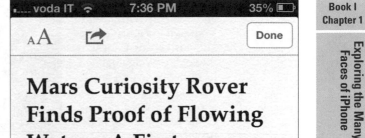

Mars Curiosity Rover Finds Proof of Flowing Water—A First

Image courtesy MSSS/Caltech/NASA

NASA's Mars Science Laboratory (aka Curiosity), as seen via self-portraits of its undercarriage.

See updated story: Mars Rover Finds Ancient Streambed >>

Figure 1-2: iPhone's great graphics make reading websites easy on the eyes.

Pocket video game console

With all the ruckus, you might think Angry Birds is the only game in town. Actually, the App Store boasts more than 100,000 games, and many are free. Take that, Nintendo DS! With iPhone, you have a video game console with you at all times. The popular game Words With Friends is shown in Figure 1-3, and with Game Center, you can play against friends online and see who has the highest score. We tell you about Game Center in Book II, Chapter 2.

Systemwide functions

The keyboard, used in any app where typing is involved, supports 50 languages. Voice Control can initiate phone calls, control Music, and tell you what time it is. Siri (iPhone 4s or later) can do those tasks and more. Accessibility settings like enlarged font sizes, custom vibration signals for incoming calls, and spoken text make iPhone easier to use. Guided Access helps those with learning disabilities stay focused on one task.

Notifications, such as text messages, Facebook status updates, reminders, and voicemails come in while you're doing

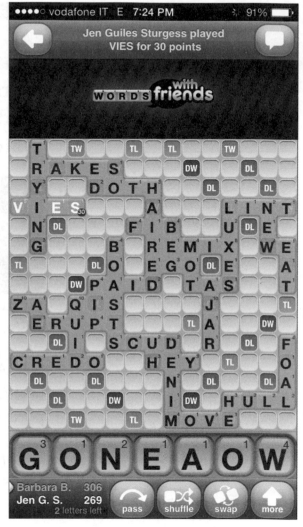

Figure 1-3: Your iPhone is also a tiny game console.

other things and you get a small indication at the top of the screen. Just swipe down the screen and you see your upcoming appointments, stock activity, and weather forecast along with a list of notifications. You choose to which and when you want to respond.

Swipe up from the bottom of the screen and you open the Control Center, as shown in Figure 1-4. Turn Wi-Fi and Bluetooth on or off, activate Do Not

Disturb, adjust brightness and volume, and shine a light on your path with the flashlight — all just a tap away.

iCloud syncs your contacts, calendars, notes, browser tabs, photos, and documents across Apple and third-party apps on all your devices, including Mac and Windows computers. With iCloud Keychain, AutoFill information such as user names, passwords, and credit card information for secure access to your favorite websites and shopping haunts is shared across all your iCloud-enabled devices.

If you want to find something, Spotlight searches the contents of your phone from within many of the apps on your iPhone.

And a thousand other things!

Even if you never add another app to your iPhone, it can do a lot, but adding third-party

Figure 1-4: The Control Center gives you instant access to often-used system controls.

apps moves the potential even higher. In the bonus content on this book's companion website, we try to knock your socks off by introducing some of the newest and most innovative problem-solving apps available. The minibook is divided into six chapters ranging from practical business solutions and creativity tools to apps for sports, cooking, and travel. (For more on how to access the companion website, see this book's Introduction.) We certainly found apps we never imagined existed when we were researching them for this book, and we hope this nudges you to do some research on your own. Figure 1-5 shows one of Barbara's favorites, StarWalk.

With that, dear reader, you should have some idea of where you want to go.

Figure 1-5: StarWalk is a location-based astronomy guide.

Chapter 2: Activating and Understanding Your iPhone

In This Chapter

✔ **Turning iPhone on and off**

✔ **Activating your iPhone**

✔ **Adjusting the volume**

✔ **Charging the battery**

✔ **Interpreting screen communications**

✔ **Making connections**

✔ **Adjusting Accessibility options for easier operation**

*A*re you itching to get started with all things iPhone? In this chapter, we tell you how to use your iPhone's hardware and understand the interface. We begin with the most obvious tasks: turning your iPhone on and off, adjusting the volume level, and charging the battery. Then we review the basic layout of iPhone's screen and define the status bar icons, notifications, and badges. We explain different types of connections you make with your iPhone — Internet and network connections, GPS connections, and printer connections. At the end of the chapter, we take a look at some of the ways you can modify your iPhone to make it easier to use if you have vision, hearing, or tactile challenges or if a young person who uses your iPhone has learning disabilities.

Turning iPhone On and Off

When you bought your iPhone, the salesperson probably showed you a few basic tasks, such as turning your iPhone on and off. For good measure, we review it here in our review of the iPhone's external buttons. But first, throughout the book we use a few terms regarding your iPhone's state of consciousness, or modes, that warrant an explanation because they could be a bit confusing:

✔ **Sleep:** Your iPhone is asleep when it's on but the screen is dark. It can receive incoming calls, e-mail, messages, and notifications, which push it into

✔ **Wake:** Your iPhone screen displays something, which could be the Lock screen (Figure 2-1) or the Home screen (Figure 2-2) or an app screen. It can receive incoming communications.

✔ **Locked (or Lock screen):** Your iPhone is awake, but you only see an image with some basic information (explained later in this chapter). You can open the Notification Center or the Control Center (Book I, Chapter 4) or slide the Camera icon up to use the camera, but you have to slide your finger across the screen or across a notification to go into

✔ **Unlocked:** Your screen is awake and active. You see either the Home screen or an app screen and interact with them with all the touch-screen gestures we explain in Book I, Chapter 3.

Figure 2-1: The Lock screen appears when you first wake your phone from its Sleep state.

Your iPhone is On in all four modes and in combination may be in Sleep/Locked mode, Wake/Locked mode, or Wake/Unlocked mode (but not Sleep/Unlocked).

The On/Off Sleep/Wake button and the Home button are found in the same place on all iPhone models, as shown in Figure 2-2. Here's how they work:

✔ **On/Off Sleep/Wake Button:** This button is on the top of iPhone, to the right, and it does two things. When you press and hold it, it turns iPhone on or off, and when you press and release it when your iPhone is On,

Book I
Chapter 2

Activating and
Understanding Your
iPhone

it wakes iPhone from sleep (and you see the Lock screen) or puts iPhone to sleep.

- To turn iPhone on, press and hold the On/ Off Sleep/Wake button. The Apple logo appears in the center of the screen. After 30 seconds or so, the Lock screen appears (refer to Figure 2-1). Depending on your iPhone model, you see one of the following:

5s: the Touch ID screen. Hold your finger on the Home button to unlock your iPhone; we explain how to set up this function in Book I, Chapter 4.

4, 4s, 5, 5c: the helpful words *Slide to Unlock*. Drag your finger

Figure 2-2: External switches turn iPhone on and off, and wake it from a restful sleep.

from left to right across the screen and the Home screen opens. If you assign a passcode to your iPhone, which we explain in Book I, Chapter 4, a keypad appears, and after you enter the correct passcode, the Home screen opens.

If you have a Subscriber Identity Module, better known as a SIM card, with a PIN or Personal Identification Number, a message comes up with two buttons: OK and Unlock. Tap the right button to open a keypad where you enter the PIN code of your SIM card to unlock it. Tap the left OK button, and you can use iPhone apps but not any of the phone, message, or Internet features.

- To turn iPhone off, press and hold the On/Off Sleep/Wake button until the red bar appears with the message *Slide to Power Off.* Drag your finger from left to right across this bar to turn iPhone off. Tap the Cancel button at the bottom of the screen if you change your mind.

- To put iPhone to sleep, press the On/Off Sleep/Wake button once.

- To wake iPhone, press either the On/Off Sleep/Wake button or the Home button, which is the round button below the screen that we explain in a couple of paragraphs. Slide your finger across the Lock screen, — or press the Home button to use the touch recognition on an iPhone 5s — and the Home screen, or the app you were using before your iPhone went to sleep, opens.

- iPhone goes to sleep and locks (not to be confused with the SIM lock) automatically when you don't touch the screen for one minute. You can change this setting to up to five minutes or never in Settings⇨General⇨Auto-Lock. (That means tap Settings, tap General, tap Auto-Lock.) This saves battery power and keeps you from unintentionally opening an app or making a call by accidentally touching the Home screen. When iPhone is asleep or locked, you still receive phone calls, messages, and alerts — unless you have the Do Not Disturb function activated — and can listen to music. You can also adjust the volume of a call or music with the volume buttons on the side of the phone.

- Incoming communications such as a phone call, text message, or notification from an app like Facebook or Mail also wake your iPhone and present an action to take on the Lock screen.

✔ **Home Button:** This is the round, central button on the front of iPhone, below the screen.

- Press this button once to return to the Home screen at any time from any app. Pressing this button once when iPhone is locked wakes iPhone the same way as the On/Off Sleep/Wake button does.

- Quickly press the Home button twice, also known as a double-click, to open the open apps carousel and switch from one app to another. More about that in Book I, Chapter 3.

If you have an iPhone 5s, the Home button performs both of the above functions and houses the Touch ID sensor, which uses your finger to authorize iPhone access and purchases in place of a passcode or Apple ID.

Activating Your iPhone

Even though your iPhone has lots of other applications besides calling, many of them don't work until your iPhone is connected to a cellular network through your cellular service provider, and, if it's a GSM phone, has a SIM card installed. You can purchase an iPhone with a cellular network contract or without a contract, which is called an *unlocked* iPhone — not to be confused with the Unlocked/Wake mode. Here's the difference:

- ✔ **Contract:** iPhone is activated when you sign up for a service plan with an iPhone service. In the U.S., your cellular network carrier choices are AT&T, which uses the GSM (Global System for Mobile Communications) cellular communications protocol; Verizon; and Sprint, which use the CDMA (Code Division Multiple Access) cellular communications protocol. We explain both GSM and CDMA in the "Making Connections" section of this chapter. You register your phone with the network and pick a plan for the calling minutes, text messages, and Internet service usage you want.

- ✔ **Unlocked:** iPhone 5 or later arrives without a nano-SIM (that's the little chip inside that gives you access to the cellular network), while iPhone 4 and 4s have a micro-SIM, which is a bit smaller than a normal SIM and a bit bigger than the nano-SIM. You purchase a nano-SIM from a service provider and then purchase prepaid calling minutes in a pay-as-you-go option. Cellular broadband Internet access may be sold separately or bundled with the calling minutes and text message allotment. You can use an unlocked iPhone with a contract; in that case, you bought your iPhone outright so the monthly contract should be less than iPhone plus a cellular service fee. T-Mobile provides national pay-as-you-go service and about 30 regional carriers offer pay-as-you-go service. Unlocked iPhones work only with carriers who use the GSM cellular communications standard (AT&T and T-Mobile in the U.S.). If you spend a lot of time overseas, say in France, you can purchase a prepaid SIM in France, which you put in your iPhone when you're there. (Check with your U.S. service provider to see if unlocking has to be performed stateside first.) When you're in the U.S., you put the U.S.-based SIM in your iPhone.

If you bought your iPhone with a cellular service contract, it's already activated when you bought it; if, for example, you bought it at an Apple Store, an AT&T store, or other retail outlet such as Wal-Mart or Best Buy. If you bought your iPhone through the online Apple Store and selected a carrier, you only need to turn your iPhone on and follow the onscreen instructions.

If you bought an unlocked iPhone, you must purchase and insert a GSM nano-SIM. To insert the nano-SIM, do the following:

1. **Insert the end of a paper clip into the hole on the SIM card tray (refer to Figure 2-2) on the right side of your iPhone.**

   The SIM card tray pops open.

2. **Place the SIM card in the tray, matching the cut corner of the SIM card to the cut corner in the tray.**

3. **Push the SIM card tray closed.**

When you turn on your iPhone for the first time, the Setup Assistant takes you through a series of screens where you type in the requested information or choose from a list and tap Next or Done. You have to have a Wi-Fi or cellular network data connection to complete activation; otherwise, you must connect your iPhone to your computer with the USB connector cable. The Setup Assistant asks for the following information:

✔ **Language:** Tap your selection in the list.

✔ **Country:** Tap your selection in the list.

✔ **Wi-Fi network:** A list of available Wi-Fi networks appears. Click the one you use and type in the password. If Wi-Fi is unavailable, you can connect your iPhone to your computer with the USB to Dock connector cable and choose Connect to iTunes.

✔ **Location Services:** We recommend that you choose Enable Location Services, which lets various iPhone apps such as Maps and Reminders to use your location to better perform operations.

✔ **Set Up iPhone:** If this is your first iPhone, you can choose Set Up as New iPhone or you can restore from a backup of your iPad or iPod touch, which puts your apps, data, and media on your iPhone. If you are moving from an older iPhone to a newer model, first backup your old phone and then choose Restore from iCloud Backup or Restore from iTunes Backup (whichever you use). Learn all the details of syncing, restoring, and using iCloud in Book II, Chapter 1.

✔ **Sign in or create an Apple ID:** Although you can choose to skip this step, your Apple ID lets you

   • Store your iPhone backup on iCloud, Apple's remote storage site.

   • Make purchases from the iTunes Store and the App Store.

   • Sign in to FaceTime.

✔ If you have separate Apple IDs for iTunes and iCloud, follow the onscreen instructions to sign in to both. iCloud requires ID with an e-mail format, such as babsboyd@icloud.com, so you may have to create a new account to activate iCloud. The Setup Assistant asks you to create an ID and password and set up a security question — a question only you know the answer to that Apple asks if you forget your password or if you call for customer service and the technician wants to verify your identity.

If you don't have an Apple ID and aren't sure what we're talking about, skip this step and go to Book II, Chapter 1, where we explain how to create and use an Apple ID in more detail.

✔ **Set Up Touch ID (iPhone 5S):** Tap Set Up Now to go through the process that allows an iPhone 5s to memorize your fingerprint as shown in Figure 2-3. (Tap Set Up Later if you prefer to postpone this action; we show you how in Book I, Chapter 4.) After setting up Touch ID, touching the Home button unlocks your iPhone and can also be used in place of your Apple ID password to authorize purchases.

✔ **iTunes Store Sign in:** Type your Apple ID and password and Agree to the Terms and Conditions when asked.

●●○○○ AT&T 🔋   10:38 AM   94% 🔋⚡

Success

Touch ID is ready. Your print can be used for unlocking your iPhone.

Continue

Figure 2-3: Touch ID uses your fingerprint in place of a passcode to open the Lock screen.

✔ **iCloud Set up:** You can choose to use iCloud or decline and then set up iCloud later, as explained in Book II, Chapter 1.

✔ **Messaging:** Choose which phone number and e-mail address other people can use to reach you on iMessage, iPhone's text messaging service, and FaceTime, iPhone's audio and video calling service that uses cellular data or Wi-Fi.

✔ **Diagnostics:** We recommend you choose Automatically Send. Tap Start Using iPhone after you complete the setup procedure.

Turning Up the Volume

When you're in a noisy place and don't want to miss a call, you might want to have the ringer at full volume. On the other hand, if you're in a meeting but waiting for an important call, you may want to keep your iPhone silent and choose to respond only to that one not-to-be-missed call. Likewise, you may want to increase the speaker volume to better hear the person you're speaking with on a call in a noisy place. Here we explain how the three buttons on the left of your iPhone control volume:

✔ **Volume Buttons:** You find the volume buttons — two round, slightly raised buttons — on the left side of iPhone. The button on top with the plus sign increases volume; the lower button with the minus sign lowers volume. When iPhone is awake, but not otherwise engaged in a noisy activity, these buttons control the volume of both the ringer and alerts, unless you've turned that feature off within the sound settings, as we explain in Book I, Chapter 4. When you are engaged in a call or using an app that has volume, be it music, a video, or a game, these buttons control the volume of the thing you are listening to, watching, or playing.

Both volume buttons double as shutter buttons for the Camera. (Refer to Book V, Chapters 1 and 4 to learn about using your iPhone's camera and video recorder.)

✔ **Silent/Ring Switch:** The switch above the volume buttons is a mute button. Push it to the back and you see a red bar. This is the Off or silent position. Pushed to the front is the On or ring position. When iPhone is in silent mode, it vibrates when calls or alerts come in. If your iPhone rings and you prefer not to answer, you can turn the Silent/Ring switch off. Your caller continues to hear the phone ring until he decides to hang up or leave a voicemail message, but your iPhone will be silent although it will continue to vibrate. See Book III, Chapter 1 for information about declining calls.

When iPhone is in silent mode, alarms are still audible. The audio for Music and some games will be heard through the speaker or earphones, if you happen to have those plugged into your iPhone (and into your ears, of course).

Charging Your iPhone Battery

Like all battery-powered gadgets, your iPhone is useless with an uncharged battery. The good news is that iPhone recharges in less than an hour, and you can charge the battery in several ways, which we describe here. Even though it recharges quickly, sometimes you want to conserve that charge for as long as possible; check out the sidebar at the end of this section for tips on helping your iPhone hold the battery charge for a longer length of time.

The battery icon in the status bar indicates roughly how much battery power you have. If you want to see a specific percentage, tap Settings➪General➪Usage and turn on the Battery Percentage switch toward the bottom of the screen.

Plugging into the USB charger

Your iPhone comes with a USB connection cable and a USB power adapter. To charge the battery, plug the dock connector into the dock port at the base of your iPhone — with any model iPhone 5's Lightning connector, you don't have to worry about which way is up as it can be plugged in either way. Plug the USB end into the USB power adapter and plug the power adapter into an electrical outlet. iPhone beeps, which lets you know it's actively charging.

The power adapter automatically adjusts to 110 or 220 voltage, based on the voltage for the location you're plugging into. If you are using your iPhone outside the U.S., you have to purchase an adapter that changes the plug conformation to meet the outlet style of the country you're visiting. You can find a kit at the Apple Store (store.apple.com/us) or single adapters at TravelProducts.com (www.travelproducts.com/). Or you can charge your iPhone with your computer's USB port, as we explain next.

Charging with your Mac or PC's USB port

When you connect your iPhone to a USB port on your computer to sync or transfer photos, the battery automatically begins taking a charge. Again, iPhone beeps, which lets you know this is going on. If your computer is turned off or is sleeping, your iPhone battery may drain instead of charge, so make sure your computer is on whenever you connect your iPhone to it.

Although plugging your iPhone into any recent or new Mac can charge your iPhone, the same isn't necessarily true for recent or new Windows desktop and notebook computers or older Macs. Apple explains that's because the USB ports on certain of those models don't pass through enough wattage to charge your iPhone. If connecting your iPhone to your USB port doesn't yield a charge — you know it's charging because it beeps and there's a lightning bolt next to the battery in the status bar — try plugging into a port dock on a powered USB hub. If that doesn't work, you'll have to plug into a charger to charge your iPhone.

Don't pull the cable to detach your iPhone from your computer. Always grasp the hard, square part of either end of the USB cable to remove it.

If iPhone's battery charge drops very low or runs down completely, your iPhone automatically shuts itself off. To bring your iPhone back to life, you must attach the USB cable to a power source (your computer or an electrical outlet). When your iPhone shuts itself off because the battery charge is too low or nearly empty, you won't be able to use your iPhone until the battery reaches a minimal charge level. Usually you only have to wait a few minutes before your iPhone turns itself on again.

To preserve the overall life, you should cycle the battery on a monthly basis. *Cycling* is letting the battery completely discharge and then charging it fully.

More charging options

Apple and other third-party vendors make charging accessories. You can use an iPhone dock, which is a type of base that you set your iPhone in to charge the battery, and it's convenient to have on your desk to keep your iPhone close at hand. Make sure you purchase the dock that's appropriate for the iPhone model you use. You can also purchase battery packs that attach to your iPhone to get a longer charge. And, if you spend a lot of time in your car, another option is a USB adapter that plugs into the cigarette lighter to charge your iPhone. Many newer car models come with a built-in USB port that both charges your iPhone and lets you listen to audio from your iPhone through the car's stereo speakers.

You can replace standard electrical outlets with USB-enabled outlets, so all you have to do is plug in the cable. We've seen USB outlets more frequently in hotels and airplanes too, which makes charging while travelling super easy.

Tap Settings➪General➪Usage to see how much time has passed since your last charge. Usage is how much you've used it. Standby is how much time your iPhone spent sleeping.

Changing the battery

If you keep your iPhone for many years, sooner or later, you'll need to replace the battery. Despite our DIY (do-it-yourself) world, you can't replace the battery yourself. You have to send it in to the Battery Replacement Program. For $85 (at the time of publication), you send your iPhone to Apple or take it to an Apple store, the battery is replaced, and Apple takes care of disposing of the old one. This service is covered if your iPhone is still under the one year warranty or you extended the warranty to two years with the AppleCare protection plan, which we explain Book I, Chapter 5.

Keeping the battery charged

Technically, you should get about eight hours of talk time on an iPhone 5 on the 3G network. Realistically, if you play games and go on the Internet, you probably get less. Here are some tips for keeping the battery charged longer and for maintaining long battery life.

- ✔ **Turn Off Location Services:** Go to Settings⇨Privacy⇨Location Services. (Remember though that the apps that use it do so only when you're using them.)

- ✔ **Turn Off Wi-Fi:** If you have Wi-Fi turned on and there's no Wi-Fi network, your iPhone keeps searching and searching and consuming battery power. To turn off Wi-Fi, tap Settings⇨Wi-Fi⇨Off or swipe up from the bottom of the screen to open the Control Center and tap the white Wi-Fi button so it's dimmed.

- ✔ **Turn Off 4G:** If 4G isn't available where you are or you don't need to access the 4G network, turn it off. Sometimes this actually improves access to your cellular calling network. It doubles your battery charge. Tap Settings⇨ Cellular⇨Enable 4G Off.

- ✔ **Turn Off Siri:** If you don't need Siri's assistance, may as well send her out to lunch since she's a power hog. Tap Settings⇨General⇨Siri Off.

- ✔ **Turn On Airplane Mode:** If you happen to be out of your network range, your iPhone consumes a lot of battery power as it continually searches for the cellular network. Eventually the words *No Service* appear instead of the carrier name and your

iPhone settles down and stops searching. Consider putting your iPhone in Airplane mode: Tap Settings⇨Airplane Mode On or swipe up from the bottom of the screen to open the Control Center and tap the Airplane Mode button. Both cellular and Wi-Fi are turned off but you can still use other apps that don't need those services.

- ✔ **Use Fetch Instead of Push:** Rather than having your iPhone constantly check for new information with Push, you can set your iPhone to sync with whichever cloud service you use, such as iCloud, Yahoo! Mail, or MS-Exchange, at set time intervals, or sync manually. Tap Settings⇨Mail, Contacts, Calendars⇨Fetch New Data⇨Push Off.

- ✔ **Use Auto-Brightness:** Dimming your screen also improves the length of a charge. The ambient light sensor dims or brightens your screen based on the light it senses. You can turn the automatic adjustment on by going to Settings⇨Wallpapers & Brightness⇨Auto-Brightness On.

- ✔ **Bluetooth:** Tap Settings⇨Bluetooth⇨Off if you don't have any Bluetooth devices connected and don't plan to use any for a while or swipe up from the bottom of the screen to open the Control Center and tap the Bluetooth button so it's dimmed.

- ✔ **Cellular Data:** Tap Settings⇨Cellular⇨ Cellular Data Off. You can still use the phone and Wi-Fi connection.

Gaming, watching videos, and surfing the web use big chunks of battery power. Playing a game helps pass the time on a long trip, but make sure you leave enough battery power to call your ride when you arrive at your destination, or that there's a power source into which to plug your iPhone.

Interpreting the (Visual) Signs

Icons have been a big part of Apple products since the creation of the Lisa computer and advent of the Mac, and sometimes looking at the status bar can be like trying to interpret Egyptian hieroglyphics. Then, a couple iterations ago, the Notification Center was added to iOS as a sort of catchall for incoming communications and updates. In this section, we explain what you see on the Home screen, how to interpret the status bar icons, and how to read and respond to notifications iPhone sends you when it has something important to communicate.

Home screen

The point of departure for everything iPhone is the Home screen, which features three basic parts (or zones), as you can see in Figure 2-4. At the very top is the *status bar*, which we get to in just a few paragraphs. The bulk of screen of the iPhone 5 or later holds up to 20 app buttons and folders (16 on earlier iPhone models). Four of the Home screen's apps stay tacked at the bottom of the screen in what's called the *dock*, which makes it easy to get to your four most-favorite apps no matter which Home screen you're viewing.

Figure 2-4: The Home screen is the point of departure for iPhone.

When a Home screen is filled with 20 (or 16) apps and/or folders, a new Home screen is added, up to 15 Home screens in all. Between the last row of apps and the dock is a line of dots (one of which is white, the others are gray). These represent the number of Home screens you have. The white dot tells you which of the Home screens you're on. In Figure 2-4, you see the first dot is white followed by three gray dots, which means this is Home screen one of four. Flick the current Home screen to the left, and the screen moves one screen to the left; flick the Home screen to the right, and the screen moves one screen to the right. Touch the dots toward the left, and the screen moves one screen to the left; touch the dots to the right, and the screen moves one screen to the right.

Tap any of the app icons on the Home screen, and the associated app opens. If you tap a folder, it opens. Then you tap the app inside the folder that you want to launch. Double-click the Home button and the apps that are open appear in the open apps carousel.

Staying informed with status bar icons

The status bar runs across the very top of your iPhone in either portrait or landscape view, in apps that support landscape view. Its icons give you information about your cellular and/or wireless network connection, battery life, and auxiliary functions you may have turned on, such as Do Not Disturb and the alarm clock. Here is an explanation of each one. Remember, you won't see them all at once on your iPhone, and some you may never see:

✈ ✓ **Airplane Mode:** You see this icon if you've turned Airplane mode on in Settings. See Book I, Chapter 4 for more details on Airplane Mode.

⏰ ✓ **Alarm:** Appears if you set an alarm using the Clock app, we explore the Clock app in Book IV, Chapter 2.

🔋⚡ ✓ **Battery:** Indicates how much charge remains on the battery. It's green if the battery is between 100 and 20 percent charged. It changes to red and shows just a tiny portion on the left when less than 20 percent charge remains. It has a lightning bolt next to it when the battery is being charged. You can read more about charging the battery later in this chapter.

✱ ✓ **Bluetooth:** Shows that Bluetooth is turned on. When it's blue or white, you are connected to another Bluetooth device such as a headset. When it's gray, Bluetooth is on but no device is connected. You may be surprised to learn that Bluetooth is named after a Danish king; read more about this connection protocol in the "Making Connections" section of this chapter.

(→ ✓ **Call Forwarding:** On GSM models (an unlocked Apple iPhone or an AT&T iPhone, refer to the "Considering iPhone Carriers and Configurations" section in Book I, Chapter 1), appears when you've forwarded your calls to another phone number. The call forwarding settings are explained in Book III, Chapter 1.

•••○○ ✓ **Cell Signal:** Indicates the strength of the cellular signal your iPhone is connected to. If you have no filled-in circles or just one, the signal is weak — more solid circles, stronger signal. *No Service* appears when iPhone is unable to pick-up a signal from your cellular provider. If Airplane Mode is turned on, you see the airplane icon instead of the cell signal circles.

✔ **Do Not Disturb:** Reminds you that you have activated the Do Not Disturb feature.

✔ **EDGE (E):** Appears when iPhone is connected to your cellular provider's EDGE data network for accessing the Internet. GSM models support EDGE networks. Read more about Internet access later in this chapter.

GPRS ✔ **GPRS/1xRTT:** GSM models use the GPRS (General Packet Radio Service) network and CDMA models use the 1xRTT (1x Radio Transmission Technology) network to access the Internet when those networks are available. Read more about Internet access in the "Making Connections" section later in this chapter.

✔ **Location Services:** When you see this icon, an app, such as Maps or Reminders, is tracking your current location coordinates in order to provide you with nearby information or other services.

LTE ✔ **LTE:** Lets you know you have an LTE cellular connection; this icon may be 4G, depending on your carrier.

✔ **Network Activity:** Spins when iPhone is accessing a cellular or Wi-Fi network for any app that uses the Internet, such as Safari or the App Store. It also appears when iPhone is syncing iCloud information over-the-air, or sometimes when an app is performing other data-related activities.

✔ **Personal Hotspot:** This icon is active when you've connected to another iPhone or a 3G/4G iPad that is providing a Personal Hotspot.

✔ **Orientation Lock:** This reminds you that you've turned off the landscape view feature. You can turn your iPhone every which way, but the screen remains in portrait position — unless you open an app that only works in landscape position, such as some games or videos.

✔ **Syncing:** Indicates that your iPhone is syncing with iTunes or iCloud.

✔ **TTY:** Indicates your iPhone is configured to work with a Teletype (TTY) machine.

3G ✔ **UMTS/EV-DO (3G):** Indicates when GSM models are connected to the UMTS (Universal Mobile Telecommunications System) network, or CDMA models are connected to the EV-DO (Evolution-Data Optimized) network to access the Internet when those networks are available. Read more about Internet access in the "Making Connections" section later in this chapter.

VPN ✔ **VPN:** Indicates iPhone is connected to a VPN (Virtual Private Network).

 ✔ **Wi-Fi:** Indicates iPhone is connected to a Wi-Fi network. The more bars, the merrier — er, we mean, the more stable — the connection. Read more about wireless connections in the "Making Connections" section of this chapter.

Understanding status bar colors

The text of the status bar may be black or white, whichever shows up better on the background of the app or Home screen. In some situations, however, the background color changes behind the status bar when you are engaged in one activity, such as a phone call, and begin another activity, such as opening Notes to jot down something your caller is telling you. These are what the different colors mean:

- ✓ **Green:** A phone or FaceTime call is active but you are doing something else. You can continue to converse while you do the other activity; it's helpful to put the call on speakerphone before opening another app.

- ✓ **Red:** Voice Memos is recording while you're doing other things. Tap the red bar to return to the Voice Memos app and stop recording.

- ✓ **Blue:** Your iPhone is set up as a Personal Hotspot and its Internet connection is being accessed by another device.

Noticing notification messages and badges

When iPhone wants to get your attention and tell you something, it communicates via badges and messages. These are different from alerts, alarms, and reminders that you set on your iPhone in that they contain information iPhone wants to give you. You see badges as shown on the Podcasts and Mail buttons in Figure 2-4:

- ✓ White numbers inside a red circle that appear in the corner of certain app icons, such as Mail and Facebook. The number indicates how many unread messages or status updates await you in those apps.

- ✓ When a new app has been installed or an existed app updated, a blue dot appears to the left of the app name under the app icon.

There are also two kinds of notification messages. The first kind requires a response and appears when you want to do something but iPhone needs something else to happen before it can complete the task. These messages appear in rectangular boxes in the middle of the screen and typically display buttons you can tap to respond to with a certain action. In the example in Figure 2-5, for instance, you have the choice of acknowledging the notification message by tapping Cancel, or by tapping Disable to turn off Airplane mode.

The second kind of notification is when you're doing one thing, say reading an article on a website, and another thing happens, say, you get an incoming e-mail. You see a notification banner across the top of your iPhone's screen. You can choose to respond or ignore it. If you ignore the banner, it disappears in a few seconds. iPhone saves all your notifications in the Notification Center, as shown in Figure 2-6, which you can see by swiping down from the top of the screen. You choose which apps you want to see in the Notification

Center in Settings, which we cover in Book I, Chapter 4. You also choose whether alert-generating apps display alerts, banners, badges, or none of the three.

Making Connections

Anymore, it seems staying connected is the whole point of technological devices and your iPhone has the ability to connect to a variety of signal sources: to the Internet via your cellular carrier's data network or via a Wi-Fi network, or to other devices like printers, keyboards, and hands-free headsets using Bluetooth, and to other iOS devices using AirDrop, which also transmits over Bluetooth. To help you understand all of your iPhone's many connection options, we've organized those options into three sections: cellular and wireless connections, Personal Hotspot, tethering, and AirDrop, and lastly, Bluetooth and GPS connections.

Figure 2-5: Notification messages often have buttons that give you a choice of actions to take.

Cellular

When you activate your iPhone with a carrier, you gain access to that carrier's cellular voice and data network. iPhone uses two types of cellular connection protocols: the CDMA type used by Sprint and Verizon in the U.S., and the GSM type used by AT&T and T-Mobile in the U.S. and in most countries outside the U.S. Without boring you with too many technical details, your iPhone typically connects using one or more of the following protocols:

✔ **LTE/4G:** Long Term Evolution is the most recent cellular communications protocol. Both GSM and CDMA model iPhones can access the LTE network where it's available. This may be referred to as 4G when a GSM carrier accesses the 4G UMTS network.

✔ **GSM (Global System for Mobile Communications) models**

- **3G/UMTS:** 3G is the third generation protocol standard that uses the UMTS (Universal Mobile Tele communications System) cellular frequency. This protocol is faster than EDGE, but consumes more battery power. If 3G is on but unavailable, iPhone defaults to EDGE.

- **EDGE:** Enhanced Data for GSM Evolution is the first-generation

Figure 2-6: iPhone keeps all your notifications in one place, the Notification Center.

protocol standard for connecting to the Internet over the cellular carrier network. EDGE often offers a more stable, albeit slower, connection than 3G because it offers wider network coverage.

- **GPRS:** General Packet Radio Service supports both second- (2G) and third-generation (3G) cellular telephony. Usage is based on volume rather than time. If neither EDGE nor 3G is available, iPhone defaults to GPRS.

✔ **CDMA (Code Division Multiple Access) models**

- **EV-DO:** The Evolution-Data Optimized is a 3G or third generation protocol, similar to UMTS for access speed.

- **1xRTT:** 1x Radio Transmission Technology is an alternative 3G protocol.

Unlike GSM-model iPhones, if you have a CDMA iPhone and are actively transferring data over your carrier's cellular network — to check your e-mail or browse a web page, for instance — you cannot also engage in an active phone call while those data-related activities are underway. Any calls you may receive while using your cellular carrier's data connection are sent directly to your voicemail. You can make and receive calls while doing those data-related things on your CDMA iPhone if you are connected to a Wi-Fi network.

When your iPhone is connected to the Internet with one of these protocols, the associated icon appears in the status bar, as mentioned earlier in this chapter.

If you happen to be outside your carrier's network, you can try to access the Internet through another carrier. This is called Data Roaming and is enabled by tapping Settings⇨Cellular and flipping the Data Roaming switch to On.

Data Roaming, especially if you're out of the country, can rack up sizeable surcharges. Check with your carrier for Data Roaming fees before being surprised with a whopping bill at the end of the month.

If your cellular carrier contract has a data transfer limit, you want to keep track of how much data you're consuming. Your carrier may have a dedicated website or app that tracks the information for you or you can monitor your cellular data usage by opening Settings⇨Cellular. Scroll down the screen to see the Call Time and Cellular Data Usage, which indicate the number of days and hours you spent on your iPhone during that period and during the total span of your relationship with your carrier plan and the amount of data you've shuttled back and forth over your cellular carrier's network. At the very bottom of the screen, you find the Reset Statistics button that resets the aforementioned stats so you can start tracking those figures.

You should tap Reset Statistics at the end of the month or on the day when your period renews. Using Wi-Fi for data access is an alternative if you have free or low-cost Wi-Fi service in places where you use your iPhone.

Wi-Fi

You may want to say that cellular is wireless, and you'd be right. But Wi-Fi is wireless, only better. Connecting to the Internet using iPhone's Wi-Fi feature is one of the fastest — and cheapest — ways to connect to the Internet. Wi-Fi networks blast their typically close-range signals from a device known as a wireless router, which is connected to a broadband modem, which in turn is typically connected to your cable or phone company's broadband Internet service (or whatever the Wi-Fi router you tap into is connected to, be it at your favorite cafe, on a train, or a public library, for example). Other people can connect their Wi-Fi enabled devices as well, making the group of you a network, as opposed to a single connection. You may need a password to access a Wi-Fi network, and some Wi-Fi services charge an hourly or daily fee to access their networks.

To join a Wi-Fi network, follow these steps:

1. **Tap Settings on your Home screen, and then tap Wi-Fi.**

   The Wi-Fi Networks screen opens.

2. **Tap the toggle switch to turn Wi-Fi on.**

   The screen expands to give you the option to Choose a Network, as seen in Figure 2-7. iPhone detects servers in the area and the Wi-Fi symbol indicates how strong the signal is: The more waves, the stronger the signal. Servers that require a password have a closed lock icon next to them.

   Some Wi-Fi networks may require you to agree to the provider's terms before you can use the network. In those cases, a prompt appears, asking for your permission to launch Safari

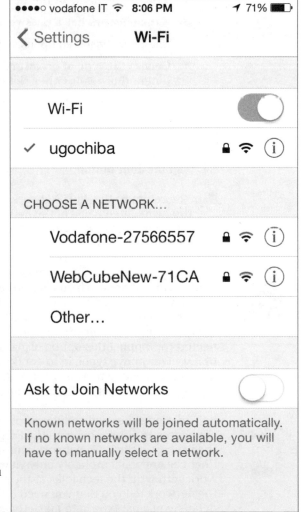

Figure 2-7: Choose a wireless network from the list of visible servers.

to view the provider's web page, where you typically tap a check box indicating you agree to the legal mumbo jumbo listed on the web page. In other cases, you have to type in a user name and password in order to agree to the provider's terms.

If you know the name of the network you want to join and it's not in the list, do this:

1. **Tap Other.**

   The Other Network pane opens.

2. **Type in the name of the network in the Name field.**

3. **If the network has a password, tap Security.**

   The Security screen opens.

4. **Choose the type of password this network uses and tap the back button that reads Other Network.**

   The Other Network screen reopens, and the cursor is blinking in the Password field.

3. **Type in the password.**

4. **Tap the Join button.**

   You return to the Wi-Fi Networks screen. A check mark appears next to the highlighted name of the network you've joined. iPhone automatically remembers any Wi-Fi network you've joined and connects to it whenever you're in its range.

iPhone remembers Wi-Fi networks you previously connected to and automatically reconnects whenever you're in range of those Wi-Fi networks, unless you're already connected to a network that has a stronger signal. Tap the disclosure triangle next to a network name and then tap the Forget this Network button to immediately disconnect from a Wi-Fi network you're connected to. Tapping this option also erases any password or other information you may have typed in to connect to the Wi-Fi network. If you have trouble connecting to a network you *know* you should be able to connect to, try forgetting the network and signing in again.

Information about and configuration options for the Wi-Fi network you're connected to appear beneath the Forget this Network button. Scroll down the list to see the Wi-Fi network's information and configuration options. Chances are you'll probably only view or change these additional Wi-Fi network settings if the tech folks at the company or organization that operates the network tell you that you need to and provide you with the necessary details you must type in to make the connection.

AirDrop

AirDrop creates a connection between your iPhone 5 or later and one or more iOS devices such as iPhones (5 or later), iPads (fourth generation or Mini), or iPod touches (fifth generation). You can then exchange documents and data from apps, such as a contact card in Contacts, an address in Maps, or an event in Calendar. To use AirDrop, follow these steps:

1. **Drag up from the bottom of the screen to open the Control Center.**

2. **Tap AirDrop.**

   When you turn AirDrop on, both Wi-Fi and Bluetooth are activated because sharing takes place with either of these types of connections.

3. **Choose one of the choices, as shown in Figure 2-8:**

   Off to turn AirDrop off.

   Contacts Only to give access to your iPhone only to people with iCloud accounts who are in your Contacts.

   Everyone to let everyone on the same Wi-Fi network with an iCloud account see your iPhone.

4. **Open whatever it is you want to share, say a photo in Photos.**

5. **Tap the Share button.**

6. **Tap the icon for the person you want to share with.**

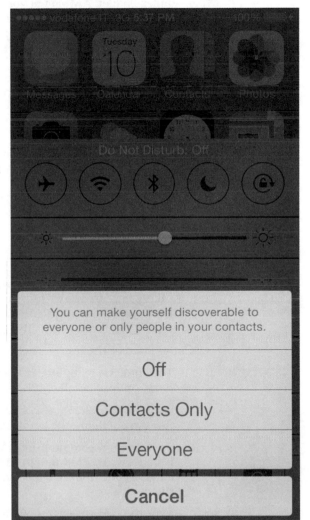

Figure 2-8: With AirDrop, you can share things with anyone nearby who has an iCloud account and an iDevice that works with AirDrop.

The person receives a notification that you want to share something with her, and she can choose to Decline or Accept your shared item.

Personal Hotspot and tethering

When another device uses your iPhone's Internet connection to connect to the Internet, that's called *tethering*. Tethering essentially turns your iPhone into a miniature Wi-Fi router that broadcasts a signal that you or a few others can tap into with your notebook computer, your iPad, or most any other Wi-Fi enabled gadget. A Wi-Fi network you can connect to is typically referred to as a *hotspot* and on your iPhone, this feature is called Personal Hotspot. You can also connect your computer to iPhone's Personal Hotspot feature using a USB cable, rather than connect using Wi-Fi.

To use iPhone's Personal Hotspot feature, you must pay your cellular service provider a separate fee in addition to your existing cellular service plan. Contact your provider for details. Personal Hotspot also quickly consumes the battery charge.

To share an Internet connection using your iPhone's Personal Hotspot feature, follow these steps:

1. **Tap Settings on the Home screen.**

2. **Choose Personal Hotspot.**

3. **Tap On.**

   Take note of the Wi-Fi Password given on the Personal Hotspot screen.

   If Bluetooth is turned off, a notification appears asking if you want to turn Bluetooth on or use Personal Hotspot only with Wi-Fi and USB. Although you can use Bluetooth, we recommend either Wi-Fi or USB because a Bluetooth connection is painfully slow.

4. **Choose one of the options below to connect:**

   • **To connect a computer using the Personal Hotspot feature's direct cable option, connect iPhone to your computer with the USB cable.**

   In Network preferences, choose iPhone. Follow the onscreen instructions to configure the connection if this is the first time.

   • **To connect a computer or other device (such as an iPad, another iPhone, or an iPod touch) using that device's built-in Wi-Fi feature, choose your iPhone from the list of Wi-Fi networks that appears on the device.**

   Type the Wi-Fi password shown in the Personal Hotspot settings.

5. **A blue band appears at the top of your iPhone screen whenever a device is connected.**

Bluetooth

The iPhone 4S and 5 use the Bluetooth 4.0 protocol. Bluetooth is a short-range (up to 300 feet) wireless protocol used to attach, or pair, devices to your iPhone. Unlike Wi-Fi, which broadcasts its availability continuously, Bluetooth has to be turned on to make your iPhone or other device discoverable so that they can see each other. A passkey or PIN (Personal Identification Number) is used to make that connection private.

One of the most common devices paired with iPhone is a wireless headset. This small device is either inserted in your ear or wrapped around it and has both a speaker to hear the person you're talking to and a microphone so they can hear you. You can have phone conversations without risking strangulation by earphone cord or, worse yet, catching the cord on something, resulting in your iPhone flying through the air and smashing on the floor. (Yeesh, just writing that makes us shudder.)

Other devices that you might want to pair with your iPhone are earphones for listening to music, a physical keyboard, or your car so you can answer calls by tapping a button on the steering wheel or radio. If you pair two iPhones, you can share photos, files, and even an Internet connection between them. To connect devices to your iPhone via Bluetooth,

1. **On your iPhone, go to Settings⇨Bluetooth and tap the Bluetooth button on.**

   The Bluetooth screen opens, as shown in Figure 2-9. Tapping On makes your iPhone discoverable, which means other devices with Bluetooth turned on can see your iPhone. The Bluetooth icon appears in the status bar.

2. **Turn on Bluetooth on the device you want to connect so it too is discoverable.**

   If the device is another iPhone or computer, you have to turn on Bluetooth on that iPhone or computer too. Active devices show up in a list on the Bluetooth screen on your iPhone.

   A Bluetooth headset only needs to be turned on. Obviously a headset doesn't have a keypad to enter a passkey, but it comes with an assigned passkey, which you need to pair with your iPhone. Check the instructions that came with the headset for the passkey code or try **0000**. (It's usually the default passcode.)

3. **In the list, tap the device you want to pair with your iPhone.**

4. **Enter the passkey on the keypad that appears on your iPhone, if requested.**

   The two devices can now communicate across the Bluetooth connection.

5. **To turn Bluetooth off and make your iPhone undiscoverable, tap Settings⇨Bluetooth⇨Off or drag up from the bottom of the screen to open the Control Center and tap the Bluetooth button.**

   The Bluetooth button on the Control Center is dimmed and the Bluetooth icon disappears from the status bar, as shown in Figure 2-10.

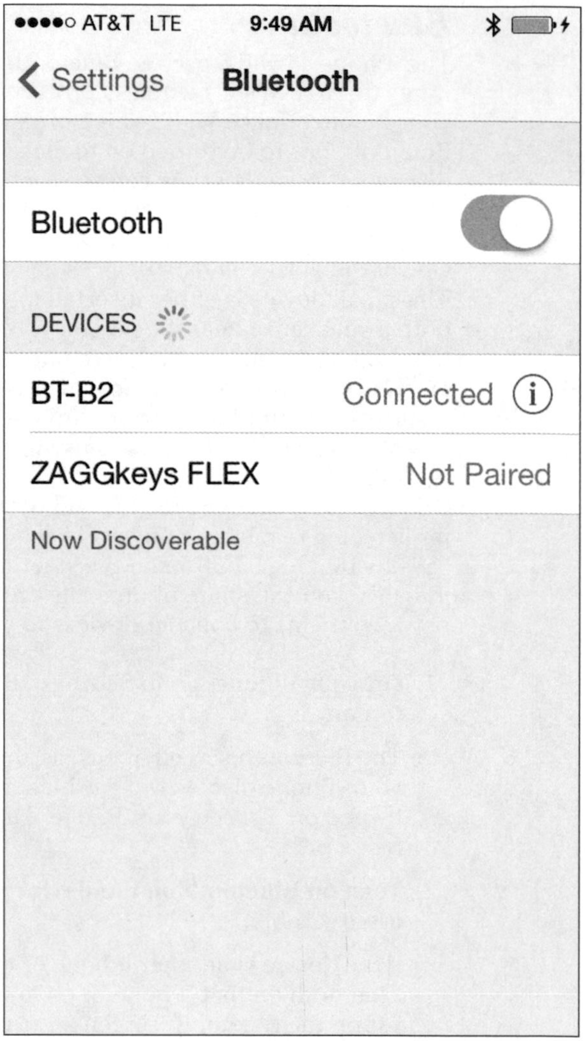

Carrier

This setting appears on the main Settings screen on GSM models (such as the AT&T iPhone or an unlocked iPhone) when you are outside your service provider's network. Tap Settings⇨Carrier ⇨Automatic for your iPhone to connect to the appropriate carrier. When Automatic is in the off position, your iPhone searches for available carriers and presents a list of those found; tap the network you want to use. You may incur Roaming Charges when you use a different network.

Many apps download and upload data with a remote server and use either Wi-Fi or the cellular data network to make those exchanges. For example, Facebook accesses the Facebook server to show you the latest status updates and let you post your own, likewise, the App Store exists in the

Figure 2-9: Bluetooth lets you connect devices to your iPhone.

virtual realm of the Internet and when you access it from your iPhone, your browsing and shopping activity travels on the cellular data network or Wi-Fi. You can better control how you consume your contractual cellular data allotment by choosing which apps use cellular data. Go to Settings⇨Cellular, scroll down to the Use Cellular Data For section, and tap On or Off the apps you want to allow cellular data access. Even if you tap an app to the off position, it can still perform its data functions when you are connected to Wi-Fi.

GPS

iPhone's built-in GPS or Global Positioning System sensor determines your location. Apps like Compass and Maps use GPS to pinpoint your location. The Camera uses GPS to do geo-tagging, which is adding the location to a photo when it's taken.

Figure 2-10: Turn Bluetooth on and off in the Control Center.

Reminders uses GPS to provide location-based alerts. The GPS is accessed when you check-in to some third-party apps or social networks.

When you turn on Location Services in Settings⇨Privacy⇨Location Services, the GPS sensor is activated. We explain the features and functions of Location Services in Book I, Chapter 4.

The Location Services icon appears in the status bar when you are using an app that uses it.

Printing from your iPhone

The utopian idea of a paperless society may be near, but it hasn't arrived yet. Words and images on a piece of paper are sometimes necessary. AirPrint enables your iPhone to print directly to an AirPrint-enabled printer. Many types of files can be printed: e-mail messages and any readable attachments, photos, web pages, even PDFs. Apps you download from the App Store may also support AirPrint. AirPrint couldn't be easier. Here are the steps to take to print from your phone:

1. **Make sure the printer you want to use is on the same Wi-Fi network that your iPhone is connected to.**

2. **On your iPhone, open the document you want to print.**

3. **Tap the Share button.**

4. **Tap the Print button.**

    The Printer Options screen opens.

5. **Tap the Printer button to select the printer you want to use.**

    Another screen opens, showing the printers that are available in the Wi-Fi vicinity.

6. **Tap the printer you want to use and then tap the Back button at the top left of the screen.**

7. **Select the number of copies you want to print by tapping the plus and minus buttons.**

    Depending on the app and the printer, you may also have the option to choose double-sided printing and/or a range of pages.

8. **Tap Print and walk over to the printer to pick up your page.**

Adjusting Accessibility Options for Easier Operation

With the Accessibility settings, Apple addresses the physical challenges that some users might have with iPhone's interface. They've created optional features that customize the interface to make iPhone more accessible. From the Home screen, tap Settings⇨General⇨Accessibility. You see the screen in Figure 2-11. We recommend that you consult Chapter 32 of iPhone's User Guide (manuals.info.apple.com/en_US/iphone_user_guide.pdf) for complete instructions on how to get the most out of the Accessibility features. The features are divided into four categories: Vision, Hearing, Learning, and Physical & Motor. Here we briefly explain each feature:

   ✔ **VoiceOver:** Turn this setting on to hear an audible description of the buttons on the screen. With some practice, vision-impaired iPhone users can learn the tapping, double-clicking, and flicking movements necessary to use apps. Within VoiceOver, you can adjust the speaking rate, attach a Braille device, select which parts of a web screen you wish to have read, and which language you want VoiceOver to speak.

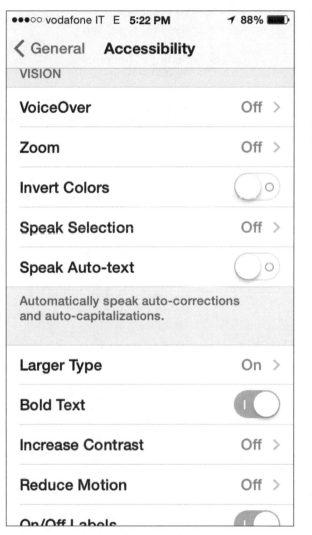

✔ **Zoom:** The Zoom feature enlarges the entire iPhone screen when you double-tap with three fingers. Use three fingers to move from left to right on the screen and one finger to move the screen up and down. Double-tap again with three fingers to return to normal size.

You can't use VoiceOver and Zoom simultaneously.

✔ **Invert Colors:** Turn this feature on and all color on the display is inverted, like a photo negative.

✔ **Speak Selection:** Turn this feature on to have iPhone read selected text out loud, even if VoiceOver is turned off.

Figure 2-11: Customize Accessibility functions to make the most of your iPhone user experience.

✔ **Speak Auto-text:** Corrections iPhone makes automatically while you're typing are spoken out loud if this function is turned on.

✔ **Larger Type:** Tap this item and then tap Larger Dynamic Type to the On position. Move the slider as shown in Figure 2-12 to choose the type size that's comfortable for you. Your choice is reflected in Calendar, Contacts, Mail, Messages, Notes, and Reader, as well as any other app that supports dynamic type. You can also tap Settings⇨General⇨ Text Size to make this adjustment.

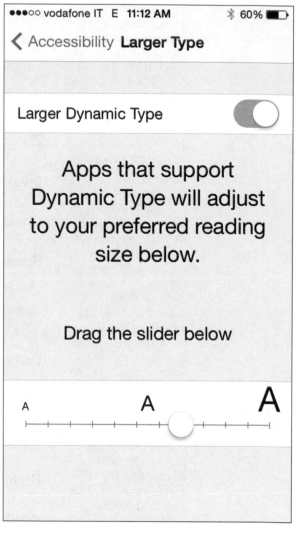

- **Bold Text:** Tap this option on and your iPhone restarts, and then all text on your iPhone shows up in a heavier, more pronounced typeface. (Figure 2-12 shows Bold Text activated.)

- **Increase Contrast:** When tapped on, the contrast on some backgrounds will be increased for better legibility.

- **Reduce Motion:** You may have noticed that as you tilt your iPhone it seems that the buttons or the background move a bit. This is called a *parallax effect* and can be turned off by tapping this option to the On position.

- **On/Off Labels:** Tap on to show the On and Off symbols on the toggle switches, in addition to the

Figure 2-12: Larger Type makes reading on your iPhone easier on the eyes.

white (off) and green (on) backgrounds and moving toggle. Refer to Figure 2-11.

- **Hearing Aids:** For those who use a hearing aid, turning this feature on may reduce interference.

- **Subtitles & Captioning:** When this option is on and subtitles or closed captioning are available, they will appear on screen.

- **LED Flash for Alerts:** When this feature is turned on, the LED next to the camera lens on the back of your iPhone flashes when iPhone is locked or asleep. It works whether the ring volume is on or not.

✔ **Mono Audio:** This feature changes the left and right sound channels into a mono channel that comes through both sides so those who can hear with only one ear hear both channels.

✔ **Phone Noise Cancelation:** When on, this functions helps reduce ambient noise when you're on a phone call and the phone is near your ear.

✔ **Volume Balance Slider:** Move the slider right or left to increase the volume on one side or another.

✔ **Guided Access:** Lets you limit iPhone use to one app and even limit features within that app so someone with attention or learning disabilities can stay focused on one task.

✔ **Switch Control:** Allows you to set up new controls and gestures for the various iPhone commands and iPhone functions with an adaptive accessory.

✔ **AssistiveTouch:** Lets you use an adaptive accessory, such as a joystick, to control your iPhone. You can also adjust tracking speed or create custom gestures to make them easier.

✔ **Home-Click Speed:** Adjust the double- and triple-click speed of the Home button.

✔ **Incoming Calls:** Lets you designate the headset or speaker as the default device for incoming calls.

✔ **Accessibility Shortcut:** You can choose to associate a triple-click of the Home button with up to five Accessibility functions: VoiceOver, Invert Colors, Zoom, Switch Control, or AssistiveTouch. If you choose more than one, when you triple-click the Home button, a menu lets you choose which option you want.

Other Accessibility Features

Although the functions controlled by the Accessibility settings are reflected across iPhone, some apps contain accessibility features that are specific to those apps. Here are some:

✔ **Custom Ringtones and Vibrations:** Create and assign unique ringtones and vibration patterns for individual contacts in Contacts. Refer to Book IV, Chapter 1 to learn about the Contacts app.

✔ **Voice Control:** Press and hold the Home button on your iPhone, the center button on iPhone's headset, or the button on a Bluetooth headset to open Voice Control. You can ask iPhone to call a person, tell you what time it is, or play a song in Music.

✔ **Siri:** On iPhone 4s or later, Siri, if enabled, performs the Voice Control functions. In addition, Siri can read messages and take dictation, adjust some settings, and do other helpful tasks. See Book I, Chapter 3 to learn all about Siri's capabilities.

- ✔ **Visual Voicemail:** This feature is explained more in Book III, Chapter 1. In a nutshell, iPhone adds pause and playback functions to voicemail messages and allows you to check your messages in any order you wish.

- ✔ **Widescreen Keyboard:** Many apps that use the keyboard let you turn your iPhone to landscape position to use a wider keyboard.

- ✔ **TTY Support:** You can add a TTY adapter to attach a Teletype machine to your iPhone.

Chapter 3: Controlling the Multitouch and Voice Recognition Interfaces

In This Chapter

➾ Learning the moves: tapping, scrolling, and zooming

➾ Leaving Home and going Home again

➾ Organizing apps and folders

➾ Talking to your iPhone

➾ Commandeering the keyboard

➾ Searching here, there, and everywhere

*I*f you activated your iPhone and explored some of the options as we discussed in the first two chapters of this book, you've already intuitively used a couple of the multitouch gestures — tap and possibly scroll. You also used the keyboard to type your Apple ID and maybe you tried talking to Siri.

In this chapter, we describe the gestures you use to control your iPhone, gestures you'll come across time and again throughout the rest of the book. We explain how the Home screen is organized and what the Home button does, and show you how to organize apps and folders on the Home screen. We then introduce you to Siri, your iPhone's voice-commanded virtual assistant, and give you examples of how to tell — ask is perhaps a better word — Siri to do something for you. For the times when you don't have Wi-Fi or if you're using an iPhone 4, we explain the Voice Control option. Although you're probably familiar with a keyboard layout, we point out how the iPhone keyboard is slightly different, and we give you some tricks that can make typing and editing easier. At the end of the chapter, we show you how to use Spotlight Search so you can find apps, phone numbers, music, and more on your iPhone and beyond.

Learning the Moves

Your iPhone's touchscreen is similar to other touchscreens you may have used, such as an ATM or the custom sandwich selector at your local mini-market. You need just a few good moves to make iPhone do all the things you're used to doing with a phone and more. These are the finger gestures that control everything on your iPhone:

- ✓ **Tapping:** A tap is lighter than pressing a button. It's a quick touch without any holding. Tap an app button on the Home screen to open the app. Tap an item in a list to select it. Variations on tapping are

    - **Double-tap:** Two quick taps zoom in on a map in Maps, and zoom in and out of a web page, e-mail message, or photo. A double-tap also changes the Shift key to a Caps Lock key if you enable that function in Settings⇨General⇨Keyboard.

    - **Two-finger tap:** On a map in the Maps app, a two-finger tap zooms out of the map; double-tap with a single finger to zoom in again.

- ✓ **Scrolling:** Scrolling is a dragging motion done with one finger, or more if that's more comfortable for you. You can even rest one finger on the screen and scroll with another one. Touch the screen and drag up or down. In some apps and websites, you can scroll left or right, too. Scrolling is most often used when reading something online or a document, to go through a list, such as Contacts, or to rotate a rotor like the one used to set the alarm clock, which we explain in Book IV, Chapter 2. Scrolling doesn't select or open anything, it only moves the list. You must tap to select.

- ✓ **Pulling:** Pulling, sometimes referred to as *swiping*, is a scroll with a specific starting point. Place your fingertip on the status bar and pull down to open the Notification Center, swipe up from the bottom of the screen to open the Control Center, or pull your list of messages down as far as they go. They refresh.

- ✓ **Flicking:** Touch your finger to the screen and quickly flick it up, or left, or right, and down. Flicking left and right on the Home screen moves to the next or previous screen. Flicking in a list, instead of scrolling, moves the list up and down more quickly. You can wait for it to stop or tap when you see what you're looking for, and then tap the item you want to select.

Your iPhone has many options to make gestures easier for people with visual, auditory, or manual dexterity challenges. You adjust those settings by going to Settings⇨General⇨Accessibility. Read about them in Book I, Chapter 2.

- ✓ **Zooming in and out:** Pinch and spread (unpinch) two fingers together or apart to zoom out and in on photos, web pages, e-mail messages, and other elements.

- ✓ **Sliding:** Slider bars show up when you want to turn your iPhone on or off. They also appear on the lock screen when your iPhone rings. Touch and hold the slider bar on the arrow on the left and slide your finger across the bar to the right. The action listed on the slider bar happens. Some sliding actions take place without a slider bar, such as when you unlock your iPhone as in Figure 3-1; just slide your finger across the screen. Sliding across an item in the Notification Center opens the item, such as a message, e-mail, or tweet.

✔ **Pressing:** Press the physical buttons on your iPhone: the Home, the On/Off Sleep/Wake, or the volume buttons. You switch the Silent/Ring switch on and off. We explain these buttons in Book I, Chapter 2.

✔ **Double-clicking:** Double-clicking the Home button reveals the open apps carousel, which shows apps that are running. You can then tap the app you want to switch to.

✔ **Triple-click Home:** Press the Home button three times to activate functions that are selected in Accessibility Settings: VoiceOver, Invert Colors, Zoom, and/or AssistiveTouch.

Figure 3-1: Use the sliding move to unlock your iPhone.

Home, Away from Home, and Home Again

The Home screen is what you see when your iPhone is awake and you aren't using an app. The Home screen is actually more than one screen. You move between one Home screen and the next by flicking or scrolling left to go to the next screen to the right and flicking or scrolling right to go back. You can have up to 15 Home screens.

The round, slightly depressed button centered beneath the screen is the Home button. When you press this button, different things may happen, depending on your point of departure:

✔ From an open app, you return to the Home screen you most recently viewed, so if you tap an app on the fifth Home screen and then press the Home button, you return to the fifth Home screen.

✔ From the second to the fifteenth Home screen (if you have multiple Home screens), you return to the first Home screen.

✔ When your iPhone is sleeping or locked, pressing the Home button wakes it (refer to Figure 3-1). Slide your finger to the right, and the last screen you were viewing appears. It could be a Home screen or a running app.

Going from top to bottom, the Home screen has a status bar that tells you about the various connections your iPhone is tapped into at the moment, as well as the current time of day. We explain the status bar icons in Book I, Chapter 2. Below the status bar are 20 spaces for apps or app folders (16 on iPhone 4s or earlier). We go over folders in the "Organizing Apps and Folders" section later in this chapter. At the bottom of the screen, you see up to four more app buttons. This area is known as the *dock*. Place four app buttons you use frequently there, and they appear in a fixed position at the bottom of every Home screen. In Figure 3-2 Phone, Mail, Safari, and Music, the preset dock apps, are in the dock.

Status bar

A folder

The Dock

Figure 3-2: The four apps in the dock remain in the same position when you move from one Home screen to another.

There's one other part to the Home screen. Those tiny gray and white dots floating just above the dock indicate how many Home screens you have. The white dot tells you which screen you're on.

Launching and Managing Apps

Apps, short for applications, are sometimes known as programs on your iPhone. Book I, Chapter 4 summarizes the apps that come with your iPhone, and other chapters throughout the book cover each app in depth. The online bonus content for this book presents some third-party apps we think you'll like. (See this book's Introduction for more about the bonus content.) Here, we tell you how to launch and close apps, and how to organize the app buttons on your Home screen.

Launching apps

To launch or open an app on the Home screen, tap the app icon. You can also ask Siri to open an app for you. You may see icons that are squares with tiny app icons on them, as in Figure 3-2; these are folders, which can contain many apps and multiple pages — you see dots at the bottom just like those that indicate the number of Home screens and flick to move between one folder page and another. To launch an app that resides in a folder, tap the folder. It opens. Tap the app button you want to launch. To close the folder, tap it or the Home screen.

Switching between apps

Instead of opening an app, closing it, returning to the Home screen, and then opening another app, you can have multiple apps open at the same time — although you just see one app at a time on your screen. When you double-click the Home button, the open apps carousel appears, as in Figure 3-3. These are the apps that you most recently used that haven't been shut down. This is especially helpful when you want to cut and paste from one app to another, which we explain in the section about using the keyboard.

Flick left and right to move through the apps. Tap the app you want to switch to.

To close an app altogether, double-tap the Home button and then swipe up the app you want to close. Or — check this out — use two or three fingers to close several apps, simultaneously.

It's a good idea to quit apps you're no longer using because they do continue consuming some of iPhone's available memory, processing brainpower, and battery, even when they aren't being used. Call us obsessively compulsive, but both of us authors regularly double-click the Home button and close apps we aren't using.

Organizing Apps and Folders

Your iPhone comes with the included apps displayed on the first two Home screens. You may want to rearrange the apps so that the ones you use most frequently are at the top of the Home screen, you may want to group similar apps in a folder, or you may want to change the apps that are in the dock. As you add new apps, you'll want to arrange them in a way that makes sense to you. You can move apps around on your iPhone and from iTunes.

Organizing apps on your iPhone

To organize apps from your iPhone, follow these steps:

1. **Press and hold any app button on your Home screen.**

   This part is fun, especially if you're new to iPhone. Try it — we'll wait.

Figure 3-3: The open apps carousel lets you switch between open apps without returning to the Home screen.

2. **Any of the apps that have circled Xs on the upper left corner can be deleted. To delete an app, just tap the circled X.**

   A message opens asking if you really want to delete that app, as shown in Figure 3-4. Tap the appropriate button: Delete, if you want to delete that app, or Cancel, if you tapped the circled X by mistake.

Don't worry — if you delete an app by mistake, the App Store maintains a copy of all your apps, free or purchased, so you can reinstall it but you could lose data or documents created with the app if they aren't backed up to your computer or iCloud.

TIP

The Apple apps that came with your iPhone can't be deleted although you can place ones you don't use in a folder so they're out of sight and some of them may be hidden by turning on Restrictions as explained later in this chapter.

3. **Touch and drag the app buttons around to arrange them in a way you like, even from one Home screen to another.**

   The Photos app button is being moved in Figure 3-5.

4. **To change the four apps that are in the**

Figure 3-4: A notification message asks for confirmation before deleting an app.

dock, you first have to drag one out, and then you can replace it with another app.

You don't have to have four apps in the dock. If you prefer three or two or none, you can move the buttons out of the dock onto a Home screen. Or you can place up to four folders on the dock instead of single apps.

Folders

Folders give you the option of putting like-minded apps together in one place so you can find them quickly and easily.

Adding folders

To add a folder, press and hold your finger on an app on the Home screen until they start a-wigglin' and a-jigglin'. Then, follow these steps:

1. **Lift your finger.**

2. **Touch and drag one app button over another app button.**

   A square is formed around both apps as shown in Figure 3-6.

3. **Tap anywhere on the screen outside of the folder.**

   The folder closes.

4. **(Optional) Touch and drag another app into the folder.**

5. **Tap the Home button to save the folder and stop the app dance.**

 If a folder has already been created but you want to add apps to it, press and hold an app to make them wiggle and then drag the app you want into the folder. To remove apps, while the apps are wiggling, tap the folder you want to change to open it. Drag apps out of the folder onto the Home screen. A folder is automatically deleted when all apps are moved out and it's empty.

Figure 3-5: Drag the app icon to the position you want.

Renaming folders

iPhone assigns a name it thinks is appropriate by default, such as Utilities, Productivity, Lifestyle, or Entertainment, based on the kinds of apps you put in the folder, but you can change the name with these steps:

1. **Press and hold an app on the Home screen.**

2. **Tap the wiggling folder whose name you want to edit.**

3. **Tap the circled X on the right of the field where the name is written.**

   The field is erased. A cursor appears at the beginning of the field and the keyboard opens.

4. **Tap out the name you wish to give this folder.**

5. **Tap the Done key on the bottom right of the keyboard.**

6. **Tap outside the folder to close it.**

   The buttons are still wiggling.

7. **Tap the Home button to save the renamed folder.**

   If your apps folder has a badge on the upper right corner, the number on the badge is a cumulative number of items that need attending to, such as unread messages, app updates, or information updates.

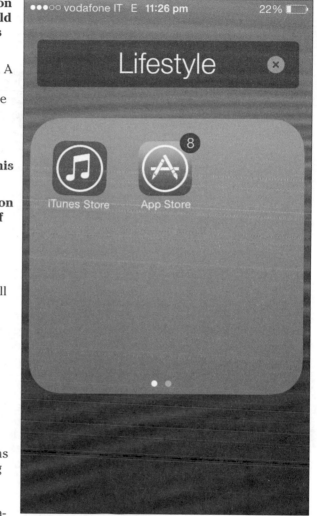

Figure 3-6: Drag one app over another to create a folder.

When you have a lot of apps and folders, moving them around from screen to screen can be tedious. Luckily, you can also organize your Home screens, apps, and folders in iTunes. (See Figure 3-7.) Connect your iPhone to your computer with the USB connector cable, select your iPhone and then Apps. Drag an app from the list to the Home screen or folder where you want it to reside and it moves from its old location to the new one. You can even move an entire Home screen to a new position in the lineup or add a blank Home screen — and you can do those maneuvers only in iTunes. After you make your changes and the Home screens are organized just the way you like, click the Sync button to sync your changes with your iPhone.

Figure 3-7: Organize your apps and folders via iTunes.

Commandeering the Keyboard

For many iPhone users, the keyboard is the hardest thing to get used to — all of a sudden you have gorilla fingers. Don't despair, with a little practice, the keyboard becomes second nature in no time. Any time you tap in a blank field, the keyboard opens and a blinking cursor appears in that empty field. If there's already text in the field, tapping the X on the right end deletes the text. This occurs in apps like Mail, Messages, Notes, or when you're filling out a form on a web page in Safari, and when you're adding contacts and calendar entries when using those respective apps.

The keyboard functions we describe here work in any app that uses the keyboard so, like most things iPhone, after you hone your skills in one app, they apply across the board in all your iPhone apps.

Keyboard settings

The default keyboard has the classic QWERTY format that you may have learned in high school typing class — we're showing our age but that's where we learned how to touch type. If you write in a language other than English, however, you'll want to add a keyboard that reflects the language you want to type in — and recognizes words in that preferred language. You'll get crazy suggestions if you type in Swedish with an English keyboard and dictionary. You also have some other optional keyboard functions that you activate, or deactivate, in Settings. Read below to learn about your options and follow these steps to change them:

1. **Tap Settings on the Home screen.**

2. **Tap General⇨Keyboard.**

   The screen shown in Figure 3-8 opens.

3. **Tap the toggle switch to turn the following functions on or off.**

• **Auto-Capitalization:** Automatically capitalizes the letter "I" when it stands alone and capitalizes the first letter after any punctuation that iPhone recognizes as a new sentence, for example a period or a return. If you use Emoji, this function also capitalizes the first letter after you insert a smiley face, heart, or one of the other myriad icons.

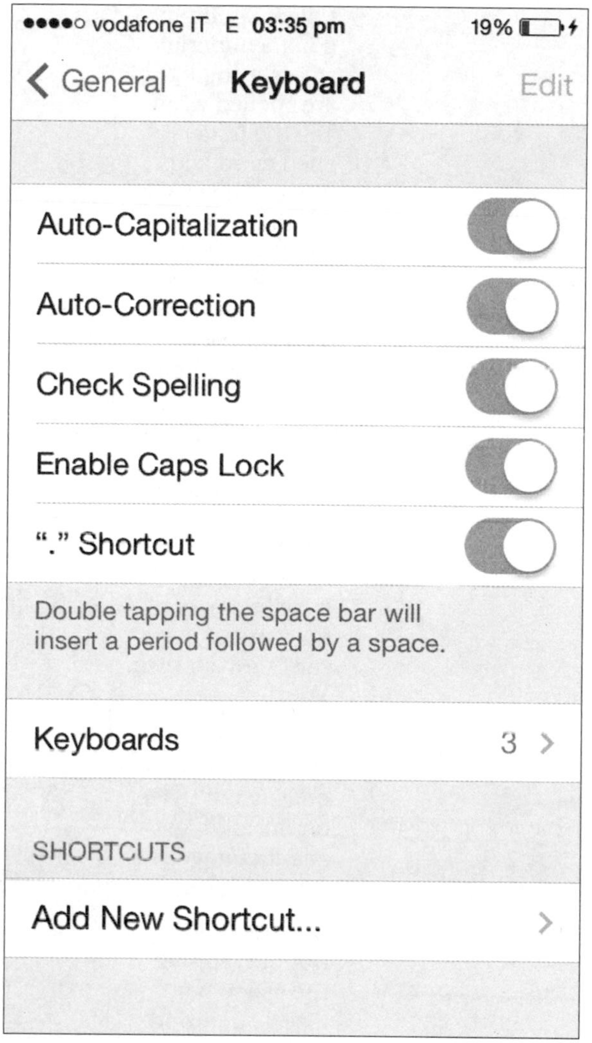

• **Auto-Correction:** Automatically corrects words as you are typing using iPhone's built-in dictionary. For example, as in Figure 3-9, if you type **jome**, "home" appears in a box above the word. If you tap the space bar,

vodafone IT E 03:35 pm	19%	
‹ General	**Keyboard**	Edit

Auto-Capitalization ⬤

Auto-Correction ⬤

Check Spelling ⬤

Enable Caps Lock ⬤

"." Shortcut ⬤

Double tapping the space bar will insert a period followed by a space.

Keyboards 3 ›

SHORTCUTS

Add New Shortcut... ›

Figure 3-8: The Keyboard settings let you control automatic keyboard functions.

the return key, or a punctuation key, the suggestion is accepted; tap the X on the box, or just keep typing to complete your word, and your typed word remains. The dictionary automatically adds names from Contacts so it recognizes many names you type. Your iPhone learns your idiosyncrasies, adding words you type frequently, that it doesn't know, to the dictionary.

- **Check Spelling:**
iPhone underlines
words it thinks
are spelled wrong.
Tap the under-
lined word and
iPhone shows you
possible replace-
ment words. Tap
the one you want
or tap elsewhere
on the screen to
decline. If iPhone
thinks the word is
spelled wrong but
doesn't have a
suggestion, a flag
reads No
Replacement
Found and you
have to correct
the word, if neces-
sary, on your own.

- **Enable Caps
Lock:** When this
is on, you can
quickly tap twice
on the shift key
and it changes to
a caps lock key.

- **"." Shortcut:**
Double-tapping
the space bar
inserts a period
and then one
space.

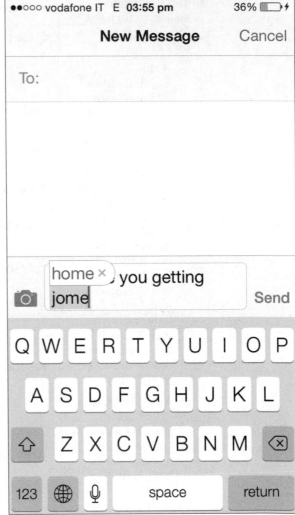

Figure 3-9: Turn Auto-Correction on to get suggestions for presumed typing errors.

4. **To change the
keyboard layout, tap
Keyboards.**

5. **Tap English or whichever language's keyboard you wish to edit.**

    Most languages have optional keyboard layouts. The screen opens and
    displays options for the Software Keyboard Layout, that is the keyboard
    on your iPhone, and for a Hardware Keyboard Layout, which is a periph-
    eral keyboard that you use with your iPhone. You can choose the
    Software Keyboard Layout you're used to using. Choose the Hardware
    Keyboard Layout that corresponds to the type of peripheral keyboard
    you use with your iPhone.

6. **Swipe right or tap Keyboards in the upper left to return to the Keyboards settings.**

7. **Tap Add New Keyboard to add another language-specific keyboard.**

   A list of languages opens. Many languages have multiple options, such as the Chinese handwriting option or the Swiss or Canadian French option.

8. **Tap the language you want to add.**

   It automatically appears in the list of keyboards.

9. **Repeat Steps 7 and 8 to add other languages or tap Keyboard in the upper left to return to the Keyboard settings.**

   To delete a language, tap Edit, and then tap the red and white minus sign to the left of the language. Tap the Delete button that appears. To rearrange the order of the languages, touch and drag the rearrange button (it looks like three stacked horizontal lines) to move the languages to the order you want.

10. **Tap Add New Shortcut.**

    Shortcuts let you type a few letters that your iPhone interprets and expands into a longer phrase. For example, type **omw** in a message and it becomes "On my way!" Type your text in the Phrase and Shortcut text fields and then tap Save.

    If you add a word or phrase to Shortcuts without typing in the shortcut, the word or phrase is added to your Personal Dictionary and iPhone won't make suggestions for correcting it.

    When you turn Documents and Data on in iCloud, your shortcuts sync between iOS devices. PDC! (That's short for "pretty darn cool.")

11. **Tap Keyboard in the upper left, General in the upper left, and then Settings in the upper left to return to the main Settings screen, or swipe right until you reach the screen you want.**

If you have more than one language activated, the keyboard includes a globe button appearing at the bottom. Tap the globe button to switch between languages. Tap and hold the globe button to see a pop-up list of languages you added and then slide to select the language, as shown in Figure 3-10. The languages are in the same order as your keyboards are listed in Settings.

Typing tips

Apple suggests, and we concur, that you begin typing with one index finger, probably that of your dominant hand, and gradually move up to two-finger or two-thumb typing. When you tap a key, the letter appears enlarged on the screen so you know which key you actually hit. If it's the letter you want, just lift your finger and that letter appears on the message, note, or field you're typing in. If it's not the letter you want, without lifting your finger, slide your finger to the key of the letter you want. As you slide, the enlarged letter changes to show which key your finger is on.

As you become familiar with the tap typing technique with your index finger, you may want to try putting iPhone on a flat surface and typing with two index fingers. In the landscape position — where the keys are slightly bigger but the typing field is smaller — you can hold your iPhone with both hands, placing your thumbs at the bottom and your middle fingers at the top. Use both index fingers to type.

For thumb-typing in either portrait or landscape position, cradle your iPhone in both hands, keeping them slightly relaxed, and use your thumbs to type. Of course there's also the I-was-born-texting position: cradling your iPhone in one hand and typing with the cradling hand's thumb. This tactic is particularly useful while standing on a moving bus (or riding in a car, but please don't text and drive).

Figure 3-10: Tap and hold the globe button to choose from languages you activate on your iPhone.

After you get going, iPhone uses an algorithm to predict the word you are typing so zones of letters imperceptibly increase in size to increase the probability that you hit the letter you want.

Keyboard layouts

Looking at the keyboard in Figure 3-11, moving top to bottom, left to right, you see the letters of the alphabet, the shift key, the delete key, the ABC/123 key, the globe key (if you've added a language), the microphone key (if you have an iPhone 4S or later and Siri is turned on), the space bar, and a return key. The keyboard changes slightly depending on what function you want to perform. When you are in a To field in Mail or in the URL field in Safari, the space bar shrinks to allow one or two more buttons next to it: an at (@) button (in Mail) and a dot (.) button (in both). This makes typing an e-mail or website address easier. The Return key becomes the Search button in Spotlight and a Go button in Safari, and sometimes it becomes a Next or Done button when you are filling out forms or signing in to a service. In addition to these visible changes that make typing easier, there are some invisible shortcuts:

- Double-tap the shift key to turn it into a caps-lock key so you can type in ALL CAPS. You have to turn this option on in the Keyboard settings.

- Tap the delete key once to delete one character to the left. Tap and hold the delete key and it begins deleting one letter after another. If you continue holding, it deletes whole words at once.

- Hold the ABC key and slide your finger to the symbol or number you wish to type. The character is typed but the keyboard reverts to letters.

- When the cursor is in the To field and you have the space, at, and dot buttons, touch and hold the dot key and a small window opens offering an assortment of the most common web suffixes: .com, .net, .edu, .org, and so on. If you've added an international keyboard, the local suffixes are included, for example .it for Italy and .eu for European Union.

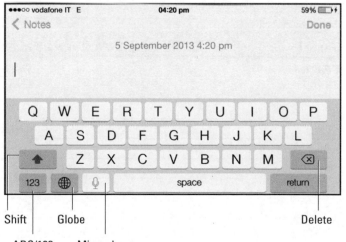

Figure 3-11: Familiarizing yourself with the keyboard layouts makes typing faster and more efficient.

✔ Tap the 123 key to change the keyboard to show numbers, as seen in Figure 3-12. The shift key changes to a symbols key; the 123 key changes to an ABC key. Tap the symbols key and the top row of the keyboard where the numbers were changes to show more symbols, as shown in Figure 3-12. Tap the ABC/123 key to return to the alphabet keyboard; tap the symbols key to switch between numbers and symbols.

Figure 3-12: The letters change to numbers when you tap the ABC/123 key and the numbers change to symbols when you tap the symbols key.

Tap the space bar after typing a number or symbol and the letter keyboard returns.

Some of the letters, when held, give non-English options, and some of the numbers and symbols give multiple options as well, as shown in Table 3-1. These options are from the U.S. English keyboard and may change when you change the keyboard language.

Table 3-1	Special Characters and Symbols
Key Pressed	*Special Character*
A or a	à á â ä æ ã å ā
C or c	ç ć č
E or e	è é ê ë ē ė ę
I or i	ì į ī í ï î
L or l	ł
N or n	ń ñ
O or o	õ ō ø œ ó ò ö ô
S or s	ß ś š
U or u	ū ú ù ü û
Y or y	ÿ

Key Pressed	Special Character
Z or z	ž ź ż
Zero (0)	0
Period	Ellipsis (…)
Question mark (?)	¿
Exclamation point (!)	¡
Apostrophe (')	` ' '
Hyphen/minus sign (–)	– — ·
Forward slash (/)	\
Dollar sign ($)	¥, €, ¢, £, ₩
Ampersand (&)	§
Quote (")	≪ ≫ „ " "
Percentage (found when you tap the symbols button after tapping the numbers button) %	‰

Editing Your Text

The longer you have your iPhone, chances are the more you'll find yourself using it for written communications that you used to create on a computer: e-mail, notes, to do lists, appointments, status updates and posts to your social network of choice, and maybe even longer documents. All this writing means a greater possibility for making mistakes, changing your mind, and wanting to move sentences around — in other words, you want to edit your text. iPhone has the basic editing capabilities of copy, cut, and paste, select or select all, even undoing and redoing. In Mail, you can stylize your text by making it bold, italic, or underlined and indented. We show you how to do each of these tasks in the following sections.

Selecting

You can tap once to insert the cursor somewhere in the middle of your text, and then make changes letter by letter or you can select a word, phrase, paragraph, or the entire text and make changes with this procedure:

1. **Tap the text you want to edit.**

    The keyboard appears and the cursor blinks more or less where you tapped.

2. **Press and hold your finger in the general area where you want to insert the cursor.**

    A magnifying loupe appears over the text with the cursor in the center.

3. **Drag your finger over the text until the cursor is at the point where you want it.**

4. **Lift your finger.**

   Two buttons appear: Select and Select All, and sometimes a third, Paste, when you have cut or copied text from somewhere else.

5. **Tap Select to select the word or portion of the text; tap Select All to select the entire text.**

   The word is highlighted in blue and there are blue grab points on the upper left and lower right corner. (Refer to Figure 3-13.)

   If you select just one word, you can *cut* or *copy* that word, or if you tap the arrow on the far right, iPhone offers to *replace* the word with its idea of auto-correct (for example, for creams, the suggested replacements were dreamy, creaky, or cream's) or *define* the selected word — just tap the appropriate button.

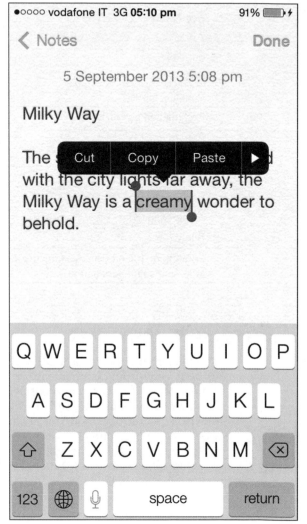

Figure 3-13: Use blue grab points to select the text you want to copy, cut, or replace with a suggested synonym.

If you don't want to use Select or Select All, tap once on the screen and proceed to edit with the delete key and keyboard.

6. **To select a portion of the text, touch and drag the blue grab points to select the text you want to cut or copy.**

7. **If you want to delete, press the cut button. If you want to copy or cut, and paste in another location, read on.**

Cutting, copying, and pasting

What if you want to copy something from an e-mail message you received and paste it onto an existing list in Notes for future reference? Here's how to copy and paste into an existing document:

1. **Following the previous steps to select the text you want to copy.**

   After you've tapped Select or Select All, a Copy button appears above the highlighted text.

2. **Open the document in the app where you want to place the copied text.**

   If, from our example, Notes is already open, then tap the Notes screen in the open apps carousel. Otherwise, press the Home button to open the Home screen and tap Notes from there.

3. **Tap and hold on the screen where you want to insert the copied text.**

   The magnifying loupe appears, allowing you to move the cursor precisely where you want it.

4. **Lift your finger.**

   A Paste button appears.

5. **Tap the Paste button.**

   Your copied text is now in a new spot.

 Copying and pasting isn't only for text within apps like Notes and Mail. You can copy a portion of a web page and paste it into an e-mail. Press and hold the part of the page you want to copy and the blue grabbers come up, along with a Copy button. Drag the grab points to select everything you want to copy, and then tap the Copy button. Open the app where you want to paste the selection. Press and hold until you see the Paste button. Tap Paste.

Undoing and redoing

To undo your edit, shake your iPhone. A message opens with the option to undo the last action or cancel. Tap the Undo button and you're home free. And if you want to redo what you thought you wanted to undo? Just shake your iPhone again and the buttons ask if you want to redo or undo or cancel, as shown in Figure 3-14.

Telling Siri What to Do

Having a personal assistant is no longer just an indispensable luxury for a few busy executives or celebrities. Siri on your iPhone is a close second to her human counterpart. After you establish a rapport with Siri, you may wonder what you ever did without her, er, or him, should you decide to give Siri a male voice. Following is a partial list of things Siri can help you with:

- Make phone calls
- Schedule meetings
- Open apps on your iPhone
- Write and read messages
- Retrieve voicemail messages
- Adjust iPhone settings such as screen brightness or Do Not Disturb
- Relay the weather forecast
- Find a restaurant and request reservations
- Use Find My Friends to see where the people you know are hanging out
- Tell you the score for last night's game and statistics for your favorite player
- Find the nearest movie theater, tell you what's playing, and buy tickets
- Play requested music
- Write your grocery list
- Set up reminders
- Make coffee and take out the trash — just checking if you were paying attention!

Figure 3-14: Shake your iPhone to undo and redo the last edit you did.

Siri requires an Internet connection. When you ask Siri to do something for you, the request is sent to the remote Siri server, which interprets your request and sends the answer back. Siri's response speed depends on the speed of your Internet connection. If you have a 3G or EDGE connection, the action will take longer (sometimes up to 30 seconds) than when you have a Wi-Fi or 4G/LTE connection.

To use Siri, first you have to turn it on by following these steps. While you're in Settings, you can adjust some of the Siri settings:

1. **Tap Settings⇨General⇨Siri.**

2. **Tap On to turn Siri on.**

3. **Adjust the following optional settings:**

   - Tap Language and then tap the language you want to use to speak to Siri.

   - Tap Voice Gender and decide if you want a male or female assistant.

   - Tap Voice Feedback to choose if you want Siri to always repeat what you say. The default is only when you are in Handsfree mode, which is when you speak to Siri while using the headset, a Bluetooth device, or holding your iPhone to your ear. Otherwise you see what you said on the screen.

   - My Info tells Siri who you are. Tap it and Contacts opens; select your Info card. Siri also uses people you indicate as related to better understand your commands. See Book IV, Chapter 1 to learn how to use Contacts.

   - Raise to Speak is a great way to use Siri in public. Tap On. When your iPhone is awake, even if the screen is locked, hold your iPhone upright in your hand and then bring it to your ear; you hear two rapid beeps to let you know Siri is ready to listen. Speak your request. It seems like you're making a phone call rather than talking to your iPhone.

4. **Swipe right or tap General and then Settings in the upper left corner to return to the main Settings screen or press the Home button to return to the Home screen.**

To talk to Siri, do the following:

1. **Press and hold the Home button, the center button on the earphones, or the button on your Bluetooth headset, until you hear the beep and the Siri screen opens.**

   You can do this from the Home screen or from within an app. Siri knows what you're doing and responds appropriately.

   Or, if you turned Raise to Speak On, press the Home button or the Sleep/Wake button to wake your iPhone and then bring your iPhone to your ear.

2. **Two rapid beeps let you know Siri is ready to listen. Following are examples of how Siri uses the apps on your iPhone. You don't have to open the app — just speak when Siri's ready:**

   - *All apps:* Say "Open StarWalk" or "Launch Mail."

   - *Calendar:* View and create events. Ask "Where is my 9 o'clock meeting?" or "Make appointment with Bill Jones for 10 am."

- *Clock:* Set alarms, start the timer, find out the time in another city. Say "Set timer for 25 minutes." You can also simply ask what time it is.

- *Contacts:* Ask for information about your contacts. Ask "What's Jim Rose's address?" If you refer to someone by first name only, Siri looks for matches in Favorites in Contacts and in Conversations in Messages, and then repeats the first and last name asking if it's the correct contact. It's quicker and easier to use both first and last names. Enter names of related people on your info card so Siri knows who "Mom" or "sister" are. Book IV, Chapter 1 is about Contacts.

- *Find My Friends:* Ask Siri where your friends are or who's near your current location.

- *Facebook/Twitter:* Ask Siri to post your status update to Facebook or Twitter, just make sure both are activated in Settings. Ask to search Twitter for a topic or person.

- *Mail:* Search and send e-mail. Say "E-mail Joe Hutsko about deadline."

- *Maps:* Get directions, find addresses. Ask "Where is the nearest Apple Store?" or "Give me directions from here to Paula's house."

- *Messages:* Read and send SMS and iMessages text messages. Say "Tell Darrin Smith I'm on my way."

- *Movies:* Ask "What movies are playing in Philadelphia?" or "What action films were released this week?"

- *Music:* Play artists, albums, playlists, songs, or the new iTunes Radio. Say "Play Blue" or "Play a reggae station."

- *Notes:* Create, search, and edit notes. Say "Note tablecloth is 104 by 84."

- *Phone:* Make a phone or FaceTime call or listen to your voicemail. Say "Call Joe Hutsko" or "Get voicemail."

- *Reminders:* Create, search, and change reminders. Say "Remind me to take book to Jen when I get home."

- *Restaurants:* Say "Make a reservation at Zuni Café for 8 pm Saturday."

- *Safari:* Search the web. Say "Search the web for cold remedies."

- *Sports Information:* Ask "Tell me Pete Rose's best batting average" or "Who won the Pac-10 game last night?"

- *Stocks:* Obtain stock info. Ask "What is the stock price for Apple?"

- *Weather:* Ask for forecasts. Ask "What is today's weather?" or "What's the forecast for Boston next week?"

- *WolframAlpha:* Answer factual, statistical, and mathematical questions. Ask "How fast is the speed of light?"

TIP

These are just a few suggestions to demonstrate Siri's vast capabilities, but we encourage you to experiment — ask Siri "What can I ask you?" to get some ideas. Speak as you would to a person and see how resourceful Siri is when it comes to finding answers and assisting you in your day to day tasks.

3. **Siri makes an audible response and displays what was done on your screen, as shown in Figure 3-15 and 3-16.**

   With the request for an appointment, going to Calendar, you'd see the appointment with Ray at 11 a.m. on the following Wednesday.

   Siri understands different ways of saying the same thing; however, if it's unsure of a command, Siri asks for clarification.

4. **If Siri doesn't understand what you say, you can make corrections by doing the following:**

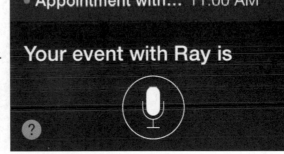

Figure 3-15: Siri reads and displays the response to your request.

- Type corrections in the bubble onscreen that shows what Siri understood or tap the microphone and dictate the correction. Tap Done when you finish.

- If a word is underlined in blue, tap the word and then choose an alternative from the choices, or tap the microphone to dictate the correction.

- Tap the microphone to speak to Siri and clarify your request.

- To correct a message or e-mail before sending, dictate the changes or say "Send it" when it's correct.

5. **If when reading your messages or relaying voicemail, Siri mispronounces a name, say "That's not how you pronounce *name.*"**

   Siri then gives three options, and you can choose the correct one.

6. **To cancel a request, say "Cancel," tap the microphone button, or press the Home button.**

In Settings⇨General⇨ Passcode Lock, you can allow access to Siri even when your iPhone is locked. Doing this, however, compromises some of the Passcode Lock's security features.

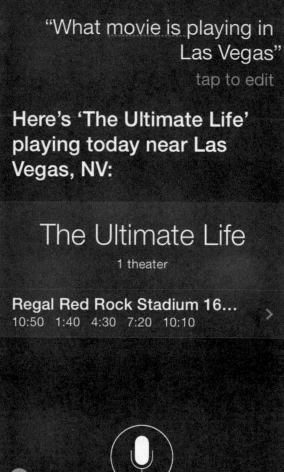

Figure 3-16: Siri finds movies and restaurants.

Siri, take a memo

Any time you want to dictate instead of type, tap the microphone key on the keyboard, dictate, and then tap Done when you finish. Siri understands your dictation best when you dictate punctuation. Pretend you're speaking to a recorder that someone will transcribe. For example, to have Siri type:

Dear John, thank you for the new iPhone 5.

Say: "dear john comma thank you for the new iPhone 5 period"

Likewise to insert paragraphs, quotation marks, and any other punctuation that might be applicable to your dictated missive.

Using Voice Control

If you have an iPhone 4 or are in an area without adequate Internet service, you can still instruct your iPhone to do simple tasks with Voice Control. Voice Control doesn't work if Siri is turned on; to turn Siri off, tap Settings⇨ General⇨Siri⇨Off. Here's how to use Voice Control:

1. **Press and hold the Home button, the center button on the earphones, or the button on your Bluetooth headset, until the Voice Control screen opens, as shown in Figure 3-17.**

   The words that appear on the Voice Control screen are suggestions for commands you can give.

   Two quick beeps let you know that Voice Control is ready to listen to your command.

2. **Speak the name of the person you want to call (or the artist you want to hear).**

   Voice Control replies with the name it understood. If it found more than one match, it reads off a list of the options. Repeat the option you want.

   If you asked for music, iPhone responds with "Playing songs by *artist's or album name*," and begins playing.

Figure 3-17: You can command your iPhone to call someone, play a song, or tell the time with Voice Control.

3. **Repeat the option that you want.**

4. **iPhone dials that person.**

    If Voice Control offers an option you don't want, say "No" or "Cancel." Voice Control closes and you have to start over.

Voice Control also tells time. Press and hold the Home button. When Voice Control opens, ask "What time is it?" Voice Control tells you.

Shining a Light on Spotlight Searches

 Spotlight is iPhone's search feature for finding things stored on your iPhone or on the web. To access Spotlight from any Home screen, flick down from the middle of the screen. Spotlight Search opens on top of the Home screen, as shown in Figure 3-18. Your search criteria can contain numbers, so you can search for a phone number, date, or address. Spotlight searches the apps, which you specify in Settings, on your iPhone for the word, phrase, or number you type. For example, if we type in the name **Bonnie**, a list appears showing all the places where that name was found: contacts named Bonnie, songs by Bonnie Raitt, the Burl Ives song "Wee Bonnie Lass," e-mails exchanged with anyone named Bonnie, appointments with Bonnie or Bonnie birthdays, and any notes we may have jotted down about Bonnie.

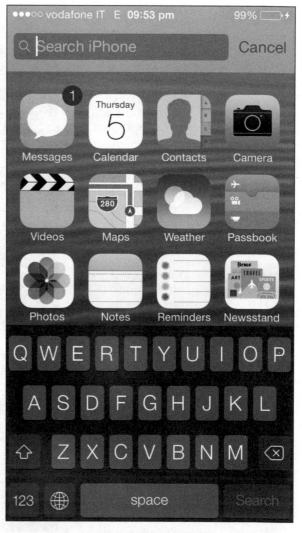

Figure 3-18: Spotlight Search searches all the apps on iPhone for occurrences of a word or phrase.

If Spotlight finds an app with the word you're searching and it's in a folder, the name of the folder is displayed to the right of the result.

You also have access to Spotlight within many apps using the Spotlight search field at the top of an app's screen. In the Mail, Messages, Reminder, or Safari apps, tap the status bar to open Spotlight. In Contacts, the Search field is always visible. In other apps, any time you see the magnifying glass icon, you can tap it to open Spotlight. To search for something within an app, do the following:

1. Tap in the Spotlight field.

If you don't see the Spotlight search field — on app screens that support Spotlight — tap the status bar at the top of iPhone's screen to make the Spotlight search field appear or pull the app screen down to unhide the Spotlight search field when you don't see it.

The blinking cursor appears and the keyboard opens.

2. Type in your word or phrase and then tap Search.

Spotlight searches within the app you're using and displays any items that match your search criteria.

3. Tap an item in the list to view that item's contents.

When you search from within an app, iPhone searches only in that app.

You can alter the Spotlight settings to limit your searches to certain apps or priority order in which the apps are searched. To change Spotlight settings,

1. Open Settings⇨General⇨Spotlight Search.

The Spotlight Search list opens, as seen in Figure 3-19.

2. Tap the name of the app in the list to make the check mark on the left appear or disappear.

A check mark means Spotlight will search that app when looking for something from the Spotlight search screen or within that app.

3. To change the order of the apps, press and hold the rearrange icon to the right of the app, and then drag up and down to move it.

Spotlight searches in the apps at the top of the list first when doing a search.

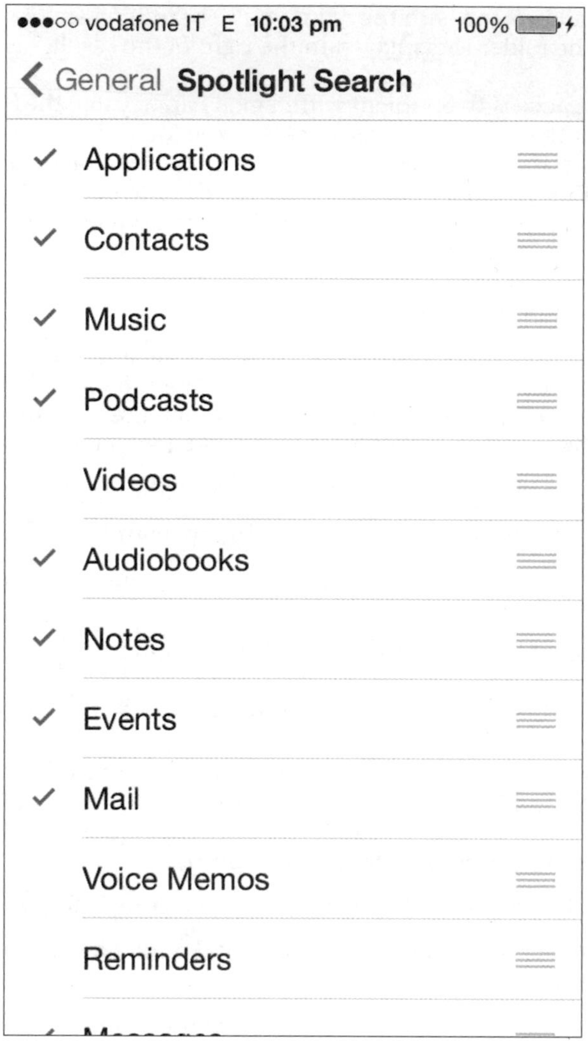

●●●○○ vodafone IT E **10:03 pm**   100% ▭ ▪ ⚡

❮ General **Spotlight Search**

✓   Applications   ☰

✓   Contacts   ☰

✓   Music   ☰

✓   Podcasts   ☰

     Videos   ☰

✓   Audiobooks   ☰

✓   Notes   ☰

✓   Events   ☰

✓   Mail   ☰

     Voice Memos   ☰

     Reminders   ☰

Figure 3-19: Change the priority of your searches in the Spotlight Search settings.

Chapter 4: Touring iPhone's Preloaded Apps and Settings

In This Chapter

✔ Getting to know preloaded apps

✔ Adjusting basic settings to suit your style

✔ Invoking iPhone's security and privacy features

✔ Setting up Touch ID

✔ Averting panic in case your iPhone is lost or stolen

As the name implies, your iPhone is first and foremost a cellular phone. Given its Internet capabilities of browsing the web and juggling e-mail, it's also a first-class smartphone. But you're probably starting to realize — if you didn't already know — that it's so much more. The apps that come with your iPhone make it a time and task manager, an address book, a photo album, an e-reader, and a GPS navigator. This chapter introduces you to those apps, as well as every other preloaded app. We also tell you about a few free iPhone apps that don't come preloaded on your iPhone that we think should.

We close this chapter by showing you how to adjust your iPhone's basic settings to suit your personal style, explaining how to activate security features, including the Touch ID fingerprint sensor on iPhone 5s, to protect your iPhone from prying eyes, and introducing you to steps you can take to track down your iPhone (and even remotely erase your personal information) if your beloved gadget is ever lost or stolen.

Tapping into iPhone's Pre-installed Apps

Right out of the box, your iPhone is preloaded with a gaggle of great apps that can do just about everything except fold your laundry or take your dog for a walk. After you're familiar with your iPhone's user interface and multitouch gestures, getting acquainted with the basic purpose and features of iPhone's apps can help you choose which apps you want to use right away.

When you turn on your iPhone for the first time, you see iPhone's apps arranged on the first Home screen page in a way Apple's iPhone designers figured probably makes sense for most people, as shown in Figure 4-1. We write about how to organize the Home screen in a way that makes sense to you, in Book I, Chapter 3.

Here's a roll-call rundown of your iPhone's apps, with bite-size descriptions of what each app can do, and pointers to the chapters you can read to learn more about each app:

Figure 4-1: iPhone's main Home screens display built-in apps and app folders.

- **Messages:** Use this app to send, receive, and manage SMS (Short Message Service) text messages, MMS (Multimedia Message Service) messages, and iMessages that can include photos, videos, contact information, web links, and map locations. (See Book III, Chapter 2.)

- **Calendar:** Create, manage, and share calendars that you can keep in sync with calendars you maintain on your Mac or Windows PC, your other iOS devices, and with any online calendars you access using iCloud, Microsoft Exchange, and Google Calendar accounts. (See Book IV, Chapter 2.)

- **Contacts:** Contacts helps you create, view, and manage contact information to keep track of people and company names, addresses, phone numbers, e-mail addresses and instant messaging account names, birthday and anniversary dates, and other contact-related bits of information. (See Book IV, Chapter 1.)

✔ **Camera:** Take normal, square, and panoramic photos and instantly add special effects filters (iPhone 5 models) and record videos. Share the results with others via Messages, Mail, Facebook, Twitter, Flickr, or Vimeo. (See Book V, Chapter 1.)

✔ **Photos:** View, share, manage, add filters, and edit photos and videos captured with your iPhone, copied from your computer, saved from other apps, or downloaded from Photo Stream. Printing photos, viewing photos as a slideshow, assigning a photo to a contact card, or choosing a photo as your iPhone's wallpaper are just a few things you can do with Photos. (See Book V, Chapter 1.)

✔ **Videos:** Watch and listen to music videos, movies, and TV shows; stream video content to your AppleTV or connect your iPhone to a monitor or HDTV with the Lightning Digital AV adapter. (See Book V, Chapter 4.)

✔ **Maps:** Locate and view your current location on a map, and get turn-by-turn directions from one place to another with traffic conditions and information about a location. Bookmark, or save as a contact, or share locations. (See Book IV, Chapter 3.)

✔ **Weather:** View current weather conditions, including humidity level, real and perceived temperature, and wind direction, a 12-hour hourly forecast, plus a five-day forecast for one or more locations around the world. (See Book IV, Chapter 3.)

✔ **Passbook:** Manage your store cards, coupons, and boarding passes. Present the bar code in Passbook at the cashier or check-in counter to earn points, pay for purchases, and take advantage of discounts. (See Book II, Chapter 2.)

✔ **Notes:** Create, view, and manage text notes you can sync over the air using your iCloud, Gmail, Yahoo!, or Microsoft Exchange account. Copy and paste text to and from notes with other apps and share and print Notes. (See Book IV, Chapter 4.)

✔ **Reminders:** Create and manage an interactive to-do list. Add deadlines and locations, and set up alerts so you know when you have to be somewhere. (See Book IV, Chapter 2.)

✔ **Clock:** View the current time in your present location and other locations with World Clock; use Alarm to wake you up; tap Stopwatch to track a timed event, and use Timer to count down the hours, minutes, and seconds remaining 'til the cows come home. (See Book IV, Chapter 2.)

✔ **Newsstand:** Keep your magazine, newspaper, and journal subscriptions in one place. Connect to the Newsstand store to download the periodical's app and then subscribe in-app. (See Book II, Chapter 2.)

✔ **iTunes Store:** Browse, search, preview, and purchase music, movies, TV shows, ringtones, and audio books; rent movies; Genius makes recommendations for music, movies, and TV shows. iTunes Match upgrades existing music to better quality audio files, and iTunes Radio offers customized listening. (See Book V, Chapter 2.)

✒ **App Store:** Search, browse, and read reviews of thousands of apps that you can download for free or a fee. Review and download updates to installed apps you already own. (See Book II, Chapter 2.)

✒ **Settings:** Not really an app, but the place to go to customize features for all the apps on your iPhone, not to mention the functions and features of the iPhone itself.

✒ **Calculator:** Add, subtract, multiply, and divide with the basic keypad, or turn iPhone sideways to reveal a wider-ranging scientific calculator keyboard; copy and paste numbers to and from the calculator display. (See Book IV, Chapter 3.)

✒ **FaceTime:** Use this app to make audio and video calls to your friends with iDevices or Macs using the cellular data or Wi-Fi service. (See Book III, Chapter 1.)

✒ **Game Center:** View and compare your game score rankings and achievements with friends and leaderboard top scores; invite friends and new opponents from around the world to compete in multiplayer games; and find Game Center-savvy games to play. (See Book II, Chapter 2.)

✒ **Utilities (folder):** Not an app, the Utilities icon is actually a folder containing other apps, as shown in Figure 4-2. The following apps may be in the Utilities folder or on the Home screen:

• **Compass:** Find out which direction you're facing, view your longitude and latitude coordinates, and switch between True North and Magnetic North bearings. Swipe across the Compass to open a level. (See Book IV, Chapter 3.)

• **Voice Memos:** Record and replay spoken or other in-the-moment sounds you want to capture and listen to again; share your recorded ramblings or even convert them to ringtones. (See Book IV, Chapter 4.)

• **Stocks:** Stay on top of stock prices, track trading summaries, and view detailed market data and news. (See Book IV, Chapter 3.)

✒ **Phone:** Use this app to place and answer calls, and even block callers you don't want to contact you. Create, search, and edit Contacts, record your voicemail personal greeting and listen to, reply to, and manage voicemail messages. (See Book III, Chapter 1.)

✒ **Mail:** Send, receive, and manage e-mail messages for multiple e-mail account types, including Microsoft Exchange, Gmail, Yahoo!, AOL, and Outlook.com. Send, receive, and download media attachments. (See Book III, Chapter 2.)

✒ **Safari:** Access and view websites; share links you like; create a reading list that you can return to when you have more time; read without distraction in Reader; switch between web page windows; create and manage bookmarks, and sync your bookmarks and tabs between iPhone and Safari or Internet Explorer on your computer or other iDevices; view, save, and print web pages, photo files, PDF and other document files. (See Book III, Chapter 3.)

✔ **Music:** Listen to your music and audio books through your iPhone speaker, earphones, Bluetooth speakers, or external speakers connected to your iPhone. (See Book V, Chapters 2 and 3.)

✔ **Nike + iPod:** This app icon won't appear until you turn on the Nike + iPod feature in Settings (tap Settings⇨Nike + iPod, and then tap the On/Off button.) Use this app to record and monitor your walking and running workouts when linked to the Nike + iPod sensor tucked into the foot bed of your Nike+ running shoes (sensor and shoes sold separately); upload your workout data to the Nike+ website to view past workouts and track progress toward your running goals.

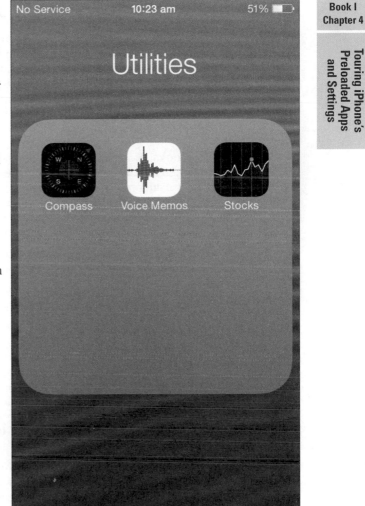

Figure 4-2: Tapping the Utilities folder reveals more apps stored inside the folder.

✔ Want the same Nike + iPod workout goodness, minus having to spend big bucks to buy the sensor and sneakers? Head over to iPhone's App Store and install the "Nike+ Running" app (free), which uses your iPhone's built-in GPS feature to track your location, pace, and distance instead of relying on the Nike+ sensor and shoe combo. Although math was always Joe's worst subject, the way he sees it, if $E = MC^2$, then Nike+ = Nike + iPod - $100 = :-).

Downloading Extra Apple iPhone Apps

While we're talking about apps, we want to introduce you to a few free Apple apps that aren't pre-installed on your iPhone. The first three apps work with media you can download from the iTunes Store so it seems fitting that we mention them. The first time you use the App Store app, a notification asks "Would you like to download free Apple apps?" so you may already have some of these apps. If not, you can download them from the App Store, which we explain in Book II, Chapter 2.

- ✔ **iBooks:** iBooks acts as your virtual doorway to Apple's iBooks Store, where you can download free classics in e-book form, like *Great Expectations* and *War and Peace*, as well as purchase the latest bestsellers and other e-books. You can also read PDF and e-pub documents downloaded from other sources such as Project Gutenberg (www.gutenberg.org/). (See Book V, Chapter 2.)

- ✔ **Podcasts:** Browse the podcast catalog to find audio and video podcasts that interest you and stream, download, and subscribe. (See Book V, Chapter 3.)

- ✔ **iTunes U:** iTunes U manages all your coursework materials, such as videos, podcasts, e-books, and presentations. iTunes U links to the iTunes Store so you can find, subscribe to, and download iTunes U lectures you want to learn from. (See Book V, Chapter 2.)

- ✔ **Find My iPhone:** In the unhappy event your iPhone is lost or stolen, all may not truly be lost if you have the Find My iPhone feature turned on. The Find My iPhone app is not required to use the Find My iPhone feature, but lets you manage and track other iPhones or iPads. It's just so handy to have on hand to see those other gadgets, or to help a friend who may have misplaced or lost his iPhone. We tell you how to use the Find My iPhone feature and app at the end of this chapter.

- ✔ **Apple Store:** Browse and order Apple products online and have them shipped to your doorstep — or reserve them at your nearest Apple Store and then drop in to fetch your new goods in person, with directions to the store brought to you by your iPhone's own Map app. The Apple Store app also lets you make a date for One on One training, or reserve a seat at the genius bar or at upcoming events and training workshops.

- ✔ **Remote:** Taps into your home Wi-Fi network to turn your iPhone into a remote control for browsing and playing content stored in your computer's iTunes library or controlling AppleTV with a better user interface than the remote that ships with Apple TV.

 If you bought a new iPhone with iOS 7 (after September 2013), you can download complimentary copies of Apple's iWork apps — Pages, Keynote, and Numbers — and iLife apps — iMovie, GarageBand, and iPhoto. If you updated an existing iPhone from iOS 6 to iOS 7, you can still purchase those apps separately from the App Store. We talk about iWork apps in Book IV, Chapters 3 and 4 and iLife apps in Book V, Chapters 1 and 4.

Adjusting iPhone's Settings

We mention the non-app customize-your-iPhone button previously: Settings. Here you adjust iPhone's numerous settings to suit your style, including date and time, screen brightness, default ringtone, and background wallpaper image options (to name a few). Turn various networking features on and off; tweak individual app settings and choose which ones can access your location or send you notification messages; create and manage e-mail, contacts, calendar, and notes accounts; manage iCloud syncing and backup; and view information about your iPhone's system software, usage, and capacity. Settings is command central for just about everything your iPhone does.

Throughout this book's many chapters, we show you how to access and adjust iPhone's individual app settings on a need-to-know basis. For instance, in Book III, Chapter 1, we show how to adjust iPhone's Phone settings to turn on (or off) features like call forwarding and whether your Caller ID is displayed when you place calls to others.

Some settings, such as the image that appears behind the buttons on the Home screen — referred to as *wallpaper* — can be changed in more than one way. For instance, when you capture a photo with Camera, you can then choose that snapshot as your Home screen or Lock screen (or both) wallpaper image. Using the Photos app to browse images you copied from your computer is another way to change iPhone's wallpaper setting.

In the rest of this chapter, we show you how to change the basic settings you may want to change now or later, straight up, no stumbling-upon necessary.

Tap Settings to display iPhone's list of settings, as shown in Figure 4-3, and then scroll up and down the list and tap on one you want to change. We go through each setting here in order of appearance, and where we don't go into detail, we direct you to the chapter in which it's discussed.

From the first Settings screen, you tap into a specific options screen and from there you often tap again. You see the disclosure triangle (>) symbol that, when tapped, displays the selected setting's individual options (and, in some cases, additional sub-settings options for that selected top-level setting). There are two ways to back out of those screens:

- ✔ **Tap** the button in the upper left corner, it displays the name of the previous screen and you can tap, tap, tap until you reach the very first Settings screen.

- ✔ **Flick** right, as if turning back pages in a book with an index finger.

Airplane Mode

Airplane Mode is a top-level setting that features a single On/Off button.

Think of the Airplane Mode setting as your one-stop, instant-cut-off switch for immediately disconnecting every one of your iPhone's wireless connection "cords" in one fell swoop. You find an Airplane Mode button in the Control Center, too.

When turned on, the airplane icon appears in the status bar, indicating Airplane Mode's "no fly" zone is in effect.

This setting is called Airplane Mode because nearly every airline requires that you turn off all wireless devices while your journey is underway—they may request you turn all electronic devices completely off during take-off and landing. In the case of your iPhone, hitting the Airplane Mode switch turns off the following wireless connection features:

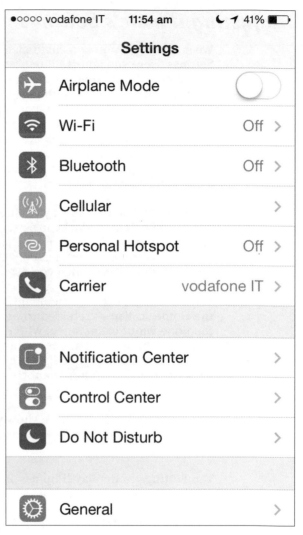

Figure 4-3: Tapping into iPhone's list of Settings.

- ✓ **Cellular voice and data**
- ✓ **Wi-Fi**
- ✓ **Bluetooth**

When Airplane Mode is on, you can't make or receive phone calls or messages, or browse the web or check your e-mail. Nor can you use wireless Bluetooth accessories like Apple's Bluetooth Wireless Keyboard, headsets, and headphones.

But that doesn't mean you can't use your iPhone to do things like listen to music or watch a movie (with wired earphones so as not to disturb fellow passengers, of course), read an e-book in iBooks, or play a favorite game.

Although most airlines require you to turn off wireless features on devices like notebook computers and smartphones like your iPhone, some airlines that offer in-flight Wi-Fi networks do let you turn on your gadget's Wi-Fi option to connect to the network while you're high in the sky. In those instances, you can turn on Airplane Mode to turn off your iPhone's wireless features, and then turn the Wi-Fi setting back on, individually.

Wi-Fi, Bluetooth, Personal Hotspot, Carrier

These settings are presented in the "Making Connections" section of Book I, Chapter 2.

Notifications

The upside, or downside, of the devices and gadgets we surround ourselves with is that we can learn about every tidbit of every person or event that interests us seconds after something happens. On your iPhone, Notifications offer a combination of sounds, alert messages, and badges that can appear on the Lock screen, the Home screen, over the status bar while you're using an app, and in the Notification Center. For each app that is somehow connected with the world, you can select how, when, and where you want to be alerted when something happens or you can choose not to be alerted at all. The great thing about notifications is they grab your attention even if the app that's doing the attention-grabbing isn't running, as illustrated by Figure 4-4.

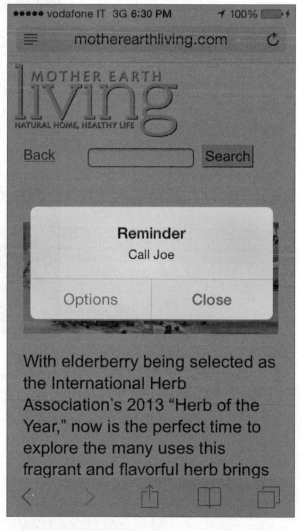

Figure 4-4: Notifications update you about apps even when you're using other apps.

The Notification Center is a central location where all notifications are saved until you remove them. Hidden from view but always available, it appears when you pull or swipe down from the very top of the screen from the Lock screen, any Home screen, or app. If the app is in landscape view, swipe down from the top of that view.

Notice the three tabs across the top of the Notification Center as shown in Figure 4-5, tapping each one displays information based on the settings you choose:

- ✔ **Today:** Tap to show the items you have selected for the Today View, such as the weather forecast, any appointments you have scheduled for the day, and the current stock activity.

- ✔ **All:** Tap to display all notifications, read or unread, from the apps you have associated with the Notification Center.

Figure 4-5: The Notifications Center keeps all your notifications in one place.

- ✔ **Missed:** Tap to see only the unread notifications from apps you show in the Notification Center.

We explain responding to notification messages in Book I, Chapter 2; here, we explain how to designate the type of notifications you want to receive for each app that offers notification options. With so many options, it can seem somewhat complicated at first, but after you set your preferred notification settings for the first few apps, you get the hang of it.

1. **Tap Settings⇨Notifications.**

   The Settings are divided into sections.

2. **Select what you wish to see in the Notification Center when you access it from the Lock screen. You can choose one, none, or both of the following:**

   - *Notifications View:* Shows any notifications or alerts received from apps such as Messages, Mail, or Facebook.

   - *Today View:* Shows the items you want to see when you tap the Today tab.

   If you turn both options on, you see the Notification Center tabs as in Figure 4-5; if you turn only one option on, you see only that information, without the tabs.

3. **In the Today View section, tap the items you want to see On or Off:**

   - *Today Summary:* Displays the weather forecast and the next appointment you have as scheduled in Calendar.

   - *Next Destination:* Referring to locations you assign to appointments in Calendar, tells you where your next appointment will be.

   - *Calendar Day View:* Displays the entire day from Calendar, even if it's blank.

   - *Reminders:* Shows you Reminders you have designated for today.

   - *Stocks:* Displays current market activity for stocks and markets you follow, as designated in the Stocks app.

   - *Tomorrow Summary:* Tells you what events are scheduled for the next day.

4. **Tap either Manually or By Time in the Notifications View section to choose how notifications are sorted in the Notification Center.**

5. **Refer to Figure 4-6, and notice how apps on your iPhone are divided into two sections: Include and Do Not Include.**

6. **Tap the name of each app in the list to choose if and how you want that app to send you notifications.**

   A screen similar to the one in Figure 4-7 opens. Do the following:

   1. Choose the Alert Style you wish the app to use:

      - *None* means you don't want any alerts from this app.

      - *Banners* appear across the top of the Home screen or app you are using, and then automatically disappear after a few seconds.

      - *Alerts* appear in the center of the screen and require an action before they disappear.

2. Tap the Badge App Icon On if you want to see the numbered badge on the right shoulder of the app's icon on the Home screen. Those numbers tell you, for example, how many unread e-mail messages you have in Mail or how many missed calls and unprocessed voicemails you have in Phone.

3. Tap Notification Center On if you want to see alerts from this app in the Notification Center.

   The app then appears in the Include list on the previous screen.

   Tap Include, which appears only if Notification Center is On, to choose how many items from this app you want listed in the Notification Center. For example, if you choose 5 for Mail, you see the five most recent messages you received in Mail listed in the Notification Center.

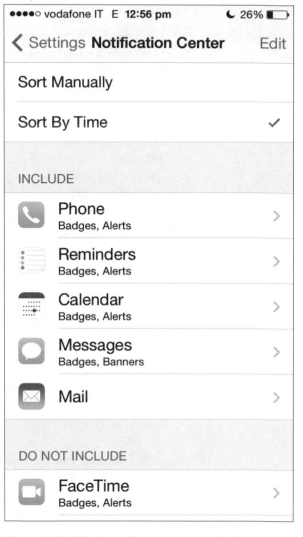

Figure 4-6: Notification settings on a per-app basis.

4. Show on Lock Screen (scroll down to see this option), when On the alert style you chose will appear on the Lock Screen when you wake your iPhone.

   Apps in the Include section appear in the Notification Center when something happens, but you can still receive alerts (badges, banners, or alerts) from apps in the Do Not Include section. For example, if you turn Notification Center Off for Messages but leave badges and banners on, when a new message arrives, you will see the numbered badge on the Message button on the Home screen and a banner will appear on the screen for a few seconds. No record of the message appears in the Notification Center.

5. (Optional for some apps.) Tap Sounds (Ringtone in Phone, Text Tone in Messages, Alerts in Reminders and Calendar) to choose what you want to hear when something new happens in that app. Choosing different sounds for different apps helps you identify which app wants your attention. Some things to know:

   • Apps like Phone, Messages, Reminders, and Calendar offer more options. We review these in the "Sounds" section later in this chapter.

   • If both vibration and tone is available you can have one, both, or none.

   • Almost all apps that have just a Sound option play the pre-established sound that came with the app, a few allow you to choose it. You can turn it On or Off.

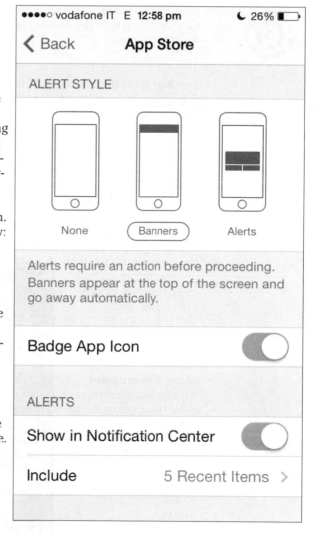

Figure 4-7: Set notifications for each app that has a notifications option.

6. You may see other Notifications options, which vary from app to app. For example, Messages and Mail have a Show Preview option, which, when turned On, displays a few lines of the message in the notification. Photos includes Photo Stream Alert options.

7. Tap the Notifications button in the upper left corner to return to the previous screen, and then scroll through and tap the apps in both the In Notification Center and Not in Notification Center lists, repeating steps 1 through 6.

Some apps offer additional notification settings options that you find by tapping the app in the first level of Settings and then tapping Notifications.

7. **Tap the Edit button.**

8. **Tap and hold the rearrange button to the right of the app name, and then drag the app up or down to reorder the list as it will appear in the Notification Center.**

9. **Tap Done.**

10. **Tap Settings in the upper left or flick right to return to the Settings screen.**

Some apps and widgets behave in a particular way in the Notification Center:

✔ **Weather:** Shows the local weather based on your location (as long as Location Services are turned on).

✔ **Stocks:** Displays a ticker tape of the stocks that you follow.

✔ **Show Government Alerts:** Some carriers offer this option in selected areas. In the U.S., on an iPhone 4S or later you can choose to receive presidential alerts, AMBER alerts, and/or Emergency Alerts.

Control Center

The Control Center gives you quick access to the most commonly used Settings such as Airplane Mode, Do Not Disturb, screen brightness, play-back volume, and several apps, including a nifty flashlight and the Camera app. The Control Center, as shown in Figure 4-8,

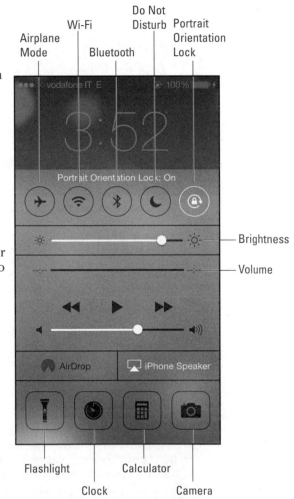

Figure 4-8: Just drag and tap to turn on settings from the Control Center.

appears when you swipe up from the bottom of the screen, and tapping the buttons that appear activates that setting or opens the app. Pull down from the arrow at the top to close the Control Center. In these settings, you can choose to access the Control Center from the Lock Screen and from within apps; just tap the switch On next to both options.

Do Not Disturb

Barbara uses Do Not Disturb on a daily, er, nightly, basis. Living in one time zone and working in another means messages and calls sometimes come in at 3 in the morning; she sets Do Not Disturb to enjoy an interruption-free night's sleep. Incoming calls are forwarded to voicemail and alerts for incoming Messages or other apps that audibly vie for your attention are silenced. You can adjust Do Not Disturb settings to allow calls to come through while blocking other alerts.

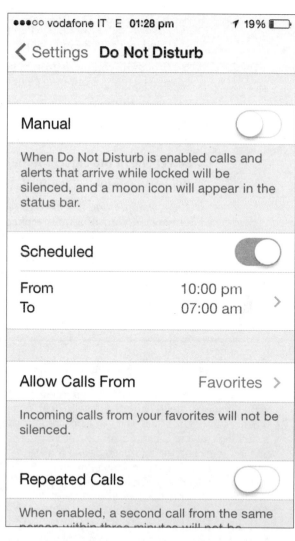

You can also manually turn on Do Not Disturb when you need some time without any intrusions or disruptions from your iPhone. Simply tap Settings➪Do Not Disturb➪Manual ON or swipe up from the bottom of the screen to open the Control Center and tap the Do Not Disturb button. To automatically activate Do Not Disturb at a scheduled time every day, follow these steps:

1. **Tap Settings➪Do Not Disturb to reach the screen as shown in Figure 4-9.**

Figure 4-9: Schedule automatic Do Not Disturb times.

2. **Tap Scheduled to the On position and then tap the From/To field to open a Quiet Hours (love that!) rotor where you choose the starting and ending time for Do Not Disturb to automatically activate.**

3. **Tap Back in the upper left to return to the previous screen.**

4. **Tap Allow Calls From.**

   A list of options appears that include

   - *Everyone:* This lets calls come through but blocks other alerts, such as incoming messages and Facebook updates.

   - *No One:* Silences all incoming calls and messages.

   - *Favorites:* Allows calls to come through only from people you've identified as Favorites in Contacts (see Book IV, Chapter 1).

   - *Groups:* If you have groups set up in Contacts, you can choose to receive calls from people in one or more group.

5. **Tap Back in the upper left to return to the previous screen.**

6. **Tap Repeated Calls On if you want to let a second call from the same number within three minutes to come through.**

7. **Select one of the choices in the Silence section (scroll down to see it):**

   Always to activate Do Not Disturb whether you're using your iPhone or not.

   Only while iPhone is locked to silence incoming calls and notifications only when your iPhone is locked. For example, if someone calls while you're looking something up on Safari, your phone will ring.

8. **Tap Settings in the upper left, or swipe right, to return to the Settings screen.**

 A quarter moon icon rises in the status bar to indicate Do Not Disturb is on.

Switching between portrait and landscape views

You might have noticed that if you rotate your iPhone 90 degrees to the left or right, the screen rotates too. This is considered switching between a portrait, or vertical, view and a landscape, or horizontal, view. Many games, as well as movies viewed in Videos, work only in landscape view. Some apps and the Home screen work only in portrait view. The pre-installed apps that can be viewed in both portrait and landscape are Safari, Mail, Messages, Maps, Notes, Contacts, Stocks, Photos, Camera, Calculator (changes to a scientific calculator in landscape view), Calendar (changes to a multiday calendar in landscape view), and Music in playback mode.

You can lock your iPhone so it stays in portrait view by tapping the Portrait Orientation Lock button in the Control Center. A lock appears to show that Portrait Orientation Lock is on and the same icon appears in the status bar to remind you it's on. See Figure 4-8.

Repeat the steps to turn Portrait Orientation Lock off.

General

The General setting screen shown in Figure 4-10 is actually a catch-all for more than a dozen individual settings — most of which we write about in greater detail in the chapters where those settings are called into play. Instead of giving you tap-by-tap instructions, the following list provides details for settings you won't find explained elsewhere in this book and points you in the right direction for the settings that are fully explained in other chapters.

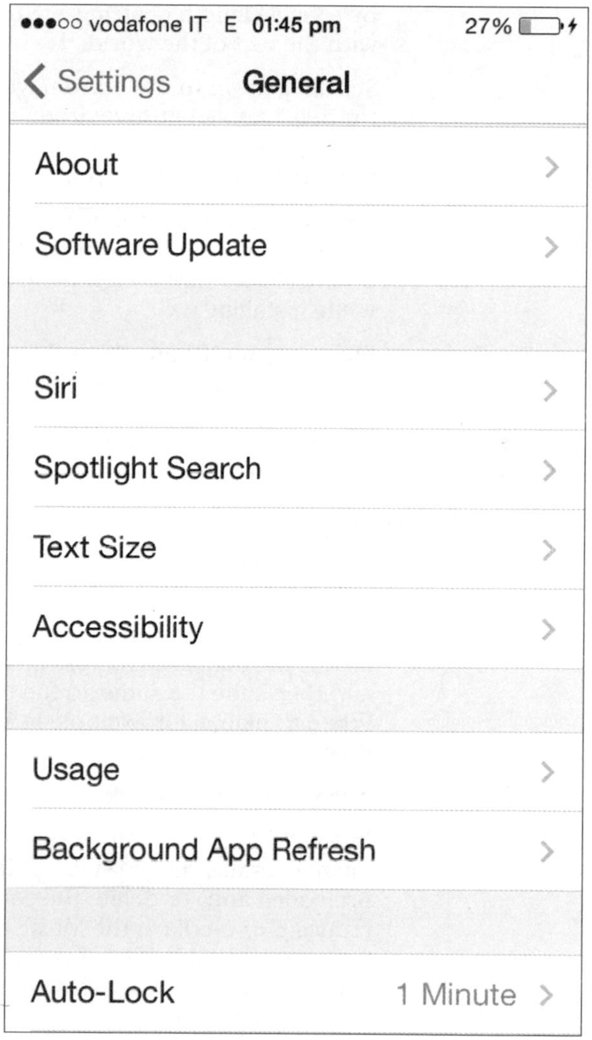

Many settings in Settings have multiple levels. Tap the arrow, also known as the disclosure triangle, to the right of the item to go to a deeper level and see more options; tap the button in the upper left of the screen, or flick right, to return to the previous screen.

●●●○○ vodafone IT E 01:45 pm   27% ⬛▸⚡

❮ Settings   General

About   ❯

Software Update   ❯

Siri   ❯

Spotlight Search   ❯

Text Size   ❯

Accessibility   ❯

Usage   ❯

Background App Refresh   ❯

Auto-Lock   1 Minute ❯

Figure 4-10: Speaking of General settings.

✔ **About:** Tap Name to change your iPhone's name. Beneath that, view detailed information about your iPhone that includes serial number, phone carrier, hardware model and software versions, the number of songs, photos, videos, and applications, the total amount of memory space storing all of those things is gobbling up (and how much memory space remains), a bunch of interesting-looking regulatory logos and glyph-like symbols that are sort of like virtual passport stamps, and page after page of tiny legal gobblygook describing a panic-inducing laundry list of permissions, rules, regulations, warnings, disclaimers, and outright threats that, were you to actually read all of it, would probably scare you so badly you'd wind up ditching your phone contract, selling or giving away your iPhone, and switching to tribal bongos or tin cans connected by a single length of string as your preferred mode of communicating with the rest of the world.

Scrolling down to the bottom, you find Diagnostics & Usage. If you want to "help" Apple improve products by letting them know how you use your iPhone, tap Automatically Send. If you'd rather keep your business to yourself, tap Don't Send.

✔ **Software Update:** If a new version of the operating system, also known as iOS, is available, tapping this button downloads and installs it to your iPhone. Make sure your iPhone is connected to a power source and Wi-Fi while installing.

✔ **Siri (Only on iPhone 4S and later):** Turn Siri On or Off and choose how you interact with Siri. See Book I, Chapter 3.

Siri can adjust many of your iPhone settings but needs to be on to enable dictation and receive requests.

✔ **Spotlight Search:** For choosing which apps (and app contents) Spotlight searches, and the order in which they will be searched. See Book I, Chapter 3.

✔ **Text Size:** Certain apps support something called Dynamic Type, which means the text size changes based on your preferences. Tap this option and then slide the slider to the text size that's comfortable for your eyes. When available, for example in Mail, Messages, Contacts, and Reader, the text will appear in the size you set.

✔ **Accessibility:** See Book I, Chapter 2.

✔ **Usage:** Lists how much storage each app on your iPhone uses and how much overall storage remains. Tap an app to delete the app (if it isn't a preloaded app) or delete the contents of an app, such as courses in iTunes U or media in the Music app. If you activated iCloud, you see the total and available iCloud storage amounts (refer to Book II, Chapter 1 to learn about iCloud). Discloses how long you've used your iPhone since its last full charge.

The most useful button is, perhaps, the Battery Percentage setting. When you turn this setting on, it pins an estimated-percentage-remaining figure alongside your iPhone's pretty vague battery charge level indicator in the status bar or on the Lock Screen when the battery is being charged.

✔ **Background App Refresh:** When On, apps that pull information from the Internet, such as Weather or Stocks, or use Location Services, for example Reminders, will refresh even when they aren't open so you have up to date information when you do open them or so they can send you location-based updates. You can turn the function on for specific apps, which helps conserve both battery and cellular data usage.

✔ **Auto Lock, Passcode Lock (Passcode and Fingerprint on 5s), and Restrictions:** We cover these in the next section, but in a nutshell, you use this trio of settings for choosing the length of time your iPhone waits before automatically locking the screen, for creating a secret passcode that must be keyed in to unlock your iPhone, for setting up fingerprint recognition on an iPhone 5, and for activating and managing a slew of options for blocking (we mean, ahem, restricting) functions with a password.

✔ **Date & Time:** See Book IV, Chapter 2.

✔ **Keyboard:** See Book I, Chapter 3.

✔ **International:** Choose the written and spoken language you wish to use with your iPhone. Tap Region Format to set how dates, times, and phone numbers are displayed in apps that use that information.

✔ **iTunes Wi-Fi Sync:** To sync your iPhone with iTunes without using the USB connector cable, tap Wi-Fi Sync and then tap Sync Now. See Book II, Chapter 1.

✔ **Reset:** See Book 1, Chapter 5.

Sounds

With the number of notifications and alerts you can receive, assigning different sounds to each one can help you distinguish which ones need immediate attention and which can be attended to later. The most obvious sound your iPhone makes is that of an incoming call. By default, your iPhone is set to vibrate whenever a call comes in. You can choose whether you want that good vibration when your phone rings or when it's in silent mode or both or none, as shown in Figure 4-11.

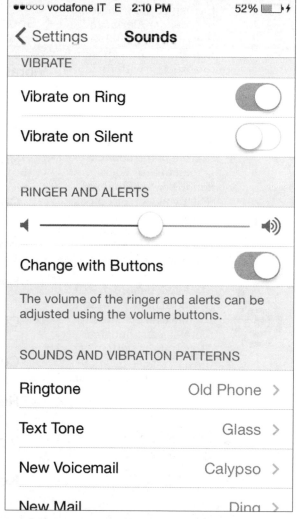

Figure 4-11: Checking out your Sounds settings options.

In the Ringer and Alerts section, dragging the volume slider left or right to decrease or increase ringtone and alert message sounds has the same effect as pressing your iPhone's actual volume buttons up or down. Turn off Change with Buttons if you don't want your iPhone's physical buttons (or, if plugged in, headset volume buttons) to change ringtone and alert volume levels. The volume buttons still let you increase or decrease the volume level of other sound-related output, such as music you're listening to, videos you're watching, and games you're playing as well as the voice of anyone you're speaking with on the phone.

In Sounds and Vibration Patterns, tap the alert in the list, such as Ringtone or Calendar Alerts, and then choose the vibration and sound you want to associate with that type of alert. You can also choose None for either or both vibration and sound; see Figure 4-12. Scroll to the bottom of the Sounds screen to turn Lock Sounds (what you hear when you lock or unlock your iPhone) and Keyboard Clicks (what you hear when you type) Off or On.

 iOS 7 added more than two dozen new sounds. If you have an old favorite that you can't find, tap Classic at the bottom of the list to open a list of the sounds from previous iOS versions.

Wallpapers & Brightness

You can control the screen brightness in the Control Center, or here, in Settings. Drag the slider left or right to decrease

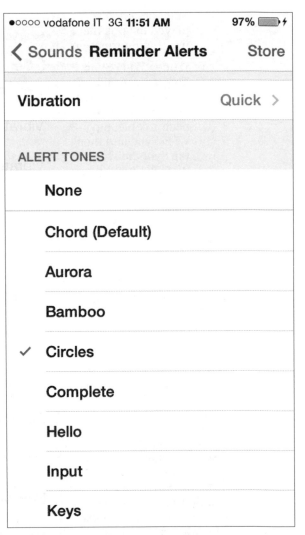

Figure 4-12: Each alert can have a different vibration pattern and sound.

or increase your iPhone's screen brightness. Auto-Brightness adjusts the iPhone's brightness level based on your environment. *Wallpaper* is the term used to describe the screen you see when your iPhone is locked, and the background image displayed behind app icons on the Home screen. You can choose the same image for both wallpaper choices, or you can choose a unique image for each choice. If you have an iPhone 4S or later, iOS 7 offers dynamic wallpaper, which means the image moves, both on its own and in response to movements you make with your iPhone.

Some iOS 7 users have reported feeling seasick while using their iPhone and the dynamic wallpaper seems to be to blame. If you're having this problem, go to Settings⬧General⬧Accessibility⬧Reduce Motion⬧On, which disables the so-called parallax effect (a fancy way of saying movement) of icons and alerts.

To change the wallpaper on your iPhone, tap the double-thumbnails button showing your current wallpaper choice to display the locations you can choose to pick your new wallpaper. Tap one of the categories to see the images stored in that category. Apple Wallpaper contains pretty pictures that came preloaded on your iPhone. Photos is where you find any snapshots you captured using Camera, or any images you may have saved from web pages, e-mail, or text messages. You can also choose from photos on Camera Roll or My Photo Stream as well as albums, events, and faces. (See Book V, Chapter 1.)

Tap an image to preview what your choice will look like as a wallpaper image. If you choose an image from Photos, you can move or zoom the image in or out to adjust the image to your liking. Tap Cancel if you don't want to use the image and return to your choices. Or tap Set to choose the image, and then tap Set Lock Screen, Set Home Screen, or Set Both to set the image as your wallpaper of choice for either or both screens. You'll see a preview of how your wallpaper will appear in the thumbnails, as shown in Figure 4-13.

Privacy

Privacy has become a hot button for many. Some say it's useless to try to maintain privacy because Big Brother knows all. We say, do what you can and don't do anything you wouldn't want your grandma to see. In this Settings section, you find Location Services, which gives your location information to apps that use it to perform their functions. Obviously, apps like Maps and Weather use your Location but so do Reminders (to give you location-based alerts) and Camera (to geotag your photos).

Here, you also find a list of apps that have accessed information from other apps that are share-able such as Contacts, Calendar, and Photos as well as Twitter and Facebook.

To adjust your privacy settings, tap Privacy⬧Location Services to display the main Location Services setting switch and a list of all the apps that tap into your iPhone's Location Services features, as shown in Figure 4-14. Tap the On/Off button to turn your iPhone's Location Services feature on or off. The app list disappears when you turn the main Location Services feature off, and reappears when you turn Locations On again.

Scroll down the list of apps and tap the switch to turn an app's Location Services setting on or off. If you spot the Location Services icon beside an app in the list, that means the app tapped into your iPhone's Location Services some-time over the last 24 hours (refer to Figure 4-14).

Scroll to the bottom of the Location Services screen and tap the System Services button. These system-wide ser-vices use your location to perform functions such as calibrating the com-pass or providing traffic conditions in Maps. If you don't want any of these

Figure 4-13: Wallpaper choices you can live with.

services to access your location or information about your iPhone use, tap the toggle switch to the Off position. Scroll further down the System Services screen to turn the Location Services Status Bar Icon On or Off. When On, the arrow appears in the status bar whenever System Services accesses your location. Tap the back button in the upper left corner twice to return to the Privacy settings screen.

Tap any of the apps in the Privacy list to see a list of other applications that have accessed information from that app. You can turn access to those apps on and off from this second-level screen.

At the very bottom of the Privacy settings screen, you find Advertising. Tap that to then tap Limit Ad Tracking to the On position. This blocks apps from seeing what you do with your iPhone, which is information they use to send you targeted ads.

Other Apple and third-party app settings

After the Privacy button, you see four sections that list other apps. We explain the settings for each app in the first three sections in other chapters of this book. The fourth section contains Apple and third-party apps that you installed. Tapping the app in the list opens a settings or information screen. There's no set rule for the type of settings options an app offers, so you have to poke around when you download a new app — or read the app's instructions either on your iPhone or on the app's website.

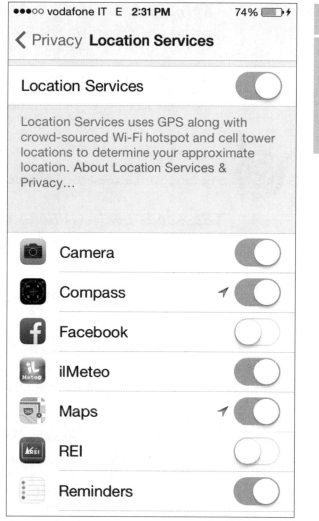

Figure 4-14: Location Services helps your iPhone find its way — and yours.

Activating iPhone's Security Features

This section is all about taking advantage of your iPhone's security and privacy options to ensure your personal data stays that way — personal, for your eyes only, or for others you may choose to share your iPhone with. (We talk about Safari's online security features in Book III, Chapter 3.) To access the settings that follow, tap Settings, and then tap General.

Auto-Lock

Locking your iPhone's screen helps conserve power and guards against unintentional screen taps, like when you're toting your iPhone in your pocket.

Tap Auto Lock and then choose the amount of time you want your iPhone to wait before it automatically locks the screen. Your choices range from one to five minutes, or you can choose Never, which means it's up to you to remember to press the Sleep/Wake button to lock your iPhone.

Even when locked, your iPhone can still receive calls, text messages, and inbound communications — unless you activated Do Not Disturb — and you can still listen to music or other audio.

Passcode Lock (iPhone 4, 4s, 5, and 5c)

Requiring a passcode to unlock your iPhone can help prevent others from viewing your personal data or making calls on your dime. To set it up, do the following:

1. **Tap Settings**⇨**General**⇨**Passcode Lock**⇨**Turn Passcode On.**

   (Optional) Simple Passcodes are four digits. If you prefer to use a more complicated passcode, such as an alpha-numeric combination, tap Simple Passcode Off, then tap Turn Passcode On.

2. **Type in a four-digit passcode, or a longer passcode if you turned off Simple Passcodes, and then type in the code a second time to verify your code.**

   You can change your secret code anytime by tapping Change Passcode, entering your old passcode, and then entering a new passcode.

3. **Tap Require Passcode and then tap Immediately if you want your iPhone to require your passcode whenever you unlock it. Or choose one of the time-out options if you want your iPhone to require your code after the chosen amount of time has passed.**

4. **Tap Voice Dial On if you want to require the passcode to make voice-controlled calls.**

5. **Tap Siri, Passbook, and/or Reply with Message to the On position if you want these functions to work from the Lock screen.**

When Siri is accessible from the Lock Screen, security features such as the Passcode Lock are overridden and, therefore, compromised — even though your iPhone is locked, you (or someone else) can make a phone call or take another action via Siri.

And, if you use AutoFill in Safari (see Book III, Chapter 3) to store passwords and credit card information for certain websites, without a passcode that information is readily available to anyone who might casually use your iPhone to visit, say, the Amazon shopping site. Interestingly, Apple doesn't allow you to store your Apple ID password with AutoFill.

6. **Tap Erase Data On to protect your personal information in the event your iPhone falls into the wrong hands.**

   Erase Data erases everything stored on your iPhone if the correct passcode isn't entered after ten tries.

On GSM model iPhones, such as an unlocked iPhone or one with an AT&T contract, you can activate and change a PIN (personal identification number) to lock your iPhone's SIM card (some SIM cards come with a preset PIN). When activated, you must type in the PIN code whenever you turn iPhone off then on again. But unlike the Passcode Lock feature, which generously offers up to ten tries in the game of Guess Your Secret Code, the SIM Pin lock feature is less forgiving — after three failed attempts to crack the SIM code, unlocking the SIM pin may then require a unique Personal Unlocking Key (PUK) code to unlock your iPhone (which rightful owners may obtain by contacting their cellular carrier's customer service department). You can change the SIM pin or turn it off completely by tapping Settings⇨Phone⇨SIM Pin⇨Off/Change Pin.

Passcode & Fingerprint (iPhone 5s)

The Home button on the iPhone 5s houses the Touch ID sensor, which can use your fingerprint in place of a passcode to verify authorized access to your iPhone from the Lock screen and instead of your Apple ID and password to authorize purchases from the iTunes, App, and iBook Stores. We predict it will be used by other websites and apps as use of this technology spreads.

You may have set up Touch ID when you set up your iPhone (refer to Book I, Chapter 2). If not, follow these steps to add your fingerprint or that of someone else, like a child or significant other. We also tell you how to name or delete fingerprints.

1. **Tap Settings⇨General⇨Passcode & Fingerprint⇨Fingerprint.**

   If you previously assigned a Passcode to your iPhone, you have to enter it before you can access the Fingerprint set up.

2. **Tap Add a fingerprint.**

3. **Place your finger, or thumb, on the Home button.**

   The fingerprint on screen begins to redden as the whorls and swirls of your finger are memorized.

4. **Lift and replace your finger on the Home button and roll it around so the Touch ID sensor can memorize the edges of your finger.**

5. **When your fingerprint is successfully read, tap Fingerprints in the upper left corner.**

6. **Choose when you want to use your fingerprint to authorize actions by tapping on Passcode in Lock (to use Touch ID to unlock your iPhone) and/or App and iTunes Store (to authorize purchases with Touch ID).**

7. **(Optional) Tap Edit, and do one of the following:**

   • *Name the fingerprint:* Tap the fingerprint and then type a name, such as "Barbara's Index" or "Lucy's Paw."

   • *Delete the fingerprint:* Tap the red and white button next to the print you want to delete, and then tap Delete.

8. **Tap in the upper left corner or swipe right until you reach the main Settings screen, or just press the Home button to return to the Home screen.**

 Even when a passcode or fingerprint is required to open the Lock screen, you, or more likely someone who wants to use your iPhone because you're incapacitated, can make an emergency call by tapping the Emergency button in the bottom left corner of the passcode screen.

Restrictions

If you share your iPhone with another person (or you're a parent or guardian who holds the keys to iPhone's kingdom), you can allow or restrict access to apps and features, or block access to content, such as songs containing explicit lyrics, or movies or TV shows based on their MPA rating. You can also allow or restrict changes to specific apps such as Contacts and Calendars as well as accounts. Scroll down to list to find a Volume Limit setting and Game Center limits.

To activate and adjust iPhone's restriction settings, tap Settings⇨General⇨ Restrictions. Tap the Enable Restrictions button and then type in a secret four-digit code, and then type in the code a second time to verify your code. Tap the apps and features you want to turn off or on as shown in Figure 4-15. App icons for any apps you restrict disappear from iPhone's Home screen.

 Although you'd think turning off access to a certain app such as Safari, for instance, totally blocks your iPhone from accessing web pages, that isn't one-hundred percent true. Although the app icon disappears from the Home screen and browsing the web with Safari is therefore disabled, certain apps you may have installed on your iPhone can *still* access the web using their own web browser features. For instance, tapping a web page link that appears in the Facebook, Twitter, or Google apps opens those apps' built-in web browsers to display the content of a web page link. There are also other browser apps, such as Google Chrome, which can't be restricted with this setting.

 If you want to "hide" some of the pre-installed apps that can't be deleted from your iPhone, you may be able to restrict them, which removes the app button from the Home screen. The app is still on your iPhone but you don't see it.

Taking Steps if Your iPhone Is Lost or Stolen

Your worst iPhone nightmare: Your beloved iPhone is lost or stolen. Don't panic — even though your iPhone may be gone for good (er, bad), all may not be totally lost. If you back up regularly or better yet, use iCloud, a good portion of the apps and data on your iPhone is in safekeeping in a remote location.

 iCloud doesn't back up video that isn't in your Camera Roll so you'll want to back up video files to a photo management app on your computer as soon as possible after shooting them or consider using iTunes as your backup of choice.

As for the risk of untoward characters accessing your data on your iPhone, we have potentially good news, possibly great news, and maybe even fabulous news. First the potentially good news: If you

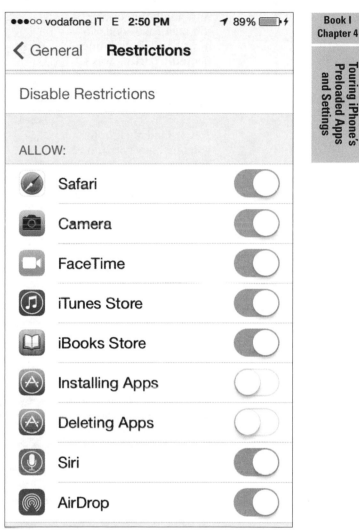

Figure 4-15: Pick and choose apps and features you want to block access to.

turned on the Passcode Lock or Fingerprint feature described in the previous section, whoever found or "borrowed" your iPhone must type in your secret passcode or have your live and attached-to-your-body finger before they can even unlock your iPhone and start snooping around. Second, the possibly great news: If, in addition to turning on the Passcode Lock feature, you also turned on the Erase Data option, your iPhone develops a sudden case of permanent amnesia and erases everything stored on it if, after the tenth try, the interloper fails to guess your secret code. And because you regularly backup with iCloud or iTunes, erasing what's on your iPhone isn't such a big deal.

And finally, what may be the best-case-scenario news of all: Before unexpectedly parting ways, hopefully you configured the Find My iPhone feature we explain here.

To use Find My iPhone, you must have an iCloud account, and then turn on the Find My iPhone option in Settings⇨iCloud, as seen in Figure 4-16.

With Find My iPhone activated, you may be able to track down your iPhone's general location on a map using a web browser on your computer or other web-savvy gadget, or by using the Find My iPhone app installed on another person's iPhone, iPad, or iPod touch, which in turn may jog your memory as to where you may have lost or misplaced your iPhone (like between the sofa cushions in the den, or your gym locker).

When you turn on Find My iPhone, even without a Passcode lock, the Activation Lock is automatically activated: If the person who got his hands on your iPhone tries to thwart your efforts at finding it with Find My iPhone, he must enter your Apple ID and password to do so, information he's unlikely to have or easily guess.

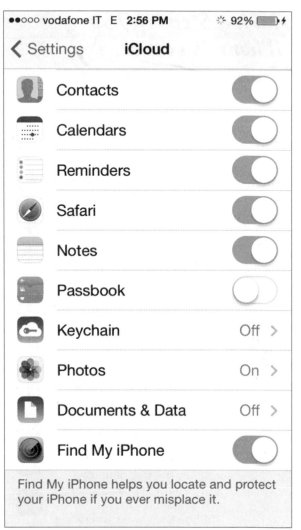

Figure 4-16: The Find My iPhone setting.

Because of Activation Lock, when you sell or give away your iPhone at some future date, it's a good idea to back up your iPhone, and then sign out of your iCloud account, which deactivates Find My iPhone and all the other iCloud services on your iPhone.

What's more, you can command your iPhone to play a loud bleating sound to help guide you (or anyone nearby) to wherever it's hiding. You can lock your iPhone with a secret passcode you create on the fly in the event your iPhone wasn't already protected using the Passcode Lock feature before it vanished.

And finally, if you still can't find your iPhone, you can issue a "self-destruct" command that instructs your iPhone to erase everything stored on it. That way, you lose only your iPhone — which you can replace — but not your personal data and identity information.

To track down a missing iPhone, tap the Find My iPhone app on a friend's iPhone (or iPad or iPod touch), or visit www.icloud.com with your computer's web browser, and then log in using your iCloud user name and password. A map appears and shows your iPhone's current location, give or take a few — or a few hundred — feet, depending on the service's ability to accurately home in on your missing iPhone. Click the information button or Devices list button to display more information and options, shown in Figure 4-17.

Figure 4-17: Locating your iPhone.

Choose one or more of the following actions, which take place immediately if your device is online. Otherwise, the action(s) occurs as soon as the device comes online:

- **Play Sound:** Click the button to play a sound on your device. The sound plays at full volume even if your device is muted.

- **Lost Mode:** When you click this button, you're asked to create a four-digit passcode. Type the digits two times, as asked, and then enter a phone number where you can be reached, which will be displayed on the screen. Click Next and then type in a message that will appear on the screen of your lost iPhone. Click Done. The phone number and message appear on your iPhone's screen and the passcode must be entered to unlock the device. You receive an e-mail confirming that your lost device has been locked and another e-mail with the device's location.

✔ **Erase:** If repeated attempts to reach out and touch someone who may be in possession of your iPhone go unanswered, this may be your last gasp option, especially if you have sensitive personal information on your iPhone and you have no luck retrieving it. Click Erase, and then enter your Apple ID password. Confirm by clicking Erase.

Chapter 5: Anticipating and Tackling iPhone Troubles

In This Chapter

✓ Avoiding common iPhone problems

✓ Troubleshooting Q&A

*Y*ou might think that near the beginning of a book is a strange place for the troubleshooting chapter. We decided to do things a little differently.

Often, when something goes awry, you panic — it's human nature. No one likes a glitch, or feeling unprepared or stupid. That's why we put this chapter up front. You can skim through the topics so if one of the problems we mention occurs, you won't be surprised or panicked. You'll know where to look to resolve the problem calmly and quickly.

We include some information here to help you avoid problems, along with the traditional troubleshooting question-and-answer format. In each chapter, we include some warnings of things that could happen and tips for how to resolve problems specific to the chapter at hand.

Avoiding Common iPhone Problems

With iCloud syncing, your version of iOS and your apps should always be current. If you're having problems, however, tap Settings➪General➪Software Update just to be sure your iOS is current. If a badge appears on the App Store icon, chances are the Automatic Downloads option isn't on for Apps. Go to Settings➪iTunes & App Store and tap Apps to the On position under Automatic Downloads. Refer to Book II, Chapter 2 to learn about the App Store.

Make sure the SIM card is properly installed (if your iPhone uses one). If you dropped your iPhone, the SIM card may be slightly dislodged. Carefully insert the end of a paper clip in the hole of the SIM tray to open the tray. Take out the SIM card and re-insert it and then gently push the tray closed.

Here are a few other things to consider if you have a problem:

✔ **The headset is plugged in but you can't hear anything.**

Make sure the headset is plugged in all the way — it makes a little "click" when it is. It may not be compatible with the cover or bumper (those colored frames that go around iPhone's outer edge) you use; that is, the cover keeps the plug from going all the way into the hole. Although 1/8-inch plugs work most of the time, the specifications call for a 3.5 mm plug.

Make sure the jack is clean. If you use your iPhone in a dusty workshop or in the yard, or eat toast while texting, crumbs and particles can build up and block the audio jack. Ever-so-gently tap your iPhone on a not-too-hard surface (a placemat on a table, for example, or a mousepad) or use a hand pump with the nozzle for inflating a basketball to blow into the jack.

✔ **The words** *No Service* **appear where your carrier's name usually appears.**

First, make sure you aren't in Airplane Mode. Try moving closer to a window or going outside. Then, try turning 3G/4G on or off. Try turning Airplane Mode On and then Off. Try turning your iPhone off and on again. Lastly, go to Settings⇨General⇨Reset and tap Reset Network Settings. If you have a weak signal, turning 3G/4G on can bring a stronger signal. If you're in a crowded area with lots of other cell phone users, turning 3G/4G on gives you access to a larger network.

✔ **You don't have Internet access.**

Assuming you have data service as part of your cellular contract, make sure you have a cellular data signal or are in a Wi-Fi zone. You see the icons in the status bar (see Book I, Chapter 2). Without one of these options, you can't get online. Try these tactics to solve the problem:

- Disconnect and reconnect to the network. Drag up from the bottom of the screen to open the Control Center. Tap Wi-Fi Off, wait a minute, and then tap Wi-Fi On.

- Try forgetting the network and joining again. Tap Settings⇨Wi-Fi, and then tap the name of the network. Tap Forget This Network and then sign in again.

- Try renewing the Dynamic Host Control Protocol (DHCP) lease, which is the access point that allows your iPhone to access a Wi-Fi network. Tap Settings⇨Wi-Fi. Tap the Info (i) button to the right of the connected Wi-Fi network, and then tap the DHCP tab. Scroll down the screen and tap the Renew Lease link, as shown in Figure 5-1.

- Reset network settings by tapping Settings⇨General, and then scroll down to Reset, which is the last button on the screen. Tap Reset Network Settings.

- Look for interference from devices like walkie-talkies or baby monitors.

- If you know Wi-Fi should be available because, say, you're home, and none of these procedures work, the problem could be with the Wi-Fi router, modem, or incoming DSL line. Try turning your router off and on again or call your service provider.

✔ **You can't send text messages.**

For SMS and MMS messages, make sure you have cellular service. iMessage requires a Wi-Fi or cellular data connection, and iMessage has to be turned on via Settings➪Messages➪iMessage➪On. Check that the recipient's phone number has an area code and that you typed your message in the message field and not the subject line. Refer to Book III, Chapter 2 to find out more about text messaging.

✔ **You can send SMS but iMessage doesn't work.**

Go to Settings➪General➪Reset and tap Reset Network Settings.

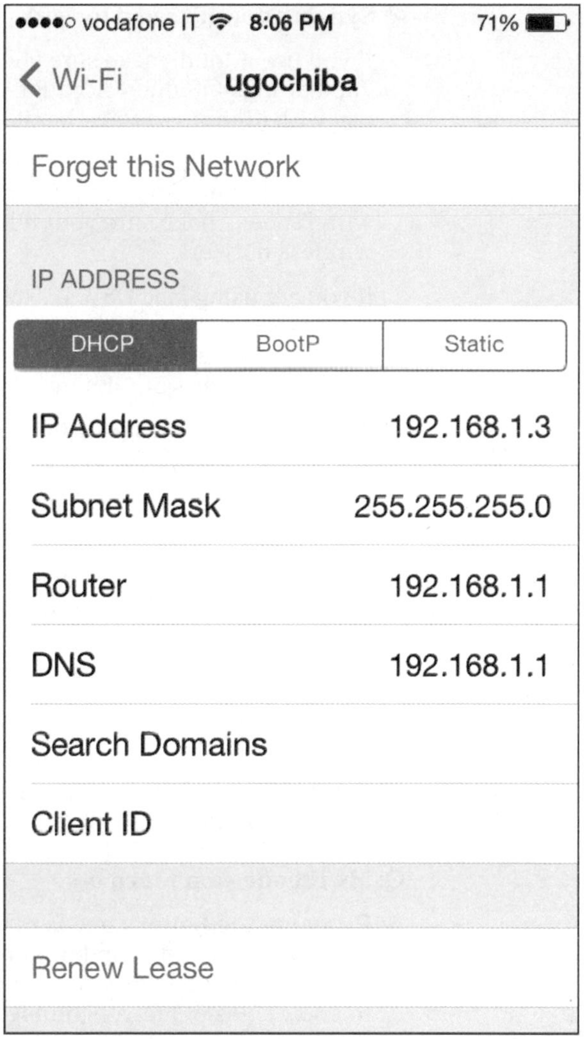

●●●●○ vodafone IT 🔶 8:06 PM		71% 🔋
‹ Wi-Fi	**ugochiba**	

Forget this Network

IP ADDRESS

DHCP	BootP	Static

IP Address	192.168.1.3
Subnet Mask	255.255.255.0
Router	192.168.1.1
DNS	192.168.1.1
Search Domains	
Client ID	

Renew Lease

Figure 5-1: Sometimes your lease is up and you have to renew to get Wi-Fi.

✔ **You can't receive or send e-mail or you see messages but you can't open them.**

Make sure you have an Internet connection, either through your cellular data network or Wi-Fi.

Try re-entering your password. Tap Settings➪Mail, Contacts, Calendars➪Account Name➪Account. Delete and retype the password. See Book III, Chapter 4 for information about the Mail app.

Turn your phone off and back on.

✓ **Syncing doesn't seem to work.**

If you use iCloud, make sure you are signed in to the correct account: Tap Settings⇨iCloud⇨Account and enter the Apple ID and password you use with iCloud — remember it must be in the form of an e-mail address.

If you use iTunes, make sure the USB connector cable is properly inserted in both your computer and your iPhone. If you sync wirelessly with iTunes, make sure your iPhone and computer are on the same wireless network.

If you are using Mac OS X 10.9 Mavericks, iTunes syncing is different than syncing with earlier versions of OS X or with Windows. Refer to Book II, Chapter 1 for full details on syncing with either computer operation system and your iPhone.

✓ **The battery drains faster than usual, especially after an iOS update.**

Double-click the Home button to see the apps in the open apps carousel. Swipe up on each one, or two or three at a time, until you've closed all of them.

Tap General⇨Reset and then choose Reset All Settings. This "clears out" some of the cobwebs in your iPhone's memory and may fix battery charge problems.

Troubleshooting Q&A

Here are some of the most common difficulties you may encounter with your iPhone and how to handle them:

Q: My iPhone won't turn on.

A: Probably the battery needs to be charged. Connect your iPhone to the USB connector cable and power adapter and begin charging. It takes about ten minutes for a completely dead battery to have enough charge to show signs of life. A lightning bolt appears on the screen, followed by the Apple logo, and you can turn your iPhone on at that point.

If you take your iPhone to the beach and leave it in your bag hanging on the back of your lounge chair (as Barbara's friend's teenage daughter did and then called in tears because her beloved iPhone wouldn't work), you risk overheating your iPhone. Likewise, leaving it out in the cold can send your iPhone into hypothermia. Signs of iPhone heat stroke, or frostbite, are a dimmed screen, weak cellular signal, and in the case of heat stroke, a temperature warning screen as your iPhone tries to cool itself. You cannot use your iPhone — except for an emergency call — when the temperature warning screen is visible. If your iPhone can't cool or warm itself, it goes into a deep sleep, a sort of iPhone coma, until it cools off or warms up. Put your iPhone in a cooler or warmer location. It will wake up once its internal temperature returns to normal.

Q: An app is frozen on my screen. Nothing closes it, the Home button doesn't work — it just sits there.

A: Force-quit the app. Hold down the Sleep/Wake switch until the Slide to Power Off message appears, and then hold the Home button until the frozen program quits and you return to the Home screen. The app should be fine the next time you open it.

Q: Um, force-quitting the app didn't work.

A: Force-restart your iPhone. Hold down the Home button and the Sleep/Wake switch simultaneously for about 10 seconds. Release when you see the Apple logo, which means your iPhone is restarting.

Q: The same app or apps keep giving me trouble.

A: Check if there's an update for the app or apps. If you aren't using automatic downloads for the App Store, a badge on the App Store button indicates you have apps to update, tap App Store and then tap the Updates button. Scroll through the list to see if the offending app is there, and if so, tap Update and then Open.

Try removing and reinstalling the troublesome app or apps. Press and hold any app on the Home screen until they begin to wiggle, and then tap the X on the app you want to remove. Even after you remove an app, you can install it again because the App Store keeps a record of all the apps you installed.

Q: An app or a pps stopped in the middle of an installation or update, and it neither opens nor allows me to remove it.

This may happen when you try to use the Update All function of the App Store, and you have more than a few apps to update. Connect your iPhone to your computer with the USB connector cable and open iTunes. Select your iPhone from the pop-up menu in the upper right of the window, and then click the Apps tab. Click the Remove button next to the offending app or apps and then click Sync. Install the app while connected to iTunes by clicking the Install button next to the apps you want to install and then clicking Sync. Alternatively, click the eject button next to your iPhone on iTunes, and disconnect your iPhone from your computer. Open the App Store from the Home screen, and tap Updates at the bottom of the screen, tap Purchased, and then tap Not on This iPhone. Tap the download icon (it looks like a cloud with a downward pointing arrow) to download the app to your iPhone. See Book II, Chapter 2 to learn more about the App Store and installing and updating apps.

Q: I'm still having problems.

A: Try resetting your iPhone settings. Tap Settings⊏>General⊏>Reset⊏>Reset All Settings, as shown in Figure 5-2. This takes your settings back to how they were when you took your iPhone out of the box, or if upgrades have been released since you bought your iPhone, to the default settings for the most recent upgrade you performed. It doesn't remove any data, but you do have to redo any settings you had altered.

Q: Nope, that didn't help.

A: Tap Erase All Content and Settings. This does just what it says. This resets all settings and erases all your information and media by removing the encryption key to the data (which is encrypted using 256-bit AES encryption).

Make sure you back up your iPhone with iCloud or iTunes before tapping Erase All Content and Settings so you can sync after.

Q: Nothing seems to work.

A: Restore your phone. Restore erases your iPhone and return it to the state it was in out of the box, but better than new because the most recent operating system (the software that makes your iPhone work) will be installed. All con-tacts, photos, music, television shows, cal-

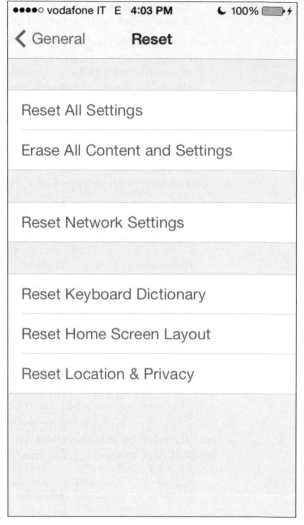

endars, e-mails, notes, bookmarks, and third-party apps are deleted. This sounds like a drastic measure, and in a way it is, but it's not as bad as it seems. If you use iCloud to back up, you can restore from your iCloud account. If you use iTunes, try to sync with iTunes before restor-ing your iPhone. Even if you can't sync, your most recent backup is stored on iTunes on your computer. See Book II, Chapter 1 to learn about backing up with iCloud and iTunes.

●●●●○ vodafone IT E 4:03 PM   ☾ 100% ▭▸⚡

❮ General   **Reset**

Reset All Settings

Erase All Content and Settings

Reset Network Settings

Reset Keyboard Dictionary

Reset Home Screen Layout

Reset Location & Privacy

Figure 5-2: Sometimes resetting is your best option for solving a problem.

When you Reset All Settings or Erase All Content and Settings or Restore, you repeat the activation process as explained in Book I, Chapter 2.

Q: iTunes doesn't recognize my iPhone.

A: Do a Device Firmware Upgrade (DFU). DFU wipes out the old OS (but not your content) and installs a new one. You can then sync and restore as explained previously. The DFU procedure is

1. Turn off your iPhone.

2. Connect your iPhone to your computer.

3. Open iTunes.

4. Press and hold the Sleep/Wake and Home buttons for exactly ten seconds.

5. After ten seconds, release the Sleep/Wake button, but continue to hold the Home button for another ten seconds.

6. After ten seconds, release the Home button. iTunes now recognizes your iPhone.

7. Click OK. iTunes asks you to confirm.

8. Click Restore and Update.

Getting More Help

The preceding tactics usually fix typical iPhone problems. If you have a problem we didn't talk about or none of the previously discussed tactics work, you can still find more help on the Internet. Chances are someone else has encountered the same problem. Your first stop should be Apple's iPhone Support page at www.apple.com/support/iphone. You can contact Apple's technical support group for personalized attention. If your iPhone is your sole connection to the Internet, ask to use a friend or relative's computer or return to the store where you purchased your iPhone.

You can also search the discussion forums, as shown in Figure 5-3, where questions and answers are submitted by other iPhone users. Type in a few words that describe your problem and peruse the discussions. If you don't find a discussion pertinent to your problem, you can submit your question and usually an answer from another user is available within a day.

If you still don't find a satisfying answer, type a few key words about your problem in to one of the Internet search engines like Google (www.google.com) or Yahoo! (www.yahoo.com).

Wherever you search, you may be surprised to find that you aren't the first person to have the problem you're having.

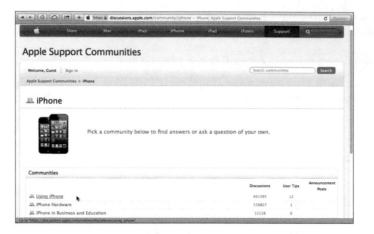

Figure 5-3: iPhone users exchange questions and answers on the discussion forums at the Apple website.

Getting Repairs if You Need Them

We are always impressed with the seriousness and efficiency of Apple's warranty and repair service. Your iPhone includes a one-year limited warranty and 90 days of complimentary support. You can get two years of coverage and support if you buy AppleCare+ ($99), which now includes no-fault insurance that covers up to two accidental damage incidents, so if you accidently drop your iPhone in the fish pond at the park, as long as you can scoop it out and take it to your local Apple Store, it will be repaired, or replaced, for a $79 deductible. You have to purchase AppleCare+ within 30 days of your iPhone purchase date. If anything goes wrong with your iPhone, call Apple or take it to an Apple Store.

If you can, back everything up before you leave your iPhone with Apple so you can re-sync on the repaired, or new, iPhone.

If you can't be without a cellular phone for two or three days, the Apple Store offers what's called the Express Replacement Service (ERS). If your iPhone is covered under AppleCare or AppleCare+, ERS is included. If your iPhone is not covered, you have to pay a fee that's somewhere between the value of your broken phone and the value of a replacement phone. Apple gives you a replacement iPhone, or sends one if you call instead of going to the Apple Store. You just have to insert your SIM card and sync what was on your broken iPhone to the replacement iPhone.

Book II

Stocking iPhone with iTunes Apps and Add-ons

Contents at a Glance

Chapter 1: Syncing and Backing Up Your iPhone

In This Chapter

- ✓ Creating an Apple ID
- ✓ Understanding the syncing relationship
- ✓ Syncing and backing up with iCloud
- ✓ Keeping documents in the cloud
- ✓ Syncing and backing up with iTunes
- ✓ Buying more iCloud storage

The information in this chapter is essential to using your iPhone. Even if you only manage a bit of data like phone numbers and appointments, losing them can be a digital nightmare and sharing them with your other devices and computers is a digital dream. We explain the theory behind syncing, and then go through, step-by-step, how to sync the data between your iPhone, your computer, and other iOS devices such as an iPod touch or iPad using iCloud or iTunes. We outline how to back up everything on your iPhone and then use the backup should you lose everything on your iPhone. Lastly, we give you the steps you need to keep your iPhone up-to-date with the latest version of its operating system, fondly known as iOS.

Creating an Apple ID

Your Apple ID is your entry ticket to just about everything iPhone. You need it to sign in and make purchases at the iTunes Store, the App Store, the iBook Store, and the online Apple Store, as well as to sign in and set up iCloud, Apple's remote syncing and storage service. Chances are you created an Apple ID when your phone was activated at the Apple Store or the retailer where you bought your iPhone or if you activated your iPhone yourself, you may have created one as part of the Setup Assistant procedure. If you skipped that step, make sure your iPhone is connected to the Internet and create an Apple ID by doing the following:

Mail

Contacts

Calendars

Reminders

Safari

1. **On the Home screen, tap Settings⟳iCloud.**

2. **Tap Get a Free Apple ID.**

   The Create an Apple ID screen opens.

3. **Scroll through the rotor to choose your birth date.**

   You have to be at least 13 years of age to create an Apple ID and if you are between 13 and 18, you have to have parental consent.

4. **Tap Next, and then enter your first and last name in the fields.**

5. **Tap Next. This screen establishes the e-mail address that will be used with your Apple ID. You can do one of the following:**

   - *Use your current email address:* Type in the e-mail address you want to use as your Apple ID.

   - *Get a free iCloud email address:* Choose this and you then create an e-mail address that will have an @icloud.com suffix. You cannot change your iCloud e-mail address after you create it, so choose carefully.

6. **Tap Create to confirm your choice.**

   If someone else already uses that ID, you'll be asked if it's yours or to cancel to create another choice.

7. **Create a password that has at least eight characters and contains at least one each of upper and lower case letters. Tap Next.**

8. **Add three security questions.**

   Select a question from the options and then type in the answer. Tap Next to go to the next question.

9. **Add an optional Rescue Email (different than the iCloud address you created) that will be used if you forget your password.**

10. **Turn on or off e-mail updates, which are communications from Apple about software updates and new products and services.**

11. **Tap Agree to agree to the Terms and Conditions of your iCloud e-mail and Apple ID.**

    Your account is created and you are automatically signed in.

12. **Tap next.**

13. **You are asked if iCloud can use your location; we suggest you tap OK, as it will be needed to activate Find My iPhone.**

14. **Tap the features you want to use with iCloud.**

    We explain more about that later in this chapter.

15. **Make note of your @icloud.com e-mail address and keep your password in a safe place.**

16. **Press the Home button to return to the Home screen.**

If you are more comfortable working from a computer, you can create your Apple ID from the iCloud System Preferences on a Mac or the iCloud Control Panel for Windows on a computer with Windows 7 or 8.

Understanding Syncing versus Backing Up

Syncing — short for synchronizing — is keeping your data on two or more devices, like your iPhone and your computer and other iOS devices such as an iPad or iPod touch, up-to-date and mirrored on all devices. When you sync your devices, data is evaluated and compared and when two pieces of data are different, the newer data replaces the older data.

Backing up is creating a copy of the data that's on your device and storing it somewhere else, be it your computer or a remote server.

You can choose either iCloud or iTunes to perform the backup function, but each syncs different types of data, which might make you want to scream "Why can't I do it all in one place?!" but it helps eliminate duplicate records and is easier done than said. We give you step-by-step instructions here so you can manage your data and meet all your backing up and syncing needs.

Syncing and backing up with iCloud

iCloud is Apple's over-the-air syncing, sharing, and storage service. Your data is stored in a remote Apple location, somewhere in North Carolina (at the time of writing), which is a good thing because if disaster or thieves strike your home and your computer breaks or disappears, your data is safe and sound. You sign in to the iCloud service with your Apple ID, and then choose which types of data you want iCloud to sync, so you have it on all your iCloud-enabled devices, and backup, so you can restore it if you lose it. iCloud offers an e-mail account and 5GB of free storage for the following:

- **Mail settings and messages**
- **Contacts settings and content, including Phone Favorites**
- **Calendar settings and content**
- **Reminders**
- **Notes**
- **Documents and data from iCloud-enabled apps**
- **Passbook**
- **Messages, iMessage, SMS, and MMS**
- **Keychain account names, passwords, and credit card information**
  (This service is scheduled to be activated by Apple in Autumn 2013 and will appear on one of the iOS 7 updates.)

- ✓ **Photos and videos in your Camera Roll**

- ✓ **App data and documents**

- ✓ **Ringtones**

- ✓ **Device data and settings such as wallpaper, Home screen, and app organization**

- ✓ **Safari bookmarks, tabs, Reading List, and history**

Purchased apps and media including music, iTunes Match content, TV shows, and books, which are all part of iTunes in the Cloud, as well as photos stored in Photo Stream don't count toward the 5 GB. If you need more storage space, you can purchase an additional amount on a yearly basis directly from the iCloud settings on your iPhone, which we explain later in this chapter.

iCloud does *not* back up the following:

- ✓ **Media that wasn't purchased in iTunes**

- ✓ **Audiobooks** (even if you purchased them in the iTunes Store, although the store remembers your purchases and you can download them again)

- ✓ **Podcasts** (again, these are available to re-download from the iTunes Store)

- ✓ **Photos and video that you transferred from your computer to your iPhone** (not such a big deal because you have the original on your computer)

- ✓ **Photos and video that are not in the Camera Roll** (unless they are stored in an app that you designate for iCloud backup, as explained in the upcoming steps)

iCloud comes with Mac OS X 10.7.2 Lion or later, and the iCloud Control Panel 3.0 for Windows (Windows 7 or Windows 8) is available for download at support.apple.com/kb/DL1455.

Follow these steps to use iCloud to sync documents and data between your devices:

1. **Tap Settings⤳iCloud.**

   If you see the e-mail you used to set up your Apple ID, go to Step 5.

2. **Type in your Apple ID and password, as shown in Figure 1-1, and then tap Sign In. Your account is verified.**

   iCloud only works with e-mail style Apple IDs. If your Apple ID is something like *johnsmith*, you must create a new one as explained at the beginning of this chapter.

TIP

You can still use your existing Apple ID and password for purchases in the iTunes, App, iBooks, and online Apple Stores but the Apple ID that uses *yourusername*@iCloud.com will control the iCloud functions.

3. **iCloud asks if you want to merge Safari data on your iPhone with iCloud. Tap Merge.**

4. **iCloud asks to use the location of your iPhone, which enables the Find My iPhone feature. Click OK.**

5. **The iCloud screen appears, as shown in Figure 1-2.**

The switches you tap On indicate which data you want to sync with iCloud. Any changes you make on your iPhone are pulled into iCloud and pushed to the other devices, and vice versa, when your devices are

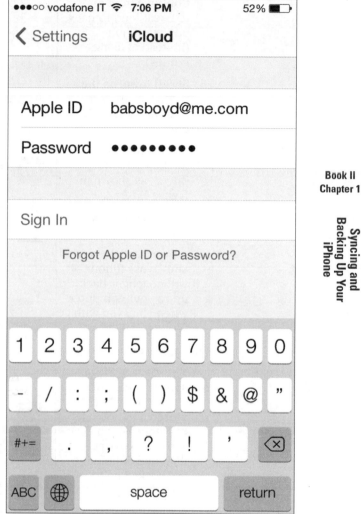

Figure 1-1: Use your Apple ID to sign in to iCloud.

signed in to iCloud and connected to the Internet. iCloud keeps all your devices in sync. When you tap out of iCloud Settings and open an app that you use and has content on another device or computer, such as Contacts or Safari, you find the information on your iPhone.

The exception is Photo Stream, which automatically uploads as many as 1,000 photos taken in the last 30 days from your iOS devices — your iPhone, iPad, or iPod touch — or imported into iPhoto or Aperture on your Mac, and pushes them to the other devices and your computer.

Continue from above to use iCloud to back up your iPhone (instead of using iTunes).

6. **Scroll towards the bottom of the screen and tap Storage & Backup.**

   The Storage & Backup screen opens, as shown in Figure 1-3.

7. **Tap iCloud Backup On.**

   A message lets you know your iPhone will no longer back up to your computer when you sync with iTunes. Tap OK.

8. **Tap Manage Storage.**

   The Manage Storage screen opens, which shows you what is stored on iCloud, as in Figure 1-4. You can see that Barbara's iPad and old iPhone are backed up to iCloud.

   Notice the Documents & Data section, as shown in Figure 1-4. The iCloud-enabled apps installed on your iPhone are listed. You may have their counterparts on your computer. See the next section, "Keeping documents in the cloud," for more information about this feature.

9. **Tap your iPhone.**

   The Info screen opens, as shown in Figure 1-5.

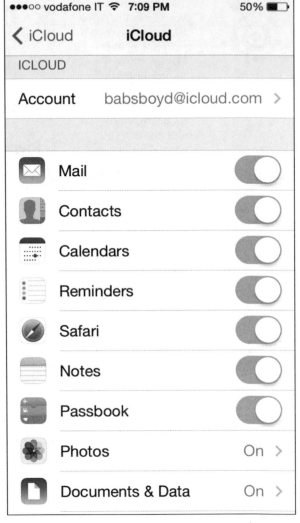

Figure 1-2: Choose the type of data you want to share with other devices using iCloud.

10. **The apps on your iPhone appear listed in the Backup Options section. Tap the switches On or Off to select which kind of data you want to back up. For example, tap a drawing app On to back up sketches you make.**

If, at some time in the future, you want to delete your backup, scroll to the bottom of this screen and tap Delete Backup, which both deletes your iCloud backup and turns it off.

11. **Tap Back in the upper left corner, or swipe right to return to the previous screen and repeat to reach the Storage & Backup screen.**

12. **Scroll to the bottom of the screen and tap the Back Up Now button.**

The button is grayed if you aren't connected to a Wi-Fi network. Swipe up to open the Control Center and tap Wi-Fi on if you're in the vicinity of a Wi-Fi network you connected to in the past; otherwise, tap back to the main Settings screen, tap Wi-Fi On and the sign in to a known network. Return to the iCloud Storage & Backup screen, and then tap Back Up Now.

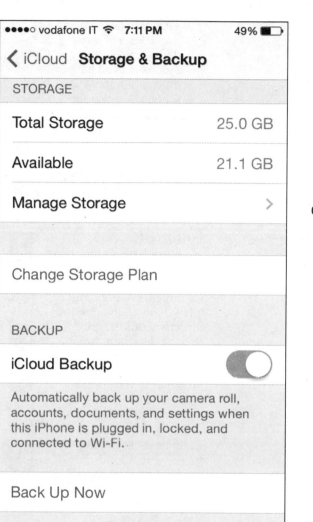

Figure 1-3: Turn on iCloud back up on the Storage & Backup screen.

The first backup may take a few minutes, depending on how much data you have on your iPhone. Your iPhone is backed up to iCloud. Subsequent backups take place once a day when your iPhone is attached to a power source, connected to Wi-Fi, and locked.

Keeping documents in the cloud

Documents in the Cloud lets you save documents directly in iCloud and then access them from all your devices that have the same app installed, and from your computer either in the app or from the www. icloud.com website. Documents in the Cloud works with iCloud-enabled apps, such as Pages, Numbers, and Keynote, as well as iA Writer, Autodesk Sketchbook Pro, Preview, and Day One. We use Pages as our example of how Documents in the Cloud works, but you

Figure 1-4: See what you have stored in iCloud from your iPhone.

could use another iCloud-enabled app in the same way. Follow these steps:

1. **Tap the iCloud-enabled app on your iPhone.**

   The first time you open the app, a message asks if you want to use iCloud to store documents from this app rather than storing them on your iPhone. Tap Use iCloud.

2. **Create a new document or open an existing one from those shown, as in Figure 1-6.**

3. **Type, draw, edit, whatever you want with the document.**

4. **Close the document.**

    You may see the words "Updating 1 Document" or something similar at the top of the screen.

5. **Press the Home button to exit the app.**

On other iOS devices such as an iPad or iPod touch, follow the same steps as for your iPhone. On your computer, do the following:

1. **Open the iCloud-enabled app that you used to create or edit your document.**

2. **Click the iCloud tab.**

    The documents stored in iCloud for that app are listed in a window similar to that in Figure 1-7.

Figure 1-5: Choose the data you want to back up to iCloud.

3. **Double-click the document you want to open.**

4. **Edit the document.**

5. **Save the document as you normally would, but save it to iCloud.**

    You have the option to replace the existing document with the same name or save the edited document as a new document.

Backing up and syncing with iTunes

If you use a Mac with OS X 10.9 Mavericks, you can use iTunes to back up the data on your iPhone to your computer but iTunes only syncs media. You can also choose to sync a selection of your media, instead of syncing everything. iTunes syncs the following:

- Music (unless you use iTunes Match, in which case music syncs with iTunes in the Cloud)
- Movies
- TV Shows
- Audiobooks
- Podcasts
- Books
- Photos from your computer to your iPhone (to copy photos from your iPhone to your computer you use a photo management app such as iPhoto or Aperture)
- Apps

Figure 1-6: Share documents on all your devices with iCloud.

Data from Contacts, Calendar, Notes, Reminders, Passbook, Safari bookmarks, Mail, and phone settings are synced only by iCloud, although you can back them up to iTunes.

If you use a Mac with an OS version earlier than Mavericks or use Windows, please refer to the sidebar at the end of this section, Syncing with the Big Cats and Windows, which explains additional syncing information for those operating systems.

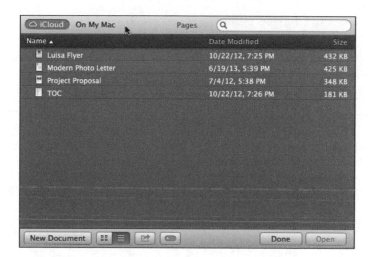

Figure 1-7: Open Documents in the Cloud on your computer directly from the app.

The first sync with iTunes

Now, you're ready to connect your iPhone to your computer and iTunes. You can set up a daily wireless sync, which is called iTunes Wi-Fi Sync, or you can physically connect your iPhone to your computer with the USB connector cable and run the ITunes Sync feature. However, even if you plan to use iTunes Wi-Fi Sync, you must connect your iPhone to your computer one time.

The first time you connect your iPhone to your computer, iTunes opens and you can set up and perform your first automatic sync. In this section, we go through those initial operations and then explain manual syncing. We also look at establishing the criteria for future syncing operations. These instructions are for iTunes 11.1 (126), which you can download for free from the Apple website, www.apple.com/itunes/. iTunes is available in both Mac and Windows versions. Click either the Get iTunes for Windows or Get iTunes for Macintosh link (although it's highly unlikely you would have a Mac without iTunes) and then click Download Now. The download begins automatically. Follow the on-screen instructions to install iTunes on your computer.

To begin syncing your iPhone with your computer, follow these steps:

1. **Connect your iPhone to your computer with the USB connector cable, using a port that is on your computer rather than one on the keyboard or hub (unless you have a powered hub).**

    iTunes opens. If iTunes doesn't open, open it manually.

2. **If this is the first time you connect an iPhone to iTunes, you probably want to choose Set Up As New iPhone. However, if you backup an iPod touch or iPad to iTunes, you can put that data on your iPhone.**

3. **Click Get Started on the next screen. The iPhone Summary window appears as shown in Figure 1-8.**

   In subsequent connections, select your iPhone from the pop-up device menu at the top right of the window.

   If iTunes doesn't recognize your iPhone, make sure the USB connector cable is firmly seated in both your iPhone and computer ports and that your iPhone is turned on.

   If iTunes still doesn't see your iPhone, choose iTunes⇨Preferences on a Mac or Edit⇨Preferences in Windows. Click the Devices icon at the top of the window that opens. Deselect the box next to Prevent iPods, iPhones, and iPads from Syncing Automatically. Click OK to activate the new setting.

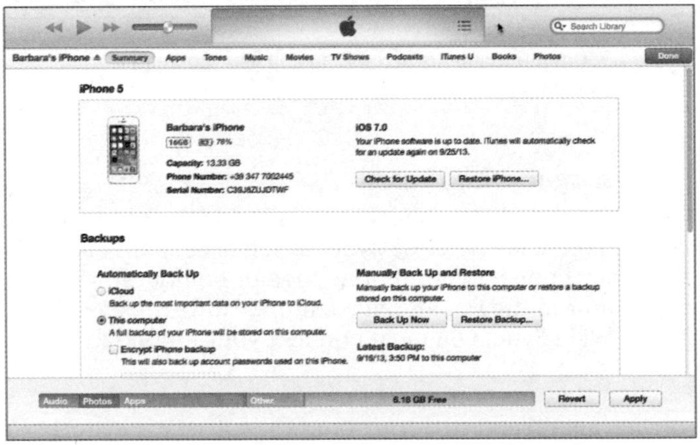

Figure 1-8: Select syncing and backup options on the Summary window.

Choose one of the following in the Backups section:

- **iCloud:** Select this choice to use iCloud as your backup destination.

- **This Computer:** Select this choice if you want to keep your iPhone backup on your computer. You have a subchoice of Encrypt iPhone Backup. Type a password in the dialog that appears. When you restore a backup to your iPhone, you'll be asked to enter the password.

4. **Select from the following in the Options section:**

   - **Automatically sync when this iPhone is connected:** Automatically launches iTunes and begins syncing when you connect your iPhone to your computer with the USB connector cable. When this box is not checked, you sync manually by clicking the Sync button in the bottom right corner.

If the Prevent iPods, iPhones, and iPads from Syncing Automatically option in the Devices pane of iTunes Preferences (iTunes⇨Preferences on a Mac; Edit⇨Preferences on a PC) is checked, this option appears dimmed and unavailable.

- **Sync with this iPhone over Wi-Fi:** Your iPhone syncs with iTunes once a day when both your computer and iPhone are connected to the same Wi-Fi network, and iTunes is open on your computer. Apple recommends that your iPhone is connected to a power source and we concur. Although you can sync without power, it significantly drains the battery.

- **Sync only checked songs and videos:** Only songs and videos that you manually check are synced. If you sync a playlist that contains unchecked songs and sync the playlist, the unchecked songs are not included in the sync. This means going through your iTunes library and manually selecting or deselecting all the songs and videos you have stored on your computer.

- **Prefer standard definition videos:** Standard definition videos occupy less memory than high definition videos, so you may prefer to sync SD videos to your iPhone.

- **Convert higher bit rate songs to 128/192/256 kbps:** iTunes automatically creates smaller audio files so you can squeeze more music onto your iPhone.

- **Manually manage music and videos:** Select this if you want to click and drag music and videos from iTunes to your iPhone. If you want to limit the music or videos stored on your iPhone, this may be a good option to choose.

- **Reset Warnings:** Click this button if, in the past, you've asked iTunes to stop showing you purchase and download warnings but you would like to see those warnings again.

- **The Configure Accessibility button:** Click this button to turn on the various Universal Access functions, such as VoiceOver and Speak Auto-Text. We explain Universal Access in Book I, Chapter 2 and also recommend you refer to Chapter 31 of iPhone's User Guide (manuals. info.apple.com/en_US/iphone_user_guide.pdf) for complete instructions on how to get the most out of the Accessibility features.

5. **Click Apply and proceed with the next sections to make choices for which data will sync.**

You can override the automatic syncing on an as-needed basis by launching iTunes before you connect your iPhone to your computer. Press and hold ⌘ +Option (Mac) or Shift+Ctrl (PC) and connect your iPhone. Hold the keys until your iPhone appears in right end of the navigation bar below the toolbar. Your iPhone won't sync automatically, but the settings you previously established remain unchanged.

Your syncing options in iTunes

Across the top of the iTunes window are eleven tabs: Summary, Apps, Tones, Music, Movies, TV Shows, Podcasts, iTunes U, Books, Photos, and On This iPhone. (A twelfth tab, Info, appears in Mac OS X 10.8, or earlier or in Windows). We take a look at each of these in the following sections. When you have set up the options as you wish, click the Sync button and your iPhone will have all the media you want it to.

Summary

The Summary pane is divided into three sections. The first section, iPhone, tells you about your iPhone, the name and total storage capacity, the version of the operating system you're using, iPhone's serial number, and your iPhone's phone number.

You can see if your iPhone is up-to-date and the next date iTunes will automatically check for an update. The Check for Update button gives you the option of checking for software updates before the date shown. If you know Apple has released an iPhone operating system software update, you can manually check and download that update by clicking this button.

The Restore iPhone button is used when you have problems with your iPhone or if you want to reset it to its original factory settings — say when you're giving or selling it to someone. All the contents are erased, and your iPhone wakes up restored as if it were fresh from the factory with the latest iOS.

Apps

You use the Apps pane, shown in Figure 1-9, to sync apps you buy in the Apps Store. If you set up automatic downloads for apps, you'll use this section only for rearranging apps and folders. In this pane, you can also copy documents between your iPhone and your computer with the Share Files feature.

Figure 1-9: Manage your apps and share files in the Apps pane.

Select the Automatically Install New Apps box to sync new apps to your iPhone that you downloaded to your computer or another device, like an iPad.

On the left side, you see a list of all the iOS apps you have on your computer. Scrolling through the list, notice that it's sorted by kind: iPhone, iPod touch, and iPad Apps, and iPhone and iPod touch Apps. With the pop-up menu, you can also sort by name, category, date, or size. Click Install next to the apps you want on your iPhone or click and drag the icon from the list to the Home screen (on the right) where you want the app to reside.

On the right side is an image of your iPhone's Home screens and folders. This is a scrollable pane within a scrollable pane; move the pointer to the pane or scrollbar with the Home screens to scroll down and see the folders, including Newsstand and any other folders you created. You can drag the buttons from the list on the right to the destination screen or folder, which can be easier than doing so on your iPhone when you have a lot of apps and folders. Use the slider at the top of the section to zoom in or out of the screens and folders window. Follow these steps:

1. **Click and drag the Home screens to rearrange them until they are in positions that you like and find useful.**

2. **Click the plus sign (+) next to the Home Screens title to create additional Home screens.**

3. **Click and drag an app icon from the list on the left to a new position on a Home screen on the right.**

   The button will move to the new position.

4. **Create folders by dragging one app icon from the app list over another app on the Home screen.**

   The button is replaced by a highlighted square in which you see two or more tiny representations of the apps inside. A rectangle (the folder) opens beneath showing the apps that are in the folder. iPhone names the folder based on the kind of apps that are in it, but you can rename it by typing in the field.

5. **Click the plus sign (+) by a specific folder to add another screen to that folder.**

6. **To delete an app, click Remove in the apps list so it will be deleted from your iPhone during the next sync.**

7. **After you've made the changes you want and your Home screens are neatly organized, click the Apply button to sync your changes with your iPhone.**

In the lower half of the Apps pane, as seen in Figure 1-10, you see File Sharing, which lets you share documents, created with apps that support file sharing, to and from your computer and iPhone. On the left are the apps you have that support file sharing; on the right are the files on your iPhone. To transfer files from your iPhone to your computer:

1. **Connect your iPhone to your computer and open iTunes, and then click the Apps tab.**

2. **From the list on the left, select the app that supports the document you want to share. We selected iA Writer in Figure 1-10.**

   A list of available documents appears on the right. If you use iCloud to share documents, such as those in Pages or one of the other iWork apps, they won't appear in the documents list of iTunes.

3. **Click the document or documents you want to transfer from your iPhone to your computer.**

4. **Click the Save to button at the bottom of the list.**

   Select the destination where you want to save the documents.

5. **Click Open (Mac) or OK (Windows).**

   The file is transferred to your computer.

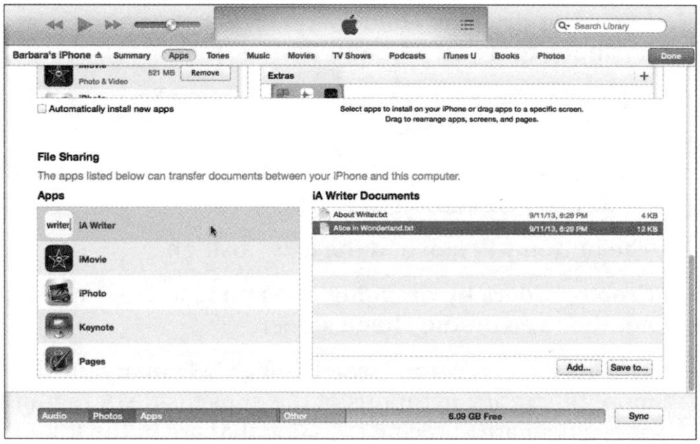

Figure 1-10: Manage file transfers from the Apps pane.

To transfer files from your computer to your iPhone:

1. **Repeat Steps 1 and 2 of the previous list.**

2. **Click the Add button at the bottom of the list.**

   Select the file from your computer that you want to transfer from your computer to your iPhone.

3. **Click Open (Mac) or OK (Windows).**

   The file is transferred to your iPhone and can be opened with an app that supports that type of document. Select additional files to transfer more than one.

To delete a file from your iPhone, select the file in the list and then tap the Delete key (Backspace in Windows) on the keyboard.

Tones

If you download ringtones from the iTunes Store or create them with GarageBand, they are saved to iTunes and you see the Tones section. To sync those ringtones with your iPhone, click the Tones tab and then choose your syncing options. Select the box next to Sync Tones, and then choose All Tones or Selected Tones. If you choose Selected Tones, another box appears that lists all the ringtones you have in iTunes. Select the ones you want to sync to your iPhone.

Music

You have three choices for syncing music from iTunes to your iPhone. The first two are selected from the Music pane:

Book II
Chapter 1

Syncing and
Backing Up Your
iPhone

✔ You can sync the Entire music library, which is a great and easy choice if you have enough storage on your iPhone to hold your entire music library.

✔ You can sync selected playlists, artists, albums, and genres. Make the selections you want in the boxes, as seen in Figure 1-11. This is a good solution if you don't have enough, or don't want to usurp, iPhone memory, or if you only want to listen to certain types of music on your iPhone.

Figure 1-11: Manage your music from the Music pane.

You have three other considerations on the Music pane:

✔ **Include Music Videos:** Any music videos you have will be synced to your iPhone from iTunes.

✔ **Include Voice Memos:** Voice memos from your iPhone are synced to iTunes.

✔ **Automatically Fill Free Space with Songs:** iTunes will sync as many songs as space on your iPhone allows. If you choose Selected Playlists, Artists, Albums, and Genres, and also choose Automatically Fill Free Space with Songs, *and* there's enough room for your entire song library, all your songs will be copied to your iPhone. Be forewarned, however, this option greatly limits space on your iPhone for other media, such as new photos or video you capture with Camera.

The third choice, made on the Summary pane, is to sync only checked songs and videos. If you have a lot of music, this can be a long and tedious operation. The upside is that you have exactly the music you want on your iPhone. Here's how to do it:

1. **In the Summary pane, select Sync Only Checked Songs and Videos.**

   If this item is unavailable, go to iTunes⇨Preferences⇨General and select Show List Checkboxes under Views, and click OK.

2. **Click Apply and then click Done.**

   If iTunes begins syncing, drag the Slide to Cancel slider on your iPhone to interrupt the sync.

3. **Click Music in the pop-up menu on the left of the window.**

4. **Check all the songs and videos you want to sync to your iPhone. Uncheck any you don't want to sync, if they are checked.**

   You can also select a playlist from the Source list and check the songs in the playlist.

5. **When you finish your selection, click your iPhone in the pop-up device menu on the upper right.**

6. **Click the Sync button on the bottom right corner.**

   Only songs and videos you checked are synced to your iPhone. The selection of checked music completely replaces the music on your iPhone, meaning that if a song is on your iPhone but remains unchecked on iTunes, it is deleted during the sync.

If you have selected Manually Manage Music and Videos on the Summary pane, you can click and drag media — songs, videos, podcasts, or playlists — from your iTunes library to your iPhone. Click the On This iPhone tab, and then click the media type you want to add to your iPhone from the list on the left. Click the Add To button in the upper right corner; the window splits into two panes. The pane on the left is iTunes on your computer and the pane on the right is your iPhone. Click and drag the items you want to move to your iPhone. You can navigate through different media types as well as change the views with the tabs at the top of the page. Click Done when you finish your selection.

When you choose to Manually Manage Music and Videos, you also have access to Autofill settings. Click Music from the list on the left. At the bottom of the window, you see a pop-up menu next to Autofill From; choose where you want iTunes to choose songs to automatically fill empty space on your iPhone, such as your entire Music library or a specific playlist. Click the Settings button and choose the criteria you want iTunes to use for Autofill, as shown in Figure 1-12, as well as how much space you want left for other things. Click OK, and then click Autofill.

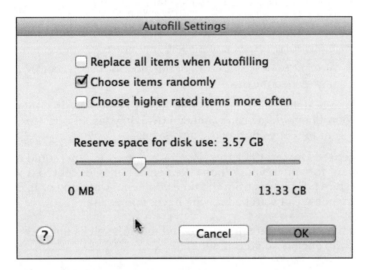

Figure 1-12: The Autofill Settings dialog.

The content will sync immediately. However, if/when someday you deselect Manually Manage Music and Videos, the content you added manually will be removed when you automatically sync. This won't make a difference if the media you manually transferred is included in the automatic sync; however, it is a hassle if you have a lot of music on your iPhone that you copied from other sources.

You can choose to convert songs to 128 Kpbs AAC by selecting that option on the Summary pane.

Movies

With iPhone's increased storage space and fabulous display, watching movies on your iPhone has become a realistic choice. Syncing gives you the option of downloading and beginning to watch a movie on one device and then syncing and watching through to the end on the other device. If you fall asleep watching a movie on your computer in the evening, you can sync it to your iPhone and watch the end during your train commute the next morning. If you sign in to your iCloud account on both your iPhone and your computer, you can begin watching on one device, pause or stop the video, and then pick up where you left off on another device. If you click the Movies tab at the top of iTunes, you have a couple of options:

- ✓ **Click the Sync Movies check box only:** Movies you have on iTunes appear in the Movies box. Manually select the movies you want to sync by selecting the box next to the name of the movie to select.

- ✓ **Click the Sync Movies and the Automatically Include check boxes:** A pop-up menu is activated, which lets you choose

  - All or all unwatched movies

  - A quantity of 1, 3, 5, or 10 watched movies

  - A quantity of 1, 3, 5, or 10 of the most or least recently added unwatched movies.

  An unwatched movie is one that hasn't been seen on either iTunes or your iPhone. After you watch a movie on your iPhone, this information is sent to iTunes during the next sync.

- ✓ **Rented Movies:** Click the Move button next to any rented movie you want to sync to your iPhone. Remember, movies rented from iTunes expire in 24 hours from the time you begin watching or in 30 days, even if you haven't watched it, whichever comes first.

If you have begun watching the rented movie, it picks up where you left off when you open it on your iPhone.

Music videos are downloaded and imported into the Movies library of iTunes. If you want the music video in the Music library, click the video, and then click Get Info. Under the Kind list, choose Music Video, and then click OK. iTunes moves it from Movies to Music, although it will be in Videos on your iPhone.

TV Shows

With iTunes, you can download free or purchased episodes and watch them when you want — on your computer or your iPhone. Watch out, though: A single half-hour episode takes about 250MB of storage, so your iPhone fills up fast if you don't manage the sync process. Alternatively, if you're connected to your Wi-Fi network, you can use Home Sharing to stream the show from your computer to your iPhone. Here's what you need to know:

1. **Click the box next to Sync TV Shows at the top of the pane to activate the other options.**

2. **Click the box next to Automatically Include and the criteria you choose in the two adjacent pop-up menus will be applied to all the shows you have on iTunes.**

3. **Choose one selection from each of the two pop-up menus, as shown in Figure 1-13:**

   Left menu:

   • All, which includes watched and unwatched episodes

   • All unwatched episodes

   • 1, 3, 5, or 10 of the newest episodes, watched and unwatched

   • 1, 3, 5, or 10 of the oldest unwatched episodes

   Right menu:

   • Apply your choice to either *all shows* in your iTunes library or *selected shows*, in which case the Shows section appears, and you click the box next to those you want to apply your choices to.

   Or

4. **To pick and choose manually among the shows you have in your library, deselect the box next to Automatically Include.**

5. **Click the representative show icon in the Shows box.**

   The episodes appear in the Episodes box on the right.

6. **Select the check box next to the episodes you want to sync to your iPhone.**

You can check the options under Include Episodes in Playlists to sync those found in your Purchased or Recently Added playlists.

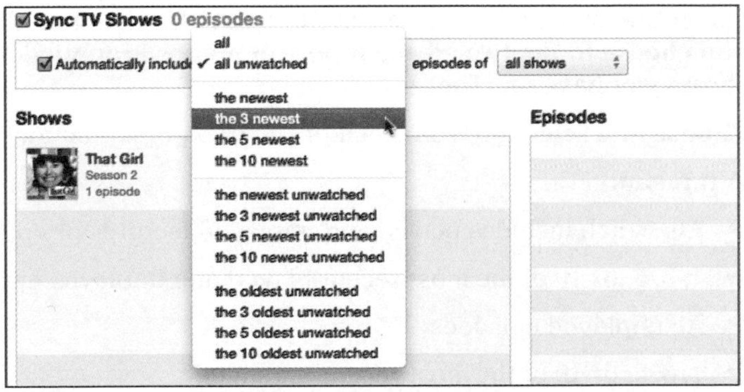

Figure 1-13: Sync only the episodes you want to watch on your iPhone.

If you want to include or exclude a watched or unwatched episode without changing your syncing options, click TV Shows in the drop-down Source menu or, if you show the Sidebar, in the Library section of iTunes' Source list. Control+click or right-click the episode and choose Mark as Unwatched or Mark as Watched (whichever you have already done and want to change).

Podcasts and iTunes U

Although these are two different types of media, the sync procedure is the same, so we grouped them together. Plus, both are great ways to learn about new things in every field imaginable. Although podcasts are a mix of talk radio and documentaries, iTunes U gives you access to grammar and high school lessons and lectures from universities and colleges around the world, as well as professional development courses. You find videos and audio books, post-graduate seminars, and presentations from museums like the Metropolitan Museum of Art and organizations like the American Society of Clinical Oncology that give lifelong learning a whole new definition. Printed material associated with iTunes U courses is found in the Books section of iTunes.

Both the Podcasts and iTunes U apps can be downloaded at the iTunes Store and you want to have them on your iPhone in order to enjoy that type of content. (See Book II, Chapter 2 to learn about downloading apps and then hop over to Book V, Chapters 2 and 3 to learn about using the iTunes U and Podcasts apps, respectively.)

The steps to sync from iTunes to your iPhone are as follows:

1. **Click the tab you want: Podcasts or iTunes U.**

2. **Select the check box next to Sync Podcasts/iTunes U at the top of the pane to activate the other options.**

3. **Select the check box next to Automatically Include and the criteria you choose in the two adjacent pop-up menus is applied to all the shows you have on iTunes.**

4. **Choose one selection from each of the two pop-up menus:**

   Left menu:

   • All, which includes played and unplayed lectures or episodes

   • 1, 3, 5, or 10 of the most recent played and unplayed episodes

   • All unplayed episodes

   • 1, 3, 5, or 10 of the most recent unplayed

   • 1, 3, 5, or 10 of the least recent unplayed

   • All new episodes

- 1, 3, 5, or 10 of the most recent new episodes
- 1, 3, 5, or 10 of the least recent new episodes

Right menu:

- Apply your choice to either all collections in your iTunes library or selected collections, in which case a check box appears next to each item in the list. Select the check boxes next to the shows you want to apply your choices to.

Or

5. **To pick and choose manually among the lectures you have in your library, deselect the box next to Automatically Include.**

6. **Click Episode in the Collections box.**

   The episodes appear in the Items box on the right.

7. **Select the check box next to the episodes you want to sync to your iPhone.**

In Movies, TV Shows, Podcasts, and iTunes U, when you set your sync options using one of the numbered selections (5 most recent unplayed, or 10 least recent unwatched), the selection changes as you download new media to iTunes. If you choose a specific episode or movie, it remains selected for subsequent syncs until you deselect it (or it expires, in the case of a rented movie).

Books

Books manages e-books, PDFs, and audiobooks. Audiobooks are great commute and workout companions, and the Internet holds myriad titles of every genre, which you can download to your computer.

E-books, or electronic books, have been on the scene for a couple decades now, too. Your iPhone can function as both an audiobook listening device and an e-book reader — cool! You do have to download the iBooks app from Apple or one of the other reader apps to view e-books in the ePub or PDF format on your iPhone; we talk about those other apps in the bonus content on this book's companion website. (For more on the website, see the Introduction to this book.) Syncing the written word from iTunes to your iPhone to read in iBooks works pretty much the same as for other media, but we show you what to do anyway:

1. **Select the check box next to Sync Books at the top of the pane to activate the other options.**

2. **If you click All Books, all the e-books that you see in the Books box are synced to your iPhone.**

   Or

3. **Click Selected Books, and then set your criteria by choosing from the pop-up menus in the Books section:**

   - **Books and PDF files, Only Books, or Only PDF files**

- **Sort by Authors or Sort by Title:** This doesn't change your syncing option, but can make finding the books you want to sync easier.

4. **Click the boxes next to the books you want to sync, as shown in Figure 1-14.**

Figure 1-14: Make syncing selections for e-books and audio books from the Books pane.

To sync e-books or documents that are neither ePub nor PDF files, you have to use the File Sharing section of the Apps sync panel.

The Audio Books section works the same way:

1. **Click the box next to Sync Audio Books at the top of the pane to activate the other options.**

2. **If you click All Audio Books, all the audio books that you have on iTunes are synced to your iPhone.**

   Or

3. **Click Selected books, which opens the Audio Books and Parts boxes.**

4. **Select the check boxes next to the items you want to sync in the Audio Books and Parts lists.**

Photos

The Photos pane lets you move photos from your computer to your iPhone. (From one computer only; if you try to move photos from a second computer, the originals are erased from your iPhone.)

To do the reverse (that is, move photos from your iPhone to your computer), you use your photo management program such as iPhoto or Photoshop Elements, which considers your iPhone a digital camera or external drive with images. Photos are synced with photo management software.

Another option is the Photo Stream feature of iCloud, where your photos are stored in Photo Stream on iCloud and then pushed to your devices, such as your iPhone or your computer.

We talk about Photos and Photo Stream in Book V, Chapter 1. To move copies of photos from your computer to your iPhone, follow these steps (refer to Figure 1-15):

1. **Select the check box next to Sync Photos From and choose the photo management application or folder where your photos reside.**

2. **Click Include Videos at the top if you want videos included in your selection.**

3. **Click All Photos, Albums (Events and Faces are visible if you use iPhoto or Aperture on a Mac) to copy every photo in that application. However, photos that are in a format that is incompatible with your iPhone won't be copied.**

   Or

4. **Click Selected Albums, (or Events or Faces on a Mac), and Automatically Include.**

   Boxes appear for Albums and Events. Mac users who work with iPhoto or Aperture have the Faces option too.

   If you choose a single folder in Step 1, a selected button appears which reads All Folders. You can't deselect this button.

   If you choose a folder that holds other folders, your options are All Folders or Selected Folders, and you can choose from the subfolders from the list that appears.

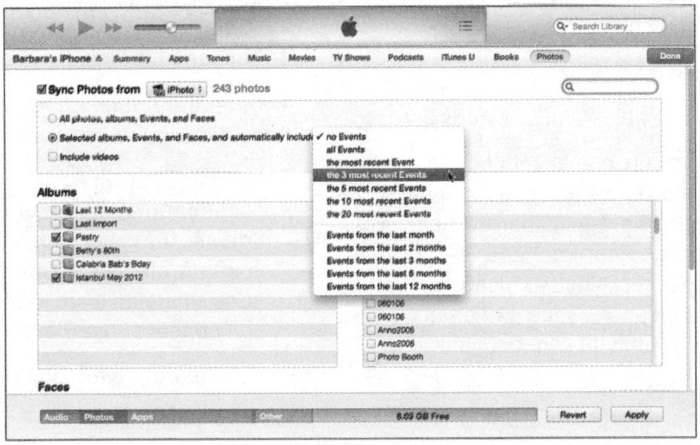

Figure 1-15: Move photos from your computer to your iPhone in the Photos pane.

Book II
Chapter 1

Syncing and
Backing Up Your
iPhone

5. **Define what you want to automatically include by choosing one of the following from the pop-up menu:**

   - **No events:** Only photos you choose from the boxes below will be included. Nothing is synced automatically.

   - **All events:** Selects and syncs all the events in the events box.

   - **The most recent 1, 3, 5, or 10 events:** Selects and syncs from one to 10 of the most recent events, which you see at the very bottom of the Events list. You may have to scroll down to see them.

   - **Events from the last 1, 2, 3, 6, or 12 months:** Selects all events that took place in the time period you select.

6. **In addition to defined events, you can choose albums and faces to sync by selecting them in the corresponding boxes.**

   The number of photos included in the selection appears in gray next to the selection.

Responding to a dialog to copy your photos or videos

If you've taken any photos with your iPhone since the last sync, your photo management software may automatically open and ask if you want to import the photos from your iPhone. To turn this function on, or off, do the following:

On a Mac:

1. Choose Finder⇨Applications or click Launchpad on the Dock.

2. Open Image Capture.

3. Click your iPhone in the Devices list.

4. In the pop-up menu entitled Connecting this iPhone Opens, choose No Application if you want no application to open when you connect your iPhone to your computer. Alternatively, you can choose from one of the applications shown to open that application when you connect your iPhone.

5. Choose Image Capture⇨Quit Image Capture to exit Image Capture. The new setting is saved and occurs the next time you connect your iPhone.

On Windows 7 or 8:

1. Choose Start⇨Control Panel.

2. Choose Hardware and Sound.

3. Choose AutoPlay.

4. Open the Apple iPhone list in the Devices section.

5. Choose Take No Action if you want no application to open when you connect your iPhone to your computer. Alternatively, you can choose from one of the applications shown to open that application when you connect your iPhone.

We talk more about photo management in Book V, Chapter 1.

iPhone supports many common image file types including GIF, PNG, JPG, although iTunes doesn't sync exact copies of your photos but files that have been converted to fit iPhone's screen size. This conversion gives you better viewing quality and uses less storage space on your iPhone.

iTunes works with the latest, and many older, versions of the iPhoto and Aperture photo management apps on the Mac and Photoshop Elements on Windows. Consult the Apple iTunes website to determine if older versions are compatible.

The iTunes sync

Now that you've set the criteria for your sync, all that remains is to click the Sync or Apply button in the bottom right corner. Sync changes to Apply when you make changes to your Sync options.

When you connect your iPhone to your computer in the future, choose your iPhone from the devices list at the top of the iTunes window, and then click Sync to perform a sync that uses the criteria you established. If you select Automatically Sync When This iPhone is Connected on the Summary pane, the sync happens without clicking the Sync button. If you also select Sync with This iPhone Over Wi-Fi, your iPhone syncs with iTunes once a day when both your computer and your iPhone are connected to the same Wi-Fi network and to a power source. The spinning sync icon in the status bar of your iPhone lets you know syncing is happening.

Book II
Chapter 1

Syncing and Backing Up Your iPhone

When you click Sync (or Apply), iTunes syncs the categories where you have selected the Sync check box at the top of the pane. If you deselect the Sync check box at the top of the Music pane, for example, when you sync, all the music on your iPhone will be deleted, although it remains on iTunes.

Disconnecting iPhone

To disconnect your iPhone from your computer, click the eject button next to your iPhone's name in the upper part of the iTunes window, and then disconnect the cable. If the sync is taking longer than you thought, and you have to go somewhere and take your iPhone with you. You can disconnect your iPhone and go where you need to go. When you're ready, reconnect your iPhone to your computer, and iTunes and iPhone take up syncing where they left off. If you get a call while you're syncing, your iPhone is so smart that it pauses the syncing session when the phone rings and picks up when the call is finished.

When the Automatic Downloads function is on, music, apps, books, and podcasts that you download or purchase from the iTunes Store or App Store from any device are transferred to the other devices. On your iPhone or other iOS device, go to Settings⇨iTunes & App Store and tap Music, Apps, and/or Books to the On position. For Podcasts, go to Settings⇨Podcasts and tap Auto-Downloads, and then select the All or Most Recent. On your computer, go to iTunes⇨Preferences⇨Store and click Music, Books, and/or Apps in the Automatic Downloads section.

Syncing with the Big Cats or Windows

If you use Mac OS X 10.7 Lion or 10.8 Mountain Lion, or Windows, you have a choice to sync data from Contacts, Calendar, Notes, and Safari using iTunes or iCloud. To use iTunes, connect as explained previously and then click the Info tab, which is second from the left. The following figure shows iTunes in Windows. Here are a few caveats:

✔ If you use iCloud, you'll see the options outlined here and can even select them, but you will also see a warning that reminds you that you sync your iPhone with iCloud; syncing with iTunes as well may result in duplicate data.

✔ If you use Microsoft Outlook on a Mac, you must first turn on Sync Services in Outlook by clicking Tools⇨Sync Services and then selecting the items you want to sync, such as Calendar, Contacts, Tasks, and Notes. This syncs anything in Outlook with iCal/ Calendar and Address Book/Contacts on your Mac, which you then sync with your iPhone with iTunes.

Refer to the following to set up syncing with iTunes:

✔ **Contacts:** Choose which app you want to sync with, and if your contacts are divided into groups, you can choose to sync all your contacts or only subsets or groups of contacts. This is useful if you use your work computer to sync but don't want the company directory on your iPhone. Refer to Book IV, Chapter 1 to learn about the Contacts app.

There is also an option to instruct iTunes what to do if, when syncing, it finds a new contact that's been created on your iPhone but hasn't been assigned to a group. Next to Add Contacts Created Outside of Groups on This iPhone to, choose a location from the pop-up menu.

✔ **Calendar:** You can sync calendars from more than one application including iCal, Calendar, and Microsoft Outlook 2011 (on a Mac), Microsoft Outlook, 2003, 2007, or 2010 (on a Windows computer), and Google Calendar. Windows users must have Outlook installed in order to sync Calendars. If you have more than one calendar created, you can pick and choose which to sync with your iPhone. You can also establish a cut-off date for old syncs, such as not syncing events older than 15 days. No sense clogging up your iPhone with the past. Refer to Book IV, Chapter 2 to learn about the Calendar app.

Sync Calendars also syncs Reminders. If you want to pick and choose which calendars to sync, you can choose Reminders from the Selected Calendars list.

✔ **e-mail:** Only your account settings are synced, not the actual messages. You can choose which accounts you want on your iPhone.

On Mac, when you check the Sync Mail Accounts box, iTunes automatically checks the box next to the first account on the list. You can deselect that one and choose one or more other accounts. Say, for example, that you have an e-mail account for your golf league. You may not want to receive those messages on your iPhone, but just on your computer. Don't check the box next to that e-mail account name in the accounts list.

On Windows, check Sync Selected Mail Accounts From and then choose Outlook or Outlook Express from the pop-up menu.

Your password may or may not be synced with the account information. If you find iPhone asks for your password, you can add it permanently by tapping Settings⇨Mail, Contacts, Calendar. Tap the account name and then type your password in the appropriate field.

Account settings move in one direction only: from your computer to your iPhone. If you set

up e-mail accounts on your iPhone (as explained in Book III, Chapter 4), they must be set up manually on your computer, if you want them to be on your computer.

✔ **Other:** Choose to sync bookmarks that you have in Safari on a Mac, or Safari or Microsoft Internet Explorer on Windows — the check boxes reflect the possible choices. You may want to delete old bookmarks you don't want any more before syncing.

✔ **Advanced:** Checking any or all of these boxes will *replace*, instead of syncing, information on your iPhone with the information that's on your computer. Why would you do this? Say you tried to organize your contacts on your iPhone and made a mess. You could rework everything — with a full-size keyboard — on your computer and then overwrite everything on your iPhone. Obviously, if you mainly use your iPhone to add or make changes to any of these apps, don't check this box.

If you want to connect your iPhone to two computers using iTunes, do the following:

1. Follow the instructions outlined previously in this chapter, sync your iPhone and one of your computers, for example, a notebook.

2. Connect and sync your iPhone with the other computer, say, a desktop. Set the same preferences in the Info pane as you did on your notebook. iTunes give you two options:

   • **Merge Info:** iPhone keeps the information from your notebook and merges it with the information on your desktop.

   • **Replace Info:** The information that was synced from the first computer is replaced by the information on the second computer.

Gauging Your Storage Needs

There are two considerations you have to think about with regard to storage. One is how much space is available on your iPhone for syncing your apps, media, documents, and data. The second is whether your backup location offers enough storage. If you use iTunes and back up to your computer, this probably isn't a concern; if you use iCloud, you may need to purchase storage beyond the complimentary 5 GB. We talk about both here.

Checking your iPhone's storage capacity

When you're ready to sync, make sure you have enough room on your iPhone before actually hitting the Sync button. Your iPhone's storage capacity depends on which version of iPhone you have.

Considering that the operating system itself takes up about one gigabyte of memory and another half a gigabyte is kept as a reserve for apps running in the background, that leaves you with 14.5 gigabytes on a 16GB phone, 30.5 on a 32GB phone, or 62.5 on a 64GB phone. That sounds like a warehouse of storage, until you start loading apps, movies, TV shows, podcasts, games, photos, and videos, when you find out it fills up fast. There are two ways to know how much space you have on your iPhone:

- **On iPhone:** From the Home screen, tap Settings⇨General⇨Usage. The list shows you how much memory is occupied by Videos, Photos & Camera, Music, and other apps with the biggest space hogs at the top of the list and tells you how much storage is Available and Used, as shown in Figure 1-16.

- **On iTunes:** When your iPhone is connected to iTunes and selected in the source list, you see a colored bar near the bottom of the iTunes window that illustrates how much space each type of data will occupy on your iPhone when you perform the sync you've set up. If you are in the Music pane and you deselect the Sync Music box, the blue section of the bar that represents audio files shrinks. If your iPhone is nearly full, you can play with your syncing options and see how they affect the storage capacity. Click once on one of the titles under the chart and the number of items in each category is displayed. Click a second time and it displays how long it will take to listen to all the audio and video in your library. Click a third time to return to the gigabyte numbers.

If you have more media than memory, you have a couple of choices for managing and choosing which data to sync:

- Manually select which music, videos, and podcasts you want on your iPhone and sync only those.

- Subscribe to iTunes Match to listen to music in streaming, which we explain in Book V, Chapter 3.

Adding storage capacity to iCloud

iCloud gives you 5 GB storage for mail, contacts, calendars, documents, and backup. Media purchased from iTunes and photos stored in Photo Stream don't count toward that limit. If you find the 5 GB isn't enough, you can delete some of the things you store in iCloud or purchase more storage. Here's how to do both:

1. **Tap Settings⇨iCloud.**

2. **Tap Storage & Backup at the bottom of the screen.**

3. **Tap Manage Storage.**

4. **Look at the apps in the Documents & Data list.**

   If you see an app that's taking up a lot of memory, tap that app to see a list of documents stored on iCloud, as shown in Figure 1-17.

5. **If there are documents you can delete, tap Edit in the upper right corner, and then tap the minus sign next to the document you want to delete or tap Delete All to eliminate all the documents from that app in iCloud.**

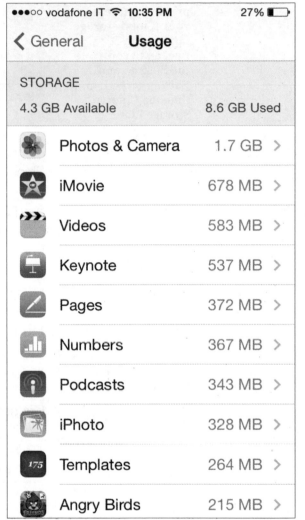

Figure 1-16: See what bits are occupying the gigabytes on your iPhone.

●●●○○ vodafone IT 🛜 10:35 PM   27% 🔋

〈 General   **Usage**

STORAGE

4.3 GB Available   8.6 GB Used

Photos & Camera   1.7 GB >

iMovie   678 MB >

Videos   583 MB >

Keynote   537 MB >

Pages   372 MB >

Numbers   367 MB >

Podcasts   343 MB >

iPhoto   328 MB >

Templates   264 MB >

Angry Birds   215 MB >

If the documents you delete are only stored in iCloud, you lose them completely. Open and save the documents on your computer, upload (using the Share Sheet) them to another remote storage server, or e-mail them to yourself before deleting them from iCloud if you want to keep a copy.

6. **If you want to keep the documents and prefer to increase your iCloud storage, tap Storage & Backup to return to the Storage and Backup screen, and then tap Change Storage Plan.**

   The Buy More Storage screen opens, as shown in Figure 1-18. You see your current plan and both upgrade and downgrade options.

7. **Tap the plan you wish to purchase, and then tap the Buy button.**

8. **Enter the password for your Apple ID, if requested, and then enter your payment information.**

9. **Tap Done.**

   Your credit card is charged for the amount indicated immediately and on an annual basis until you downgrade, as we explain next.

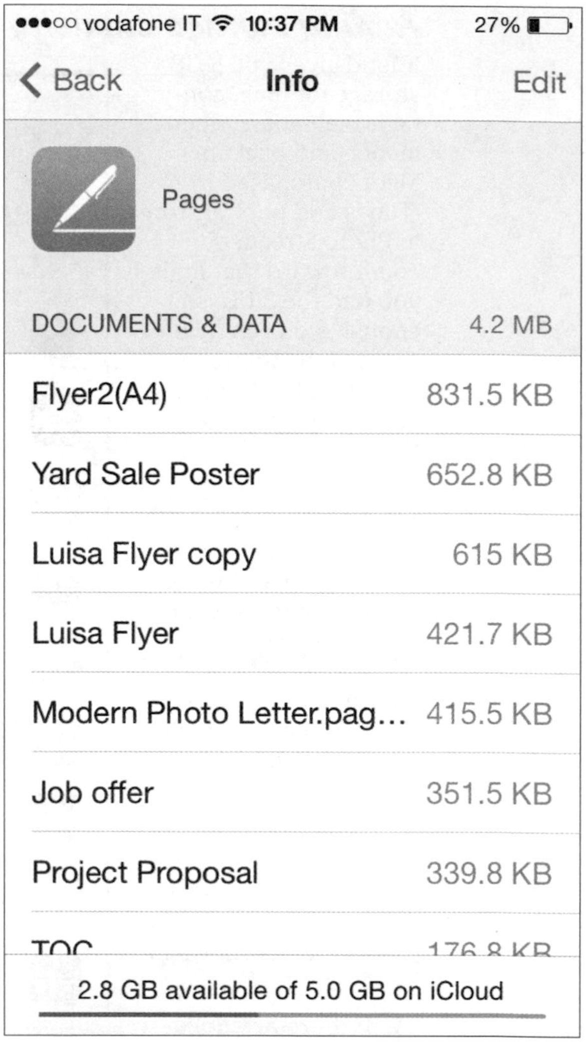

●●●○○ vodafone IT 🛜 10:37 PM		27% 🔋
‹ Back	**Info**	Edit

Pages

DOCUMENTS & DATA	4.2 MB
Flyer2(A4)	831.5 KB
Yard Sale Poster	652.8 KB
Luisa Flyer copy	615 KB
Luisa Flyer	421.7 KB
Modern Photo Letter.pag…	415.5 KB
Job offer	351.5 KB
Project Proposal	339.8 KB
TOC	176.8 KB

2.8 GB available of 5.0 GB on iCloud

Figure 1-17: See the documents stored in iCloud for each app.

You can also purchase iCloud storage through the System Preferences⟳iCloud on your Mac or by clicking Start⟳Control Panel⟳iCloud in Windows.

If you purchase more storage and then find you don't need it, you can downgrade at any time so your credit card will be charged less or not at all when the renewal date arrives. Do the following:

1. **Tap Settings⟳iCloud⟳Storage & Backup⟳Buy More Storage.**

2. **Tap Downgrade Options.**

   You may be asked to enter your Apple ID password.

3. **Tap the storage plan you want when your current plan expires.**

4. **Tap Done.**

5. **Tap the back button to return to the main Settings screen, and then press the Home button to close Settings.**

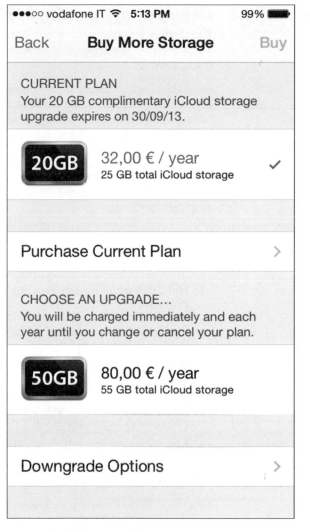

Syncing with More Than One iPhone or iTunes Computer

Used to be that you had one computer every two and a half households and the only music you heard through the phone was your father singing "Happy Birthday" to you. Today, you probably have a computer at home and one at work, and maybe a notebook computer, too. Perhaps you share your home computer with your significant other or children and each of them has an iPhone. Apple has lightened up on its one iPhone-one computer monogamy policy. Here

Figure 1-18: Purchase additional storage on iCloud.

we give you a way to use multiple computers with one iPhone as well as multiple iPhones with one computer, too.

One iPhone, multiple computers

The fact is, different pieces of our lives often overlap. You want the contacts on your notebook and desktop computers and your iPhone and iPad to be the same, and you want the option of making changes in either of those places and syncing with the other two. The simplest solution is an over-the-air, or OTA, syncing and storage service, like iCloud as explained at the beginning of this chapter. Just sign in to the same iCloud account on all your devices and everything is kept in sync.

One computer, multiple iPhones

Your family members share one computer and each of you has an iPhone. You can sync more than one iPhone with the same computer. Each device is recognized by its unique name.

On a Mac, each iPhone can use different sync settings; on Windows, each phone has to use the same settings. Each person has a separate Apple account because each iPhone has an Apple account associated with it. You probably each have different media that you'd like to sync with your respective iPhones.

The ideal solution — the one we highly recommend — is to set up separate user accounts on the Mac or Windows computer for each user, who in turn would have his own iTunes library for media and iCloud account for data to sync to his iPhone.

If for some reason the idea of separate user accounts doesn't work for you, you can sync different sets of media by setting up a different iTunes library for each family member:

1. **Hold down the option key (Mac) or the shift key (Windows) and open iTunes.**

   A dialog gives you the options of creating a new library or choosing which you want to open.

2. **Select Create Library.**

   Type in a name and location for the library.

3. **Whenever you start up iTunes, hold down the Option (Mac) or Shift (Windows) key to open your personal library.**

4. **Sync your iPhone with your library.**

Make sure you uncheck Copy Files to iTunes Media Folder When Adding to Library. On Mac, this is found under iTunes⇨Preferences⇨Advanced; on Windows, Edit⇨Preferences⇨Advanced.

Perhaps you have an iPhone for business and another one for your personal use. You can sync more than one iPhone with the same account and even sync different things to each. Give each iPhone a different name and when you open iTunes, choose the phone you want to sync from the pop-up source menu and then sync as outlined previously. iTunes remembers which sync goes with which phone.

Banking on Backups in Case Things Go Kerflooey

Sooner or later the backup you created using either iCloud or iTunes might come in handy. You may have to erase and reset your iPhone because it's gone haywire or maybe you had to send your iPhone in for repairs. (Refer to

Book I, Chapter 5 for troubleshooting tips.) The best case scenario is you got a new iPhone and want to restore your old data to your new phone. To load the backup file onto your iPhone, old or new, from iCloud:

1. **Choose Settings⇨General⇨Reset.**
2. **Tap Erase All Content and Settings.**
3. **When the Setup Assistant opens, tap Restore from iCloud Backup.**
4. **Sign in to iCloud with your Apple ID and password.**

   iCloud pushes the most recent backup to your iPhone.

If your backup is on your computer, and you use iTunes to restore the backup to your iPhone:

1. **Connect your iPhone to the computer you usually use to sync.**
2. **Open iTunes, if it didn't automatically open (depends on how you set it up).**
3. **Click iPhone, or whatever you named it, in the devices pop-up menu in the upper right.**
4. **Click the Summary tab.**
5. **Click Restore Backup.**

   iTunes gives you a chance to back out of your choice or go ahead. Clicking Restore iPhone will erase your iPhone and re-install the most up-to-date operating system. You then must restore from a backup or start over with your iPhone. Choosing to set up as a new iPhone is a good option if you plan to give your iPhone to someone else and want it to have a clean slate.

6. **If you see multiple backup files, choose the most recent one associated with your iPhone.**
7. **Sync your music, videos, podcasts, and books as we explained earlier in this chapter.**
8. **Tap Settings⇨iCloud and sign in to your iCloud account to sync your Contacts, Calendar, Notes, bookmarks, and all the other data that iCloud manages.**

If you backed up an old iPhone to iTunes and want to restore that existing data to a new iPhone, connect the new iPhone to your computer and open iTunes. Choose Restore from Backup, and then select the most recent backup from the pop-up menu. If you like to keep things minimalistic, you can delete older backups. Go to iTunes⇨Preferences (Edit⇨Preferences on Windows), and click Devices. You see a list of your backups. Just clock the one or ones you want to delete then click Delete Backup. Poof! Gone.

Chapter 2: Apps 411: Browsing, Installing, and Managing Apps

In This Chapter

✓ Searching for and installing apps

✓ Reviewing apps

✓ Updating apps

✓ Deleting apps

✓ Managing store cards with Passbook

✓ Stopping by the Newsstand

✓ Playing around in the Game Center

Since 2008, when third-party software developers were given the possibility to create apps for iPhone, the number of things you can do with your iPhone has increased exponentially, limited more by imagination than the hardware itself. To give you an idea, you can find apps for recipes, games, electronic readers, home banking, photo enhancement, conversion tools, and music identification, not to mention profession-specific apps such as radiation dosage calculators for oncologists or turbine calculators for mechanics. You find all those apps in the App Store.

In this chapter, we tell you how the App Store works, give you tips for reading reviews to help you choose apps, show you how to install and delete apps and reinstall them if you deleted them by mistake. iOS 7 lets you set up automatic updates so you always have the most current version of the apps you use. We introduce you to three Apple apps that organize other apps: Newsstand, which organizes apps for purchasing, subscribing, and reading periodicals on your iPhone; Passbook, which organizes apps for store cards, airlines, coffee shops, and the like; and Game Center, which puts all your games in one place and piques your competitive nature with multiplayer games and published leaderboards.

This book's online bonus content gives a smorgasbord of apps that we recommend. Refer to the introduction to learn how to access the bonus content.

Discovering the Joy of Apps: "There's an App for That!"

A couple dozen apps — many included with your iPhone and the rest available to download, some for free — are developed by Apple, and the other 899,976, give or take a few, are developed by third-party developers. You download apps from Apple's App Store, which you access either via your iPhone or other iOS device or via iTunes on your computer. The nice thing about the App Store is that it offers one-stop shopping. You don't have to shop from website to website for the best price or the latest version; everything is in one place. And Apple reviews the app before it goes up on the App Store, so it's been tested to work with your iPhone.

What's more, if you replace your iPhone with a newer model, acquire additional iOS devices, lose your iPhone, or your iPhone or computer crashes before you've had a chance to back up the apps you've downloaded, the App Store has a record of everything you've downloaded and you can download your apps again (if they're still available) — without paying for them a second time. That's why you need an Apple ID to sign in to the App Store or iTunes, even to download free apps.

Free or for a price?

There are two kinds of apps: free and paid. Many, many apps are free although we have noticed a trend toward paid apps or in-app purchases. App developers continue to sprout like mushrooms, and the relative ease with which an app can be written and distributed makes app programming, for some developers, a relaxing pastime. Rarely do you get somethin' for nothin'; apps that are free to download are often supported by ads, so after you take your turn in Words With Friends Free, a commercial for FootLocker occupies your screen for 15 seconds before you can go on to your next turn, or an advertising banner may scroll across the bottom of your favorite recipe app. There's usually a paid, ad-free version available.

Nonetheless, we've divided the free apps into four types:

- **Stand-alone apps:** Found in all categories, these apps work on their own and can be games, financial management, recipes, or just about whatever you can think of. They may or may not have ads.

- **Teaser or intro apps:** Pared-down versions of fee-based apps. Here, too, they may or may not have ads.

- **Support apps:** Vendors who provide an app that either is an iPhone version of their website or gives specific information. Home banking apps and real-time public transit information apps are two examples. Often, you find a link to the App Store on the website of the vendor or service provider. These usually only promote their own products.

✔ **Revenue-generating apps:** These apps provide frameworks for the real meat of the app. The app is free, but you pay for the content or to activate special features or purchase accessories.

We think of paid apps in two categories:

✔ **Low-priced:** Most are just 99 cents and the highest runs $5. Many ad-free apps are in this category and we find the price justified for apps we use a lot — those ads can get old fast. They run the gamut of categories.

✔ **Higher-priced:** More than $10. For the most part, these apps, such as scientific journals or productivity tools, give access to costly, copyrighted information or research and development investment on the part of the developer.

Double- (or triple-) duty apps

Look around and most people you see have one gadget or another in their hands. Having the same apps and the same information about those apps on each device makes work, and life in general, easier. *Universal apps* make working on multiple devices a breeze because they work on all iOS devices (iPhone, iPad, iPod touch). A plus sign in the upper left corner of the price button indicates a universal app (see the Rome Metro Free app in Figure 2-2). When you look at an app's Info screen, which we explain in just a few paragraphs (refer to Figures 2-3 and 4), tap the Details tab and scroll down to the Information section. Next to Compatibility, you see which devices the app is compatible with.

Many iOS apps also have a Mac counterpart, often with more features, and are iCloud-enabled, which means you can create documents on one device, save them to iCloud, and open and edit them on another device. If you're a Windows user, you don't have to feel left out: You can access some of your documents through the www.iCloud.com website.

Searching for and Installing Apps

Now that you know a bit about what you're looking for, we tell you how to get your hands on some apps. You can enter the App Store through iPhone or iTunes doors.

Searching the iPhone App Store

With the number of apps soon to hit one million, it's hard to know where to begin, let alone actually choose an app. Apple helps you by making some recommendations for apps, showing you bestsellers, best earners, and some Apple favorites. To begin navigating through the sea of apps on your iPhone, tap the App Store button on the Home screen. A screen like Figure 2-1 appears.

If you're familiar with the iTunes Store on a computer, you notice that the App store looks very similar on your iPhone. Across the bottom, you see five buttons:

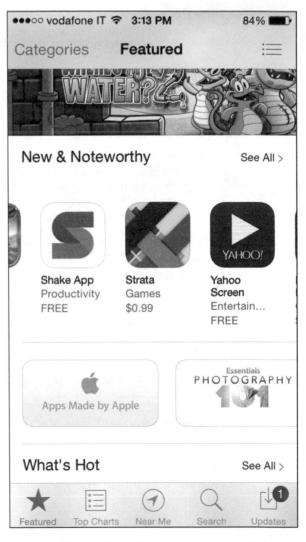

Figure 2-1: The App Store gives you many ways to find apps.

- ✔ **Featured:** Shows Apple-recommended apps divided into sections. Ads automatically scroll across the top. You can scroll down to see the following:

    - **New and Noteworthy:** Scroll horizontally through the icons or tap See All to see a complete list.

    - **What's Hot:** Here you find the most popular — that is, the most downloaded — apps, regardless of whether they are free or paid.

    - **Collections:** In between the sections that show individual app icons, you see rectangular icons that link to app collections. For example, tap on the Apps Made by Apple collection to find those or Photography 101 to see a list of apps that you might find interesting if you take a lot of photos.

    - **Other Sections:** Scroll down to see other sections such as Editors' Choices or seasonal or theme-based suggestions, such as Back To School or Puzzles.

- ✔ **TopCharts:** Tap one of the tabs — Paid, Free, Top Grossing — to see a list of apps sorted by those criteria.

TIP

You see apps under Top Grossing that are free, and you may wonder how a free app can be top-grossing. Two ways:

- **Free App a Day:** Free App a Day lets you make a wish that an app is free. If a single app gets enough wishes, it can be downloaded free for a limited time. The idea is that word gets out about how great the app is and people pay for it anyway after the free period is over.

- **In-App Purchases:** The app is free, but you then buy things within the app. For example, a poker game is free, but you buy 25 gold chips for $1.99.

Both the Featured and Top Charts screens have a Categories button in the upper left corner. Tap it to see a list of categories. Tap on one of the categories to see a list of apps in that category, which you can view by Paid, Free, or Top Grossing from the Top Charts view. Some apps fall into more than one category, in which case it shows up on two different lists. Some categories are divided into subcategories. Games and Newsstand are divided into subcategories.

✓ **Near Me:** Tap to see a list of apps that are popular based on your location. At first glance this may seem like a wasted toolbar space, but it's particularly useful if you want to find apps for local transportation, travel guides, stores, or restaurants. (Refer to Figure 2-2.)

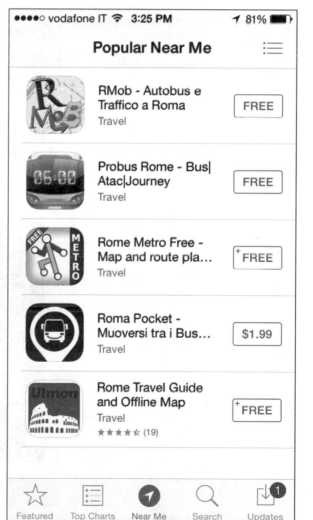

Figure 2-2: Near Me makes recommendations for you based on your location.

✔ **Search:** You can search by the name of the app, if you know it, or by key words. The more words you type in the search field, the narrower your search results.

✔ **Updates:** Because the App Store knows which apps you've purchased and downloaded, it automatically sends you a notification when an update is available. The number you see in the badge on the Updates button is the number of apps that have updates. With iOS 7, you can choose to have your apps updated automatically, in which case you never see the update notification. We talk about updates a little further along in this chapter.

To learn more about an app, tap either an icon on the Featured screen or an item in a list in the To Charts, Near Me, or Search screens. An Info screen opens, as seen in Figure 2-3. At the very top, you see the name of the app, the developer's name, the star ratings, and a button that displays either the price or "free." Three tabs let you view

✔ **Details:** Scroll horizontally through screenshots of the app, or scroll vertically to read a description, information about the app such as the version and age rating, which indicates the minimum age considered appropriate for this app, as well as which devices it's compatible with, as mentioned earlier. You also find developer information, in-app

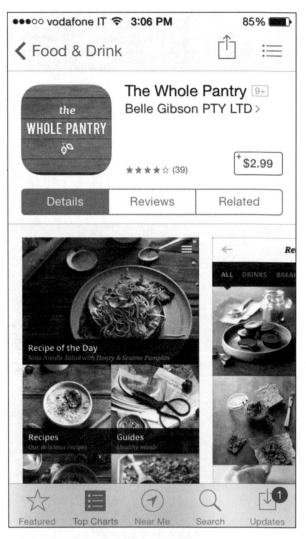

Figure 2-3: The app's Info screen gives detailed information about the app, including a description, screenshots, and reviews.

purchases, the version history, and privacy policy. You may have to tap More or a disclosure triangle to read everything in the section, as shown in Figure 2-4.

✔ **Reviews:** You see the number of ratings and the average stars the app's been given as well as written reviews. If available, you can Like the app on Facebook. You can also write a review yourself or tap a link to go to the app support page.

✔ **Related:** Scroll horizontally through a selection of other apps by the same developer or other apps that were purchased or downloaded by customers who purchased or downloaded this app. Tap any of the icons to reach that apps' information screen.

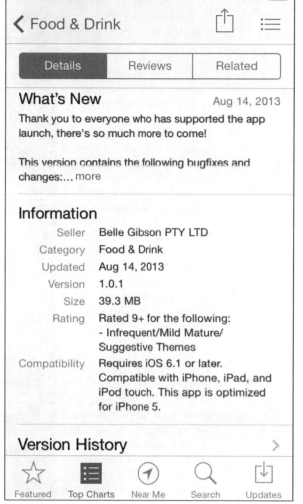

Figure 2-4: Scroll down to see more information at the bottom of the Info screen.

When you're choosing apps, read the description, which is written by the developer, to understand exactly what you should expect from the app. Then read the reviews with a discerning eye as to whether the app does what the description says it does, whether it's buggy, whether it's lame. Some reviewers write a bad review because they expected the app to do something that it never claimed to do. Look for a positive or negative consensus in reviews to help you make a downloading decision. And if it's free, just try it — you can always delete it if you don't like it.

Installing from the iPhone App Store

If you decide to download the app, tap the Free or price button on either the Info screen or directly on the app in the list format. The button changes to Install or Buy. Tap the button. If you have an iPhone 5s, you confirm your purchase with Touch ID by pressing the Home button. Otherwise, you may be asked to confirm the old-fashioned way by entering your Apple ID and password, as shown in Figure 2-5. (See Book II, Chapter 1 for more on setting up an Apple account if you haven't done so already.)

If you chose a paid app, you have to enter your credit card or PayPal account information, have your on-file charge card charged, redeem an iTunes or Apple Store card, or have a credit balance in your iTunes account. If this is the first time you've purchased something with this iPhone, you have to verify the account and payment information. A screen appears that asks for your payment

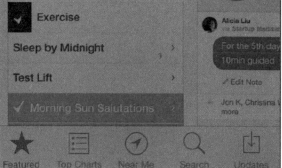

Figure 2-5: Confirm your purchase with Touch ID or type in your Apple ID and password when asked.

information, where you must enter your credit card or PayPal information. Otherwise, you may tap None in the selection of credit card options, redeem an iTunes or Apple Store card, and then purchase items against the iTunes account balance. A second screen may ask your security questions to verify that you are who you say you are. After you enter this information the first time, you don't have to do it again until your credit card expires, your iTunes balance reaches zero, or you change devices.

TIP

If you frequently download items from the iTunes store, you can associate a credit card with your iTunes account or purchase iTunes or Apple store cards. Scroll to the bottom of the Featured screen and tap Redeem, as shown in Figure 2-6. If asked, sign in with your Apple ID and password. If the code on the back of the iTunes or Apple store card has a box around it, you can scan it with your iPhone's camera by tapping Use Camera, pointing the iPhone lens at the code, and then tapping the camera button in the upper right corner. Otherwise, tap You Can Also Enter Your Code Manually, and then type in the code. Whatever your payment method, you always have a chance to Confirm or Cancel your purchase after you hit the price button.

After the App Store has the information it needs from you, and you have confirmed that you want to buy the app, the price or Free button becomes a

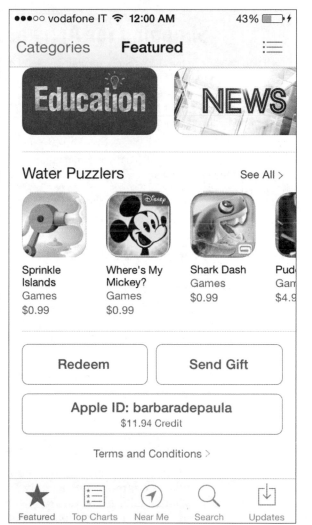

Figure 2-6: Scroll to the bottom of the Featured screen to find the Redeem button.

circle that rotates and when the app is downloaded, the button reads Open. You can continue shopping or tap the Home button and the button of the new app appears. Across the bottom, a Waiting or Loading progress bar appears beneath the app, although if you're downloading with a Wi-Fi or LTE connection, your app will download so quickly it will probably be finished by the time you get to the Home screen.

Shopping for Apps at the iTunes Store

If you do shop at the iTunes Store on your computer, you want to turn on Automatic Downloads so any purchases you make on one device, such as your computer or iPhone, are automatically downloaded to other devices linked to the same Apple ID.

To shop for iPhone apps from your computer, follow these directions:

1. **Open iTunes on your computer.**

2. **Click iTunes Store button in the upper right corner.**

3. **Click the App Store tab at the top of the window or click and hold the tab to open a pop-up menu from which you can click a specific app category.**

4. **Browse and shop as you would for other media.**

Here's how to set up Automatic Downloads:

1. **Open iTunes on your computer.**

2. **Choose iTunes⇨Preferences and click the Store tab.**

3. **Under Automatic Downloads, check the type of media (Music, Apps, and/or Books) you want downloaded simultaneously to all devices.**

4. **Click OK.**

5. **On your iPhone, tap Settings⇨iTunes & App Store and then tap On next to the items you want activated for Automatic Downloads (Music, Apps, and/or Books).**

There are a few more things you should know about shopping at the App Store:

✔ You can't use store credits to give an app to someone as a gift. If you have both a store credit and a credit card on file and gift an app to someone, it will automatically be charged to your credit card.

✔ Although you can window-shop the App Store from your iPhone to your heart's content, you can only download apps up to 50MB in size from your cellular network. To download apps larger than 50MB, you have to have a Wi-Fi connection on your iPhone or go through the iTunes Store on your computer and then sync the apps to your iPhone.

✔ If you lose your Internet connection or for some reason the download is interrupted, the next time you have an Internet connection, the download starts again. If, instead, you open iTunes on your computer and sign in to your account with the same Apple ID you used to begin the download that was interrupted, iTunes completes the download.

Sharing apps

Like many other iPhone apps, you can share what you find at the App Store. Tap the Share button at the top right of an app's info screen to open the Share Sheet. From there, tap one of the sharing options: AirDrop, Message, Mail, Twitter, or Facebook to send a link via one of those methods. You can also copy the link and paste it in another app. With paid apps, you have two more choices: Add to Wish List, to keep track of apps you want, or Gift, to send the app to another person.

To see your Wish List, tap the Wish List button in the top right corner of the Featured, Top Charts, or Near Me screens. Apps listed are the same as in other lists: tap the price to install the app as described previously. After an app is installed, it's removed from your Wish List. To delete an item from your wish list without installing it, tap Edit, and then tap the circle next to the app to select it, and then tap the Delete button in the upper left corner.

Apps that find you

Sometimes an app finds you. A lot of information providers, like newspapers or radio broadcasts, service providers, such as banks and FedEx, and social networks, like Facebook or Pinterest, caught on to the power of apps right from the beginning and developed slimmed-down versions of their Internet offerings.

If you visit the FedEx website via Safari on your iPhone, you'll be prompted to download the FedEx app so you can track deliveries or request pickups. Barbara's bank sent her an e-mail invitation to download its online banking app. These apps give you direct access to the iPhone versions of their websites, which allow you to access the essentials without the extemporaneous fluff that takes a long time to load across a cellular data network.

Another way you can find apps for products and services you use frequently is to scan 2D barcodes, which are those one-by-one inch square graphic images that look like a labyrinth. You have to download a 2D barcode scanning reader such as QR Reader for iPhone or i-nigma QR. (QR stands for Quick Response.) After you have the reader app, you open the app and hold it over one of those barcodes. You are automatically sent to a mobile web page for the product or service associated with that barcode.

Deleting Apps

You may tire of an app or find you downloaded an app that's a dud and you want to delete it. We explained this in Book I, Chapter 3, but here's a quick review. To delete apps from your iPhone, do the following:

1. **Press and hold any app on the Home screen until all the apps start wiggling.**
2. **Tap the X in the corner of the apps you want to delete.**
3. **Press the Home button when you're finished and the apps stand still.**

You can also go to Settings⇨General⇨Usage and in the Storage section tap Show all Apps to open a list of all the apps on your iPhone. Tap the app you want to delete and then tap Delete App.

You can't delete the apps that came preloaded on your iPhone.

After you download an app, it remains associated with your Apple ID on iTunes. If you accidentally delete an app from your iPhone, you can download again from the App Store, as explained in later in this chapter.

Updating and Upgrading Apps

It seems almost every day there's an app or two that's been updated. Prior to iOS 7, a badge showed up on the App Store button on the Home screen indicating how many apps were waiting to be updated. You had to open the app store and manually update the apps. Now, update badges are no more — unless you want them. In the App Store settings, you can choose to have apps automatically update as updates become available. Pretty cool, huh? To make things even better, updates are free.

Upgrades, on the other hand, may have a fee attached. For example, if you download the free, barebones or ad-laden version of an app but then want to upgrade to the full or ad-free version, you'll probably have to pay for it. Here we tell you how to put updates on automatic and how to find and install upgrades.

Setting up automatic updates

With iOS 7's automatic updates, you always have the most recent release of an app. You aren't obligated to use automatic updates but we highly recommend you do. Follow these steps to turn on this feature:

1. **Tap Settings on the Home Screen.**

2. **Scroll down and tap iTunes & App Store.**

   The screen as shown in Figure 2-7 appears.

3. **Tap Updates to the On position in the Automatic Downloads section.**

   While you're there, tap Apps On as well so whenever you download an app on one device, it's automatically downloaded on other devices on which you signed in to the same Apple ID.

4. **Tap Use Cellular Data (scroll down to see it) On to download and update apps over the cellular data network.**

   Downloads and updates over the cellular data network are limited to 50 MB; any apps larger than that have to be downloaded or updated using Wi-Fi or syncing with iTunes.

Add the App Store to the Notification Center to see when apps have been updated. Go to Settings⇨Notification Center⇨App Store⇨Show in Notification Center On.

Using iPhone's App Store to update

If you want to continue to manually update your apps, ignore the previous instruction set and do the following when you see a numbered badge on the App Store button:

1. **Tap App Store on the Home screen.**

2. **Tap the Updates button on the bottom right corner of the App Store.**

   A list of apps that have updates appears. The version number is shown under the name of the app.

3. **Tap What's New (it's written quite small under the version number) to see what changes or fixes the update made or tap the app icon to open the Info screen.**

   A list of changes pops open.

4. **Tap the Update button on the Updates list or the Info screen.**

   OR

5. **Tap Update All on the Updates screen.**

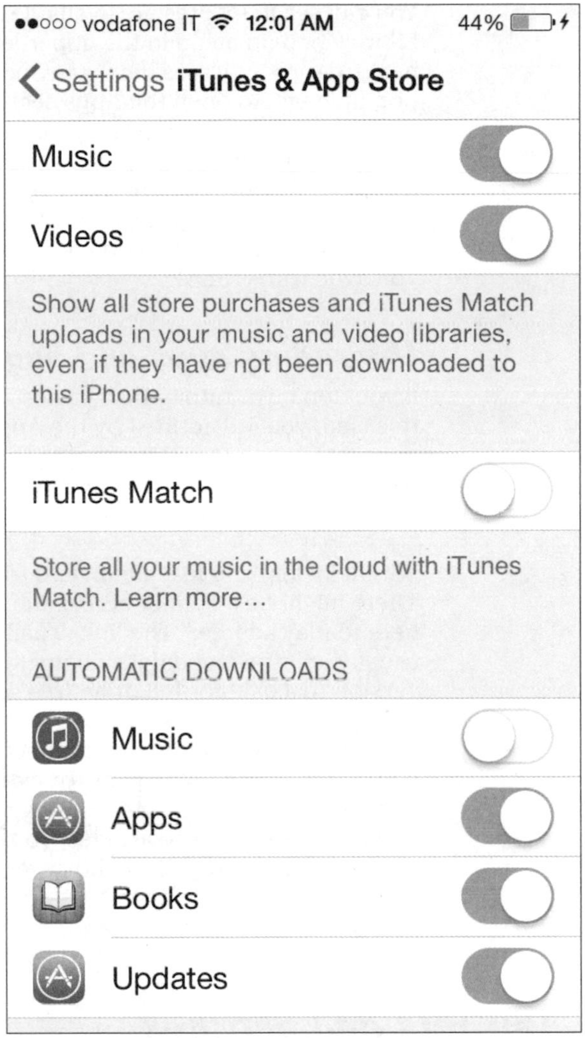

   If you turned Apps On in Settings⇨iTunes & App Store in the Automatic Downloads section, the apps in iTunes are updated as well.

●●○○○ vodafone IT 📶 12:01 AM   44% 🔋⚡

❮ Settings iTunes & App Store

Music ⬤

Videos ⬤

Show all store purchases and iTunes Match uploads in your music and video libraries, even if they have not been downloaded to this iPhone.

iTunes Match ◯

Store all your music in the cloud with iTunes Match. Learn more…

AUTOMATIC DOWNLOADS

🎵 Music ◯

Ⓐ Apps ⬤

📖 Books ⬤

Ⓐ Updates ⬤

Figure 2-7: Automatic Updates means you always have the most current version of an app.

Using iTunes to update

You can see if updates are available from iTunes on your computer. Click the Library pop-up menu in the upper-left of the iTunes window and the number next to Apps indicates how many updates are available. Select Apps from the pop-up menu to open the Apps section of iTunes. A button at the bottom of the window tells you how many updates are available. Click the Updates tab at the top of the window. The My App Updates window opens, where you can tap the Get Update buttons next to each individual app or click Download All Free Updates to get all the updates at once. If you didn't update the apps directly on your iPhone, they will be updated the next time you sync with iTunes.

Upgrading apps and buying content

If you don't use automatic updates, when a new version of an app is released, you are notified by the App Store on your iPhone and iTunes. Some apps let you know within the app that a new version is available. You might be playing a game and a notification appears telling you that a new version is available. Simply click the link that appears to get the new version.

Within an app you may be invited to upgrade to the full or ad-free version. There might be a banner across the bottom that says something like "Click here to play ad-free." The link usually takes you to the App Store, and there's usually a fee involved if it's an upgrade, from either a barebones or ad-free version to a paid-for full or ad-free version.

Earlier in this chapter, we mentioned in-app purchases that could be chips you buy to play a poker game or extra tools to defend your avatar in a game or special effects in a video editing app. In-app purchases can also be content such as recipes or articles. To keep things simple, in-app purchases are managed by the App Store, however, you make the purchase directly from within the app. Some apps have a Store button in their in-app settings or info screens, which we tell you about. . . right now.

App Info and Settings

After an app is installed, you may want to find out more about the app or adjust some of the settings. On your iPhone, information such as the version number and links to the support site are usually found within the app by tapping an "i", a help button, or one of the common icons such as a gear or list. Some app settings are managed on your iPhone under Settings. Tap Settings on the Home screen and scroll down to the bottom. The last section you see is the list of apps that have settings you can change. Each app has different settings so click through and play around with the settings for the apps that you have.

Other app settings are managed from within the app. There's no cut-and-dried rule to follow. You can visit the support page for an app to learn where the settings are and what they do. Again, we recommend playing a bit with the apps you have and trying different settings to make the app useful and enjoyable for you.

In iTunes on your computer, select Apps from the Library pop-up menu to display all your apps. Click an app icon, and then select File⇨Get Info. The app Info window opens, which has several tabs across the top. You're probably most interested in the Summary screen where you can see the version number of the app, its size and age rating, and when it was downloaded. You can also see what kind it is to determine if it works on both iPhone and iPad.

Reviewing Apps and Reporting Problems

Purchase decisions today are often based more on what someone else has to say about a product than on what the company says about its product. App reviews can help you decide whether, or not, to purchase an app. After you purchase and use an app, you can contribute to the improvement of the app world by writing honest, objective reviews and, when necessary, reporting problems. Your fellow app users will thank you and, at least in our experience, developers thank you, too, obviously for good reviews but also for a heads up when there's a problem. When you have a good or bad experience, write a quick review or at least give the app the appropriate number of stars. If you encounter a recurring problem, let the developer know. Here's how to submit reviews and problem reports on your iPhone and through iTunes.

On your iPhone

Open the App Store from the Home screen. Tap Updates and then tap Purchased at the top of the screen (tap the Status Bar if you don't see Purchased). Scroll through the list of your purchased apps, which also includes Free apps. You can only write reviews for apps that you have downloaded, whether free or purchased. Tap the app you want to review to open the Info screen and then do the following:

1. **Tap the Reviews tab.**
2. **Tap Write a Review.**

   You may be asked to sign in to your Apple account.

3. **Tap the number of stars you want to give the app, and then fill in the form and write your review.**
4. **Tap Send to submit your review.**

If you're having a problem with the app, tap the App Support button, which opens the developer's website. Follow the links there to contact the developer about any problems you are having.

On iTunes

To write a review from iTunes, locate the app in the App Store section of the iTunes Store and click the Write a Review button just under Customer Reviews. Fill in the form that appears and click Submit. To contact the developer about a problem, click Report a Problem on the Write a Review form or click the App Support button next to the Write a Review button.

If you are having a problem downloading or launching an app you recently downloaded, first try deleting it from your iPhone and installing it again. If that doesn't work and you want to report a problem to Apple, go into your purchase history from Store⇨View Account. Click See All in the Purchase History section and then click the arrow to the left of the app that's giving you trouble. Click Report a Problem and then follow the onscreen instructions.

Reinstalling Apps You Already Own

Mistakes happen. Computers crash. iPhones fall out of windows of moving cars. The result may be that you accidentally lose an app, could be a favorite game that you purchased or your online banking app. In any case, if you lose one app or all of them, the App Store knows what apps you already bought and lets you download them again (if they're still available from the App Store), free of charge. Here's how to do it on your iPhone:

1. **Tap App Store on the Home screen.**

2. **Tap the Updates button at the bottom right of the screen.**

3. **Tap Purchased at the top of the screen.**

   A list of apps you purchased appears.

4. **Tap All to see all apps you purchased or Tap Not on This iPhone to see apps you purchased that aren't on this iPhone.**

   There are three buttons you might see, as shown in Figure 2-8:

   • **Open** which opens the app

   • **Update** which means an update is available for the app

   • **iCloud icon** which means that you previously purchased the app but it isn't on your iPhone

5. **Tap the iCloud icon next to the app you want to reinstall.**

   The button changes to a circle while the app is downloading and reads Open when the installation is complete. The app button appears on the Home screen.

When you reinstall an app, you automatically install the latest version even if you originally installed a prior version.

On iTunes, the procedure is similar:

1. **Open iTunes on your computer and click iTunes Store.**

2. **Sign in to your account if you aren't already signed in.**

3. **Click Purchased in the Quick Links list.**

4. **Click the Apps tab and then click the iPhone tab.**

5. **Click Not on This Computer to see which apps are missing.**

6. **Click the iCloud button to download the app to your computer.**

   The app is downloaded to iTunes and automatically downloaded to your iPhone too, if you have activated Automatic Downloads in iTunes preferences; otherwise, sync your iPhone with iTunes and the apps will be added to your iPhone.

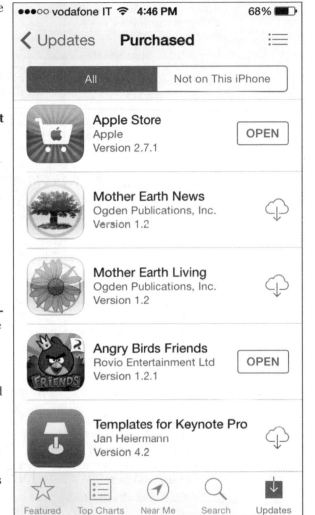

Figure 2-8: Access a list of purchased apps from the Updates screen.

Reading the News with Newsstand

With the quality of iPhone screens and the accessibility settings that let you adjust the type size, reading on your iPhone has become a viable option to staying current with your reading material of choice. Newsstand isn't really an app but a folder in disguise that neatly organizes all your periodical subscriptions in one place. You find a publication's app (usually for free) by tapping the Newsstand button and then tapping Store. The Newsstand category of the

App Store opens. (You can also reach it by opening the App Store, tapping Categories, and tapping Newsstand.) Scroll through as you would for any other kind of app as we explained previously. Tap the publication that interests you and tap Free to install the app.

The app icons appear like magazine covers or newspaper front pages on the Newsstand bookshelf, as shown in Figure 2-9. There are two ways to obtain issues:

- Tap Newsstand, and then tap the publication. Not all periodical apps are equal; to see a list of subscription options similar to those shown in Figure 2-10, tap the Library, Subscriptions, or Read button. Often you have the option of purchasing single issues or 3-, 6-, or 12-month subscriptions, as well as special issues.

Figure 2-9: Newsstand stores your newspaper and magazine subscriptions in one place.

- In the App Store, find the publications app, and then scroll to the bottom of the Info screen. Tap Top In-App Purchases to see what issues are available. Tap the issue you want to buy.

Press the Home button to exit the publication and return to the Newsstand shelf.

The first time you tap the publication, a dialog asks if you want to allow Push notifications. Allowing Push will send new issues to your iPhone immediately. Even if you don't allow new issues to be pushed, when new issues are released, a badge on the Newsstand icon indicates their availability. Click the publication on the Newsstand shelf to download and read the latest issue.

Because each publication app is just that, an app created by a third-party developer, there's no set rule for the publication interface. Different publications use different buttons, and you'll have to poke around and see what you can do and how the app works. The first time you open a publication after you subscribe, you may have to enter login information, which may be your Apple ID or may be a different user ID and password the publication asked you to create. Some publications give you a free iOS subscription if you subscribe to the print edition, and you would enter your subscriber information, usually culled from the mailing label on the print edition, in the Settings screen. You may have other options within the publications on Newsstand, as you can see in Figure 2-10, there's a Search and Settings option.

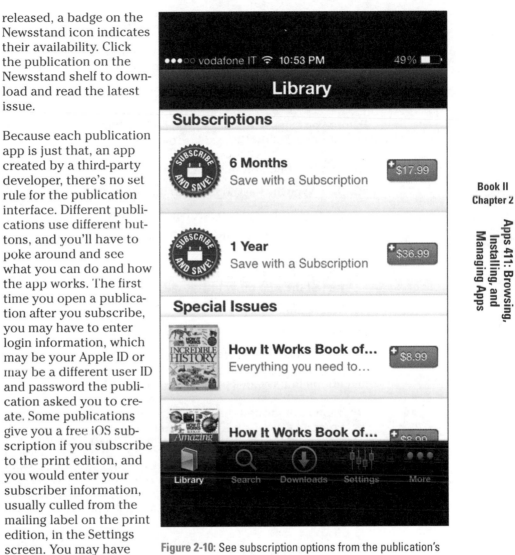

Book II
Chapter 2

Apps 411: Browsing, Installing, and Managing Apps

Figure 2-10: See subscription options from the publication's app.

Newspapers usually show articles in streaming, meaning they are frequently updated, and if you want to download an article to read later, you add it to a reading list in the app. Magazines, on the other hand, are usually downloaded to your iPhone, which means they occupy space. If you find you're running out of storage, see if the app offers an Auto Remove option, which deletes the issue after you read it and frees up storage space. As a subscriber, you can download it again at a later date.

Checking in with Passbook

In the ongoing effort to eliminate paper, Passbook steps in to provide electronic versions of boarding passes, movie tickets, coupons, and store cards.

Obtaining passes

Before you can use Passbook, you have to install Passbook-enabled apps on your iPhone. Follow these steps to do that:

1. **Tap Passbook on the Home screen.**

2. **Tap Apps for Passbook at the bottom of the screen.**

   A list of apps that support Passbook appears.

   If you don't see the Apps for Passbook button, tap Passbook at the bottom of the screen.

3. **Tap the Free button next to the Passbook apps that interest you to install the app on your iPhone.**

4. **Tap Install.**

5. **Type in your Apple ID Password if requested.**

   The app is downloaded and the button now reads Open.

In addition to Passbook apps, there are two other ways to add passes:

✔ Tap Passbook and then tap the Scan Code button. The camera opens. Point it at the bar code on a product or a QR code in an ad to scan it; the pass or discount coupon is then added to passbook.

✔ You may receive e-mail with a link or find URLs on websites that download coupons (www.coupons.com has many) or special offers to Passbook. Tap these links and the associated barcode or QR code is downloaded to Passbook, as shown in Figures 2-11 and 2-12.

Getting on board

The fun and practical side of Passbook is using the passes. When you're ready to use one of the Passbook-enabled apps, tap the app on the Home screen and do one of the following:

✔ Tap the Add to Passbook button and then tap the Add button on the coupon or follow the onscreen instructions to insert your username or number and password.

✔ For boarding passes, proceed with online check-in and then tap Download Boarding Pass to Passbook option.

After the passes are in Passbook, you need only tap the appropriate one and scan it at the check-in counter or cash register. This means all you need is your passport and iPhone at the airport and when you reach the cash register at your favorite store, instead of shuffling a deck of store cards, just tap Passbook and then tap the appropriate card. In no time, you're on your way down the tarmac, points are added to your account, or discounts are applied to your purchase.

Managing passes

Most of the passes in Passbook have options for automatic updates as well as some information about how the pass works. Tap the Information button in the lower right corner of the pass to see the "back side" of the pass. Go to Settings⇨Notification Center⇨Passbook to choose to see Passbook on the lock screen and the Notification Center. Then location and time based passes, such as boarding passes or theater tickets appear on the lock screen when you get to the airport or theater (as long as Location Services is on and you have a data connection). You can also eliminate a pass by tapping the Delete button in the upper left corner of the pass.

Tap the Share button to send the pass to someone via AirDrop, Mail, or Messages.

Figure 2-11: You find Add to Passbook button in apps and on websites and online order forms.

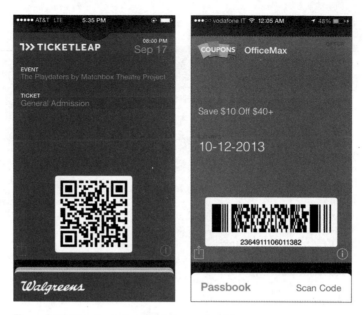

Figure 2-12: Theater tickets and discounts all in one app.

Playing Around in the Game Center

Like Newsstand and Passbook, the Game Center gathers like-minded apps — in this case games — in one place and then enhances how you use those apps. Game Center is part social network and part competitive playing field. When you sign in, any Game Center-enabled games you have on your iPhone are accessed by Game Center, and your playing history is recorded. The app buttons remain on the Home screen but you can play your games directly from Game Center too. There are two types of games:

- ✔ **Single player:** You play by yourself, but Game Center tracks your scores for the entire game and individual levels and posts them on the leaderboard if you choose to go public with your playing habits. There are also achievements, which are specific actions within a game, such as unlocking a character, that garner points in Game Center.

- ✔ **Multiplayer:** You play with other people either across a Wi-Fi or Bluetooth network. Some games are immediately interactive, whereas others can be played leisurely, each playing taking her turn when she wants, although this does hold up the progression of the game.

Signing in and making friends

Sign in to the Game Center with your Apple ID, and then choose a username or nickname for your Game Center profile that will appear as your moniker when you play multiplayer games or on leaderboards, sort of like choosing the tophat in Monopoly or calling yourself Curly at the bowling alley. You have to choose one that no one else is using and you can change it in the Game Center settings if you decide you want a new gaming identity.

The Game Center screen opens, and you find five buttons across the browse bar at the bottom of the screen. Here's a quick rundown of what each one does:

✔ **Me:** From this screen you can type in a status update and add or edit an image that represents you. Bubbles on the screen tell you how many games, turns, challenges, friends, and requests you have. Tapping the bubbles opens the same screens as tapping the buttons in the browse bar.

✔ **Friends:** Here's where the social part of Game Center comes in. When you first sign in, Game Center lists friends who use Game Center and asks if you want to add them as Game Center friends. You can choose who you want to add. To add more friends, scroll through the list of recommendations and tap one you'd like to add as a friend. An info screen opens that tells you the person's username and shows his or her photo or image, which can help you make sure it's the person you thought. Tap the Send Friend Request button, and when your request is confirmed you can then see the games and scores of that friend, send challenges, and play multiplayer games together. You can also add friends by:

- *Typing a name* in the Search field to find a specific friend and, if the person you want is found, sending a friend request.

- *Tapping the Add button* in the upper right corner, which opens an e-mail friend request. Type the email address or nickname of the person you want to send a friend request to.

- *Get more recommendations* by going to Settings⇨Game Center and tapping Contacts and Facebook on in the Friend Recommendations section.

Tap the name of a friend to see that player's profile as shown in Figure 2-13. Tap the bubbles to see more information. Friends shows that player's friends, and Games and Points show the games that player plays and the points he or she has racked up. If the player plays games you don't have, tapping the game in the Games or Points list opens a screen where you can download the game (after purchasing if it's not free). If you ever want to remove someone as a friend, tap the ellipsis in the upper right corner of that friend's Info screen, and then tap Unfriend in the popup menu.

✔ **Games:** Displays a list of the Game Center-enabled games on your iPhone. You also see how many achievement points you have for that app under the name. Tap a game to open the game information screen, as shown in Figure 2-14. Do the following from this screen:

- *Play or share* the game by tapping the ellipsis at the top right corner.

- *Rate the game* by tapping the dots under the game icon.

- *Like the game* on Facebook by tapping the Like button.

- *Review the leaderboards* by tapping the Leaderboards tab, and then tapping the leaderboards for the total game score or top scores for a specific level. Tap a name in the leaderboard to view the player's profile and send a friend request.

- *See your achievements* by tapping the Achievements tab. Tap the achievement to share your accomplishment with your friends or challenge friends to master the same achievement.

Figure 2-13: Learn about new games from a friend's profile.

- *See who's playing* when you tap the Players tab you see friends who are playing the game.

✔ **Challenges:** Lists challenges you send to and receive from other players. You have to be friends with a player in order to exchange challenges.

✔ **Turns:** Lists the games you're playing with others, along with the score and whose turn it is.

Challenging a friend

You can send challenges for a level you've already achieved, essentially challenging your friend to beat your score, or for an achievement. To send a challenge:

1. **Tap Games in the browse bar.**

2. **Tap the game you want to send a challenge from.**

3. **Tap a level on a leaderboard or an achievement on the achievements list.**

4. **Tap the Challenge Friends bubble.**

   The Challenge screen opens and is addressed to friends who play this game but haven't completed the level or achievement to which you are challenging them.

5. **Type a message to accompany the challenge, if you wish.**

6. **Tap Send.**

When you receive challenges, you see the number of challenges received in the Challenges bubble on the Me screen and a list of challenges on the Challenges screen. Tap the challenge to take. When you meet the challenge, your result is shared with your friend.

Figure 2-14: Access leaderboards and achievements from the game information screen.

Taking your turn

If you want to play a multiplayer game, you have to invite friends to join in. Tap Friends in the browse bar or on the Me screen, tap their Games bubble, and then tap a game you have in common. Tap the ellipsis in the upper right corner to invite the friend to Play, and then tap Next to add more players. After all the invitations have been accepted, you can begin playing. Tap Turns in the browse bar to see who's up next or when it's your turn to play.

Playing with the Game Center settings

Like most iPhone apps, Game Center has a few settings that customize how you use the app. Tap Settings⇨Game Center and turn the following on or off by tapping the switch next to the item:

- ✓ **Allow Invites:** When on, friends can invite you to play games. If you have a lot of fun, gaming friends, but want to limit your distractions, it might be a good idea to turn this off — but that kind of defeats the purpose of Game Center.

- ✓ **Nearby Players:** Lets Game Center users who are physically near you, invite you to play multiplayer games on Wi-Fi or Bluetooth.

- ✓ **Friend Recommendations:** Tap Contacts or Facebook On to receive friend recommendations based on who you know in those two apps.

You can adjust the types of notifications Game Center sends you in Settings⇨Notification Center⇨Game Center.

Chapter 3: Enhancing and Protecting iPhone with Add-ons

In This Chapter

↳ Protecting iPhone with screen protectors and cases

↳ Tuning in to headphone and headset options

↳ Pumping up the volume with external speakers

↳ Touring in-car helper gizmos

Accessories for your iPhone are like jewelry or tablecloths or fancy car mats: They aren't necessary but they enhance the aesthetic aspect and sometimes protect it. (Yes, even jewelry can protect — remember Wonder Woman's bracelets?) iPhone accessories and add-ons cover the gamut from just-for-looks to how-did-I-live-without-this. With every new iPhone Apple releases, new (and usually improved) add-ons and accessories hit the market, too. So instead of trying to cover every possible accessory category and type, we've selected just a few of our favorites to illustrate some of the most popular types of add-ons and accessories for your iPhone.

Let's go shopping!

Although many iPhone (and iPod touch) cases, cables, docks, and other accessories may *look* similar or just seem like they'd work with some or all of the I-device products, they rarely do. This explains why Apple created the Made for iPhone label, which is what you want to look for when you're shopping for iPhone accessories. What's more, you want to note *which* iPhone model (or models) a particular product is designed to work with, so you can be sure the product works with *your* iPhone.

Taking Protective Measures

Whether you have an iPhone 5c, 5s, or an older model, your iPhone is made from resistant material, be it plastic, glass, or aluminum. Nonetheless, scratches occur and iPhones get dropped and bumped sometimes. Screen protectors and protective cases give added assurance against those potential dings.

Screen protectors

The iPhone screen is made of hardened oleophobic glass that's so strong you can drag your car key back and forth across it and you still won't be able to scratch the glass.

Still, some iPhone owners swear by those sticky-backed screen protectors you can stick to your iPhone's screen to protect it from scratches. And while neither of us uses a screen protector on our iPhones, we both agree with two potential byproduct benefits of using a screen protector, which are

- **Minimizing smudges:** Certain screen protectors minimize how much of the finger and face oil smudges you see.

- **Preventing bits of glass from falling free if you shatter your iPhone's screen:** Joe can attest to this fact when, a few years ago, his iPhone 3G's screen shattered to bits when he knocked it off his desk and it landed face down on the floor. The screen was still able to function and respond to his finger taps, thanks to the ZAGG invisibleSHIELD screen protector he'd previously applied to the screen. Luckily, he could continue using the smashed-screen iPhone until he was able to replace it with a new iPhone. (Of course, had Joe enclosed the befallen iPhone in a protective case that offered cushioning around the front edges, the screen probably would have survived the short fall intact, screen protector be damned — more on protective cases in a moment.)

Screen protectors are made of pliable, adhesive-backed plastic, or flexible glass, film. Some come with a special cleaning wipe or liquid to prepare the screen before applying the protector as well as a tool for smoothing out air bubbles. We recommend cleaning the screen so you don't permanently trap dust particles and fingerprints under the protector. Our favorite screen protector picks are

- **TrueClear Anti-Smudge Screen Protector (**www.belkin.com**):** Smooth anti-smudge finish means obsessive types won't need to constantly polish their iPhone's screen to keep it looking clear and clean.

Because some iPhone cases include a plastic screen protector, consider buying one of those two-for-one options if you're planning on buying a case as well, rather than laying out cash to buy both add-ons separately.

✔ **Zagginvisible SHIELD (**www.zagg.com**):** Joe has applied the invisibleSHIELD — based on a clear, thin, and very durable military film originally made to protect U.S. military helicopter blades from high-speed damage — to numerous iPhones and iPads and has always been happy with the results. Choose from four different grades and full-body or screen-only options (as shown in Figure 3-1), all of which come with a spray bottle of fluid used to help position the film, and a squeegee to squeeze out fluid and air bubbles.

Figure 3-1: Zagg offers screen-only or full-body invisibleSHIELD options.

Cases

Of course, a screen protector won't protect your iPhone's screen from breaking if it's struck with considerable force — or even just on a corner or edge. To protect your iPhone's screen from breaking, your best bet is to buy a protective case or at the very least (for minimalist types), a bumper.

Protective cases generally come in five styles:

✔ **Bumper case,** which is sort of like a semi-rigid rubber-band that wraps the frame of your iPhone. The edges are well protected, and the case has holes for the volume buttons and connector ports. The bumper extends slightly beyond the front and back so that if your iPhone falls flat on its face, the bumper hits the ground first.

✔ **Hybrid case,** which is a bumper with a thin, clear plastic back that protects the back of your iPhone from scratches. Some, such as the Ringke Fusion (www.rearthusa.com), let you customize the back with a photo.

✔ **Minimal case,** which covers the back and sides of your iPhone, and usually the four corners, but not always the front face, which may leave your iPhone's screen vulnerable to breakage if it endures a forceful fall or impact.

- ✔ **Surrounded case,** which covers the back, sides, corners, and front edges of your iPhone and offers the best protection for your iPhone, with choices ranging from lightweight (yet still offering full protection) to thicker, heavier weight models designed to endure the most rugged conditions or environments — including falling from the sky, or landing in a puddle of water, as some of the choices below illustrate.

Both minimal and surround-type cases generally come in two styles:

- • One-piece construction that you squeeze your iPhone into.

- • Two-piece, or "slider" construction that you slide onto either end of your iPhone until the inner edges meet in the middle (or nearly in the middle in some cases); or two-piece "snap" case construction that's typically a larger, fuller back and sides half, and a second front "frame" that snaps to the front of the back half to seal the full-case protection deal . . . er, design.

- ✔ **Wallet case,** which is styled like a miniature folio and typically features a few slots inside the front cover for stashing your ID, credit cards, and cash. (In addition to the two cases in the following section, be sure to check out Joe's favorite — the BookBook case for iPhone — in "Bonus Chapter 5: The Well-Informed Listener and Reader," which you can download from the companion website. For more on the website, see this book's Introduction.

Some minimal protection cases — which are so thin, they're sometimes referred to as *skins* — don't provide corner or front screen edge protection for your iPhone. As such, choosing one of those types of cases is more of a fashion over function purchase. To each his or her own!

Apple introduced model specific cases for both iPhone 5c and 5s, but they're not the only game in town. A few of our favorite third-party cases include the following:

- ✔ **Scosche bandEDGE** (www.scosche.com): The bandEDGE bumper provides reasonable peace of mind in the event you drop your iPhone and it lands on one of its vulnerable front edges — or even facedown. At the same time, the bandEDGE's lack of a back cover makes this case feel close to going naked — from your iPhone's point of view, of course.

- ✔ **Incase Slider** (www.goincase.com): The Slider does just that. Top and bottom pieces slide onto your iPhone and snap together to provide surround protection. Choose from the standard slider or one of the stylized finishes such as chrome or crystal, as shown in Figure 3-2.

Figure 3-2: The Crystal Slider Case offers full protection, minus the bulk and weight.

✔ **Grove Bamboo Case** (www.grovemade.com): Beautiful and better for the environment — that's what you get when you go with one of these handmade cases. Choices include plain or engraved, as shown in Figure 3-3. You can also send your own custom design.

Figure 3-3: The eco-friendlier Grove Bamboo Case for iPhone.

✔ **Griffin Survivor + Catalyst Waterproof Case for iPhone 5 (**www. griffintechnology.com**):** This case does double-duty: It protects your iPhone and turns it into an underwater camera, as shown in Figure 3-4. You can attach a wrist strap so your iPhone doesn't float away while you're swimming from reef to reef.

Figure 3-4: Your iPhone stays dry when you take it for a swim with a Griffin case.

✔ **Moshi Overture (**www.moshimonde.com**):** A stylish wallet style case that has card and cash holders, roomy enough to step out for a coffee with just your iPhone and house key. A washable microfiber cleaning cloth that attaches to the inside of the wallet is included.

✔ **Lenmar Meridian iPhone 5 Battery Case (**www.lenmar.com**):** Although recent and new model iPhones feature rechargeable batteries that are mighty enough to see you through at least a full day of typical usage, some heavy-usage iPhone owners may have to carry their chargers so they can plug in and juice up their iPhone when the battery is running low. Or you can leave the charger home and opt for the Lenmar Meridian iPhone 5 Battery Case juice pack, shown in Figure 3-5, which offers 2300 mAh and pulls double-duty as both a protective case and an extra power source that can greatly extend your iPhone's uptime.

Figure 3-5: A protective case and battery booster in a single package.

Most of the companies we mention here make an assortment of iPhone accessories, not just the single ones we mention. Take a look around their websites for other cool stuff.

Discovering Headphones, Headsets, and Handsets

The EarPods with mic that are included with your iPhone offer pretty good sound quality and the added bonus of letting you control a bunch of your iPhone's features, like answering and controlling phone calls and playing and pausing music and video. For most people, that's good enough.

But for some folks, spending extra to replace the bundled headphones is a must: for instance, audiophiles who want higher quality sound output or the comfort of over-ear headphones. And ditto for anyone who enjoys (or depends on) listening to their favorite musical performers to help push them harder when they're working out or running without those dangling wires to get in the way of their own performance. Frequent phone-callers might like the hands-free convenience of a Bluetooth headset to have phone calls without wires getting in the way.

Some of our favorite headphone and headset choices include the following:

- **Bose SIE2i sport headphones** (www.bose.com): For outdoorsy types or runners (like Joe), they're sweat- and weather-resistant, stay comfortably yet securely in place without wobbling or bouncing no matter what terrain you're traversing. An included Reebok fitness armband holds your iPhone in place, and the built-in remote and mic make it easy to answer that important call you're waiting for, or control music playback and volume. Work it!

- **Beats by Dr. Dre** (www.beatsbydre.com): It used to be just wearing white iPhone headphones made you stand out in a crowd. Nowadays, the standard iPhone headphones are commonplace, and a new eye-catching brand has become the in sound "thang": Beats headphones. Designed for sound engineers, musicians, and those who take sound seriously, Beats are the brainchild of legendary artist and producer Dr. Dre and chairman of Interscope Geffen A&M Records Jimmy Iovine.

- **WoodTones** (www.griffintechnology.com): WoodTones headphones, shown in Figure 3-6, take a cue from the wood ceiling and walls of the world's best symphony halls to reproduce acoustic accuracy. We love the sound — and look — of these headphones. Both the over-ear and in-ear versions have a built-in mic so you can conduct calls and get Siri's attention.

Figure 3-6: Acoustics sound better with wood.

✔ **Jawbone Icon HD** (www.jawbone.com): Small and light enough to stay in your ear without one of those annoying loops, the Jawbone Icon HD Bluetooth headset, shown in Figure 3-7, is equipped with advanced, military-grade noise cancellation technology that eliminates unwanted background noise when you talk on the phone. What's more, the headset's battery level appears in your iPhone's status bar — or tap the Icon HD's control button to get a spoken report on how much battery juice is left for handsfree chitchat.

✔ **iRetrofone** (www.etsy.com/shop/iRetrofone): If you work at a desk, and prefer to cradle a handset rather than use a headphone, this combination iPhone charger dock handset, as shown in Figure 3-7, is the solution. Download the companion app to add a (digital) rotary dial to your iPhone.

Figure 3-7: If you long for the good old days of landlines, consider iRetrofone.

The online Apple Store, which you can access from the Apple Store app, sells many of the accessories we present here and more.

Pumping Up the Volume

Headphones are great for private conversations and listening but when you want to share the sound or rock out at full volume, speaker docks are a great iPhone accessory. Combined with your iTunes library, iTunes Radio or even podcasts and audiobooks, your iPhone in a speaker dock is a great alternative to a home stereo system. Speakers come in many sizes and prices, so here we list choices across a price and features range.

✓ **Philips Soundshooter SBT30/00** (www.usa.philips.com): Smaller than your iPhone itself, this portable speaker, as shown in Figure 3-8, produces a lot of sound and boasts up to eight hours of battery charged playing. Connect your iPhone with Bluetooth and even make hands-free calls because there's a built-in mic too, which we think would be great for group calls.

Figure 3-8: Soundshooter fills a room with music or conversations.

✓ **iHome iPL10** (www.ihomeaudio.com): This speaker dock takes the traditional clock-radio cube to a new level. Insert your iPhone 5 or later into the Lightning adapter and charge your iPhone while you listen. A USB port lets you charge other devices at the same time. A simple but nifty feature syncs the clock to the time on your iPhone.

✓ **Bose SoundDock Portable** (www.bose.com): The SoundDock series offers four options but we particularly like the portable version for its style and sound quality. A discrete built-in handle makes taking the speakers with you easy, although a travel bag is available, as well as an extra rechargeable battery.

✓ **Band & Olufsen BeoPlay A8** (www.beoplay.com): If you want to go top of the line, the BeoPlay is a good choice. The A8 offers both USB and wireless AirPlay connections and the design is as outstanding as the sound. A position switch adjusts the sound output based on where you place the speakers, for example, in a corner or freestanding in the middle of a room.

Hooking up with cables

You can never have too many connections, especially iPhone-friendly ones that enhance your iPhone's features. They let you do things like connect your iPhone to your TV to watch photo slideshows or videos you shoot with iPhone — or movies you buy or rent from the iTunes Store — just to name a few scenarios. You make a lot of connections with Bluetooth or Wi-Fi, but for those times you don't, there are two adapter cables you might want to keep on hand:

✔ **Lightning to 30-pin adapter** (www.apple.com): Happy you bought a new iPhone 5c or 5s to replace your earlier iPhone, but bummed your plug-in accessories won't work with iPhone 5's new Lightning connector? No worries, you can buy one of two types of Lightning to 30-pin Adapters: a compact adapter or a cabled adapter. With these adapters, you can use those 30-pin accessories you already own.

✔ **Apple AV adapter and cables** (www.apple.com): Plug the Lightning Digital AV adapter or the Lightning to VGA adapter into your iPhone, and then connect the adapter to your HDTV with an HDMI cable (sold separately) or your VGA TV or monitor, and va-va-voom: Your iPhone can now entertain the entire room on the big-screen. Show off what you see on your iPhone screen (be it a game of Angry Birds, or the latest blockbuster you rent or buy from the iTunes Store), while keeping your iPhone juiced to last through the entire performance, thanks to a second port on the adapter that accommodates your iPhone's charger cable.

Taking It Away with Car and Travel Accessories

Until iOS in the Car is released sometime in 2014 — and you buy a car that is iOS-enabled — you might want to use your iPhone while driving. It goes without saying (but we'll say it anyway) that you must use the EarPods or another headphone or Bluetooth headset. Neither of us advocates using your iPhone to text (!) conversations while driving — and we mean never, ever. If you need to send or reply to a text message, or make or answer a call, please use Siri or Voice Control to do so. And if you can't, do yourself — and everyone in your car or on the road — a favor and pull over. (This public service announcement brought to you by "Common Sense.")

That unsaid rule said and out of the way, here are a few accessories that will make your travels safer:

✔ **Koomus Windshield Dashboard Car Mount** (www.koomus.com): With handsfree portrait or landscape viewing, the holder's suction cup can be mounted to your windshield or dashboard to keep your iPhone at eye-level for quick glances at Maps while following navigation directions. With EarPods or another headset, you can make voice-controlled calls and Siri can also read and reply to your messages.

✏ **IOGEAR Solar Bluetooth Hands-Free Car Kit** (www.iogear.com)**:** Pair your iPhone with IOGEAR's Solar Bluetooth Hands-Free Car Kit (refer to Figure 3-9) for hands-free placing and answering calls while keeping your eyes on the road and your hands on the wheel. A built-in solar panel harnesses the power of the sun for easy recharging.

Figure 3-9: The IOGEAR Solar Bluetooth Hands-Free Car Kit lets you make and answer calls while keeping your hands on the wheel.

Figure 3-10: Kenu Airframe is easily installed and removed.

✔ **Kenu Airframe Portable Car Mount (**`www.kenu.com/products/` `airframe`**):** This holder, as shown in Figure 3-10, attaches to any car's air vent and is great if you travel and use rental cars. It's small, light-weight, and easily mounted and dismounted — just remember to take it with you when you return the car.

Book II
Chapter 3

Enhancing and
Protecting iPhone
with Add-ons

Book III
Communications Central: Calls, Messages, and the Web

Visit www.dummies.com/extras/iphoneaio for tips on creating ringtones.

Contents at a Glance

Chapter 1: Managing Phone and FaceTime Video Calls

In This Chapter

✔ **Making and receiving calls**

✔ **Blocking unwanted callers**

✔ **Audio and video chatting with FaceTime**

✔ **Taking note of Phone notifications**

✔ **Listening to and managing voicemail messages**

✔ **Perusing and adjusting phone-related settings**

✔ **Juggling call options and conference calls**

*W*e're guessing you've already made and received phone calls with your iPhone before you arrived at this chapter. You may have listened to voicemail messages for calls you were unable to answer, and thought about changing the ringtone that plays when calls come in. And you really want to try FaceTime.

Even if you have done some or all of those things, this chapter is all about maximizing your up-close-and-personal relationship with iPhone's phone-related features.

In this chapter, we introduce you to the Phone app you use to place a call or answer one. We also tell you how to politely decline a call that you can't respond to at that moment or block callers that have become a nuisance. We explain both types of FaceTime calls — voice and video — that you can have with other iOS devices or Mac users. We then show you how to listen to and manage your voicemails, and about the different ways iPhone notifies you when you miss a call. We review the phone-related settings you may want to familiarize yourself with before you start making calls — especially if you're traveling overseas. At the end of the chapter, we tell you about two Phone features: call waiting and conference calls.

Lucy Blue

iPhone ★
347 7002445

FaceTime

home
37 Bone Street
˙ˑbletown IN 12063

Homing in on Phone

Tapping the Phone icon on the Home screen is indisputably the most obvious way to use your iPhone as, well, a phone. When the app opens, you see the screen associated with the phone-calling method you most recently used. The image in Figure 1-1 shows the Favorites list screen but if you made a call with the keypad and then switch to another app, when you return to Phone, the keypad appears.

Some not-so-obvious ways that can also land you on Phone screen include answering an incoming call, tapping a phone number in an e-mail or web page to call that number, tapping a number in the Contacts app, or by speaking the name or number you want Siri or iPhone's Voice Control feature to dial on your behalf.

●●●○○ We assume that your iPhone currently enjoys an active connection with your provider's cellular network, as indicated by the cell signal strength icon in the top left corner of iPhone's status bar. The more filled in circles you see, the better the signal. If instead of circles you see No Signal or No Service or the Airplane Mode icon, you won't be able to make or receive calls until you're once again in range of your provider's cellular network signal or Airplane Mode is disabled. To familiarize yourself with other icons you see in the status bar, check out Book I, Chapter 2.

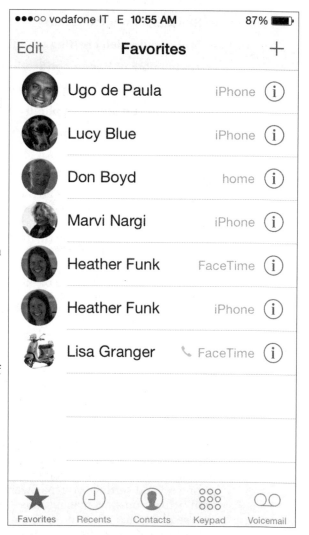

Figure 1-1: The Phone app: More ways to make calls than meets the eye.

However you reach the Phone screen, you always see the following icons at the bottom of the screen that activate Phone app's main features:

 ✔ **Favorites:** iPhone's version of speed dial, offering quick, one-tap dialing or FaceTime access to the 50 people you call the most.

 ✔ **Recents:** A roll-call list displays up to 75 of the most recent calls you placed, answered, missed, or hung up on.

 ✔ **Contacts:** Your personal phonebook stored in the Contacts app. See Book IV, Chapter 1 to learn about the Contacts app.

 ✔ **Keypad:** An on-screen keypad that works like the physical keypads introduced in the 60s for dialing phone numbers.

 ✔ **Voicemail:** Your inbox for listening to, replying to, managing, deleting, and getting more information about voicemail messages you receive.

We write about the first four of these Phone features (as well as using Voice Control) in the next section and cover Voicemail in the section "Visiting Voicemail."

Making Calls

You can tap out numbers on your iPhone's keypad, but there are a number of other ways iPhone lets you make calls. You can even say the number or name of the person you want to call out loud without having to bother touching the screen at all.

To simply make a phone call, tap the Phone app on the Home screen, and then tap one of the five buttons at the bottom of the Phone screen (refer to Figure 1-1).

Here's a quick rundown of the ways to make calls (all of which we cover in depth in the following sections):

 ✔ Tap Favorites, and then tap the contact you want to call.

 ✔ Tap Recents, and then tap the name or number you want to call.

 ✔ Tap Contacts, find and tap the contact you want to call to display his contact card, and then tap the phone number you want to dial.

 ✔ Tap Keypad, type the number you want to call, and then tap Call.

 ✔ Tap Voicemail, tap the name or number you want to call, and then tap Call Back.

 ✔ Press and hold the Home button to activate Siri or Voice Control, and then say the name or number you want to call.

Book III Chapter 1

Managing Phone and FaceTime Video Calls

Using Favorites

Tapping Favorites displays the names of up to 50 people and organizations you deem important enough to score a spot on what is essentially iPhone's version of your speed-dial list, as shown in Figure 1-1. Each number counts as one, so if you have a work number and a home number for the same person, that equals two favorites, same goes for FaceTime and phone numbers. You can add, edit, rearrange, remove, and — most importantly— make phone calls with Favorites.

Add a Favorite

1. **Tap the + (plus sign) button to display your contacts, and then search or scroll through your contacts to find the one you want to add.**

2. **Tap the contact you want to add to your favorites list. (See Book IV, Chapter 1 to learn about Contacts.)**

   If you have only one number for that contact, the dialog in Figure 1-2 appears immediately. If you have more than one number, the contact card opens so you can tap the phone number you want to add to Favorites.

3. **A dialog asks if you want to add the number as a Favorite for Voice Call, FaceTime Audio, or FaceTime (Video), as shown in Figure 1-2. Tap the one you want.**

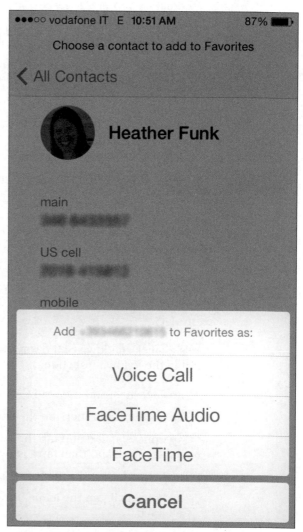

Figure 1-2: A number can be assigned as a FaceTime or Voice Call Favorite.

The person's name is added to your Favorites list. A label indicates the type of number it is, referring to the label used in Contacts, such as *mobile, home,* or *iPhone.* FaceTime means a FaceTime video chat will be initiated, whereas a phone icon next to FaceTime (refer to Figure 1-1) means tapping that Favorite will initiate a FaceTime audio call. We explain FaceTime just a bit later in this chapter.

Add Favorites directly from Contacts by scrolling down a contact's info card and tapping Add to Favorites. If there are multiple numbers for the contact, a menu prompts you to choose the number you want to add, and then you select Voice, FaceTime, or FaceTime Audio.

Call a Favorite

Tap a name in the list and the outgoing call is placed.

Delete or rearrange Favorites

1. **Tap the Edit button in the upper left.**

2. **Tap the red button to the left of a name you want to delete, and then tap the Delete button that appears to the right, as shown in Figure 1-3.**

   Your out-of-favor contact's name only vanishes from your Favorites list, but her card is not deleted from your saved Contacts.

3. **Next to a name you want to move to a new position in the list, tap and drag the rearrange button up or down your list and then let go to save your favorite in its new location.**

4. **Tap the Done button when you finish.**

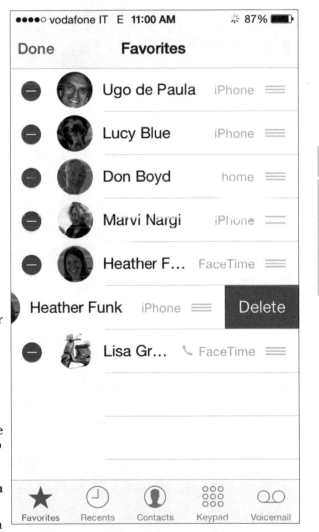

Figure 1-3: The Favorites edit screen.

You're limited to 50 favorites, so the + (plus sign) button doesn't appear after you've reached the limit. You'll need to delete an existing favorite from your list to make the + appear again so you can tap it to add a new favorite.

Get More Info/Edit a Favorite

Tap the Info button to display a favorite's contact Info screen. The person's contact card displays any information you filled in for that contact, including phone numbers and e-mail addresses. We explain Contacts more in Book IV, Chapter 1, but you'll notice two things in Contacts after you add a person to your Favorites list:

- A star appears next to the phone number that's been saved in your Favorites list. Tap another number for that contact to add a second favorite number for that contact (for instance, one for Mom's mobile number, a second for her home number).

- Contacts without phone numbers or those already added to your favorites list with no second or remaining phone numbers to add appear dimmed in your contacts list when adding new contacts to Favorites (because you've already added them).

Using Recents

Tapping Recents displays a chronological list — also referred to as your phone's call log — of up to 75 of the most recent numbers your iPhone has called, received, or missed calls from, or hung up on (more than one call from the same number counts as one of the 75), as shown in Figure 1-4. Tap the All tab to view every kind of incoming and outgoing call or tap Missed to see only those calls you didn't respond to for one reason or another.

Here's how to interpret the information you find on the Recents list:

- Names indicate calls to or from people whose numbers are saved in Contacts.

- Phone numbers aren't associated with a contact card. (That doesn't mean you can't save a phone number in Contacts without a name — you can. But why you'd want to is anyone's guess.)

  Because the Recents lists doesn't retain Caller-ID (for numbers that aren't in Contacts), you can download the ReversePhone app to look for the identities of incoming calls, particularly missed calls when you didn't have a chance to see the Caller-ID.

- The label under the recent caller/callee's number — such as home, mobile, or other — is displayed if you assigned that label to the number in Contacts or the contact management app from which you imported the contact.

Outgoing call

Outgoing FaceTime

Missed incoming calls

Info

Figure 1-4: Recents displays a list of all incoming and outgoing phone activity.

✔ Calls you place are marked with the outgoing phone call icon.

✔ Missed calls are hard to miss on your list because they're the items displayed in red type.

✔ Incoming and outgoing calls from or to the same phone number are displayed together as one item in the list, although FaceTime or missed calls from the same number are each their own item. The number in parentheses next to the name or number (refer to Figure 1-4) tells you how many calls were placed.

✔ The time of calls from today and the day of other calls is shown to the right of the name.

Tap the Info button to see detailed information about the call activity: the day and time (or consecutive times) a contact or phone number reached out to you (or you reached out to them), as shown in Figure 1-5. You also see any additional phone numbers, e-mail or street addresses, and other details from the contacts card in Contacts. A star appears next to any of that contact's phone numbers you designated as favorite.

To remove items from the list, one at a time:

✓ Swipe across an individual call and then tap the Delete button that deletes only that recent call from the list.

✓ Tap the Edit button in the upper right. Tap the red and white minus sign that appears to the left of the call you want to delete, and then tap the Delete button.

To remove all the items from the Recents list, tap Clear in the upper left, and then tap Clear All Recents in the dialog that appears.

Tapping the Clear button clears *all* items from the Recents list even if you tap Clear while viewing only Missed calls.

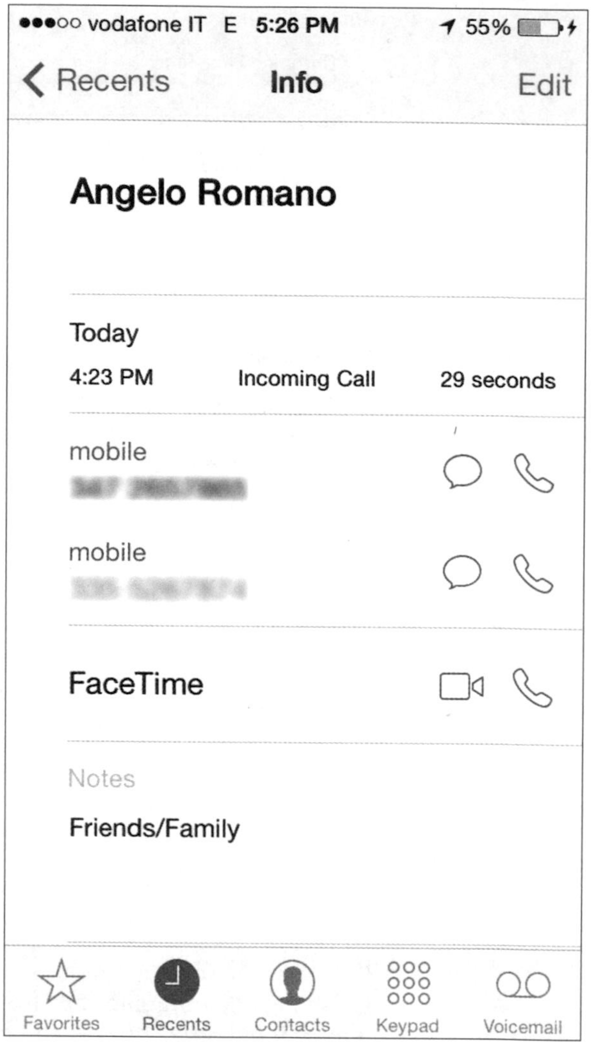

●●●○○ vodafone IT E 5:26 PM   1 55% ▭ ⚡

‹ Recents   **Info**   Edit

Angelo Romano

Today
4:23 PM   Incoming Call   29 seconds

mobile
○ ☎

mobile
○ ☎

FaceTime   ▭◁ ☎

Notes
Friends/Family

☆   ◔   ☻   ⦙⦙⦙   ◠◠
Favorites   Recents   Contacts   Keypad   Voicemail

Figure 1-5: Tap the Info button to see the time and duration of calls from the same number.

Make sure to tap the Info button when you want more information in either the Favorites or Recents list because tapping the name will initiate a call.

Using Contacts

Tapping Contacts displays your iPhone's central directory for storing and managing contact "cards" containing the names, phone numbers, e-mail and street addresses, and other information, as shown in Figure 1-6. The Contacts you see in the Phone app are the same as those in the Contacts app.

Tap a contact card to display the contact's Info screen, as shown in Figure 1-7, and then tap the phone number you want to call to dial that number.

You can search your contacts from the Contacts list three ways:

- ✔ Scroll up or down the list until you see the contact you want.

- ✔ Tap a letter in the A to Z index on the right edge to jump to contact names beginning with that letter, and then scroll through the list until you see the contact you want.

- ✔ Tap the Search field (tap the clock in the Status bar if you don't see it) and begin typing the name of the person or company you're searching for to display any contacts that match what you type, and then tap the contact that matches the one you're looking for, as shown in Figure 1-8.

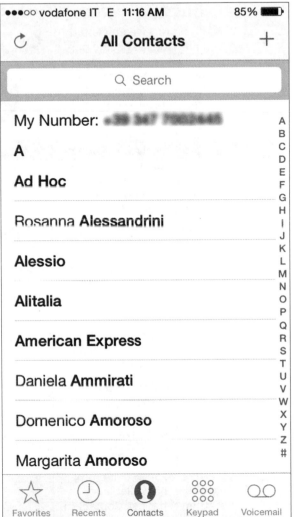

Figure 1-6: Contacts lists every contact "card" saved on your iPhone.

Book III Chapter 1

Managing Phone and FaceTime Video Calls

From the Home screen, you can also search for your contacts using Spotlight search, which you access by pulling down the middle of the screen; we tell you everything you need to know about using Spotlight in Book I, Chapter 3.

When you tap the Info button next to an unknown phone number (in the Recents list), you can create a new contact or add the number to an existing contact, and when you tap it for a Contact (in Favorites or Recents), you can edit the contact information by tapping the Edit button.

Blocking callers

If you receive unwanted calls from a specific person or entity, you can block incoming calls. The information remains in Contacts and you can make outgoing phone or FaceTime calls, but you won't receive any incoming communications via phone, FaceTime, or Messages. Open the contact in one of the following ways:

✔ Tap Contacts on the Home screen, and then tap the undesired contact in the list.

✔ Tap the Info button next to the person in the Favorites list.

✔ Tap the Info button next to the person or number in the Recents list.

Scroll to the bottom of the Info screen and tap Block this Caller, and then tap Block Contact in the menu that appears as in Figure 1-9. Incoming phone calls and messages from any number associated with that contact will be blocked.

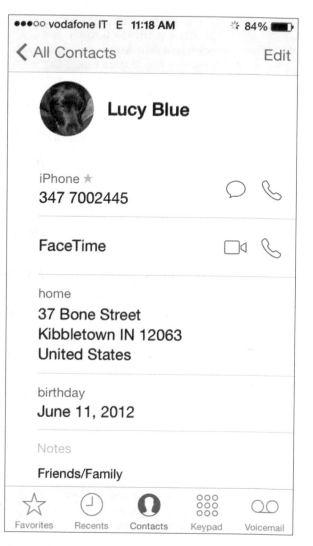

Figure 1-7: Tap a contact's phone number to call that number.

Using the Keypad

Tapping the Keypad button displays the onscreen keypad. Tap the numbers of the phone number you want to call and then press Call to dial your number, as shown in Figure 1-10.

Tap the delete button to backspace over a number (or numbers) you mistyped.

Some nifty things you can do (and see!) when you're using Keypad include the following:

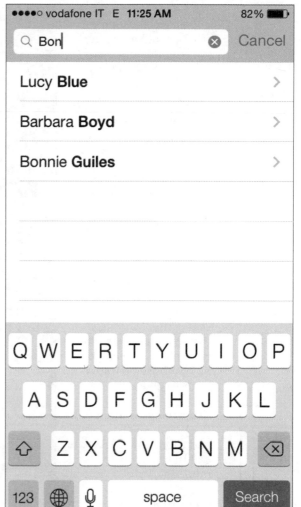

Figure 1-8: Homing in on contacts with the Search feature.

✔ Enter a "soft" pause by pressing and holding the * key until a comma appears in the phone number display. A soft pause is two seconds. You could use this feature if you call in for your voicemail at work and have to call the phone number, and then enter an access code, and then perhaps a passcode. Putting a soft pause between the phone number and each code gives the system time to receive the information and go to the next step.

✔ Enter a "hard" pause by pressing and holding the # key until a semicolon appears in the phone number display. A hard pause waits for your confirmation (tap the Call button) before transmitting the next series of numbers. For example, when calling a company, you have to wait for the line to be answered before entering an extension.

✔ Paste a phone number you copied from another app into Keypad by holding your finger on the display zone above the numeric keys, and then tapping Paste when it appears.

✔ Press Call to bring up the last number you dialed, and then press Call again to dial it.

✔ See the contact name magically appear beneath a number you tap in if that number is on any contact's card.

✔ Tap Add to Contacts under the number you enter to either create a new contact card with the phone number you're typing, or to add the phone number to an existing contact.

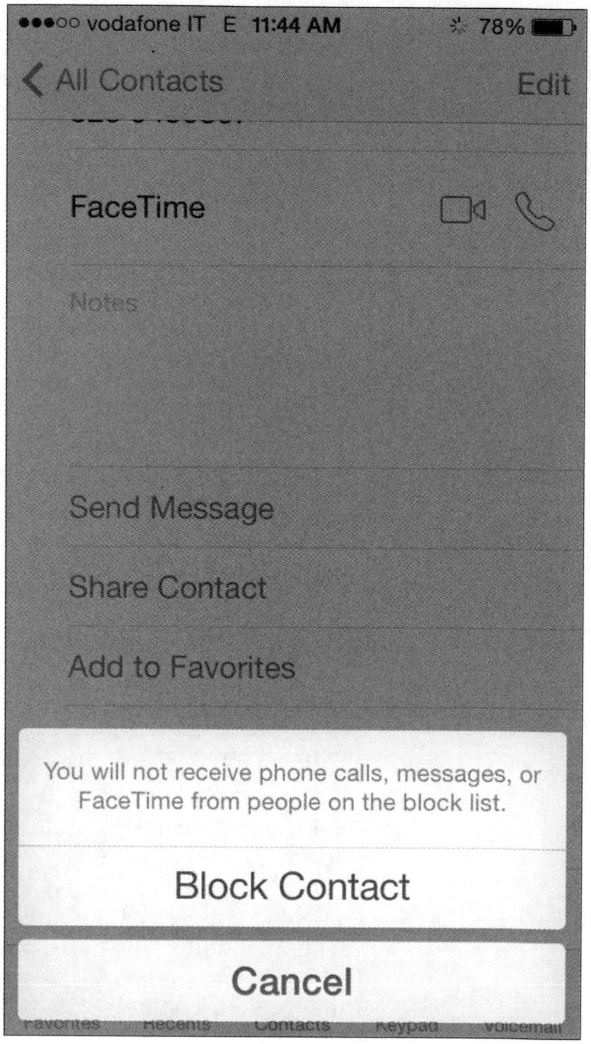

Using Voicemail

One of our favorite things about the Phone app's Voicemail feature is how *seeing* those messages in the voicemail inbox helps to remind us to call back any of those people we want to chat with.

Tap a name or number in the Voicemail list screen and then tap Call Back to call that person or phone number.

To learn about the other things you can do on the Voicemail screen besides returning phone calls, check out the section "Visiting Voicemail," later in this chapter.

Figure 1-9: Block unwanted incoming communications from specific contacts.

Using Siri or Voice Control

Both iPhone's Voice Control and Siri (iPhone 4s or later) features are all ears when it comes to using your voice to make your iPhone do things for you — including making phone calls. In Book I, Chapter 3, we explain all the other things Voice Control and Siri can do for you. Here, we explain phone calls.

You can use Voice Control or Siri but not both at the same time, and you need either a cellular data or Wi-Fi Internet connection to use Siri.

Siri

Siri is a bit more intelligent than Voice Control, or perhaps she's just a better listener. Do one of the following to solicit Siri:

✔ Press and hold the Home button until the Siri screen opens

✔ Press and hold the center button on the EarPods controls until you hear a double-beep

✔ Press the Attention button on your Bluetooth headset

✔ Bring your iPhone to your ear, if you activated the Raise to Speak function, until you hear a double-beep

Speak your command, more or less as if you were talking with a person. You can give simple instructions, like "Call

Figure 1-10: Dialing phone numbers the "old-fashioned" way.

Lucy," or more complex commands such as "Call my sister at work." Siri looks for matches in Favorites and Contacts. When a match is found, Siri responds along the lines of "Calling Lucy Blue's iPhone." If there is no match or if there's more than one phone number for the contact you want to call, Siri asks for more information, as shown in Figure 1-11. When there are multiple choices for the phone number, Siri reads the label and the number for the contact, you can then repeat the label or say "the second one" and the call will be put through. Speak the requested information and Siri makes the phone call when she finds the number. If the person you want to call isn't in your Contacts or somewhere else on your iPhone, Siri can search the Internet for the number, and then connect you. You get the picture. If the person isn't available, you can ask Siri to send the person an e-mail or text message.

Siri requires a Wi-Fi or cellular Internet connection and can be slow to respond to your request — at times up to 30 seconds — depending on the type of Internet connection you have and because your request is sent to Apple's server, which processes the request and then instructs Siri how to respond. If you use Siri only for making phone calls, Voice Control will probably be faster and more accurate.

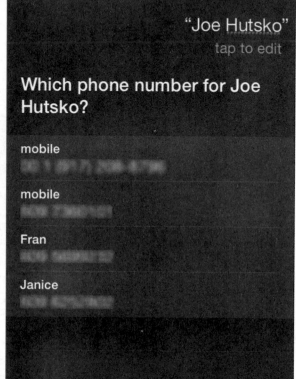

Figure 1-11: The Siri calling screen.

Voice Control

Press and hold the Home button to activate Voice Control. The screen shown in Figure 1-12 opens (you'll also hear a double-tone sound). Say "Call" or "Dial," followed by the name of the person or phone number you want to call. A slightly robotic voice repeats your request aloud and then places your call for you.

Ways Voice Control may respond to your request include the following:

✔ **No Match Found:** That's what the Voice Control robot says (followed by three tone sounds) if it can't find a phone number in Contacts that matches the name you said; or if it can't understand the phone number you gave it to dial for you. Either way, you can try again by immediately repeating the name or number (perhaps more slowly this time).

✔ **Multiple Numbers:** If a contact you're calling has more than one phone number, the Voice Calling robot says the contact's name aloud, and then rattles off the different phone numbers it finds for that contact, such as "home, mobile, or work." After listening to the choices, you can repeat the label or say, "the first number" or "the second one," and your call is placed to the correct number.

✔ **Multiple Matches Found:** That's what Voice Control tells you if it finds multiple numbers for a name you say, such as "Call Joe;" Voice Control lists the names of contacts with the same name so you can pick one, or it asks you to be more specific.

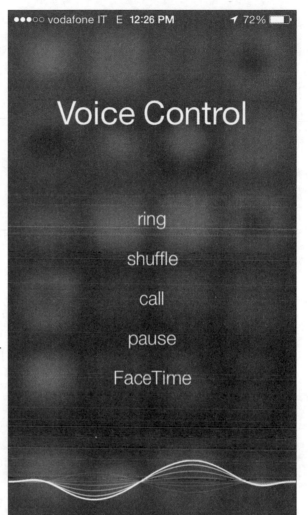

Figure 1-12: The Voice Control screen.

Book III
Chapter 1

Managing Phone
and FaceTime Video
Calls

Calling tips

Add relations to your card in Contacts so you can say "Call Dad" or "Call my sister" or to other contact cards, so you can request things like "Call Skip Johnson's brother" when you have a hard time remembering a name. Whether you're talking to Siri or Voice Control, when saying a person's name, you can differentiate between people who have the same first name by adding their last name, as well as say the specific phone number you want to call if you have more than one phone number for the person:

✔ Say "Call" or "Dial," and then say

- "Joe Smith"
- "Joe Smith at work"
- "Joe Hutsko, mobile"

Sometimes your iPhone has trouble understanding you in a crowded place with a lot of ambient noise such as a party or street corner.

When saying phone numbers you want to call, remember the following:

✔ Speak each number clearly and separately; for instance, if you want to call 555-6666, you would say "Call five five five, six six six."

✔ If you're calling an 800 number, you can say "eight hundred," followed by the rest of the number you are calling.

The Voice Control and Siri features work even if your iPhone is locked, which is a handy feature—unless you misplace or

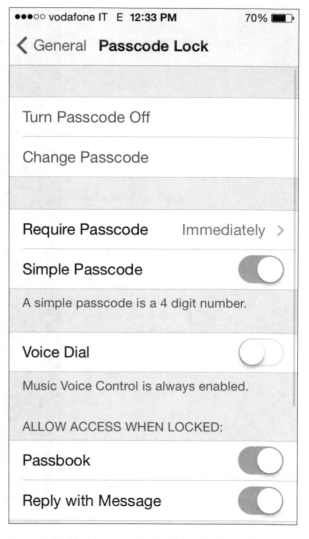

Figure 1-13: Disable or enable the Voice Dialing or Siri feature when iPhone is locked.

lose your iPhone and someone picks it up and starts making international calls. To turn off the ability to make Voice Control calls when your iPhone is locked, go to Settings➪General➪Passcode Lock and turn off the Voice Dial option, as shown in Figure 1-13. (It will only be active if you have set up a Passcode.) When the Voice Dial feature is off, you can still use Voice Control or Siri when your iPhone is locked to do things like play or pause music or say "What time is it?" to hear the local time. If you say "Call Joe Hutsko," however, the ever-watchful genie that lives inside your iPhone politely responds, "Voice dialing is disabled."

Even more ways to make calls

Besides using the Phone app, Siri, or Voice Control to make calls, you can also initiate calls by tapping phone numbers that appear on web pages you're browsing, in e-mail, notes, or text messages you receive, and in other near and possibly faraway places like the search results you turn up when you use Maps to locate a restaurant, business, or other organization. To make a call from Maps, tap the arrow next to the name on the map to open up an information screen, and then tap the phone number to make the call. Tapping a phone number in any app displays a dialog, which gives you the option to call the number, whereas pressing and holding on a number serves up even more options for doing things besides just calling the number, including sending a text message to the number, creating a new contact card for the number, or adding the number to an existing card already saved in Contacts.

Answering Calls

Because you never know when you might get a call, mastering the art of answering calls (or rejecting ones you're unable or not in the mood to answer) is a useful iPhone talent to acquire sooner than later.

When you receive a call, your iPhone displays one of the incoming call screens shown in Figure 1-14, depending on whether your iPhone is locked (left) or awake (right). You'll hear your chosen ringtone and, if your iPhone is on your person — depending on how sensitive you are — you may feel it vibrating. If the information of the person calling you is saved in Contacts, you'll see the person's name (and photo, if you assigned a photo to that person's contact card). If the caller isn't one of your contacts, you either see the caller's phone number and name, or "Unknown" or "Blocked" if the caller has chosen to block their Caller ID from appearing when they place calls.

**Book III
Chapter 1**

**Managing Phone
and FaceTime Video
Calls**

To answer an incoming call

- Drag the Slide to Answer button to the right (if your iPhone is locked)
- Tap Answer

To instantly quiet your iPhone's ringtone when you receive an incoming call, tap either volume button once, or press the Sleep/Wake button once. You can still answer the call but the ringing is muted. Double-click the Sleep/Wake button to send the call directly to voicemail.

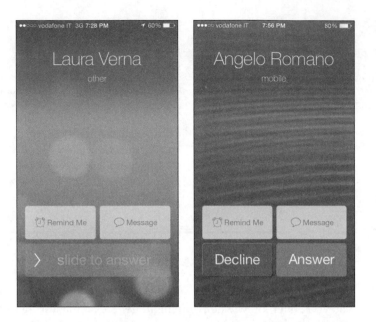

Figure 1-14: Two incoming call screens: One locked (left), the other not (right).

When you answer an incoming call, the active call screen appears. We give you the full 411 on your options in the section "Managing Calls" a little further along in this chapter.

Declining Calls

Sometimes, you just can't respond to a call or don't want to talk to the caller. There are several ways to decline phone calls and two ways to respond, other than answering: You have the option of declining a call but sending a message to the caller that reads "I'll call you later" or something to that effect, or you can opt to be reminded in an hour to call the person back. Here are your call-declining options:

- ✔ **Press the Sleep/Wake button twice (which sends the call to voicemail).**

- ✔ **Tap the Decline button (if your iPhone is awake).**

- ✔ **Ignore iPhone's pleas to get your attention.** After a few moments, the call is automatically declined.

- ✔ **Tap either the Remind Me or Message button on the incoming call screen, and then tap one of the choices:**

   - *Reply With Message:* Choose one of the options or tap Custom to create a specific response for that call. Go to Settings⊏➤Phone⊏➤Respond with Text to create different default replies. Tap in the field of the reply you want to replace and type your own reply, as shown in Figure 1-15.

- *Remind Me Later:* Tap one of the options:

  In One Hour. You'll receive a notification in an hour to call the person whose call you declined.

  When I Leave, and then choose either Current Location, Get Home, or Get to Work to receive a reminder based on one of those three locations. Location Services must be turned on for the When I Leave feature to appear and function.

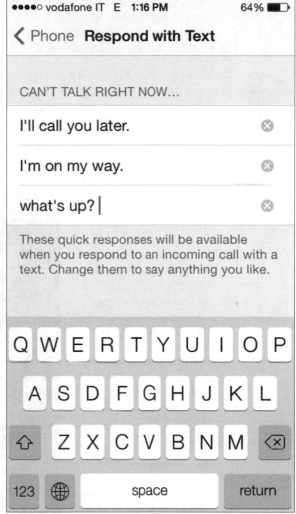

Figure 1-15: Create your own default replies to calls you decline.

Answering or declining calls while using your iPhone's stereo headphones is merely a matter of working the remote button as follows:

- Click the center button once to answer a call, or twice to decline a call.

- Put a call on hold to answer another incoming call by pressing the center button; press again to return to the caller you left on hold.

- Answer an incoming call but hang-up on the current call by pressing and holding the center button for a couple seconds; two low beeps let you know you ended the first call.

- Click the volume + or - buttons to adjust the volume level.

When you decline a call in any of the preceding ways, the caller hears your voicemail greeting, followed by the option to leave you a voicemail message. Ditto if someone tries calling you when your iPhone is turned off, Airplane Mode is turned on, or Do Not Disturb is activated.

Activate Do Not Disturb by dragging up from the bottom of the screen to open the Control Center and then tap the Do Not Disturb button. To create a scheduled uninterrupted time, tap Settings➪Do Not Disturb➪Scheduled and then select the start and ending times. See Book I, Chapter 4 for more details.

Managing Calls

In the previous sections, we tell you about (almost) every which way you can answer and make calls with iPhone. In this section, we tell you about the things you can do while you're engaged in an active call, such as adjusting the volume for your call or switching on iPhone's speakerphone, as well as neat stuff like using the active call screen to do other things while you're actively engaged in a call, and making or accepting a second call while you're on your current call, and then merging those two calls together so everyone can join the conversation.

When you make or answer a call, the active call screen appears as in Figure 1-16. The Active Call screen displays information about the person or business you're speaking with such as the phone number or name (if saved in Contacts), and the length of time you're engaged in your call from the

Figure 1-16: The Active Call screen.

moment you connected. You'll also see a photo of the person if you saved a photo with his contact card in Contacts.

The buttons you see have the following functions:

- ✔ **Mute:** Tap Mute to prevent your caller from hearing sound on your end of the conversation, even though you can still hear your caller; tap again to turn off Mute.

- ✔ **Hold:** Press and hold the Mute button; the mute button changes into the Hold button; tap Hold again to turn off Hold. When you place a call on hold, neither you nor the person on the other end can hear the other.

- ✔ **Keypad:** Tap Keypad to display the keypad, and then tap any numbers or the * and # buttons to do things like respond to options when calling automated customer service phone numbers, or check your work voice-mail inbox.

- ✔ **Speaker:** Tap the Speaker icon to hear your caller's voice through iPhone's built-in loudspeaker.

- ✔ **Audio Source:** You see this button in place of the Speaker button when you have a Bluetooth headset paired with your iPhone, which we explain in the section "Using Bluetooth headsets."

- ✔ **Add Call:** Tap Add Call to put one person on hold and call another and also to set up a conference call. We explain this in detail in the section "Making dual and conference calls."

- ✔ **Use FaceTime:** Tap FaceTime to switch your current cellular call to a FaceTime Audio or video call, which uses a Wi-Fi or cellular data connection. Refer to the section "Making a FaceTime call," later in this chapter.

- ✔ **Contacts:** Tap Contacts to browse your contact cards to do things like find and share a phone number with the person you're currently speaking with, or choose another contact's phone number that you want to call while engaged in your current call.

Using Bluetooth headsets

When you make a call while you're connected to a Bluetooth headset you paired with your iPhone, the Audio Sources screen shown in Figure 1-17 appears while your call is being connected. Tap iPhone or Speaker if you want to switch to either of those audio sources instead of your Bluetooth device; or tap Hide Sources to display the active call screen, which automatically appears after your call is connected. (We tell you how to set up and manage Bluetooth devices in Book I, Chapter 2.) To change the audio source, tap the Audio Source button on the active call screen to display the Audio Sources options, tap the audio source choice you want to switch to, and then tap Hide Sources to return to the active call screen.

Press iPhone's volume up and down buttons to increase or decrease the volume level of your call. If you're using headphones or a Bluetooth headset, you can also press the volume + and - buttons on those listening devices to adjust the call volume.

Multitasking while on a call

Whenever a call is underway — whether you placed or answered the call — the active call screen is displayed (refer to Figure 1-16).

When you're engaged in an active call, you can switch to another app to do other things, like looking up recipe ingredients you jotted in Notes, or reading an e-book while you're stuck on hold. When you switch to another app while engaged in a call, the green pulsing active call banner shown in Figure 1-18 appears at the top of the screen. Tapping the active call banner returns you to the active call display.

Making dual and conference calls

While you're engaged in an active call, you can make a second call, or you can answer an incoming call (unless you've turned off your iPhone's call waiting feature, which we explain in the "Call Forwarding, Call Waiting, and Caller ID Blocking" section of this

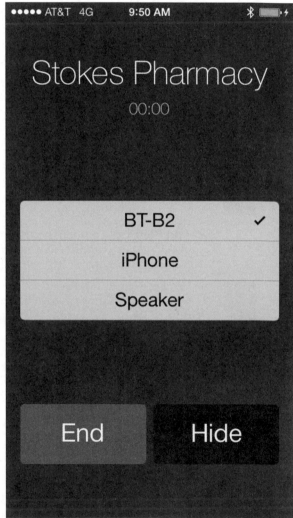

Figure 1-17: Choosing your preferred audio source while making or managing a call.

chapter). If you have a GSM-model iPhone, you can also initiate a conference call that lets you speak with up to five people at once.

Making a second call

While on an active call, you can make a second call by doing the following:

1. **Tap Add Call to display your iPhone Contacts.**

2. **Scroll to find and tap to choose the contact you want to call.**

   You can tap the Favorites, Recents, and Keypad buttons at the bottom of the screen to use any of those options to add your second call.

   When your second call is established, the active multiple calls screen appears (refer to Figure 1-19).

3. **On a GSM phone, switch between your callers to speak privately with one or the other by tapping the caller's name at the top of the screen.**

   See the section "Activating Your iPhone" in Book I, Chapter 2 to determine which type of phone you have if you're not sure.

Figure 1-18: The active call banner.

CDMA phones only allow you to switch between calls if the second call was incoming.

4. **Tap End Call to hang up on the caller you're currently speaking with. Your other caller becomes your active call, and you can press End Call when you're finished conversing with that caller.**

Answering a second incoming call

If a second call comes in while you're engaged in another call, you see the screen shown in Figure 1-20. Respond to the incoming call screen by doing one of the following:

✓ **Tap Hold Call + Answer** to put your current call on hold and answer your second incoming call. When you choose this option, the active multiple calls screen appears.

✓ **End Call + Answer** to disconnect with your current call and answer your second incoming call. Your iPhone responds differently depending on whether you have a GSM (AT&T, T-Mobile) or CDMA (Verizon, Sprint) iPhone.

- **GSM:** Tap End Call + Answer.

- **CDMA:** Tap End Call, and when the second call rings again, tap Answer.

vodafone IT   7:32 PM   54%

Ugo de Paula   HOLD

Francesca Drake   00:04

mute   keypad   speaker

merge calls   swap   contacts

End

Figure 1-19: The active multiple calls screen.

Making a conference call

You initiate a conference call by making or answering a second call as described previously. After your second call is established, the multiple active calls screen appears (refer to Figure 1-19).

To turn your two calls into a conference call, and even add more callers to your two calls and turn those calls into a conference call, do the following:

1. **Tap Add Call to add a second person to a call you initiated and then choose the person you want to add from Contacts, Favorites, or Recents.**

   Or tap Hold Call + Answer to add an incoming call.

2. **On A GSM phone, you may have up to five people on your conference call. Repeat step one to add the third through fifth person to your current group call.**

3. **Tap Merge Calls to combine your two (or more) calls into a single Conference Call in which everyone can speak and hear everyone else.**

   To merge calls on a CDMA phone, you must place the second call in order to merge with the first one.

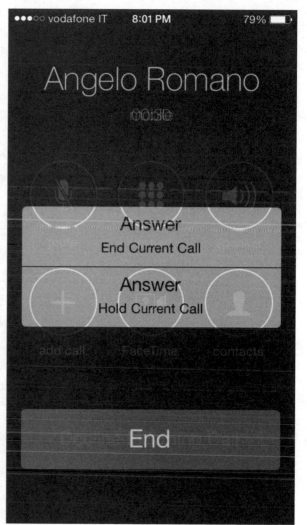

Figure 1-20: Options for responding to a second incoming phone call.

Book III
Chapter 1

Managing Phone and FaceTime Video Calls

The conference call screen shown in Figure 1-21 appears, the names of the people on the call scroll across the top of the screen.

Managing a conference call

When a conference call is underway, you can use the conference call screen to manage your conference call by doing the following:

- ✔ Tap the Info button at the top of the screen to display a list of the people on the call, as shown in Figure 1-22.

- ✔ Tap the End button under a caller's name or number to disconnect that caller from the conference call.

- ✔ To speak privately with one caller in your conference call, tap the Private button under the caller's name to speak that caller; your other callers are put on hold while you speak privately with a single caller.

- ✔ Tap the Back button to return to the Conference call screen.

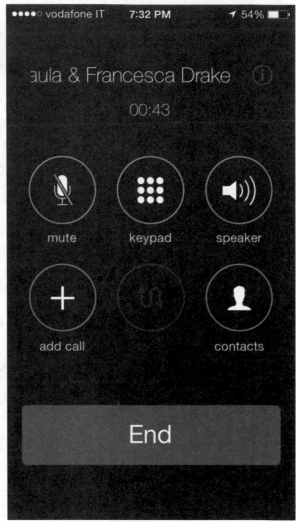

Figure 1-21: The Conference call screen.

Visiting Voicemail

For the times when you can't respond to a call, voicemail is a great way for your caller to let you know what she wants so you can respond when it's convenient for you. In this section, we explain setting up your voicemail greeting, and listening to and managing voicemail messages.

Tap Phone➪Voicemail to display the Voicemail screen, as shown in Figure 1-23.

Visual voicemail: Seen *and* heard

Visual voicemail is called that because you actually see your voice messages listed in a nice and neat list just like your e-mail messages, whereas typical "non-visual" voicemail only appears . . . well, nowhere, because only visual voicemail messages can be seen and heard. If you've never had voicemail, you may be unfamiliar with what it's like to retrieve your voicemail messages the "old-fashioned way" by dialing into your voicemail mailbox. Then pressing buttons on the keypad to skip, fast forward, rewind, and delete those messages as they rattle off one after the other — all of which visual voicemail lets you do with your fingertips. You can select the messages you want to hear and listen to them in the order you want. Better yet — ask Siri to read your list of visual voicemail messages to you.

Unfortunately, visual voicemail isn't a feature you always find on every iPhone. In some cases, you may have to pay an extra monthly fee for the feature. In other cases, the visual voicemail feature may not be offered by all carriers.

Recording and changing your greeting

If this is the first time you're visiting the Voicemail screen, iPhone prompts you to create a password and record your voicemail greeting. Repeating the same steps is how you change your voicemail greeting message whenever you want.

Tap Greeting to display the Voicemail Greeting screen shown in Figure 1-24, and then choose one of the following options:

- Tap Default if you want callers to hear your cellular provider's generic voicemail message (which says something like "the person you are trying to reach at" — your phone number — "is not available," followed by instructions on how to leave a message, yada yada yada).

- Tap Custom if you want to record (or change) a personal greeting message in your own words, and then tap Record to record your greeting; tap Play to listen to your greeting.

- Tap Save when you're happy with your choice, or tap Cancel if you've changed your mind and you want to keep the existing greeting.

Go to Settings⇨Sounds⇨New Voicemail to designate the sound and vibration pattern you want to hear when you have a new voicemail message.

Listening to and managing voicemail messages

When you tap a voicemail message in the voicemail list, the selection expands to reveal the playback controls along with a couple other message management buttons, as shown in Figure 1-25.

✔ To listen to and control playback of a voicemail message:

- Tap the Play button to listen to the message. A Pause button replaces the Play button. You can juggle between the two to play and pause playback.

- Drag the playhead in the scrubber bar to move to any location in the voicemail message.

- Tap the Speaker button to hear messages out loud through iPhone's speaker (rather than holding iPhone to your ear or listening through headphones).

✔ Tap Call Back to call the person who left you the selected message.

✔ To display more information about the caller, tap the Info button on the right side of the names in the Voicemail list to display the Info screen.

✔ Tap Delete to delete the selected voicemail message. When you delete a voicemail message, the message is removed from the Voicemail list screen, and is saved in the Deleted Messages list, which is automatically created if it isn't already displayed.

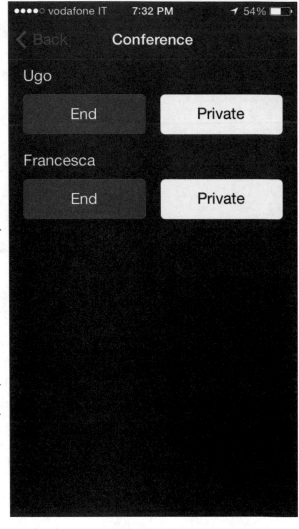

Figure 1-22: Juggle individual callers during a conference call.

Messages you've lis-
tened to remain in
your voicemail inbox
until your cellular
carrier deletes those
messages. This
means that even if
you delete a mes-
sage, it may pop
back into the Inbox
at a later date. The
length of time mes-
sages you've listened
to remain in your
voicemail box varies;
check with your
carrier.

When viewing the
Deleted screen as shown
in Figure 1-26, you can

✔ Tap a voicemail mes-
sage to open it, and
then

• Tap Play to listen
to the message

• Tap Undelete to
move the mes-
sage out of the
Deleted Messages
list and back to
the Voicemail
messages list

✔ Tap Clear All to
remove all deleted
messages from the
Deleted Messages list
and back to the Voicemail messages screen.

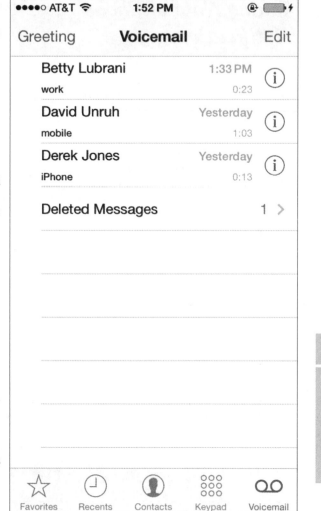

Figure 1-23: The Voicemail screen lists your voicemail messages.

With Visual Voicemail at your service, the idea of ever going back to the old
way of dialing in to your voicemail box and tapping buttons to skip through
your messages seems like torture. That said, you can relive the past by
pressing and holding the 1 button on the keypad to automatically dial into
and begin listening to your voicemail messages, or by typing your own
phone number and pressing Call, and then pressing * and entering your
password to listen to your voicemail messages. Like we said, torture!

Taking Note of Phone Notifications

Using the Phone app puts you in control of placing and answering calls and voicemail messages when you want. iPhone works behind the scenes as your personal answering service, alerting you to missed calls or voicemail messages by displaying notifications and badges, as shown in Figure 1-27. Read more about notifications in Book I, Chapter 4.

You can set how your iPhone alerts you to incoming calls by going to Settings➪Sounds, as explained in the "Perusing Phone Settings" section later in this chapter.

The different notification messages iPhone displays when you miss (or decline) calls or receive new voicemail messages include the following:

••••○ AT&T 🛜   1:53 PM   ▣ 🔋⚡
Set your outgoing message.
Cancel   **Greeting**   Save
Default
Custom   ✓
|
Play   Record

Figure 1-24: The Voicemail Greeting screen.

✔ **Missed Call:** Displays the phone number, or name of one of your contacts, whose call went unanswered.

✔ **Voicemail:** Displays the phone number or name of one of your contacts who has left you a voicemail message.

✔ **Missed Call and Voicemail:** Combines both types of notifications.

The different notification badges iPhone displays when you miss (or decline) calls or receive new voicemail messages are as follows:

✔ **Phone App Icon:** A red badge indicates the combined number of missed calls and/or new voicemail messages.

Reminder: If you declined an incoming call by tapping Remind Me Later, a reminder notification shows up on your phone an hour after you declined the call.

If your iPhone is unable to receive calls because it's in Airplane Mode, is out of your cellular network range, or is powered off, notifications messages, badges, and sounds for any missed calls or voicemail messages won't appear until your iPhone is able to receive calls again. When Do Not Disturb is on, a silent notification lets you know someone called.

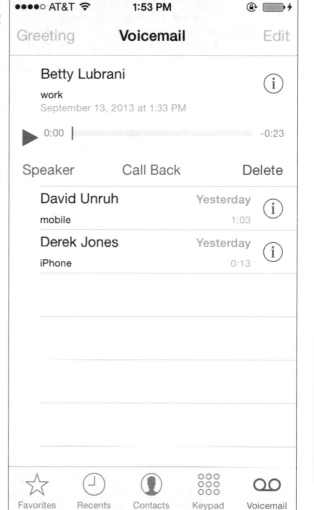

Figure 1-25: Listening to a voicemail message with the speakerphone turned on.

Perusing Phone Settings

From the moment your iPhone is activated, you can use the Phone app to make, receive, and manage calls, and to listen to voicemail messages — all without ever needing to adjust (or even know about) any of your iPhone's many phone-related settings options.

We show you how to change a few phone-related settings throughout this chapter on a "need to know" basis; however, we encourage you to take a moment to get acquainted with the full spectrum of those settings.

By touring iPhone's phone-related settings options, you can maximize your awareness of every call-related feature, and potentially minimize the risk of incurring unexpected charges on your monthly phone bill by acquainting yourself with certain options that can cost you an arm and a leg if you happen to turn them on without realizing the implications.

You find various Phone settings in the Settings app. For details on Settings⇨General, which gives you options for usage tracking and accessibility, see Book I, Chapter 4. The specific Phone settings are explained in the next few sections.

Notifications

Tap Settings⇨Notification Center⇨Phone to choose whether you want Phone notifications listed in the Notification Center and set the alert style you prefer: None, Banners (which appear at the top of the screen and then disappear automatically), or Alerts (which block your phone until you perform one of the actions). Choose whether you want the badge to appear on the Phone icon and whether you want to see notifications when the screen is locked. Read all about Notifications in Book I, Chapter 4.

Figure 1-26: The Deleted screen lists items in the Deleted Messages folder.

Sounds

Tap Settings⇨Sounds to choose your vibration, ringtone, and volume options. Choose when you want your phone to vibrate, if at all, by tapping Vibrate on Ring and Vibrate on Silent to the On or Off position. Tap Change with Buttons On so you can adjust the ringer volume with your iPhone's volume buttons. Tap Ringtone to choose the sound you want to hear for incoming calls. On the Ringtone screen, you can also select or create a vibration pattern.

Remember to choose a sound for your New Voicemail too.

TIP

See Book IV, Chapter 1 to assign special ringtones to a specific contacts. Tap Settings⊅Phone to adjust the following information, as shown in Figure 1-28.

> ✔ **My Number:**
> Displays your personal phone number. Although it's set automatically, you can tap the disclosure triangle and change it.

> ✔ **Contact Photos in Favorites:** When on, the photo you assigned to a person in Contacts appears next to the name in the Favorites list.

> ✔ **Reply with Text:** Change the default replies for calls you decline with this option. Refer to the section "Declining Calls."

Figure 1-27: iPhone lets you know when you missed a call.

> ✔ **Call Forwarding, Call Waiting, Show My Caller ID (GSM models):** Turns those features on or off. See the next section to learn how to activate these features.

> ✔ **Blocked:** Shows a list of people whose attempts to call or send you a message are blocked. Add other names to the list by tapping this item and then tapping Add New. Contacts opens and you can choose who you want to block.

> ✔ **Change Voicemail Password:** To change your numeric voicemail password.

> ✔ **Dial Assist:** To have iPhone automatically add proper prefix number when calling the U.S. from abroad.

**Book III
Chapter 1**

**Managing Phone
and FaceTime Video
Calls**

✔ **SIM PIN (GSM models):** To turn on, choose, and change the secret code you can use to lock your iPhone's SIM card; when activated, you must type in the PIN code whenever you turn iPhone off then on again.

After three failed attempts to unlock the SIM code, you may need to type in a Personal Unlocking Key (PUK) code in order to unlock your iPhone; if so, contact your cellular carrier's customer service number to find out your iPhone's PUK code.

✔ **Carrier Services (depends on iPhone model and carrier):** One-touch speed-dial access for dialing up various phone account-related information like your current bill balance, data and minutes usage, and directory assistance.

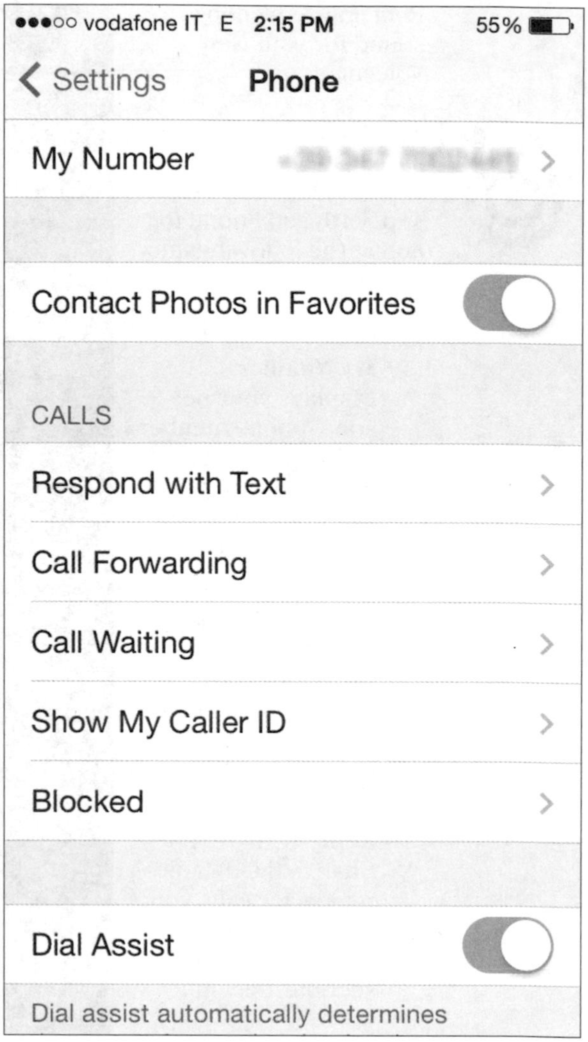

●●●○○ vodafone IT E 2:15 PM   55% ▭

‹ Settings   **Phone**

My Number   ›

Contact Photos in Favorites   ◯◯

CALLS

Respond with Text   ›

Call Forwarding   ›

Call Waiting   ›

Show My Caller ID   ›

Blocked   ›

Dial Assist   ◯◯

Dial assist automatically determines

Figure 1-28: Change the Phone app settings to suit you.

Call Forwarding,
Call Waiting, and Caller ID Blocking

Some phone-related settings you may want to take advantage of include call forwarding, call waiting, and caller ID blocking. To turn those features on or off for GSM model iPhones (like the ones that work with AT&T or the unlocked model you can buy at the Apple Store), tap Settings⇨Phone, and then tap the setting you want to turn on or off. Refer to Figure 1-28.

You have to have cellular service when you turn Call Forwarding on, which means activate Call Forwarding before you go off into the wilderness with your iPhone. If you turn on Call Forwarding, a prompt appears so you can type in the phone number you want your calls forwarded to.

The call forwarding icon appears in the Status Bar when you turn on the Call Forwarding feature on GSM model iPhones.

Don't forget to turn Call Forwarding off when you no longer want your calls sent to another number; otherwise, you'll be wondering why your iPhone doesn't ring anymore.

Caller ID blocking only works for phone calls; your ID still appears when you make a FaceTime call.

To turn these functions on or off for CMDA model iPhones like the ones that work with Verizon, use the Phone app's keypad to type in the appropriate special code below for the particular feature you want to manage:

- **Call Forwarding on:** Type *72 followed by the phone number you want your calls forwarded to, and then tap Call.

- **Call Forwarding off:** Type *73, and then tap Call.

- **Call Waiting off for a call you are about to make:** Type *70, and then type the number you want to call and tap Call.

- **Block Caller ID for a call you are about to make:** Type *67, and then dial the number you want to call and tap Call.

On CMDA model iPhones, you can only turn off call waiting and caller ID blocking on a per-call basis, but you can't turn either feature off for all calls the way you can with GSM model iPhones.

Doing FaceTime Calls

With iOS 7, FaceTime got its own app button on the Home screen along with the capability to make audio-only calls as well as video calls. This is great news for those of you who want to make FaceTime calls before you're ready for the world to see you and, more importantly, those who use the 3G cellular data network to make FaceTime calls because audio calls will consume less of the monthly data allotment than video calls.

FaceTime calls other iPhones with the phone number or e-mail address, but uses an e-mail address to call FaceTime-enabled Macs, iPod touches, or iPads. And if one of those devices is calling your iPhone, they use the e-mail address associated with your FaceTime ID. Refer to "Adjusting FaceTime settings" later in this section.

To use FaceTime, both parties need to be connected to a Wi-Fi network (iPhone 5 model users can also use FaceTime with a cellular data connection

**Book III
Chapter 1**

Managing Phone and FaceTime Video Calls

by going to Settings⇨Cellular and then scrolling down to the section Use Cellular Data For and tapping FaceTime to the On position) and meet one of the following requirements:

a. You and the person you want to FaceTime with are both using iPhone models that offer the FaceTime feature, and that feature is turned on in Settings⇨FaceTime. (The FaceTime feature is turned on by default; additionally, the FaceTime feature can also be turned off in Settings⇨ General⇨Restrictions.)

b. Your iPhone meets the preceding requirement, and the person you want to connect with is using another FaceTime-capable device, such as an iPad 2 or later or a fourth generation iPod touch or later, or a Mac with FaceTime.

Using FaceTime on the cellular network — instead of Wi-Fi — cuts into your data transfer allowance. If you have a cap on your data allowance, you'll want to keep track of how much you're consuming so you don't go over your monthly limit and incur additional charges. A 45-minute FaceTime call consumes roughly 65 megabytes.

Making a FaceTime call

With iOS 7, FaceTime got its own app. Tap the FaceTime icon on the Home screen and then tap one of the buttons in the browse bar at the bottom of the screen. They have the same functions as in the Phone app:

- *Favorites,* which shows the contacts you assigned Favorite status to for their FaceTime audio or video information.

- *Recents* shows any recent incoming and outgoing FaceTime calls.

- *Contacts* opens your Contacts list.

From either of these three screens, tap the name of the person you want to initiate a FaceTime call to, and then tap the FaceTime audio or video button, whichever type of call you want to place. You see the outgoing call screen and when the person responds, you hear his voice, and see his face if you initiated a video call.

As we mention in the "Managing Calls" section, you can also switch an existing voice call to a FaceTime call, or you can initiate a FaceTime call by first making a call using any of the methods we show you in the "Making Calls" section.

Some things to consider when making FaceTime calls:

- **During a Call:** Tap the FaceTime button in the active call screen to switch your voice call to a FaceTime audio or video call.

- **Using Favorites or Recents:** The FaceTime camera or phone icon indicates phone numbers and names that you can tap to call using FaceTime.

✔ **Using Keypad:** Type the phone number you want to call using FaceTime, and then tap Call; tap the FaceTime button after the call is in progress.

✔ **Using Voicemail:** Tap the More Information button on an item in your Voicemail list, tap the FaceTime button, and then tap the e-mail address or phone number you want to call.

✔ **Using Contacts:** Tap the contact you want to call, tap the audio or video FaceTime button.

✔ **Using Voice Control or Siri:** Press and hold the Home button and then say "FaceTime" followed by the name or number of the person to call.

✔ **Caller ID Block:** Your phone number appears when you make a FaceTime call even if you have activated your iPhone's Caller ID Block feature (which we write about in the section "Call Forwarding, Call Waiting, and Caller ID Blocking," earlier in this chapter.)

The FaceTime Failed message appears if a person you try to call isn't using a FaceTime-capable device or FaceTime is turned off on that device.

When your FaceTime call is established, the active FaceTime call screen appears as shown in Figure 1-29.

Accepting a FaceTime call

The FaceTime incoming call screen appears when you receive an incoming FaceTime call invitation, as shown in Figure 1-30.

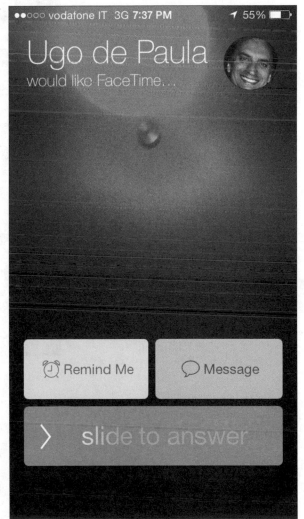

Figure 1-29: The active FaceTime call screen, live and in-person (virtually speaking).

Tap Accept or Decline to answer or decline the FaceTime invitation. You can also touch and drag the Reply/Remind button to use that feature as explained in the section "Declining Calls."

Managing a FaceTime Video Call

When you're engaged in a FaceTime video chat call — that you initiate or accept — the active FaceTime call screen appears. The person you're connected with fills up most of iPhone's screen, while your own mug appears in a tiny window that you can drag to whichever corner you want.

During an active FaceTime call, you can do a bunch of neat things, including the following:

Figure 1-30: An incoming FaceTime call invitation.

✔ **Changing to Landscape View:** Rotate your iPhone sideways to view your caller in Landscape mode.

✔ **Switch Cameras:** Tap the Switch Cameras button to switch your live video feed from iPhone's front-facing camera to the higher-resolution rear-facing camera. You can use this feature to show off things around you, like the snoozing kitty in your lap, or the snowstorm coming down outside your office window. Tap the Switch Cameras button again to switch back to iPhone's front-facing camera and its focus on you.

✔ **Mute Your Sound:** Tap the Mute icon to squelch the mic on your end of the video chat conversation. When you mute your mic, you can still hear sound from the person on the other end of your chat, and they can still see your video. Tap Mute again to allow yourself to be heard again.

✔ **Pause Your Video:**
Tapping Home and
switching to another
app puts your
FaceTime video on
hold; the person on
the other end will still
hear you, but you
won't see each other
while you're away
from the FaceTime
screen; tap the ban-
ner that appears at
the top of iPhone's
screen (as you would
in a regular phone
call) to return to your
FaceTime call, where
you'll be both seen
and heard once more.

✔ **Capture a
Screenshot:** Press
Home and Sleep/Wake
at the same time to
capture a screenshot
of your FaceTime
chat; iPhone saves
your screenshot in
the Photo app's
Camera Roll album.
(You can capture a
screenshot this way
in other apps too, not
just in FaceTime.)

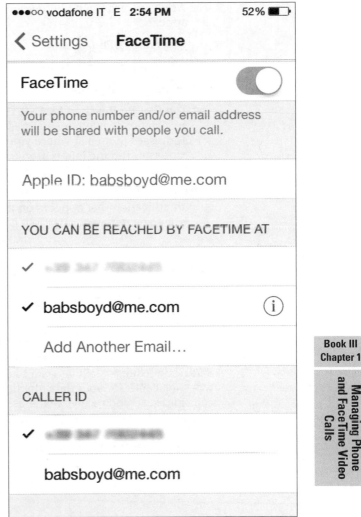

Figure 1-31: Choose the e-mail others can use to reach you via FaceTime.

Adjusting Face-Time settings

Just like Phone and most
of the other apps on your iPhone, FaceTime has a few settings that you can
adjust to your liking. Tap Settings⇨FaceTime to see the screen as in
Figure 1-31. You can do the following:

✔ **Tap** the toggle switch to turn FaceTime Off or On.

✔ **Apple ID:** You must be signed in for FaceTime to work, if you try to tap
FaceTime On and it doesn't work, tap your Apple ID, enter your password in the screen that follows, and then confirm the phone number and
e-mail address where you can be reached via FaceTime.

When you are signed in to your Apple ID account, the following choices appear:

- *Change your Location*
- *View your Apple ID account*
- *Sign Out*: If you sign out, you'll have to sign in again to use FaceTime.

✔ **You Can Be Reached by FaceTime at:** Your cellular phone number is automatically filled in and uneditable. Tap the e-mail address or addresses in the list where you want to use to receive FaceTime requests. Tap the Info button to the right to remove the e-mail completely from the list. Tap Add Another Email to do that.

✔ **Caller ID:** Choose either your phone number or e-mail address as the identification that appears on the device of the person you're calling when you initiate a FaceTime call.

International Calling Options

Depending on which iPhone model you own, you may be able to use your iPhone while you're traveling overseas. Again, using this feature is typically a very costly proposition, and again, your best plan is to contact your provider before you take off. If it turns out you can use your iPhone while traveling overseas, we recommend turning off the data roaming feature. Tap Settings⇨Cellular⇨Cellular Data to disable that feature and only use Wi-Fi, when available, for your data functions. You can still make and receive phone calls and send and receive text messages, although often with a roaming surcharge above and beyond your regular phone plan cost. For example, Barbara sends SMS for 10 cents a message when at home and 75 cents per message when overseas so she tries to limit her text messaging when travelling.

Chapter 2: Sending and Receiving Text and Multimedia Messages

In This Chapter

☞ Setting up for SMS and MMS messages

☞ Using iMessage to text iOS devices and Macs

☞ Sending and receiving messages

☞ Managing messages

*R*emember when you drove off to college and Mom, a tear in her eye, said "Call me when you get there." Now moms say, "Text me when you get there." Messages on your iPhone is your one-stop text, media, and iMessage messaging center and we tell you all about it in this chapter.

As with other apps, you have more than one way to perform the task at hand. In this chapter, we show you the different ways you can send messages — traditional SMS and MMS as well as iMessage messages, which you exchange with your i-device — and Mac — user friends. With iMessage, you can begin an exchange (called a *conversation* in Messages lingo) on one device, say your iPhone while you're at the bus stop, and then continue it on another, such as your Mac or iPad, when you get home. Because "the media is the message," we show you how to add photos, video, voice memos, and links to your messages. With all this communicating, we close the chapter with how to manage the messages you've been sending and receiving.

.ıe Guiles,

Subject

Before all that, however, we're going to give you a quick run-through of the settings for the Messages app.

Reviewing Messages Features and Adjusting Settings

To understand the Messages features and settings, you should familiarize yourself with the parts of a message, as shown in Figure 2-1.

✔ **To field:** Enter names, phone numbers, or e-mail addresses (for iMessage) of people you want to send messages to.

✔ **Contacts:** Tap the plus sign to open and choose recipients from Contacts.

✔ **Text and Subject fields:** Type your message here; the Subject field within the Text field is a feature you can turn on or off in Settings➪Messages.

✔ **Camera button:** Tapping the Camera button lets you add photos or videos to your messages.

✔ **Character count:** This keeps track of how many characters your message contains. Again, this is a feature you can

Figure 2-1: The features of a new message.

switch on or off in Settings. Some service providers limit the length of text messages (SMS or MMS but not iMessage); if yours does, this option helps you write messages within the limit.

Setting up Messages settings

By now, you're probably familiar with the Settings app. It's where you turn the features for the other iPhone apps on or off. The settings for Messages let you personalize the way iPhone alerts you that you have messages and offers some options for composing messages.

To open Settings for messages, tap Settings➪Messages. You'll have to scroll down because Messages is a little way down the list after iCloud. You see what's shown in Figure 2-2.

✔ **iMessage:** Tap this toggle switch on to activate the iMessage service, which lets you exchange messages with other iOS devices, such as iPhone, iPad, and iPod touch, as well as Macs running OS X 10.8 Mountain Lion, or OS X 10.9, Mavericks, over Wi-Fi or the cellular data network without cutting into your SMS allotment. We explain this service in the "Addressing, Writing, and Sending Text Messages and iMessages" section of this chapter.

✔ **Send Read Receipts:** When turned on, people who send you messages will be notified when you read their sent message.

✔ **Send As SMS:** If iMessage is unavailable, your message is sent as an SMS text message. Your cellular service plan may charge an extra fee for SMS.

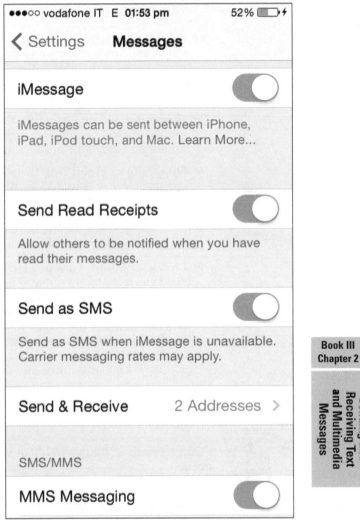

Figure 2-2: The Messages Settings screen.

✔ **Send & Receive:** Add additional e-mail addresses where you want to receive iMessages (in addition to your mobile phone number). Tap Send & Receive. The iMessage screen opens. Tap Add Another Email. The keyboard appears where you can type in the e-mail address you wish to add. Tap Messages at the top when you finish.

Scroll down to see the last five choices:

✔ **MMS Messaging:** With this feature on, you can send and receive photos, video, and voice memos and insert a subject line in the text field. You may have to enter information from your cellular service provider in the MMS section of Settings⇨General⇨Cellular⇨Cellular Data Network, and there may be an additional charge to send MMS.

✔ **Group Messaging:** If you turn this on, you can send one SMS/MMS message to several people, although responses come back only to you. This option isn't available in all areas.

✔ **Show Subject Field:** With this switch on, a subject line appears before any text messages that you write — just like e-mail. However, this turns an SMS (Short Message Service) into an MMS (Multimedia Message Service). If you're sending to someone who doesn't have MMS capabilities, they may not receive your message. If you leave the subject field blank, it remains an SMS, or you can just keep this setting off.

✔ **Character Count:** Turn this switch on in conjunction with Show Subject Field and a character counter appears to the right of the text-entry field in the New Message screen so you can keep an eye on the length of your message. iPhone conveniently splits messages longer than 160 characters into multiple messages so people with phones that have limited text capabilities can still receive messages from you. The kicker is that each section of the message counts as one message, meaning one three-part message is billed as three messages.

✔ **Blocked:** This function lets you insert phone numbers you don't want to receive calls, messages, or FaceTime from. If you set up blocked numbers from the Phone settings, they appear here as well.

Change switches from on to off, or vice versa, with a simple tap. No swiping needed.

New message notification and alert

Immediacy is one of the benefits of messages so you'll want to know when you receive one. You can pick and choose between silent visual notifications and loud attention-grabbing sounds, or some combination and variation of both.

✔ To set the type of notification you want to receive when a new message arrives, tap Settings⇨Notification Center⇨Messages. By default Messages should be in the Include section; if you don't see it, scroll down to Do Not Include and tap it there. Choose the alert style you wish to see on the screen: None, Banners, which appear on screen briefly then discretely disappear, or Alert, which remains on the screen until you take an action such as close or open message.

✔ Tap Badge App Icon on if you want to see the number of messages you have displayed on the Messages icon on the Home screen.

✔ Tap Alert Sound to change the noise you hear when a new message arrives. A list of potential alert vibrations and tones appears. (You can also tap Settings⇨Sounds⇨Text Tone to reach this list.)

- To set the vibration that occurs when a message arrives, tap Vibration and then select a vibration style from the list that appears. You can also tap Create New Vibration to create a custom vibration or tap None to hear only a text tone without a vibration when a new message arrives.

- To preview the sounds, tap the names on the list. Tap the name of the sound that you want to hear when a new message arrives or tap None. A checkmark indicates the sound you've chosen.

Swipe right to return to the previous Settings screens or tap the button in the upper left corner.

✔ Tap Show in Notification Center and Show on Lock Screen to the On position if you want to see messages on either or both of those screens.

✔ Tap Show Preview to see part of the incoming message on the alert or banner. When this option is off, alerts show the name or phone number the message is from.

✔ Tap Repeat Alerts to choose to hear the alert up to ten times at two minute intervals.

✔ Tap either Show Alerts from Everyone or Show Alerts from My Contacts, whichever you prefer.

✔ Swipe right to return to previous Settings screens, or press the Home button to return to the Home screen.

Addressing, Writing, and Sending Text Messages and iMessages

Now that you're set up, you're ready to send a text message. It's not so different than sending an e-mail, if you're familiar with that form of communication. You address you message, type it, and send it.

Here are the steps:

1. **Tap the Messages icon on the Home screen.**

2. **Tap the Compose button in the upper right corner. It's the one that looks like a pencil and piece of paper.**

   A New Message screen opens.

3. **Address and write your message as explained in the following section.**

4. **Tap the Send button.**

Book III
Chapter 2

Sending and
Receiving Text
and Multimedia
Messages

Addressing your message

When you open a New Message screen by tapping the Compose button, the keyboard is active and the cursor is in the To field, where you fill in the name or number of the person you want to send your message to. You can address your message in one of three ways:

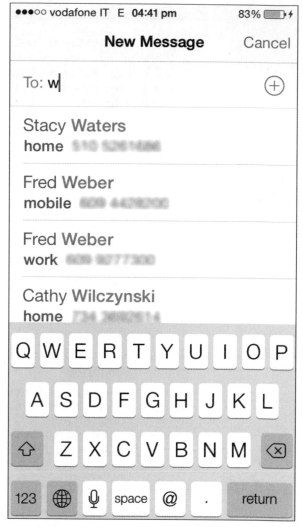

- ✔ Tap the 123 button in the lower left corner of the keyboard to change the top row of letters to numbers. Type the phone number.

- ✔ If the person you want to send the message to is stored in Contacts, begin typing the recipient's name in the To field. Names of people or companies in Contacts that contain the typed letters show up as a list from which you can choose. Your choices narrow as you type more letters. (See Figure 2-3.) The phone number is listed under the contact's name and if a contact has more

Figure 2-3: Begin typing the first letters of your recipient's name and Messages searches Contacts to find matches.

than one phone number, his name is listed with each phone number. You can see that Fred Weber has two phone numbers. Blue phone numbers indicate an iMessage-enabled number.

- ✔ Alternatively, tap the Contacts (+ plus sign) button in the upper right corner, which opens Contacts. Find the name you want by doing one of the following:

- Scroll through the list until you find the name of the person you want to send a message to.

- Tap the first letter of the name in the alphabet that runs down the right side of the screen to jump to names beginning with that letter. Scroll through that section to find the person you're searching for.

- Tap in the Search field. Type the name of the person you're looking for. As with any Search field, matches pop up when you type the first letter and diminish as you narrow your search by typing more letters.

When you open Contacts from Messages, you see your active groups. Tap the Groups button to open more groups. (You only see this button if you have groups in Contacts.)

After you've found it, tap the name of the person you want to send a message to. If the contact has just one phone number, when you tap the name, you automatically return to the New Message screen and the name of the recipient will be in the To field. If the contact has more than one phone number or also has an e-mail address, the contact information opens. Tap the number you want to send the message to, and you'll bounce back to the New Message screen.

If you want to send your message to more than one person, just tap the plus sign (+) button and repeat the preceding steps to add a person from the contact list or type in a phone number.

From Contacts, you can tap the Text Message button next to a phone number or e-mail address to open a New Message screen with your chosen contact in the To field. From your Favorites list, tap the Info button on the right, and then scroll down and tap the Text Message button, which takes you to a New Message screen.

Book III
Chapter 2

Sending and
Receiving Text
and Multimedia
Messages

Sending an iMessage

iMessage is a great way to communicate with your iDevice-toting and Mac-using friends — iMessage works with iPhones, iPads, iPod touches, and Macs (at least those running OS X 10.8 or later). iMessage automatically enters your phone number and you should associate your Apple ID to iMessage too so you can receive iMessage on your other iDevices or Mac. To set up iMessage, follow these steps:

1. **Go to Settings⇨Messages and tap iMessage On.**

2. **Tap Use your Apple ID for iMessage.**

   You see the Apple ID associated with your iPhone on the screen.

3. **Enter your password and tap Sign In.**

   Your Apple ID is verified and you are signed in to iMessage. The screen as shown in Figure 2-4 appears.

4. **(Optional) Tap Add Another Email, if you wish to do so.**

5. **Tap the phone number or Apple ID you want to use to start new conversations.**

After iMessage is activated, your iPhone takes care of everything for you. It immediately recognizes phone numbers and e-mail addresses associated with iOS devices or Macs used by people in your Contacts, and when available, Messages uses iMessage rather than traditional SMS or MMS. You know you have an iMessage connection because when you type a contact's name or phone number, it shows up blue.

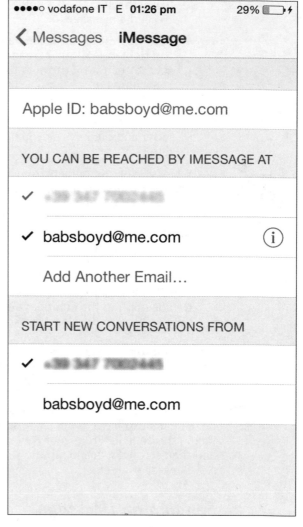

Figure 2-4: Send unlimited iMessages to other iOS devices and Macs — for free!

Instead of cutting into your text message allotment, iMessage messages travel across the Wi-Fi or cellular data airwaves (with the latter it does cut into your cellular data allotment). If an Internet connection isn't available, your message is sent as a normal SMS or MMS, as long as you turned that option on in Settings⇨Messages⇨Send as SMS On.

Writing your message

After you've entered the names of the message recipients, tap return. The cursor moves to the text field:

1. **Type your message.**

   Any features you activated for the keyboard in Settings, such as Auto-Correction or Enable Caps Lock, are active in Messages.

   Messages remembers the keyboard you use to write messages to different contacts. If you write some messages in English with the English keyboard and some in Chinese using the Chinese keyboard, after a couple exchanges in Chinese, Messages automatically "remembers" that you write in Chinese with that contact and opens with that keyboard; likewise for your English messages. It means one less tap for you.

   If you make a mistake and need to edit your message, the Text field has the same functions for typing as other apps, as explained in Book I, Chapter 3.

   Add the Emoji language in Settings⇨General⇨Keyboard⇨International Keyboards to insert smiley faces and hearts in your messages.

2. **When you've finished typing your message, tap the Send button and it's on its way.**

   You'll see a progress bar at the top of the screen and hear a whooping sound when the message has been sent.

If you use an iPhone 4s or later and have activated Siri, tap the Dictation button to the left of the space bar if you prefer to dictate your message instead of typing it. (Refer to Book I, Chapter 3.)

Receiving and Replying to Text Messages

Ding-ding! You've got a message. Or your iPhone may only vibrate and you may or may not see a banner or alert on the screen, depending on the notification and alert settings you choose, as outlined at the beginning of this chapter.

Siri can also read your messages and then send the response you dictate.

After you've received a message, you'll want to read it and maybe respond. Here's how to read your messages:

1. **If you set up a banner to appear on your Lock screen, swipe across it to open the incoming message, or tap Messages on the Home screen. An unread message has a blue dot next to it.**

In the Messages list (refer to Figure 2-5), you'll see the name or number of the person or entity who sent the message, the time, day, or date it was received (depending on how long ago it was sent), and the first two lines of the message.

After an exchange begins, you see the last message exchanged regardless of who sent it, so if you sent a response to someone, you see the first two lines of your response next to the name of who sent the message.

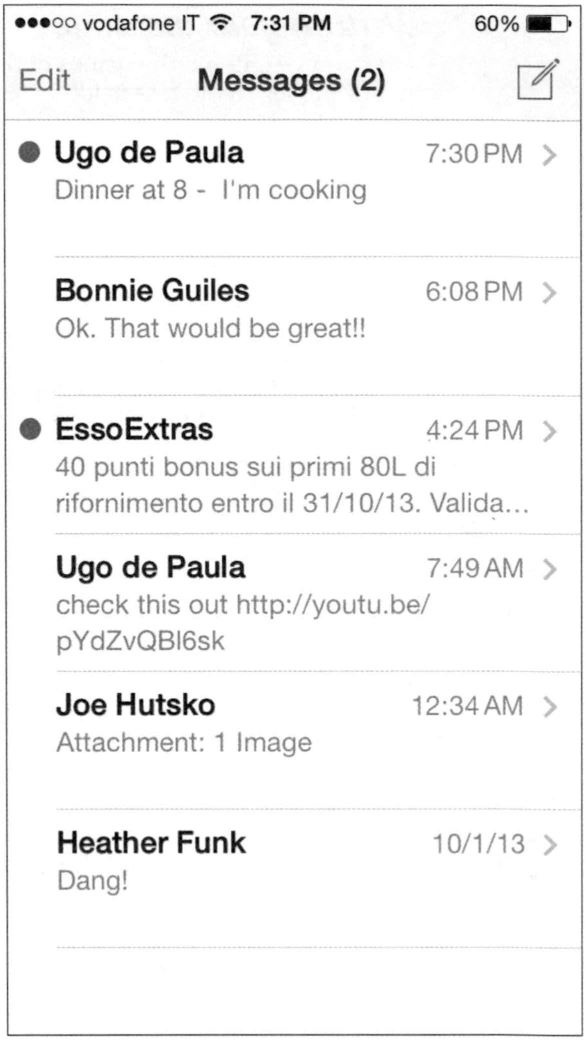

2. **Tap the message and a message screen opens, displaying the whole message. The text of incoming iMessage is in a blue bubble; that of an SMS is in a green bubble. To reply,**

3. **Tap once in the Text field.**

   The keyboard opens.

4. **Type your message.**

5. **Tap Send.**

   As with a message you initiated, you see a Sending progress bar and you hear a whoop indicating that the message has been sent — unless you have those sounds turned off.

> ●●●○○ vodafone IT 🤙 7:31 PM   60% 🔋
>
> Edit   **Messages (2)**   ✎
>
> ● **Ugo de Paula**   7:30 PM >
>   Dinner at 8 - I'm cooking
>
>   **Bonnie Guiles**   6:08 PM >
>   Ok. That would be great!!
>
> ● **EssoExtras**   4:24 PM >
>   40 punti bonus sui primi 80L di
>   rifornimento entro il 31/10/13. Valida…
>
>   **Ugo de Paula**   7:49 AM >
>   check this out http://youtu.be/
>   pYdZvQBl6sk
>
>   **Joe Hutsko**   12:34 AM >
>   Attachment: 1 Image
>
>   **Heather Funk**   10/1/13 >
>   Dang!

Figure 2-5: The Messages list shows read and unread messages you've sent and received.

Instead of responding with a message, you can choose to place a voice or FaceTime call to the person. Tap Contact in the upper right corner and do one of the following:

✔ To call, tap the Call button at the top of the screen and then choose Voice Call or FaceTime Audio, as shown in Figure 2-6.

✔ To communicate via FaceTime, tap the FaceTime button. We explain FaceTime in Book III, Chapter 1.

✔ Tap the Info button to call a number different than the one used for the message exchange or view and edit the person's information in Contacts.

If you're writing a message and need to refer to something in the incoming message, or earlier in the conversation, you can scroll through the conversation. To free up more of the screen, touch the background (a non-message part of the screen) just above the text field and flick down to hide the keyboard, giving you more viewing room to scroll through the conversation. Tap in the text field to bring the keyboard back.

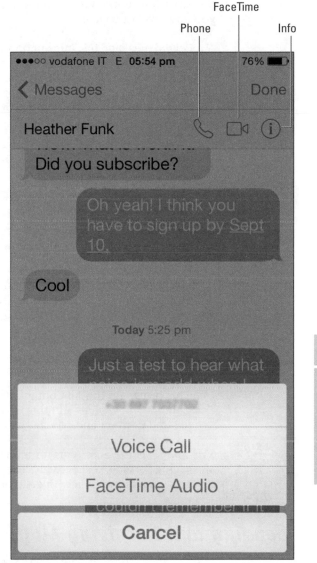

Figure 2-6: Switch to a phone or FaceTime call from Messages.

Book III
Chapter 2

Sending and
Receiving Text
and Multimedia
Messages

When your iPhone is unable to receive incoming calls, it's also unable to send or receive SMS and MMS messages. Whether it's in Airplane mode, is out of range of your carrier's cellular network, or is powered off, notifications, badges, and sounds for any new SMS or MMS messages won't appear until your iPhone is able to receive calls — and messages — again. If you try to send a message and it doesn't reach its destination, an alert badge that looks like an exclamation point appears on the Messages icon on the Home screen. (iMessage and FaceTime still work if you have Wi-Fi service.)

A received message has information about a person or company that you can store in Contacts. To add a new name and phone number or new information to an existing contact, do the following:

1. **From within the message, tap the button at the top right of the screen.**

   If the person the message is from already exists in Contacts, the button on the upper right of the screen reads Contact. Tapping that button takes you to the Contact Info screen of the person where you can edit the information.

   If Messages doesn't recognize the number the message came from, the button reads New Contact. Tapping the button gives you the option to Create New Contact or Add to Existing Contact.

2. **To add a person or entity to Contacts, choose Create New Contact.**

   You are bounced to a New Contact screen that is partially filled out with the name and number. You can fill in the other information if you like. Save by tapping Done. You are then returned to the message where you began.

   Or

   To add a new number to an existing contact, tap Add to Existing Contact.

   This brings up the All Contacts screen, where you select the name of the Contact you wish to add this information to. Tap on the name of the desired Contact and type in the new information.

SMS and MMS are acronyms for Short Message Service and Multimedia Messaging Service, respectively. These are the protocols used for transferring text and multimedia with cellular phone technology.

Sending and Receiving Multimedia Messages

You can take stunning photos and video with your iPhone, but what fun is it to keep them to yourself? MMS is a quick way to share your artistic expression and memories with the folks you know.

Most people have MMS-enabled cell phones these days, but there are some who can't receive media and MMS messages either because of the type of phone hardware or because of their cellular service contract. They'll still receive the message, but not the media. And, there are holdouts who refuse to use texting and have neither SMS nor MMS capabilities, in which case, even your text message goes undelivered.

Capturing and sending a video or photo

Say you've spent all day working in the garden and want to send a photo of your new flowers to your sister. Here's how:

1. **Tap Messages on the Home screen, and then tap the Compose button.**

2. **Fill in the To field as described in the previous section.**

   If your recipient uses iOS 5 or later, your MMS may be sent with iMessage if the iMessage requirements are met.

3. **Tap the Camera button.**

   Three buttons appear — Take Photo or Video, Choose Existing, and Cancel. See Figure 2-7.

4. **Tap Take Photo or Video to open the camera and then tap the Camera button at the bottom of the screen.**

   The photo, or video, is taken and a Preview screen opens. You have the option of retaking the photo, by tapping Retake in the lower left corner, or using the photo, by tapping Use Photo in the lower right corner.

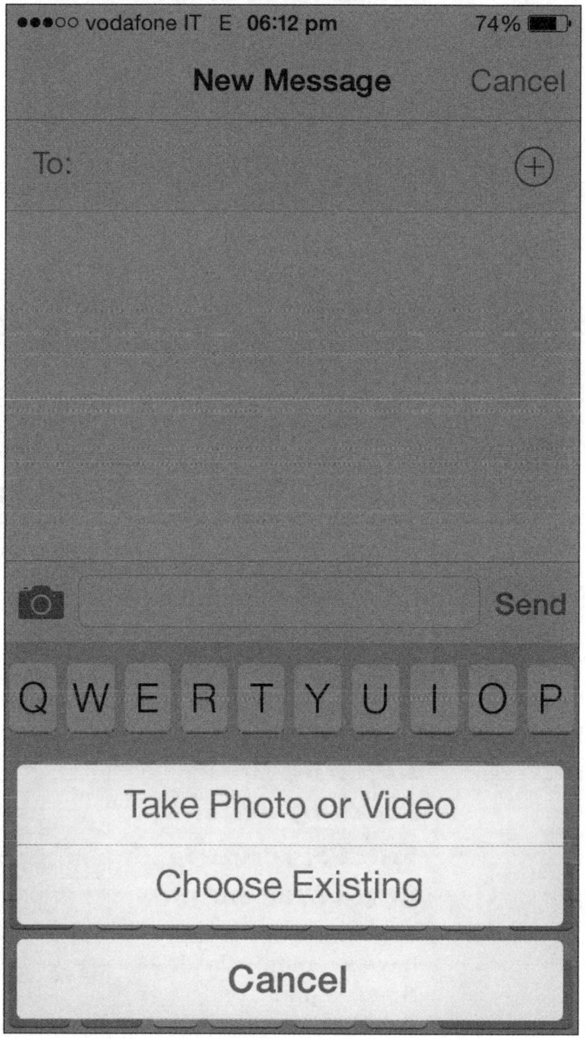

5. **If you don't like the photo, tap Retake and try again, and again, and again until you have a photo or video you like.**

6. **When you take a photo you like, tap Use Photo.**

   Messages opens and, your photo or video is in the Text field and the cursor blinking under the image, as shown in Figure 2-8.

●●●○○ vodafone IT E 06:12 pm   74% ▪️

New Message   Cancel

To: ⊕

Send

Q W E R T Y U I O P

Take Photo or Video

Choose Existing

Cancel

Figure 2-7: Tap Take Photo or Video to insert a new image.

Book III
Chapter 2

Sending and
Receiving Text
and Multimedia
Messages

7. Type your message and tap Send.

You see a Sending progress bar and you hear the whoop that lets you know the message has been sent.

If the Camera button is grayed and inactive, make sure MMS Messaging is On in Messages Settings. You can still send photos and video with iMessage when MMS Messaging is Off.

You can also open Camera, take your photo or video, and send an MMS from Camera. Full details are in Book V, Chapter 2.

Copying and sending existing videos, photos, and voice memos

Sometimes you already have a multimedia file — that is a photo, video, or voice memo — on your iPhone. There are two ways to send that file via MMS. Your first option is from within Messages; the second option is from the Photos or Voice Memos apps. The procedure is virtually the same, only your point of departure changes:

Figure 2-8: A message becomes an MMS when multimedia files are inserted.

✔ Tap Messages on the Home screen. Tap the Compose button and address your message as explained previously or tap a message exchange that's already initiated with someone. Tap the Camera button to the left of the Text field. A screen appears asking if you want to Take Photo or Video or Choose Existing. Tap Choose Existing and the Albums

screen opens show-
ing a list of your
Albums. Tap the
Album where the
photo or video you
wish to send resides,
and then tap the
photo or video you
want to send.
A Preview screen
opens, allowing you
to choose that image
or cancel. Tap
Choose and you
return to the New
Message screen; tap
Cancel and you can
choose a different
photo. Add a written
message. When the
message is ready,
tap Send.

✔ To send directly
from the Photos app,
tap Photos on the
Home screen. Tap
Photos at the bot-
tom of the screen to
see all your
Collections or tap
Albums to view the
Albums list. Tap the
Collection or Album
that contains the
video or photo you
want to send, and
then tap the photo
or video you want to
send. Two icons
appear at the bot-
tom of the screen, as

Book III
Chapter 2

Sending and
Receiving Text
and Multimedia
Messages

Action

Figure 2-9: Tap the Action button to place a photo or video
into your message.

shown in Figure 2-9. Tap the Action button, which is on the lower left,
and tap the Message button on the Share Sheet. A New Message screen
opens. Address, write, and send your message as previously explained.

✔ To send a recording from Voice Memos, tap Voice Memos on the Home
screen. Tap the memo you want to send. Tap the Action button and then
tap the Message button. The New Message screen opens. Address the
message and type in an accompanying message in the Text field, and
then tap Send.

As with most things, you have to pay a price for messaging. Depending on the phone plan you have, you may pay a per-message fee for sending and receiving SMS or MMS, usually around 20 cents, or you can opt for a bundled flat fee for a limited, or sometimes unlimited, number of messages per month. One message to 25 recipients doesn't count as one message but 25 messages, so keep your plan in mind when doing group sends to avoid unpleasant end-of-the-month invoice surprises. And remember iMessage messages don't count toward text messaging limits because they travel over the cellular data or Wi-Fi airwaves, whichever is available.

If someone sends you an image or video, you might want to save it outside Messages. When you receive an MMS, tap the image in the speech bubble. It opens on the full screen. Tap the Action button and choose Save Image (or Video). The image or video is saved to the Camera Roll on your iPhone.

Sending Map Locations, Web Page Links, and More

The Share Sheet, as shown in Figure 2-10, is accessible from many iPhone apps. You find it in Maps by tapping Share at the top of a Location information screen, in Share a Web Page from Safari, or in a note in Notes by tapping the Action button. Likewise, to share a great new find from the iTunes Store or an interesting interview from Podcasts, the Action button opens the Share Sheet. Tapping Messages

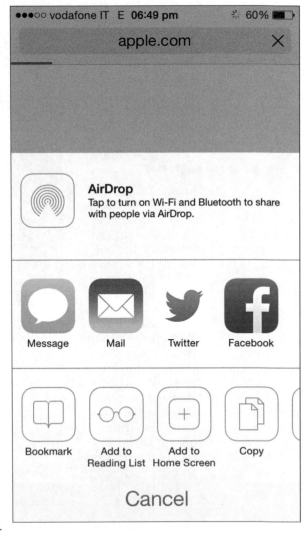

Figure 2-10: Send Messages with maps, website links, and more from the Share Sheet.

opens a New Message with the link to whatever it is you want to share. Address the message and tap Send.

Receiving links to locations or websites is just as easy as sending them. If you receive messages that have URLs embedded in them, the links are active, which means you can just tap them, right in the message, and Safari opens to the linked page or Maps to the location or iTunes to the album, and so on.

Saving and Deleting Messages

As you send and receive messages, they stack up in reverse chronological order within the Messages app — what we've been referring to as the Messages list (refer to Figure 2-5).

Ongoing conversations

Incoming and outgoing messages exchanged with the same person are called *conversations* — notice that the icon for Messages is a conversation bubble. You see the name of the person you have exchanged messages with in the Messages list. Tap on that name and you see all the messages you've exchanged with that person. Received messages are shown in grayed conversation bubbles on the left. Sent messages are on the right in green or blue conversation bubbles, as shown in Figure 2-11. If you're in the middle of an iMessage exchange, an ellipsis indicates that the other person is writing.

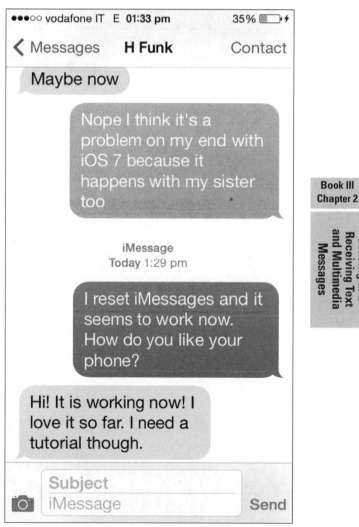

Book III
Chapter 2

Sending and
Receiving Text
and Multimedia
Messages

Figure 2-11: Received message conversation bubbles are on the left; sent messages are on the right.

Drag your finger to the left to reveal timestamps for each message of the exchange.

SMS, MMS, and iMessage messages are all listed in Messages and sometimes all three types appear in a conversation with the same person. This happens when you send a message to someone who has iMessage capabilities but you don't have a Wi-Fi or cellular data connection.

Only the most recent message is shown in the Messages list, whereas the most recent 50 messages are shown in the conversation. You can download older messages by tapping the button. The newest message is displayed at the bottom — Messages opens to show this message — so if you scroll to the top of the screen, you can read from top to bottom and follow the conversation as it occurred.

Deleting messages

Text messages often contain information of fleeting importance, so you probably don't want to keep them and clutter up your Messages list. You can delete messages that are part of the conversation or the entire conversation with all its exchanges.

To delete only parts of the conversation, press and hold the message you want to delete until you see two tabs above it: Copy and More. Tap More. A check mark appears next to the selected message and empty circles appear to the left of all the other

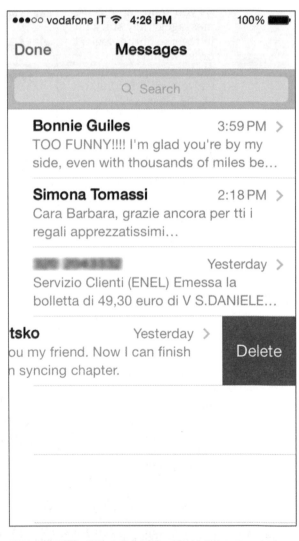

Figure 2-12: The three-step method for deleting messages.

messages of the conversation. Tap others if you want to delete more than one message, and then tap the Delete button (the trash can) at the bottom left of the screen. All the messages with a check mark next to them are deleted.

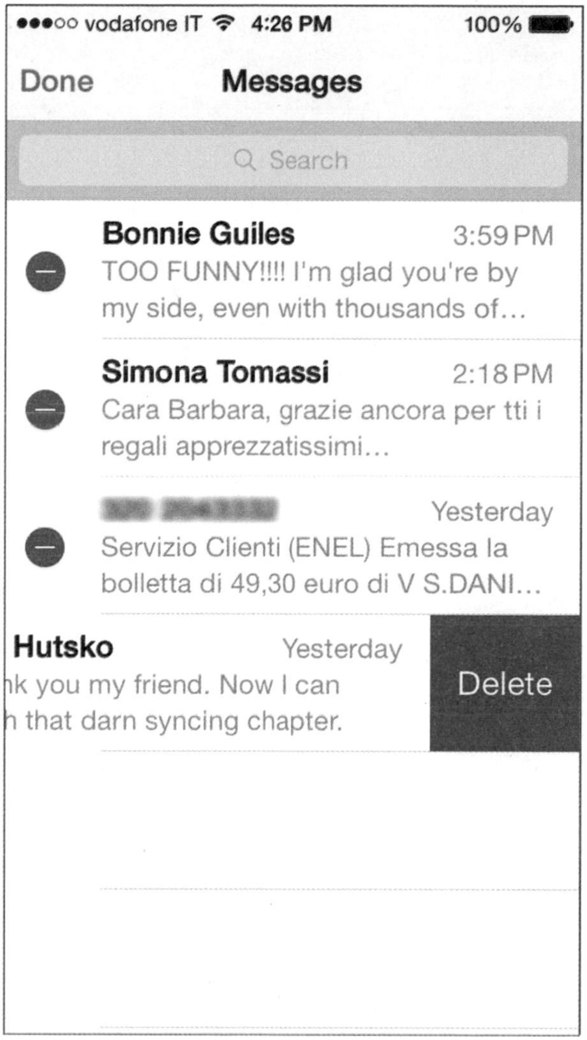

Select messages in the same way to forward them to someone else, but tap the Forward button in the lower right corner instead of the Delete button and then address the message to the person to whom you want to forward it.

There are two ways to delete complete conversations: You can use either a two-step method or a three-step method. After a message is deleted, it's gone, so if you want an extra step to think about what you're about to delete, use the three-step method:

✓ Tap Edit and red circles with hyphens appear next to each message. Tap the circle next to the message you want to delete. The circle rotates 90 degrees and a Delete button appears to the right of the message, like you see in Figure 2-12. Tap the Delete button and poof! The message is gone.

✓ If, on the other hand, you don't worry about deleting something by mistake, use the two-step method. Swipe across the entry for the message you want to delete. A Delete button appears next to that message, as in Figure 2-13. Tap the button and the message is deleted.

You can search for text within messages in the Messages list by using the Search box at the very top of the list. Just type the specific word or phrase you're searching for and tap the magnifying glass.

••••○○ vodafone IT 🔋 4:26 PM **100% ▰**

Done **Messages**

🔍 Search

Bonnie Guiles   3:59 PM
TOO FUNNY!!!! I'm glad you're by my side, even with thousands of…

Simona Tomassi   2:18 PM
Cara Barbara, grazie ancora per tti i regali apprezzatissimi…

▨▨▨   Yesterday
Servizio Clienti (ENEL) Emessa la bolletta di 49,30 euro di V S.DANI…

Hutsko   Yesterday
nk you my friend. Now I can h that darn syncing chapter.   **Delete**

Figure 2-13: The message-deleting two-step.

Chapter 3: Surfing the Web with Safari

In This Chapter

✔ Touring Safari's features

✔ Opening and viewing web pages

✔ Filling out forms

✔ Managing bookmarks

✔ Adding web apps and clips to your Home screen

✔ Adjusting general and security settings

*O*ne of the things that makes a smartphone stand out from a cellular phone is the cellular data capability, or in simpler terms, surfing the web and accessing e-mail. In this chapter we talk about the first one, specifically using Safari, your iPhone's browser app. We begin with a guided tour, pointing out basic features and ways you use Safari to browse web pages. We then walk you through actually opening and viewing pages, showing you neat things along the way to make viewing web pages easier.

After getting your feet wet with a little basic web surfing, we show you how to juggle multiple web pages you want to view, how to work with media within a web page, and how to create bookmarks for web pages you often visit so you can return to those web pages with a few taps of your finger.

Near the end of our surfin' safari, we show you the ins and outs of using Safari's Search feature to find web pages you're looking for — and to find things on those web pages you've found. And finally, we conclude this chapter by giving you a rundown of Safari settings you may want to adjust to make your web surfing experience smoother — and safer.

If web browsing is old hat to you, you may want to skip ahead to the "Playing Favorites with Bookmarks" and "Accessing Websites from the Home Screen" sections, which explain some nifty features you may not be familiar with.

Surfin' Safari Tour

There's no time like the present to take a quick tour of the Safari screen so that we'll be on the proverbial same page. The Safari screen is divided into three zones: the title bar, the web page, and the toolbar. Refer to Figure 3-1 for the following explanations:

- **Address/Search field:** Tap here to make the keyboard appear, so you can type a URL, which stands for Uniform Resource Locator and is the electronic address for a web page or type the name of a person, place, or anything you're searching for, such as a restaurant, a weather report, or the name of your favorite *For Dummies* author.

- **Stop/Reload button:** A dual-purpose button you can tap to stop a web page from loading, or to reload a web page to see any new information that may have been updated on that web page, such as breaking stories on a news web page.

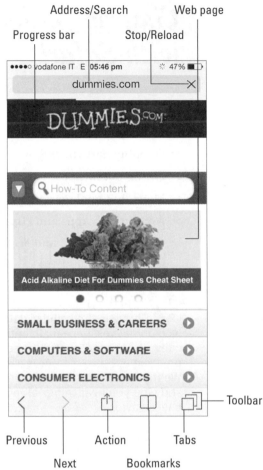

Figure 3-1: The Safari web browser screen displaying a web page.

As soon as you begin scrolling through a web page, the Toolbar disappears and the address becomes a miniscule line beneath the Status bar. Just tap the Status bar at the top of iPhone's screen or lightly swipe down the screen to make the Toolbar and Address/Search field reappear.

- **Web page:** Below the address/search field, you see the bulk of the web page content. The beauty of web pages is that no two are exactly alike — which can also be the frustrating thing about web pages.

- **Toolbar:** At the bottom of the screen, you find the toolbar that displays buttons for the following functions:

A tale of two web pages

Many websites have both full and mobile versions, so what you're used to seeing on your computer, beyond being smaller, might look completely different on your iPhone.

The notion behind "mobile" web pages is that they minimize graphics and much of the other extraneous "stuff" that normally appears on the desktop version of the web page, so as to make it easier for you to navigate those web pages on your mobile device, in this case, your iPhone. Some web pages gauge whether the web browser you're using is a desktop browser or a mobile browser, and automatically present one or the other, based on your browser. Other times, you type in a specific mobile web page address like mobile.nytimes. com to access the mobile version of that web page. Sometimes typing the mobile address for a web page using your computer's browser has no effect and the desktop version of the web page opens anyway, and vice versa: Sometimes typing the full desktop version of a web page on your iPhone ignores your wish and forces you to view the mobile version of the web page.

Other times, you get the best of both worlds: A web page that automatically opens the mobile version when it detects you're using an iPhone gives you the option to switch to the desktop version of that web page if you so desire. You usually find this at the bottom of the page with a toggle switch, Mobile Theme is shown here, or with a Full Site link.

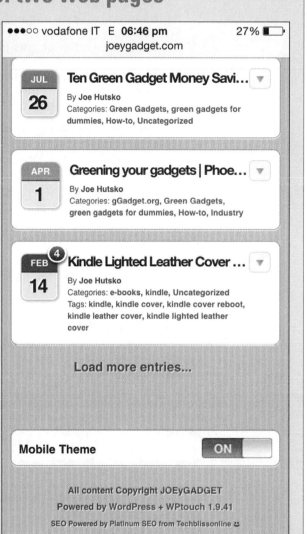

Taking the idea of an iPhone-savvy website one step further, many companies have created *web apps* — specific iPhone apps that let you view information from their website via a special app that offers other features. We discuss them toward the end of the chapter.

Book III
Chapter 3

Surfing the Web
with Safari

- **Previous/Next (arrows):** Previous goes back to the previous web page you viewed in this window or tab; Next moves you Forward to the web page you just left when you pressed Previous. One or both buttons may be dim until you navigate away from the current web page you're viewing. Previous will be dim when you haven't visited a URL earlier on this page or tab or you've tapped your way back to the first URL visited. Next is dim if you haven't tapped Previous. Even when dim, pressing and holding either button reveals the viewing history for the page, which you can tap to return to that page.

- **Action:** Opens the Share Sheet and displays options for sharing or doing something with the current web page you're viewing. See the section "Acting on Web Page Links" later in this chapter for a full explanation.

- **Bookmarks:** Displays the Bookmarks screen, which holds a list of links that give you quick access to web pages you want to revisit. Reading List, (viewing) History, and iCloud tabs are listed in Bookmarks too. We dedicate a whole section to bookmarks later in this chapter.

- **Tabs:** Lets you scroll through open web pages and move quickly from one to another.

Opening web pages

Just as there are many ways to slice a pie, there are many ways to open a web page. Here we take you through the different ways of opening web pages, switching from one to another, searching, and a bunch of other things you can do in Safari. Your iPhone needs to be connected to a Wi-Fi network or your cellular provider's data network in order to follow along with all of the Safari goodness contained within these pages. Start with these steps:

1. **Tap Safari on the Home screen.**

   The Safari screen appears, and you see either the Favorites screen with a few pre-established favorite bookmarks or the last website you viewed the last time you used Safari.

2. **Do one of the following:**

   Tap Address/Search Field: The keyboard appears as shown in Figure 3-2; type in the web address of a web page you want to view, or type a word, name, phrase, ZIP code, or whatever you're searching for, and then tap Go. As soon as you begin typing, Safari displays a list of potential matches for either a URL or a search criteria. If you see what you want in the list, you can tap that instead of tapping Go. Safari then displays the web page or search results for the text you typed in.

Tap a Favorite button: The bookmarks you've nominated as Favorites appear when you tap the Address/Search field. The first four as seen in Figure 3-2 are pre-established (and we show you how to delete, add, and rearrange them in the section "Playing Favorites with Bookmarks").

Tap the Bookmarks button: Tap a web page bookmark you want to open. Safari displays the web page for the bookmark you tapped.

3. **Interact with the web page in the following ways, which we explain in detail in the section "Navigating Web Pages," or repeat Step 2 to go to another web page:**

Scroll through the page to read it.

Tap links, buttons, or other elements that take you to another spot on the web page, to a web page on the website you're accessing, or to another web page on another website.

Tap fields to type in information.

Save images.

Tap a link to upload an image.

Tap a phone number.

Tap a street address.

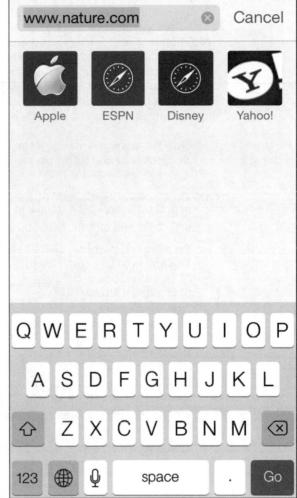

Figure 3-2: Type a URL or search criteria or tap a Favorite to open a web page.

Safari keyboard tips and tricks

Typing in and editing the Safari Address/Search field is the same as typing in any other app on your iPhone, such as Notes or Calendar: Type as you would on any keyboard, tap and hold in the field to bring up the loupe and move the cursor within the text, release your finger to bring up editing commands such as Cut, Copy, and Paste, and tap the X on the right side of the field to erase the text within. However, here are a few other tips and tricks that can help you maximize your Safari keyboard experience, while minimizing how much typing you actually have to do:

- **Skip the www:** If you know the URL, type it without the "www" in the Address field and Safari presents a list of potential matches, tap the match. Same goes for the ".com" suffix.

- **Type www sometimes:** You may *want* to type **www** when you're typing in certain website addresses in order to open the full-size versions instead of the mobile version.

- **Press to complete:** Tap and hold the dot (".") button to display a list of alternate completion options, and then drag your finger to the one you want and let go to fill in that choice (.net, .edu, .org, .com, or one of the other choices).

●●●○○ vodafone IT E	09:22 am	96% ▭ ⚡
dummies		⊗ Cancel

  Google Search

  Q dummies

  Q dummies never fail

  Keyboard with: Q W E R ... / .it .uk .eu .net / A S D ... / .edu .org .ie .co.uk .com / ⇧ Z X ... / 123 🌐 🎤 space Go

- **Landscape keyboard:** Rotate your iPhone sideways to display the wider-reaching landscape keyboard for easier, more accurate typing.

- **Use AutoFill:** Use Safari's AutoFill feature to automatically fill in common fields such as name, address, and phone number fields, e-mail address fields, and user name and password fields. We tell you about AutoFill later in this chapter.

You don't need to tap the erase button to clear the Address field before you type the web page address you want to open. Tap the Address field and begin typing the web address you want to open; the field is automatically erased. (Don't tap and hold, which inserts a blinking cursor allowing you to edit the existing URL address.)

Stopping and reloading web pages

Whichever way you choose to open a web page, after Safari actually begins loading the web page, a trio of visual cues appears to let you know Safari is processing your request. Those cues include a blue progress bar in the

Address field, the Reload button changing to the Stop button, and the twirling network activity icon in the status bar.

You can stop or reload a web page by doing one of the following:

✓ Tap the stop button if you want to instantly stop loading a web page that seems to be taking forever.

✓ Tap the reload button if you lose your network connection and Safari stops loading the page.

✓ Tap the reload button to reload the web page and display any new information that may have been added to the web page since you began viewing it (such as the latest-breaking news on a news web page).

Viewing Web Pages

When the web page appears, you're free to move about the cabin — er, we mean view the web page — in any number of free-ranging ways.

Using fullscreen and portrait views

When it comes to viewing web pages, Safari lets you use the entire real estate of your iPhone screen. As mentioned at the beginning of the chapter, as soon as you begin scrolling through a web page, the Address/Search and Toolbar go into hiding. You may want to change your point of view depending on the page you're viewing: Hold your iPhone upright for portrait orientation view (taller than it is wide) and turn it 90 degrees to use landscape orientation view (wider than it is tall), as shown in Figure 3-3.

Figure 3-3: Rotating iPhone sideways displays the landscape view, here in its full-screen glory.

Landscape view is particularly useful when you want to watch video on a web page.

If you see the Portrait Orientation Lock icon in the top right corner of the status bar, turning your iPhone on its side won't switch your web page to the wide-screen landscape view. To turn the Portrait Orientation Lock feature off or on, drag up from the bottom of the screen to open the Control Center, and then tap the Portrait Orientation Lock icon to toggle that feature on or off.

Using Reader

If you see a Reader button in the Address Field, you can view the article in Reader. Reader displays the text of the article on a plain white page without any of the ambient noise that surrounds it on the web page itself, as shown in Figure 3-4. Tap the Reader button again to return to the regular web page view.

Scrolling web pages

One thing you do a lot of when you're viewing a web page is scrolling — up, down, and sometimes all around — to see all of the information on the web page. In rare instances, you may also come across a web page that contains a scrollable frame of text *within* the web page — which is referred to as a *text frame.*

Ways you can scroll a web page you're viewing include

The Reader button

latter. There are lots of writers who tell it like it is, but only a few who, with such commitment and intensity, tell it like it isn't. King takes the weird and gives it weight. And yet, at the same time, his novels retain a lightness, a playfulness. They show us horrible things, but they also glow, I think, with King's joy—with his pleasure and exhilaration in imagining.

Illustration by Hannah K. Lee.

UP NEXT:

Build A Website From Scratch The...
smallbusiness.yahoo.com

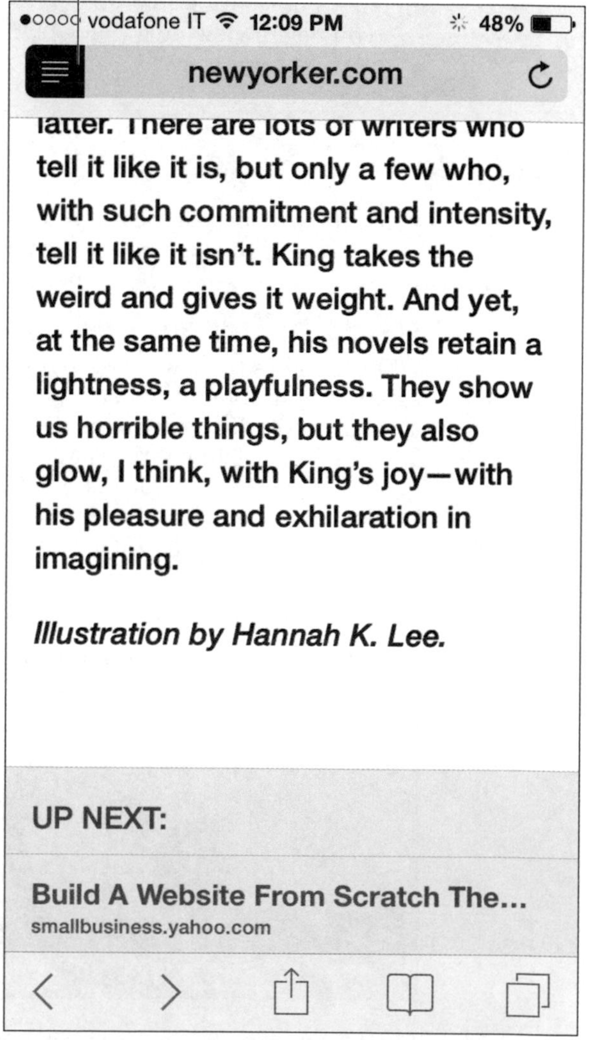

Figure 3-4: Reader makes reading web articles easier.

✔ **Scrolling carefully:** Drag a web page up or down, or sideways; don't worry about accidentally tapping something on the web page — as long as you drag your fingertip as soon as you touch the screen, Safari interprets your gesture as a scroll (or flick) rather than a tap.

✔ **Scrolling quickly:** Flick up or down to scroll in those directions more quickly.

✔ **Scrolling instantly to the top:** Tap the status bar at the top of iPhone's screen twice (the first time brings the Toolbar and Address/Search field into view) to instantly return to the top of a web page.

✔ **Scrolling inside a text frame:** Drag two fingers up or down in a text frame within a web page to scroll just the text in that frame up or down.

Zooming web pages

Using Safari's zoom view features can make scrolling web pages (and text frames within web pages) easier on your eyes — and fingertips.

Fortunately, many web pages automatically display an easier-to-read mobile version of themselves when they detect you've opened the web pages using a smartphone like the iPhone, which means you typically won't need to (or won't even be able to) zoom in or out of the contents of those web pages.

Other times, a web page may not offer a mobile viewing option, which means you're faced with viewing the full-size version of the web page that is designed to be viewed with your computer web browser program.

Thankfully, Safari's zoom in and out features make it easy to narrow your focus on just the section that you want to view.

Ways you can zoom in and out of web pages include the following:

✔ **Double-tap zooming:** Double-tap on a web page to zoom in or out, as shown in Figure 3-5. The cool thing is Safari understands what you tapped and zooms appropriately. For example, double-tap text and the text zooms only as large as the width of your iPhone so you don't have to scroll left to right to read, whereas double-tap an image and it zooms in to the maximum width the screen. For a wider view, turn your iPhone to landscape position. Double-tap again to zoom out.

✔ **Spread and pinch zooming:** Spread two fingers apart or pinch together to zoom out or in to a web page.

Double-tapping only works after the web page is fully loaded, but spread and pinch works even while the page is loading. If you have a Wi-Fi or 4G connection, this doesn't really matter, but if you have a slower connection, it can explain why double-tapping isn't active.

Although you can always zoom in and out of any full-size web page on iPhone's screen, not all mobile versions of certain websites allow zooming.

Navigating Web Pages

There's a reason it's called the World Wide Web. When you open and view a web page, more often than not, you don't stay on that one web page. Web pages contain links, which can be words or buttons or graphics, that you tap to open other web pages that contain more links and all those links weave a web of pages that seems infinite. One tap leads to another tap, and pretty soon you've spent your whole morning learning about the habits and habitats of the wild boar that decimated your neighbor's wheat field the previous evening. Barbara refers to it as the Internet vortex, but Safari's navigation features can help you stay the course as you wind your way from web page to web page, as we explain in the following subtopics.

Figure 3-5: Zooming in on a web page with a double-tap — or a pinch.

Moving from page to page

It's important to distinguish between the terms website and web page. A website comprises web pages. Web pages can contain links to other sections of the same web page, to other web pages within the same website, or to other websites, which have their own sets of web pages. Safari acts differently depending which type of link you tap.

When you tap a link to a web page within the website you're viewing, the Previous and Next buttons are activated. You can backtrack one or two or ten or more steps to return to whatever web page you started on before you wound up getting inadvertently lost (or (un)intentionally sidetracked). And, you can repeat your steps forward to the farthest web page you visited before you backtracked *away* from that farthest point. Safari gives you two ways to move backward and forward along your web page trail:

- ✓ Swipe right to go to the web page you viewed previously and swipe left to go forward to a page you were viewing before you swiped to go to the previous page.

- ✓ Tap the Previous or Next button in the Toolbar to move from one website to another.

When you tap a link to a different website, Safari moves your current screen to the tabs screen and opens the just-tapped link. You can only view one screen at a time, but think of the open web pages as tabs like you have in the browser on your computer. To move from one website, or tab, to another, tap the Tab button, and all the open web pages are displayed, as in Figure 3-6.

The New Page button

Figure 3-6: The Tabs screen.

**Book III
Chapter 3**

**Surfing the Web
with Safari**

Things you can do when viewing the Tabs screen include the following:

- **Open a new web page:** Tap the New Page button to open a new Safari web page.

- **Switch between web pages:** Scroll up and down to see tabs of other open web pages, and then tap the web page you want to view to open that web page.

- **Reorder the tabs:** Tap and hold the tab, and then drag it to a new position above or below where it was.

- **Close a web page:** Tap the X button in the upper left corner of a tab to close that web page or swipe left.

- **Open iCloud tabs:** Scroll to the bottom of the tabs to see shared tabs from other devices.

- **Close the Tabs screen:** Tap Done to close the Tabs screen.

If you tap and hold a link, a menu appears, as shown in Figure 3-7. Consider the first two options (we discuss the others a bit later on):

- **Open:** Opens the web page in the same manner as if you tapped the link.

- **Open in New Page:** The linked page opens in a new tab, even if it's on the same website.

    OR

- **Open in Background:** This option, which you activate in

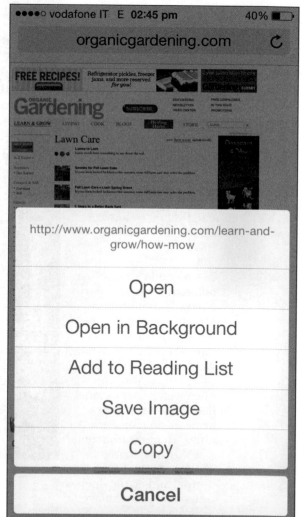

Figure 3-7: Tap and hold a link to see more opening (and sharing) choices.

Settings⇨Safari⇨Open Links, opens a new tab for the linked site but adds it to the tab screen. The page you're viewing remains on the screen.

We prefer this option. If you just tap a link to another website, a new tab opens on top of the one you were viewing, but tap and hold and a tab is opened in the background to be viewed later. You don't lose the link but you also don't interrupt what you've doing — for example, you're reading an article and there's a link that you want to open but you'd like to finish reading the article before going to the linked page.

When you see words or phrases in blue within the text of an article, those (usually) are links that open another web page related to the word or phrase you tapped.

Revisiting history with History

Sometimes you want to go back in time to a web page you viewed a few hours ago or even a few days or weeks ago. Thanks to Safari's History feature, you can do just that.

Opening previously viewed web pages

To view your Safari web page history, tap Bookmarks, and then tap History to view your web history activity, as shown in Figure 3-8. Safari lists the web pages you've visited in chronological order, with the most recent at the top of the list. Subheadings indicate the time period, such as This Afternoon, This Morning, Monday Evening, and so on. This can help you find the web page you want to revisit — book reviews, hmm must have been Sunday morning, or that sort of mnemonic trigger. Scroll through and then tap a listed item to revisit that web page.

Subheadings indicate the time period.

Figure 3-8: Revisit web pages you previously viewed in the History folder.

Book III
Chapter 3

Surfing the Web with Safari

If you don't see the History folder shown in Figure 3-8, that means you previously navigated to another Bookmarks folder; tap the Bookmarks button in the upper left corner, or swipe right, to back your way out of whatever folder you're in until you see the History folder, and then tap the History folder to view your Safari web history. Or you may be in Reading List, in which case tap the Bookmarks button at the top of the screen.

To see your most immediate viewing history, tap and hold the previous button.

Erasing your web history

On the History screen (refer to Figure 3-8), you may have noticed the Private and Clear buttons in the lower left and right corners. They have two separate but similar functions:

- ✔ **Clear:** To erase your entire Safari web page viewing history, tap the Clear button in the lower left corner. The red Clear History button appears, giving you a moment to reconsider whether you really want to wipe out your web history. Tap Clear History if you really do, or tap Cancel if you change your mind. Open pages in tabs and bookmarks remain but your history is wiped out.

- ✔ **Private:** This option cancels history before it happens. As you go from web page to web page, Safari develops instant amnesia and doesn't remember where it's been. When you tap this button, you have the option to Close All or Keep All of the open pages in tabs.

  You know Private is turned on because the Address/Search field and Toolbar background is dark gray, the Previous and Next buttons are inactive, and when you tap either Tabs or Bookmarks, the Private button in the lower left corner is highlighted. To turn the privacy function off, tap the Private button again. If you have open tabs, you are asked to Close All or Keep All.

Tapping into Web Page Links

One of the things that makes the web so amazing is the seemingly limitless options for interactivity. In this section, we tell you about interacting with the different types of links you might encounter, such as phone numbers, e-mail, and location addresses. We tell you how to view and do things with content-rich web links, such as saving photos or graphics to your iPhone's Photos app, or opening other apps to view the contents of a link, like Word or PDF documents, or a PowerPoint presentation. In addition to opening other web pages, web links can initiate the following actions, too:

- ✔ Display a graphic or photo or a photo slideshow you can tap through to view a series of photos

- ✔ Open a PDF document file

- ✔ Display a form with fields you can fill in with information, such as your shipping address on a shopping site, or your e-mail address, so you can receive a weekly newsletter from a museum you're fond of

- ✔ Play an audio file, such as a news story, a podcast, or a song

✔ Play a video file, say a movie trailer or a friend's dog catching a Frisbee

✔ Open another app, which you must exit (by double-pressing the Home button) to return to Safari

Working with basic links and forms

You can open a link with a quick tap or access more options with the tap and hold gesture. The web page link's full web address (URL) appears at the top of the dialog, and below the web address are buttons you can tap to do the following things:

✔ **Open:** Opens the web page link.

✔ **Open in New Page or Open in Background:** Forces Safari to open the web page link in a new Safari page screen or tab instead of replacing the web page screen you are viewing (see "Moving from page to page" and Figure 3-7 earlier in this chapter).

✔ **Add to Reading List:** Places the entire text in your Reading List so you can come back later and read whatever it is that interests you on this web page. Open Reading List by tapping the Bookmarks button.

✔ **Copy:** Copies the web page address to the clipboard so you can paste the web address elsewhere, like in a note in the Note app, or in a text message in the Messages app.

✔ **Cancel:** Closes the web page information and options screen.

Filling in forms and fields

When it comes to filling in forms, Safari serves up some useful helpers to make tapping out type and numbers using the keyboard as easy as possible.

Tap a field and begin typing. If you're having trouble seeing the field you're typing in, you can zoom in and out of the web page even while the keyboard is displayed. Turning your iPhone to landscape view makes the keyboard slightly larger.

When you open a field that offers a pop-up menu of choices, a rotor appears at the bottom of the screen, as shown in Figure 3-9. Scroll to your choice, tap to highlight it, and then tap Done.

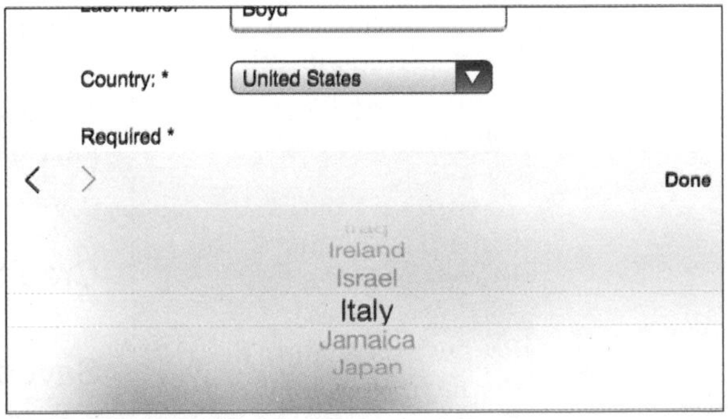

Figure 3-9: When filling out forms, Safari helps you "tab" between fields with the Next and Previous arrow buttons.

Book III
Chapter 3

Surfing the Web with Safari

Tap the arrows to move the cursor to the next or previous field in the form. Tapping either of those two buttons repeatedly quickly moves you from field to field. You can also scroll down to tap into any other fields you need to complete.

Tap Done when you finish filling in the form fields.

Using AutoFill to do the typing for you

When filling out forms you may encounter pop-up menus and pick-lists you tap and scroll through to select predetermined information such as the state you live in or a quantity of something you may be ordering. Tap these boxes or buttons to mark or unmark your selection.

For information about you such as name and address that remains constant, Safari's AutoFill feature automatically fills in common fields with your personal information with a single tap instead of requiring you to fill in those fields individually. Safari can also keep track of user names and passwords and credit card information. What's more, when you create a new account on a website, Safari asks if you want it to generate and memorize a password for you.

To turn on Safari's AutoFill feature and options, tap Home, and then tap Settings⇨Safari ⇨ Passwords & AutoFill to display the AutoFill settings screen, as shown in Figure 3-10. Here's how each option works:

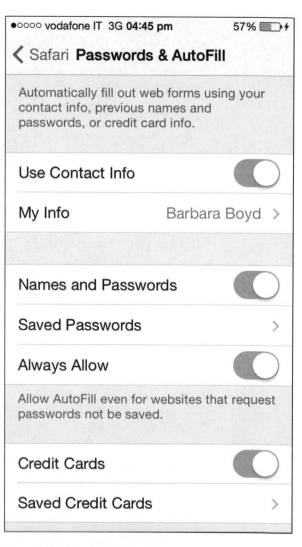

Figure 3-10: Safari's AutoFill settings screen.

✔ **Use Contact Info:** Tap On and Safari fills in online forms with your personal information. That personal information is pulled from your information in Contacts. You should see your own name in the My Info option field. When you are filling in a form, tap AutoFill on keyboard and Safari copies the information you have saved in the name, address, phone number, and e-mail address fields of your own Contacts card and pastes those bits of information into the appropriate fields.

If you don't see your name in the My Info option field, tap that field to display your Contacts, and then locate and tap your own Contacts card name to select it as the card you want to use for the My Info option.

✔ **Names and Passwords:** Tap the option On if you want Safari to remember any user names and passwords you type to access certain web pages. The first time you type your name and password on a web page that requires that information, Safari displays a pop-up message, asking if you'd like to save the password. Tap Yes if you would, Never for This Website if you never-ever-ever want to save the password for the web page, or Not Now, if you don't want to save the password right now, but you want to keep your option of saving the password open the next time you visit the web page.

Saved Passwords: Tap to see a list of websites for which you have a saved name and password, as shown in Figure 3-11. Tap the

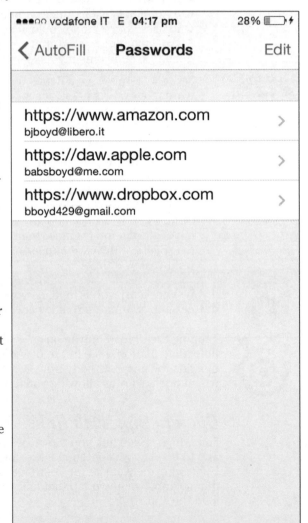

Figure 3-11: As you save names and passwords for websites, Safari stores them in Settings.

Book III
Chapter 3

Surfing the Web
with Safari

disclosure arrow to the right of the website to see the user name and password spelled out. To delete any of the websites, tap Edit in the upper right corner. Tap the radio button to the left of the website you want to delete; a check mark appears. Tap the Delete button in the upper left corner.

Always Allow: Tap on to override websites that prefer passwords not be saved. You have to have Passcode Lock turned on to enable this option and if you don't, when you tap it on, you're automatically led through the steps to create one.

If you turn off Passcode Lock, a dialog asks if you want to continue to use AutoFill in Safari since without the security of a Passcode, anyone who uses your iPhone could access any AutoFill information you keep in Safari, including your stored credit card information. Use AutoFill without a Passcode only if you keep your iPhone chained to your body.

Some websites have a Remember Me option for usernames and passwords that works if you accept cookies, in which case Safari doesn't ask if you want it to remember because the website takes care of that. (See the section "Adjusting General and Security Settings" at the end of this chapter to learn about cookies.)

✔ **Credit Cards:** If you shop frequently online, this feature can be a real timesaver. Tap on and then tap Saved Credit Cards⇨Add Credit Card to add your cardholder information to Safari. When you purchase something online, tap in the credit card field and then tap AutoFill Credit Card. Safari will automatically fill in the credit card information. If you have information for more than one credit card saved, a list of the last four digits of the card appear, as shown in Figure 3-12. Tap the card you want to pay with.

If you sync Safari with iCloud, all your auto-fill information is available on all devices and computers that sync with iCloud.

Tapping the Upload button on sites like Flickr or eBay opens two choices for uploading photos: Take Photo or Video, which opens the Camera app and uploads the image directly from Camera to the website, or Choose Existing, which opens Photos allowing you to select the image you want to upload.

Opening app web links

Sometimes a web link you tap closes the Safari screen and opens another app to display the contents of the link you tapped. For instance, you might be viewing the website for your favorite store and find they have a special iPhone app; when you tap that link, the App Store opens so you can download the app.

Whenever you leave Safari and a web page you were viewing to use another app, when you finish working with the app, Safari automatically opens. Following are examples of how Safari links to other iPhone apps:

✔ **Phone:** Tap a phone number link you want to dial, and then tap Call in the pop-up screen that appears. The Safari screen closes and the active call screen appears as your iPhone places your call.

✔ **Mail:** Tap an e-mail address you want to use to send an e-mail message, and a new message appears with the address already filled in the To field. Complete your new e-mail message and then tap Send. The e-mail message screen closes and returns to Safari.

To do other things with an phone number or e-mail address link, press and hold on the phone number or e-mail address to display the link options screen, and then choose one of the following options (options vary for phone number or e-mail):

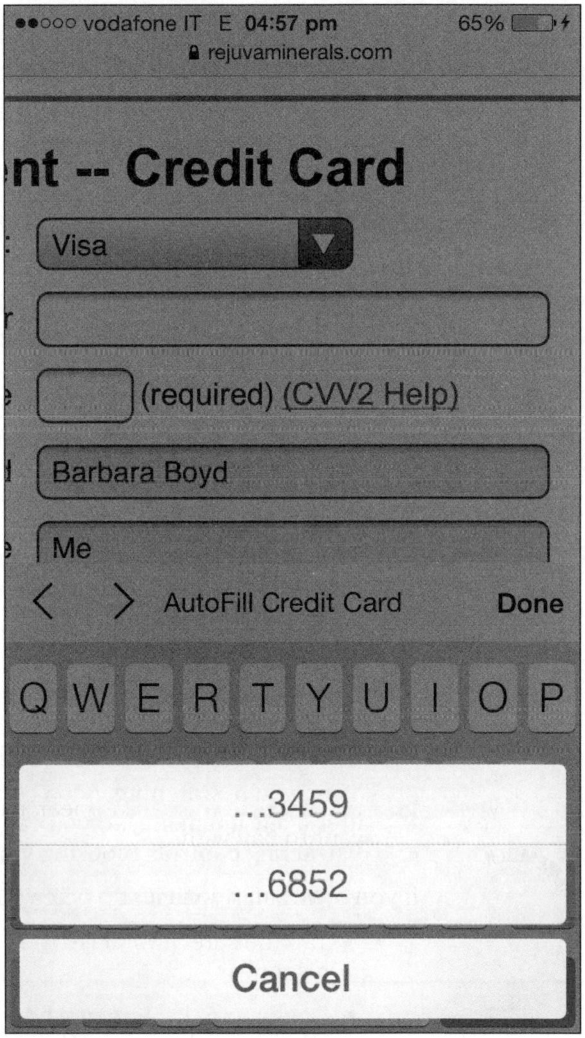

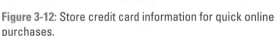

Figure 3-12: Store credit card information for quick online purchases.

- **Call:** Dials the phone number.

- **Text Message:** Opens a new text message and pastes the phone number into the To field.

- **New Message:** Creates a new e-mail message with the e-mail address you tapped already filled in the To field.

- **Add to Contacts:** Opens an Info screen in Contacts where you can choose to Create a New Contact or Add to an Existing Contact. After you choose one, either a New Contact screen opens or your Contacts list opens. Scroll through to find the contact to which you want to add the number.

- **Copy:** Copies the phone number or e-mail address to the clipboard so you can paste the e-mail address into another app such as Notes or Messages.

✔ **Photos:** Press and hold on a photo or other kind of image file to display the Safari options screen, and then tap Save Image to save that image file to the camera roll in the Photos app or Copy to place the image in the clipboard and then paste it in another app. If the image you tap is actually a link, you'll see more options, such as Open, Open in New Page, Add to Reading List, and Copy.

A bit of copyright "fine print" you ought to keep in mind: Although it's generally acceptable to save any photo or other kind of image file for your own viewing pleasure, you're generally not permitted to use those photos or other image files to share with others — on your own website, or in a magazine you write for, for instance — without the express consent/permission of the person or organization who owns the rights to those image files you may have saved to your iPhone.

✔ **Videos:** When you tap a streaming video or audio link on a web page, Safari opens and begins playing the link with its built-in video or audio player feature. The player displays all of the controls you need for starting, pausing, stopping, rewinding, fast forwarding, and adjusting the volume of the content you're watching or listening to.

When you're watching video content, those controls typically disappear after a few moments, so you can enjoy the video without having those distracting controls blocking your view.

A few things you can do when you're watching video content include

- Tap the screen to make the video controls reappear after they disappear

- Double-tap the screen when you're watching a video in portrait mode to zoom in or out

- Rotate your iPhone sideways to watch a video in landscape, fullscreen mode to enjoy the fullest possible view

Sometimes instead of seeing a thumbnail of a video on a web page, you may see a message informing you that your web browser requires Adobe Flash to view the video. Unfortunately, viewing Flash videos with Safari isn't possible because of Apple's choice to not support Flash on iPhone.

Your iPhone supports the video playing features of the web page formatting language known as HTML5, which supports embedded QuickTime video playback, or Apple's own QuickTime video feature. The good news is that more and more websites are using HTML5 to create or revise their web pages. And, Adobe has released a software tool that developers can apply to their Flash videos and games, which makes them viewable on an iPhone.

✔ **Quick Look:** This isn't an app you'll find on your Home screen, but it does open certain document files you may encounter on your web adventures. Tapping on a document link on a web page you're viewing prompts Safari to try to open the document file using its built-in Quick Look feature, as shown in Figure 3-13. The Quick Look feature can display a number of popular document file types, including Microsoft Word, Excel, and PowerPoint documents, and PDF documents.

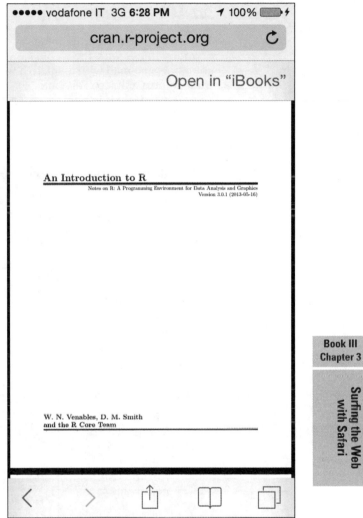

Figure 3-13: Safari's Quick Look function opens PDF and productivity documents.

✔ **Other Apps:** Sometimes you may want to open a document you're viewing using another app you have installed on your iPhone. To open a document using another app, tap the Open In *<appname>* button on the right to use the default app displayed on that button, or tap the Open In button on the left (refer to Figure 3-13) to display other apps on your iPhone that you can use to open the app. Tap the button that corresponds to the app you want to use to open the document. Safari closes and the app launches and loads the document.

Acting on Web Page Links

The action button in the toolbar at the bottom of the Safari screen lets you do many things with the web page you're viewing. Say you want to send someone an e-mail with a link to a web page you want them to look at or you want to post a link to Facebook. Or maybe you want to copy a web page link so you can paste it in another program such as Notes, for instance, where you might be creating a list of favorite recipe web pages. You can do all of those things and more directly from the web page you're browsing. Follow these steps:

1. **While viewing a web page in normal or Reader mode that you want to share, print, or copy, tap the Action button at the bottom of the screen.**

   The Share Sheet as shown in Figure 3-14 appears.

2. **Tap your sharing method of choice from the following:**

   - **AirDrop (iPhone 5 or later):** Share the web page link with other AirDrop users near you.

   - **Message:** A new text message, which may be SMS or iMessage depending on the recipient, appears with the web page address pasted into the body of the message; complete the message as usual and then tap Send.

Figure 3-14: Tap the Action button to see your sharing options and more.

- **Mail:** A new message appears with the web page address pasted into the body of the message; complete the message as usual and then tap Send.

  If you share an article from Reader, the entire article will be pasted in to the Mail message.

- **Twitter:** Write something to accompany your link, and then tap Send.

- **Facebook:** Write something to accompany your link, and then tap Post.

- **Bookmark:** Adds the URL to your bookmarks. Learn more about this function in the next section "Playing Favorites with Bookmarks."

- **Add to Reading List:** Adds the web page to your Reading List so you can view it later.

- **Add to Home Screen:** Places an icon on the Home screen that, when tapped, opens directly to the web page.

- **Print:** Select a printer if your printer isn't selected, tap the plus sign to print more than one copy, and then tap Print.

After each of these actions, your message disappears into the ether and the web page you were viewing appears front and center once more.

- **Copy:** The web address is copied to the clipboard so you can paste it to another app. Return to the Home screen or the multitasking bar to open another app and paste the link. Double-press the Home button to open the multitasking bar and tap Safari to return to the web page you were viewing.

3. **Continue what you were doing in Safari.**

You can also print other types of content you can open and view in Safari, such as PDF (Portable Document Format) or Microsoft Word docs, Excel spreadsheets, and photos — in other words, anything iPhone's QuickLook feature can open and display on the screen, you can print to an AirPrint-enabled printer.

**Book III
Chapter 3**

**Surfing the Web
with Safari**

Playing Favorites with Bookmarks

Much like their paper counterparts save your place in a book, electronic bookmarks save your place, or places, on the web — it's a way of easily returning to a website or specific web page whenever you want. Even better, as long as you turn on Safari in iCloud on all your devices, you find the same bookmarks from whichever device you access the web.

Viewing, opening, and creating bookmarks

Tap the Bookmarks button in the Toolbar to open the Bookmarks screen, (refer to Figure 3-15) where you also find tabs for Reading List and Shared Links, if you subscribe to Twitter. To view a bookmarked web page, tap the corresponding bookmark. Your iPhone comes with some pre-installed bookmarks — a few are in Favorites — to get you started. You see the following when the Bookmarks tab is selected:

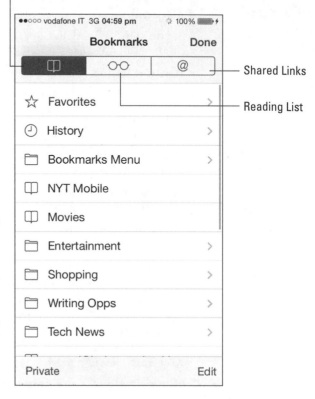

Bookmarks

Shared Links

Reading List

Figure 3-15: Bookmarks mark your favorite web pages so you can return in a tap.

- ✔ **Favorites**: In Settings⇨Safari⇨ Favorites, you can choose which folder you want to head up the Bookmarks list. The Favorites folder is the default but you can choose News or Entertainment or another folder you create. It will appear at the top of the Bookmarks list and you see buttons for the bookmarks within the Favorites folder when you tap the Address/Search field.

- ✔ **History:** Tap to see a list of web pages you viewed on your iPhone.

- ✔ **Bookmarks Menu, Folders, and (single) Bookmarks:** You can create any of these on your iPhone and, if Safari is on in iCloud, you sync with any bookmarks you have in these places on your computer or other devices.

You may need to scroll down your list or tap a folder stored in the Bookmarks list to find the bookmark you want to open.

Adding bookmarks

To create a new bookmark for a web page you're viewing, do the following:

1. **Tap the Action button to display the Share Sheet, and then tap Bookmark to display the Add Bookmark screen.**

   The keyboard appears, and the blinking cursor is positioned at the end of the web page name.

2. **(Optional.) Edit the name of the website if you don't like the name that's automatically created for the bookmark, as shown in Figure 3-16.**

   You might want to use something more descriptive or shorter so the whole name appears in the Bookmarks list.

3. **(Optional.) Tap Location to choose where to store the bookmark.**

   A list that contains Favorites and all your folders appears. Tap the location where you want to store the bookmark. Choose Bookmarks to store it at the top level, although if you store many bookmarks at the top level it can become a long, confusing list so it's often a better idea to group like-minded bookmarks in appropriately named folders, as we explain in the next section.

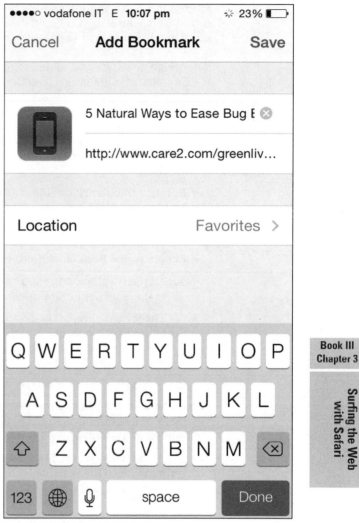

Figure 3-16: The Add Bookmarks screen.

4. **Tap Done or Save to save your new Bookmark.**

Organizing bookmarks

The number of bookmarks you have can get out of hand quickly if you want to remember and revisit many web pages. Placing bookmarks for similar web pages together in folders makes your browsing easier and saves you from scrolling through hundreds of bookmarks to find the one you want. Deleting bookmarks you don't use anymore is also a good idea. For example, if you plan a vacation to Los Angeles, you might place bookmarks about L.A.

museums, hotels, and restaurants in one folder for easy access. When you return from your trip, you could delete the whole folder or move the restaurants to a Restaurants bookmark folder and delete the rest — you get the idea.

You create new folders and delete or rearrange folders and bookmarks using the Bookmarks edit feature. Tap Bookmarks, and then tap Edit to display the Bookmarks edit screen. You can do the following:

- **Rearrange your bookmarks and folders:** Tap the Rearrange button to the right of a bookmark or folder, and then drag the bookmark up or down the list and release your finger to drop the bookmark in its new location.

- **Delete a bookmark or folder:** Tap the red – (minus) sign to the left of a bookmark or folder you want to say goodbye to, and then tap the Delete button. The bookmark or folder (and all the bookmarks filed inside) disappears.

- **Create a new bookmark folder:**

    1. Tap New Folder, and then type a name for your new bookmark folder in the Title field that appears.

       The folder lands in the top level of the Bookmarks list. To place a folder inside another folder, on the Bookmarks Bar, or Bookmarks Menu, tap Location, and then tap where you want it to go. A check mark lets you know where that folder will be placed.

    2. Swipe right to return to the previous screens.

- Rename or move an existing bookmark or folder by tapping the bookmark or folder, and then following the same steps for creating a new bookmark or folder.

- Tap Done when you're finished editing the Bookmarks list, and Safari returns you to the web page you were viewing before you started tweaking your bookmarks.

Saving to read later

If you've spent any time on the web, you probably know how many things you find that you'd like to read but you don't have the time when you find it. If you're like us, in the past, you used bookmarks to save those places you wanted to come back to later, only to find you had so many bookmarks they were no longer manageable, or that you had bookmarked a website but the content you wanted to read had changed when you returned.

The Reading List function of Safari takes care of those problems as it stores articles or web pages you want to read later. To save an article or web page to your reading list, while you're on the page, tap the Action button and then tap Add to Reading List.

To view an article in the Reading List, tap the Bookmarks button on the toolbar and then tap Reading List (if you don't see Reading List, tap the Bookmarks button in the upper left corner to return to the main Bookmarks screen). The title, source, and the first two lines of the article appear in the list, as shown in Figure 3-17, so you don't have to decipher cryptic bookmark names. Tap the All or Unread button in the bottom right corner to view everything in Reading List or only the things you haven't read yet.

Tap an article and it opens in Safari. Scroll down to the bottom and the next article on your reading list is ready to be opened under an Up Next heading. Just scroll up to see it and likewise for the article after that.

You can read articles in your Reading List offline and, like bookmarks, Reading List items sync between devices so if you put something on your Reading List on your iPhone, you find it on your iPad and computer – how great is that? Articles remain in Reading List until you remove them by swiping across and then tapping the Delete button (refer to Figure 3-17).

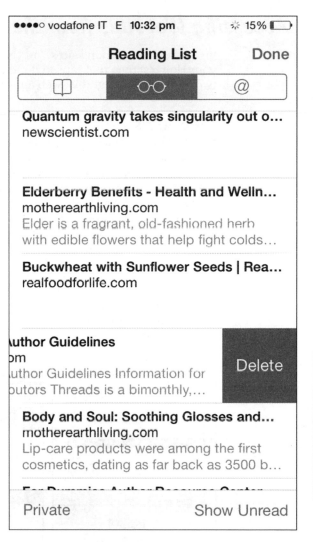

Figure 3-17: Reading list puts articles and web pages you want to read later all in one place.

If you follow folks on Twitter, tap the Shared Links tab on the Bookmarks screen to see links to web pages people are tweeting about.

Accessing Websites from the Home Screen

Instead of bookmarking sites you visit frequently, you can have a button on your Home screen that taps in directly to the website or web page. There are two ways to go about this: web apps and Web Clips. Here we explain both.

Web apps

Many websites, from those of news outlets like *The New York Times,* to stores such as Target, or your bank, display a link that reads Download the iPhone App. When you tap this button or link, the App Store opens and gives you the opportunity to download an app for that site. (See Book II, Chapter 2 to learn about downloading and installing apps.) When you use the web app, you see the content of the website, but usually see other functions as well that help you navigate and interact with the information that website provides. Or you might have a streamlined version of the main service that website offers. Like apps in general, there's no hard, fast rule for how and what they present, so the best thing to do is explore.

Figure 3-18 shows an example: Barbara can go to her bank's website and sign in to her account or use the bank's web app, which has an easier sign-in procedure and eliminates extraneous information.

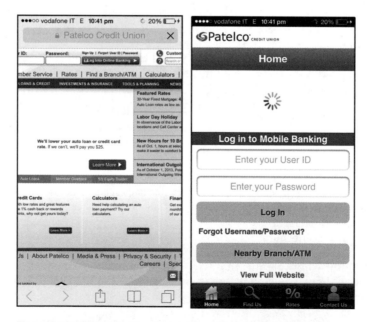

Figure 3-18: Web apps are site-specific apps that give you added features related to the services offered.

Web Clips

If you visit a particular web page often and there's no web app available, you can create a Home screen icon, called a Web Clip, for that web page. Tapping the Web Clip automatically opens the web page. If you want Safari to open to a specific Home page, create a web clip for that page.

To create a Web Clip:

1. **Open the web page for which you want to create a Web Clip.**

   You can zoom in to a particular column on the web page you want to add to your Home screen, and when you tap the icon on the Home screen, Safari opens the web page to that same section — very handy for tracking just a column of information, like the daily menu special at your favorite diner.

2. **Tap the Action button to display the Share Sheet, and then tap Add to Home Screen.**

   The Add to Home screen appears, displaying a name and icon for the Web Clip you want to add to the Home screen.

3. **Edit or type a new name for your Web Clip — nine letters is optimal if you want to see the whole name under the icon.**

4. **Tap Add.**

   Safari closes and ushers you to the Home screen where your new Web Clip has been added.

Book III
Chapter 3

Surfing the Web
with Safari

Searching Tips and Tricks

Safari's Search field is the place to go to whenever you want to find something on the web or on the web page you're viewing. When you first begin using your iPhone, Google is the search engine that Safari uses to find things you search for using the Search field but if you prefer Yahoo! or Bing, tap Settings on the Home screen, and then tap Safari⇨Search Engine and pick your preferred search engine.

To Search the web using Safari's search feature:

1. **Tap the Address/Search field to display the keyboard, and then begin typing the word, name, phrase, ZIP code, or whatever you're searching for. If you don't see the field, tap the Status Bar.**

   As you type, a list of suggested search words appears, as shown in Figure 3-19, divided by category and based on web pages you may have already visited, or bookmarked, or one that your chosen Search engine provider thinks may match what you're looking for.

At this point, you can do one of the following:

2a. **Tap one of those suggested matches if it matches your criteria.**

2b. **Ignore those suggested matches that appear and finish typing what you're looking for in the Search field, and then tap the Go button.**

Either way, Safari displays a list of search result links that you can then tap to explore any of those possibilities.

You can ask Siri to search for you if you have an iPhone 4s or later. Press and hold the Home button until you hear Siri ask how she can help you, and then speak your request or question.

Adjusting General and Security Settings

In the sections before this one, we occasionally ask you to check out or adjust a particular Safari setting, like turning on the AutoFill feature, for instance. In this section, we give you a complete rundown of Safari's settings and feature options.

Press the Home button, and then tap Settings⇨Safari to display the Safari Settings screen, as shown in Figure 3-20.

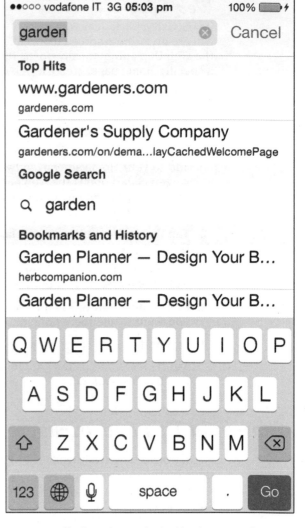

Figure 3-19: Finding what you're looking for on a web page you're viewing.

The 411 on Safari's settings is as follows:

- ✔ **Search Engine:** Tap and choose your preferred Search provider.

- ✔ **Passwords & AutoFill:** Tap to activate and adjust the AutoFill features described in the earlier section, "Using AutoFill to do the typing for you."

- ✔ **Favorites:** Choose the folder that appears at the top of the Bookmarks list.

- ✔ **Open Links:** Tap this button to choose what you want Safari to do when you tap a link in a web page. See the section "Moving from page to page" for a full explanation.

- ✔ **Block Pop-ups:** When on, Safari does its best to block pop-up ads or solicitations.

- ✔ **Do Not Track:** When on, Safari asks websites that track data about you (ostensibly to offer you more tailored information when you visit their sites) to not track your activity. It's a request, not a demand, so it is up to the website to respect your request or not.

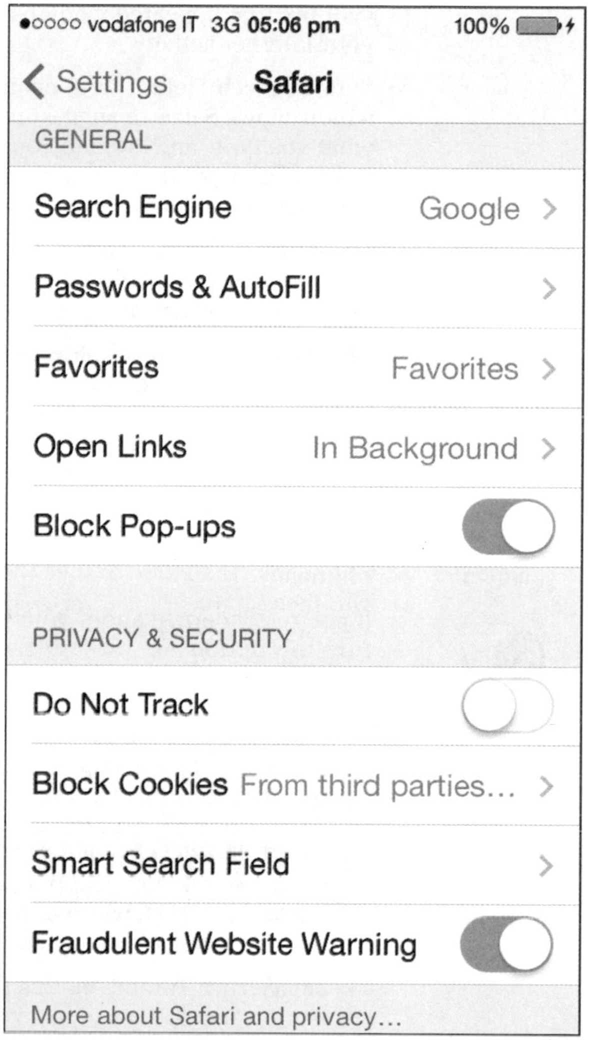

Figure 3-20: Safari's settings screen.

Book III
Chapter 3

Surfing the Web with Safari

- ✔ **Block Cookies:** Cookies are bits of information certain websites store, so those websites can know and remember certain things about you. Tap and choose whether you want to receive cookies Never, From Visited, or Always. From Visited is the choice we recommend so that websites you go to can remember things like your ZIP code for giving you the weather forecast and so on. Choosing Never may result in some websites not functioning properly, and choosing Always also allows sites you didn't visit but that appeared via pop-ups to grab and store information about your Internet activity.

✔ **Smart Search Field:** Tap to enable two options: Search Suggestions, which allows Safari to suggest matches to your search criteria based on what you type, and Preload Top Hit, which begins loading a web page in the background when a match is determined based on your bookmarks and browsing history.

✔ **Fraudulent Website Warning:** Turn this on if you want Safari to warn you if what seems like a legitimate website you want to open may in fact be a potentially harmful site.

✔ **Clear History, Clear Cookies and Data:** Tapping either of these erases their respective saved files from your iPhone. Clear History wipes out Safari's memory of any websites you visited. Clear Cookies and Data erases any crumbs of cookie information you may have typed in to certain websites, like your ZIP code.

✔ **Use Cellular Data:** Downloads articles to Reading List using your cellular data connection (when Wi-Fi isn't available) so you can read them offline.

If you're concerned about your cellular data limits and consumption, turn this option off.

✔ **Advanced:** Opens the following two choices:

- **Website Data:** Tap to view any databases that are automatically created by certain websites so those websites can speed up your web browsing experience when you use them. You may see databases for `mail.google.com`, for instance, if you use Safari to read your e-mail. The list also displays how much space that database is taking up on your iPhone. Tapping Edit allows you to delete items one by one from the list, whereas tapping Remove All Website Data at the bottom of the screen clears the list completely.

- **JavaScript:** Turned on, this feature allows websites to present information and options in fancy ways, with things like pop-up buttons, swirling graphics, and interactive features that won't appear or work if you turn this feature off.

- **Web Inspector:** Website developers turn on this feature to help them troubleshoot problems the web pages they create may run into. Average Joes like you and me can keep this option turned off.

If you want to keep advertisers' snooping eyes from gathering information about your web habits (to then offer you things they think you should buy from them), go to Settings⇨Privacy⇨Advertising, and then tap Limit Ad Tracking On.

Chapter 4: E-mailing Every Which Way You Can

In This Chapter

- ✓ Configuring your e-mail account
- ✓ Using Mail
- ✓ E-mailing from other apps
- ✓ Adjusting your e-mail account settings
- ✓ Playing Fetch with your e-mail

*A*lthough you can send text messages with Messages or through Facebook, LinkedIn, Twitter, and the myriad other social networks, good ol' e-mail is still a viable choice. It's an efficient way to send and request information, make reservations, and, yes, keep in touch with family and friends, especially when you want to keep your communication a bit more private. With a little web research, you can find the name of the CEO of your favorite company and send her a message about how much you like the latest model of the doohickey they've released. You can also complain directly to the head of research, development, and manufacturing when your beloved doohickey breaks a week after you bought it.

With your iPhone, you have e-mail at your fingertips. In this chapter, we show you how to configure your iCloud e-mail account as well as that of any other e-mail service providers you work with. Then, we explain the ins and outs of Mail — writing and sending a new message, receiving and replying to a message, and saving and deleting messages. We give you tips for managing your messages. New messages can be generated from other apps such as Notes, Maps, and Photos, so we review that too. Then we take a look at the account settings you can change. Your iPhone comes with preset choices for these features that probably are fine for 90 percent of users, but for the remaining 10 percent and the purely curious, we explain all the settings one by one.

Inbox

🔍 Search

Barbara Boyd   12:46 pm
🔲 Editing email

Hutsko   12:32 pm
son's summer camp pic

Configuring Your E-Mail Account

The first step to using Mail is setting up an account. If you established the iCloud account while setting up your iPhone, you already have a configured e-mail account — although iCloud may not be your only e-mail account.

You configure your e-mail account directly on your iPhone with a series of taps. Apple has been kind enough to insert the technical stuff needed to access some of the most used e-mail services. For the following e-mail services, you need to have your e-mail address and password handy:

- iCloud
- MS-Exchange
- Google Mail
- Yahoo!
- AOL
- Outlook.com

Setting up an iCloud account

If you set up an iCloud e-mail account when you created your Apple ID, you have an @iCloud.com account. If you're a long-time Apple user, you may have an @me.com or @mac.com account, and these both work transparently with iCloud.com. And, you may have already turned on your iCloud account when you set up iCloud syncing (refer to Book II, Chapter 1). If not, we explain it here.

Follow these steps to set up your iCloud e-mail on your iPhone:

1. **Tap Settings on the Home screen, and then tap Mail, Contacts, Calendars.**

   You have to scroll down — it's right below iCloud.

2. **If you have no e-mail account, the Add Account screen opens directly, as shown in Figure 4-1.**

   If you see iCloud in the Accounts list and Mail is listed beneath it, as in Figure 4-2, you can skip ahead to the "Using Mail" section.

   If you see iCloud but Mail isn't listed or you don't see iCloud at all but want to add it, tap Add Account and go to Step 3.

3. **Tap iCloud.**

   iCloud recognizes the @icloud.com, @me.com, or @mac.com e-mail address domains.

4. **Type in the e-mail address and password associated with your Apple ID and then tap the Next button.**

   If you don't have an Apple ID, click Get a Free Apple ID and follow the on-screen instructions to set one up.

   Your account is verified.

5. **The iCloud screen opens.**

   A message asks if you want iCloud to use the Location of Your iPhone. We suggest you tap OK. Find My iPhone is explained in Book I, Chapter 4.

   On the screen shown in Figure 4-3, you have a series of options and toggle switches that turn those options on. Turning

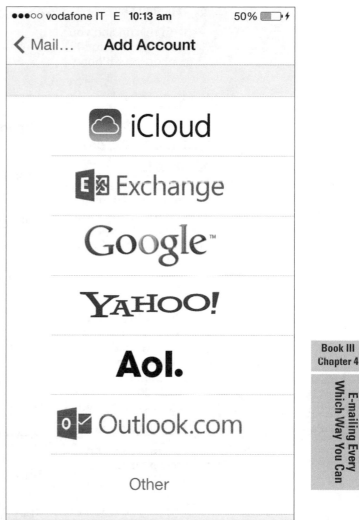

Figure 4-1: The Add Account screen.

an option on means that the information in that app is shared between your iPhone and iCloud and any other devices you access iCloud with, such as an iPad, Mac, or Windows PC. Any time you make changes to one of them on one device, the changes go up to the iCloud and rain down on the other device. We explain each option fully in Book II, Chapter 1.

6. Tap Mail On.

Turn this on and you receive your iCloud mail on your iPhone.

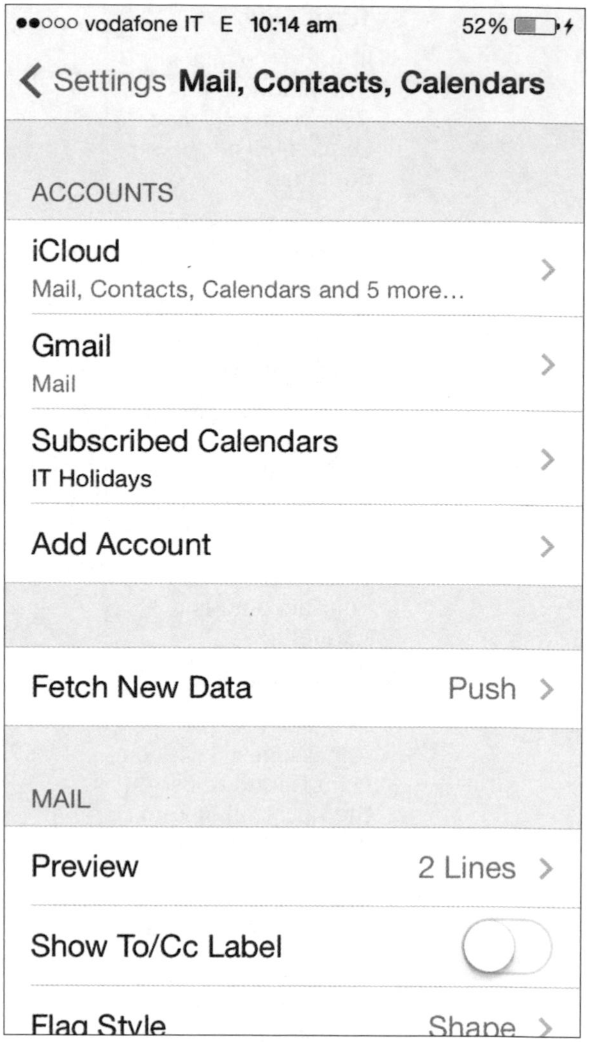

Google Mail, Yahoo!, AOL, and Outlook.com accounts

Apple has already put the incoming and outgoing server information for the most popular e-mail providers on iPhone. If you use Gmail, Yahoo!, AOL, or Outlook.com, do the following:

1. **Tap Settings on the Home screen, and then tap Mail, Contacts, Calendars. You might have to scroll down — it's right below iCloud.**

2. **Tap Add Account.**

3. **The Add Account screen opens.**

   Refer to Figure 4-1.

4. **Tap the name of the account you use; for example, Google Mail, also known as Gmail.**

5. **The Google Mail (or Yahoo! or AOL or Outlook.com) screen opens, as shown in Figure 4-4.**

   Filling in the Name field is optional (Windows Live Hotmail doesn't even have one). Type your e-mail address in the Address field and your password in the Password field.

●●○○○ vodafone IT E 10:14 am   52% 🔋⚡

‹ Settings **Mail, Contacts, Calendars**

ACCOUNTS

iCloud
Mail, Contacts, Calendars and 5 more...   ›

Gmail
Mail   ›

Subscribed Calendars
IT Holidays   ›

Add Account   ›

Fetch New Data   Push ›

MAIL

Preview   2 Lines ›

Show To/Cc Label   ⚪

Flag Style   Shape ›

Figure 4-2: The Mail, Contacts, Calendars settings show which accounts you have set up on your iPhone.

6. **Tap the Next button in the upper right corner.**

   Your account is verified.

   The Google Mail (or one of the others) screen opens. You have a few options to consider turning on or off, depending on the services you use. For our purposes, turn on Mail.

   This connects you to your e-mail account so that messages download to your iPhone in the Mail app and you can send messages from your e-mail account in Mail.

7. **Tap Save.**

   Your account is added to the Accounts list of Mail, Contacts, Calendars settings.

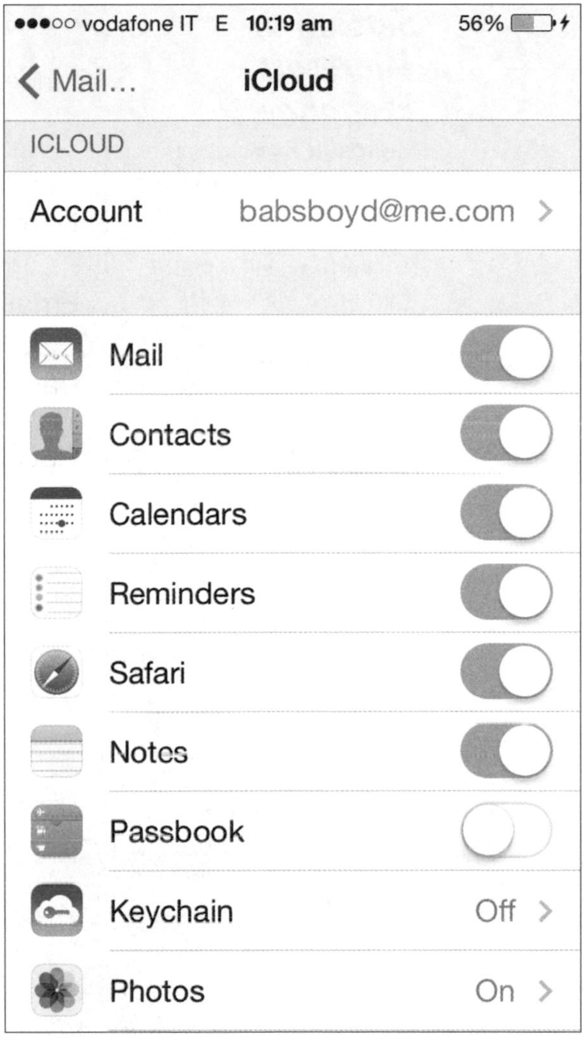

The Description field is automatically filled in with Exchange, Google Mail, Yahoo!, AOL, or Outlook.com, but if you tap there, you can change it. For example, we set up two Gmail accounts: one for personal e-mail exchanges and another for newsletter subscriptions. This way, we don't have to weed through a dozen or more daily newsletters to find more important messages. In the Description field, we named one Friends and the other Subscriptions, and then tap the mailbox in the Mailboxes list to view only those types of messages. See the "Multiple mailboxes" section for more information.

●●●○○ vodafone IT E 10:19 am	56% ▭▪
❮ Mail... **iCloud**	
ICLOUD	
Account	babsboyd@me.com ❯
✉ Mail	⬤━
👤 Contacts	⬤━
📅 Calendars	⬤━
▤ Reminders	⬤━
🧭 Safari	⬤━
▤ Notes	⬤━
📒 Passbook	━◯
🔑 Keychain	Off ❯
🌼 Photos	On ❯

Figure 4-3: Tapping Mail On to send and receive e-mail on your iPhone with your iCloud account.

Setting up Microsoft Exchange

Microsoft Exchange is often used in a corporate setting where a company-specific server manages the employees' e-mail. If you use Microsoft Exchange, you might need to ask your network administrator for the server name, and then follow these steps to set up a Microsoft Exchange account on your iPhone:

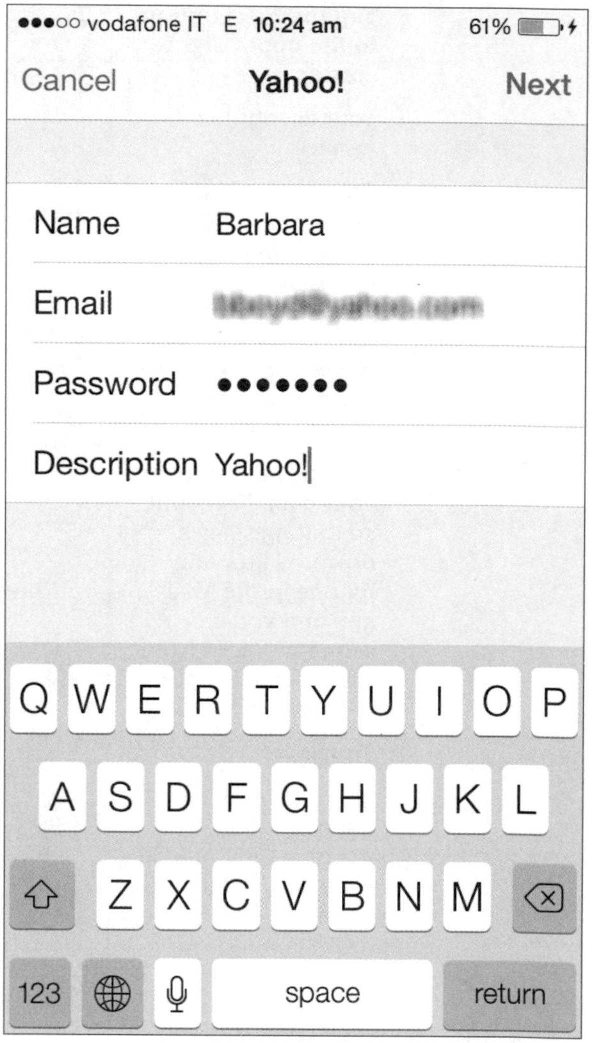

1. **Tap Settings⇨Mail, Contacts, Calendars⇨Add Account⇨Microsoft Exchange.**

   The first Exchange screen opens and requests your e-mail address, password, and a description, which is optional.

2. **Fill in the information requested and tap Next.**

3. **The second Exchange screen opens, as shown in Figure 4-5. Fill in the requested fields.**

   You may have to ask your network administrator for some of the details.

4. **Tap Next.**

   If Microsoft Auto Discovery didn't fill in the server address, type it in. It will be something like *exchange.company.com*.

●●●○○ vodafone IT E 10:24 am   61% ▭ ⊁

Cancel   **Yahoo!**   Next

Name   Barbara

Email

Password   ●●●●●●●

Description Yahoo!

Q W E R T Y U I O P

A S D F G H J K L

⇧ Z X C V B N M ⌫

123 ⊕ 🎤   space   return

Figure 4-4: Type your name, e-mail address, and password in the designated fields.

5. **The Exchange account opens with options for Mail, Contacts, and Calendars. Turn Mail on to have e-mail from your Exchange account accessible from your iPhone.**

Turn on Contacts and Calendars as well if you want to access that information from your Exchange account. See Book IV, Chapter 1 and 2 to learn more about Contacts and Calendars.

Setting up other IMAP and POP accounts

If you or your company uses another e-mail provider, it's probably an IMAP — Internet Message Access Protocol or POP — Post Office Protocol account. iOS 7 is pretty clever at finding the account and setting it up based on just your e-mail address and password, which we explain here:

Figure 4-5: Fill in the Microsoft Exchange screen to add Exchange to your e-mail accounts.

1. **Tap Settings on the Home screen, and then tap Mail, Contacts, Calendars.**

2. **Tap Add Account.**

3. **Tap Other at the bottom of the list.**

4. **Tap Add Mail Account, the first button on the screen.**

   A New Account screen opens.

5. **Fill in your name, address (your e-mail address), your password, and a description if you want something different than what is automatically entered. See Figure 4-6.**

6. **Tap Next.**

   Mail looks for your account and verifies it.

7. **Your iPhone automatically recognizes if it's an IMAP or POP account and presents the appropriate choices.**

8. **Tap the options, such as Mail or Notes, to the On position to have that data accessible from your iPhone.**

9. **Tap Save.**

   The account is added and appears in the list of accounts in Settings⇨Mail, Contacts, Calendars.

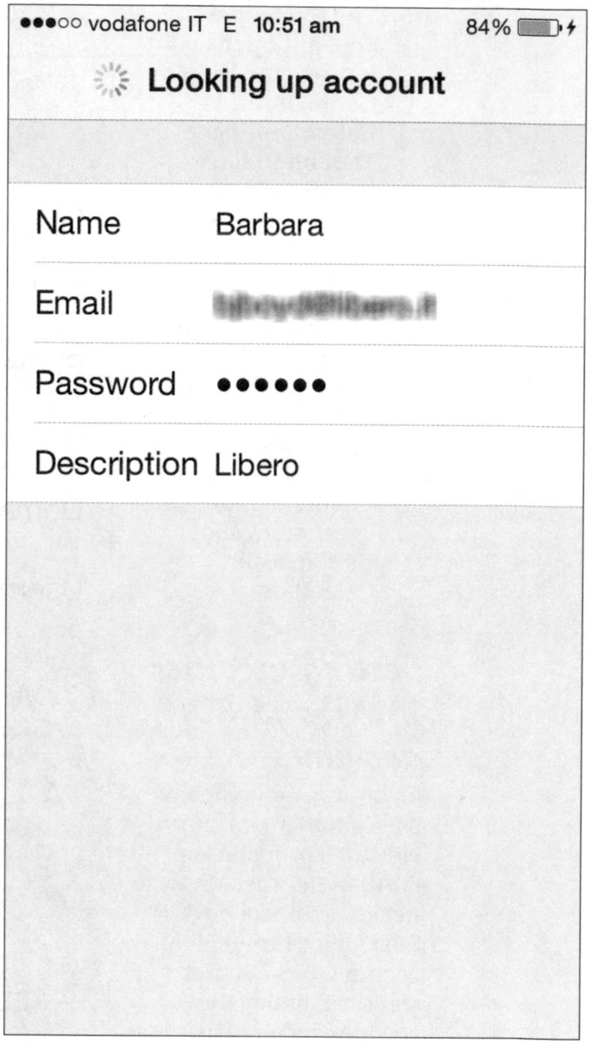

●●●○○ vodafone IT E 10:51 am   84% 🔋⚡

🔄 **Looking up account**

Name	Barbara
Email	▓▓▓▓▓▓▓▓▓▓
Password	●●●●●●
Description	Libero

Figure 4-6: Fill in the requested information in the New Account screen.

Depending on the type of service, you may be asked for other information during the setup: for example, Host Name, which is usually something like *mail.providername.com*, the User Name, which is the name you gave when you signed up for this e-mail service and is often the part of your e-mail address before the @ (at) symbol, your password, and the Outgoing Mail Server Host Name. You can find this information on the website of the provider on the page that references iPhone or smart phone setup, or ask the tech support person or the network administrator at your office.

POP goes the message

IMAP services keep your messages on the e-mail or Internet service provider server, even after you've read them, whereas POP services only store your messages temporarily. After you've downloaded them, they're no longer on the server, unless you change the settings in your Mail program that you want to leave them on the server after being downloaded.

Most web-based e-mail service providers, such as iCloud, Google Mail, Yahoo!, or AOL use IMAP. IMAP is convenient if you want to read e-mail messages on both your iPhone and from a computer in a different location, although you do need to delete messages now and then so your mailbox doesn't fill up and reject new incoming messages.

Other e-mail service providers use POP, which is convenient because the messages are literally on your iPhone or on your computer if you've downloaded them there first. After you download the messages, they reside where you first read them. You can configure both your computer and iPhone to leave the messages on the server after you've downloaded them so you can access them from the other device at a later time. We explain that just a bit further on in this chapter under "Incoming Settings."

Using Mail

iPhone's Mail app works like most e-mail programs. Terms we're familiar with for printed material (what's that?) delivered to our homes and offices — mail, inbox, carbon copy — are used to describe electronic material that is delivered to our homes and offices via computers, iPhones, and other devices. We start by explaining how to create and send a message, and follow up with replying to, forwarding, filing, and deleting messages. We also go through the ways you can view and organize messages.

Creating and sending e-mail messages

To create and send an e-mail message, just follow these steps:

1. **Tap the Mail button on the Home screen.**

   The Mailboxes screen opens, as seen in Figure 4-7.

   Notice that we added an Unread mailbox — see the section "Multiple mailboxes" to learn how to do it.

2. Tap the inbox for the account you want to send the message from.

3. Tap the Compose button in the lower right corner of the screen.

A New Message screen opens. The cursor is blinking in the To field.

 You can tap the Compose button in the lower right corner of the Mailboxes screen. The message will be sent from the default mailbox you establish in Settings➪Mail. We show you how to change the outgoing e-mail address from within the message in Step 5.

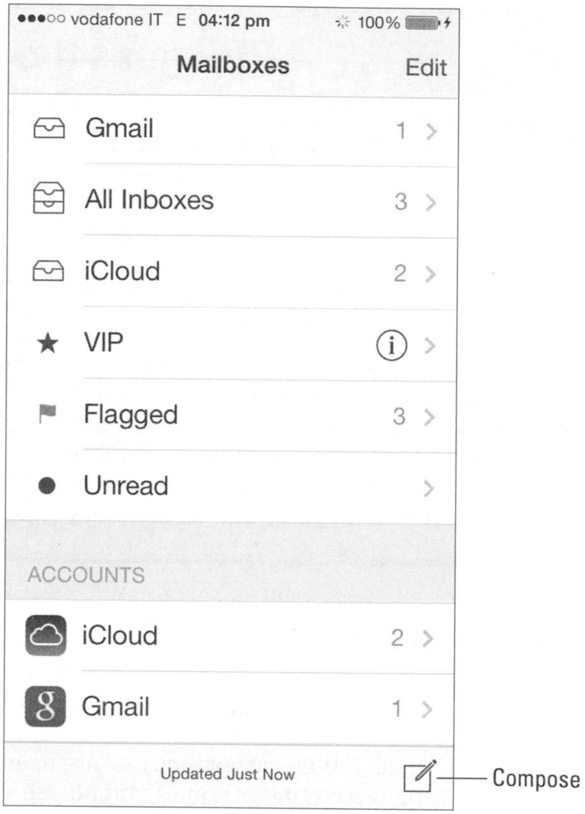

4. In the To field, type the e-mail address of the person you want to send the message to.

●●●○○ vodafone IT E 04:12 pm	⚡ 100% ▬▶⚡	
Mailboxes		**Edit**
🖂 Gmail	1	>
🖂 All Inboxes	3	>
🖂 iCloud	2	>
★ VIP	ⓘ	>
🚩 Flagged	3	>
● Unread		>
ACCOUNTS		
☁ iCloud	2	>
g Gmail	1	>
Updated Just Now	✎	

—— Compose

Figure 4-7: The Mailboxes screen lists the inboxes and accounts on your iPhone.

As you begin typing the recipient's name in the To field, names of people in Contacts or people with whom you recently (or not so recently) exchanged e-mail that contain the same letters show up as a list from which you can choose. Your choices narrow as you type more letters.

Referring to Figure 4-8, the e-mail address is listed under the contact's name and if a contact has more than one e-mail address, his name is listed with each address and the type of address appears to the left.

TIP

Entries with an info button next to them are e-mail addresses that you received messages from or sent to but who aren't in your Contacts. Tap the arrow to show the Recent screen, as in Figure 4-9. From here you can create a new contact, add the e-mail address to an existing contact, or delete the entry from the Recent history — tap the button for the task you want to do.

When you find the name you want, tap it. If you want to add another recipient, repeat the previous step.

To open Contacts and choose the recipients from there, tap the plus sign button on the right of the To field. Contacts opens. Scroll through the list and tap the names of the desired recipients. You can access all your contacts or just specific groups by tapping the Groups button.

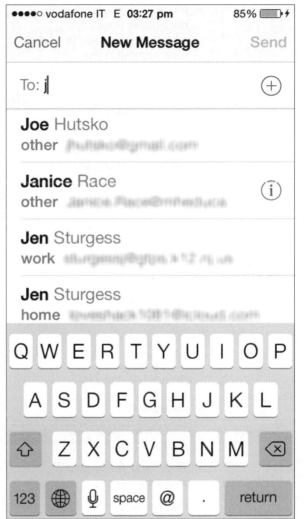

Figure 4-8: Type the first letters of the name of the person you want to send a message to find the e-mail address in Contacts.

5. **If you want to send a Cc — Carbon Copy, or Bcc — Blind Carbon Copy, to other recipients, tap the Cc/Bcc field.**

The field expands into three fields: Cc, Bcc, and From. Fill in the Cc and/ or Bcc fields the same way you fill in the To field.

If you want to change the address from which the message is sent, tap the From field and choose the account you wish the message to be sent from, as seen in Figure 4-10.

6. **When you finish addressing the message, tap Return.**

   The cursor moves to the Subject field.

You can move names from one address field to another, such as from To to Bcc, by touching and dragging them where you want.

7. **Type the subject of the message, and then tap Return or tap directly in the message field.**

   The cursor moves to the message field.

8. **Type your message and then edit it.**

   Double-tap a word to highlight it and activate grabbers. Tap Select to select the word or Select All to select the entire text

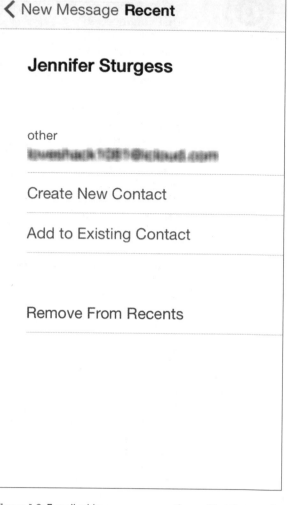

Jennifer Sturgess

other

Create New Contact

Add to Existing Contact

Remove From Recents

Figure 4-9: E-mail addresses you recently used but that aren't in Contacts appear in the list of potential addresses too.

and then, optionally, grab the blue grabbers to highlight the word or words you want to format, and then do the following:

• Tap the Cut, Copy, or Paste buttons if you want to perform those editing actions on your text.

• Tap the arrows on the right or left ends of the button bar to see more options.

- Select just one word, and tap Replace to see a list of alternate spelling corrections or tap Define to see a definition.

- Tap **B/U** to open a button bar with bold, italic, and underline options, which you tap to format the selected text.

- Tap Quote Level to open a button bar that offers an increase (indent) or decrease (outdent) option. Tap the one you want to use.

- Tap Insert Photo or Video to open the Photos app and choose an image or video to attach to your message.

Repeat the process to apply more than one formatting option to the same text or to remove the format. (Refer to Figure 4-11.)

●○○○○ vodafone IT	11:16 am	97% 🔋▸⚡
Cancel	**New Message**	Send

To:

Cc:

Bcc:

From:

Subject:

Figure 4-10: Tap Cc/Bcc to expand the field and type in an additional address or change the From address.

9. **Tap the Send button.**

The word *Sending* appears at the bottom of the screen, and then a blue sending progress bar opens. Faster than you can put a stamp on an envelope, your message is on its way. If you've turned on the Sent Mail alert under Settings⇨Sounds, the sound you chose confirms your message has been sent.

If you're composing a message and have to stop midway, you can save it as a draft. Tap Cancel in the upper left corner, and then tap Save Draft from the buttons that appear on screen. The message goes into your Drafts inbox to be opened later and modified. Tap Delete Draft if you wish to eliminate the message or Cancel to return to the message and continue writing. Tap and hold the New Message button to see a list of Drafts waiting to be completed.

Siri is happy to read as well as compose and send e-mail messages (as long as you use an iPhone 4s or later, Siri is turned on, and you have an adequately robust Internet connection). Press and hold the Home button or bring your iPhone up to your ear and tell Siri who you want to send a message to, and then start dictating. See Book I, Chapter 3 to learn more about Siri. Unfortunately, Siri can't read your messages to you — yet.

Figure 4-11: Format text with in-message editing buttons.

Sending messages from other apps

One of the great things about the Mail app is its flexibility and bandwidth. It's the backbone for sending so much more than just e-mail messages. You can access Photos directly from the message you're composing, which makes inserting photos and videos super easy. You can send a Note directly from Notes, an address or web page link from Maps or Safari, and new media or apps you like from the iTunes and App Stores. The process for each type of object is the same, as we outline here. We mention the pre-loaded apps that came with your iPhone, but other apps often have an action button that allow you to send information from Mail.

1. **Open the app you want from the Home screen.**

2. **Write the note, go to the address, web page, song, or app.**

   In Photos, open the Collection or Album you want, tap Select in the upper right corner, and then tap the photo (or photos) you want to send.

3. **Tap the Action button at the bottom of the page.**

   The Share Sheet opens.

4. **Tap the Mail button.**

   A New Message opens with the cursor is blinking in the To field.

5. **Address the message as explained previously.**

   Type a subject and write something in the message field, if you want.

6. **Tap Send.**

Size matters: Your cellular service provider may have a limit on the file size that you can send across the cellular data network. Likewise, your recipient's e-mail server may restrict the size of incoming messages (usually 5 MB) and your media won't reach its destination.

Giving VIP status

If you send and receive a lot of e-mail, there may be communications with Very Important Persons that you don't want to get lost in the electronic slush pile. Mail lets you identify people and companies to a VIP list so any incoming and outgoing messages exchanged with those VIPs go to a special VIP mailbox. Those messages will still be in the mailbox they were sent to and you'll see a star next to the VIPs name. You can also select a special alert that lets you know when a message has arrived from one of your VIPs. To give someone VIP status:

1. **Tap a message that you sent to or received from the person or business you want to give VIP status to.**

2. **Tap the name in the To or From address field.**

   The screen that opens gives you at least three options: Add to VIP, Create New Contact, Add to Existing Contact. If the person is in your Contacts, the related info screen appears with the various Contacts options (see Book IV, Chapter 1).

3. **Tap Add to VIP.**

**Book III
Chapter 4**

**E-mailing Every
Which Way You Can**

4. **Tap Message in the upper left corner to return to the originating message.**

5. **Tap the back button in the upper left corner or swipe right several times to return to the Mailboxes screen.**

6. **Tap the Info button to the right of the VIP inbox.**

   A list of your VIPs appears, as shown in Figure 4-12.

   If you eventually want to delete a VIP, tap Edit and then tap the red and white minus sign followed by the Delete button, or swipe the person and tap Delete. Tap Done when you finish demoting VIPs.

7. **Tap VIP Alerts to set the alert style, sound, and notification you wish to receive when a VIP sends a message to you.**

8. **Double-tap the Home button and then tap Mail to return to the Mail app.**

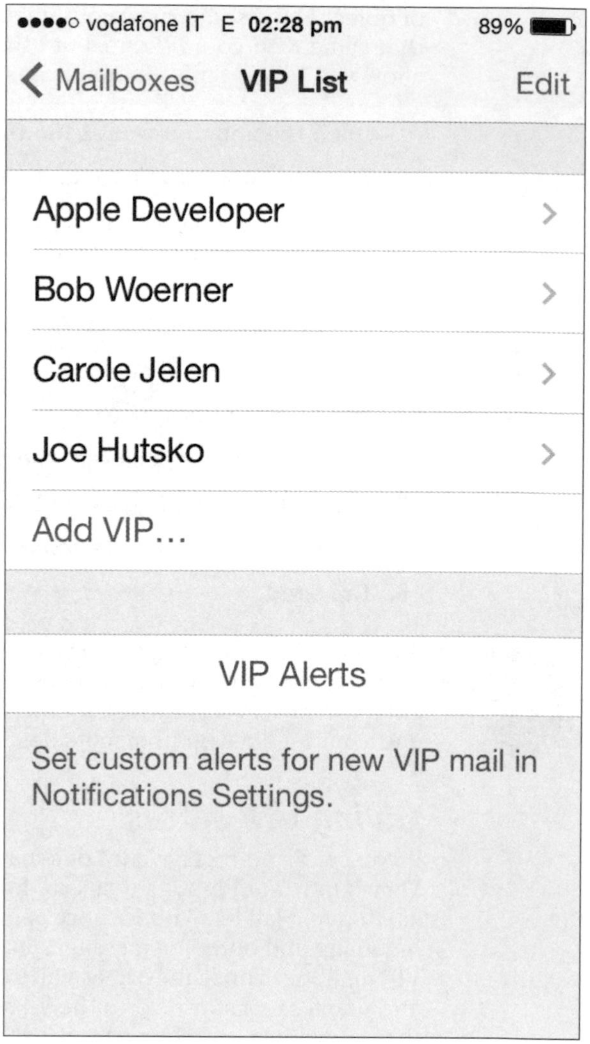

●●●●○ vodafone IT E 02:28 pm	89% ▇▇▇
‹ Mailboxes **VIP List**	Edit
Apple Developer	›
Bob Woerner	›
Carole Jelen	›
Joe Hutsko	›
Add VIP…	
VIP Alerts	
Set custom alerts for new VIP mail in Notifications Settings.	

Figure 4-12: Messages from VIPs get special attention.

To add VIPs directly from Contacts, tap Add VIP on the VIP List screen. Contacts opens and those with e-mail addresses are bold in the list. Tap the name you want to add.

Replying to, forwarding, filing, printing, and deleting messages

iPhone has several ways of letting you know you've received a message. If Badge App Icon is turned on in Settings⇨Notifications⇨Mail, the Mail icon on the Home screen wears a badge showing the number of unread messages you have. If the Notification Center and Alert Styles are selected in Settings⇨Notifications⇨Mail, you are alerted that way. Also, an audible alert plays if you turned on New Mail alerts under Settings⇨Sounds. See Book I, Chapter 4 to learn more about notifications settings.

To refresh your inboxes, drag down from the top of the screen (just below the Status Bar or you'll open the Notifications Center) a spinning gear lets you know Mail is working for you. Mail checks for any new messages. (Refer to the end of the chapter to learn how to adjust the Push and Fetch settings.)

To read your messages, tap Mail on the Home screen. The Mailboxes screen opens. (Refer to Figure 4-7.) To see incoming messages from all of your accounts, tap All Inboxes; to see those from just one account, tap the name of the inbox you wish to view. If you have only one e-mail account on your iPhone, this is the only inbox you'll see.

When you tap the inbox, a list of the messages opens, as shown in Figure 4-13. Here's how to interpret the icons:

- 🡥 Unread messages have a blue dot next to them.

- 🡥 The gray To label indicates that Barbara was a direct recipient of the message.

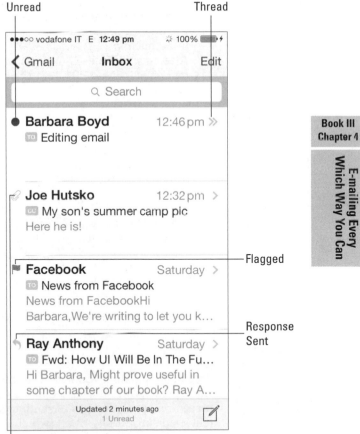

Unread · Thread · Flagged · Response Sent · Attachment

Figure 4-13: Messages are listed in reverse chronological order within a mailbox.

✔ The gray Cc means Barbara received a copy of the message. We explain how to activate this feature in the section, "Adjusting E-Mail Account Settings."

✔ A Flag indicates messages you've flagged.

✔ A double arrow lets you know this message is the most recent in a thread.

✔ The paper clip means the message has attachments. Attachments Mail can open include PDF files, images files such as JPEG, TIFF, PNG, and GIF, and iWork and Microsoft Word, Excel, and PowerPoint files. Tap attachments to download and open them on your iPhone. Tap and hold an image attachment, and then tap Save Image to save it to your Camera Roll.

✔ A star (refer to Figure 4-14) indicates the person is in your VIP list.

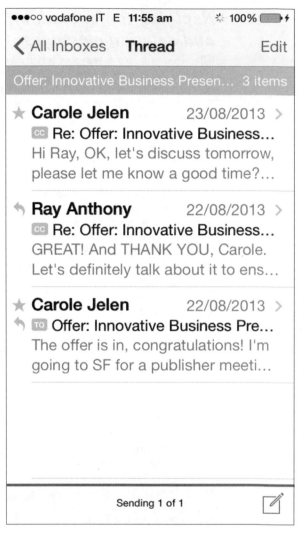

Figure 4-14: Organize by Thread groups related messages together in a sublist.

An e-mail exchange you have with the same subject line, whether with the same person or not, is called a *thread*. A thread is created when you have three or more exchanges of sending and receiving messages. Turning this feature on in Settings⇨Mail (which we get to a bit later in this chapter) puts related messages, the so-called thread, together. In the main message list, as shown in Figure 4-1, you see the most recent message of the thread — a double arrow indicates a thread. Tap that message and you see the thread of messages, as shown in Figure 4-14. The subject and number of items in the thread above the message list; a curved arrow to the left of a message means you responded to that message.

Tap on the message you want to read in either a mailbox or thread, and it opens as in Figure 4-15.

You have several options from the message screen:

- ✔ Tap the up and down triangles in the upper right corner to read the next or previous message.

- ✔ Tap the Flag button to add a colored flag to the message so it stands out in the Inbox message list (refer to Figure 4-13). Here you can also mark a message as unread, in which case the blue dot reappears next to the message in the list, as if you'd never opened it or move it to the Junk file.

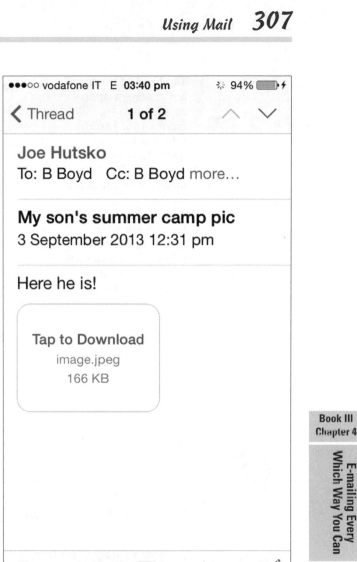

Figure 4-15: A received message.

Mail tucks away information about messages you move to the Junk folder and little by little learns who the offenders are and automatically puts messages into that folder. If you're expecting an e-mail but it doesn't show up in your inbox, check the Junk folder as it may have been erroneously sent there. Swipe the message, tap More, and then tap Not Junk.

Book III
Chapter 4

E-mailing Every
Which Way You Can

✔ Tap the File button, and a screen opens as shown in Figure 4-16. Tap the folder where you want the message to reside. To file the message in a different mailbox, tap Accounts, and then tap the folder to which you want to move the message. If you change your mind, tap Cancel.

✔ Tap the trashcan button to delete your message. Tap one of the two buttons that appear: a Delete Message button and a black Cancel button.

✔ If Archive Messages is on, you won't see a trashcan button. Tap and hold the button for an option to Archive or Trash the message. To enable or disenable the Archive Messages feature in Settings⇨Mail, Contacts, Calendar⇨ *Account Name*.

✔ Tap the Forward button, and then tap one of the following options:

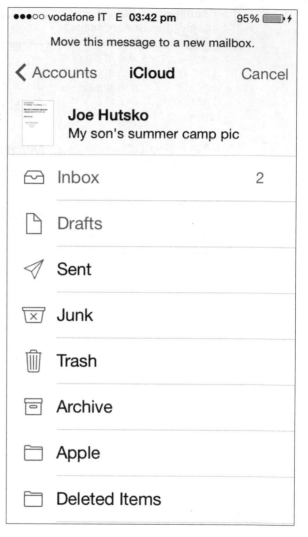

Figure 4-16: Choose the folder where you'd like to file the message.

✔ **Reply:** Tap to reply to the sender of the message. When you finish writing your message, tap Send.

✔ **Reply All (if there are other recipients besides you):** To send a reply to the sender and to all addresses in the To or Cc list, tap this button. When you finish writing your message, tap Send. The entire message is placed in the body of your reply.

If you want to include only a portion of the message you are replying to or forwarding, highlight that portion before tapping the Reply or Forward button.

✔ **Forward:** To forward a copy of the message to someone else, tap the Forward button. If there are attachments, Mail asks you if you want to include the attachments. After you make this choice, the message window opens with the cursor blinking in the To field. Address the message as explained previously. Write something in the message field, and then tap Send. The Re in the subject field changes to Fwd so the recipient knows this is a forwarded message. You can forward any kind of attachment, even those you can't open with iPhone.

✔ **Print:** To print the message, you must have access to an AirPrint-enabled printer. Tap Print, and then tap Select Printer. iPhone looks for available printers. When one is found, you return to the Printer Options screen. Tap the plus sign to print more than one copy, and then tap Print.

✔ **Compose:** The last button on the right is the compose button, which takes you to a New Message screen to write a new message.

Working with multiple messages

You may want to delete multiple messages, move several from the inbox to another folder, or flag a selection of messages or mark them as unread, all at once. Here's the way to do that:

1. **Tap Mail⇨All Inboxes or one of the account-specific inboxes.**

2. **Tap the Edit button in the upper right corner.**

   Empty circles appear to the left of each message.

3. **Tap the circle next to the messages you want to delete, move, or mark.**

   A white check mark in a blue circle appears and the number of messages selected is indicated at the top.

   Notice that although it *appears* only two messages have been selected, the first one is a thread so there are actually six messages selected because all the messages in the thread are selected. Whatever action you take will affect all the messages in the thread.

4. **After you've selected all the messages you want, tap the appropriate button: Mark, Move, or Trash, as shown in Figure 4-17.**

   Tapping Mark lets you flag the messages, in which case a little flag waves next to the message in the message list, or mark them as *unread*, which re-places the blue dot next to the message that indicates unread messages. Repeat the steps to Unflag or Mark as Read messages that are flagged or marked as unread. Tapping Move opens the filing options (refer to Figure 4-16). Tapping Trash, well, that eliminates the selected messages.

5. **You can also swipe on the message in the list to act on it.**

   Tap the More button to see the options as shown in Figure 4-18.

   Tap the Trash button to delete it.

If you swipe a thread, the action affects all messages in the thread. If you want to act on individual messages within a thread, tap the most recent message to open the thread, tap Edit in the upper right corner, and take the same actions as explained previously.

The thing is, just because you tapped Trash, your messages still aren't really deleted. They've been moved to the trash. To truly take out the trash or delete your messages from you iPhone, follow these steps:

1. **Tap the button in the upper left corner or swipe right to return to the Mailboxes list (refer to Figure 4-7).**

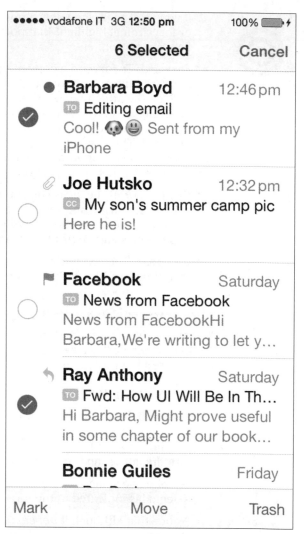

Figure 4-17: Tap Mark, Move, or Trash when managing messages.

2. **Tap the name of the account you want to work with in the Accounts list, not the Inboxes list.**

3. **Tap the Trash button, which looks like a trashcan.**

   If Archiving is on, instead of the trashcan, you see an archival box icon.

4. Tap Edit.

The Delete All button at the bottom of the screen is activated.

5. Tap Delete All.

Your messages are truly deleted.

But wait! What about that Mark All button or the grayed Move button?

1. Follow Steps 1 through 4 above.

2. Tap Mark All to mark all the messages in the list.

Or

Tap in the empty circles to the left of the messages you want to remove from the mark, move to another folder, or delete.

The buttons change to Mark, Move, and Delete.

3. Tap the Move button to put the selected messages in the folder you want or the Mark button to flag, mark the messages as unread, or move to the Junk folder. Tap Delete to delete only the selected messages.

Figure 4-18: To work with one message, or thread, at a time, swipe left.

**Book III
Chapter 4**

E-mailing Every
Which Way You Can

Likewise, you should tap into the Junk folder every now and then, tap Edit and then tap Delete All there too.

Tapping into in-message links

An incoming message contains much more than just the written message. Take a look at these features (refer to Figure 4-15):

∠ Tap the name of the sender or one of the other recipients of the message. A screen opens that gives you an option of creating a new contact or adding this e-mail address to an existing contact (see Figure 4-19).

Tap a sender's name to add that person or company to the VIP list. Any incoming messages from that address automatically go to the VIP inbox so all your most important messages are grouped together.

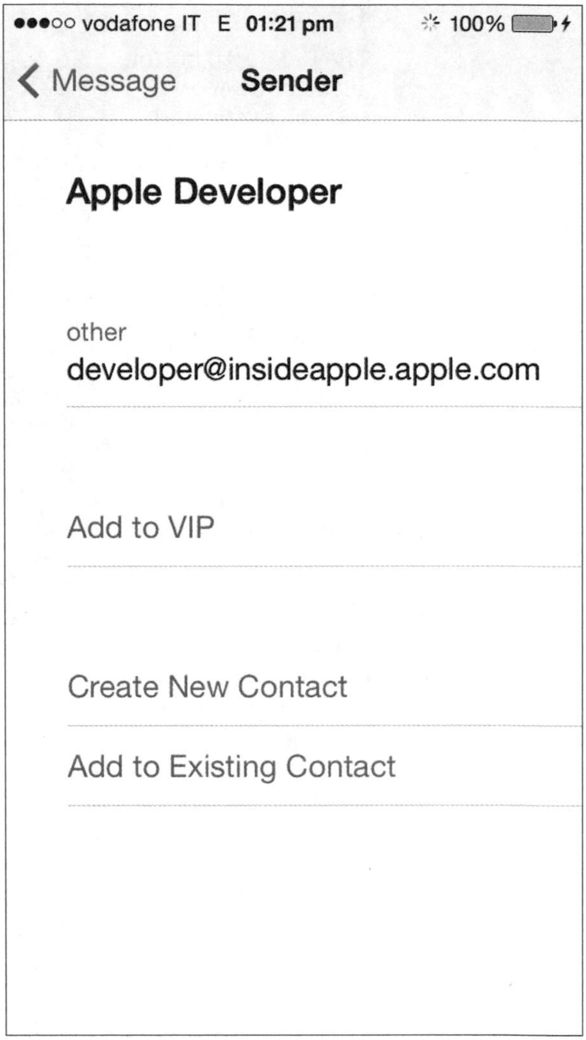

∠ Phone numbers, e-mail addresses, and website addresses that appear blue and underlined are active links. Tap the phone number, and an option of calling that number appears. Tap the e-mail address, and a New Message screen opens. Tap a website address to open the page in Safari.

∠ Tap Hide/more, next to the sender's name, to hide or show the recipients of the message. When there are a lot of recipients, it's helpful to tap Hide so you can see more of the message in the opening screen.

●●●○○ vodafone IT E 01:21 pm   ☀ 100% ▭▸⚡

‹ Message   Sender

Apple Developer

other
developer@insideapple.apple.com

Add to VIP

Create New Contact

Add to Existing Contact

Figure 4-19: The sender's address can be added to Contacts or the VIP list.

✔ If you receive an invitation from a calendar app that uses the iCalendar format, tap on the file and the Event Details open. Tap the Add to Calendar button at the bottom of the screen and then choose the calendar where the event should be inserted. For more details about sending and receiving event invitations, see Book IV, Chapter 2.

✔ Zoom in on the message by spreading two fingers on the screen.

If you follow a link and move from Mail to Safari, you can return to Mail by tapping the Home button twice to open the recent apps bar. Tap the Mail button to return to the open message you were most recently reading.

If you return to the Home screen or flip to another app with multitasking, Mail (or any app for that matter) remains where it was. Say you're reading a message and then remember a phone call you have to make. You finish the call and then tap the Mail button. Mail opens on the message you were reading, not the first Mailboxes screen. To return to the Mailboxes screen, tap the back button in the top left corner of the screen.

Multiple mailboxes

Even if you have only one e-mail account, you may want to see more than what the default Mailboxes list shows you.

When you tap Mail on the Home screen, the first screen that opens shows a list of inboxes and a list of accounts. Your account, or accounts, contain more than just the inbox. Within the account you find folders for Drafts, Sent Messages, and even Junk mail. By default, you have to tap the Account on the Mailboxes list to see those other folders but you can add them to the Mailboxes list, create other folders to group your messages by Unread or Attachments, and rearrange the order you see the mailboxes. Tap the button in the upper left corner until you reach the Mailboxes list and do the following:

1. **Tap Edit.**

   The screen appears like Figure 4-20. Blue circles with white check marks indicate the mailboxes that you see.

2. **Tap an empty circle, such as that next to Unread, to add that mailbox to the Mailboxes list.**

3. **Tap and drag the rearrange button to move a mailbox higher or lower on the list.**

4. **Scroll down to the Add Mailbox option and tap it.**

   If you have multiple accounts, you see a list of your accounts; tap the one you want to work with.

   The list of mailboxes for that account appears.

5. **Tap the mailbox you'd like to see added to the Mailboxes list, Drafts for example.**

6. **Tap Done.**

   You now see that additional mailbox in the list with a check mark next to it.

You can choose All Inboxes to see a chronological list of all the messages you've received. Tap an account-specific inbox and you see a list of messages from that e-mail account only. For example, tap iCloud to see only messages that have been sent to your iCloud address.

Searching messages

There are times when you know who sent you an e-mail, you know it arrived sometime between last Thursday and Friday, you know the subject was something about a train, but you cannot find the message. Thankfully there's Spotlight,

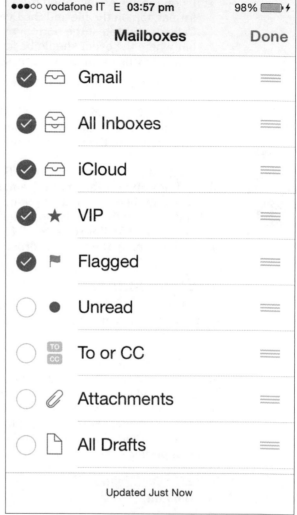

Figure 4-20: Edit the Mailboxes list to see more mailboxes or reorder the list.

iPhone's searching tool that works with Mail, as well as many other apps such as Contacts, Reminders, and Messages. To use Spotlight:

1. **From within a mailbox — it can be All Inboxes, a specific mailbox, or even the Trash box — tap the status bar at the top of the iPhone screen or scroll up until you see the Search field.**

2. **Tap in the Search field.**

3. **Type in the word or phrase you are searching for.**

   Mail searches the address and subject fields as well as content of messages within that mailbox, including the trash and junk files.

4. **Tap the message or messages you want to read from the list that appears.**

Adjusting E-Mail Account Settings

When you set up your e-mail account on iPhone, you've pretty much set up everything you need with regard to the technical information about the account. As with most things iPhone, however, there are many adjustments you can make in Settings to improve and personalize your Mail experience.

First we go through the settings that are specific to the Mail app and affect how your inboxes and messages appear and behave. Then we go through the more technical aspects of managing your e-mail account.

Settings for message presentation

These options have to do with the local management of your messages. Tap Settings⇨Mail, Contacts, Calendars and scroll to see the Mail settings, as shown in Figure 4-21. We explain each one in the following list:

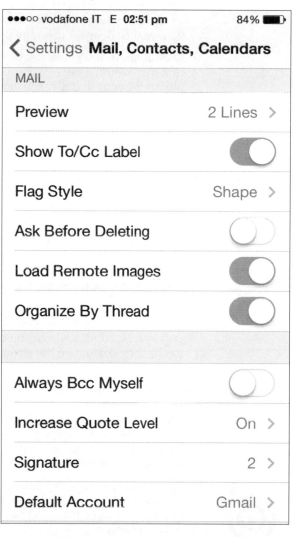

●●●○○ vodafone IT E 02:51 pm 84% 🔋

‹ Settings **Mail, Contacts, Calendars**

MAIL

Preview   2 Lines ›

Show To/Cc Label   ⬤

Flag Style   Shape ›

Ask Before Deleting   ◯

Load Remote Images   ⬤

Organize By Thread   ⬤

Always Bcc Myself   ◯

Increase Quote Level   On ›

Signature   2 ›

Default Account   Gmail ›

Figure 4-21: The Mail settings section of Mail, Contacts, Calendars screen.

Book III
Chapter 4

E-mailing Every
Which Way You Can

✔ **Preview:** Tap this button to choose how many lines of a message you want to see in the list of e-mail messages. You may choose from zero (None) to five lines.

✔ **Show To/Cc Label:** This puts a small label next to the subject line in the list of messages in your inbox. *To* means that the message was sent directly to you; *Cc* means you were sent a copy of the message whose primary recipient was someone else.

✔ **Flag Style:** Tap to choose between a flag icon (shape) or a colored dot.

✔ **Ask Before Deleting:** If you're prone to accidentally tapping the trash-can button when you don't want to, turn this on so that iPhone asks if you want to delete a message before it's actually deleted.

✔ **Load Remote Images:** Remote images reference an image on a web page that Mail would have to access, which gives the hosting site an opportunity to log your activity. You can save cellular time, and increase your privacy, by turning this off, which leaves you the option to manually open the images.

✔ **Organize by Thread:** This turns threading, the grouping of messages with the same subject, on or off.

✔ **Always Bcc Myself:** A Bcc is a blind carbon copy, meaning the recipients of your message don't see this name on the list of recipients, but the person who receives the Bcc sees all the (non-Bcc) recipients. If you turn this switch on, you receive a Bcc of every message you write.

✔ **Increase Quote Level:** Tap this option On and when you respond to a message, the original message will be indented. In an exchange, each time a response is sent, the text is indented more. You can select the text and use the quote level editing tool to manually shift it.

✔ **Signature:** This is the line (or lines) that appears at the end of e-mail messages you write. The default is *Sent from my iPhone*. Tap the button, and a screen opens where you can type a new signature line. Tap Per Account to customize the signature line for each e-mail account you use, as shown in Figure 4-22.

✔ **Default Account:** The default account is used to send messages from other apps, like Maps or Safari. This is also the account your messages will go from if you tap the Compose button on the main Mailboxes screen and don't change the From field in outgoing messages. If you have multiple e-mail accounts, tap this button and choose the account you want to be the default account.

You can't type an active link to your web page, however, you can copy one from Safari and then paste it to your signature so people who receive messages from you can access your website directly from your e-mail message.

Account-specific settings

Some settings are specific to each e-mail account and are represented in a slightly different order for each account, but the titles and functions are the same. You may have to tap through several screens to reach your final destination. For example, tap Settings⇨Mail, Contacts, Calendars⇨iCloud⇨ Account and then Mail in the Advanced section at the bottom of the screen to find the Outgoing Mail Server or Settings⇨Mail, Contacts, Calendars⇨ Gmail⇨Account, and at this level you find the Outgoing Mail Server. On either account, tap the Advanced button beneath Outgoing Mail Server to find other settings, such as Mailbox Behaviors. Any time you see an arrow in the right end of a field, you can tap it to see more information. Here are what the settings you find mean and how you might want to use them.

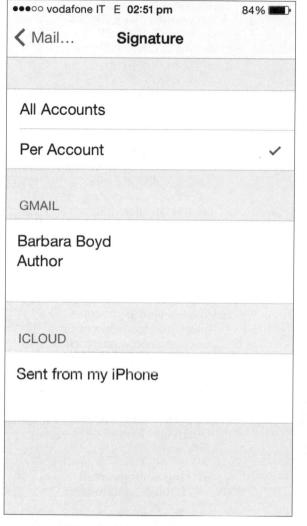

Figure 4-22: Write a custom signature line for your outgoing e-mail messages using the Signature feature.

Outgoing Mail Server

This feature controls which server your mail is sent from. If you have only one e-mail account on your iPhone, leave this alone. You can skip down to the next subheading.

If you have more than one e-mail account on your phone, each one has an assigned outgoing mail server. This is called the Primary Server for that account. You have the option of turning on the outgoing server associated with another e-mail account so that if the primary outgoing mail server of one e-mail account doesn't work, iPhone tries one of the other servers. If you look at Figure 4-23, iCloud uses the iCloud SMTP server to send mail. If that server is down and Barbara's trying to send a message, iPhone uses `smtp.gmail.com` to send it because that server is turned on in the list of Other SMTP servers.

These are the steps for managing your outgoing mail servers. If you have just one e-mail account or use preset accounts such as iCloud or Gmail, you'll probably never need to fuss with these settings. If you have more than one account and set up under Other, take a look to see how it works:

1. **Tap Settings⇨Mail, Contacts, Calendars.**

   The Mail, Contacts, Calendars screen opens.

2. **Tap the name of the account you want to work on under the Accounts list.**

3. **Tap the Account button.**

4. **Tap the SMTP button under Outgoing Mail Server.**

   The SMTP screen opens, and you see which outgoing servers are used for sending your mail. (Refer to Figure 4-23.)

5. **Tap Add Server at the bottom of the list of servers.**

   An Add Server screen opens.

Figure 4-23: If your primary server is down, iPhone attempts to send messages with a secondar server.

6. **Type in the Host Name, for example,** `smpt.verizon.com`. **Then type in your user name and password.**

7. **Tap Save.**

The From address on your e-mail is the one associated with the server that sends the message. For example, if your work server is down and you've set your personal Gmail account as the secondary server, the e-mail is sent from your Gmail account. Your colleagues, clients, or CEO see the e-mail as coming from `hotdiggitydog@gmail.com` rather than `johnsmith@ab4.org`.

Mailbox Behaviors

This setting controls where your draft and sent messages are stored, either on iPhone or on the mail server. Depending on your e-mail service provider, you may also have the option of when the deleted items are ultimately deleted; for example, immediately, a week after they've been removed, or once a month. In iCloud, you have four options for deleting messages from the server:

- **Never:** Messages remain on the server after you've deleted them manually. This means you may access them on another device.

- **After One Day/Week/Month:** Messages are deleted from the server after one day, seven days, or one month, whether you've read them or not.

Gmail only lets you choose where drafts are stored but doesn't let you choose when deleted messages are removed. Other accounts may or may not give you the same choices — you have to poke around in the deeper levels of the settings screens.

Even if your provider lets you manage different mailboxes, the process is the same:

1. **Tap Settings⇨Mail, Contacts, Calendars.**

   The Mail, Contacts, Calendars screen opens.

2. **Tap the name of the account you want to work on.**

3. **Tap the Account button.**

4. **Tap the Advanced button.**

   The Advanced screen opens and is similar to Figure 4-24. There may be fewer (or more) options depending on your service provider.

5. **Tap Drafts Mailbox.**

   This setting controls where your draft messages are kept.

6. **Tap Drafts under On My iPhone if you want to keep your draft messages on your iPhone.**

   A check mark shows up next to Drafts.

**Book III
Chapter 4**

**E-mailing Every
Which Way You Can**

7. **Tap Drafts (or another folder if you want) in the list under On the Server if you want your draft messages to be stored on the server.**

   If you have large draft files, perhaps with multimedia attachments, it may be more convenient to store them on the server so as not to deplete the memory on your iPhone.

8. **Repeat Step 7 for Sent Mailbox and Deleted Mailbox.**

9. **(Optional) Tap Remove under Deleted Messages to set how soon messages are removed from the server after you delete them.**

10. **Tap the button in the upper left corner to return to the previous level. Continue tapping the upper left button until you reach the Settings screen. Tap Done if you see it along the way and have made changes. Press the Home button to go to the Home screen.**

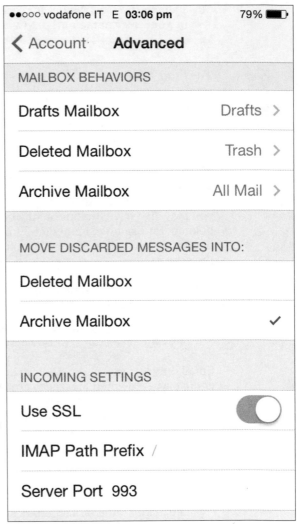

●●○○○ vodafone IT E 03:06 pm   79% 🔋

‹ Account·   **Advanced**

MAILBOX BEHAVIORS

Drafts Mailbox   Drafts ›

Deleted Mailbox   Trash ›

Archive Mailbox   All Mail ›

MOVE DISCARDED MESSAGES INTO:

Deleted Mailbox

Archive Mailbox   ✓

INCOMING SETTINGS

Use SSL   ⬤

IMAP Path Prefix /

Server Port 993

Figure 4-24: The Advanced features allow you to manage where your draft and deleted messages are stored and adjust the pathway for incoming mail.

The S/MIME option, which you may see, lets you add certificates for signing and encrypting outgoing messages. To install certificates, you need a profile from your network administrator or from a certificate issuer's website on Safari or sent to you in an e-mail. If you want to send encrypted e-mail without going through the certificate process, you can download an app like iPGMail in the App Store.

Configure your computer e-mail program to leave messages on the server as well. Go to the Preferences or Tools menu and follow the instructions for your particular e-mail program.

Incoming Settings

The Incoming Settings section (refer to Figure 4-24) gives you limited options for encrypting incoming e-mail and changing the path it comes in on. You probably shouldn't change these settings unless instructed to do so by a technical support person from your cellular provider or a network administrator at your place of employment. In fact, iCloud doesn't even give you the option of changing them because they're preset by Apple. Here, we go through the settings briefly, but remember: You probably don't want to change them.

1. **Tap Settings⇨Mail, Contacts, Calendars.**

2. **Tap the name of the account you want to work on.**

3. **Tap the Account button.**

4. **Tap the Advanced button.**

5. **Turn Use SSL (Secure Sockets Layer) on or off.**

   Ideally, this setting is on as it encrypts incoming messages, making them unreadable to shady types who want to "eavesdrop" on your e-mail conversations.

6. **The last two, IMAP Path Prefix and Server Port, should really be left alone unless you are instructed to change them by a technician.**

7. **Tap the back buttons in the top left corner to return to the Settings screen you want or press the Home button to go to the Home screen.**

Using Push and Fetch

Going back to the Mail, Contacts, Calendars screen, you see a button called Fetch New Data. Think of the Mail app as the dog and your incoming e-mail messages as the ball. The mail server throws — the terminology is *pushes* — your messages and iPhone catches — or downloads — them. Alternatively, the messages are on the server and Mail goes and fetches them when told. Once again, you have the option of turning Fetch and Push on or off. Here's how to activate or deactivate Fetch:

1. **Tap Settings⇨Mail, Contacts, Calendars⇨Fetch New Data.**

   The Fetch New Data screen opens, as seen in Figure 4-25.

2. **Turn Push on and new data is pushed to your iPhone from the server.**

   Whether Mail is open or not, messages arrive in real-time in your mailbox and you hear an audible alert as they arrive, if you've established one.

3. **Set Push or Fetch for each account. Tap the name of an account.**

A screen opens with the schedule options available. iCloud also lets you assign Push to specific mailboxes, such as Inbox or Drafts and the others remain Fetch.

4. **Tap the option you want:**

Push: To automatically retrieve new messages as they arrive in your inbox on the server.

Fetch: To check for messages at the interval you previously established.

Manual: To check for messages only when you open the Mail app or when you drag down below the status bar to refresh your inbox.

5. **Choose a frequency for Fetch. (Scroll down to see your options.)**

If you turn Push off or use an application that doesn't support Push, your iPhone automatically downloads messages at the frequency you chose.

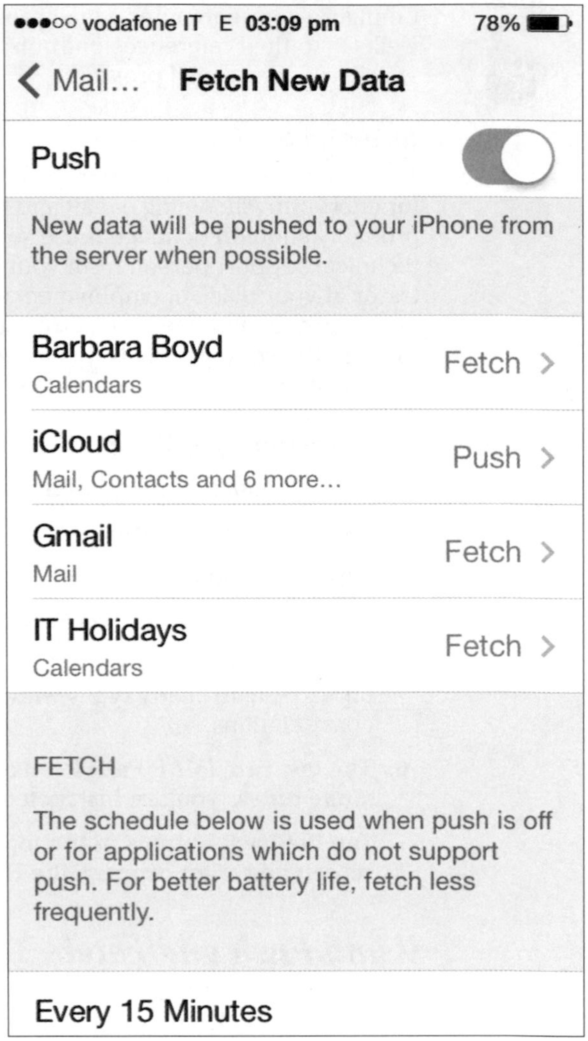

6. **Tap the back buttons in the top left corner or swipe right to return to the Settings screen you want or press the Home button to go to the Home screen.**

●●●○○ vodafone IT E 03:09 pm   78% ▬▬▷

‹ Mail…   Fetch New Data

Push   ⬤▭

New data will be pushed to your iPhone from the server when possible.

Barbara Boyd   Fetch ›
Calendars

iCloud   Push ›
Mail, Contacts and 6 more…

Gmail   Fetch ›
Mail

IT Holidays   Fetch ›
Calendars

FETCH

The schedule below is used when push is off or for applications which do not support push. For better battery life, fetch less frequently.

Every 15 Minutes

Figure 4-25: Fetch New Data lets your iPhone play catch with incoming e-mail messages.

Book IV
Making iPhone Your Personal Assistant

●●●○○ vodafone IT E **02:12 pm**   100% ▮▮▮▮

　　　　　Q Search   Done

Sat 24 Aug
all-day   ~~Rita compleanno~~

Mon 26 Aug
all-day   🎁 Nancy Kelly's 50th Birth...

06:30 pm   Lucy's dental appointment
07:30 pm   Dr. Plack

Tue 27 Aug
all-day   🎁 Lucy Blue's 1st Birthday

Wed 28 Aug
12:30 pm   Lunch with Olive
02:30 pm

Thu 5 Sep
all-day   Rosh Hashanà

Thu 19 Sep
all-day   S. Gennaro

Today   Calendars   Inbox

Contents at a Glance

Chapter 1: Perfecting Your People Skills with Contacts

- ✒ **Adding existing Contacts**
- ✒ **Creating new Contacts**
- ✒ **Accessing friends from social networks**
- ✒ **Viewing Contacts**
- ✒ **Searching Contacts**
- ✒ **Contacting a Contact**

*E*ven if your iPhone is your only device, Contacts is a sort of hub for your iPhone activities. Many of the apps on your iPhone retrieve data from Contacts to perform their functions: Phone accesses Contacts to call a stored phone number or FaceTime address, while Messages and Mail rely on Contacts to send messages to stored mobile phone numbers and e-mail addresses. Contacts use isn't limited to communication apps; for example, both Calendar and Reminders access Contacts for information about people or places with whom you have appointments. Third-party apps may use the information in Contacts, too.

If you already have an iPhone-compatible electronic address book, one of the first things you'll want to do is transfer the data to your iPhone by syncing your iPhone and your computer. We begin this chapter by explaining how to sync your existing electronic address book with Contacts on your iPhone. We discuss syncing in Book II, Chapter 1, but we go through the specifics for Contacts here. We then explain the editing procedures for a single contact: adding a new contact, making changes, even deleting a contact. We show you how to search for a contact, too. We conclude this chapter with the interactive aspects of Contacts, including adding your Twitter and Facebook friends to Contacts, sharing your contacts with someone else, and communicating with your contacts via phone, FaceTime, e-mail, and text messages.

Adding Existing Contacts

You probably have some form of electronic address book on your computer or another device such as a tablet, you may also access a company directory through Microsoft Exchange or IBM Lotus Notes. If you don't — or if you prefer to keep contacts on your iPhone separate — skip over this section and go directly to the section Creating New Contacts, in which case you create your address book in the Contacts app on your iPhone. Your existing contacts could be in one or more of the following places:

- On your Mac in Contacts, Address Book, Entourage, or Outlook.

- On your PC in Microsoft Outlook, Windows Address Book, or Windows Contacts.

- Online in Microsoft Exchange, Yahoo!, Google or a social network such as Facebook or LinkedIn.

- On the SIM card of a previous cell phone (refer to the sidebar at the end of this section).

To transfer your contacts from an old iPhone to a new iPhone simply sign in to your iCloud, Gmail, Yahoo!, or Exchange account on the new iPhone. With the exception of iCloud, this holds true if you're migrating from another smartphone that uses Android. Your new iPhone accesses anything you already have saved to any of those accounts automatically. In this section, we explain how to sign in to these different applications on your iPhone. We also give specific steps for imports from Microsoft Exchange, Google, Yahoo!, LDAP or CardDAV formatted data, and a SIM card. At the end of this chapter, we explain adding contact information from incoming phone calls, voicemail, messages, and vCards attached to e-mail.

If you use IBM Lotus, you can use IBM Sametime, Lotus Notes Traveler, or a third-party contact management app such as DejaOffice (`www.dejaoffice.com`) to sync your contacts to your iPhone. Consult with your network administrator for the necessary passcodes.

If you use Windows, you can sync with just one application. On a Macintosh, you can sync with multiple applications.

Accessing your contacts from iCloud

We explain how to set up an iCloud account in Book II, Chapter 1. Essentially, iCloud stores your data, such as contacts, calendar information, your iTunes media library, photos, and documents on a remote server — called a *cloud* — that pushes data updates to your iPhone and any other computers or devices with iOS 5 or later you have associated with your iCloud account. To sync Contacts on your iPhone with your computer and other iOS devices via iCloud, do the following:

1. **Tap Settings⇨ iCloud.**

2. **Tap Contacts ON, as shown in Figure 1-1.**

   If your screen doesn't look like Figure 1-1, go to Book II, Chapter 1 to set up an iCloud account.

   Any changes you make in Contacts on your iPhone or on other devices associated with iCloud, such as your computer, iPad, or iPod touch, are automatically pushed to all devices. You will never have conflicting information again!

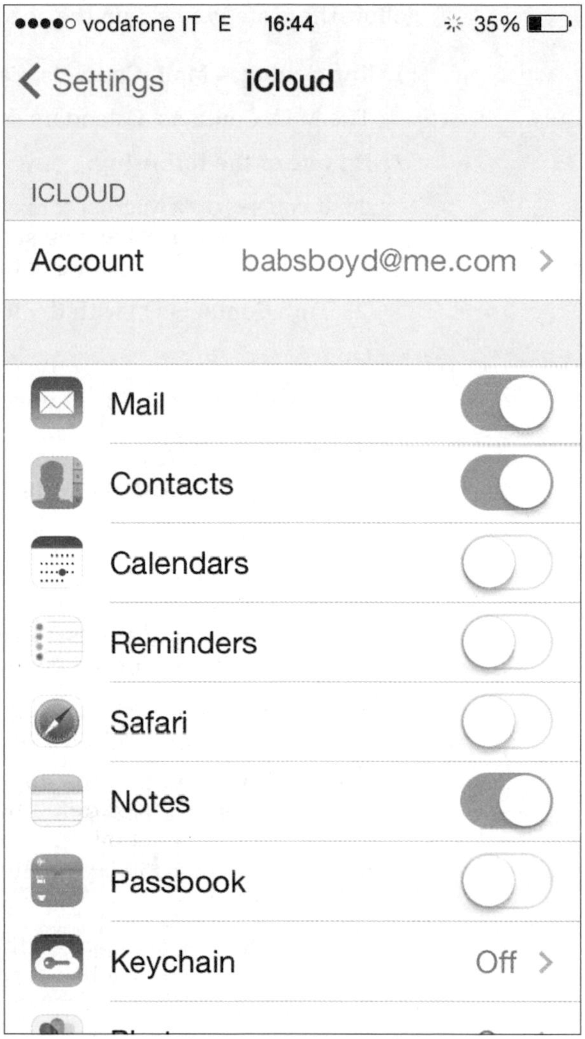

   TIP If you want to use iCloud with your Windows PC, download the iCloud Control Panel for Windows app from Apple (www.apple.com/icloud/setup/pc.html).

Figure 1-1: Turn Contacts On in iCloud to automatically sync Contacts on your iPhone with other devices using iCloud.

Adding and syncing Microsoft Exchange contacts

Particularly in a corporate setting, some of your contacts, such as the company directory, may be in Microsoft Exchange. As long as the technical support folks in your office will give you the access information, you can sync the contacts from Microsoft Exchange with your iPhone. Microsoft Exchange uses over the air (or OTA) syncing to import and exchange information between the Contacts app on your iPhone and the contact data stored in the Microsoft Exchange cloud.

Follow these steps to set up the account on your iPhone:

1. **Tap Settings⇨Mail, Contacts, Calendars.**

   The Mail, Contacts, Calendars screen opens.

2. **Do one of the following:**

   1. If you set up a Microsoft Exchange account when you first set up your iPhone or when you set up e-mail as explained in Book III, Chapter 4, tap the name of that account in the list that appears.

   2. Turn Contacts On with the toggle switch in the account screen.

   Or

   1. Tap Add Account to set up a new account.

   2. Tap Exchange.

   3. Fill in the requested information.

   4. Tap Next.

      After the information you entered is verified, you'll be asked to turn on a series of switches to establish which types of things you want to sync. Turn on Contacts. (Turn on the others such as Mail, Calendars, Bookmarks, or Notes if you want to sync those with Exchange.)

   You now see Microsoft Exchange in the list of accounts on the Mail, Contacts, Calendars settings screen.

3. **Tap the Save button in the upper right corner and you return to the Mail, Contacts, Calendars settings screen.**

4. **Tap Fetch New Data.**

5. **Tap Push On.**

   Anytime changes are made to the contacts on the server now associated with your Microsoft Exchange account, those changes are pushed to your iPhone.

6. **If your server doesn't support push, or you want to conserve battery power, select a default fetch interval — every 15 or 30 minutes, or hourly.**

   Your iPhone contacts the server for new data at the interval you select.

Importing Google, Yahoo!, AOL, and Outlook contacts

Apple has made importing your contacts from the most frequently used e-mail service providers simple. By configuring your iPhone to recognize your account from one or more of these providers, you can access the contact information you store with them. And, you can have more than one account. For example, if you use Google for your personal contacts but

Outlook for work, you can have both on your iPhone. Later in this chapter we explain how to manage several accounts in Contacts. To set up an account for one of these providers on your iPhone, follow these steps:

1. **Tap Settings on the Home screen, and then tap Mail, Contacts, Calendars.**

2. **Tap Add Account.**

3. **Tap the name of the service provider you use — Google, Yahoo!, AOL, or Outlook.com — on the Add Account screen.**

   If your service provider is not one of those listed, for example Comcast or Verizon, tap Other, and then tap Add Mail Account. A New Account screen appears where you can type in your e-mail address and password, and then tap Next. Your iPhone will search the Internet for that service provider and set up an account for you. It's almost like magic!

4. **The Add Account screen opens.**

   Filling in the Name field is optional. Type in your e-mail address in the Address field and your password in the Password field. An identifier is automatically entered in the Description field; however, you can tap and hold on the text to replace it with something that helps you remember the account, such as "work" or "golf team."

5. **Tap the Next button in the upper right corner.**

   The next screen shows a list of available services.

6. **Tap the Contacts switch On.**

Some services, such as Yahoo!, store your address book on a remote server, so you have to have an Internet connection to access it.

If you use iCloud, changes are synced automatically and a backup is created when your iPhone is connected to a power source, to the Internet via Wi-Fi, and in sleep mode.

Configuring LDAP or CardDAV contacts accounts

LDAP (Lightweight Directory Access Protocol) and CardDAV (Card Distributing Authoring and Versioning) are Internet protocols that allow access to data on a remote server. Multiple users can access the same information, so it is often used in business and organization settings. The difference between the two is that LDAP data remains on the server — you access it from your iPhone via an Internet connection, but it isn't synced to your iPhone. CardDAV data is synced over the air (and copied) to your iPhone, and, depending on the way the server is set up, you may be able to search the server for contact information.

If your employer uses a contacts program that uses the LDAP or CardDAV formats, which you want to access or sync with your iPhone, you can add an

LDAP or CardDAV account. You'll need some account information from your IT department or network support person:

- ✔ **Server:** This has your company or organization information.
- ✔ **User Name:** This is your identification.
- ✔ **Password:** A password is required.
- ✔ **Description:** This name shows up on the list of accounts on the Mail, Contacts, Calendars settings screen.

After you've gathered the necessary information, set up the account on your iPhone by following these steps:

1. **Tap Settings⇨Mail, Contacts, Calendars.**

2. **Tap Add Account.**

3. **Tap Other.**

4. **In the Contacts section, tap Add LDAP or Add CardDAV Account, whichever is indicated.**

5. **Type in the information requested.**

6. **Tap the Next button in the upper right corner.**

   After your account information is verified, make sure Contacts is turned On, and the contacts data are added to your iPhone.

7. **Tap the Save button in the upper right corner and you return to the Mail, Contacts, Calendars settings screen.**

   When you open Contacts, your contacts are automatically synced.

8. **Tap Fetch New Data.**

   The Fetch New Data screen opens.

9. **If your server supports push notifications, Tap Push On.**

   Anytime changes are made on the server where the contacts reside, that change is pushed to your iPhone, and vice versa.

10. **If your server doesn't support push or you want to conserve battery power, select a default fetch interval — every 15 minutes, every 30 minutes, or hourly.**

    Your iPhone contacts the server for new data at the interval you select.

 If your contacts are in another program, you can try exporting them as vCards (the file will have a .vcf suffix) and then importing them into Address Book (OS X 10.7 or earlier), Contacts (OS X 10.8 or later), or Entourage or Outlook 2011 on the Mac or Outlook or Windows Address Book on a Windows PC. Follow the previously outlined procedure for syncing.

Copying SIM card contacts the SIM-ple and not-so-SIM-ple way

Although your iPhone doesn't store information on the SIM card, if you are transferring to iPhone from another cellular phone, you may have contact information on the old SIM card that you want to transfer.

If your old device is an Android or other non-iPhone smartphone that uses a micro SIM card, you can typically pop out your new iPhone 4 or 4s's micro-SIM and pop in your old one to copy those contacts to your new iPhone. (Go to Settings⇨Mail, Contacts, Calendars⇨Import SIM Contacts.) Ditto if your old device uses a nano-SIM card and you're moving to a new iPhone 5 or later, which also uses a nano-SIM card.

If your old phone's SIM card isn't the same type of SIM card in your new iPhone — regardless of iPhone model — you may still be able to copy any contacts from your old smartphone by connecting it to your computer and using special data export software that may either come with your old phone, or is available to download from the phone manufacturer's website, or by using a third-party smartphone data transfer program. Check your smartphone's manual or search the manufacturer's support site to see if they offer a software application you can download to export your contacts from your old phone so you can copy them to your new iPhone.

A DIY solution for making your too-big micro-SIM fit in your much smaller nano-SIM slot is to carefully cut the micro-SIM down to nano-SIM size. Search Google on those terms, and you'll turn up a slew of how-to videos on how to do exactly that.

Another option: Check out the nifty third-party program PhoneView for Mac (www.ecamm.com), which offers super-simple drag-and-drop backing up and transferring of contacts (and all sorts of other iPhone data) between old iPhones and new iPhones, and even between iPhones and iPads (handy for transferring your Angry Birds progress between iOS devices so you don't have to replay all those levels you already beat).

Adding your social network contacts

Both Twitter and Facebook have been integrated since iOS 6 and Flickr and Vimeo have been added in iOS 7. Instead of opening the profile of each member of your high school class to copy and retype their e-mail addresses and phone numbers, with just a few taps, you can import the information to Contacts directly from any of these social networks. Follow these steps:

1. **Tap Settings⇨Facebook/Twitter/Flickr/Vimeo.**

   The appropriate settings screen opens.

   If you don't have the app installed, tap the Install button to download it from the iTunes Store.

2. **Tap in the User Name field and type in your user name.**

3. **Tap in the Password field and type in your password.**

4. Tap Sign In.

A disclaimer appears that explains what happens on your iPhone when you sign in to the social network. Essentially, information about your friends will be downloaded to Contacts; events will sync to your Calendar; you can post status updates and images directly from the Photos app; and apps enabled to work with your account have your permission to do so.

5. Tap Sign In again to accept these conditions. You can change the settings after you sign in if you don't want these things to happen.

6. The settings screen reappears with Calendar and Contacts options, as shown in Figure 1-2.

The apps enabled to work with your account are listed as well, and you can tap the switch to turn access on or off. (Refer to Figure 1-2.)

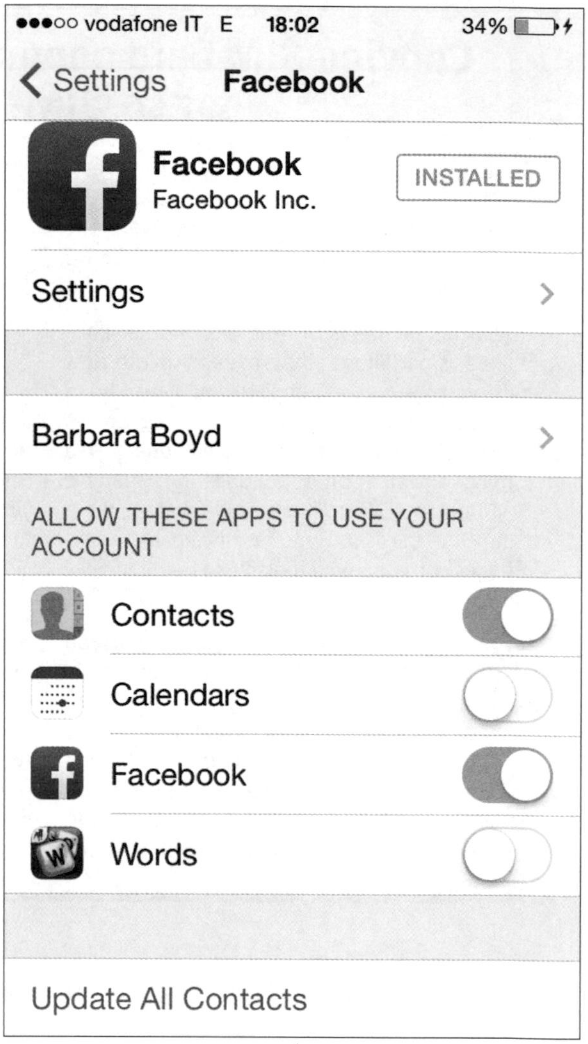

7. Tap Contacts On.

8. Tap Update All Contacts to provide Facebook with information from your Contacts, which allows it to update matching contacts.

●●●○○ vodafone IT E   18:02   34% ☐ᐅ⚡

‹ Settings   **Facebook**

Facebook   INSTALLED
Facebook Inc.

Settings   ›

Barbara Boyd   ›

ALLOW THESE APPS TO USE YOUR
ACCOUNT

Contacts   ⬤

Calendars   ◯

Facebook   ⬤

Words   ◯

Update All Contacts

Figure 1-2: Turn Contacts on in Facebook settings to see your Facebook friends in Contacts.

Unifying contacts

When you import or access contacts from different sources, you may find you have more than one information record for the same contact. Contacts links contacts that have the same name, and creates a unified contact. A unified contact doesn't merge the information but does display all the information for one person on one record. If the names aren't exactly the same, two records appear but you can manually link contacts and change which one is the top unified contact by doing the following:

1. Tap a contact that has more than one record, and then tap Edit.

2. Tap the Link Contact field at the bottom of the Info screen.

   Your list of contacts opens.

3. Tap the name of the contact you want to link to the first contact.

4. Tap the Link button in the upper right corner.

5. Tap Done.

6. To unlink contacts, tap Edit, and then tap the minus sign next to the source you want to unlink.

You can link two or more contacts with the same name or with different names, such as a personal card and a company card or two partners at the same business, but when you link two or more contacts, only the primary contact appears in the Contacts list and the linked contacts are listed on the contact they've been linked to. To use a different name for the unified card, tap the name you want to use and then tap the button that reads Use This Name for Unified Card. The names on the individual contact records don't change but the unified card shows the name you selected.

If you make changes to one record, that information syncs with the source it came from, but doesn't change on records from other sources. This means if you change the e-mail on a contact in Google, the information is updated on the Google server and on your devices that access the Google server, but it isn't changed on the record that comes from Facebook.

Creating New Contacts

When you're out and about, chances are you'll add new friends, colleagues, and acquaintances to Contacts on your iPhone. If you use iCloud, the new information syncs automatically to your computer and other iOS devices you use with iCloud. Contacts stores much more than just names, addresses, and phone numbers. You can add a photo of the person, a birthday or anniversary — which nicely links to Calendar — e-mail addresses, websites, and whatever kind of field you want to invent, like favorite color or namesake holiday date. In this section, we show you how to create new contacts, fill in the contact info with everything you know about the person, make changes, and, well, delete them if things go bad in the relationship, for whatever reason.

Book IV
Chapter 1

Perfecting Your
People Skills with
Contacts

Filling in name, address, phone number, and more

Follow these steps to fill in basic information about your contacts:

1. **Tap Contacts on the Home screen or in the Dock within the Phone app.**

   1. If you want the new contact to be part of a group, tap the Group button at the top of the screen. You won't see this button if you don't have any groups.

   2. Deselect all but the group you want the new contact to be part of. You can only add to a group that resides on your iPhone not a remote group such as Facebook.

      A check mark indicates which group is active, as shown in Figure 1-3. Even if you add a contact to a group, it is part of both All Contacts.

   3. Tap Done.

Despite the outcry of many Contacts users, Apple has still not added a create groups function within the iOS Contacts app. Groups you create in other contact management apps that you access from Contacts are reflected. If you use iCloud, you can sign in to www. icloud.com from a computer, sign in to your account, click Contacts, and create groups there.

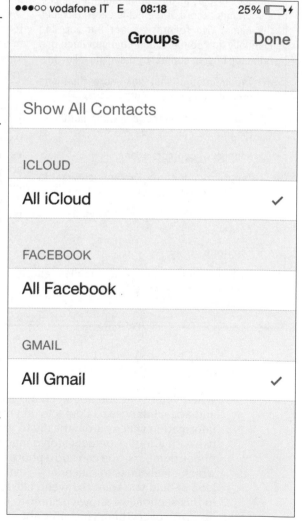

Figure 1-3: The Groups screen lets you choose which contacts you want to view and where to add new contacts.

2. **Tap the plus sign in the upper right corner.**

   A New Contact screen opens.

3. **Tap in the field that reads First.**

   The cursor appears in that field and the keyboard opens.

4. **Type in the first name of your new contact.**

   Not all contacts have first and last names and you are not obligated to fill in any field that you don't have information for. If you just have the name and phone number of a company, you can fill in only those fields.

5. **Tap Return to move from one field to the next.**

   Continue typing in the information you have for your contact.

If you have contacts from more than one account, for example a Microsoft Exchange account as well as contacts on your iPhone, select the default account where new contacts will be saved by tapping Settings➪Mail, Contacts, Calendar and then tap Default Account in the Contacts section. Tap the account you want to use or On My iPhone to automatically place new contacts on your iPhone.

The following sections describe fields that have specific functions.

Phone, E-mail, and URL fields

The Phone, E-mail, and URL fields behave the same way, but their behavior may seem a bit peculiar at first. Here we give you a few tips to help you understand them:

- ✔ As soon as you begin typing in the first field, say, phone number, a minus sign appears to the left and a new field is added beneath it. You can type a second phone number in this new field. As soon as you begin typing in the second phone number field, a third one appears. This happens with the Phone, E-mail, and URL fields. Don't worry: Those empty fields won't clutter up the final view of your contact's info screen. You only see the blank field in Create or Edit mode.

- ✔ Notice that there's a line between the field name and the empty field for Phone, E-mail, and URL. You can change the field name of these fields by tapping on the field name to the left of the line. A Label list opens. Click the label you want to associate with the phone number, e-mail, or URL that you type in the adjacent field.

- ✔ Scroll down to the bottom of the Label list and you see Add Custom Label. Tap this and you can enter a label of your own for the field.

You can memorize a phone number with an extension so when you dial from Contacts you don't have to enter the extension. Type the phone number, tap the +*# button, and then tap Pause. The keypad returns and you can type the extension. When you tap Done, a comma appears between the phone number and extension. You can add more than one pause if the system needs more time between dialing the number and typing the extension. If you tap Wait and enter the extension, when you make the call, you have to tap Dial again at the appropriate time after the initial call is made and the extension will then be dialed.

Ringtone, Vibration, and Text Tone fields

You can assign a special sound or vibration so that when a contact calls or sends a text message, you know by the sound who is calling or who the message is from:

- **Tap Ringtone.** A list opens from which you choose the ringtone you want to hear when that contact calls.

- **Tap Text Tone.** A list opens to choose the sound you hear when that contact sends you a text message. Tap Buy More Tones to access the ringtone section of the iTunes Store and download tones that can be used for ringtones or text tones.

- **Tap Vibration.** A list gives you options for the vibration you want associated with a text message that arrives from that contact. Click Create New Vibration to record your own custom vibration.

You can only have one of each per contact. You can't assign a different ringtone, text tone, or vibration for each number associated with a contact.

Add Address

You can tell how little importance is given to our physical addresses anymore. This field is at the bottom of the list like a rarely used option. To add an address, tap the plus sign to the left of the field or in the blank field. The field expands as shown in Figure 1-4. Type in the address.

Here, too, as soon as you begin typing a second field opens, so you can add a second address. And, tapping on the field name to the left, you can change the field name so it reflects which address it's associated with, like work or home or even a custom field, like cabin or boat slip.

Tap an address in Contacts, and Maps opens to show the location. See Book IV, Chapter 3 for more information about Maps.

Birthday and Date fields

The neat thing about Contacts is that it not only manages information about *how* or *where* to contact someone but also information *about* the person, like a birthday or other important date. If you link your Facebook friends to Contacts, information from their profiles flows into Contacts. This information can also be accessed by Calendar so you don't forget to call, or send a dozen roses, on the important date.

- **Birthday:** Tap birthday and a rotor opens, as shown in Figure 1-5, so you can choose the month, day, and year of the contact's birth date. A birthday that is added to a contact appears in Calendar if you activate the Birthday calendar. Read more about Calendar in Book IV, Chapter 2.

- ✔ **Date:** The first field name that comes up is Anniversary for this field, after which you can add as many other important dates related to this contact as you want. Use the rotor to put in the date you want. Like the Phone, E-mail, URL, and Address fields, as soon as you add this field, a blank one appears beneath it. You can also edit the name of the field by tapping on it and choosing other or adding a custom label.

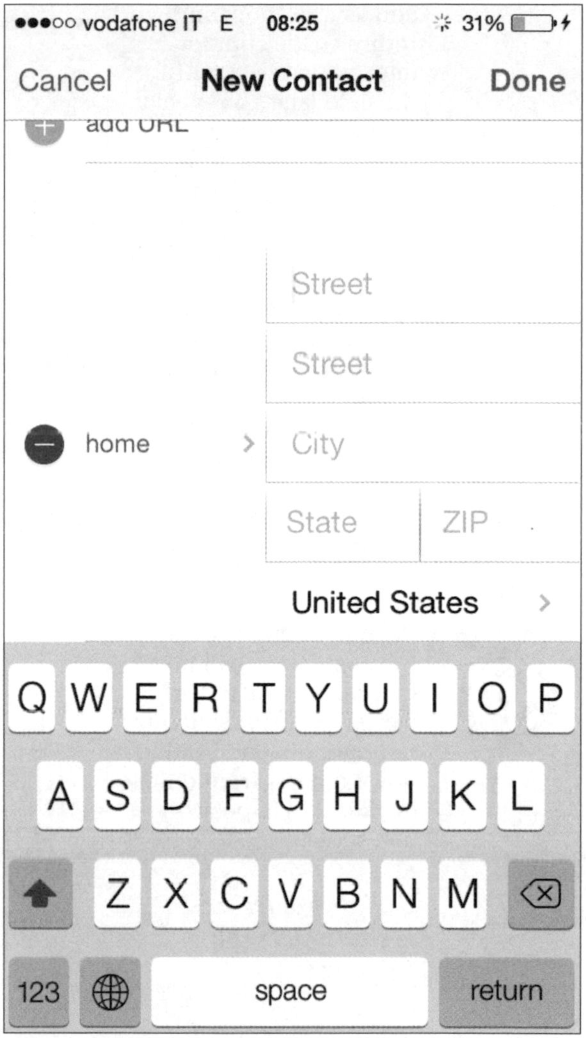

Add Related Name

This is one of our favorite features of Contacts. For example, before this feature was added, Barbara would create a custom field for the phone number of a colleague's secretary and add him to the contact info of the colleague. You can imagine the confusion this caused, not to mention the ever-growing list of custom fields. Now, she creates a separate contact for the secretary and then links it to the known colleague. If she can't remember the secretary's name, she can go to the colleague's contact and access the relationship. This is also a great tool for linking spouses or parents and children.

Figure 1-4: The Add Address field expands so you can type in the street address, city, state, ZIP, and country.

To add people who are related to the Contact, such as parent, spouse, sibling, partner, assistant, or manager, tap Add Related Name, and then tap the Info button on the right. The Contacts list opens; tap the name you want to add as a relation, and you return to the contact information screen. Tap the field label to reveal a list of choices for the type of relation, and tap the appropriate one.

If you want to cancel the relation, tap Edit in the upper right corner. Tap the minus sign that appears to the left of the relation, and then tap Delete, which appears on the right. This action only deletes the relation between the two contacts; it doesn't delete any contacts.

 Related Names are not the same thing as Linked Contacts. Refer to the earlier sidebar, "Unifying Contacts" to understand how contacts from different sources appear on one screen.

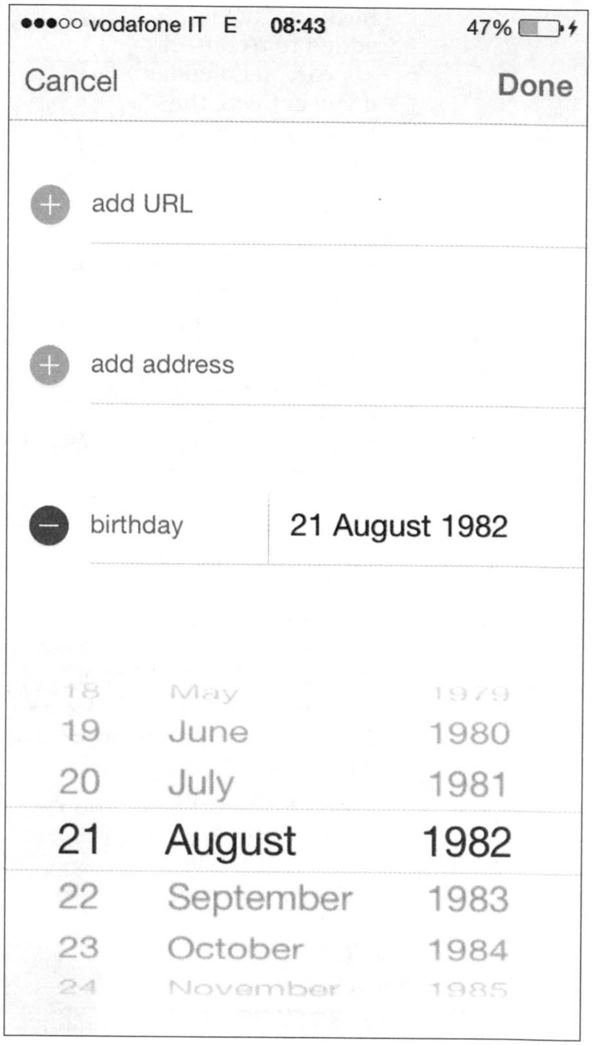

Social Profiles and Instant Message Addresses

If you allowed Contacts to access information from your social network accounts (in Settings⇨ Twitter/Facebook/Flickr/ Vimeo), this information is automatically added to Contacts. If you want to limit promiscuous sharing between Contacts and your social networks or your friends have set up their social network accounts to not share this information, you can manually add multiple social network profile user names to each contact. Tap Add Social Profile, and then tap the field label to the left to choose which social network you want; Twitter, Facebook, Flickr, LinkedIn, Myspace, Sina Weibo, or a custom service. After tapping the service, the Info screen re-opens. Tap the Social Profile field to the right and type in the profile name.

••••○○ vodafone IT E	08:43	47% ⬛▸⚡

Cancel   Done

⊕ add URL

⊕ add address

⊖ birthday   **21 August 1982**

18	May	1979
19	June	1980
20	July	1981
21	**August**	**1982**
22	September	1983
23	October	1984
24	November	1985

Figure 1-5: Use the rotor to set your contact's birthday.

Likewise, you can enter instant message addresses for services such as Skype or MSN Messenger. Tap Add Instant Message, and then tap the service field on the left to reveal a list of ten IM services plus an option to add a custom service. Tap the service you use to instant message with this contact. After tapping the service, the Info screen re-opens. Tap the Instant Message field to the right and type in the contact's IM address.

Notes

The Notes field is a catchall for additional information you want to keep about a contact. Tap the field and the keyboard appears so you can type, or dictate if you use Siri. Here are a few ways that we use this field:

- Business hours
- Club membership numbers for airlines
- Favorite wines or dishes at restaurants
- Tags that are used to create groups in Contacts on the Mac

Add Field

The last field provides options related to the name of the contact. Tap Add Field and the list of field options opens. After one of the options is used, it no longer appears in the Add Field options list.

- **Prefix:** Adds a field before first name where you can type in a title such as Mr. or Princess.
- **Phonetic First Name, Phonetic Middle Name, and Phonetic Last Name:** Are inserted immediately after the First, Middle (if added), or Last name fields so you can type in a phonetic spelling of the names that are pronounced differently than they are spelled.
- **Middle:** Adds a field between the First and Last for a middle name.
- **Suffix:** To add common suffixes like M.D. or Jr.
- **Nickname:** Comes right before company.
- **Job Title and Department:** Are inserted before Company.

Create a New Contact for yourself including your own related people and then specify which is your card by going to Settings⇨Mail, Contacts, Calendars⇨My Info, which opens Contacts. Choose the contact you created for yourself. The My Info card is used by Siri, Reminders, and other apps to understand commands like "Remind me upon arriving Home" or "Call my sister." Specify the My Info card for Siri by going to Settings⇨General⇨Siri⇨My Info.

Each time you add a custom label, that label is added to the list beneath whatever options Contacts gives you for that field. If you add a lot of custom labels, the Add Custom Label button is all the way at the bottom — just scroll down to find it. You can delete custom labels from the list by tapping the Edit button. Tap the minus sign that appears next to the label you want to delete, and then tap the Delete button. If the custom label was being used on a contact, it will be replaced by a generic label.

Adding photos

The first thing you see on the New Contact screen is a field in the upper left corner called Add Photo. This lets you add a photo of the contact and when a call comes in from any of the phone numbers of that contact, the photo appears on your Home screen. You have three ways to add photos:

✔ **From Social Networks:** If you give Facebook, Twitter, or one of the other social networks access to contacts, the profile photo for your contact is automatically added to the contact info.

✔ **Tap Add Photo:** A dialog appears, which gives you the option to take a photo or choose an existing photo.

- **Tap Take Photo:** The Camera app opens. Book V, Chapter 1 talks all about the Camera, but here's a quick rundown.

  1. Aim the camera at the subject you want to photograph, and tap the Switch Camera button if you see yourself instead of your subject. When you're satisfied, tap the white camera button.

  2. If you like the shot, you can resize it by pinching or spreading your fingers on the image and drag to move it to a pleasing position.

  3. If it's just not right, tap Retake, and try again. Refer to Figure 1-6.

  4. When you like the result, tap Use Photo.

  You see the photo you took in the photo field on the Contact Info screen.

  Or

- **Tap Choose Photo.**

  The Photos app opens.

  1. Tap the album where the photo you want to use is stored.

  2. Tap the photo you want to use.

  3. Move and scale as explained in Step 2 previously.

  4. When you like the photo, tap Choose.

     The photo is saved to the New Contact screen.

The data in Contacts in the Phone app is the same data as in the Contacts app — just two ways to reach the same information.

Adding contacts from phone calls and messages

If you receive or initiate a phone call, text message, or e-mail from a number or address that isn't in Contacts, you may want to add that information to an existing contact or create a new contact. Here's how:

1. **After you finish a conversation, tap Phone⇨Recents.**

   A list of recent incoming and outgoing calls appears.

2. **Tap the Info button to the right of the number you want to add, it can be from a call you received or one you initiated.**

   An Info screen opens, as shown in Figure 1-7.

3. **Tap Create New Contact.**

   A New Contact screen opens. Type in the information you have and select a special ringtone if you want.

   Or

4. **Tap Add to Existing Contact.**

   The Contacts screen opens.

5. **Search for the contact you want to add the number to and add the number in the appropriate field.**

6. **Tap Done.**

Move and Scale

Retake   Use Photo

Figure 1-6: Take a photo of your contact and adjust it until it's just right.

With iOS 7, you can block incoming calls from specific numbers by tapping the Info button next to the undesired caller, scrolling down to the bottom of the screen that opens, and tapping Block this Caller.

To create a new contact or add a number to an existing contact from the keypad, when you call a new number:

1. **Tap Phone⇨Keypad.**

2. **Enter the number you want to call, but don't tap Call.**

3. **Tap + Add to Contacts at the top of the screen just under the number.**

   A dialog gives you three choices:

   - Create New Contact

   - Add to Existing Contact

   - Cancel

4. **Tap the button for the action you want to take.**

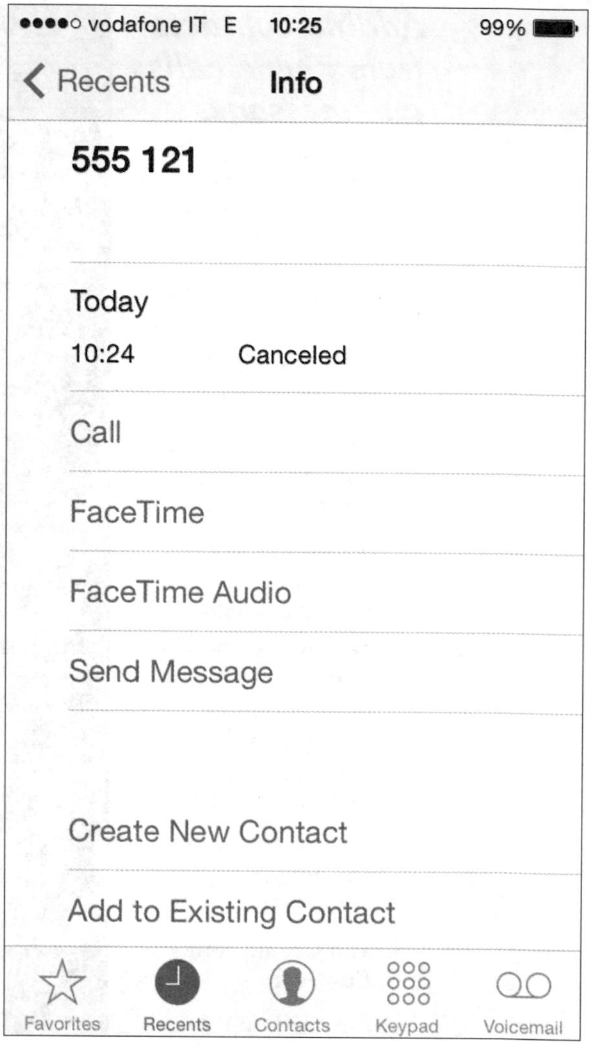

5. **Follow the procedure for creating a new contact or adding a number to an existing contact.**

6. **Tap Done.**

vodafone IT E 10:25 99%
‹ Recents   Info
555 121
Today
10:24   Canceled
Call
FaceTime
FaceTime Audio
Send Message
Create New Contact
Add to Existing Contact
Favorites   Recents   Contacts   Keypad   Voicemail

Figure 1-7: Add the phone number from a recent call to an existing contact or create a new one.

To create a new contact or add a number to an existing contact from a received message:

1. **Tap Messages on the Home screen.**

2. **Tap the message that came from an unidentified number.**

3. **Tap Contact, and then tap the Info button.**

4. **Follow Steps 3 through 6 as outlined previously.**

To create a new contact or add a number to an existing contact from an e-mail:

1. **Tap Mail on the Home screen.**

2. **Tap the message that has the e-mail address you wish to add and do one of the following:**

   In the address fields, tap the sender's or recipient's address and then choose Create New Contact or Add to Existing Contact on the screen that appears.

   On an address within a message, tap and hold the address and then choose Add to Contacts, and then choose Create New Contact or Add to Existing Contact on the screen that appears.

3. **Follow Steps 3 through 6 as outlined previously.**

If you have numbers that you call frequently, you can add them to the Favorites list on the Phone app. Open the contact you call frequently and tap the Add to Favorites button at the bottom of the Info screen. If there's just one phone number, choose the type of call you want to add to Favorites: Voice Call, FaceTime, or FaceTime Audio. If there are multiple numbers, a dialog shows all the numbers and you tap on the number you want to add to the Favorites list in Phone, and then choose the type of call. Refer to Figure 1-8.

Editing and Deleting Contacts

People move, change jobs, phone numbers, and names, and you want to keep Contacts current with the state of affairs. The point of departure for editing and deleting contacts is the same:

1. **Tap Contacts on the Home screen or in the dock of the Phone app.**

2. **Tap the name of the contact you want to edit or delete.**

3. **Tap the Edit button in the upper right corner.**

4. **Tap in the field you want to edit.**

   The keyboard opens so you can make your change.

   Scroll to the next field you want to edit and make any other changes.

5. **To delete a field, tap the red and white minus sign to the left of the field, and then tap Delete, which appears to the right.**

   If you want to delete a field that you added from the Add Field selections, tap that field, tap the X that appears to the right, and then tap

Done. When the field is empty, it will no longer appear on the Contact Info screen.

6. **To add an additional phone, e-mail, website, or address, tap in the blank field below the last filled-in field.**

7. **To add a field, tap the Add Field field at the bottom of the screen and proceed as explained previously in the "Creating New Contacts" section.**

8. **Tap Done in the upper right corner.**

The corrected contact info screen appears.

To delete a contact, tap the name of the contact, tap edit, and then tap the Delete Contact button at the bottom of the edit screen.

Changes, additions, and deletions you make are automatically pushed to your computer and other devices logged in to the services you use such as iCloud or Google.

Figure 1-8: When adding Favorites, choose the number and type of call for speedy dialing.

Sorting and Displaying Contacts

You can adjust the sort order and the display options in the Contacts section of Settings⇨Mail, Contacts, Calendars (refer to Figure 1-9). The settings apply to groups and All Contacts. You can mix and match the options in four different ways; for example, you can sort by last name and then display by first name, whatever makes the most sense to you.

- ✔ **Sort Order:** Tap to open options for choosing to sort your contacts by first name and then last name, or vice versa.

- ✔ **Display Order:** Tap to open options for viewing your contacts by first name followed by last name, or vice versa.

- ✔ **Short Name:** Tap to open the screen that gives the option to turn on and define how you want names to appear when there isn't enough space to display the whole first and last name of a contact. The choices are first name and last initial, first initial and last name, first name only, or last name only. From this screen you can also turn on the Prefer Nicknames option. Contacts will display the nickname and you can use it with Siri and Voice Control.

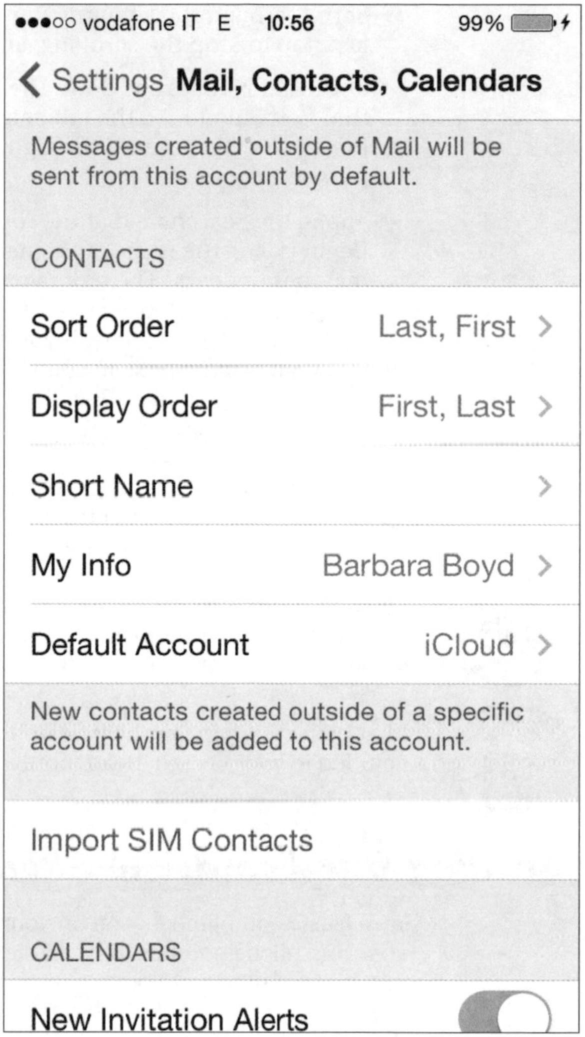

●●●○○ vodafone IT E	10:56	99% ▭ ⊁

‹ Settings Mail, Contacts, Calendars

Messages created outside of Mail will be sent from this account by default.

CONTACTS

Sort Order	Last, First ›
Display Order	First, Last ›
Short Name	›
My Info	Barbara Boyd ›
Default Account	iCloud ›

New contacts created outside of a specific account will be added to this account.

Import SIM Contacts

CALENDARS

New Invitation Alerts

Figure 1-9: Sort and display contacts in the order you want.

Book IV
Chapter 1

Perfecting Your
People Skills with
Contacts

Searching Contacts

You can search Contacts in three ways. Each time you open Contacts from another app, which we talk about in the next section, the search and find process is the same. Tap Contacts on the Home screen and choose either Show All Contacts or the group you want to search in:

✓ Scroll through the list until you see the name you want. If you scroll very fast, tap to stop the scrolling, and then tap on the name you want.

✓ In the index that runs down the right side of the screen, tap the letter that corresponds to the initial letter of the name of the person you're looking for. Then scroll through that section of the alphabet to find the person.

✓ Tap in the Search field at the top of the screen to open the keyboard. Begin typing the name of the person you want to find. A list of possible matches appears. The more you type, the fewer the choices. Contacts looks at the first letters of first names, last names, and words that are part of a company name. If you type "Jo," first names like **Jo**e or **Jo**anne come up, last names, like **Jo**hnson and **Jo**nes appear, and companies or organizations such as **Jo**lly Ice Cream and Association of Writers and **Jo**urnalists show up as well.

Whichever way you choose to search, when you find the name you are looking for, tap on the name to either open the Contacts info screen or to add that name to the To field in the program you're sending from.

If you are searching for a contact that you know is in Contacts but can't find it, make sure you are looking in the right group or switch to the All Contacts view to search your entire address book.

When you search in Spotlight Search from the Home screen, Contacts is included in your search. Read more about Spotlight Search in Book I, Chapter 3.

Sending One Contact to Another

Say a friend compliments you on your new haircut and asks for your stylist's name and phone number. You can dictate the name and number or write it down on a scrap of paper, or you can send the information directly from Contacts:

1. **Open the contact you want to share.**

2. **Tap the Share Contact button at the bottom of the screen.**

3. **Tap one of the choices to send the information:**

   AirDrop: Share with other iDevices that have AirDrop turned on and are on the same WiFi network or close enough for a Bluetooth connection.

   Message or Mail: Fill in the address and tap Send. The information is sent in vcf or vCard (Versit Consortium Format), which is a file format for electronic business cards.

A Share Contact button on the Info screen also opens when you tap the Info button on the Recent Calls list.

Calling and Messaging from Contacts

Although you use Contacts to manage information, you can also generate communications directly from a contact info screen. Tap the contact you want to connect with and then do one of the following:

✏ Tap a phone number to call the person.

✏ Tap an e-mail address to open a pre-addressed New Message in Mail. Type in a subject and message, and tap Send.

✏ Tap FaceTime to initiate a FaceTime video chat.

✏ When a phone number or e-mail address can be used by more than one service, buttons appear to the right, as shown in Figure 1-10. Tap the Messages or Phone button to send a text message or call a mobile number; tap the video or phone button to make either type of FaceTime call; tap the Messages or Mail button to send an iMessage or e-mail to an address.

✏ Tap Send Message at the bottom of the Contact Info screen, and then choose the correct phone number or e-mail address if sending to a device with iMessage to send a message. A New Message in Messages opens, addressed to the contact. Type your message and tap Send.

You can access Contacts from communication apps that use the information in Contacts — Phone, FaceTime, Mail, and Messages. Contacts also appears when you want to send things from non-communication apps like Photos and Safari. We take you through the process for each one in their respective chapters, but after you learn to

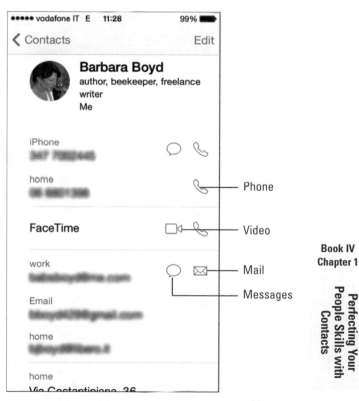

Figure 1-10: When more than one option is available, appropriate buttons appear.

send things to a contact from one app, you pretty much know how to send them in any app. Ah, the beauty of iPhone!

Read about each of the apps that use Contacts in the following chapters:

- ✔ **Mail:** Book III, Chapter 4.
- ✔ **Messages:** Book III, Chapter 2.
- ✔ **Notes and Voice Memos:** Book IV, Chapter 4.
- ✔ **Photos:** To send still images and video, see Book V, Chapter 1.
- ✔ **Safari:** To send links to web pages, see Book III, Chapter 3.
- ✔ **Maps:** To send links to a specific map or directions, see Book IV, Chapter 3.

Chapter 2: Managing Your Time with Calendar, Reminders, and Clock

✔ **Adding and syncing existing Calendars**

✔ **Viewing and hiding Calendars**

✔ **Creating, changing, and deleting Calendar events**

✔ **Sharing Calendar through iCloud**

✔ **Remembering with Reminders**

✔ **Using Clock to help pass the time**

Sometimes it seems the more technology advances in the name of making our lives easier, the more complicated and busy our lives become — or maybe we just take on more because we can. Whatever the reason, we all have a lot to remember and the three apps explained in this chapter can help.

The Calendar app on your iPhone helps you keep track of appointments, birthdays, and deadlines along with fun things like parties and vacations. Calendar syncs with calendars on your computer and other iOS devices as well as remote calendars you subscribe to. When you receive invitations, Calendar inserts the event on the right date and time. We begin this chapter by explaining how to add your existing electronic calendars to your iPhone. Then, we show you Calendar's different views and settings. Next, we look at creating and editing events on your iPhone, how to respond and send event invitations, and how to search for an event.

The second app we explain is Reminders, the list-making, automatic reminding app that's great for simple shopping lists as well as projects that have tasks with deadlines. Both Calendar and Reminders work with Notifications, which means your events and time commitments are viewable when you open the Notifications Center. (See Book I, Chapter 4.) While we're on the subject of time, we explain the Clock app too. You learn that it's not just your ordinary clock but a world clock, alarm, stopwatch, and timer.

Adding and Syncing Existing Calendars

The Calendar app consists of one or more calendars and events on those calendars. You can create blank calendars on your iPhone and then fill in the events as you schedule them. Calendar connects with calendars kept on other services, such as Google, Yahoo!, Facebook, or a Microsoft Exchange calendar that resides on your company's server and is shared among colleagues at work. First we explain how to create a calendar on your iPhone, and then, for those of you who do use one or more other calendar services, we explain how to access calendars from your iPhone and keep all your calendars synced in the future.

Adding a calendar on your iPhone

You probably have your iPhone with you almost all the time, so it makes sense to use Calendar as your time management system. You can create one calendar that has everything or, which we recommend, create a separate calendar for each area of your life, which could be as simple as work and play, or a more complex setup with separate calendars for doctor appointments, sporting events, entertainment, and deadlines. Calendar lets you view one, some, or all of your calendars so you could view all of them when setting up a new appointment but then view just one to see how many times you went to the dentist in the last year. To create a calendar, follow these steps:

1. **Tap Calendar on the Home screen.**

2. **Tap the Calendars button at the bottom of the screen.**

   A list of your local and remote calendars appears.

3. **Tap Edit in the upper left corner.**

4. **Tap Add Calendar.**

   If you turned the Calendar option on in iCloud, you find this in the iCloud section, otherwise it's under the On My iPhone heading.

   The Add Calendar screen opens.

5. **Type a name for the calendar and then tap a color you want to use to identify events in this calendar, as shown in Figure 2-1.**

6. **Tap Done.**

   The Edit Calendars screen appears and you see your new calendar in the list.

7. **Tap Done in the upper left corner to return to the main Calendars list.**

8. **Tap Done — once more — in the upper right corner to view your events.**

   See the section "Viewing and Hiding Calendars" later in this chapter for more information.

Using Calendar with iCloud

We explain how to set up an iCloud account in Book II, Chapter 1. Essentially, iCloud stores your media, documents, and data on a remote server — called a *cloud* — that pushes data updates to your iPhone and any other computers or iOS devices you have associated with your iCloud account. Even if you only use Calendar on your iPhone, it makes sense to use iCloud so you have a remote copy of your Calendar in the unfortunate event that something happens to your iPhone. To turn on iCloud, do the following:

1. **Tap Settings⇨iCloud.**

2. **Tap Calendars on.**

Any changes you make in Calendar on your iPhone or on other devices associated with iCloud, such as your computer, iPad, or iPod touch, are automatically pushed to all devices. You will never have conflicting information again!

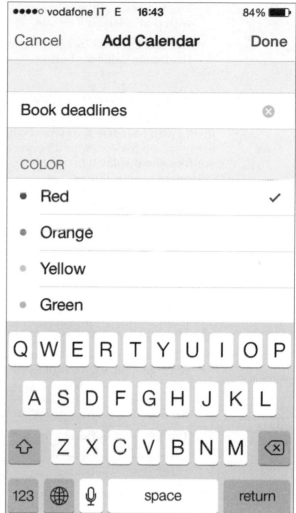

Figure 2-1: Create new calendars directly on your iPhone in the Calendar app.

You can edit the name and color and delete iCloud calendars on your iPhone. Tap the Calendar app on the Home screen and then tap Calendars at the bottom of the screen. Tap the red info button to the right of the calendar, do one of the following, and then tap Done:

✔ *Edit* the name of the calendar by tapping in the first field, selecting the text, and typing a new name.

Book IV
Chapter 2

Managing Your
Time with Calendar,
Reminders, and
Clock

✔ *Edit* the color of the calendar by tapping the color you want to associate with that calendar's events.

✔ *Delete* a calendar by scrolling to the bottom of the screen and tapping the Delete Calendar button.

Adding calendars from other sources

You may have discovered the ease of Google Calendar to share appointments with colleagues, or your company might use MS-Exchange to keep everyone up-to-date. Your iPhone can access the data from all these remote sources and display it in one place — Calendar. Follow these steps to add calendars to your iPhone:

1. **Tap Settings on the Home screen.**

2. **Tap Mail, Contacts, Calendars.**

3. **Tap Add Account.**

   If you already set up an account for mail or contacts, tap the name of the account in the list and then tap the Calendar switch On.

4. **Tap the service you use: Exchange, Google, Yahoo!, or Outlook.com.**

5. **The Add Account screen opens.**

   Filling in the Name field is optional. Type in your e-mail address in the Address field and your password in the Password field. An identity is automatically entered in the Description field, however, you can tap and hold on the text to replace it with something that helps you remember the account, such as "work" or "golf team."

6. **Tap the Next button in the upper right corner.**

   After your account is verified, a screen opens showing a list of available services.

7. **Tap the Calendars switch On.**

8. **Swipe back to the first Mail, Contacts, Calendars settings screen and you now see the added account in the Accounts list and the activated services appear under each account name, as shown in Figure 2-2.**

If you want to use iCloud with your Windows PC, download the iCloud Control Panel for Windows app from Apple (www.apple.com/icloud/setup/pc.html).

You have to sign in on your iPhone with the same account information you use on your computer to have the same information in both places.

Configuring CalDAV calendar accounts

CalDAV is an Internet standard that allows access to data in the iCalendar format on a remote server. Multiple users can access the same information so it is often used in business and organization settings. If your employer uses a CalDAV supported calendar program, and you want to access that calendar from your iPhone, you can add a CalDAV account. You'll need some account information from your IT department or network support person:

- ✔ **Server:** This has your company or organization information.
- ✔ **User Name:** This is your identification.
- ✔ **Password:** A password is required.
- ✔ **Description:** This name shows up on the list of accounts on the Mail, Contacts, Calendars settings screen.

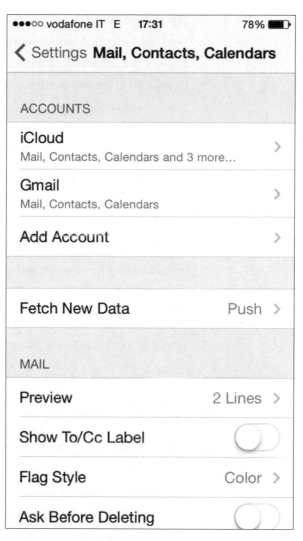

Figure 2-2: See which services are activated from each provider in Settings.

Book IV
Chapter 2

Managing Your
Time with Calendar,
Reminders, and
Clock

Armed with this information, set up an account on your computer as explained at the beginning of this section. Next, set up the account on your iPhone by following these steps:

1. **Tap Settings⇨Mail, Contacts, Calendars.**

2. **Tap Add Account.**

3. **Tap Other.**

4. **Tap Add CalDAV Account in the Calendars section.**

5. **Type in the information requested.**

6. **Tap the Next button in the upper right corner.**

   After your account information is verified, the calendar data is added to your iPhone.

7. **Tap the Save button in the upper right corner and you return to the Mail, Contacts, Calendars settings screen.**

8. **Tap Fetch New Data.**

9. **If your server supports push notifications — and you want to use it, Tap Push On.**

   Anytime you make a change to the calendar on your computer that's associated with your iCloud or Microsoft Exchange account, that change is pushed to your iPhone, and vice versa.

10. **If your server doesn't support push (or you want to conserve battery power ⇨ Push is power hungry), select a default fetch interval — every 15 minutes, every 30 minutes, or hourly.**

   Your iPhone contacts the server for new data at the interval you select.

Adding Facebook events to Calendar

Whether you're a Facebook addict or just an occasional user, linking Facebook to Calendar can be an easy way to keep track of friends' birthdays and other events posted on Facebook such as class reunions and store promotions. This is optional, so follow these steps to activate this feature, or not:

1. **Tap Settings⇨Facebook.**

   The Facebook settings screen opens.

   If you don't have the Facebook app installed, tap the Install button to download it from the iTunes Store.

2. **Tap in the User Name field and type in your user name.**

3. **Tap in the Password field and type in your password.**

4. **Tap Sign In.**

   A disclaimer appears that explains what happens on your iPhone when you sign in to Facebook. Essentially, information about your Facebook friends is downloaded to Contacts; Facebook events sync to your Calendar; you can post status updates and images directly from the Photos app; and Facebook-enabled apps work with your permission.

5. **Tap Sign In again to accept these conditions. You can change the settings after you sign in if you don't want these things to happen.**

6. **The Facebook setting screen reappears with Calendar and Contacts options.**

7. **Tap Calendar On.**

   Even if you turn this feature on, you can hide the Facebook Events calendar, as explained in the later section, "Viewing and Hiding Calendars."

Subscribing to iCalendar (.ics) calendars

One of the strong points of Calendar is the ability to access calendars created by other people and see those events on your iPhone. You may learn about these events through electronic invitations — invitations that are sent via e-mail — or from a public calendar site where you can search for published calendars.

An iCalendar or .ics file is the standard file type for exchanging calendar information. Calendar, Outlook, and Google Calendar support the .ics standard.

If you receive an e-mail with an invitation to an event attached, the invitation probably has the .ics suffix. You simply click that attachment, either from the e-mail message or your iPhone, and then choose one of the following responses:

✔ **Accept** the invitation and the event is automatically added to your calendar. The event is synced to any other devices signed in to the same calendar account.

✔ **Decline** to refuse the invitation.

✔ **Maybe** to postpone your decision to attend the event or not.

Whichever response you choose is sent to the person who sent the invitation.

If you receive a list of events in Mail, tap the calendar file within the message. When the list of events appears, tap Add All. Choose the calendar where you want to add the events, and then tap Done.

If you receive an invitation to a calendar, you can choose to Decline or Join Calendar. If you decline, an e-mail informs the sender of your decision. If you join, an e-mail informs the sender of your decision and the calendar is added as one of your calendars in Calendar. You can choose to view or hide that calendar's events by selecting or deselecting it in the calendars list.

To subscribe to published, public calendars, you can search a site like `http://icalshare.com/` or Google Calendars and subscribe to the

Book IV
Chapter 2

Managing Your
Time with Calendar,
Reminders, and
Clock

calendars that interest you. Some organizations post a subscription link on their website so you can automatically receive notifications of their events. To add a calendar subscription on your iPhone, do one of the following procedures:

1. **Tap Safari on the Home screen.**

2. **Type the URL for the calendar sharing site you want to use, for example,** `http://icalshare.com/`.

3. **Find the calendar you want to add, and then tap the Subscribe to Calendar button.**

4. **Tap the appropriate response, such as Open, Subscribe or Add Calendar, in the dialogs that appear.**

5. **The calendar is automatically added to Calendar and appears on the calendar list.**

If the calendar you want to add isn't part of a service like iCalShare, have the URL of the shared calendar handy and follow these steps:

1. **Tap Settings⇨Mail, Contacts, Calendar.**

2. **Tap Add Account.**

3. **Tap Other.**

4. **Tap Add Subscribed Calendar (near the bottom of the screen).**

5. **Type in the server address for the calendar on the Subscription screen, as seen in Figure 2-3.**

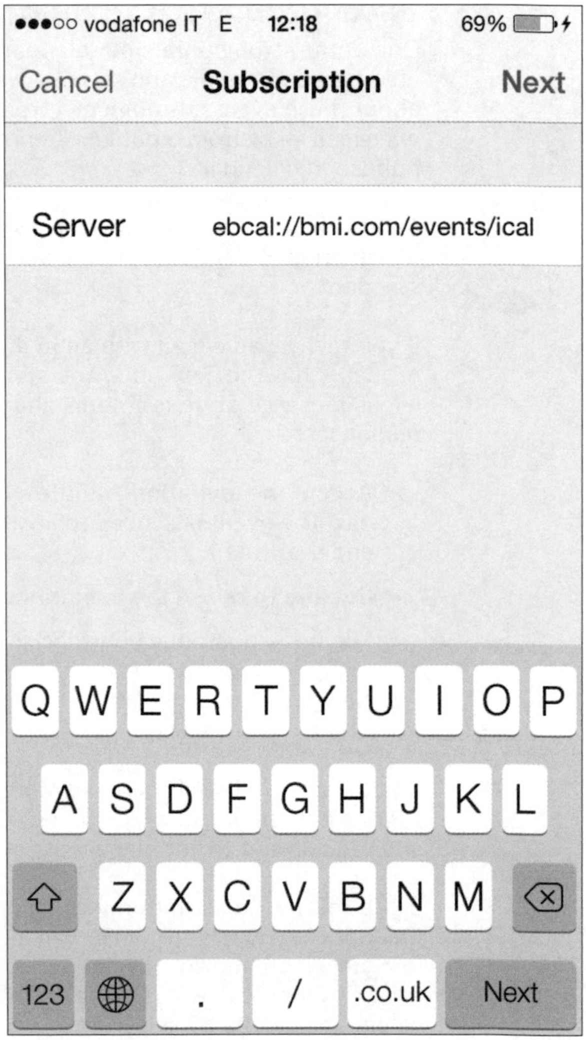

Figure 2-3: You can subscribe to public calendars that use the iCalendar standard.

6. **Tap Next.**

   The server address is verified and a Subscription screen appears. You may have to enter a username and password to have access to the calendar. Some calendar providers ask you to use SSL (secure socket layer) for security reasons. See Book III, Chapter 4 to learn how to turn SSL on in Mail.

7. **The calendar appears on the calendar list in the Calendar app.**

You can make changes to the event in a subscribed calendar in Calendar, but the changes are not reflected on the source calendar (such as Google Calendars), which is stored on a remote server and accessed on the Internet.

Deleting calendars

There are different ways to delete calendars, depending on the source.

- ✓ **iCloud calendars:** Tap Calendars, tap the info button to the right of the calendar you want to delete, and then tap Delete Calendar at the bottom of the screen. If you only have one iCloud calendar, this option doesn't appear because you have to have at least one iCloud calendar.

- ✓ **Third-party calendars (Google, MS-Exchange, and so on):** Tap Settings⇨Mail, Contacts, Calendars⇨Account and turn off the Calendars option.

- ✓ **Subscribed calendars:** If you want to delete a calendar you subscribe to, go to Settings⇨Mail, Contacts, Calendars⇨Subscribed Calendars. Tap the calendar you want to delete, and then tap Delete Account.

Viewing and Hiding Calendars

You now have one or multiple calendars on your iPhone. Calendar neatly presents the data in four formats: in portrait (vertical) view, Calendar displays a year-at-a-glance, a month-at-a-glance, a day-at-a-glance, which displays the dates of the associated week across the top of the screen, and a scrollable list of your events and appointments. Turn your iPhone to the landscape (horizontal) position to see several days at-a-glance — 5 on an iPhone 5 or later, 3 and a half on earlier models. To choose which calendars you want to see:

1. **Tap Calendars on the Home Screen.**

2. **Tap the Calendar button at the bottom of the screen.**

   A list of your calendars opens, as shown in Figure 2-4.

3. **Tap the name of the calendar you want to see or hide.**

   If there's a check mark next to the name of the calendar, events in that calendar show up in the four views. Note that the Calendars are

**Book IV
Chapter 2**

Managing Your
Time with Calendar,
Reminders, and
Clock

color-coded. Events shown in List and Day views are color-coded to respond to the calendar they come from.

4. **Tap Show All Calendars if you want to see all events.**

5. **Tap Done.**

Calendars opens to the view you most recently used.

Calendar views

When you open Calendar from the Home screen, you see one of the screens as shown in the upcoming figures. The buttons on the screen, from top to bottom, work as follows:

✔ **Year/Month:** Think of Calendars as being arranged hierarchically: the top view shows the entire year; tap a month and you move down a layer to see the entire month; tap a date to see the detail of a day's appointments. Tap in the upper left corner to move back to a higher level: the month's name to move from day view to month view; the year to move from month view to year view.

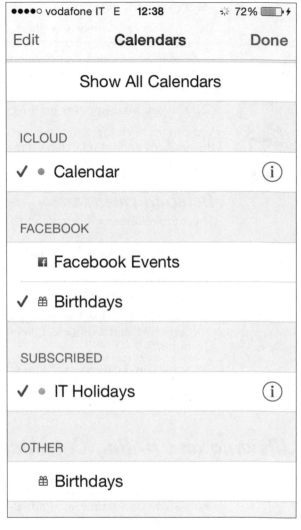

Figure 2-4: The Calendar list shows you the calendars you sync with and those you subscribe to.

When in year or month view, scroll up and down to move to the past or future month or year. In Figure 2-5, you can see the end of 2013 and the beginning of 2014.

When in day view, tap a date in the week displayed at the top to move to that date; scroll up and down in the day to move between morning to evening hours and scroll left and right to move backward and forward in time to select a different day. All-day events are displayed between the week and hour sections, as shown in Figure 2-6. Notice the current day is in red (August 25) and the birthday is indicated by a gift icon.

To view several days of your calendar together rotate your iPhone to landscape view and you see a multiday calendar. Swipe left and right to scroll to previous and upcoming days. Swipe up and down to scroll from morning to evening. All-day events are posted at the top of the day. Multi-day events are highlighted across all the days of the event.

●●●●○ vodafone IT E	13:54	93% ▬
		🔍 +
29 30	27 28 29 30 31	24 25 26 27 28 29 30
JUL	**AUG**	**SEP**
1 2 3 4 5 6 7	1 2 3 4	1
8 9 10 11 12 13 14	5 6 7 8 9 10 11	2 3 4 5 6 7 8
15 16 17 18 19 20 21	12 13 14 15 16 17 18	9 10 11 12 13 14 15
22 23 24 25 26 27 28	19 20 21 22 23 24 ㉕	16 17 18 19 20 21 22
29 30 31	26 27 28 29 30 31	23 24 25 26 27 28 29
		30
OCT	**NOV**	**DEC**
1 2 3 4 5 6	1 2 3	1
7 8 9 10 11 12 13	4 5 6 7 8 9 10	2 3 4 5 6 7 8
14 15 16 17 18 19 20	11 12 13 14 15 16 17	9 10 11 12 13 14 15
21 22 23 24 25 26 27	18 19 20 21 22 23 24	16 17 18 19 20 21 22
28 29 30 31	25 26 27 28 29 30	23 24 25 26 27 28 29
		30 31

2014

JAN	**FEB**	**MAR**
1 2 3 4 5	1 2	1 2
6 7 8 9 10 11 12	3 4 5 6 7 8 9	3 4 5 6 7 8 9
13 14 15 16 17 18 19	10 11 12 13 14 15 16	10 11 12 13 14 15 16
20 21 22 23 24 25 26	17 18 19 20 21 22 23	17 18 19 20 21 22 23
27 28 29 30 31	24 25 26 27 28	24 25 26 27 28 29 30
		31
APR	**MAY**	**JUN**
1 2 3 4 5 6	1 2 3 4	1
7 8 9 10 11 12 13	5 6 7 8 9 10 11	2 3 4 5 6 7 8
14 15 16 17 18 19 20	12 13 14 15 16 17 18	9 10 11 12 13 14 15
21 22 23 24 25 26 27	19 20 21 22 23 24 25	16 17 18 19 20 21 22

Today	Calendars	Inbox

Figure 2-5: Scroll up and down to move from one year to the next in year view.

WARNING!

Multi-day view doesn't work when you have the orientation lock turned on. To permit week view, drag up from the bottom of the screen to open the control center and tap Orientation Lock off. Drag down to close the control center and week view appears when you turn your iPhone to the horizontal position.

✏ **Search (the magnifying glass icon):** Opens the List view as shown in Figure 2-7. You see five or six events. If you have a busy day, you may see only one day. If you have just one or two things each day, you see more days. The colored line to the left of the event corresponds to the calendar it comes from. You can scroll up and down this list to see what you did or what's coming up.

Tap in the search field at the top to look for an event. Calendar searches in the title, location, notes, and invitees fields of calendars that are active; if you don't find an event, tap Calendars at the bottom of the screen, tap Show All Calendars, and then try your search again.

- **Plus Sign:** Tap this button to add an event to your calendar. We explain that in detail in the next section.

- **Today:** Tap on the Today button at the bottom of the page in any of the views, and today is highlighted (refer to Figure 2-5) in that view.

- **Calendars:** Takes you to the list of your calendars.

Figure 2-6: Day view shows the week that contains the day, all-day events, and the day's appointments.

- **Inbox:** Shows invitations you've received from other calendars. The number in parentheses indicates how many invitations you've received. Click on the button and a list of invitations opens. We talk about responding to invitations in the "Responding to meeting invitations" section later in this chapter.

Showing birthdays

If you use Contacts, you probably know that you can include a birthday as part of the contact information. (We explain Contacts in Book IV, Chapter 1.) Calendar links to Contacts and can display the birthdays on your calendar.

Scroll to the bottom of the Calendars list screen. You find the Other section and Birthdays. A check mark indicates that Birthdays is selected; tap Birthdays if it isn't selected. Tap Done. Birthdays are automatically inserted as all-day events. If you turned Calendar On in the Facebook Settings, you also see a Birthdays option in the Facebook section of the Calendars list screen (refer to Figure 2-4).

You now see birthdays in the search and day views and a dot on the date in month view. The gift icon is next to the event so you know it's a birthday.

Figure 2-7: Tap the search button to see a list of your appointments and events.

Book IV
Chapter 2

Managing Your
Time with Calendar,
Reminders, and
Clock

You can set a default alert time for birthdays by tapping Settings➪Mail, Contacts, Calendars➪Default Alert Times➪Birthdays and choosing when you want to receive an alert that someone's birthday is near (from a week before to the day of).

If you use birthdays from Contacts and add the birthday as an event, it shows up twice on your calendar.

Creating, Changing, and Deleting Calendar Events

As work and life styles evolve, we tend to use Calendar on our iPhones more than our computers. (Of course, every entry is synced to our computers and devices with iCloud.) In this section, we show you how to create new events and change or delete existing ones. We explain setting up repeating events and alerts so you don't miss any important scheduled encounters, and we discuss how to send and respond to invitations.

Filling in who, what, where, and when

If you're familiar with Calendar on a Mac (iCal in OS X 10.7, and earlier), creating events in Calendar will be a breeze. Even if you use Outlook or another calendar program, Calendar is pretty straightforward. Here's how to add an appointment or event:

1. **Tap Calendar on the Home screen.**

2. **From day, month, or year view, tap the plus sign button in the upper right corner to open the Add Event screen.**

   In Day view, press and hold the time at which you want to add an event until an Add Event screen appears.

3. **Tap the first field, where you see Title.**

   The keyboard appears.

   If you like working with a slightly bigger keyboard, turn your iPhone to the horizontal position — or use an external keyboard connected via Bluetooth.

4. **Type in the name of the event or appointment in the Title field.**

5. **Tap Return, and then type in a Location or something else pertinent to the appointment. This field is optional.**

6. **Tap the field with Starts, Ends, and Time Zone.**

   The time and date rotor opens, as in Figure 2-8.

7. **Using the rotor, set the date and time the appointment begins.**

   Your iPhone keeps track of your movements and places you frequently visit, as long as Frequent Locations is turned on in Settings⇨Privacy⇨Location Services⇨System Services⇨Frequent Locations. iPhone uses your location history to calculate travel time to your appointments and then adds that information to the Today view of the Notification Center.

8. **The ending time is automatically set for one hour later. To change it, tap the Ends field. Set the date and time the appointment ends.**

   Tap the Ends field again to close the rotor.

9. **If it's an all-day event such as a meeting or anniversary, tap the All-Day switch to On.**

   The rotors change and show only the month, day, and year. If the event is more than one day, say a conference or vacation, choose the beginning and ending dates.

   The advantage to using the all-day feature instead of setting the beginning time to 8 a.m. and the ending time to 8 p.m. is that in Day view, the event shows up at the beginning of the day rather than as a highlighted event over the course of the whole day. This way, you can add specific appointments during the course of the all-day event. In List view, All-Day appears next to the event title.

10. **Tap the Time Zone field if you want to set the event in a time zone other than your own.**

    A field opens where you type in the name of a large city that resides in the time zone you want to use. Tap the city from the list when a match appears. You return to the Add Event screen.

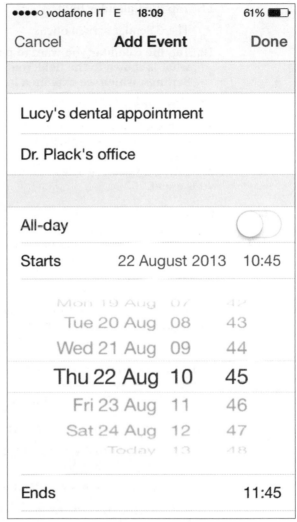

Figure 2-8: Use the rotor to set the starting and ending date and times for your event.

Book IV
Chapter 2

Managing Your
Time with Calendar,
Reminders, and
Clock

11. **Tap the Calendar field.**

    The Calendar screen opens.

12. **Tap the calendar you want to put this event on if it's different than what is shown in the field. You choose the default calendar under Settings, which we explain a few sections ahead.**

13. **Tap Done.**

You can stop here or you can add some more details to your event with the remaining fields: Repeat, Alert, and Notes. If you use an over-the-air calendar like iCloud or Microsoft Exchange, you also have the options of indicating if you're busy or free during the event and of inviting people to your event.

If you receive text or e-mail messages with time and date references — even things like "Meet me at 6" or "Dinner next Thursday," the reference is highlighted and underlined and tapping it opens a pop-up menu that lets you create an event or show the time or date in Calendar.

Setting up a repeating event

The default repetition setting for a new event is Never. If your event is one-time only, skip this. For yearly events like an anniversary, or weekly events, such as a tennis lesson, the repeat function is handy.

You only have to enter the information once and Calendar takes care of the rest, saving you the hassle of both remembering to re-enter the event the next time it's coming around and of re-typing the information. Here's how:

1. **Tap Repeat on the event you created.**

    If it's an event that you created previously, open that event and tap Edit in the upper right corner.

2. **Choose the frequency with which you want the event to repeat.**

    You return to the Add Event screen but another field is added under Repeat: the End Repeat field.

3. **Never is the default, which you probably want to leave for events such as anniversaries. Your tennis lesson may be seasonal, so tap the End Repeat field and then tap On Date.**

4. **Use the rotor to choose the date the event ends.**

5. **Tap Add Event or Edit in the upper left corner to return to the event screen.**

6. **Tap Done.**

If you use Calendar on a Mac, you find more flexibility for creating complicated repeating events, which then sync to your iPhone.

Adding Alerts

If you have a lot on your plate — and who doesn't? — alerts can be a big help. Your iPhone beeps (or vibrates if the Ring/Silent switch is set to Silent) and sends a notification message at the interval you select, from five minutes to two days before your event.

Even if your iPhone is sleeping and/or locked, Calendar wakes your iPhone if you turn on Show on Lock Screen in Settings⇨Notification Center⇨Calendar. You hear the beep, or whatever sound you choose for Calendar alerts, and the notification appears, as shown in Figure 2-9. Slide the notification to view the event. If you are actively using an app, a banner appears across the top of the screen at the appointed alert time. When you sync your calendars, alerts sync to the corresponding calendar on your computer, and vice versa.

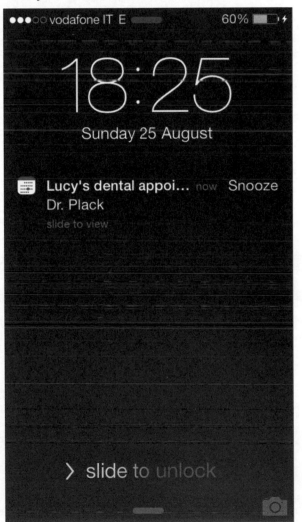

You can even receive two alerts, so you can be reminded of your dear Aunt Sybil's retirement dinner two days before the event, giving you time to get a gift, and then again, the day of the dinner. Follow these steps:

1. **Tap Alert on the Add Event screen or the Edit screen, if you want to add an alert to an event you already created.**

2. **Tap how long before the event you want to receive an alert.**

   You return to the Add Event screen, but another field is added under Alert, the Second Alert field.

Figure 2-9: Alerts are received even if your iPhone is locked or sleeping.

Book IV
Chapter 2

Managing Your
Time with Calendar,
Reminders, and
Clock

3. **Tap Second Alert if you want to receive two alerts for the same event.**

4. **Tap how long before the event you want to receive a second alert.**

   You return to the Add Event screen.

5. **Tap Done.**

The Notification Center Settings work with Calendar in two ways:

✓ View Calendar events in the Notification Center by turning on Settings⇨Notification Center⇨Calendar Day View and/or Tomorrow Summary On.

✓ Choose the alert sound and style in Settings⇨Notification Center⇨Calendar⇨Calendar Alerts. Tap the sound you want to hear or None for one or both types of alerts if you don't want to receive a visual or audible notification. To learn more about the Notification Center, go to Book I, Chapter 4.

You can set default alerts for events or all-day events by tapping Settings⇨Mail, Contacts, Calendars⇨Default Alert Times. Then tap Events or All-Day Events and choose when you want to receive an alert. This gives you an alert for all of those kinds of happenings, so if you have a lot of events, setting up default alerts may be more a cause of confusion than a reminder. In that case, you may want to only assign individual alerts to your most important events.

If you have an alert scheduled during a time that Do Not Disturb with the Always option is turned on, you won't receive the alert.

Adding Notes

Adding a URL and a note to an event is a great way to remember things associated with that event: For example, if you're scheduling a video conference or a webinar attendance, adding the URL for the call gives you instant access at the scheduled time and add any other useful information about the appointment in the Notes field, such as the phone number of the person you're going to meet or the confirmation number for a flight. To add a URL and/or note:

1. **Tap URL on the Add Event screen, or Edit screen if you want to add to an event you already created.**

2. **Type the URL.**

   Open Safari and go to the web page you want to add to the event, tap and hold in the URL field, copy the address, and then switch back to Calendar. Tap and hold the URL field and paste the copied address.

3. **Tap Notes.**

4. **Type in the information you want.**

   Or

   Copy and paste to the Notes field from a contact, website, note, or an e-mail: Switch to the app that contains information you want to copy.

   Copy that information. Double-click the Home button to see the open apps and tap Calendar. You return to the Notes screen where you left off. Press and hold in the field until the magnifying loupe appears. Lift your finger, and then tap Paste. Voilà The information you copied is now in the note of your event.

5. **Tap Done.**

Indicating your availability

If you post an event to an over-the-air calendar such as one in iCloud, Google Calendar, or Microsoft Exchange, you can indicate that you are free, or busy, during the event that you post by tapping Show As on the Add Event (or Edit) screen, and then tapping Busy or Free, as appropriate.

Inviting people to your event

If you use an over-the-air calendar, like iCloud or Microsoft Exchange, or use Mail on a Mac, you can invite people to your event directly from Calendar. Make sure you accurately complete the details of your event before sending it to the invitees. Then follow these steps:

1. **Tap Invitees.**

   The Add Invitees screen opens.

2. **Type in the e-mail addresses of the people you want to invite or tap the plus sign on the right.**

   Contacts opens. Scroll the list or tap the letters down the right side or use the Search function to find the name you're looking for.

3. **Tap the name of the person you want to invite.**

   You return to the Add Invitees screen and the name appears in the space at the top.

4. **Repeat Steps 2 and 3 to add more people.**

5. **Tap Add Event (or Edit if you are inviting people after an event has been created) in the upper right corner.**

6. **Tap Done.**

   An event invitation is automatically sent to your invitees.

Figure 2-10 shows a completed Add Event screen.

**Book IV
Chapter 2**

Managing Your
Time with Calendar,
Reminders, and
Clock

Of course one of the easiest ways to add an event is to call on Siri. Press and hold the Home button until Siri appears and then speak the details of your event, such as "Set up a meeting with Joe on Thursday at 3 p.m." or "Create a repeating event every Tuesday from 10:15 to noon." Siri asks the necessary questions to send invitations, add locations, and even edit events at a later date.

Editing and deleting events

Meetings get cancelled, appointment times and dates get changed, and in the old pen and paper calendar world, we used a lot of correction fluid. You can swiftly edit or delete appointments and events on your iPhone without inhaling those nasty fumes.

1. **Tap Calendar from the Home screen.**

2. **Locate the event you want to change or delete from one of the views. We find the list view accessed by tapping the search button easiest.**

3. **Tap the event you want to work on.**

   An Event Details screen opens, as you see in Figure 2-11.

4. **Tap Edit in the upper right corner.**

   The Edit screen opens, which looks like the Add Event screen except it's filled in.

●●●●○ vodafone IT E 19:04		92% ⬛)⚡
Cancel	**Add Event**	Done

Lucy's birthday party

Bow Meow Chow

All-day	⚪
Starts	30 August 2013 16:00
Ends	19:00
Time Zone	New York >

Repeat	Yearly >
End Repeat	Never >

Invitees	3 >

Figure 2-10: A completely filled-in Add Event screen.

5. **Tap in the field you want to change.**

6. **Make changes using the same techniques you use to enter data in a new event.**

7. **Tap Done.**

If you want to delete the event, instead of editing as in Step 5, tap the red Delete Event button at the bottom of the screen. Two buttons pop up, Delete Event and Cancel. Tap the appropriate one.

Responding to meeting invitations

Meetings are a fact of life in large and small businesses. Once upon a time, we used the phone to invite people to meetings, but e-mail and electronic calendars have changed that. You can receive and respond to meeting invitations on your iPhone if you have enabled calendars on Microsoft Exchange or iCloud.

You receive up to three types of notifications when someone sends you an invitation. The first one is optional, the other two are automatic:

●●●○○ vodafone IT E 19:06	93% ▭ ▸ ⚡
❮ Back · **Event Details** · Edit	

Lucy's dental appointment
Dr. Plack

Monday, 26 Aug 2013
from 18:30 to 19:30

Calendar	● Calendar >
Alert	30 minutes before >

Figure 2-11: The Event Details screen shows information about events you created.

✔ **Notification box:** An alert beep sounds and a notification box gives you minimal details about the event and the choice to close the box or view the complete details of the event. You can turn New Invitation Alerts off in Settings➪Mail, Contacts, Calendar➪New Invitation Alerts.

Book IV
Chapter 2

Managing Your
Time with Calendar,
Reminders, and
Clock

✔ **On the Calendars screen:** A numeric alert badge appears in the inbox on the lower right corner.

✔ **On the Home screen:** A numeric badge appears on the Calendar button.

Tap the inbox on the Calendars screen to view invitations received. Tap on the invitation to open the details, see Figure 2-12. You have three response choices:

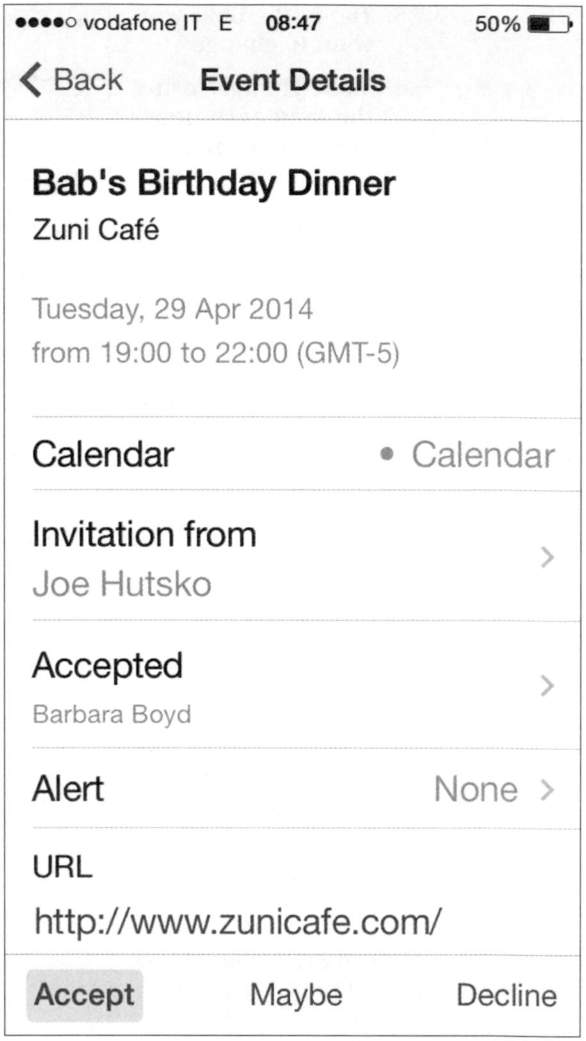

✔ **Accept:** This puts the meeting on your calendar at the indicated date and time. Your name is added to the list of attendees.

✔ **Maybe:** On both your calendar and the sender's calendar, the meeting appears tentative if you select Maybe.

✔ **Decline:** This sends a response to let the person know you won't be attending. Nothing is added to your calendar. The invitation is deleted from your iPhone

●●●●○ vodafone IT E 08:47	50% ▬▭

‹ Back   **Event Details**

Bab's Birthday Dinner
Zuni Café

Tuesday, 29 Apr 2014
from 19:00 to 22:00 (GMT-5)

Calendar	• Calendar

Invitation from	›
Joe Hutsko	

Accepted	›
Barbara Boyd	

Alert	None ›

URL
http://www.zunicafe.com/

Accept	Maybe	Decline

Figure 2-12: You can Accept or Decline an invitation, or choose Maybe while you think about it.

unless you switch on the Show Declined Events option on the Calendars screen. This is a good option because you can go back and accept an invitation if you change your mind.

If you receive an invitation in an e-mail, it shows up as an attachment with an .ics suffix, which indicates the iCalendar standard. Tap on the attachment and the Event Info screen opens. You can then add the event to your calendar and respond.

Sharing Calendars

Just as you can subscribe to other's calendars on servers like iCalshare. com, you can share calendars you create on iCloud with other people. Private calendars can only be seen by people who have an iCloud account, whereas Public calendars can be shared with anyone with an Internet connection and browser. Sharing calendars lets others know what you're up to and in some cases gives others the possibility to post events on your calendar. Follow these steps to activate sharing:

1. **Tap Calendar on the Home screen.**

2. **Tap the Calendars button at the bottom.**

3. **Tap the red info button to the right of the calendar you want to share. It must be an iCloud or Microsoft Exchange calendar**

   Tap Edit➪Add Calendar if you want to create a new calendar, and then tap Done.

4. **To share the calendar with one or more specific persons, tap Add Person.**

   An Add Person message screen opens; it looks like an e-mail message.

5. **Type in the name of the person you want to share the calendar with or tap the plus sign to choose someone from your Contacts list.**

   Add as many names as you wish.

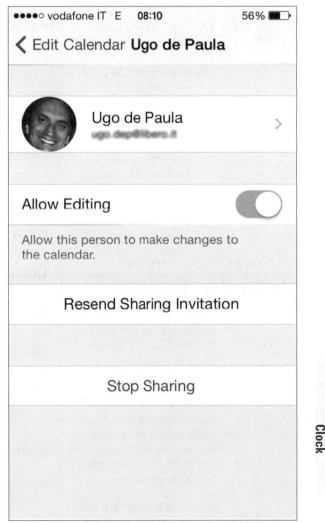

Figure 2-13: Grant editing privileges to people with whom you share your calendar.

Book IV
Chapter 2

Managing Your
Time with Calendar,
Reminders, and
Clock

6. **Tap Add.**

   The Edit Calendar screen appears and the name or names of the people you share with appear in the Shared With list.

7. **Tap View and Edit to grant or remove calendar editing privileges to the person, as shown in Figure 2-13.**

8. **Tap Edit Calendar to return to the previous screen.**

9. **Scroll to the bottom of the screen to find the Public Calendar option.**

10. **Tap On to allow anyone to subscribe to a read-only version of your calendar.**

11. **Tap Share Link to open the share sheet and send an e-mail or message to people you want to invite to subscribe to this calendar. Alternatively, copy the link to post it elsewhere such as Twitter, Facebook, or your blog.**

12. **Tap Done.**

Adjusting iPhone's Calendar Settings

You can change Calendar settings from the main Settings app on your iPhone. To access them, tap Settings ⇨Mail, Contacts, Calendars. Scroll down to the bottom of the screen. The Calendars settings are in the last section, as shown in Figure 2-14. You can adjust seven items:

✔ **New Invitation Alerts:** When this is set to On, you receive an alert when

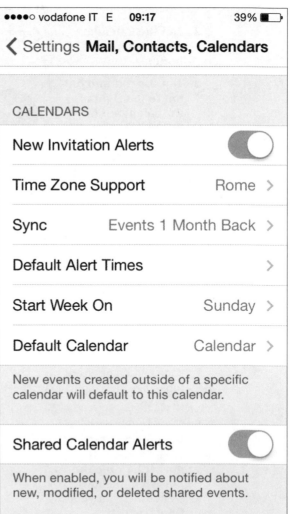

Figure 2-14: Customize Calendar to your liking in Settings.

a new invitation arrives from a remote calendar, such as Outlook. If you're feeling overwhelmed by the number of meeting invitations you receive, tap this setting Off.

✔ **Time Zone Support:** Time Zone Support is turned On when you first use your iPhone. The time zone that your iPhone is set to appears next to the Time Zone Support button. Events and alerts you enter in Calendar maintain the time you enter, regardless of what time zone you're actually in. We recommend that you leave it that way because switching between On and Off changes the times on events you already created.

To change your time zone, tap Time Zone Support on the Mail, Contacts, Calendar Settings screen. The Time Zone Support screen opens. Tap the switch On and then tap Time Zone. The Time Zone screen opens with a keyboard. Begin typing the initial letters of the city or country of the time zone you want to use. A list of potential cities appears and the results narrow as you type more letters. Tap a city that's in the time zone you want. You return to the Time Zone Support screen. Tap the Mail button in the upper left corner to return to the Settings screen.

Turn Time Zone Support off and your events reflect the local time of your current location. The times for events you already created change. For example, an event at 9:30 a.m. in London changes to 2:30 a.m. when you land in Atlanta.

✔ **Sync:** Choose how much event history you want to include when you sync your events. Tap to open the Sync screen and choose 2 Weeks Back; 1, 3, or 6 Months Back; or All Events.

✔ **Default Alert Times:** Set alerts for all birthdays, all events, or all all-day events. Tap the type of event you want an alert for — Birthdays, Events, or All-Day Events — and then, from the list that opens, choose when you want to be alerted to the event.

✔ **Start Week On:** Tap to choose which day you want Calendar to display as the first day of the week.

✔ **Default Calendar:** Choose which calendar you want as the default. Any new events you create automatically are placed on the default calendar, unless you change it on the Add Event screen. Tap Default Calendar. The Default Calendar screen opens, which displays the calendars that are available. Click the calendar you want. A check mark appears to the right of the selected default calendar.

✔ **Shared Calendar Alerts:** If you share calendars and events with others, turn this feature on to be notified when changes or new events occur.

Control other Calendar alerts in Settings⇨Notification Center.

Book IV
Chapter 2

Managing Your
Time with Calendar,
Reminders, and
Clock

Remembering with Reminders

Reminders is a catch-all for your To Do lists, neatly divided into categories you establish. Create lists of tasks and then have Reminders send you an alert based on a time or location. So you never forget a task regardless of the device you have at hand, Reminders automatically syncs via iCloud with the Reminders app on your other iOS devices or Mac and with Outlook on your Mac or Windows PC. Just remember to turn Reminders on in Settings⇨iCloud.

Creating Reminders lists

Reminders comes with one list: Reminders. You add other lists and then add tasks to the lists. To add a list, follow these steps:

1. **Tap Reminders on the Home screen to open Reminders, as shown in Figure 2-15.**

2. **Tap New List at the top of the screen.**

   A New List appears with the keyboard at the bottom of the screen.

   If you see an open reminder, tap the white strip at the bottom of the screen to open the list of reminders and the New List option (refer to Figure 2-15).

3. **Type a title for your new list.**

4. **Tap the color you want the list to be.**

5. **Tap Done.**

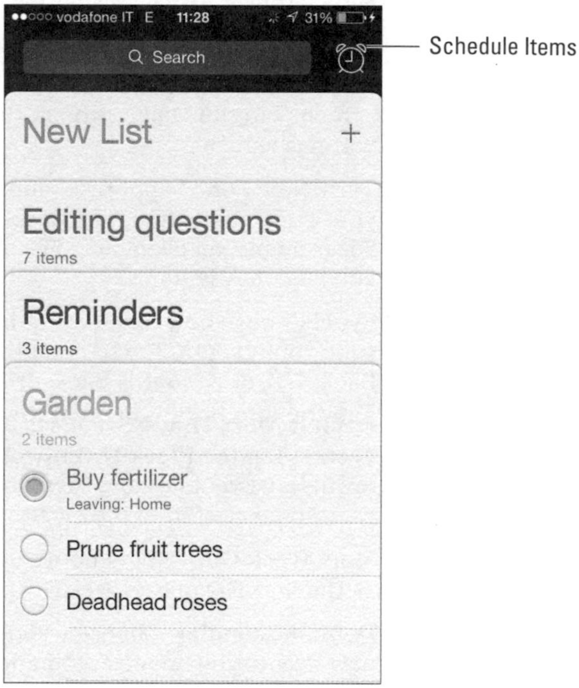

Schedule Items

New List +

Editing questions
7 items

Reminders
3 items

Garden
2 items

⦿ Buy fertilizer
   Leaving: Home

◯ Prune fruit trees

◯ Deadhead roses

Figure 2-15: Reminders shows your lists like neatly stacked index cards.

Reorder your lists by touching and dragging them up and down the screen until they are displayed in the order you like.

Tap a list and then tap the Edit button in the upper right to do the following:

- **Rename the list:** Tap and hold to select the name and then type a new one.

- **Change the list color:** Tap Color and choose a new hue.

✓ **Delete the list:** Tap Delete List at the bottom of the screen.

Search in Reminders by tapping the Search field. Type a few words of the task you're looking for in the search field or use Spotlight Search from the Home screen. Or just ask Siri to find a reminder for you.

To see a list of your scheduled tasks, tap the alarm clock to the right of the Search field. If you don't see the search field and alarm clock, pull down lightly on the stack of lists. Likewise, push up to hide it.

Creating new Reminders tasks

We prefer to ask Siri to add new tasks to our Reminders lists (see Book I, Chapter 3), but if you don't have an Internet connection or your connection is slow, you can create them by yourself. Here's how to "manually" create new Reminders:

1. **Tap Reminders on the Home screen.**

   The Reminders screen opens. The first time you open Reminders, you see a blank list.

2. **Tap the lined piece of "paper."**

   The keyboard appears.

3. **Type the task you want to remember.**

   The task appears in the list with a radio button to the left and an info button to the right.

4. **Tap the info button to open the Details screen.**

5. **Tap each item to specify how you want Reminders to help you remember this task.**

   • *Remind Me On a Day:* Tap On and tap the date to open a rotor that allows you to specify the date and time. You also have the option to Repeat at an interval you select.

   • *Remind Me At a Location:* Tap On, then tap Location. Tap one of the choices that appear: Current Location or Home, or tap in the Search field to enter a specific street address or the name of a person or business that you have stored in Contacts. Tap the address you want to use and a map showing the address appears in the bottom half of the screen. A pin indicates the address and a circle indicates the *geofence*, which is the distance from your address at which the Reminder will be activated; drag to increase or decrease the geofence. Tap either When I Leave or When I Arrive to hear an alert when one of these actions occurs. Tap Details in the upper left corner, as shown in Figure 2-16. The Location option only works with iPhone 4 or later and doesn't sync with Outlook or Exchange calendars. It works better if you use a street address, and you do need a GPS connection when you're at the location for location-based Reminders to work.

**Book IV
Chapter 2**

Managing Your
Time with Calendar,
Reminders, and
Clock

Go to Settings⇨ Notifications to choose the alert tone and style you want Reminders to use and while you're there, choose whether to include Reminders in the Today view of the Notification Center.

- *Priority:* Tap the exclamation points to set the task's level of importance.

- *List:* Tap to choose which list you want to keep the reminder. See the next section, "Creating Reminders lists."

- *Notes:* Tap to type in any additional details about the reminder.

6. **Tap Done to return to the list.**

Go to Settings⇨Reminders and choose the Default List so when you create new reminders outside of a list, for example in Outlook or another app that syncs to Reminders, they are added to the chosen list.

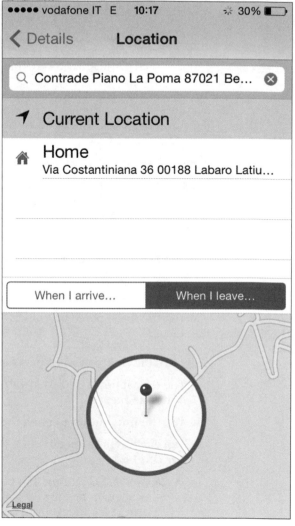

Figure 2-16: Choose when and where Reminders should prod you to your task.

To rearrange, edit, or delete items in a list do the following:

- To rearrange the order of items in your list, tap the Edit button in the upper right corner and then tap and drag the list button to the right of each item to move it up or down in the list.

- Edit a task by tapping the item and then tapping the info button to the right of the task to open the Details screen. Edit the task following the steps you use to create a task.

✓ Edit a task by swiping across the task and then tapping the gray More button.

✓ Delete an item by swiping across the task and then tapping the red Delete button.

✓ Delete an item by tapping Edit and then tapping the red and white minus sign to the left of the item.

When you complete a task, tap the circle to the left of the task on the list as shown in Figure 2-17. You can hide or view completed tasks for a specific list by tapping Edit then Hide Completed or Show Completed at the bottom of the list.

Using Clock to Help Pass the Time

Your iPhone has not one but four time tools: a world clock, an alarm, a stopwatch, and a timer. If you keep your iPhone by your side, you can pretty much eliminate wrist-watches and most clock-like gadgets in your home (although you're still stuck with the blinking numbers on the DVR, VCR, and microwave). With the Clock app, you can do things like use the world clock to make sure you don't call your cousin in Mongolia at 2 a.m. Or, set an alarm to wake you up in the morning and separate alarms to wake your children in time for school. Help your friend track trial times for the 100 meter dash. Set a timer for the cake you've put in the oven and to turn off your iPhone's Music, Video, or Podcasts app when you fall asleep. We take you through each of these marvelous clock features, one by one.

Tap here to see all lists

Figure 2-17: Hide or show completed tasks on your lists.

Book IV
Chapter 2

Managing Your
Time with Calendar,
Reminders, and
Clock

Take a close look at the Clock app icon on the Home screen — yup, it shows the actual time and the red second hand moves continuously.

Adding clocks from around the world

When you tap the Home button to wake your iPhone, you see the time on the screen. You set that time on the World Clock function of your iPhone's Clock app. You can also set up clocks from other time zones to keep you informed of what time it is in your overseas office or in the country where your sister is studying.

You only see four or five clocks at a time (depending on your iPhone model), but you can scroll down the list and have as many clocks as there are time zones.

Follow these steps:

1. **Tap Clock on the Home screen.**

2. **Tap the World Clock button in the bottom left corner.**

3. **Tap the plus sign in the upper right corner.**

   A search field and a list of cities appears.

4. **Scroll through the list of cities or begin typing the city or country that you want to add a clock for.**

   If I type **S**, both Scotland and San Rafael come up, as does Detroit, U.S.A. The more letters you type, the narrower your search results.

5. **Tap the city you want to add.**

   If you don't see the exact city you were searching for, tap one that's in the same time zone.

6. **The World Clock screen returns, as shown in Figure 2-18.**

   You see the city you chose added to the list. In Figure 2-18 the time for each city is shown. Tap on the time to reveal analog-style clocks instead of a digital readout. The clock has a white face if it's daytime in that city and a black face if it's night.

7. **Tap the Edit button in the upper left corner to do one or both of the following:**

   Rearrange the list order: **Tap and hold the reorder button on the right, and then drag the clock to the position you want.**

   Delete a clock: **Tap the red button on the left and then tap the Delete button that appears to the right.**

8. **Tap Done after you finish.**

Turn 24-hour time on or off in Settings⇨General⇨Date & Time.

Setting Alarms

Some of the things we like about the Alarm function are that you can have multiple alarms, choose the days an alarm should repeat, select the sound you want it to have, and add a snooze function. If you want the alarm to vibrate only, leave your iPhone in Ring mode but turn the volume completely down.

REMEMBER

Keep in mind that the alarm sounds even when your iPhone is in Silent mode.

Here's how to set alarms:

1. **Tap Clock on the Home screen.**

2. **Tap the Alarm button at the bottom of the screen.**

3. **Tap the plus sign in the upper right corner.**

   The Add Alarm screen opens.

4. **Use the rotor to set the time you want the alarm to sound.**

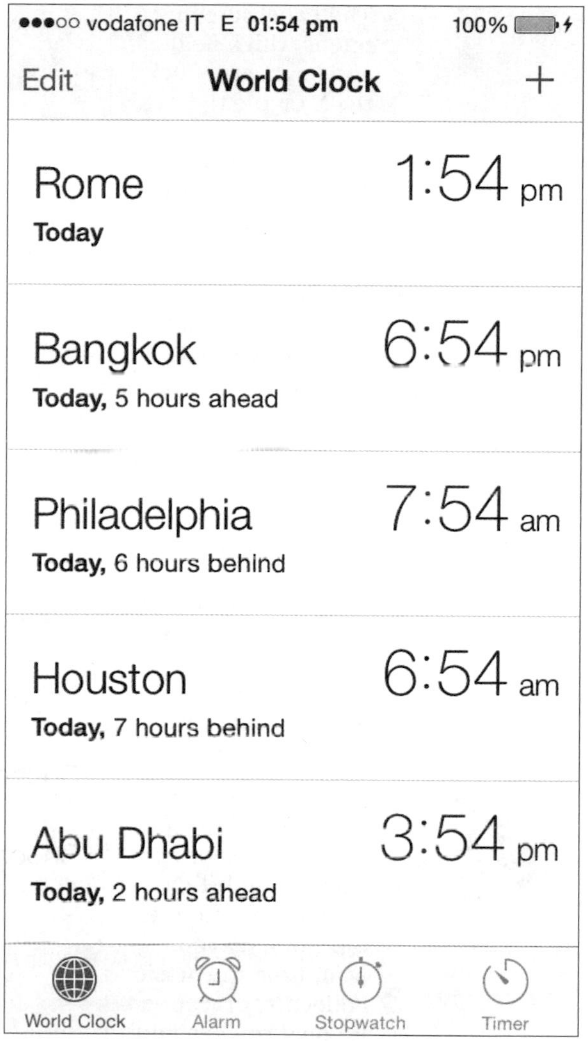

5. **(Optional) Tap Repeat if you want to create a repeating alarm.**

   You can choose any day of the week or a combination of days, which means you can have a Monday through Friday alarm, which is labeled Weekdays on the alarm list, whereas a Saturday/Sunday alarm is labeled Weekends, as shown in Figure 2-19.

6. **Tap Back after you choose the days you want the alarm to repeat.**

7. **(Optional) Tap Label to name your alarm.**

●●●○○ vodafone IT E 01:54 pm   100% ▭ ⚡

Edit   **World Clock**   +

Rome
Today   1:54 pm

Bangkok
Today, 5 hours ahead   6:54 pm

Philadelphia
Today, 6 hours behind   7:54 am

Houston
Today, 7 hours behind   6:54 am

Abu Dhabi
Today, 2 hours ahead   3:54 pm

🌐   ⏰   ⏱   ⏲
World Clock   Alarm   Stopwatch   Timer

Figure 2-18: World clock shows clocks from multiple time zones.

Book IV
Chapter 2

Managing Your
Time with Calendar,
Reminders, and
Clock

The Label screen opens with a field and keyboard. Click the X on the right end of the field to delete the default Alarm label, type the name you want, and then tap Back.

8. **Tap Sound to choose the sound you want for your alarm.**

Choose a sound from the list — scroll down to see all the options, which include ringtones you purchased or created. You can buy more tones by tapping the button at the top of the list, which takes you to the iTunes store.

A neat new feature of iOS 6 or later is using a song for an alarm sound. Tap Pick a Song and then tap the song you want from the music collection on your iPhone. You can add more than one song and assign a different song to different alarms.

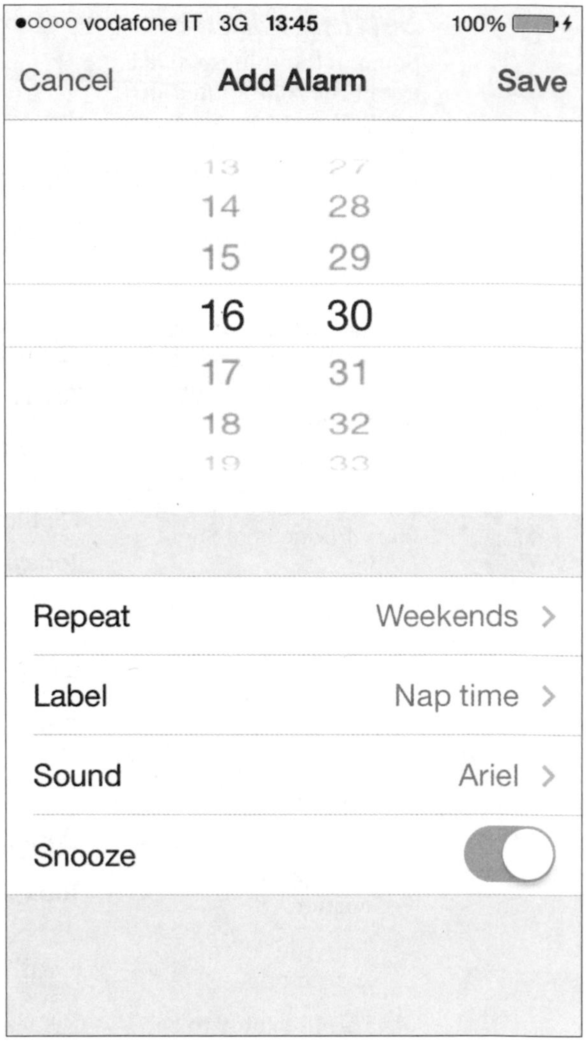

●○○○○ vodafone IT 3G **13:45**		100% 🔋 ⚡
Cancel	**Add Alarm**	Save

13	27
14	28
15	29
16	**30**
17	31
18	32
19	33

Repeat	Weekends >
Label	Nap time >
Sound	Ariel >
Snooze	🔘

Figure 2-19: Set a repeating alarm for selected days of the week.

9. **Tap Snooze On or Off.**

Snooze lets you tap the alarm off when it sounds. After ten minutes, it sounds again.

10. **Tap Save.**

The alarm is added to the list of alarms on the Alarm screen. Use the switch on the right to turn the alarm on or off so you don't have to add and delete alarms you use frequently.

11. When the alarm goes off, just tap the screen to turn it off.

To make changes to an existing alarm, tap the Edit button on the top left of the screen, and then tap the name of the alarm you want to change. The Edit Alarm screen opens, which is the same as the Add Alarm screen but has the information of the selected alarm.

To delete an existing alarm, tap the Edit button. Tap the red button to the left of the alarm time, and then tap the Delete button that appears on the right. Tap Done after you finish.

When you set an alarm, the alarm icon, which looks like a clock, appears in the status bar at the top of your iPhone's screen.

Timing events with Stopwatch

You can use the Stopwatch to time single events such as a speech or laps. Tap Start to start counting.

To time one thing, let it run until the action stops, and then tap Stop.

To time laps, tap Lap each time the runner or swimmer or bicycle rounds the bend. The large numbers continue giving a cumulative time; the smaller numbers above show the lap's duration. When you tap Lap, the laps are listed with each lap's time. If you tap Start again, the count resumes from where it left off.

Tap Reset to zero the count and erase the lap times.

Counting down to zero with Timer

While the Stopwatch starts counting from zero, the timer counts down to zero. You can set the time from one minute up to 23 hours and 59 minutes, after which, you're better off setting an alarm. After you set the timer, you can go on to do things with other apps, even press the Sleep/Wake button. The timer continues to countdown in the background and sounds when the time's up. To set the timer:

1. **Tap Clock on the Home screen.**

2. **Tap the Timer button in the lower right corner.**

3. **Turn the rotor to set the length of time you want to pass before the timer sounds.**

4. **Tap When Timer Ends to choose the "time's up" sound.**

   Scroll through the When Timer Ends list and tap the sound you want. Tap Buy More Tones at the top of the list to go to iTunes and buy additional sounds.

5. **Tap the Set button in the upper right corner.**

**Book IV
Chapter 2**

Managing Your Time with Calendar, Reminders, and Clock

6. **Tap the green Start button on the Timer screen.**

   Tap Pause to interrupt the timer and then Resume to restart it or tap Cancel to turn off the Timer.

To use the Timer as a Sleep Timer while you're listening to audio or watching a video:

1. **Tap When Timer Ends.**
2. **Scroll to the very bottom of the screen and tap Stop Playing.**
3. **Tap Set.**

   The Time screen appears.
4. **Turn the rotor to set the length of time you want to enjoy your media.**
5. **Tap Start.**

   The countdown begins.
6. **Click the Home button.**
7. **Tap Music, Podcasts, or Videos depending on the type of media you want to listen to or watch.**
8. **Tap your selection.**
9. **Tap the Play button to begin playback.**
10. **Whatever you are listening to or watching is turned off when the timer stops.**

Chapter 3: Tapping into Maps, Compass, Weather, Calculator, Stocks, and Numbers

- Adjusting iPhone's location settings and services
- Seeking, finding, and sharing points of interest
- Getting directions
- Talking about the Weather
- Staying on course with Compass
- Keeping things on the Level
- Doing the math with Calculator
- Tracking investments with Stocks
- Summing it up in Numbers

The apps we talk about in this chapter are best described as tools that help you do something you already do, but with more ease and sometimes better performance.

The apps in the first part of the chapter help you navigate to a destination, find out ahead of time how to dress for where you're going, and get your bearings once you get there. What are we talking about? With Maps, just type in beginning and ending points and a mapped out route appears turning your iPhone into a GPS navigator that guides you to your destination.

The Weather app can help you decide whether you ought to wear a raincoat or apply sunscreen. The Compass app can be a handy ally when you want to know which way is north by northwest, and the flip side of Compass is a level that shows the inclination of surfaces where you rest your iPhone.

The last part of the chapter is dedicated to number crunching apps: Calculator and Stocks. Whether you want to tackle basic math problems or complicated scientific equations, Calculator helps you find the solutions. The Stocks app is a great tool for checking daily price quotes and tracking the historical performance of your investments.

Because the apps we cover here are stand-alone tools, don't feel obliged to read this chapter from start to finish (although we're always happy if you do). We go through them one by one and give you all the ins and outs, tips, and tricks so you get the most out of each app.

Adjusting iPhone's Location Settings and Services

Location Services is auxiliary to a lot of apps — Camera uses it to geotag photos, that is to add information about where the photo was taken in addition to putting a time and date stamp on it, and Reminders uses it to alert you to a task when you arrive at or leave a specified address. For Maps and Compass, however, Location Services is essential in order to get the most out of the app. Without Location Services, Maps can give you directions from one address to another and the Compass can give you magnetic north. If you want to know where you are, or want true north, you have to turn on Location Services in Settings. Maps uses your location to give you the best local information available, whereas the Compass uses your location to identify true north. We give you a simple explanation about the difference between true north and magnetic north when we talk about Compass.

The first time an app wants to use Location Services, a notification message appears asking if you want to allow the app to use your location. You can choose yes or no. For example, if you don't want the Camera to put your location on your photos, just tap no when Camera asks to use your Location. You can change these settings at any time, as explained in the third step here:

1. **Tap Settings on the Home screen.**

2. **Tap Privacy⇨Location Services, and then tap the toggle switch On.**

   The Location Services list, as seen in Figure 3-1, opens and displays all apps that can use your location in one way or another.

   When Location Services is being accessed by an app, its icon appears in the status bar.

3. **Turn Location Services on or off for each app.**

   The Location Services icon next to apps indicate the following:

   - *Purple icon* the app has recently used your location.

   - *Gray icon* the app has used your location in the last 24 hours.

- *Purple outlines icon* the app uses a geofence, which is a limit to the location and is used by apps like Reminders to alert you when you leave or arrive at a specified address.

 Location Services must be on for Find my iPhone to work. This should be a strong incentive to use a passcode to lock your iPhone. Otherwise, whoever "finds" your iPhone could just turn off Location Services and render Find My iPhone useless.

Getting There from Here with Maps

With Maps, you can do normal things that maps do — like find out where you are, if you're curious (or lost); or scope out an address you want to visit before you go. Maps becomes particularly useful when used to chart a course from your office to a potential client's office because it provides the travel time and alternate routes. If you use Maps to plan leisurely jaunts, you can find rest stops, outlet malls, historic sites, and hotels along the way.

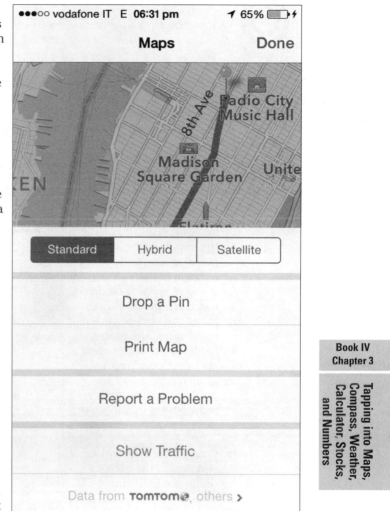

Figure 3-1: You can turn Location Services on for specific apps.

**Book IV
Chapter 3**

Tapping into Maps, Compass, Weather, Calculator, Stocks, and Numbers

In this section, we tell you how to find your present location and locate an address you know. Then we'll show you how to find a service, such as a restaurant or bookstore, near a location. We talk about how to get directions from one place to another, and finally, how to share or save the locations and directions you use.

TIP

If you use a Mac running OS X 10.9 (Mavericks), you can find an address or directions in Maps, bookmark it, and then open it on Maps on your iPhone.

Finding yourself

With Location Services on, Maps can tell you where you are. Tap Maps on the Home screen to open Maps, and then tap the Tracking button in the lower left corner. If you have Location Services turned off, a notification message gives you the option of turning it on so Maps can find you.

Your exact location is the blue dot on the map, like you see in Figure 3-2. If there is a pulsing circle around the blue dot, your location is approximate; the smaller the circle, the more precise your exact (or nearly exact) location. If you're walking or driving, the blue dot moves along the map as you move along the road (or hiking trail or beach surf — you follow our point). A compass appears in the upper right corner to show the direction you're facing.

Change the orientation and size of the map by doing the following:

- Double-tap the Tracking button and a flashlight beam shines from the blue dot, lighting the way your iPhone is oriented. The Tracking button at the bottom of the screen changes to a flashlight icon, as in Figure 3-3.

- Use the spread and pinch gestures with

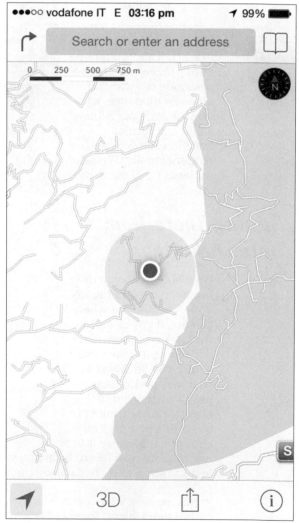

Figure 3-2: The blue dot indicates your present location and follows your every move.

your thumb and forefinger (or the two fingers that are comfortable for you) to zoom in and out of the map. When your fingers are on the screen, a scale appears in the upper left corner (refer to Figure 3-2) to help you understand distances; it disappears when you lift your fingers.

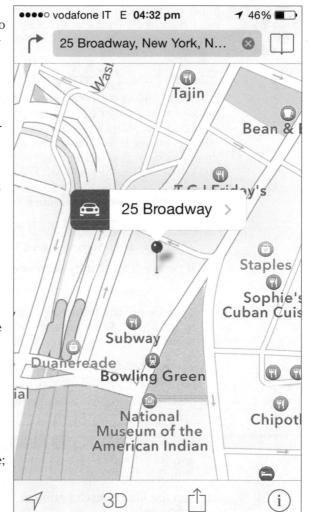

- Double-tap with one finger to zoom in.

- Double-tap with two fingers to zoom out.

- Drag two fingers up the screen or tap the 3D button to switch to 3D mode.

Single-tap the map with one finger to hide the search and command bars at the top and bottom of the screen to see as much map as possible; single-tap again to bring them back into view.

Figure 3-3: A red pin and flag indicate the sought-after address.

The following gestures cancel Tracking if you are using it, although the zooming and 3D gestures work with or without Tracking:

- Use two fingers to rotate the map.

- Tap the Compass button that appears in the upper right corner to return to a north-facing orientation.

- Drag one finger around the screen to move the map up, down, or sideways.

**Book IV
Chapter 3**

Tapping into Maps, Compass, Weather, Calculator, Stocks, and Numbers

Maps combines the GPS (Global Positioning System), Wi-Fi, and cellular network data to determine your location and then uses TomTom and other mapping services to display locations and calculate routes.

Seeking and finding locations

Instead of finding a street name on a list, and then flipping a large unwieldy piece of thin, easily ripped paper, otherwise known as a map, to look for quadrant K-5, Maps lets you type in the address you seek. As fast as your Internet connection allows, the equivalent of quadrant K-5 appears on your iPhone screen. You can also find addresses from Contacts and from bookmarks that you set up in Maps. Follow these steps to map-folding freedom:

1. **Open Maps from the Home screen.**

2. **Tap the Search field at the top of the screen.**

   The keyboard opens and a list of your recent searches appears.

3. **If you seek a recently searched for address, tap it in the list.**

   Or

   Type one of the following in the search field (if an address is already in the search field, tap the X at the right end of the field to delete the text):

   • *An address* in the form of a street name and number or an intersection, with the city and state or just the name of a city or town.

   • *A neighborhood or landmark.*

   • *The name* of a person or business that's stored in your Contacts.

   A list of potential matches from Contacts and the Maps database appears; if you see the address you seek in the list, tap it to open a map showing that location.

4. **Tap the blue Search button in the bottom right corner of the keyboard.**

   A red pin on the map indicates the address you seek. The address is written on a flag attached to the pin, as shown in Figure 3-3. If the location is near your current location, you also see the travel time under the driving button.

If you want to keep the found address for future use, tap the right end of the flag, and then tap Add Bookmark, to store the address in Maps or tap Create New Contact or Add to Existing Contact to store the address and associated information in Contacts.

To view and use an address you've recently used, bookmarked, or from your Contacts list, do the following:

1. **Open Maps from the Home screen.**

2. **Tap the Bookmarks button to the right of the Search field.**

3. **Tap the Bookmarks button at the bottom left of the screen to use a bookmarked location.**

   A list of bookmarks opens.

   Or

   Tap the Recents button at the bottom in the center of the screen to use an address you've recently accessed.

   A list of recently used addresses opens.

   Or

   Tap the Contacts button at the bottom right of the screen to choose a person or business from Contacts.

   Your All Contacts list appears. Scroll through the list to open the Info screen that contains the address you seek.

4. **Tap the address you wish to use.**

   A map opens and a red pin indicates the address or location you're looking for.

If you want a clean slate, you can clear your bookmarks by opening the list and tapping Edit, and then tap the red and white minus sign followed by the delete button, or simply swipe across the bookmarked address and tap Delete. Although bookmarks can be removed singly, removing recent locations is an all or nothing deal: Tap Recents and then tap the Clear button and the list is emptied. If you want to save a Recents address, open it, and then save it as a bookmark or an addition to Contacts.

You can blunder around an unfamiliar city looking for a place to eat until you stumble upon an appealing restaurant, or you can rely on Maps, which uses Yelp! to make suggestions for eateries and the like. Follow these steps to find sites and services quickly and easily:

1. **Open Maps from the Home screen.**

2. **Tap the Tracking button to find something near your current location; otherwise, Maps searches for something near the last location you worked with.**

3. **Tap the Search field at the top of the screen.**

   The keyboard opens so you can type what you're looking for, say, *books* or *museums Prague*.

4. **Type your criteria in the Search field.**

As you begin typing, Spotlight lists potential matches of locations (which have a red pin next to them) and words, which have a magnifying glass icon next to them.

5. **If your desired search word appears before you finish typing, you can tap that. If not, finish typing and then tap the Search button in the bottom right corner.**

Red pins appear on the matches in your vicinity or in the city you specified, as shown in Figure 3-4.

6. **Tap one of the pins to see a flag with the name of the result.**

Or

Tap the List button at the bottom of the screen to see a list of names, addresses of all the results. Tap a result to see it on the map (or tap Done to return to the map).

7. **Tap the arrow on the right end of the flag in Map view or tap the Info button in List view to see information about the location.**

A Location screen opens that shows the distance of the location from your current location (determined by Location Services), along with information like the phone number and address of the selected site, the site's web address, or a link to Yelp!, as seen in Figure 3-5. When available, you'll also see a Reviews and Photos button that give you reviews to read and photos to look at of the location.

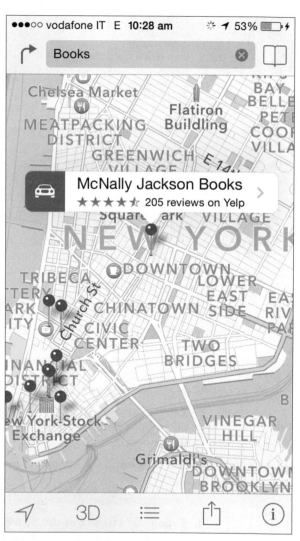

Figure 3-4: Use Maps to find services in a city or near a specific address.

Tap the web page address to find out more about the location you found, such as the menu of a restaurant or special exhibits at a museum, or tap the phone number to call. (If you search for an eating establishment, Maps also integrates with the OpenTable app (free to download at the App Store) to make reservations.)

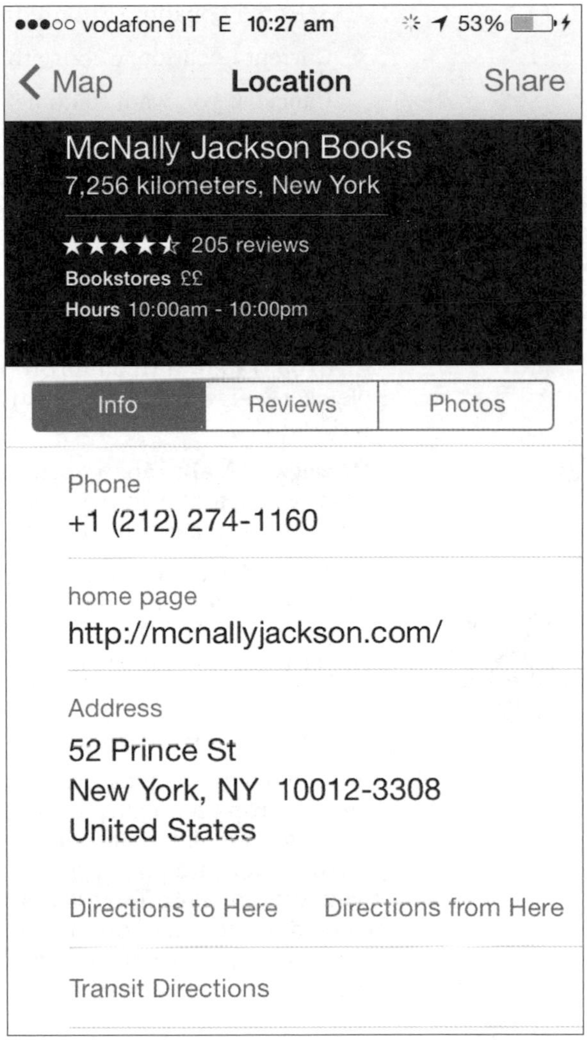

TIP

Scroll down the Location screen to find the Add Bookmark, Create New Contact, and Add to Existing Contact buttons to take those actions on the address you've found.

REMEMBER

If you have an iPhone 4s or later, press and hold the Home button and ask Siri to find whatever you need for you.

Sharing points of interest

When you find a great restaurant or want to share the address for a party, you can share it in several ways directly from Maps. Here's how to share locations:

●●●○○ vodafone IT E 10:27 am ☀ ◀ 53% ▭ ⚡

< Map **Location** Share

McNally Jackson Books
7,256 kilometers, New York

★★★★⯪ 205 reviews
Bookstores ££
Hours 10:00am - 10:00pm

| Info | Reviews | Photos |

Phone
+1 (212) 274-1160

home page
http://mcnallyjackson.com/

Address
52 Prince St
New York, NY 10012-3308
United States

Directions to Here   Directions from Here

Transit Directions

Figure 3-5: The Location screen shows information about a location you select.

1. **Find the address you want to share with someone, either by searching or choosing from a bookmark or Contacts.**

2. **Do one of the following:**

   1. Tap the Action button at the bottom of the screen.

   2. Tap one of the three choices that appear:

**Book IV
Chapter 3**

Tapping into Maps, Compass, Weather, Calculator, Stocks, and Numbers

Selected Location: Choose this to share the location you found.

Current Location: Choose this to share where you are.

Cancel: If you want to do neither of the above.

Or

1. Tap the right end of the location's flag on the map.

2. Tap Share at the top of the Location screen that opens.

    The Share Sheet opens.

3. **Tap one of the sharing options:**

    AirDrop: Tap to turn on AirDrop and share the location with other people near you who use AirDrop. (See Book I, Chapter 4 to learn about AirDrop.)

    Message or Mail: Tap to open an outgoing message that contains the location. Fill in the address for one or more recipients and then tap Send. (See Book III, Chapters 2 and 4 to learn about Message and Mail.)

    Twitter or Facebook: Tap to post to either of these social networks. You must be logged in to your account.

You can also tap Add Bookmark to add the location to Maps' Bookmarks.

Dropping a pin

If there's no pin on the location you want to save or share, tap the Info button and tap Drop Pin. A purple pin shows up on the map with a flag that reads *Dropped Pin*. If the pin isn't exactly where you want it, zoom in on the map (double-tap with one finger), drag the pin, and then let go on the exact spot you want to mark. Tap the right end of the flag to display a Location screen with the standard options. To remove the pin, tap Remove Pin. That's exactly what happens when you return to the Map screen — out of sight, out of mind.

If you still prefer your maps on paper, tap the Info button and then tap Print Map. See Book I, Chapter 2 for details about printing.

Getting directions

Rather than asking a stranger at a gas station where the intersection of First and Pine is, only to find he said "left" when he should've said "right," you can ask Maps to show you the way. With iOS 6 or later and an iPhone 4S or later, Maps provides voice-guided navigation just like a GPS navigator — one less gadget to cart around. Follow these steps for getting directions:

1. **Find an address in one of the three ways detailed previously.**

    The pin with the flag indicates the sought-after address.

2. **To get directions to the address from your current location, tap the Quick Driving Directions button on the left end of the pin's flag.**

   Or

   Tap the right end of the flag and go to Step 3.

   Or

   Tap the Directions button to the left of the Search field in the upper left corner and go to Step 4.

   An Info screen opens.

   A quick way to get directions from your current location is to search for the address you want to go to and when the map is pinned, tap the Driving directions button on the left end of the flag. A route is immediately calculated; skip ahead to Step 6.

3. **You can obtain directions to and from this location by tapping one of the buttons:**

   Directions to Here: The Directions screen opens as seen in Figure 3-6. Current Location is the default for the starting point.

   Directions from Here: The Directions screen opens; however, Current Location is the default ending point or destination.

   To use an address different than your Current Location as a starting or ending point, tap in the field that contains Current Location.

   Current Location is highlighted.

   1. Tap the circled X on the right end of the field to clear the field.

   2. Type in the address you wish to use.

   3. Tap the Next button on the bottom right.

      The cursor moves to the other field, which has the previously established address. You can change it with the keyboard if you want.

   Swap the Start and End points of the Directions by taping the Swap button.

   If you want directions and travel time for walking between destinations, tap the pedestrian button at the top of the screen. Tap the bus button, or the Transit Directions button on the Location screen, to open the App Store and see a list of apps associated with the public transportation available for the area of your chosen directions, which you can download and use to search for a public transportation solution.

4. **Tap the Route button in the upper right corner or on the lower right corner of the keyboard.**

   The screen displays a map showing the route from your starting point to your destination, or from your destination back to your starting point, if you prefer.

The distance and estimated travel time are displayed above the map. If more than one route is available, Maps displays alternate routes, assigning a number to each. Tap the route you want to follow.

5. **Tap the Info button to select and change how you see the map.**

   You see the screen shown in Figure 3-7.

6. **Choose one of the following views:**

   • **Standard** shows you a map. This is the default view.

   • **Hybrid** shows the street names on a satellite view.

   • **Satellite** shows a satellite view.

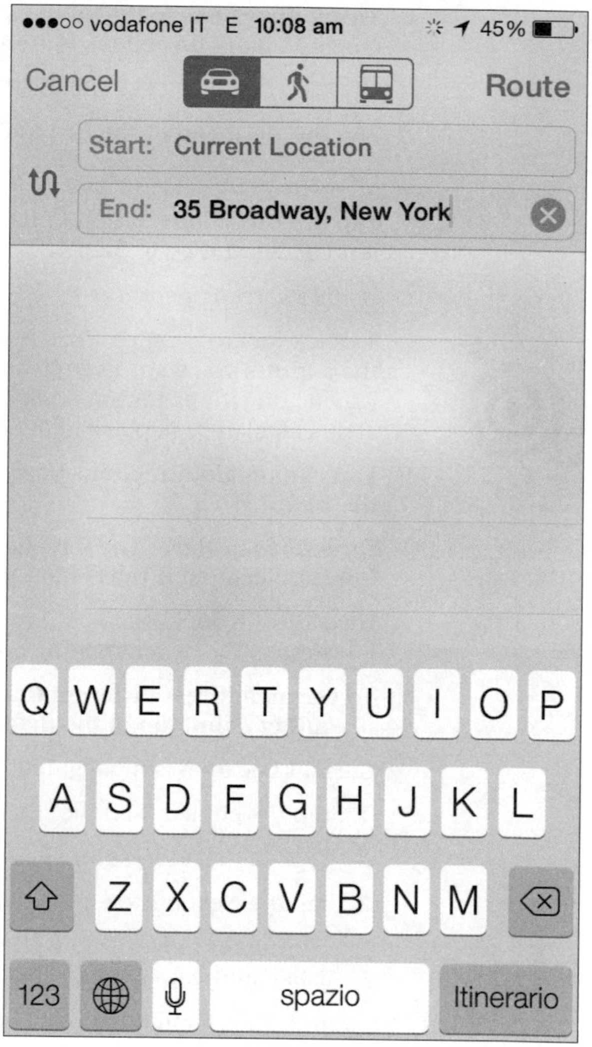

If you ever wanted to take flight like a bird and swoop among the tall buildings of some of the world's most famous cities, tap the 3D or Flyover button next to the Tracking button to see the your standard view map in 3D or a hybrid or satellite view in Flyover mode (requires iPhone 4s or later). Zoom in until the 3D or Flyover button is active, as shown in Figure 3-8. The 3D or Flyover button is gray if the services are unavailable.

7. **Tap Show Traffic.**

This feature is only available in some locations.

The roads on the map show you traffic conditions as in Figure 3-9:

• **Red** dashes shows where traffic is heavy and stop and go.

Figure 3-6: Fill in the starting point and destination you want on the Directions screen.

- **Orange** dots means traffic is moving slowly.

- **Road Closed** icons mean what they show — road closed.

- **Men At Work** icons indicate road work.

8. **Tap the Start button in the upper right corner.**

   If you have an iPhone 4s or later and an active Internet connection, point-to-point directions are dictated to you as you move along the route.

   In Map, Satellite, or Hybrid view, Maps zooms in to the first step of the list.

9. **Swipe across the indicators at the top of the screen to move from one step to the next.**

   A white arrow indicates the intersection of the turn or road change at each step. The following taps give you different views along the way:

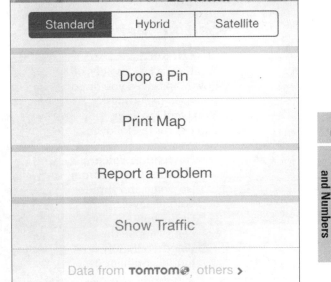

Figure 3-7: You have three map views to choose from.

Book IV Chapter 3

Tapping into Maps, Compass, Weather, Calculator, Stocks, and Numbers

- Tap the Overview button to see the indications from starting point to destination on the map.

- Tap the List button (next to the Tracking button in Overview) to see a list of the point-to-point directions.

- Tap any item in the list to see that point on the map.

Tap Overview, and then tap Resume to return to the point-to-point instructions.

10. **If you want to change your starting point or destination or the whole route, tap the End button in the upper left corner and start over.**

When you're looking for directions during the dark hours of the day, Maps automatically switches to Night mode, which shows light text on a dark background.

Setting Maps' settings

You have a few choices of how Maps gives you directions. Go to Settings⇨ Maps and tap your choices for the following:

Figure 3-8: Flyover gives you a 3D satellite view.

- **Navigation Voice Volume:** Choose from No Voice and three volume levels. Unfortunately, you can't choose the voice itself, only how loudly you hear it.

- **Distances:** Choose miles or kilometers.

- **Map Labels:** Turn the toggle switch On to see labels in English or Off to see labels in the local language.

- **Preferred Directions:** Choose Driving or Walking for your default directions.

On the Info screen, fields that appear are active and information that's available on your iPhone is filled in. For example, if an address you are using is associated with a person in Contacts for whom you also have a phone number and e-mail, those fields appear. If the location is unknown, only the Directions to Here, Directions from Here, and Transit Directions buttons appear, along with the Add to Contacts, Share Location, and Add to Bookmarks. Activate these options by tapping on the associated button:

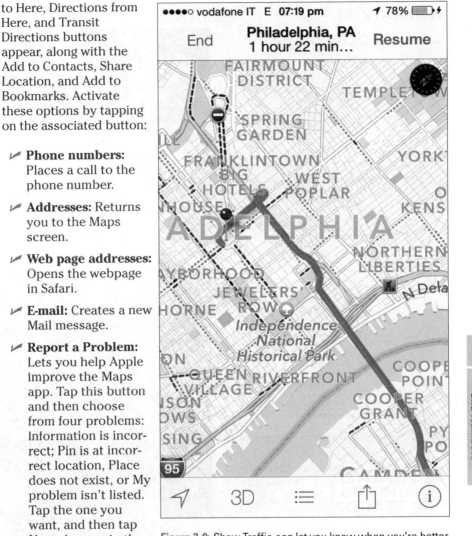

✔ **Phone numbers:** Places a call to the phone number.

✔ **Addresses:** Returns you to the Maps screen.

✔ **Web page addresses:** Opens the webpage in Safari.

✔ **E-mail:** Creates a new Mail message.

✔ **Report a Problem:** Lets you help Apple improve the Maps app. Tap this button and then choose from four problems: Information is incorrect; Pin is at incorrect location, Place does not exist, or My problem isn't listed. Tap the one you want, and then tap Next. Answer in the associated questions on the subsequent screen, and then tap Send.

Figure 3-9: Show Traffic can let you know when you're better off choosing a different route.

Book IV
Chapter 3

Tapping into Maps,
Compass, Weather,
Calculator, Stocks,
and Numbers

Talking about the Weather

Fresh air is good for your physical and mental health, but it's nice to know how to dress for the occasion, and for that you have Weather on your iPhone. Brought to you by Yahoo! and The Weather Channel, iPhone's Weather app is updated hourly and gives you the current temperature and conditions and a five-day forecast for cities across the country and around the world.

Adding, removing, and reorganizing cities

Weather uses Location Services to provide the forecast for your current location, but you may want to add other cities and locales too. Say you have to go on a multi-city book tour and want to know what the weather will be like in each city. You can add the cities you'll be going to and then quickly flip through each day to see whether to expect sunny skies in your upcoming stop. Follow these steps:

1. **Tap Weather on the Home screen.**

2. **Tap the List button in the bottom right corner.**

   A screen similar to that in Figure 3-10 opens.

3. **Tap the F or C button if you want to switch between Fahrenheit and Celsius temperature readings.**

4. **Tap the plus sign to add locations where you want to track the weather.**

   A screen opens with a search field and keyboard.

Figure 3-10: Add, delete, and reorder the cities you want Weather forecasts for.

5. **Type in the name, ZIP code, or airport code of the city or town you want to add.**

   A list opens with possible matches.

6. **Tap the name of the city you want to add.**

   The city now appears in your list.

To delete a city from your list:

1. **Tap Weather on the Home screen.**

2. **Tap the List button in the bottom right corner.**

3. **Swipe left across the city you want to delete.**

   A Delete button appears to the right of the name.

4. **Tap the Delete button.**

   The city disappears from the list.

   If you swiped by mistake, tap anywhere but the Delete button to cancel.

5. **Tap a city in the list to return to the weather screen.**

To rearrange the order of the cities in the list, which in turn affects the order they're displayed on the weather screen, touch and hold a city, and then drag it to the position you want on the list. Drag the names of the cities around until they are in the order you like.

Viewing current and upcoming conditions

After you've added and organized the cities and tapped Done, the weather screen returns, as shown in Figure 3-11. Each city on your list has its own weather forecast screen.

●●●●○ vodafone IT   E   08:55 pm   69% ▭+

Philadelphia

Humidity	67%
Chance of rain	4%
Wind ENE	9 mph
Feels like	82°

| **Thursday** Today | | 81 | 66 |

Now	3pm	4pm	5pm	6pm	7pm
☁	☀	☀	☀	☀	☀
81	81	81	81	79	77

Friday	☀	82	68
Saturday	⛅	84	72
Sunday	⛈	82	72
Monday	⛈	84	72
Tuesday	⛈	79	61

Figure 3-11: Weather gives you the current temperature and a five-day forecast.

**Book IV
Chapter 3**

Tapping into Maps,
Compass, Weather,
Calculator, Stocks,
and Numbers

Flick left or right to move between screens. If you have Location Services on for the Weather app (Settings⇨Privacy⇨Location Services), the first screen shows the forecast for your current location. The white dots at the bottom of the screen tell you how many cities you have forecasts for. Notice that the Location Services icon appears to the left of the dots.

The dynamic background (available on iPhone 4s or later) reflects the current weather so you may see the Milky Way with an occasional shooting star or cumulus clouds drifting across a blue sky. Under the city name you see either the current temperature or conditions, tapping on that area of the screen toggles between the two pieces of information. The day's hourly forecast, including sunrise and sunset times, runs horizontally across the middle of the screen and below that a list of the next five-days' forecast with the weather symbols we're used to: sunny, partly sunny, cloudy, thunderstorms, and so on. Swipe the hourly forecast left to see the conditions for later in the day. On an iPhone 4s or earlier, swipe down on the daily forecast to open an hour by hour forecast for the next 12 hours.

When you pull down the Notification Center, you'll see the local forecast. Tap on the forecast in the Notification Center and the Weather app opens.

If you want more information, tap the Yahoo! button in the bottom left corner. This opens the Yahoo! weather page in Safari and gives you more detailed weather information along with links to websites with news and other information about that city.

Staying on the Straight and Level with Compass

iPhone uses a built-in magnetic field sensor — a magnetometer — to give compass readings. The first thing we explain is how to calibrate the Compass to cancel any interference and get Compass back on course. We show you how to read the Compass, and explain the difference between true and magnetic north and how to select one or the other.

Calibrating your iPhone for greater accuracy

When you first open Compass — it might be in the Utilities folder if you don't find it on your Home screen — a notification message appears indicating that you should calibrate your iPhone. Any time iPhone detects some interference, usually something with a magnetic field or an electronic device like a cell phone or stereo, you see a message asking you to calibrate your phone. As instructed on-screen, simply tilt your iPhone around until the circle is completed filled in and the Compass itself appears.

Getting your bearing

Whether to determine the direction you're facing, for example to make sure your plants are on the east side of your house to get the morning sun, or find the direction you want to go, Compass is a great tool. After the Compass is calibrated, hold your iPhone (face-up, of course) so the back of your hand is parallel to the ground.

The red arrow on the Compass points north, the direction your iPhone is pointing is written in white above the compass. Move around, and the compass rotates and the headings change. When you have Location Services turned on, your geographic coordinates and sometimes the town name are displayed below the compass, as shown in Figure 3-12.

What's really helpful is that Compass links to Maps. If you want to see where you are on a map, tap the coordinates at the bottom of the screen. Maps opens and the tracking flashlight indicates your location and the direction you're facing. If you want to know the address, drop a pin and the address appears in the attached flag.

Figure 3-12: The Compass shows both the heading and the geographic coordinates for your location.

Choosing between true north or magnetic north

Compass gives accurate readings of both true north and magnetic north, and both are valid indications. True north, which is a GPS bearing linked to the geographical location of the North Pole, works when Location Services is turned on.

Magnetic north, on the other hand, depends on the Earth's natural magnetism, which changes based on your physical location. It works when Location Services is both on and off. Because magnetic north changes at different latitudes, it can be a few to many degrees different than true north and even south of your latitude. This difference is called *declination*. In some places, declination is less than one degree so it barely alters your bearings. Keep in mind, however, if you're hiking in the wilderness on a trail with 10 degrees of declination, those seemingly minor ten degrees can result in you being miles off course after several hours of continuous hiking. Technically speaking, to achieve the most accurate results, you have to know the actual declination degrees you're traversing for your current location to calculate the difference between magnetic north and true north. Localized trekking maps often have declination degrees on them, so you can adjust the orientation of your map when using true north. To turn on true north, tap Settings➪Compass and then tap Use True North on.

Keeping things on the Level

The Compass is really two, two, two tools in one! (Anybody but me remember the old Certs commercial?) Swipe left from the Compass screen and you find an electronic spirit level. Instead of having an air bubble that must fall between two lines to indicate a level horizontal surface, two white bubbles, um, circles must line up when you place your iPhone on a horizontal surface. The degree of inclination appears in the circles, as shown in Figure 3-13, and when your iPhone is in a perfectly level position, the whole screen turns green and zero degrees show in the center circle. If you use the edges of your iPhone, instead of circles, you have a horizontal line across the center that divides the white top from the black bottom. When your iPhone is in a position of zero inclination, the black turns green.

Figure 3-13: Make sure your surfaces have the inclination you want with the Level.

Doing the Math with Calculator

The Calculator app on your iPhone is really two calculators: a basic four-function calculator that you use for addition, subtraction, multiplication, and division, and a scientific calculator that is capable of performing trigonometric calculations, logarithms, square roots, and percentages.

Doing basic addition, subtraction, multiplication, and division

Even if you remember your times tables, there are times when you reach for a calculator and you don't have to reach any farther than your iPhone. The basic four-function calculator opens when you tap Calculator. Follow these steps:

1. **Tap Calculator on the Home screen or you might find it in the Utilities folder on the Home screen.**

   The Calculator opens, as shown in Figure 3-14.

2. **Tap the numbers and operations you want to perform.**

   A white outline appears around the operation key you tap to remind you which operation is active.

 The percentage key has moved to the four-function calculator in iOS 7 (it was on only the scientific calculator in earlier versions). To subtract a percentage, type in the total amount and then the minus sign, followed by

Figure 3-14: The four-function Calculator adds, subtracts, multiplies, divides, and calculates percentages.

the amount of the percentage off and the percent sign. A quick press of the equals sign, and you have the reduced amount: for example, 45000 — 3.475% = 43,436.25. To add a percentage, just tap the plus sign instead of the minus sign.

You can copy and paste numbers from the Calculator results display to another app by pressing and holding on the display until the Copy/Paste button appears. You can also paste a number from another app into the calculator display to use it in a calculation. See Book I, Chapter 3 to learn about editing functions and commands.

Switching to a scientific view

Most cell phones have calculators today, but iPhone offers a full-function scientific calculator too. To open the scientific calculator, turn your iPhone to landscape view, as seen in Figure 3-15. (If you have locked your iPhone in Portrait view, this won't work until you unlock it: swipe up from the bottom of the screen to open the command center and tap the Orientation Lock button.)

Here you'll find the memory commands:

- ✔ **mc** clears any numbers you have in memory.
- ✔ **m+** adds the number on the display to the number in memory.
- ✔ **m-** subtracts the number on the display from the number in memory.
- ✔ **mr (memory replace)** uses the number you put in memory in your current calculation. The button is outlined in black when a number is stored.

Two keys on the calculator toggle the other keys:

- ✔ **2nd:** Tap to change trigonomic (sin, cos, tan) and hyperbolic functions to the inverse. The button is outlined in black when active.

- ✔ **Rad/Deg:** Tap to switch between Radians and Degrees for trigonomic functions. Deg or Rad in the left corner of the number display tells you what mode you're in.

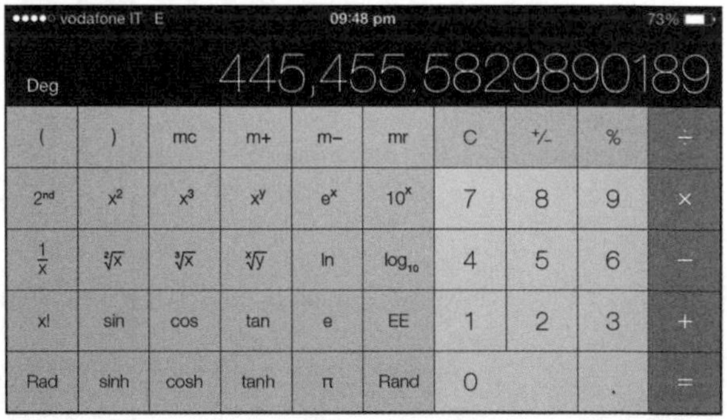

Figure 3-15: Turning your iPhone to landscape view opens the scientific calculator.

You find keys that calculate square, cube, and other roots, decimal and Naperian logarithms, and factorials, as well as generates random numbers.

Tracking Investments with Stocks

Whether you have a single mutual fund or a sizeable portfolio managed by a financial advisor, keeping an eye on your investments is usually a good idea. And that's exactly the idea behind iPhone's Stocks app, a simple yet powerful tool you can tap into to display and track activity for the stocks and funds you're interested in for the time interval you want. First we show you how to add the companies you want to watch and put them in an order that you like. Next, we show you how to manage the viewing options Stocks offers.

Adding, deleting, and reordering stocks, funds, and indexes

Stocks comes with an assortment of U.S. and foreign index listings along with share activity of a few publicly traded companies already specified, as seen in Figure 3-16.

**Book IV
Chapter 3**

Tapping into Maps, Compass, Weather, Calculator, Stocks, and Numbers

Figure 3-16: Stocks shows market activity for U.S. and foreign indexes as well as individual corporate share prices.

The first thing you want to do is add your personal stock or fund holdings or those that you're interested in watching for potential investments and delete any loaded ones that don't interest you. Here are the steps to follow:

1. **Tap Stocks on the Home screen.**

2. **Tap the List button in the bottom right corner.**

   The Stocks screen opens.

3. **Tap the plus sign button in the upper left corner.**

   A search field opens with a keyboard.

4. **Type a company name or a stock identification code.**

   Stocks searches and a list of possible matches appears.

5. **Tap the stock you wish to add to your list.**

   The screen returns to the list. The stock or fund you chose is added to the bottom of the list.

6. **Repeat Steps 3, 4, and 5 to add as many stocks as you wish.**

7. **Tap the Done button in the upper right corner.**

   The current price screen returns.

To delete a stock or index from your list:

1. **Tap Stocks on the Home screen.**

2. **Tap the List button in the bottom right corner.**

3. **Tap the minus sign to the left of the name.**

   A delete button appears to the right of the name.

4. **Tap the Delete button.**

   The stock or index disappears from the list.

   If you tapped the minus sign by mistake, tap it again to cancel.

5. **Tap the Done button in the upper right corner.**

   The current price screen returns.

You can arrange the stocks and indices in any order you want, such as putting those you're most interested in at the top.

Touch and hold the reorder button, and then drag the stock to the position on the list. Drag the names of the stocks around until they are in the order you like.

The three buttons at the bottom of the Stocks screen let you choose how you view market fluctuations: by percentage changes, by price changes, or by market capitalization.

The market fluctuations appear on a green background if there's been a price increase and on red if there's been a decrease. The information lags about 20 minutes behind actual market activity.

Scrolling through views and news

After you establish the stocks and indices you want to follow, you may want to look at some historic data or see what the press has said about that company today.

Referring to Figure 3-16, the screen is divided into two zones: The top holds the list of stocks and indices you follow (six appear at a time, but you can scroll to see the other companies on your list).

The lower zone shows information about whichever stock or index you select from the upper zone. This zone scrolls left to right. After the price activity section, there's a graph that shows historic activity from one day up to two years. Scroll to the next screen to see a vertically scrollable list of news stories related to the stock or index highlighted in the upper zone — tap a news headline to open the complete article in Safari or tap and hold to add the article to Reading List. That's one information-packed screen!

Turn on Stocks in Settings⇨Notifications and list of the status of your chosen markets, stocks, and funds appears in the Notification Center.

Monitoring investment performance over time

But wait, there's more. Go back to the graph that shows historic activity. There are seven time intervals at the top. Tap any of those intervals and the graph expands or contracts to show price fluctuations from today back to the date that corresponds with the interval you chose.

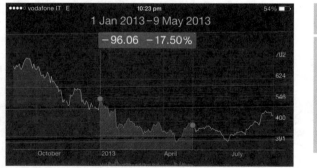

Figure 3-17: Turn Stocks to landscape view and the share price fluctuation graph becomes interactive.

To display a more detailed view, turn your iPhone to landscape view, as in Figure 3-17. The graph for the interval you were viewing in portrait view appears with the greater detail that increased landscape size allows. This screen is interactive. For example, tap the one week view, and then touch and drag the blue line left and right. You see price fluctuations at intervals throughout the day. If you knew an announcement was made at a certain time on a certain day, you could see how soon after the announcement a change in the share price appeared.

Touch and hold on the screen to bring up the blue line, and then drag left and right to see the price for different days. In the three month, six month,

Book IV
Chapter 3

Tapping into Maps,
Compass, Weather,
Calculator, Stocks,
and Numbers

and one year views, the detail gives the daily closing price; in the two year view, the daily closing price is given for every other day; in the five year view, every year; and in the 10 year view, every other year.

If you put two fingers on the screen at once, two vertical, blue lines bracket a time interval and the share price change in that period is shown.

Move your fingers in and out to shorten and lengthen the time interval. In landscape view, when you flick from left to right, you see the graph for the same interval for each of the stocks and indexes on your personalized list.

Summing It up with Numbers

Numbers could be a chapter, if not a mini-book of its own, but here we present a quick introduction. We take you through creating a simple spreadsheet with a few formulas, a graph, and several formatting tweaks. We encourage you to poke around the app to discover more features or review the in-app tutorial by tapping the Charting Basics template on the main Numbers screen.

Numbers, and its iWork sibling apps Pages and Keynote, work with iCloud, which means that if you go to Settings⇨iCloud⇨Documents & Data and turn on Numbers, your documents automatically sync with other iOS devices and Macs that use Numbers with the same iCloud account. You can also share your Numbers spreadsheet with other people through the iCloud.com website.

Creating a spreadsheet with formulas

Numbers comes with 30 templates and one blank, and these are the same templates as in the Mac version of Numbers. Templates make it really easy to create a new document and just type in your data and substitute the placeholder text with your own. Even if you don't use a template, looking at them gives you a good idea of the power of Numbers — granted, if you want to get fancy, you probably want to create your spreadsheet on an iPad or a Mac and use your iPhone to access your data, make minor corrections, or project it on a computer or monitor.

Here are the steps for creating a spreadsheet:

1. **Tap Numbers on Home screen.**

   For our purposes, Numbers is turned on in iCloud so we can share the spreadsheet after it's created.

2. **Tap Create New (it's the first icon on the top left with the plus sign on it).**

   If you already save Numbers spreadsheets to iCloud from another device or Mac, you see them here and can tap to open them. Likewise if you saved Excel documents in Numbers on your Mac; they have an "E" on them in the Numbers chooser until you open them and then you see a preview on the icon on the Numbers screen.

3. **Tap Create Spreadsheet.**

4. **Tap Blank.**

A sheet, named . . . drumroll please . . . Sheet 1, is created and contains one blank table.

In addition to the 30 templates that come with Number, you also find free and fee-based template apps in the App Store.

5. **Double-tap in any field to enter data. Tapping the buttons at the top changes the keyboard to reflect the type of data you want to enter:**

   - Tap the value button (42) to enter a number value. Tap the button on either side of the keypad to assign a value type, such as dollar or percent. Tap the star to create a ratings box or the check to create a check box.

   - Tap the clock to enter a date or time.

   - Tap the calendar or hourglass by the keypad to switch between months and numbers.

   - Tap the text button (T) to enter text.

   - Tap the formula button (=) to enter a formula, as shown in Figure 3-18. You can see the formula in the field at the top of the screen. To use a cell to create a formula, tap the

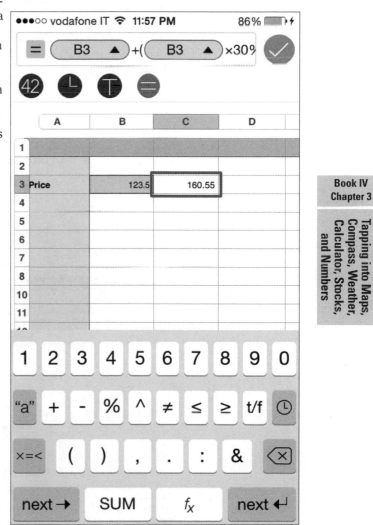

Figure 3-18: Type your own formulas cell by cell.

Book IV
Chapter 3

Tapping into Maps,
Compass, Weather,
Calculator, Stocks,
and Numbers

cell and it appears in the field. Tap the operator you want to use and then tap another cell or a number. In the figure, you see the formula for cell C3 equals B3 + 30 percent. Tap the check mark on the right end of the field when you finish entering the value, date, text, or formula you want.

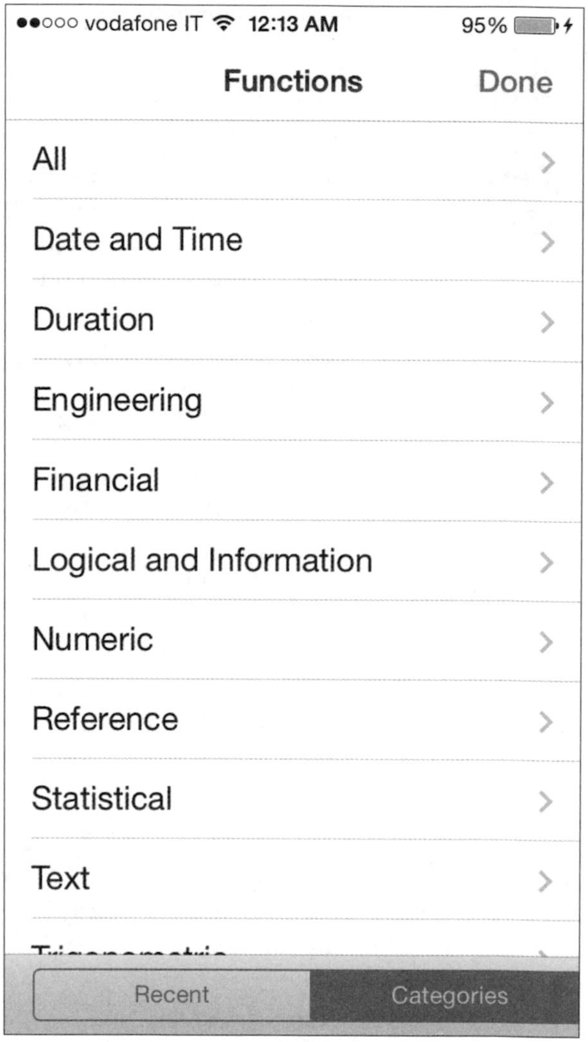

An easier way to enter a formula is to use Numbers' functions. Tap the function key (next to the SUM key, refer to Figure 3-18) to open the list of function categories, as shown in Figure 3-19. Tap Categories at the bottom of the screen if it isn't selected, and then tap a category from the list. A list of functions in that category

Functions	Done
●●○○○ vodafone IT 🛜 12:13 AM	95% 🔋⚡

All	>
Date and Time	>
Duration	>
Engineering	>
Financial	>
Logical and Information	>
Numeric	>
Reference	>
Statistical	>
Text	>

| Recent | Categories |

Figure 3-19: Use Numbers' predefined functions to create complex, hardworking spreadsheets.

opens, and you can tap each function to read a definition of the function, how it operates, as well as an example of how it's used. Tap the category name in the upper left corner to return to the function list and then tap the function you want to use. It's pasted into the cell you had selected.

All keyboards have a delete button. The value, clock, and formula keyboards have tab buttons, which move the cursor on cell to the right, and return buttons, which move the cursor to the beginning of the next line, whereas the text keyboard only has a Next button, which moves down one cell. The formula keyboard has a clock and text ("A") button, which switches to those keyboards to you can insert those types of variables in your formulas; tapping Done takes you back to the formula keyboard. The formula keyboard also has a symbol shift key, which toggles between different mathematical symbols to give you more choices, much like the numbers and globe keys on the text keyboard toggle between different keyboard layouts and languages.

6. **Tap the Add Column button in the upper right corner of the sheet to add a column or the Add Row button in the lower left corner of the sheet to add a row.**

7. **Tap the Add Sheet button (the plus sign next to the left of the Sheet 1 tab) to add another sheet to the spreadsheet.**

8. **Double-tap the name of a sheet to select it and type a more descriptive name.**

Formatting tables

The formatting button (it looks like a paint brush) opens up the options to customize the parts of your sheet, as shown in Figure 3-20. Select a portion of the sheet by tapping and dragging on the table, and then tap through the tabs to format the parts of your table:

✔ *Table:* Tap a table style to apply it to your table, for

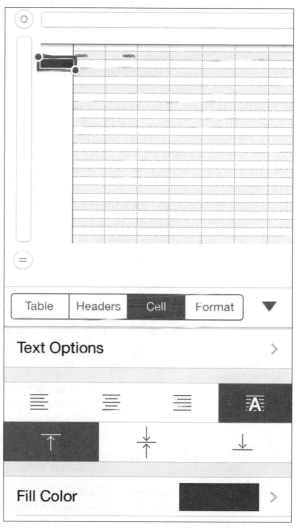

Figure 3-20: Make your table more attractive with the formatting tools.

example, choosing a table with row and column headers and alternating row colors. Tap Table Options to see more choices, such as naming your table, selecting a font for the name, and defining where you want grid lines placed.

✔ *Headers:* Set from zero to the first five rows and/or columns as headers. Freeze them in position so they don't move when you scroll vertically or horizontally through the sheet.

✔ *Cells:* The options here affect all the selected cells so you probably want to select the headers and format those cells and then select the data cells to format in a different way. The type can be formatted as bold or italic, and tapping Text Options lets you choose the font family, size, and color. Scrolling down, you also have choices for how to align the data within the cell and the option of adding a background (fill) color and cell border style.

✔ *Format:* A list of character types appears. Tap a type, such as Currency or Number, and then tap the Info (i) button to better define your choice — for example, currency format or the number of decimals. You can also designate a cell or group of cells as Checkboxes, Star Ratings, or a Pop-up Menu. If you choose Text, numeric characters do not have a numeric value.

Adding tables, charts, and media

Numbers doesn't just calculate and tabulate your data; it makes it meaningful and compelling with charts, images, even songs. Use these steps to add elements to your sheet:

1. **Tap the Plus button.**

   A screen similar to Figure 3-21 appears.

2. **Tap the tab for the type of element you want to add:**

   Media inserts photos, movies, and audio from the Photos and Music apps.

   Tables offers a selection of table styles in color schemes that coordinate with the template theme you chose.

   Charts takes data from a table and displays it as a graph or pie chart, 2D, 3D, or interactive. After you insert a chart, follow the onscreen instructions to select the data it will represent. As with Tables, the color scheme coordinates with the template theme.

   Shapes gives you a choice of simple line drawings that can be combined with text boxes to liven up your spreadsheet or highlight a specific point.

   Text inserts a text box where you can type parenthetical information or lists. The text box grows to accommodate the text but you can change the size and shape with the resizing handles.

3. **Tap the element style you want to insert, such as a photo, a pie chart, or an arrow.**

The element appears on your sheet.

Tap the triangle on the right end of the tabs to leave this area without adding anything.

4. **Tap the element and then do one or more of the following:**

   • Drag the resizing handles to shrink or enlarge photos or shapes.

   • Tap the Cut, Copy, or Delete buttons in the pop-up menu to take those actions.

5. **Tap and drag the element around to place it where you want.**

6. **Tap the element on the sheet, and then tap the Format button (the paintbrush).** **Tap the tabs to see the options for changing the appearance or modifying the typeface family, size, and color of any text. Again, choices will be in keeping with the template theme.**

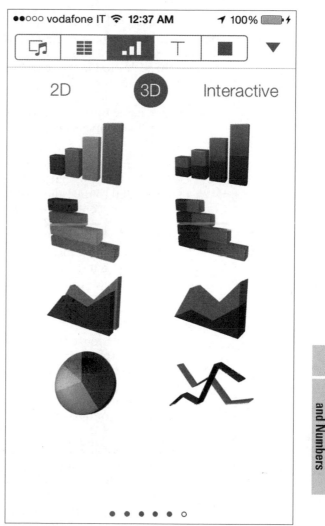

Figure 3-21: Add interest to your sheet with charts, shapes, text, and media.

When you see the Arrange tab, use that to create the hierarchy between overlapping elements.

Renaming, sharing, and deleting spreadsheets

When you want to take an action that affects the whole spreadsheet, as opposed to an element of it, which we explained up until now, tap the Spreadsheets button in the upper left corner to return to the opening Numbers screen. You can do the following:

- ✏ Tap the name under a spreadsheet on the Numbers screen to rename it. The keyboard opens and you can give the spreadsheet a meaningful name.

- ✏ Tap edit, and then tap a document, or documents, you want to copy or delete. Tap the copy button in the upper left corner, and a copy is immediately added to the Numbers screen. Tap the delete button (the trash-can), and then confirm that you want to delete the document(s).

- ✏ Tap the Share button and choose the action you want to take:

  - *Share Link via iCloud*, which will send only a URL link that will open the document on iCloud.com. People with this kind of access can make changes to your document and it will be syncing on all your devices.

  - *Send a Copy*, which will do just that, send a copy of the document.

    After you choose the method, tap the document you want to share, and then the Share Sheet opens with the options that work with your chosen sharing method: AirDrop, Message, Mail, Facebook, and Twitter for links; AirDrop, Message, and Mail for sending copies. You can also copy the link when you share via iCloud and send as an iTunes or WebDAV format when you send a copy. Tap the vehicle you want to use to share the link or copy and then proceed as usual.

  - *Open in Another App*, asks you to select the spreadsheet you want to open elsewhere, then choose a format — Numbers, Excel, CSV, or PDF. Numbers saves your spreadsheet in the chosen format and then opens the Share Sheet with choices of apps that can read that format. Tap the app and your spreadsheet opens there. You can also upload to remote storage servers like Dropbox with this method.

You can paste your Numbers spreadsheet in another app, such as Pages or Keynote, by either selecting and copying the tables or charts or by sharing the whole spreadsheet as a PDF file.

Chapter 4: Creating and Sharing Notes and Voice Memos

In This Chapter

- Creating, viewing, managing, and sharing notes
- Adding accounts to Notes
- Recording, playing, managing, and sharing voice memos
- Syncing Voice Memos with iTunes
- Publishing with Pages
- Making your point with Keynote

*A*re you the note-taking type who goes through multi-colored sticky notes faster that a chimp in a peanut factory? Do ideas pop into your head that you don't remember later because those sticky notes and a pen aren't within reach? And even if they were close at hand, you wouldn't be able to use them, anyway, because you're doing something like driving or working out?

If you answered yes to any or all of those questions, you're in good company. This chapter is all about using two of your iPhone's most useful apps — Notes and Voice Memos. Using this dynamic duo, you can capture your every thought on the fly, as neatly typed out notes that you type or dictate to Siri, or as recorded audio files captured using your iPhone's built-in mic (or your stereo headphone's mic) that you can listen to later.

Taking Note of Notes

Notes is a super-simple app you can use to make lists, jot down ideas, and record anything you'd normally scribble down on a sticky pad or cocktail napkin. Notes you create are stored on your iPhone and, optionally, synced with your computer and other iOS devices through iCloud, Gmail, or another IMAP account.

To get started, tap the Notes app icon on the Home screen to launch Notes. The main Notes screen shows a list of any notes already saved in Notes, as shown in Figure 4-1.

You may see one or more notes listed even if you hadn't previously created a single note using the Notes app. That's because Notes can also come from e-mail accounts set up on your iPhone for which you've turned on Notes. We write about syncing Notes and e-mail accounts in the section "Setting up multiple Notes accounts" later in this chapter.

Creating a new note

Tap the New button to create a new note. The keyboard appears, ready to capture your every thought or idea, as shown in Figure 4-2.

Turning your iPhone sideways displays the landscape mode keyboard, which can help increase your typing speed and accuracy —

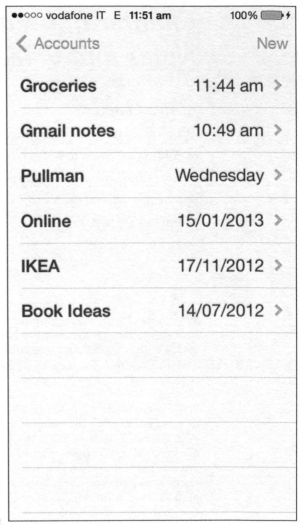

●●○○○ vodafone IT E 11:51 am   100% ▭ ▸ ✦

❮ Accounts   New

Groceries   11:44 am ❯

Gmail notes   10:49 am ❯

Pullman   Wednesday ❯

Online   15/01/2013 ❯

IKEA   17/11/2012 ❯

Book Ideas   14/07/2012 ❯

Figure 4-1: A list of notes you have saved in the Notes app.

although it does decrease the number of lines you see as you write your note. If the wider keyboard doesn't appear when you turn your iPhone sideways, flick up from the bottom of the screen to open the control center, and then tap the orientation lock button to unlock the orientation lock feature and flick down to close the control center.

Tap Done to save your note and hide the keyboard.

Tap Notes to return to the notes list.

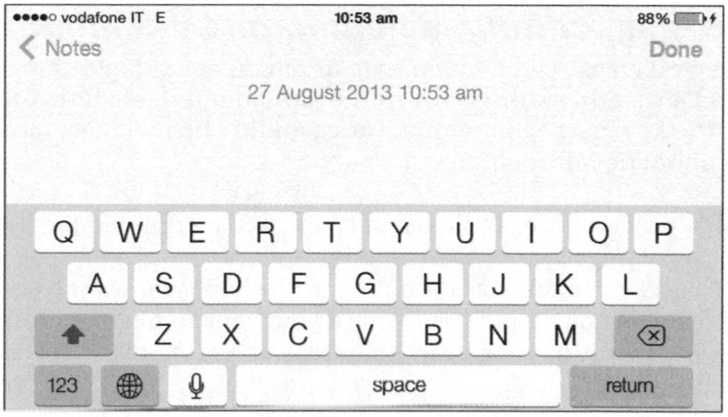

••••○ vodafone IT E   **10:53 am**   **88% ⬛◗ɬ**

‹ Notes   **Done**

27 August 2013 10:53 am

Figure 4-2: Typing with a narrow focus, or a wider point of view.

Press and hold the Home button to activate Siri. When Siri is ready, just say "create a note" and when asked, dictate your note.

Searching and managing your Notes list

Notes are listed in chronological order, with the newest (or most recently edited) note appearing at the top of the list, and the least recently modified note relegated to the bottom of the list. Notes titles are automatically generated based on the first 29 characters of each note's first line; if you enter a return in the first line, only the word (or words) before the return appear in the title.

When viewing the Notes list, you can do the following:

✔ Swipe left across a note title to display the Delete button, and then tap Delete to delete the note. If you swipe by mistake, just tap anywhere except the Delete button to cancel the action.

✔ Tap a note to view, edit, share, or delete the note.

✔ When viewing a list of notes, tap the status bar at the top of iPhone's screen or drag your finger down the list to reveal the Search field, and then type in the first few characters of whatever you're looking for. Note titles and contents are searched and the titles of any notes containing matches to your search criteria are displayed; tap the note title to view that note.

If you have selected Notes in Settings➪General➪Spotlight Search, any searches you perform from the Spotlight Search Home screen will search in Notes too.

Browsing, editing, deleting, and e-mailing Notes

Notes you create can contain regular and accented letters, numbers, and symbols (in other words, any of the alphanumerical stuff you can type with the keyboard), but not pictures, audio clips, videos, or other non-alphanumeric information.

When viewing a note, as shown in Figure 4-3, you can do the following:

- ✔ To add more text or edit a note, tap where you want to begin typing or touch and hold where you want to begin editing, and then type or edit to your heart's content. (See Book I, Chapter 3 for editing tips.)

- ✔ Shake your iPhone to display the Undo message; tap Undo to, well, undo what you just did. Shake again to display the Redo option and tap Redo to redo what you undid.

- ✔ Tap Notes at the top of the screen to return to the Notes list.

- ✔ Tap the Delete button (the trashcan) to delete your note.

- ✔ Tap the New Note button to create a new note.

- ✔ Tap the Action button to open the share sheet as shown in Figure 4-4, and then tap the action you want to take:

  - • **AirDrop (iPhone 5 or later):** Tap to turn on AirDrop and share your note with other people who use AirDrop. (See Book I, Chapter 4 to learn about AirDrop.)

  - • **Message or Mail:** Tap to open an outgoing message that contains your note. Fill in the address for one or more recipients and then tap Send. (See Book III, Chapters 2 and 4 to learn about Message and Mail.)

  - • **Copy:** Tap to copy the contents of your note to the clipboard, which you can then paste in another app.

  - • **Print:** Tap to choose an AirPrint printer connected to a Wi-Fi network in the vicinity and print one or more copies of your note.

Setting up multiple Notes accounts

You can keep your Notes notes on your iPhone only or sync Notes with your computer and other devices from multiple sources, including iCloud or another Notes-enabled service such as Gmail or Yahoo!.

Notes you choose to sync with iCloud appear on any computers or other iOS devices logged in to your iCloud account with the Notes option turned on. Those you sync with your e-mail accounts appear on both your iPhone and on your computer's e-mail program (Outlook, Gmail, or Yahoo!). If you are using a Mac OS prior to Mountain Lion, Notes will continue to sync with

Mail. Activate syncing as follows:

- ✔ **iCloud:** Tap Settings⇨iCloud and tap the switch by Notes to On.

- ✔ **Gmail/Yahoo!/AOL/ Outlook:** Tap Settings⇨Mail, Contacts, Calendars, and then tap the account you want to sync Notes with. Tap the switch next to Notes On to automatically sync your notes over-the-air.

Tap Accounts on the upper left corner of the Notes list (refer to Figure 4-1) to display any of the notes you sync with iCloud or e-mail accounts for which you turned on the Notes sync setting in Settings⇨Mail, Contacts, Calendars. (If you only use iCloud, instead of Accounts you see Folders.) When viewing the Accounts list, as shown in Figure 4-5, you can do the following:

> ●●●○○ vodafone IT E **11:56 am**   100% ▬▬
>
> ‹ Notes
>
> 17 November 2012 1:38 pm
>
> IKEA
>
> Photo shelf
> Bedside lamps? Pink or green glass
> Magnetic strip €13
> Filing cabinet 41 x 50 x 104.
> 3 drawers €99

Figure 4-3: Take action or delete your note.

- ✔ Tap All Notes to display a list of all of your notes saved and synced with all of your e-mail accounts or on your iPhone.

- ✔ Tap Notes under an e-mail account name or On My iPhone to display only the notes stored and synced in that location. Under the iCloud section you see top level Notes but not the Notes stored in Folders. Tap All iCloud to see all Notes stored on iCloud, including those in folders.

- ✔ Tap a folder in the iCloud section to see Notes in that folder. (This option is available if you use Notes on a Mac with iCloud.)

If you want to store some Notes only on your iPhone, create at least one note before turning Notes on in iCloud (or turn Notes off in Settings⇨iCloud, create a note, and then turn it back on). You then see an On My iPhone section in the Accounts list (refer to Figure 4-5).

If you have multiple accounts, go to Settings⇨Notes⇨Default Account, as shown in Figure 4-6 to choose the account you want new notes to be created in if you create a new note from the All Notes list. If you are viewing notes from one source, such as On My iPhone or Gmail and create a new note, the new note is stored in that source.

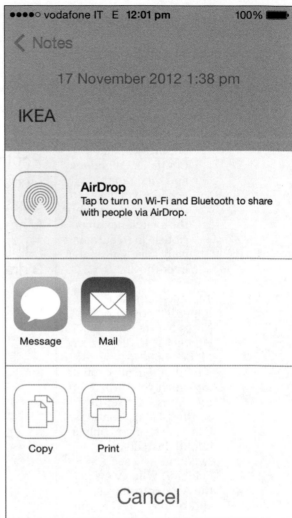

Figure 4-4: Print, copy, or share the contents of your note.

Speaking of Voice Memos

With iPhone's Voice Memos app, you can record, listen to, edit, and share out-loud sounds all with the tap of your finger. And so, because we're big believers in the adage "actions speak louder than words," rather than listening to lengthy introductory words by yours truly, why don't you act on recording and listening to *your* spoken words and other sounds with Voice Memos?

Tap Voice Memos on the Home screen (it may be in the Utilities folder) to launch the app.

Recording voice memos

The recording function is handled by your iPhone's built-in mic, or by the mic built into the EarPods that came with your iPhone if you have those plugged in.

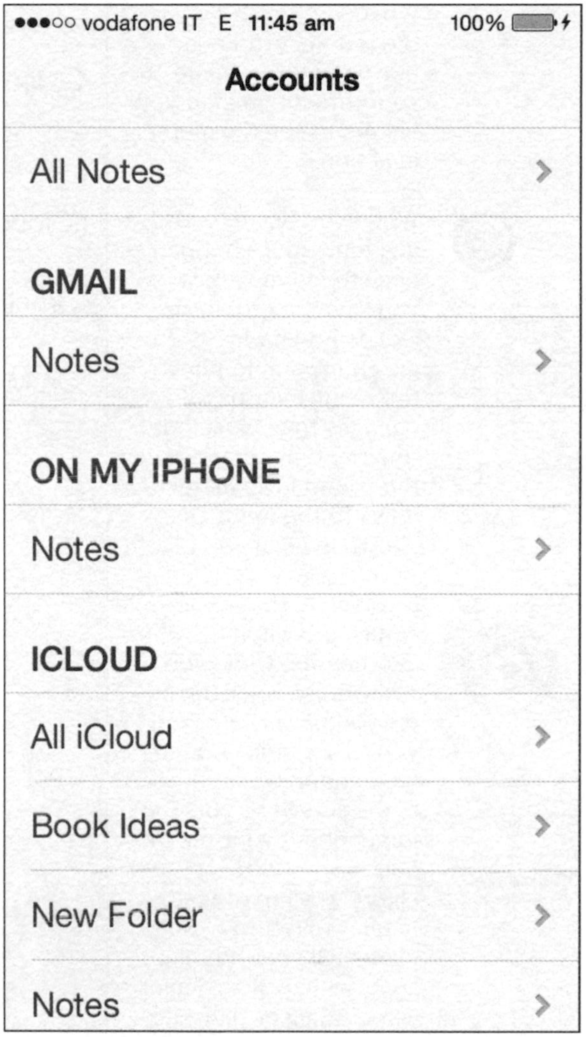

Other mic-enabled options for recording audio with Voice Memos include external mics designed to plug into your iPhone's Lightning or Dock Connector, and wireless Bluetooth headsets and headphones that let you cut the proverbial cord altogether (thus freeing your hands for flailing, gesticulating, or whatever).

Center stage of the Voice Memos screen is the sound level meter. As you speak or record other sounds around you, the sound waves expand vertically to indicate the decibel level of your recording. The waves appear in response to any sounds the mic picks up, whether you're actually recording those sounds or not.

•••○○ vodafone IT E 11:45 am   100% ▭▪⚡
Accounts
All Notes ⟩
GMAIL
Notes ⟩
ON MY IPHONE
Notes ⟩
ICLOUD
All iCloud ⟩
Book Ideas ⟩
New Folder ⟩
Notes ⟩

Figure 4-5: Accounts displays e-mail accounts for which you have Notes turned on.

For optimal recording quality, Apple recommends a recording level between the -3 and 0-decibels (dBs) zone. Translation: As you're speaking, move your iPhone (or headphone mic) closer or farther from your mouth, or lower or raise your voice, or use a combination of both, to try to keep the recording level in or as close to that optimal-quality sweet spot between the -3 and 0.

When you're ready, tap the red Record/Pause button and say "hello" to your iPhone or snap your fingers to see the meter in action.

When you begin recording, four things happen at once to let you know your live recording session is underway: A single-chime sound plays, the record button changes to a pause button, the timer starts, and the sound level meter flows to the right, as shown in Figure 4-7.

If you go to the Home screen or switch to another app while you're recording a voice memo (or you pause a memo you're recording), a red banner appears at the top of the screen so you don't forget about your recording, as shown in Figure 4-8. Tap the red banner to return to Voice Memos. If your iPhone locks while Voice Memos is recording or paused, when you press the Home button to unlock it, you see the sound level meter in action, even if you have another app open and Voice Memos is recording or paused in the background.

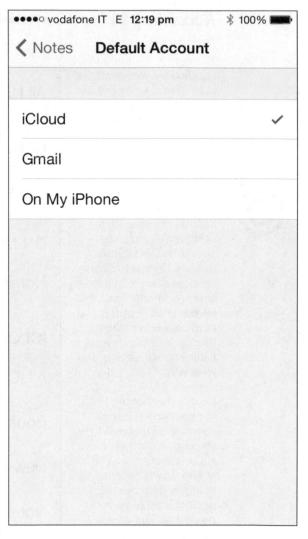

Figure 4-6: If you have multiple Notes accounts, choose the default account for new Notes created from the All Notes view.

To pause recording, tap the Record/Pause button. If you switch to another app or go to the Home screen, the red banner pulses at the top of the screen but reads "paused."

To resume a paused recording, tap the Record/Pause button. Recording resumes; you can repeat this process of pausing and resuming your recording as many times as you want until you decide to tap Done, to end your recording session.

To stop recording, tap Done. A double-chime plays, and a New Voice Memo dialog opens, as in Figure 4-9. Backspace over the text or hold on it until the editing tools appear, and then type a name for the voice memo. Tap OK. Your newly recorded voice memo appears in the list of recordings.

You *shouldn't* hear the chime and double-chime sound effects that play when you start and stop recording a memo if iPhone's ring/silent switch is switched to silent mode. We say *shouldn't* because in some countries or regions, the recording sound effects play even when the ring/silent switch is set to silent. Our guesstimate as to why those sound effects may still be heard even when iPhone is set to be quiet? To offer some kind of audible warning to anyone within earshot that you may be recording anything they say. (However, whether anything hypothetical persons may say can or will be held against them in a court of law, is not for me to say. We can only speculate.)

Figure 4-7: Live, from New York! (Or wherever are!)

Listening to voice memos

The voice memo list appears on the lower half of the screen and displays your voice memos in chronological order, from newest to oldest, refer to Figure 4-10. Below the title you see the date the voice memo was made and the length of the recording. To listen to, pause, and control playback of a voice memo, tap it in the list and then do the following:

Book IV
Chapter 4

Creating and
Sharing Notes and
Voice Memos

Figure 4-8: Voice Memos keeps recordi22ng even if you switch apps or lock your iPhone.

> Tap — you guessed it — the Play button to hear your voice memo.
>
> When your voice memo begins playing, the play button turns into a pause button and the playhead moves forward on the scrubber bar.

> Tap the Pause button to pause listening to your voice memo, as shown in Figure 4-10, and then press Play to resume.

> Drag the playhead left or right in the scrubber bar while the voice memo is playing or paused to move backward or forward.

> Tap the Speaker button if you want to hear your voice memos out loud through your iPhone's built-in speaker. (By default, voice memos play through your iPhone's receiver speaker, or through your headphones, if you have those plugged in.)

> To select another voice memo, tap the list to close the open voice memo then tap the one you want to listen to. Use the play, pause, and scrubber playhead buttons as previously described to listen to your selected voice memo.

You can rename your voice memo when you tap it for playback. Press your finger on the voice memo title until the editing loupe and keyboard appear. Lift your finger and then edit the title as you would any other text on your iPhone, tap return when you finish.

Trimming a voice memo

When possible, we suggest leaving a bit of air time at the beginning and end of your recording to give you leeway for trimming your voice memo. Then there are the times that you begin recording something and forget and find yourself with a ten-minute voice memo of a three-minute conversation. To trim your voice memo, follow these steps:

1. **In the voice memo list, tap the voice memo you want to trim.**

2. **Tap Edit.**

   The playback editing screen displays the sound waves of your recording, as shown in Figure 4-11.

3. **Tap Play.**

   The blue line indicates the time of the playback and the recording flows behind it.

4. **Tap Pause when the playback is just past where you want your recording to begin.**

Figure 4-9: Identify your new voice memo with a descriptive name.

5. **Tap the Trim button and you find the blue line where you positioned it in Step 4.**

   The red lines at the left and right sides of the recording are the trim grabbers. (Refer to Figure 4-12.)

6. **Touch and hold the left red grabber and drag it toward the middle to shorten your recording to the point you want it to begin, slightly**

before the blue line.

Refer to the timers to precisely position the grabber.

7. **Tap the Play button.**

The blue line moves to the right as the recording plays so you can see the exact point at which you want to trim.

8. **When the blue line is just past the point you want your recording to end, tap the Pause button.**

9. **Drag the right grabber to a few seconds after the position of the blue line.**

10. **When you're pleased with the position of the trim grabbers, tap the Trim button to save your edited selection (or tap Cancel if you change your mind and you don't want to trim your voice memo after all).**

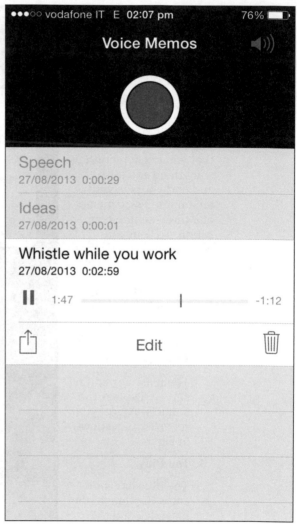

Figure 4-10: Pausing a voice memo.

Three choices appear:

Trim Original: Replaces the original recording with the trimmed recording.

Save As New Recording: Creates a new voice memo without the trimmings — that's a trimmed recording. This choice is our recommendation — you can always delete the original later but you can't bring it back after it's replaced.

Cancel: Returns to where you left off working.

Sharing or deleting a voice memo

Some recordings are better left unsaid, or even deleted, and others you'll want to shout out to the world. Both actions are just a tap away in Voice Memos.

To share a voice memo:

1. **Tap a voice memo to open it.**

   The screen appears as in Figure 4-10.

2. **Tap the Action button to open the share sheet, and then tap the action you want to take:**

   AirDrop (iPhone 5 or later): Tap to turn on AirDrop and share your note with other people who use AirDrop. (See Book I, Chapter 4 to learn about AirDrop.)

   Message or Mail: Tap to open an outgoing message that contains your voice memo. Fill in the address for one or more recipients and then tap Send. (See Book III, Chapters 2 and 4 to learn about Message and Mail.)

3. **Tap another voice memo to return to the list.**

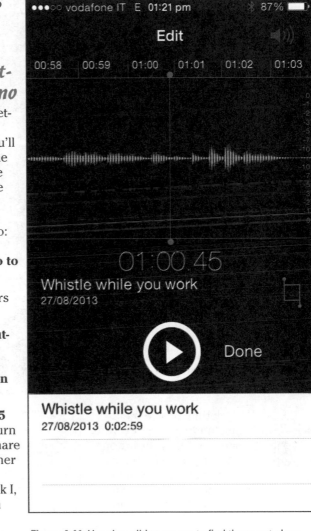

Figure 4-11: Use the editing screen to find the exact place you want to trim your recording.

If a message saying your voice memo file is too large to send appears, you need to trim your voice memo using the trim tool (see the previous section) before you trying to send your message again.

To delete a voice memo swipe left across the voice memo in the list and tap the Delete button that appears to the right, or

1. **Tap a voice memo to select it, and then tap the Delete button.**

   Delete and Cancel buttons appear, giving you a moment to consider whether you really want to delete your selected voice memo.

2. **Tap Delete to say goodbye to your selected voice memo, or tap Cancel if you've had a sudden change of heart and you want to keep your voice memo.**

Deleting a voice memo instantly erases the voice memo from your iPhone. But that doesn't necessarily mean the voice memo is gone forever — if you've turned on the voice memos sync option in iTunes, which copies all of your recorded voice memos to your computer's iTunes library and stores them there even if you later decide to delete those synced voice memos from your iPhone. Of course, voice memos you record and then delete before syncing with iTunes are gone forever. We tell you how to sync your voice memos with iTunes next.

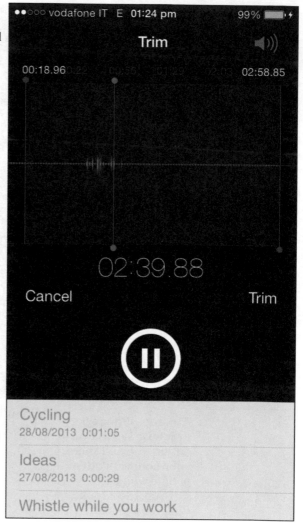

Figure 4-12: Trimming a voice memo down in size.

Syncing voice memos with iTunes

Capturing voice memos on the fly is handy for remembering things you don't want to forget. After you've dealt with whatever your voice memos remind you to do, you can then delete those voice memos from your iPhone.

Other voice memos, like a gang of friends and family singing "Happy Birthday" at your mom's 80th, or an interview with a fast-talking politician you recorded for an article you're writing, may be ones you want to (or must) keep for personal or professional reasons.

But you probably don't need to keep those kinds of audio files on your iPhone, where they consume storage space you'd rather free up. The solution? Sync any voice memos you want to keep with iTunes on your computer, and those voice memos remain safe and sound, so to speak, until you want (or need) to hear them anew.

Because we give you the full lowdown on how to pick and choose the kinds of information and files (including voice memos) you want to sync between your iPhone and your computer using iTunes in Book II, Chapter I, we won't repeat ourselves here. Not completely, anyway. We would be remiss if we didn't take a moment to at least mention a few points worth knowing about when you're thinking about syncing your voice memos with iTunes, including

- ✔ iTunes automatically creates a playlist named (drum roll, please. . .) Voice Memos on your computer, and that's where you can track down new, not so new, and downright ancient voice memos you recorded and synced with iTunes syncs.

- ✔ Voice memos you delete from your iPhone remain safely backed up in your iTunes library.

- ✔ If you delete a voice memo from iTunes that you have saved on your iPhone that voice memo will be deleted from your iPhone the next time you sync with iTunes.

You can use a voice memo as a ringtone by trimming the file to shorter than 30 seconds, e-mail it to yourself then change the file extension to .m4r and open it. The file imports into iTunes as a ringtone, which you can then sync to your iPhone. If you use a Mac, you can trim and edit the file in GarageBand and save it as a ringtone.

You can also e-mail the voice memo to yourself and avoid iTunes syncing altogether.

Publishing with Pages

If you bought an iPhone 4, 5c, or 5s with iOS 7, you're eligible to download the iWork suite of apps, Pages and Keynote, which we discuss here, and Numbers, which we talk about in Book IV, Chapter 3. Pages is two apps in one: a powerful word processor for creating documents that can go on for, well, pages and pages, and a page layout app for creating mixed media documents such as newsletters, posters, flyers, invitations, and more. We give you the down and dirty here, but encourage you to get creative, have fun, and spread your words around.

Creating a Pages document

As we mentioned, Pages can manage both word processing and page layout tasks, so before you create your document, you should think about which you need. After you create your document in one type of template, you can't change over to another without a bunch of copying and pasting — yuck! Pages makes it pretty easy to choose because the templates are divided by document type. Do the following to create a new document and start creating:

1. **Tap Pages on the Home screen.**

2. **Tap the Create New icon in the upper left corner (it has a plus sign).**

3. **Scroll through the template categories and choose one that most closely matches the type of document you want to create.**

   You can also choose blank if you want to start from scratch and do everything yourself. We chose Modern Report for our example because it has both text and images.

   Many third-party developers make templates for Pages and Keynote too. Search the App Store to see them and go to Bonus Chapter 2 online to read about some of our favorites.

4. **Tap the template you want to use.**

   Your chosen template appears on the screen.

5. **Tap the placeholder text and begin typing your own words.**

   This is a situation where a Bluetooth keyboard would come in handy.

   Because this is a report, even if the text goes beyond the placeholder space, it flows onto successive pages.

6. **Tap the Add Image button (the plus sign) on the first placeholder image.**

   Your Photos library opens. Tap through the Camera Roll and your other libraries and albums to find the photo you want to insert.

   If you have a lot of photos in Photos, it helps to go through and flag those you might want to use beforehand or even put them all in an album so you can quickly find the one's you want to place in your document. See Book V, Chapter 1 to learn about working with Camera, Photos, and iPhoto.

7. **Tap the image you want to insert.**

   It shows up in your Pages document, replacing the placeholder text. You can drag it around or resize it if you want but that may cause some of the other parts of the document to shift around.

8. **Double-tap the image to bring up a slider so you can scale, pan, and crop the photo, as shown in Figure 4-13. Tap Done when you're happy with the size and position.**

9. **Repeat Steps 5 through 9 until your document is complete.**

Fine-tuning your text and images

Templates make creating documents quick and easy because the creative legwork is done for you, you need only supply content. You might find you want to tweak some of the elements of your document, however. Tap the text or image you want to fine-tune, and then tap the Format button (the paintbrush). These are the options you have:

- ✔ **Text:** Three tabs let you alter the Style of the typeface and paragraph, (as shown in Figure 4-14); scroll down to see the paragraph styles associated with the templete. The List tab defines how bulleted or numbered lists are formatted, and the Layout tab lets you change the number of columns and increase or decrease the line spacing. Tap each tab and then play with the options. You see the changes immediately in the document. Tap on the document and then tap Undo or shake your iPhone and tap Undo if you don't like how it looks.

- ✔ **Image:** Here, the Style tab offers frames, borders, and shadow effects. Tap the Image button to edit or reset the original cropping (called a Mask) or use the Instant Alpha effect, which, when selected, makes areas of the same color that you drag your finger across

Figure 4-13: Scale, pan, and crop images to add the most impact to your document.

transparent. Instant Alpha makes parts of your image stand out and works best when you have two or more contrasting colors. You can also tap Replace to choose a different image to substitute the existing one. The third tab, Arrange, lets you flip the image horizontally or vertically and also moves it backward or forward in relation to other elements on the page. This is helpful when you layer several images or elements and one is larger than the other. The larger one should be moved backward so the smaller one can be seen on top.

Tap the triangle to the right of the tabs to exit the Format screen without making changes.

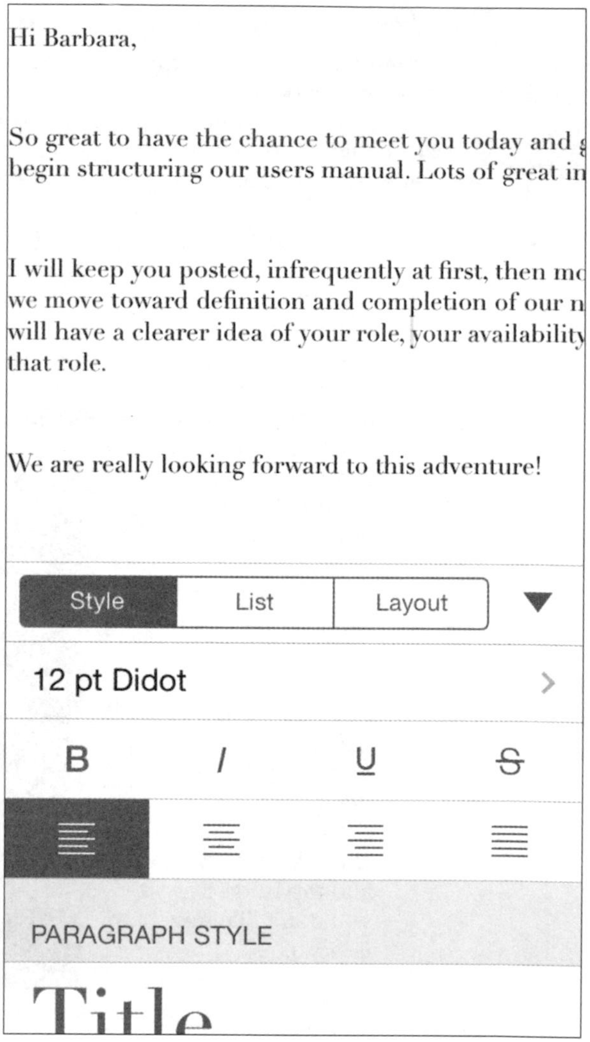

Adding other design elements

You can copy and paste elements and objects from other apps, for example a chart you create in Numbers, or you can create the chart directly in Pages. The charts, tables, shapes, and text styles are in keeping with the style of the template you are working in, although you can edit them as just explained for text and images. Follow these steps to use the design elements in Pages:

Hi Barbara,

So great to have the chance to meet you today and
begin structuring our users manual. Lots of great in

I will keep you posted, infrequently at first, then m
we move toward definition and completion of our n
will have a clearer idea of your role, your availability
that role.

We are really looking forward to this adventure!

| Style | List | Layout | ▼ |

12 pt Didot   >

B   *I*   <u>U</u>   S̶

PARAGRAPH STYLE

Title

Figure 4-14: The Format tabs give you options for customizing the style of your text and images.

1. **Tap the Add Element button (the plus sign).**

   A screen similar to Figure 4-15 appears.

2. **Tap the tab for the type of element you want to add:**

Media inserts photos, movies, and audio from the Photos and Music apps. Tap the type of media you want to insert and then scroll through the apps' libraries to find the piece you want.

Tables offers a selection of table styles in color schemes that coordinate with the template theme you chose.

Charts takes data from a table and displays it as a graph or pie chart, 2D, 3D, or interactive. After you insert a chart, follow the onscreen instructions to select the data it will represent. As with Tables, the color scheme coordinates with the template theme.

Shapes gives you a choice of simple line drawings that can be combined with text boxes to liven up your spreadsheet or highlight a specific point.

Text inserts a text box where you can type parenthetical information or lists. The text box grows to accommodate the text but you can change the size and shape with the resizing handles.

3. **Tap the element style you want to insert, such as a photo, a pie chart, or an arrow.**

The element appears on your sheet.

Figure 4-15: Spice up your document with charts, shapes, text, and media.

Tap the triangle on the right end of the tabs to leave this area without adding anything.

4. **Tap the element and then do one or more of the following:**

   • Drag the resizing handles to shrink or enlarge the inserted element.

   • Tap Edit Data in the pop-up menu of a chart. Tap in the fields, as shown in Figure 4-16, to type in the data you want displayed in the chart, and then tap Done.

   • Double-tap a field in a table and type in the information you want.

   • Tap the Cut, Copy, or Delete buttons in the pop-up menu to take those actions.

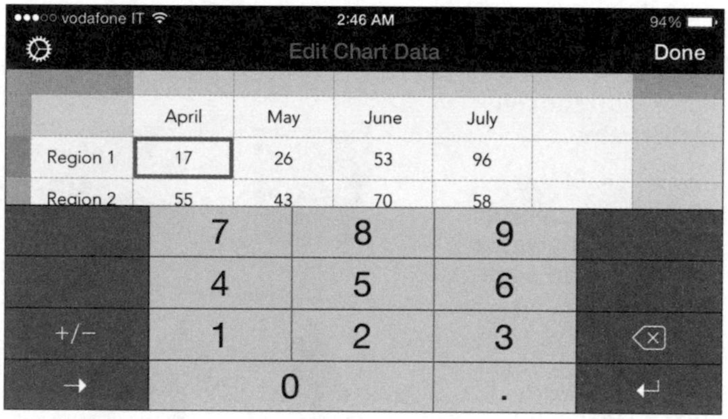

Figure 4-16: Substitute the placeholder data with your own.

5. **Tap and drag the element around to place it where you want.**

6. **Tap the element on the sheet, and then tap the Format button (the paintbrush). Tap the tabs to see the options for changing the appearance or modifying the typeface family, size, and color of any text.**

   Again, choices will be in keeping with the template theme.

   Tables have the same Table, Header, and Arrange options that they do in Numbers. Tap through here or see Book IV, Chapter 3 for details.

   Charts give you options for labeling the X and Y Axes and stylizing the gridlines an tick marks.

REMEMBER

Use the Arrange feature of the Formatting tabs to properly layer overlapping elements such as a text box on a shape.

Checking your spelling

In addition to the Auto-Correction and Check Spelling options in Settings⇨General⇨Keyboard, Pages has a spelling option. Tap the Tools button in the upper right corner of the document screen, and then tap Settings in the list of tools. (You can check out the others too, such as Ruler or Document Setup.) In the Settings screen, tap Check Spelling to the On position and, while you're there, tap on Word Count, if that's information that would be useful for you to see while you're working on your documents. Although you adjust the settings within a specific document, they will be applied across all the documents you work on in Pages.

Making Your Point with Keynote

Your iPhone might not seem like the ideal place to design a presentation — and it's probably not — but with a little patience (and maybe a pair of reading glasses), you can pull together a nice message and you can then project your presentation on a larger screen with Apple TV and AirPlay.

Creating a new presentation

Like the other iWork apps, Keynote comes with a bevy of themes that you use as the jumping off point for the creation of your presentation. Each theme is applied to a dozen or so slide layouts. The steps are the same as for Pages:

- ✔ Tap the app, Keynote, on the Home screen. Tap Create New, and then tap the theme that best reflects the style and tone you want your presentation to have.

- ✔ Double-tap text placeholders to type in your text — headers, bulleted lists, quotes, and so on.

- ✔ Tap the add media (the plus sign) on the image placeholders to insert your own photos.

- ✔ Tap the Add Elements button to insert media, charts, text, and shapes, as explained in the previous section, "Adding Other Design Elements."

- ✔ Tap the Add Slide button (the plus sign at the bottom left of the screen) to choose the slide layout you want to use for a new slide, as shown in Figure 4-17. Tap the layout, and it appears in the main part of the screen.

Book IV
Chapter 4

Creating and
Sharing Notes and
Voice Memos

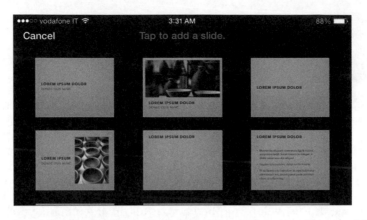

Figure 4-17: Tap the slide layout you want to use when you add a new slide.

Adding transitions between slides

With Keynote, you can use transitions to jolt your audience when you move from one slide to the next. Keynote comes with many types of transitions, and you can experiment to find those that you like. To add transitions between slides, do the following:

1. **Tap the presentation you want to work on in the Keynote opening screen.**

2. **Tap the slide that will come before the transition.**

3. **Tap the Tools button, and then tap Transitions and Builds.**

   The effects and options list opens as shown in Figure 4-18.

4. **Tap the Effects tab at the top, and then tap the type of transition you want.**

   Magic Move moves an object from a location on one slide to a location on the next slide. Follow the onscreen instructions to create this effect.

5. **Tap the Options tab, and then scroll through the tools to set the duration, direction, and delay of the transition and when you want it to begin.**

6. **Tap Play to see a preview, and then tap Done.**

7. **To create an animation, tap an object or element of the slide.**

8. **Tap the plus sign to add the first part, the build in, of the animation.**

   A list of possibilities opens. Tap the Effects and Options tabs to choose the type of animated effect you want.

9. **Repeat Step 8 for the second, build out, part of the animation.**

   Tap the Order tab to rearrange the order in which the animated effects occur.

10. **Tap Play to see a preview, and then tap Done.**

●○○○○ vodafone IT 🤖	4:04 AM	84% 🔋
Play	Effects Options	Done

None

Magic Move...

Clothesline   ✓

Cube

Dissolve

Doorway

Figure 4-18: Choose transitions from the list.

Tap an object or element, and then tap the Format button (the paintbrush) to see the editing options available for that object.

Using interactive links

Keynote has some nifty tools to help you put on a great show, like the transitions and animations we just outlined. We want to highlight one other. Tap the Tools button at the top of the presentation editing screen, and the list of tools opens. Tap Presentation Tools and then tap Interactive Links. With the Interactive Links tool, you select an element of a slide and then link it to another slide or a web page or e-mail message. For example, there are technical aspects of your presentation that may or may not need further explanation, depending on the audience's expertise. Set up a link to a more detailed slide that you use only if you need it.

Tap Interactive Links in the Presentation Tools list, and then tap the slide where the technical information is introduced. Tap a diagram on the slide and the Link options appear as in Figure 4-19. Tap Link To Slide and then choose a slide from the list where more detailed information is stored.

You won't use this slide unless your audience needs to see it, but you have it ready to go rather than fumbling with your computer looking for the explanatory image and losing the moment. You can also link to a web page by tapping the Webpage tab and then inserting the URL, or to an e-mail, which is a great tool for self-playing presentations that you share with others. When the viewer finishes watching, he taps the linked object and an e-mail opens with your address filled in so the viewer can contact you. Tap Done after you assign the link. Tap the Tool button to add more.

Book IV
Chapter 4

Creating and
Sharing Notes and
Voice Memos

Figure 4-19: Links can help you customize the same presentation to different audiences.

As you're preparing your presentation, you can type up notes, or the parts of your speech that go with each slide. Presenter Notes in the Tools list. Tap the slide in the thumbnail view on the left and then type your notes in the white space that appears. If you use your iPhone as the remote control when you give your presentation (download Keynote Remote from the App Store), you see your notes on your iPhone, but the audience only sees your slides.

Renaming, sharing, and deleting documents

Document management is the same for both Pages and Keynote (for Numbers too, so some of this may be repetitive if you read Book IV, Chapter 3). You can do the following:

- Tap the name under a document on the opening Pages or Keynote screen to rename it. The keyboard opens and you can give the spreadsheet a meaningful name.

- Pull or flick down in the upper third of the screen to see sort tabs: Date or Name. Tap one or the other to sort your documents by that criteria.

- Tap edit, and then tap a document, or documents, you want to copy or delete. Tap the copy button in the upper left corner, and a copy is immediately added to the screen. Tap the delete button (the trashcan), and then confirm that you want to delete the document(s).

- Tap the Share button and choose the action you want to take:

  - *Share Link via iCloud,* which will send only a URL link that will open the document on iCloud.com. People with this kind of access can make changes to your document and it will be syncing on all your devices.

  - *Send a Copy,* which will do just that, send a copy of the document.

After you choose the method, tap the document you want to share, and then the Share Sheet opens with the options that work with your chosen sharing method: AirDrop, Message, Mail, Facebook, and Twitter for links; AirDrop, Message, and Mail for sending copies. You can also copy the link when you share via iCloud and send as an iTunes or WebDAV format when you send a copy. Tap the vehicle you want to use to share the link or copy and then proceed as usual.

* *Open in Another App,* asks you to select the document you want to open elsewhere, and then choose a format — Keynote, PDF, or PowerPoint for Keynote; Pages, PDF, Word, or ePub for Pages. Your document is converted to the chosen format and then the Share Sheet opens with choices of apps that can read that format. Tap the app and your document opens there. You can also upload to remote storage servers like Dropbox with this method.

Book IV
Chapter 4

Creating and
Sharing Notes and
Voice Memos

Book V

Letting iPhone Entertain You: Photos, Videos, Music, and More

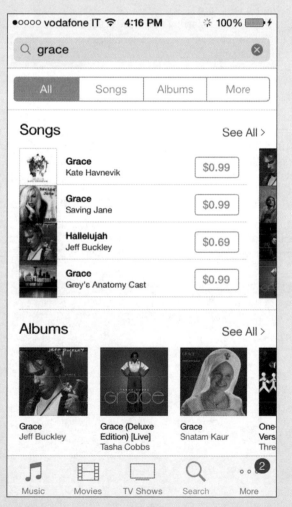

Visit www.dummies.com/extras/iphoneaio to find out how to create albums with iPhoto.

Contents at a Glance

Chapter 1: Capturing, Editing, and Sharing Photos

In This Chapter

- ✓ Snapping a picture with Camera
- ✓ Taking in the panorama
- ✓ Focusing, flashing, and zooming
- ✓ Turning the lens on yourself
- ✓ Editing photos
- ✓ Storing and sharing with iCloud

The Camera app on your iPhone takes advantage of two objective lenses on your iPhone. The iSight camera is the 8-megapixel still and video camera (on iPhone 4s or later) on the back that takes regular photos and 240-degree panoramic photos plus high definition videos. All iPhone models have an LED flash, but the 5s sports a True Tone flash, which combines two LED lights — one white and one amber — to produce natural skin tones as well as crisper photos in low-light conditions. The 5s also has burst mode, which takes 10 photos per second in rapid succession, and a slow motion video option. The other is the FaceTime camera, a 1.2-megapixel still camera that also shoots 720 pixel HD video on the front of your iPhone so you can take self-portraits and use FaceTime, your iPhone's video and audio chat app. All the functions work in portrait and landscape position.

In this chapter, we explain how to use the still cameras, front and back. (We explain the video functions along with the Video app in Book V, Chapter 4.) We talk about focusing, flashing — er, using the flash — and zooming in on your subject. You can also apply a filter to your photo before or after taking it (options vary between iPhone models). After you capture photos in Camera, you probably want to edit them, so we show you how to use the Photos app to enhance the photo quality, crop photos, and cure that terrible red-eye disease. At the end of the chapter, we give you all your options for sharing your photos between your own devices with Photo Stream and with others via AirDrop and iCloud's photo sharing feature, e-mail, text messages, Twitter, YouTube, Flickr, and good old-fashioned slideshows and printing.

 TIP If you purchased an iPhone with iOS 7, you're entitled to download a complimentary copy of Apple's iPhoto app. On the Web Extras for this book at www.dummies.com/extras/iphoneaio, you'll find an article on how to use it.

Camera Features and Controls

The first time you open Camera, a message appears asking if Camera can use your location. Tapping OK lets Camera geotag your location. A geotag uses GPS (Global Positioning System), Wi-Fi, and cellular access to add the longitude and latitude of the location of the photos and videos you shoot. (In some situations, say, if you're standing in a lead-walled bunker, your iPhone may not be able to activate geotagging.) Like the date and time, a *geotag* is a piece of information about your photo that's kept in the metadata; that is, data you don't see that describes your data. You can then sort and search for photos based on the location — more about that later in this chapter.

If at some point you want to turn geotagging off, tap Home⇨Settings⇨ Privacy⇨Location Services. You can turn Location Services off completely or turn Location Services off for specific apps, in this case, Camera.

Previewing through the viewfinder

We think the easiest way to learn about taking photos with your iPhone is to snap a few shots. The two basic "parts" of any camera that you need to know are the viewfinder and the shutter button. Like some digital cameras, your iPhone doesn't have a viewfinder. Instead, you point your iPhone at your subject and then look at the screen to see how it will be framed.

As for the shutter button, your iPhone actually has three:

- **Camera button:** Tap the button on the bottom of the screen in the center to snap a photo. The button is a red circle when you switch to video mode.

- **Volume buttons, either one:** Press one of the volume buttons on the left side of your iPhone to snap a photo or to start and stop video recording.

If your iPhone is locked, when you click the Home button or press the on/off sleep/wake button, a Camera button appears in the bottom right corner, as shown in Figure 1-1. Touch and drag the Camera button up (as if you want to push the lock screen out of the way) to open the Camera app, and then take photos as explained next.

Taking photos with the iSight camera

The iSight camera is located on the back of your iPhone. Here's how to take a photo with it:

1. **Tap Camera on the Home Screen or, if your iPhone is locked, unlock it by clicking the Home button and then drag the Camera button up.**

   A shutter opens, revealing a screen as shown in Figure 1-2.

   The words above the onscreen shutter button indicate the type of photo you're going to take:

   Slo-Mo (iPhone 5s): Used to take slow motion video.

   Video: Used to shoot video, which we discuss in Book V, Chapter 4.

   Photo: To take a standard rectangular photo.

   Square: To take a square "Polaroid" or Instagram style photo, as shown in Figure 1-3.

   Pano: Use to take panoramic photos; we explain how to use this function in the next section.

2. **Flick across the middle of the screen to move from one photo style to another. The one you choose is highlighted.**

3. **Point your iPhone at whatever you want to photograph.**

Figure 1-1: Access the Camera from the Lock screen by dragging the Camera button by the unlock slider.

4. **(Optional, iPhone 5 or later)Tap the Filters button, and then tap a special effect you'd like to apply to your photo.**

You see the effect onscreen immediately, as shown in Figure 1-4, before you take the photo, but you can also add an effect when you edit the photo in Photos after it's taken.

5. **Tap the Camera button or press one of the Volume buttons.**

A clicking noise lets you know the photo was taken. You can mute the shutter sound by moving the ring/silent switch to silent.

If you have a hard time holding the phone still when tapping the onscreen button, you can press on the shutter button, steady the camera, and then lift your finger.

Figure 1-2: Your iPhone screen is your viewfinder.

6. **A thumbnail preview of the photo you took appears in the lower left corner (in landscape mode, the lower right or upper left corner, depending on which direction you rotate your phone).**

Bursting on the scene

If you have an iPhone 5s, you can take a rapid succession of photos by holding the onscreen shutter button or one of the volume buttons to activate Burst mode, at ten frames per second, is great for catching stills when there's a lot of action going on. A counter will tell you how many photos you took.

Taking a panoramic view

A fun Camera feature is the possibility of taking 240 degree panoramic photos so you can capture the full width, or height, of your subject at hand. Here's how it works:

1. **Tap Camera on the Home screen.**

2. **Tap Options at the top.**

3. **Tap Panorama.**

4. **The arrow you see in the center, as shown in Figure 1-5, is a nifty tool that uses iPhone's built-in gyroscope to help you capture better images.**

5. **Tap the camera button and begin slowly but continuously moving your iPhone in one direction. Keep the arrow on the plumb line as you move in the direction of the arrow.**

   Left to right is the default but just tap the arrow, before beginning to take the photo, to go the other way.

6. **Tap Done when you finish capturing the panorama.**

   Your photo is saved in Camera Roll.

7. **Tap Done to return to normal Camera mode.**

Figure 1-3: Choose square to take an Instagram-style photo.

Turn your iPhone to landscape view and take a vertical panoramic shot. This is great for capturing tall buildings or boat masts in a single photo.

Setting the exposure and focus

The buttons, as shown in Figure 1-2, appear when you open Camera. The first thing you want to do is choose where you want Camera to focus its attention. Your iPhone's default autofocus is the center of the image on the screen, where you see the yellow box.

iPhone 4s or later use face detection and focus on the most prominent face. Face detection balances exposure across up to ten faces. If you want the Camera to focus on a subject that isn't in the center, tap that area on the screen. You see the focus and exposure change to put your chosen subject in the best light. (Unless you want the subject in the center, in which case you should move your iPhone until you see the subject in the center of the screen.)

You can change the exposure (that is, the amount of light that is allowed through the lens) and then focus on a different area. Tap and hold on the area on the screen that has the amount of light you want the photo to have. A yellow box blinks to indicate that the exposure lock is on and the words "AE/AF Lock" (Auto Exposure/Auto Focus) appear at the top of the screen. Move iPhone to the subject you want to photograph, and then tap the Camera button. Tap elsewhere on the screen to unlock the AE/AF Lock.

Figure 1-4: Tap to choose the filter you want to apply to your photo.

For example, if you point your iPhone out a sunny window and activate the AE/AF lock, the natural light needs less exposure. Then point your iPhone at a subject indoors, and take the photo. The exposure needed for the natural light is applied to the indoor setting and the photo comes out dark, even if the room seems well-lit.

Lighten up

Depending on the model, your iPhone has one LED light, two on the 5s, next to the objective lens on the back camera that functions as a flash. You see the flash button at the top left of the screen. Auto is the default position, meaning your iPhone turns the light on if it senses there's not enough light for the photo. Tap the flash button to turn the flash on or off manually, as shown in Figure 1-6.

Figure 1-5: Keep the arrow on the line to capture captivating panoramic photos.

In addition to the flash, the Backside Illumination Sensor perceives low light conditions and makes adjustments to compensate. You can tap on areas that are too dark or too bright to adjust the lighting. The sensor corrects the contrast of the image as a whole. Figure 1-7 shows the difference between two photos.

To zoom or not to zoom

To zoom in on a portion of the subject you want to photograph, use the pinch and spread technique. iPhone's zoom is a digital zoom, which means it zooms by enlarging the image, not by getting closer to the subject. Digital zooming compromises the quality of the final image, so physically moving closer to your subject is by far the better choice. Try taking zoomed and normal photos to see if you can live with the compromise.

Macro mode kicks in automatically when you're about two inches away from the person or object you want to photograph. Tap the object you are focusing on to create a special effect where the main object is crisp and the background is blurry, as shown in Figure 1-8.

To help you visualize the distribution of objects in your photo and use the photographer's rule of thirds, turn on the Grid feature that puts a three-by-three grid overlay on your screen, dividing the screen into nine sections (refer to Figure 1-6). To activate this option, go to Settings⇨Photos & Camera and tap Grid to the on position.

Figure 1-6: Tap the Flash button to show the options: Auto, On, or Off.

Turning on iPhone's HDR

Digital photography is terrific in bright to shady situations, but in overly bright or very low light conditions, the quality can be poor and result in overexposed or underexposed photos. Using iPhone's High Dynamic Range option can help you get better shots when the conditions aren't perfect. HDR is off by default; tap it at the top of the screen to turn it on.

Figure 1-7: The Backside Illumination Sensor perceives areas that are too dark or too light and corrects the contrast.

When High Dynamic Range is on, Camera takes three photos with different exposures and superimposes them to create a better image. Taking images with HDR takes a few seconds longer than shooting normal photos, so try to hold iPhone steady and ask the subject to remain still. And, the iPhone 5s has a larger light sensor that provides greater light sensitivity, which means brighter, crisper photos.

The LED flash doesn't work when HDR is on.

You can save both a normal version and an HDR version. In Settings⇨Photos & Camera, tap Keep Normal Photo on. If you turn this off, only the HDR version is saved.

Figure 1-8: Camera activates Macro mode when the subject is closer than two inches.

Turning the lens on yourself

The Switch Camera button in the upper right corner of the screen switches the active objective from the iSight camera on the back of your iPhone to the FaceTime camera on the front so you see yourself on the screen. This camera has lower resolution, no flash or zoom, but it can take advantage of the

Backside Illumination Sensor and takes both still photos and video. It's handy for self-portraits (or if you find yourself without a mirror and some lettuce in your teeth) and FaceTime.

To use the front camera — that's the one above the screen:

1. **Tap Camera on the Home Screen.**

2. **Tap the Switch button in the upper right corner.**

   You see yourself on the screen. The objective is at the top of your iPhone (or the side if you rotate to the landscape position), so playing around with tilting, raising, and lowering your iPhone for the most favorable photo.

3. **Switch to Square and add a filter if you'd like that style of selfie. Tap the onscreen shutter button or press one of the volume buttons.**

Browsing and Editing Photos

As soon as you take a photo with the Camera app, the photo is stored in the Photos app in the album called Camera Roll. After you've taken some photos, you probably want to see them and you do that by simply tapping Photos on the Home screen, tapping the Albums button on the bottom right, and then tapping Camera Roll in the Albums list. In the thumbnail view that opens, tap the photo you want to view. Flick left or right to move from one photo to the next and back again.

Other ways to obtain images

Taking photos with Camera isn't the only way to add images to your iPhone. We can think of at least five other ways:

✔ **Screenshot:** If you have an image on your screen — even during a FaceTime conversation — that you want to save or maybe send to a friend, tap the Home button while holding the On/Off button. You hear the shutter click and the image is saved to your Camera Roll in Photos.

✔ **Mail or Messages:** Tap the photo or video in the message that someone has sent to you. The photo opens in QuickView. Tap the Share button and choose Save Image from the options.

✔ **Image Capture:** In Safari, tap and hold on an image on a web page. Tap Save Image from the options that appear. The image is automatically copied into the Camera Roll album in Photos.

✔ **Photo Stream:** If you activate Photo Stream, photos taken with other iOS devices or added to iPhoto or Aperture on a Mac connected to iCloud's Photo Stream will be in the Photo Stream album on your iPhone. See the section "Photo Stream and Shared Streams" for more information.

✔ **From your computer:** Use iTunes to sync photos from your photo management software (see Book II, Chapter 1).

TIP You can tap the Preview button in the Camera app to see Camera Roll but you can't view your other albums from Camera, only from the Photos app.

Photos stores your photos in three ways, which you access by tapping the associated button in the browse bar at the bottom of the Photos screen:

- **Photos:** These are photos you take with your iPhone or sync from Photos on your computer using iTunes. The photos are organized hierarchically by year, each year or group of years is a Collection, which is divided roughly by month. Each Collection is divided into Moments, as shown in Figure 1-9. Moments are grouped more or less by a time period or place. If Location Services for geotagging was on when the photo was taken, when you tap on the location, a map shows where the photos were taken, as in Figure 1-10.

- **Shared:** Stores the Photo Streams you create to share with others. See the Photo Stream section later in this chapter.

- **Albums:** Here you find the Camera Roll album that holds all the photos you take with your iPhone.

Figure 1-9: The browse buttons at the bottom of the screen give you sorting and viewing options.

You also find the My Photo Stream album, which contains photos in Photo Stream from your iPhone but also from other devices. You see albums synced from iTunes including Events and Faces as well as albums you create on your iPhone. Events shows collections of photos divided by event, as set up on your computer, and Faces, which is supported only by photos imported from iPhoto or Aperture on a Mac via iTunes, sorts photos by identifying people in the photo.

When you take a burst photo, you don't see all of the 47 or 86 or however many photos you took in Camera Roll; you just see one. Tap the preview thumbnail and then tap Choose Favorites to see the series of photos. A gray dot under some of the photos indicates those images that Photos thinks are the best quality. Tap the photos you want to save to Camera Roll and the circle on the lower-right corner of the photos becomes a check mark. Tap Done and those photos are moved to the Camera Roll. You can tap any of the saved photos to see the entire burst. Alternatively, select the photos you

Figure 1-10: Find geotagging information when viewing Moments in Photos.

want to save and then tap the trash can; a dialog asks if you want to save the selected photos to Camera Roll and delete the rest. Tap Delete Photos to eliminate the unwanted ones and save the selected ones.

Creating albums

You can create albums on your iPhone to make finding and viewing photos easier. You can place photos in an album from Camera Roll as well as from Photo Stream or from Collections, which include the photos you sync from your computer. You can sync albums from your computer to your iPhone, but albums you create on your iPhone don't sync to your computer.

The original photos remain where you copy them from. Albums lets you put related photos together for easier viewing. To create a photo album, follow these steps:

1. **Tap the Photos icon on the Home screen to open Photos.**

2. **Tap Albums at the bottom of the screen.**

3. **Tap the Add button that appears in the upper left corner.**

   The New Album dialog opens.

4. **Type in a name for your new Album.**

5. **Tap Save.**

   The Add Photos screen opens.

6. **Tap Photos or Albums in the browse bar to find the photos you want to place in the new album.**

   In Photos, tap a Collection to see thumbnail images of the Moments it contains. Tap Select next to a Moment to choose all the photos it contains or tap individual thumbnails to select them.

   In Albums, tap Camera Roll or another album to see thumbnails of the photos in that album, and then tap the thumbnails of the images you want to include in the album.

7. **Tap all the photos you want to include in the new album from various sources, and then tap Done.**

8. **Your new album appears in the Album list.**

9. **(Optional.) To add more photos to the album, tap the album in the Album list to open the thumbnail view. Then tap the Select button in the upper right corner. Tap the Add button at the bottom and repeat Steps 6 and 7.**

10. **(Optional.) To Delete photos from an album, tap the album in the Album list, and then tap Select in the upper right corner. Tap the photos you want to remove from the album and then tap the Delete button (the trash can).**

11. **(Optional.) To delete an album, tap Albums at the bottom of the Photos screen. Tap the Edit button, and then tap the red and white minus sign to the left of the album name. Tap Delete, and then tap Done.**

12. **(Optional.) To change the order of albums on the Album list, tap the Edit button, and then touch and drag the Rearrange button to the right of the album name to move it to the position you want in the list, and then tap Done.**

Editing photos

The quality of the photos you take with your iPhone is pretty good, but you may want to edit your photos to make them even better. Here's how to use Photos' editing options:

1. **Tap Photos on the Home screen.**

2. **Tap Camera Roll, an album, Photo Stream, Events, Faces, or Places — wherever the photo you want to edit resides.**

3. **Tap the photo you want to edit.**

4. **Tap the Edit button.**

   Five buttons appear at the bottom of the screen, refer to Figure 1-11:

   Rotate: Tap to rotate 90 degrees at a time. Tap Save when you like the orientation.

   Auto-Enhance: Tap to adjust the sharpness and contrast of the photo, and then tap Save. Auto-enhance also automatically looks for red-eyes and adjusts them. Tap Save to keep the correction or Cancel to leave the photo alone.

   Filters: Tap to apply one of the color filters. A strip across the bottom shows you how each effect will affect your photo; tap the one you like and then tap Apply in the upper right corner, or tap Cancel in the upper left corner to leave the photo as is.

Figure 1-11: You have five photo-editing options in Photos: Rotate, Auto-Enhance, Filter, Red-Eye Removal, and Crop/Constrain.

Red-Eye Removal: Tap the tool and then tap the red eye to correct the werewolf effect of your subject's eyes. If you like the result, tap Apply, and then tap Save. If not, tap on the eye-again to remove the black spot.

As handy as it can be, red-eye removal isn't perfect. If it doesn't recognize the red-eye, a message appears at the bottom which reads "Did not find red-eye to correct." Try zooming in and tapping again. Sometimes it finds more eye than you want and puts a black mark on the face of the person. Tap near the eye again to remove the extra black mark and try using Auto-Enhance or, better yet, another photo-retouching app such as iPhoto or Photoshop Express.

Crop/Constrain: Use your fingers to zoom, pan, and rotate the image until it appears as you wish. Drag the corners of the crop grid to set the area you want to crop or tap the Aspect button to choose one of the preset aspect ratios. Tap Crop to see the edits, and then tap Save. Your image is saved with the changes you made.

Tap Cancel if you don't want to Save your changes.

5. **Tap the previous button in the upper left corner to return to the album where the photo resides.**

6. **Tap a button at the bottom of the screen to go to another album or press the Home button to leave Photos.**

Bonus Chapter 4 (online) suggests photo enhancement apps that you can download to your iPhone, and the Web Extra for this minibook talks about the iPhoto app specifically. For more on how to access the online bonus content, see this book's Introduction.

Sharing the (photo) wealth

After you're happy with your photos, you might want to share one or more electronically or as an old-fashioned print. Photos lets you copy, print, and send photos and videos to others by AirDrop or as e-mail attachments or multimedia messages (MMS or iMessage), or upload them to Twitter, Facebook, Flickr, or YouTube. You can also delete photos and videos from Camera Roll or Photo Stream. First, we look at how to do things with a single photo, and then we explain managing batches of photos.

To share one photo:

1. **Tap Photos on the Home screen.**

2. **Tap the collection, moment, or album where the photo you want to share, copy, or print resides.**

   The thumbnail view opens.

3. **Tap the photo you want to use.**

   At the top of the screen, you see

- **Collections, Camera Roll, or "Album Name" button:** In the upper left corner, this tells you where this photo resides. Tapping this button takes you back to the album where you began. From there, you can tap one of the browse buttons at the bottom of the screen to go to another source (Photos, Shared, or Albums).

- **Photo number:** Indicates where in the lineup this photo or video falls (such as 4 of 12).

At the bottom of the screen, you see the Share and Delete buttons.

4. **Tap the Share button to open the Share Sheet and then tap the action you want to take, as shown in Figure 1-12:**

- **AirDrop:** Send the photo to someone nearby who has AirDrop turned on and who is in your Contacts. Just tap the person's name or image and the photo is sent to them. From their iPhone, they can accept or decline the photo.

- **Message:** Pastes the photo in a New Message, which will be sent as an MMS or iMessage. Fill in the recipient and tap Send. (Refer to Book III, Chapter 2.)

- **Mail:** The photo is pasted into a new message. Type in the address and a message if you wish, and tap Send. (See Book III, Chapter 4.) You are asked to choose what size file you want to

Figure 1-12: The Share Sheet displays all available sharing options.

send: Small, Medium, Large, or Actual Size. The approximate megabyte size is indicated; if your e-mail service has size limits for attachments, choose an image that is about half the size of the limit.

- **iCloud:** Add the photo to a Shared Stream that you created, or you can create a new one. See the "Photo Stream" section for more information.

- **Twitter:** Sends your photo to your Twitter account. You must be signed in to Twitter to use this feature.

- **Facebook:** Posts your photo to your Facebook profile. Add a comment and location if you like and tap Post. You must be signed in to Facebook to use this feature.

- **Flickr:** Posts your photo to your Flickr account. Add a comment and tap Post. You must be signed in to Flickr to use this feature.

- **Copy:** Puts a copy of the photo in the clipboard, which you can then paste in another app such as Notes or Pages.

- **Slideshow:** Opens a slideshow of the images in the album or begins playing the video. See the section "Viewing slideshows" for the steps to take.

- **Assign to Contact:** Assigns the photo to a person or entity in Contacts. See Book IV, Chapter 1 for complete details.

- **Use as Wallpaper:** Uses the photo as the background for your lock or Home screen. We explain how to do this in the section "Using a photo as wallpaper" later in this chapter.

- **Print:** Prints the photo to a printer on your wireless network. See Book I, Chapter 2 for details about wireless printing.

If you want to share more than one photo, you can select others from the thumbnails at the top of the screen just by tapping them, and then tap the action you want to take.

Tap Cancel in the upper left corner if you don't want to share the photo after all.

5. **After you tap your choice, the Share Sheet closes.**

If you want to delete a single photo, select it as above and then tap the Delete (the trash can) button.

Batches

Sometimes you have more than one photo that you'd like to print or e-mail, or even delete. Photos lets you choose a group of photos and then take the same action for all of them at once. Do the following:

1. **Tap either Photos or Albums in the browse bar. Slightly different things happen depending on which you tap:**

Photos: Tap a Collection to see the Moments it contains and do one of the following:

If the photos you want to share are in one Moment, tap the Share button next to the Moment that has the photo or photos you want to share, and then, as shown in Figure 1-13, choose Share this moment, which shares all the photos in the Moment, or Share some photos, which opens another thumbnail view of the moment where you tap each photo you want to share.

If you want to share photos from several Moments, tap Select in the upper right corner and then tap the photos you want to share.

Albums: Tap the album that has the photo or photos you want to share. Tap Select in the upper left corner and then tap the photos you want to share.

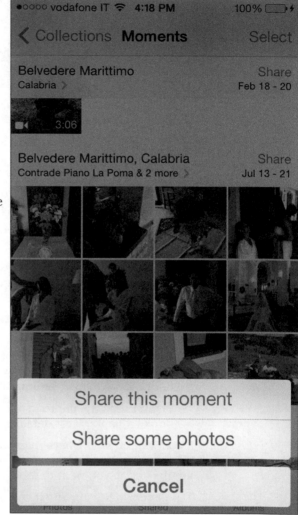

Figure 1-13: Send entire Moments or batch photos from an album to take an action on a group of photos.

2. **Tap the Share button at the bottom of the screen. The actions that can be taken have active buttons. If you exceed the photo limits, the option doesn't appear in the Share Sheet:**

   Mail: Up to five photos

   Message: Up to two photos

   iCloud, Facebook, Flickr, Print, or Copy: Unlimited, although Flickr and Print don't support Moments selected as a group. They must be selected using the Select button and then tapping the photos individually.

3. **(Optional.) Add the selected photos to a new or existing album by tapping Add To at the bottom of the screen.**

A list of albums created on your iPhone opens.

Tap the album you want to add the photos to or scroll to the bottom and tap New Album, in which case the New Album dialog opens where you type a name and tap Save.

The selected photos are added to the existing or new album.

4. **(Optional.) Delete the selected photos by tapping the Delete button.**

When you Delete a photo from an album, other than Camera Roll, the photo remains on your iPhone in Camera Roll, but is removed.

Using a photo as wallpaper

You can customize the wallpaper, or background image, that appears on your lock screen and your Home screen. We explained how to do this from Settings in Book I, Chapter 4. Here we explain how to assign wallpaper directly from Photos:

1. **Select the photo you want to assign from any of the albums on Photos.**

2. **Tap the Share button in the bottom left corner.**

3. **Tap Use as Wallpaper.**

The Move and Scale screen opens.

4. **Pinch and spread the photo to zoom to the size you want and pan, or move, the photo around until the image is just how you want it on the screen.**

5. **Tap the Set button.**

6. **Choose one of the options that appear:**

   - **Set Lock Screen:** To use the image for the Lock screen.
   - **Set Home Screen:** To use the image for the Home screen.
   - **Set Both:** To use the image for both the Lock and Home screen.
   - **Cancel:** If you decide to leave things the way they are.

Viewing slideshows

Gone are the days of 35 mm slides and overstuffed guests falling asleep while you try to figure out which way to put the slide in the projector so it doesn't display upside-down and out of focus. With its larger Retina display, either iPhone 5, 5c, and 5s shows off your photos beautifully, but earlier iPhones are nothing to sneeze at. You can also connect to a television or monitor to play your slideshow, which we explain in Book V, Chapter 4. To view a slideshow on your iPhone, follow these steps:

1. **Open the photo or album where you want the slideshow to begin.**

2. **Tap the Share button and then tap Slideshow.**

   The Slideshow Options screen opens.

3. **Tap Transitions.**

   Choose the type of transition you want from the list. A transition is what happens on the screen between one photo and the next.

4. **Tap Play Music On or Off.**

   If you want music to accompany your slideshow, tap On. The Music app opens so you can make a selection from any of the lists. After you tap your selection, you automatically return to where you were in Photos.

5. **Tap Start Slideshow.**

   The slideshow plays from the photo where you begin through to the end of the album.

The Slideshow settings give you a few viewing options. Tap Settings➪Photos & Camera. In the Slideshow section, set the following:

- **Play Each Slide For:** Choose the duration of each image on the screen, from 2 to 20 seconds.
- **Repeat:** Plays the slideshow in a continuous loop.
- **Shuffle:** Plays the images in a random order.

Moving photos from your iPhone to your computer is handled by your photo management software. On a Mac, this might be Image Capture, iPhoto, Aperture, or another application that you prefer. On Windows, you may use Photoshop Elements (8 or later), Live Photo Gallery, or Pictures Library. When you connect your iPhone to your computer with the USB connector cable, the photo management application you use recognizes your iPhone as it would any other digital camera. If import photo choices don't appear automatically, you may have to go to a command such as File➪Import and choose to import all the photos or select only some of the photos you want to import.

Photo Stream and Shared Streams

Photo Stream is an incredible alternative to connecting your iPhone to your computer with the USB connector cable. Photos from all devices that are signed in to the same iCloud account with Photo Stream turned On are synced. Photos taken with your iPhone or other iOS devices and those uploaded to your computer appear here and can be saved to your iPhone if you want. As part of iCloud, Photo Stream both stores and lets you share your photos. Here we look at both functions.

Photo Stream storage

Photo Stream automatically uploads photos you take with your iPhone or other iOS devices to iCloud. Then, Photo Stream pushes, or downloads, them to the other devices and your computer. We've found this to be a priceless tool and timesaver in taking the screenshots for this book, seconds after capturing a screenshot on our iPhones, upon opening iPhoto they show up in the Photo Stream section under Recents as well as in Events on our Macs — no cable required.

Photo Stream also uploads photos from your computer. For example, if you take photos with a digital camera, and then move them to your computer, those photos are automatically uploaded to iCloud and pushed to your iOS devices, including your iPhone. You can view them on your iPhone for 30 days, giving you time to save a copy on your iPhone, too, if you like. Only photos uploaded after you turned Photo Stream on will be placed in Photo Stream.

The most recent 1,000 photos from all sources are stored in Photo Stream on iCloud for 30 days. As you add new photos beyond the 1,000 limit, the oldest ones are deleted.

Photos are downloaded and stored in full resolution on your Mac or Windows PC, but are optimized for download speed and storage for your iOS devices.

To start using Photo Stream, do the following:

- ✔ **On your iPhone**, go to Settings➪Photos & Camera and tap My Photo Stream On, as shown in Figure 1-14. You must be connected to Wi-Fi for Photo Stream to function.

- ✔ **On your Mac (OS X 10.7.5 or later)**, go to System Preferences➪iCloud and click the check box next to Photos. Click Options and check both boxes in the dialog: My Photo Stream and Photo Sharing.

  In your Mac's photo management program, do the following:

  Go to Preferences and click the iCloud tab. Check the box next to My Photo Stream to turn it on, and while you're there, click the box next to Photo Sharing, which we cover in a few paragraphs. Then choose how you want Photo Stream to handle your photos:

  Automatic Import Photos that are pushed to the Photo Stream library on your Mac are automatically imported to iPhoto or Aperture. With this box checked, your photos are permanently stored on your computer in

Events, Faces, and Places when they enter Photo Stream from another device.

Automatic Upload, which sends all new photos from your computer to Photo Stream. Deselecting this box means you manually drag photos into the Photo Stream library or select the photos and then choose Photo Stream from the pop-up Share menu at the bottom of the window. Although Photo Stream makes sure you don't exceed the storage space on your iPhone, manually managing photos that go from your computer to Photo Stream limits the number of photos pushed to the Photo Stream library on your other devices.

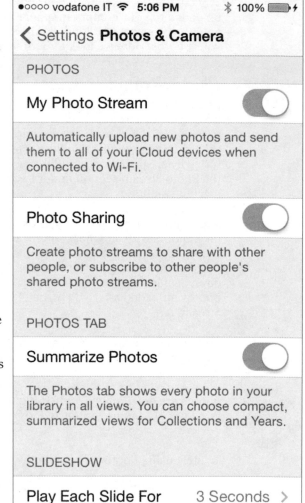

✔ **On a Windows PC (7 or 8)**, download the iCloud Control Panel for Windows at `support.apple.com/kb/DL1455.` Open the iCloud Control Panel and click the check box next to Photo Stream.

Figure 1-14: Activate Photo Stream on all your devices to share photos seamlessly.

On Windows, the process is manual: drag photos you want in Photo Stream from your photo management application to the designated Photo Stream folder. The default folder is C:\Users\<user name>\Pictures\Photo Stream\My Photo Stream, which you can change by clicking the Options button next to Photo Stream in the iCloud Control Panel.

Photo Sharing

Passing your iPhone around the table from friend to friend isn't the only way to share photos. Photo Sharing lets you invite people to view specific photos grouped in a stream. It's called a stream because photos can flow into it on an ongoing basis. You create a stream and invite specific people to see it. As you add more photos to the stream, the invitees are notified that new photos have been added and can go view them. You can also make your stream public. For example, if you're a realtor, you could take photos with your iPhone, create a Homes For Sale stream, and then share that stream by listing the Photo Sharing URL for that album for people to view properties. Here we explain both private and public sharing.

Keeping shared streams private

Access to a private shared stream is by invitation only. First, make sure Photo Sharing is On in Settings⇨Photos & Camera, and then do the following:

1. **Tap Photos on the Home screen.**

2. **Tap the Moment or Album that has the photos you want to share.**

   To share just one photo, open the photo and then tap the Share button and go to Step 6.

3. **Tap the Select button.**

4. **Tap the photos you want to share.**

5. **Tap the Share button.**

   If you want to share all the photos in a Moment, tap the Share button above the Moment, and then tap Share this moment.

6. **Tap iCloud.**

   A dialog opens as shown in Figure 1-15. Type an optional comment then do one of the following:

   - If the Stream that appears next to Stream is the one you want to add photos to, simply tap Post.

   - If you want to add the photos to a different existing Stream, tap Stream and then tap the one you want to use.

   - If you want to create a new Stream, tap Stream and do the following:

     1. To add a new shared stream, tap New Shared Stream and type in a Stream Name. Then tap Next.

     2. Tap the To field and type the e-mail address of the person you want to invite to view your photos, or tap the Add button (it looks like a plus sign) to access your Contacts and choose recipients from there.

     3. Repeat Step 8 to add more recipients.

     4. Tap Next and you return to the opening dialog.

7. **Tap Post.**

   Addressees receive an invitation to subscribe to your Shared Stream.

8. **After someone joins your shared Photo Stream, they'll be notified when new images are added.**

The people you invite to view your shared stream have to have an Apple ID, which they use to sign in to it. Otherwise, follow the steps in the next section to turn Public Website On, and the e-mail they receive will contain a link to the Shared Photo Stream. Figure 1-16 shows an example of a Shared Photo Stream viewed in iCloud.com.

Another way to create Shared Photo Streams is to tap the Shared button at the bottom of the screen to open the Shared Streams list. Tap the plus sign in the upper left, name the Shared Stream, address invitations to view it, and then tap Create. Tap the new Shared Stream from the list of Shared Streams and tap the plus sign to add photos. Select photos from Photos and Albums and then tap Done.

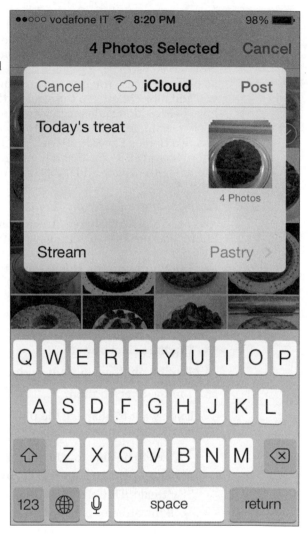

Figure 1-15: Post photos to your shared streams on iCloud.

Publishing shared streams

To make a shared stream available to the public through a URL, you have to first create the stream in one of the two ways explained previously and then go into the stream's settings. Follow these steps:

1. Tap the Shared button at the bottom of the Photos screen.

A list shows Shared Streams, which contain all the shared streams you created. The first stream, called Activity, shows the history of everything you've done with shared streams.

2. Tap the stream you want to make public.

You see all the photos that are in the stream and two tabs at the bottom: Photos and People.

Figure 1-16: Shared Photo Streams are viewed on iCloud.com.

3. Tap People.

You see the screen as in Figure 1-17 and can do the following:

Tap the disclosure triangle to the right of a name of a subscriber to resend the invitation or remove the subscriber.

Tap Invite People to invite others to see this shared stream.

Tap Subscribers Can Post to the On (or Off) position if you want invitees to be able to add photos or videos to this stream.

Tap Public Website On (or Off) to change the status of this Photo Stream. This creates a URL on iCloud so anyone — who knows the link — can view it.

Tap Share Link, to share the link of a publicly Shared Photo Stream via Mail, Message, Twitter, or Facebook or to copy the link so you can paste it elsewhere, such as a newsletter or website.

Tap Notifications if you want to receive alerts in the Notification center when subscribers interact with the stream by liking, commenting, or adding photos.

Tap Delete Photo Stream to delete this Shared Photo Stream.

Should you ever want to delete your entire Photo Stream from your iPhone, go to Settings⇨Photos & Camera and turn My Photo Stream Off. To completely empty Photo Stream, go to iCloud.com and sign in to your account. Click your Name in the upper right, click Advanced, and then click Reset Photo Stream. All photos are removed from iCloud but remain on the devices and computers they originated from.

Making More Adjustments with iPhoto

If you purchased a new iPhone 4s, 5c, or 5s after the announcement of iOS 7, you're eligible to download the iPhoto app for free from the App Store. iPhoto now gives you many more options and finer control. Limited print space keeps us from going through every single feature, but we explain the major functions and, once you understand those, we're sure you'll be comfortable exploring the iPhoto app on your own.

Viewing your photos

iPhoto accesses photos from Photos on your iPhone, so if you have iCloud's Photo Stream feature turned on, you will also see photos from iCloud on iPhoto. When you tap iPhoto on the Home screen, you have two viewing options in the browse bar: Photos, which displays all the photos on your iPhone in chronological order, and Albums, which displays the albums in your Photos library, including Camera Roll, your current Photo Stream and shared Photo Streams from iCloud, Albums you created in Photos, and Faces, as shown in Figure 1-18.

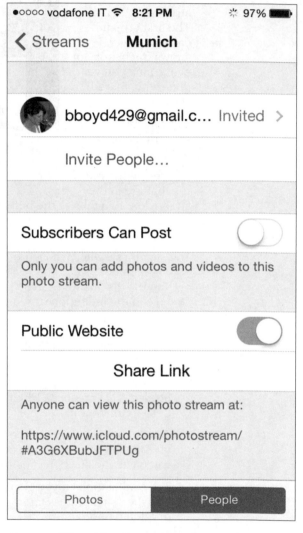

Figure 1-17: Go public with your shared streams.

Flagging, tagging, and liking photos

The double-edged sword of digital photography is that you can take a lot of photos without the expense of film and processing, giving you many to choose from and sometimes too many to choose from. To help you keep track of photos you like or want to group together, or even print, iPhoto gives you three markers:

- ✔ *Flags* are a great tool for marking photos that you want to put together in an album or group together in some other way.

- ✔ *Tags,* which are words you associate with the photos and can use to search.

- ✔ *Hearts,* which are the symbol for designating your favorite photos — similar to liking it on a social network.

When you tap a photo to open it in the photo editor, you see the flag, heart, and tag buttons In the browse bar, as shown in Figure 1-19. Tap the button for the marker you want to place on the photo (you can use all three if you like). After you mark a photo, iPhoto creates Flagged and Favorites albums and adds them to the iPhoto Library. Tags albums go in a Tags library, and as

Figure 1-18: iPhoto accesses photos from Photos and iCloud.

you place the same tag on other photos, they are added to that tag's album. The first time you use a tag, it's added to the tags list and when you tag another photo, you can create a new tag or tap an existing one. A photo can have more than one tag and photos that have been marked have the relative icon(s) on the images in the thumbnail grid below the photo editor. (If you don't see the thumbnail grid, tap the second button in the toolbar at the top of the screen.)

Editing photos

iPhoto on your iPhone offers a full palette of tools and effects that you can apply singly or together to your photos. There are also some handy viewing features so you can see your original photo next to your edited photo and remove effects if you decide you don't like them. Tap a photo you want to play with, and then tap the Tools button on the left end of the browse bar. The following buttons appear and tapping each opens another set of tools; tap the Tools button to return to the previous browse bar, and tap Browse to return to the first browse bar. Try these editing tricks:

Figure 1-19: Marking with a flag, tag, or as a favorite is a way to quickly sort and find photos.

- **Crop:** Drag the corners of the grid to resize the overall size, or tap the ellipsis to see a variety of cropping sizes and ratios; each one shows a photo preview. Use a two-finger pinch and spread to zoom in and out of the image or to rotate it. For more precision, use the wheel to rotate the image to a specific degree.

- **Exposure:** Drag your finger along the slider to increase or decrease the exposure, which can change the brightness and contrast of your photo.

- **Color:** Experiment with the color options by tapping a color circle and then seeing the effect it has on your photo: warmer, cooler, black and white, sepia, and so on. Tap the White Balance at the far right of the Color tools to use different effects such as bright sun, clouds, or shadow.

✔ **Brushes:** These tools beg for experimentation. Tap the Brushes button and a list of brush types opens. Here you find the redeye removal tool, which you use to paint over red eyes. There are also brushes to lighten, darken, saturate, and desaturate the image or sharpen or soften It. For example, if you tap the desaturate brush and then rub your finger over part of your photo, that part loses color. A handy eraser tool at the far right lets you cancel parts of what you brushed over.

✔ **Effects:** Tap this button to open a chooser that displays nine groups of effects such as black and white, camera filters, or artistic, which makes your photo look painted or drawn. Tap a group and then tap the buttons to see how the effect will look on your photo. Tap the button at the far right to see all the effect groups again.

Figure 1-20: Three tools were used to change a photo into a sketch.

After you use an effect, a blue dash appears over the button. To see the original, tap the Original button in the toolbar (second from the right). Your original is always saved and edited versions are saved to an Edited album in the iPhoto Library.

To add a second effect, tap the Tools button and then tap the next effect you want to try. The effect is applied to the original photo and then if you tap to the first effect, you see both effects there — think of the effects as being layered one on top of the other. Figure 1-20 was rotated and cropped, the dogs color was sharpened slightly with a brush, and then an artistic effect was applied.

To remove an effect, tap the effect button and then tap ellipsis in the upper right corner; tap Reset. From this menu, you can also copy the effect and paste it on another photo. To remove all effects, tap Tools and then Browse to reach the first browse bar, and then tap the ellipsis in the upper right corner and tap Revert. All your changes are cancelled and the edited version is removed from the Edited album.

 Auto-enhance (the button to the left of the flag in the browse bar) is a quick fix for photos that adjusts contrast, brightness, and red eyes.

When you take a photo, it's not just the image that's captured but also information about when, where, and how it was taken. Tap the Info (i) button at the left end of the browse bar to see details about the photo and add a caption if you like.

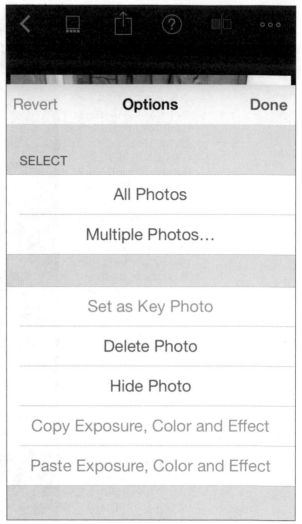

Figure 1-21: Tap the ellipsis at the top of the screen to see options for selecting and deleting photos.

 You can share your edited images by tapping the Share button in the toolbar at the top of the screen, and then choosing how you want to share: Mail, Message, social media, AirDrop, or Beam, which searches for beam-enabled iOS devices in your vicinity and lets you send the photo directly to them.

Deleting photos

Each time you edit a photo, a copy is saved to the Edited album and your storage can fill up quickly. Eventually, you might want to delete some photos. To do that, follow these steps:

1. **Tap Albums, and then tap the album that holds the photos you want to delete.**

   It has to be the Camera Roll or an album in iPhoto, not in iCloud.

2. **Tap the ellipsis in the upper right corner, as shown in Figure 1-21.**

3. **Under Select, tap All Photos, if you want to delete the entire album, or tap Multiple Photos.**

4. **The photo browser opens.**

   Drag the main photo up to see more thumbnail images.

5. **Tap the photos you want to delete.**

   Tap Range, and then tap the first and last photo of the range; all the photos in between will be selected, too.

6. **Tap Done when you complete your selection.**

7. **You see a group preview of the photos you selected.**

8. **Tap the ellipsis again.**

9. **Tap Delete Photos.**

Chapter 2: Acquiring and Browsing Music, Videos, Movies, and More

In This Chapter

✓ **Just browsing and sampling**

✓ **Making your purchases**

✓ **Matching your existing media**

✓ **Tracking down free iTunes promotional music and other goodies**

✓ **Reading up on iBooks**

✓ **Learning about iTunes U**

As the App Store, which we talk about in Book II, Chapter 2, is where you go to download apps, the iTunes Store, is the place to be to download music, movies, TV shows, tones, and audiobooks.

In this chapter, we take a close look at the iTunes store, both on your iPhone and on your computer, and show you the ins and outs of browsing, sampling, and buying media. With the latest version of iTunes, there's little difference between the two. If you think iTunes is just for music, think again. We explore iTunes' other offerings, including movies, TV shows, audiobooks, and free promotional music. After you have media to enjoy on your iPhone, go to Chapter 3 to learn about using the Music and Podcasts apps and Chapter 4 to get clued in on Videos and iTunes U.

New Releases

Here to You

Wise Up Ghost (Deluxe)
Elvis Costello &...

Self Made, 3
MMG

Matching Your Media to iTunes

We explained how to sync your iPhone with media stored on your computer in Book II, Chapter 1, but not all of your media is necessarily in iTunes. If you have a collection of CDs, you might not have copied them onto your computer because you didn't have any reason to. Or you may download music from other online sources. Wouldn't it be great to put some of that music onto your iPhone to listen to when you're away from your computer or stereo system? First you have to move that music into iTunes on your computer, and here we explain the different ways to do that.

Media that's already on your computer

Moving media that you downloaded from another site like Amazon (www.amazon.com) or GoMusic (www.gomusic.com) is simple — just drag those files into your iTunes library. To make that task even easier, choose the Automatically Add to iTunes folder when selecting the destination for saving a downloaded file, and the file shows up in your iTunes library.

An alternative to moving all your music into the iTunes app on your computer is to subscribe to iTunes Match. For a yearly fee of $24.95, iTunes Match "matches" up to 25,000 songs you have that are available from the iTunes Store and puts it in your iTunes in the Cloud library as an iTunes item. It also upgrades songs that are available in the iTunes Store to 256 Kbps (unavailable songs remain in the format you have them in). The upgrades alone could be good reason to purchase it, but since anything in your iTunes library is also in iTunes in the Cloud, with iTunes Match, even songs you didn't purchase through iTunes are available across all your devices. After the media is in iTunes, and you activate iCloud, you're just a syncing step away from having everything in your iTunes library accessible on your iPhone.

Media on a CD

To import media from a CD, follow these steps:

1. **Open iTunes.**

2. **Insert the CD you want to copy into the disc drive on your computer.**

   If the CD doesn't appear under the Library pop-up menu, go to iTunes⇨Preferences⇨General. Toward the bottom of the screen, you see the When You Insert a CD pull-down menu. Choose Show CD to see the CD under Devices. You can also change the default Settings here.

3. **Click on the CD in the pop-up menu on the top left of the window.**

   The songs are listed and selected by default. If you only want to import some of the songs, deselect those you don't want.

4. **Click Import CD.**

   The Import Settings window opens. Click the pop-up menu next to Import Using to change the default settings. (See the sidebar for details about import settings.)

5. **Click OK.**

   The status display at the top of the screen displays the songs that are being copied and the time remaining.

   When finished, the songs are stored in the Music library.

6. **Click the Eject button to remove the CD from your drive.**

If you have an active Internet connection when you copy a CD to iTunes, click the Options button and choose Get Track Names. iTunes will automatically scan the Gracenote Internet music database for any information related to the CD and copy it into the Info about that CD. After copying a CD to iTunes, download any album artwork that's available in iTunes by clicking File⇨Library⇨Get Album Artwork. You have to have an Internet connection and sign in to your Apple ID account to use this feature.

---

iTunes encoding music settings

When iTunes imports music, it automatically compresses the file with the iTunes Plus encoder, which plays at 256 Kbps in stereo (128 Kbps in mono). However, iTunes also gives you the option of using a different encoder to compress music you import. Click Import Settings at the bottom right of the iTunes screen to change your settings for the active import (set your own default import settings by going to iTunes⇨Preferences⇨General and clicking the Import Settings button). You have five choices, each of which has an Auto setting, and four have custom settings.

Considering that CD quality audio is around 44,000 KHz per second with 16 bits of data over two channels for stereo listening, one minute of music requires 10MB of storage. Compressing makes the file smaller so you can fit more songs on your personal listening device; that is, your iPhone. AAC and MP3 encoders compress the data by removing audio you wouldn't be able to hear unless you have bionic ears. AIFF, WAV, and Apple Lossless Encoders transform the data without removing any audio, so it can be played on your computer or iPhone.

Here's a brief explanation of the settings to help you choose if you decide to change the encoder you use to import music:

✔ **AAC (Advanced Audio Coding) Encoder:** Offers better sound quality and more flexibility at the same bit rate as MP3. The Custom settings are iTunes Plus, High Quality

(128 Kbps in stereo and 64 Kbps in mono), and Spoken Podcast (64 Kbps in stereo and 32 Kbps in mono). Files are compressed and tags identify information about the song, such as artist, CD, and title.

✔ **AIFF (Audio Interchange File Format) Encoder:** Custom settings let you choose a sample rate between 8,000 and 48,000 KHz (the DVD standard); a sample size of 8 or 16 bit, and mono or stereo channels. AIFF and WAV offer the highest listening quality but don't copy tag information, such as the name of the artist, CD, or song (although iTunes does track that in its database, it won't show up if you burn to another CD), and the files are large because they aren't compressed. AIFF files can be read and created on iTunes on both the Mac and Windows, but they are more commonly used in the Mac environment.

✔ **Apple Lossless Encoder:** Offers only an automatic setting. Apple Lossless compresses files without removing (or losing) any audio so you have audio quality similar to AIFF/WAV but with slightly smaller files. It also sets tags like AAC and MP3 encoders. The downside is that most non-Apple devices don't support Apple Lossless.

✔ **MP3 Encoder:** Choose Good Quality at 128 Kbps, High at 160, or Higher at 192. Custom settings offer Stereo Bit Rates between 16 and 320 Kbps; seven settings for Variable

---

continued

continued

Bit Rate (VBR) encoding, ten choices for the Sample Rate between 8,000 and 48,000 kHz, mono or stereo channels, and normal or joint stereo mode. You also have an on/off option for Smart Encoding and Filter Frequencies Below 10 Hz. Files are compressed and tagged. This is the choice to make for non-iOS MP3 players or if you want to burn an MP3 CD to play in a portable CD player or car stereo.

✔ **WAV Encoder:** Offers the same custom settings as the AIFF encoder. iTunes on both Mac and Windows reads and creates WAV files. They are widely used with Windows and other operating systems.

To convert a song from one format to another, click on the song and then click Advanced ⇨ Create Version, where the version will be what you established in the Import Settings. Keep in mind there's no sense converting a lower quality file to a higher quality, for example, converting an MP3 file to AIFF. The encoder can't add in audio that was removed. You can go from one encoder to another of similar quality, such as AIFF to WAV or Apple Lossless to MP3 with good results, albeit slight additional detail loss.

Your choice depends on how sensitive your ears are and what kind of output device you'll be using to listen to your music.

Browsing, Sampling, and Buying Music, Movies, and More at the iTunes Store

Have your Apple ID — or your finger if you have an iPhone 5s — handy when you want to use iTunes because that's what you use to sign in and confirm your purchase. If you haven't yet created an Apple ID, see Book II, Chapter 1 for instructions.

When you first open the iTunes Store, it can seem overwhelming, and in a way it is: It offers more than 14 million songs. Besides all the music, iTunes also carries thousands of movies and TV shows, plus ringtones and audiobooks. Luckily, the iTunes Store, on your computer and iPhone, is organized to help you narrow your choices. If you're familiar with the App Store, which we covered in Book II, Chapter 1, you'll recognize the iTunes Store setup.

On your computer

There's not much difference between the iTunes Store on your computer and on your iOS devices, including your iPhone. The Home tab presents an opening screen with offers in each category, and tabs across the top of iTunes correspond to different types of media: Music, Movies, TV Shows, App Store (refer to Book II, Chapter 2), Books, Podcasts (Book V, Chapter 3), and iTunes U (Book V, Chapter 4). On the top left, you see your Apple ID, which is a tab, too. (The Apple ID in Figure 2-2 is barbaradepaula.) Tap a tab to see what's available in that media category. See Figure 2-1.

**Book V
Chapter 2**

**Acquiring and
Browsing Music,
Videos, Movies, and
More**

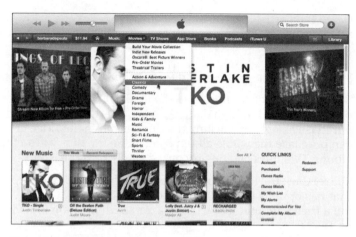

Figure 2-1: The iTunes Store lets you browse for music, movies, TV shows, and more.

In each category, you see rotating banner ads across the top. Below the ads are sections along the lines of This Week or New & Noteworthy as well as seasonal and themed sections. You can scroll horizontally and vertically, and clicking any of the ads or icons in this smorgasbord of offers takes you to an information screen about that item.

When you click on a song or album icon or name from anywhere in the iTunes store, the album information window opens. Click on a TV show and the season information screen opens. Click on a movie and a movie information screen opens. Figure 2-2 shows an example. These are the parts of an information screen:

Figure 2-2: Information about the media item is displayed in iTunes.

- **Name** (and artist if in the Music category): Click the arrow next to the artist's name to see more songs and albums by the same artist.

- **Release date.**

- **Star Ratings:** The number of ratings appear in the parentheses.

- **Buy button:** Click to download the media. Each option, for example rent or buy, standard or high-definition, has its own button. Songs can be purchased singly by clicking the Buy button in the Price column or you can purchase the whole album by clicking the Buy button under the album; TV shows can be purchased singly or by season.

- **Share:** Click the triangle next to the Buy button to open a pop-up menu that has options to gift the item to a friend, add it to your own wish list, tell a friend about it, copy the link, or share the item info via Facebook or Twitter.

You can't use a store credit to pay for a gift. You must pay with a credit card or PayPal account.

- **Ratings:** For movies only. The ratings are the usual G, PG, PG-13, R, and so on for U.S. markets. Foreign films may have different ratings.

Three tabs give you different information:

- **Songs** (Music), **Details** (all other categories): The first few lines of the description of the item are visible. If the description is longer, click More on the right to expose the complete description. This is where you find the song list if you're viewing an album, the episode list for TV Shows and Podcasts, Chapters for Books, and lessons or lectures for iTunes U.

- **Ratings and Reviews:** Users can give a simple star rating, from zero to five, or write a review. Reviews help your downloading or purchasing decisions.

- **Related:** Lists items by the same performers and other items purchased by people who bought that particular item. A fourth tab appears when bonus items such as iTunes Extras or LP are available.

Tap the History button next to the Library button at the top of the window to see a list of items you previewed recently in any category. Here you'll also find your Wish List and your iTunes Radio history.

Finding music when you know what you're looking for

If you have a specific song or movie in mind, you can skip the rotating banner ads and lists of recommendations and search for the media you seek.

⌘+F takes the cursor to the Search field. Type the name or a couple key words in the Search field at the top right of the window, and then press return. A list of matching results appears. The results are culled from the entire iTunes Store but are divided by category. If you click Media Type in the list on the right, you'll only see that type of media.

Book V
Chapter 2

Acquiring and
Browsing Music,
Videos, Movies, and
More

You can also click one of the media type tabs at the top of the screen —
Music, Movies, TV Shows — to see a greater selection in just one type of
media. Click and hold to open the pull-down menu that displays genres or
categories within a type of media.

Downloading media from iTunes

When you find something you like, click the Buy (or Rent) button and it's
downloaded to iTunes. Either way, you have to sign in with your Apple ID
account and pay the price. This happens two ways:

- **Credit card:** Insert your credit card information into your Apple ID
  account. You did this either when you opened it, or you can do it by
  clicking Edit to the right of Payment Type. A window opens where you
  can choose the type of credit card you want to use (or PayPal) and type
  in the necessary information: account number, expiration date, billing
  address, and so on.

- **Redeem:** You can redeem Apple or iTunes gift cards, gift certificates, or
  allowances. (You can set up a monthly allowance for yourself or someone else. A set amount is charged to your credit card or PayPal account
  and credited to the designated iTunes account.) Click your Apple
  ID⇨Redeem or click Redeem in the Quick Links section. Type in the code
  from the card or certificate or click Use Camera and hold the card up to
  your computer's camera. The amount of the card or certificate is added
  to your account and appears to the right of the Apple ID account tab.

After you download the item, close the iTunes store by clicking the Library
button in the upper-right corner — It changes to iTunes Store when you're
viewing your iTunes library. You return to iTunes library, which is non-store
iTunes on your computer. Click the pop-up menu to choose the category for
the type of media you downloaded (Music, Movies, and so on) to see your
media. Click a tab at the top to choose the viewing style you want, and then
click an item. Clicking an album shows you the album contents, as shown in
Figure 2-3.

You can select Automatic Downloads so that whenever you download something on your computer or device, it's automatically downloaded to other
computers or devices using the same Apple ID. On your computer, in iTunes,
go to iTunes⇨Preferences and click the Store tab. Check the boxes next to
the media you want automatically downloaded to other devices: Apps or
Music (Books as well on Windows). Books are managed by iBooks on a Mac
running OS X 10.9 Mavericks; go to iBooks⇨Preferences and click the Store
tab and then choose Download New Purchases Automatically. On your
iPhone, tap Settings⇨iTunes & App Store and tap the switches next to Music,
Apps, or Books On. While you're there, you can choose to use the cellular
network to download purchases by tapping the switch by Use Cellular Data
On, although there are size limits for downloading on the cellular network.
Use a Wi-Fi connection to download larger files.

Weighing renting versus buying options

Online rentals and purchases give you another option for watching movies.

Two things you have to consider when deciding whether to rent or buy a video from the iTunes Store:

✔ **How often do you want to watch the video:** If you think you'll only want to watch it once, renting is probably fine. At the time of publication, movie rentals cost between $3.99 and $4.99. You have thirty days to begin watching the movie and 24 hours to finish watching once you begin. If you think it's a classic or a keeper, you probably want to buy.

✔ **How much do you want to spend:** Rentals are $3.99 for a standard version and $4.99 for high definition. iTunes runs specials to purchase films for as low as $4.99 and new releases in high definition go for around $14.99.

With iCloud, you can access rented or purchased media from all your devices. When you start watching on one device, you can pause there, and begin playback on another device from where you paused on the first device. We explain viewing video on your iPhone in Book V, Chapter 4.

Figure 2-3: The Music section of the Library shows which songs, albums, and music videos you have in iTunes.

iTunes isn't just about music and movies: You can also find podcasts, audiobooks, and even university courses and K-12 lessons. While you browse, purchase or subscribe, and download those items from the iTunes Store on your computer, or your iPhone, you still find audiobooks in the iTunes app but after you download the associated apps podcasts are acquired through the Podcasts app and iTunes U courses have their own iTunes U app. (If you don't download the apps, you still find them in the iTunes app on your iPhone.) See Chapters 3 and 4 of this minibook to learn about each, respectively.

**Book V
Chapter 2**

**Acquiring and
Browsing Music,
Videos, Movies, and
More**

Authorizing iTunes to play your purchased music, videos, books, and apps

When you open an iTunes account or Apple ID, you automatically authorize that computer to open videos, books, and apps purchased from the iTunes Store with your account. The media and the computer have to have the same authorization. You can authorize up to five computers, which means you can access your iTunes account from each of those five computers. Follow these steps to authorization:

1. **From iTunes, click Store⇨Authorize This Computer.**

   A pane opens asking you to type in your Apple Account name and password. That's what you established when you set up your account on iTunes.

2. **Click Authorize.**

   A message appears telling you how many computers are authorized with this account.

At some point, you may want to deauthorize an account, say, if you buy a new computer and donate your old one to the local homeless shelter. Instead of clicking Authorize This Computer, click Store⇨Deauthorize This Computer. Type in your Apple Account name and password, and then click Deauthorize. Any videos, books, or apps associated with that computer are no longer available.

On your iPhone

iTunes on your iPhone is a streamlined version of the iTunes Store. Banners run across the top of the screen and then sections such as New and Noteworthy or This Week appear along with seasonal and media-specific sections. The recommendations are all there, but because of the smaller screen space, you see less of it at once — which might be a good thing. You have to have a Wi-Fi or cellular data connection to use iTunes on your iPhone. When you tap the iTunes button on the Home screen, the screen shown in Figure 2-4 opens. The first time you open iTunes, the Music section appears, but if the last time you looked in iTunes you were browsing movies or audiobooks, when you re-open, that's what you'll see.

Tapping any of the buttons in the browse bar at the bottom of the screen takes you to the corresponding section of iTunes. Tap More to open a list of sections that aren't displayed in the browse bar. To search for media, do the following:

1. **Tap any of the media browse buttons: Music, Movies, TV Shows, or Audiobooks or Tones from the More menu to look for that type of media.**

2. **Tap Genres to see a list of genres for that media (called Categories in the Audiobooks section).**

   Tap a genre and you see specific selections in either the Featured or Charts view.

3. **Tap the Featured tab at the top center to see the banner ads and icon; tap Charts to see the most popular items in each media category.**

   If you want to see the Featured or Charts for all genres in a media category, tap All Genres at the top of the list.

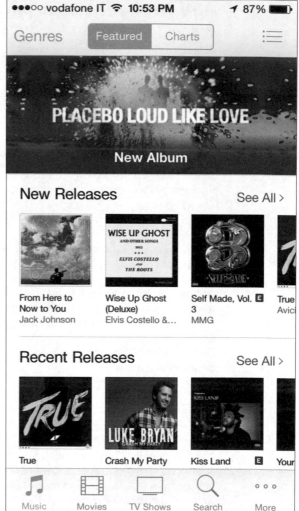

Figure 2-4: The iTunes screen on your iPhone.

Tap the History button in the upper-right corner to see your browsing history. This new feature is a great way to go back to something you had to think about before purchasing.

Scroll down to the bottom of any Featured screen to access the following:

Redeem: Opens a screen where you enter the code from any gift card or iTunes codes you have; the amount is added to your Apple ID account.

Apple ID: Click to sign in if you don't see your Apple ID there. If you have a store credit, the credit balance appears under your account name.

If you're looking for e-books, you find them as in-app purchases in the iBooks app.

Book V
Chapter 2

Acquiring and
Browsing Music,
Videos, Movies, and
More

Downloading to your iPhone

When you reach the center of the iTunes vortex and find the song, movie, or TV show you want to download, tapping the item opens an information screen. On items that have more than one component, such as an album that comprises songs, or a TV show that has multiple episodes, the information screen shows a list of each component, as shown in Figure 2-5. By the name and graphic of the item you see information such as the genre, release date and star ratings. Below there are three tabs that give you the following information:

Figure 2-5: An iTunes information screen on your iPhone.

- ✔ **Songs** (in Music) or **Details** (Movies and TV Shows) to see a description of the item and a list of songs or other details such as plot and actors for movies or a list of episodes for TV shows.

- ✔ **Reviews:** Shows star ratings, the total number of rankings, and written reviews. You can also write a review yourself by tapping Write a Review here.

- ✔ **Related:** Shows other items by the same artist or in the same genre and media, as well as other items people who bought this item bought.

To preview an item, simply tap it in list. The Preview button transforms to a loading button and then a piece of the song or video plays.

 You can preview video via Airplay on Apple TV by tapping the Airplay button.

To download an item:

1. **Tap on the price or Free button to the right of the item.**

   The price button transforms to read Buy Song/Album/Movie/Episode/ Season; Free becomes Download.

2. **Tap Buy Song/Album/Movie/Episode/Season or Download.**

   If you tap Buy by mistake, tap somewhere else on the screen, and it disappears.

   To purchase items, you must have credit or credit card information in your Apple ID account. Free items begin downloading immediately.

   Go to Settings➪iTunes & App Stores and turn on Use Cellular Data to process automatic downloads and iTunes Match through your cellular data service when Wi-Fi isn't available. Note that items larger than 50MB cannot be downloaded over the cellular network. For those you must connect to Wi-Fi to download large files or you can download them on your computer. TV shows and rented movies begin playing as soon as enough data has been downloaded to launch the video.

   Bonus songs and video download to your iPhone; iTunes Extras, iTunes LP, and digital booklets can only be downloaded to your computer. In iTunes, choose Store➪Check for Available Downloads to retrieve these items.

3. **Downloaded items appear in the Purchased section found by tapping More.**

   Purchases are sorted by type: Music, Movies, and so on.

To add an item to your Wish List or share it on one of the social networks or in a message, tap the Share button at the top of the screen to open the Share Sheet. Tap the sharing method you want to use and let your friends know about the great new artist you discovered on iTunes.

The last browse button

You'll see a few other options for iTunes on your iPhone. The default browse bar contains:

✔ **Search:** Tapping the Search button opens a search field. Tap in the field to open the keyboard. Tap type in the title or subject of the item you want to find, and then tap the Search button. iTunes lists potential matches to your search words sorted by media category, which you can scroll through or tap a tab at the top to see the result for only one type, as shown in Figure 2-6.

The More screen

There are three more choices on the More screen that help you manage your iTunes experience. If you find you use one of them often, check out the Tip at the end for rearranging the buttons you find on the browse bar.

**Book V
Chapter 2**

**Acquiring and
Browsing Music,
Videos, Movies, and
More**

✔ **Purchased:** Choose the media type: Music, Movies, or TV Shows and then choose to display by All, which is everything you've purchased on iTunes, or Not On This iPhone, where iTunes compares the media you've purchased and the media on your iPhone and shows you things that haven't been synced to your iPhone yet. Click the download button to download those items to your iPhone.

✔ **Genius:** Genius makes recommendations based on your iTunes purchasing history. To use Genius, tap iTunes⇨More⇨Genius. Tap the media you want recommendations for Music, Movies, or TV Shows. Genius gives you a list of results it thinks you'll like. Tap any of the results to go to the information screen. Purchase and download as instructed earlier in this section.

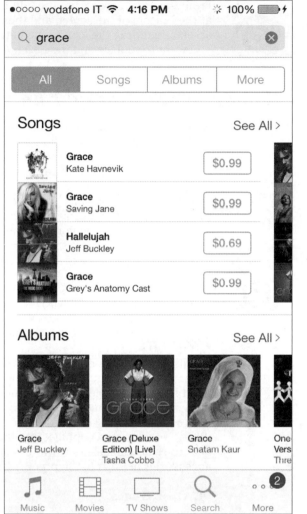

Figure 2-6: Search looks through iTunes' entire media database to find matches.

✔ **Downloads:** Shows a status list of pending and in-progress downloads. Tapping the Pause button pauses the download until you start it again. If you lose your Internet connection, iPhone starts the download when the connection re-opens, or iTunes on your computer completes the download the next time you sign-in to iTunes. Pre-ordered items remain in the list until they are available and you download them. Tap the item for release date information. When it's available, tap the item and then tap the Download button.

From the More screen, tap the Edit button to rearrange the buttons you see at the bottom of the screen and those that appear in the secondary More screen. Just drag the icon of the button you want on the bar over the one you want to replace and they exchange places.

Managing and Transferring Purchases

Now that you've purchased and downloaded different types of media, you probably want to put them in a useable order. iTunes, on its own, puts the media into libraries so the songs and music videos are in the music library, movies are in the movie library, and so on.

One way you can organize your media is with playlists. Here, we explain how to create Playlists on your computer, which sync with your iPhone. You can also create playlists on your iPhone in the Music app, see Book V, Chapter 3.

 Change the media type of an item by clicking on the song or video and going to File⇨Get Info⇨Options. Choose a different media type from the Media Kind pop-up menu. This is handy, for example, if a podcast from another site ends up in your Music library.

Playlists

Playlists are groups of songs that you want played together in a certain order. Playlists are nice for listening to music on any device, but they're great for putting together a sequence of songs for your yoga practice or a dinner party — no more running to the stereo to change the CD or listening to the same CD repeat for an entire evening. Instead, just connect your iPhone to your stereo, plug it into the dock of your iPhone speakers, or connect to remote speakers with AirPlay. (We tell you about these kinds of accessories in Book II, Chapter 3.) To create a playlist on your computer,

1. **Open iTunes.**

2. **Click the Playlist tab at the top of the window.**

3. **Click the plus sign at the bottom of the window and choose New Playlist.**

   Or click File⇨New Playlist. Either way, the window is divided into two panes: Your music library is on the left and the empty playlist on the right.

4. **Type the name of your playlist.**

   Click the playlist to highlight it and type a new name.

5. **Drag songs you want in the playlist to your music library. Click a tab at the top of the window to change the view.**

6. **Click and drag the songs up and down to rearrange the order or click the sort menu and choose another way to sort, such as Name or Artist.**

Your playlists are copied to your iPhone when you sync.

**Book V
Chapter 2**

**Acquiring and
Browsing Music,
Videos, Movies, and
More**

You can also let iTunes do the work for you. There are two types of playlists that iTunes creates. Smart Playlists are based on criteria you set, whereas Genius playlists are created with songs iTunes thinks go well together. Genius also suggests new songs it thinks you'll like based on your purchase history and what you have in your library. Here's how to create these two types of playlists:

- **Smart Playlists:** Choose New Smart Playlist from the pop-up menu at the bottom of the window or click File⇨New Smart Playlist and set the criteria for the type of media, songs, videos, and podcasts you want put together in a playlist. iTunes creates a playlist based on that criteria. When you add a new song or video to iTunes, if it meets the criteria of an existing smart playlist, the new song or video is automatically added to the appropriate smart playlist. You can edit the criteria of an existing smart playlist by clicking the playlist, and then clicking File⇨Edit Smart Playlist (or Control+playlist name).

- **Genius:** Click Store⇨Turn On Genius. Sign in to your Apple account and agree to the Terms of Use. iTunes accesses the iTunes Store so it can review your interests in music, movies, and TV shows and make informed suggestions about media you might like. Click a song you like in any view and then click the action button, which is the arrow to the right of the song — not to be confused with the playback triangle. Choose Create a Genius Playlist from the menu that appears. A playlist is created from your music library with songs that iTunes thinks go well with the song you selected.

If you've created many playlists, you can organize them into folders. Click File⇨New Playlist Folder. A folder appears under the Playlist category. Name that folder and then click and drag the playlists you want into the folder.

Tracking purchases

One of the nice things about iTunes is how it keeps a history of everything you ever downloaded, free or paid. This is really useful if your computer is stolen or irreparably damaged. You can transfer media directly from iTunes to a new computer, without having to re-purchase items you already bought.

Follow these steps to retrieve items you already downloaded:

1. **Open iTunes and click iTunes Store.**

   Sign in to your account if you aren't signed in.

2. **Click Purchased in the Quick Links list.**

3. **Click Not on This Computer in the upper-right section.**

   A list of the items that you purchased in the past but that aren't on your computer appears with a little cloud Download button next to them.

4. **Click the Download button for the item you want to retrieve or click Download All at the bottom of the screen.**

5. **The items are downloaded to the appropriate iTunes library.**

You can also view purchased and free items you've downloaded by clicking Purchase History on the Account Information screen of iTunes.

On your iPhone, tapping Purchased in the browse bar opens a list of the media you purchased. You can view all or only those that haven't yet been added to your iPhone.

Getting the Goods for Free

You probably noticed the word "free" floating around on iTunes. Some things, like lectures from iTunes U and podcasts, are always free. Temporarily free items are iTunes promotions. You can find them in different places:

- ✔ **iTunes Store Home page:** Take a look around. There's usually at least one link to something free in the banner ads. Scroll through the other sections. Free and discounted items are marked with a yellow triangle on the upper right corner of the icon. At the very bottom of the page, there's a section called Free on iTunes. Tap See All to view the entire selection.

- ✔ **Music and TV Shows:** Click the Free link under Quick Links. Pilot episodes of new television series are often free.

- ✔ **Books:** Click the free button in the Top Charts section on the right side. Only electronic books are offered; audiobooks don't have a free section.

Reading Bestsellers in iBooks

You might think the screen is too small, but with its high definition and storage capacity, your iPhone is a good substitute for an iPad or Mac when it comes to reading e-books on iBooks. Think of those times when you're waiting for an appointment or your plane is delayed — having a good book at hand can help pass the time. And, if you don't have a book already downloaded, you can find one on the spot. Here we walk you through the stacks of the iBook Store and show you how to adjust the iBook settings to best suit your eyes.

iBooks syncs across your iOS devices and Macs. You can also go to Settings⇨iTunes & App Store, and tap Books to the On position in the Automatic Downloads section to simultaneously download books purchased on other devices to your iPhone.

Book V
Chapter 2

Acquiring and
Browsing Music,
Videos, Movies, and
More

Finding something to read

Like any major brick and mortar or online bookstore, the iBook Store has a huge offering of fiction and non-fiction books on just about any subject you can think of and for different ages. To find a book that suits your fancy, just follow these steps:

1. **Tap iBooks on the Home screen.**

   Your Library opens, as shown in Figure 2-7, although your shelves will be empty if you haven't downloaded any books.

   If you haven't yet downloaded iBooks, go to the App Store and do so and then come back here.

2. **Tap the Store button in the upper right corner.**

   The iBook Store opens, which has the same layout as the iTunes and App Stores with promotional banners and buttons filling the main part of the screen. The buttons in the browse bar — Featured, Top Charts, Top Authors — as well as the Categories button in the upper left corner, help you narrow your search and the Search button opens search field so you can look

Figure 2-7: iBooks displays your e-books on virtual shelves.

for a book with a specific title, by a specific author, or on a specific subject. The last button in the browse bar, Purchased, opens a list of all purchases you've made at the iBook Store on any device, as well as a list of those not on your iPhone.

3. **Tap through to a category or Top list that interests you and then tap a book that you might like to read, or tap a promotional button on the Featured screen.**

   The info screen opens and shows the usual information: Details, Reviews, and Related tabs, and Price and Sample buttons to either purchase the book or download a sample, respectively.

4. **After you find something you want to try or purchase, tap Sample, to download a sample to your iPhone, and then if you like it, you can purchase it later. Or, tap the price button, confirm that you want to purchase the book, and then either type in your Apple ID and password or touch your finger to the Home button to approve the purchase with your fingerprint (iPhone 5s only).**

   The book is downloaded to your iPhone, and your Library opens. Your recently downloaded book is on the shelf with a "New" or "Sample" banner across it (refer to Figure 2-7).

iBooks can store PDF documents. Tap the Books button at the top of your Library shelves, and then tap PDF to access any PDF documents you downloaded or synced to your iPhone.

For your reading pleasure

Now that you have one or more books on your iBook shelves, you'll want to read it. Tap a book on the shelf and you can then do the following:

✔ The book opens to the Table of Contents. Tap the chapter where you want to begin reading.

✔ Tap the Font Size button in the upper right corner, and a window opens as shown in Figure 2-8.

   • Use the slide to adjust the screen brightness and tap the letters to shrink or enlarge the font on the page.

   • Tap Fonts to change the typeface.

   • Tap Themes to change the page and type colors.

✔ Tap the Search button to look for a specific word or phrase or jump to a page number.

✔ Tap the bookmark in the upper right corner to virtually dog-ear a page so you can find it later.

✔ Tap and hold a word to select it. Drag the grabbers to select a phrase if you want, and then tap one of the tabs above the selection: Copy, Define, Highlight; tap the arrow at the end of the menu to see the remaining options: Note, which lets you write a note in the virtual margin of the page, Search, or Share, which perform those tasks.

✔ Tap the Contents button (it looks like a list next to the Library button) to view the Table of Contents, as shown in Figure 2-9. Tap the Bookmarks or Notes tabs to see any of those you added to the book. From the Contents screen, tap the Resume button to return to the book or the Library button to return to your bookshelves.

✔ Go to Settings➪ iBooks to turn on options such as full justification and auto-hyphenation, and to set your syncing preferences.

To delete books or PDF files, tap the Edit button at the top left of the Library screen, tap the items you want to delete to select them, and then tap the Delete button in the upper right. Tap Done when you finish.

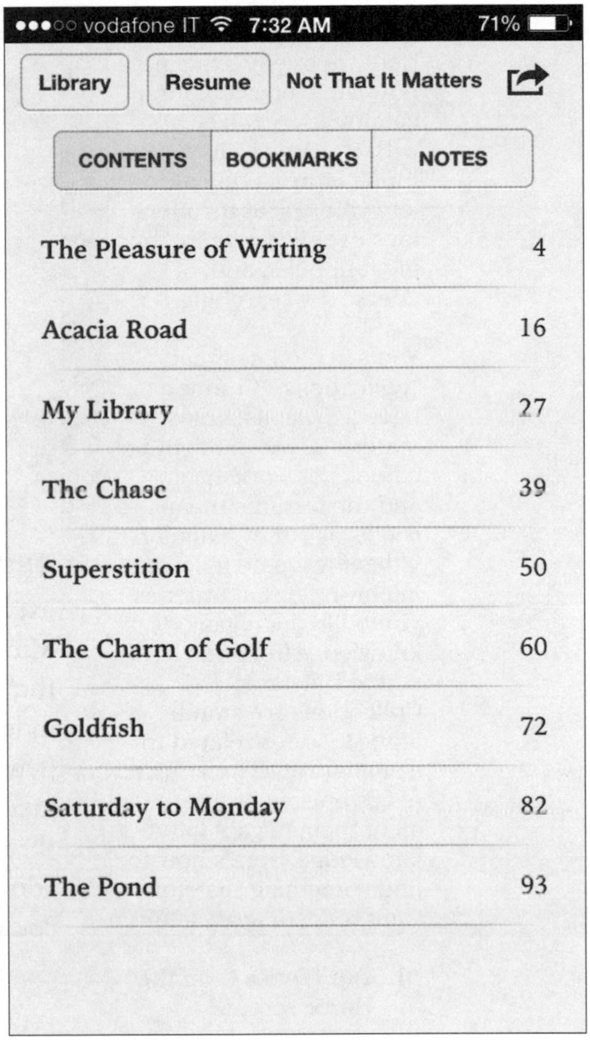

●●●○○ vodafone IT 🛜 7:32 AM		71% 🔋
Library	**Resume**	**Not That It Matters** ➦

CONTENTS	BOOKMARKS	NOTES

The Pleasure of Writing	4
Acacia Road	16
My Library	27
The Chase	39
Superstition	50
The Charm of Golf	60
Goldfish	72
Saturday to Monday	82
The Pond	93

Figure 2-8: Adjust the typeface style, size, and color to make for comfortable reading.

Enrolling in iTunes U

Although the iTunes U app doesn't come preinstalled on your iPhone, we highly recommend you download this free app and take advantage of all the interesting and informative media available in the iTunes U catalog.

Divided into 16 genres (think faculties), iTunes U features audio and video lectures from seminars and courses at universities around the world. iTunes U isn't limited to universities, however. You find lectures and presentations from professional meetings and conferences, such as TED and the Prostate Health Conference, as well as K through 12 and professional certification material. Aside from the vast selection of topics and the quality of the presentations, the best part is that the lectures are free!

Choosing courses

Here we briefly explain how the iTunes U course catalog is organized. As with the App, iTunes, and iBook Stores, iTunes U lets you look at its offerings overall, by genre, by most popular, and, of course, by searching.

You see "courses" and "collections." Courses have a syllabus, study materials, which might be e-books or worksheets, and the lectures themselves as either audio or video files to be followed in chronological order as you build upon gained knowledge from one lesson to the next. Collections are standalone lectures related to a similar topic; you don't need to listen or watch all of them to gain full knowledge. Here's how to find something that you want to learn more about:

1. **Tap iTunes U on the Home screen.**

   The iTunes U catalog opens. The opening screen is probably familiar by now.

Figure 2-9: Contents accesses the book's Table of Contents and any bookmarks or notes you add.

Banner ads scroll across the top, New Courses and other categorical sections follow, and all are tappable buttons that lead to more information about that course. The other buttons are

- **Genres (Upper left):** Genres opens a list of the 16 "faculties" you can choose from. Tapping one of those then opens a selection of courses on that topic displayed like the opening screen — banners, buttons, and the like. Choose All Genres from the Genres list to return to the full catalog selection.

- **Library (Upper right):** Library takes you to your collection of downloaded courses. We talk about that in the next section.

**Book V
Chapter 2**

Acquiring and
Browsing Music,
Videos, Movies, and
More

The browse buttons at the bottom are

- **Featured:** You see the latest course additions and then, scrolling down, find the most popular courses in the What's Hot section and the courses that Apple likes the most in Staff Favorites. This same type of selection appears when you select a specific Genre.

- **Charts:** Divided into Courses and Collections, this view lists the most popular — the most downloaded — courses and collections.

- **Browse:** Choose the level you want: Higher Ed, K-12, or Other, and then scroll through the alphabetical list of institutions offering courses at that level.

- **Search:** Tap to open the search field. Type your criteria and then tap the Search button. You can then view the results by collections, courses, or all, which includes collections and courses as well as a list of episodes (lectures) and materials that meet your search criteria.

2. **Tap a course or collection that interests you, and the Info screen opens, as shown in Figure 2-10.**

   - **Tap Details** to see descriptions, the course outline (if it's a course), and a list of lectures and materials. Tap More to see the complete information.

   - **Tap Reviews** to see what others have to say about the course or collection.

   - **Tap Related** to see other courses and collections on a similar topic that might interest you.

   - **Tap the Share button** to share a link to the course via Mail, Messages, Twitter, or Facebook, or copy the link to another app.

3. **When you find a course or collection you want to watch or listen to, you have the following options:**

   - **Tap Subscribe** to subscribe to the entire course. Links to the materials are added to your Library and updates are added as they become available (this is the default setting that we show you how to change later).

Figure 2-10: Subscribe to courses or single episodes from the Info screen.

- **Tap the download button** next to a single episode or material. The icon next to the download button indicates the type of file it is: A filmstrip icon means video; a speaker icon indicates audio; and a piece of paper icon means written materials, usually a PDF file.

4. **Tap the back button in the upper left to return to the iTunes U screen where you were before.**

If you scroll to the bottom of the screen, you see your Apple ID, a Redeem button for adding iTunes Store card credit, your credit balance, and a button that says Enroll. Some courses have limited enrollment and you must request an enrollment code from the instructor to subscribe and attend. You can find more information about the instructor in the course description.

Attending class

After you subscribe to one or more iTunes U courses or collections, they're stored in your iTunes U library. Follow these steps to playback a podcast:

1. **Tap the Library button in the upper right.**

   The faux-wood grained bookshelf displays the courses and collections you subscribed to. The number tells you how many new episodes have been added since you first subscribed.

2. **Tap a course or collection to open it and begin learning.**

   Collections display a simple list of the video or audio comprised, as in Figure 2-11. Tap the disclosure arrow next to the collection title to see more information, tap the "i" to see more information about a specific episode, or tap the download button to download an episode. Tap the Search button to search within the collection or a specific episode. Tap the Edit button to delete episodes you no longer want or remove the collection entirely.

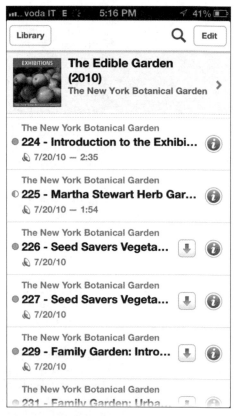

Figure 2-11: Collections display a list of episodes.

Book V
Chapter 2

Acquiring and
Browsing Music,
Videos, Movies, and
More

Courses are interactive and you can access several different types of material and views, as shown in Figure 2-12.

The buttons at the top do the following:

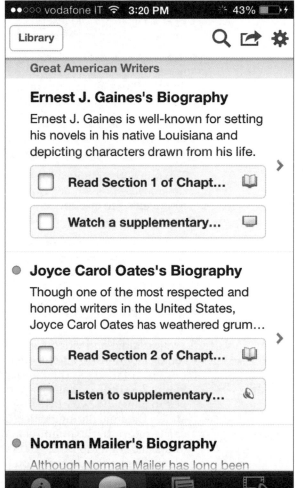

- Tap the Search button (the magnifying glass) to search throughout the course or within a specific episode.

- Tap the Share button to share a link to the course via Mail, Messages, Facebook, or Twitter, copy and paste the link in another app, or print what you see on the screen.

- Tap the Gear button to change the settings for that individual course: turn Subscription On to receive updated information automatically; turn Auto Download On to download new episodes and materials automatically.

- At any time, tap the button in the upper left corner to return to the previous screen.

Figure 2-12: Courses offer diverse types of material and options.

The browse buttons along the bottom contain the following:

- **Info:**

  - Tap Overview to read a description of the course including the types of materials, what you can expect to learn, how long the course usually takes, and what education level it's appropriate for. Tap the Info button in the upper left to return to the previous screen.

- Tap Instructor to read about the professor. You may find a link to send an e-mail as well.

- Tap Outline to see the syllabus for the course.

✔ **Posts:** These are the lessons and any supplementary material the instructor has provided.

✔ **Notes:** Notes you take are neatly organized here. You can view all your notes together or your course notes, audio/video notes, or book notes. Tap the Plus sign at the top if you want to add a note from this screen. You can also add notes while you are listening or watching an episode.

✔ **Materials:** Lists all the course materials (which sometimes must be purchased) and gives you the option to view by type: Audio, Video, and Books. Some books are readable only on an iPad.

Tap one of the choices to see the list of materials. See more information, download, and listen or watch the episodes the same way as you would for an episode of a collection. Tap Edit in the upper right corner to remove downloaded episodes.

3. **Tap the episode to begin listening or watching, or tap a book if you want to begin reading course material. (Although, many of the interactive textbooks can be read only on an iPad.)**

The playback controls are similar to those you find for audio or video in other apps. You can go back 30 seconds, rewind, fast forward, jump back or forward an episode, and control the playback speed.

Course audio and video has the added feature of Notes. While you're listening or watching an episode, tap the Notes button in the upper right corner and then tap the Plus sign. The keyboard opens (refer to Figure 2-13) so you can type a note related to the lecture, which continues to play while you take your note unless you tap Pause. The note shows the time during the lecture that the note was taken so you can easily return to the point related to your note. Tap Notes to see all your notes and then tap Done to return to the lecture. The red lines on the scrubber bar show where you took notes.

Figure 2-13: Take Notes while listening to or watching a lecture.

Book V
Chapter 2

Acquiring and
Browsing Music,
Videos, Movies, and
More

4. **Tap the back button to return to the episode list for this course, and then tap Materials to see the materials list.**

5. **Tap Library to return to your iTunes U library shelf; tap Catalog in the upper right corner to browse more courses.**

6. **(Optional) To rearrange the icons on the iTunes U shelf, touch and hold an icon until it gets a bit bigger, and then drag it to a new position.**

In addition to the individual settings that you find when you click the disclosure triangle next to the name of a course or collection in your Library, you can sync your courses and notes with other iOS devices by going to Settings➪iTunes U and turning on Sync Courses and Notes.

Chapter 3: Listening to Music and Audio

In This Chapter

- ✓ Meeting and mastering the Music App
- ✓ Tuning in to iTunes Radio
- ✓ Searching Music for media
- ✓ Creating Playlists
- ✓ Controlling music and audiobook playback
- ✓ Customizing Music's settings
- ✓ Listening to podcasts

*W*hether you want some easy listening while you work or you need to block out the jackhammer on the sidewalk outside your window, the Music and Podcasts apps can help — especially if you pair them with the EarPods that came with your iPhone or one of the headsets we talk about in Book II, Chapter 3.

In this chapter, we talk about Music, the app you use to listen to music and audiobooks and to tune in to iTunes Radio, Apple's new custom streaming service. We also talk about Podcasts, the app you use to listen to or watch — you guessed it — podcasts, which are free informational or entertaining episodes on just about every topic under the sun.

Meeting and Mastering the Music App

Music gives you the joy of listening to your favorite singers, bands, and audiobooks whenever you have your iPhone with you. First, we take you through the general layout of Music and then show you the basic commands for listening to music and creating playlists. Then we explain how to listen to your favorite type of music with iTunes Radio.

Tap Music on the Home screen and you see a screen as shown in Figure 3-1. You see five browse buttons across the bottom of the screen:

✔ **Radio:** Streams music from more than 250 genre-based stations or custom-built stations based on your music tastes.

✔ **Playlists:** Displays a list of playlists you have either created on your iPhone or synced from iTunes, including Genius playlists. (You have to activate Genius on iTunes on your computer and then sync your iPhone with iTunes to see Genius on your iPhone.)

✔ **Artists:** Displays an alphabetical list of artists.

✔ **Songs:** Shows a list of songs, or spoken monologues or routines, in alphabetical order by title. Tapping the Shuffle button at the top of the screen begins playing all the songs on your iPhone in a random order.

✔ **More:** Brings up a list of additional viewing options:

- **Albums:** Shows a list of the albums the songs on Music come from. Even if you have only one song from an album, that album appears in the Albums list.

- **Genres:** Shows a list of genres. Tapping the genre opens a list of media in that genre.

- **Audiobooks:** Opens a list of audiobooks, if you have any on your iPhone.

Figure 3-1: The Music screen.

- **Compilations:** Shows a list of compilations, which are often songs from different albums or artists put together as one.

- **Composers:** Displays an alphabetical list of composers. Tapping the name of the composer opens a list of songs written by that composer.

- **Shared:** Shows devices that are on the same Wi-Fi network and can share libraries or playlists that have been selected for streaming or can be seen by Home Sharing. Tap a different device to access music stored on that device. Home Sharing allows not only listening but also copying the content to the computer of the listener.

Tapping the Edit button in the top left corner of the More screen opens a Configure screen. Tap and drag a button from the main part of the screen over one of the browse buttons. The two buttons exchange places. Tap Done when they're arranged as you like. This lets you put the buttons you use most in the browse bar.

iTunes Radio

This new addition to iOS 7 and iTunes 11.1 is a good way to discover new artists in the genre you prefer and explore different types of music without making the immediate commitment to purchase. To use iTunes Radio, do the following:

1. **Tap Radio in the browse bar at the bottom of the Music app.**

2. **Tap Start Listening the first time; subsequent times you see the screen as in Figure 3-2.**

Figure 3-2: With more than 250 stations, you're sure to find something you want to hear.

You see two scrollable sections: Featured Stations, which scrolls horizontally and shows you iTunes created stations, and My Stations, which scroll vertically.

3. **Tap a button that reflects the type of music you want to listen to.**

    The station opens with either a brief introduction audio that will be following by a song or goes right into a song.

    You can ask Siri to play a station for you.

4. **Tap the Back button to return to the iTunes Radio screen.**

The playing screen, as shown in Figure 3-3, has a lot of options for playing the song and managing your stations. Here's how they work:

- **Back:** Returns to the iTunes Radio screen but the song continues playing.

- **Info:** Tap to get more information about or purchase the song.

- **Price:** Tap to purchase the song from the iTunes Store. The price becomes a Buy Song button; tap that button and then enter your Apple ID password or press the Home button to authorize your purchase.

- **Star:** Tap to then add the song to your Wish List, play more songs like the one you're listening to, or block the song from ever being played again on that station.

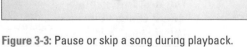

Figure 3-3: Pause or skip a song during playback.

✔ **Pause:** Tap to interrupt playback; tap again to play.

✔ **Skip:** Tap to go to the next song on the station.

✔ **Volume:** Drag your finger along the slider to increase or decrease volume. The volume buttons on your phone or headphones control the volume too.

If your phone locks during playback, the song artwork and playback controls appear on the Lock screen.

What's more, when you tap Info, you get several options for finding more stations, as shown in Figure 3-4. Tap Done when you finish with this screen to return to the playback screen.

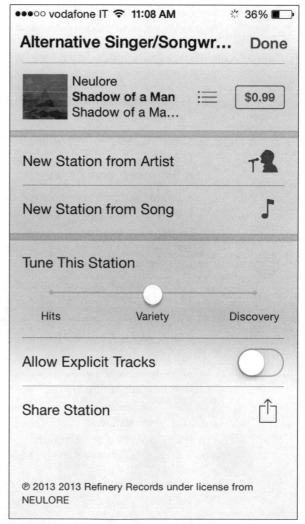

✔ **Info:** Tap to the song's info page in the iTunes Store.

✔ **Price:** Tap to purchase the song from the iTunes Store.

✔ **New Station from Artist:** Adds a new station based on songs from different artists similar to this artist.

✔ **New Station from Song:** Adds a new station based on songs similar to this song.

✔ **Add to My Stations** (visible when you choose a station from the Featured Stations): Tap to add the current station to My Stations.

Figure 3-4: Use the playing song or artist as the basis for your favorite station.

✔ **Tune This Station** (visible when listening to one of your stations): Tap Hits, Variety, or Discovery to hear those kinds of songs in the genre of your station.

✔ **Allow Explicit Tracks:** Tap On or Off to include or exclude songs that use explicit language.

✔ **Share Station:** Tap to open the Share Sheet and let others know about the station either with AirDrop, a message, or social network.

Adding new stations

Besides creating new stations based on a song or artist you like and are listening to, you can also create a station based on a genre you like. When you have different stations on iTunes Radio, you can hear the kind of music you're in the mood to listen to with just a tap. Here's how to add stations to your Favorites:

1. **Tap the Radio button in the Browse Bar of the Music app (refer to Figure 3-2).**

2. **Tap New Station. You might have to scroll down to see it.**

3. **If you have something in mind, tap in the search field and type an artist, genre, or song title.**

   A list of matches appears. Tap the one you want and a station is created based on your choice.

   We're sorry to say if you type a specific song, that song doesn't play but songs in the same genre or by the same artist begin to play. And, like any radio, you can't replay a song.

4. **A list of music genres appears. Tap the type of music you want to hear, for example Classic Alternative.**

5. **Another list of genre types opens. Tap one you like, such as New Wave, under Classic Alternative.**

   A song begins playing in the genre you chose and other songs in that genre will follow it until you choose a different station or stop playback by pausing the song or closing the Music app.

Editing your stations

iTunes Radio lets you customize your stations in ways that make sense to you. Tap the Edit button on the Radio screen, and then do the following:

✔ To manage the station list, tap Edit and then

   Change the order of your station list: Press and drag the reorder button to the right of the station name to move it up or down the list.

   Delete a station: Tap the red and white button to the left of the station name and then tap Delete, or without tapping Edit, drag across the station name and then tap Delete.

✔ To manage or delete a station, tap the station name. The screen as in Figure 3-5 opens. Do the following:

Rename the station: Tap in the Station Name field, tap the X at the right end of the field, and then type in a name that you like.

Tell your friends: Tap the Share button to open the Share Sheet and spread the word about the station in the usual ways.

Customize your station: In Play More Like This or Never Play This, tap Add Artist, Song, or Genre and then type in the artist, song, or genre you want to add to or avoid on this station. Your choices appear listed below each heading. Except for the first item in the Play More Like This section, you can swipe across your entries to delete them.

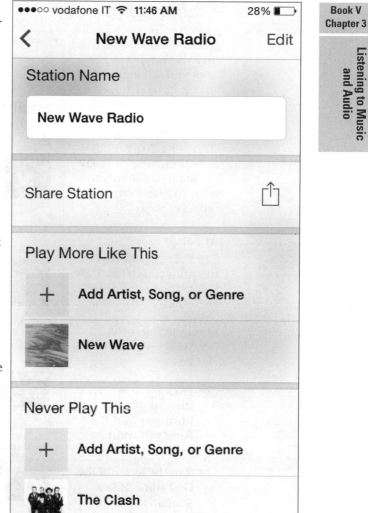

Figure 3-5: Customize your stations.

Delete the station: Tap Delete Station at the bottom of the screen to eliminate it from your My Stations selections.

Tap the back button to return to the My Stations list, and tap Done to return to the iTunes Radio screen in Music.

To see a list of what you've listened to or added to your wish list, tap the History button in the upper left corner of the Radio screen. Your listening history is sorted by station, and tapping any song in the list plays a sample. You can purchase directly from the History list by tapping the price button.

Finding songs

Chances are you have a great collection of music that you synced from your computer to your iPhone. There are times you want to listen to your absolutely familiar favorites rather than iTunes Radio's random selections. You can play the song or album you want to hear from different views.

In Songs

Tap the Songs button in the browse bar; tap More if you don't see it there, and choose it from the list that appears, as shown in Figure 3-6. Now you have three choices:

Figure 3-6: Songs shows an alphabetical list of all the songs on your iPhone.

- ✔ **Flick up to scroll through the list until you find the song you want to hear.**

- ✔ **Tap the letter of the first word of the song in the alphabet that runs down the right side of the screen.** "The," "A," and "An" don't count as first words.

- ✔ **Type the name of the song in the search field at the top of the screen.** If you don't see the search field, tap the status bar at the very, very top of the screen or the magnifying glass at the top of the alphabet that runs down the right side.

In Artists

Tapping Artists in the browse bar opens an alphabetical list of artists, sorted by first name. Find the name of the artist you want by using the search field or flicking through the list, or tapping the letter that corresponds to the artist's first name in the index that runs down the right side. The number of albums and songs by that artist in your Music collection appears beneath the artist's name. Tap the name of the artist to see a list of songs by that artist.

In Albums

Tapping Albums in the browse bar opens a list of albums; tap More if you don't see it there, and choose it from the list that appears. Tap the album that has the song you want to hear and you see a list of the songs on that album. The name of the artist and the album name appear to the right of the album cover image. The number of songs and album playing time are shown as well. The playing time for each song appears to the right of the song name.

With Search

From a screen in Music in any category (except Radio), you can open Search and look for a song, artist, or album. Tap the status bar at the very top of the screen and the Search field appears. Tapping in the Search field opens the keyboard. Begin typing the name of the artist, album, or song, and a list appears divided by category: artist, album, and song. The more letters you type, the narrower your search results. Search looks at all the words in a title, not just the first word and gives you results for songs that are part of an album name that matches your search criteria. For example, search for "blue" and the results include all the songs on Joni Mitchell's album *Blue,* Diana Krall's version of the song "Almost Blue," as well as all the songs by the band Blue Sage, if you have those on your iPhone.

You can also search the iTunes Store: Scroll to the bottom of the result list to tap Continue Search in Store. The iTunes Store opens and displays songs, albums, and other media, such as audiobooks, ringtones, or movies, that matches your search words.

You can find media from outside Music, too. Open Spotlight Search by pulling down in the center of any Home screen, and type in a few letters or a word of the song or artist you seek. The results appear by App, so if a match is found in Music, it appears in the results list under the Music app.

Playing songs

When you find the song you want to hear, tap the song. The song begins playing and you see the Now Playing screen as shown in Figure 3-7. If you have any other songs in your library that are from the same album, those subsequent songs play until they're finished or you tap the pause button.

The main controls — Play/Pause, Previous/Rewind, Next/Fast Forward, and Volume — are at the bottom of the screen.

  ✔ **Play/Pause:** Tap to begin playing the song or to pause. When the song is paused, it stays at that paused point even if you do other things on your iPhone. When you return to the song that was playing, it picks up where it left off.

✔ **Previous/Rewind:** Tap to jump to the beginning of the playing song, unless you are in the first three seconds of the song, in which case you jump to the previous song. The numbers above the album image tell you which song in the lineup you're listening to. Tap and hold to rewind.

✔ **Next/Fast Forward:** Tap to jump to the next song. Tap and hold to fast-forward the song you are listening to.

You can also fast-forward or rewind in a song by dragging the playhead (the red line on the bar) along the scrubber bar. Slide your finger down to use half-speed scrubbing or keep your finger on the scrubber bar for high-speed scrubbing.

Figure 3-7: The Now Playing screen shows the album cover of the song that's playing along with the Music controls.

When you tap a song from the Songs list, the Now Playing screen opens. The Previous and Next buttons take you to the song before or after the playing song in your songs list. Shuffle randomly plays all the songs in your songs list.

If you only want to hear songs from a specific album or a particular artist, tap the Album or Artist browse button and choose your first song from there. The Previous and Next buttons function within the limits of the album. Shuffle randomly plays the songs in that album. You see three buttons under the volume bar, which are

✔ **Repeat:** Tap to open a pop up menu and choose Repeat Off, Repeat Song, which plays the same song continuously, or Repeat Artist, which plays consecutive songs by the same artist. Tap Cancel if you don't want to use the Repeat feature.

✔ **Create:** Tap to open a menu that lets you create a Genius Playlist, which is a playlist that goes well with the song you're listening to, or Create a New Station from Artist or Song in iTunes Radio. Tap Cancel if you touched the Create button when trying to pause the song. (If you don't see the Genius button, and you want to, go to iTunes on your computer and select Store⇨Turn Genius On and then sync your iPhone with iTunes.)

✔ **Shuffle:** Tap once and music plays the songs of the album, playlist, or your entire song library in a random order (the button is highlighted and reads Shuffle All); tap again to turn off shuffle and hear the songs in the order they appear on the album or playlist (the button is white again). You can also shake your iPhone to Shuffle, unless you've deactivated that function in Music settings, which are explained a little later in this chapter.

Tap Repeat Artist and Shuffle together to hear the album, playlist, or your song library continuously in a random order.

The Back button at the top left of the screen returns you to the spot where you chose the song, which could be the album itself, the Songs list, the Artists list, and so on. You can also swipe to the right to go back.

The Track List button in the upper right switches between the Song Playing view, as shown in Figure 3-7, and the Album Playing view, as seen in Figure 3-8.

In the Album Playing view, you can assign a rating of one to five stars to each song. iTunes can then use your ratings to create a playlist based on your ratings; for example, a playlist of songs that have four or five stars. Red bars indicate the song that's playing. Tap Done to return to the Song Playing view.

Playing albums

You can go directly to an album by tapping Albums in the browse bar (tap More in the browse bar if you don't see it) and then choosing the album you want to hear from the list. Tap the first song and the album begins playing. You can also start the album from another song or tap the shuffle button to let Music choose a random playing order.

From the Now Playing screen, turning your iPhone to a horizontal position opens the Cover view, as seen in Figure 3-9. Flick from left to right to scroll through your album collection. Tap on an album cover to open the track list. Tap a song to begin playing. You can tap the Play/Pause button in the lower left corner to use those two controls; however, you have to turn your iPhone to the vertical position to use the other playback controls.

Playlists

Playlists are sort of like creating your own personal radio station that plays songs you like all the time. Oh, wait, isn't that iTunes Radio? Not quite, Playlists are limited to songs in your library; you mix and match the songs you want to listen to together, in the order you want to hear them, and save it to listen to again and again.

Tap the Playlists button in the browse bar. The first two items in the list are Genius Playlist and Add Playlist. A playlist that iTunes creates for you using the music in your collection is a Genius playlist. A simple playlist is one you create yourself.

	●○○○○ vodafone IT 🛜 1:13 PM	66% 🔋⚡
Rating		**Done**
	The Civil Wars **Barton Hollow** 14 songs	46:32
1	**20 Years**	3:02
2	**I've Got This Friend**	3:24
▫️	**C'est la mort**	2:30
	★ ★ ★ ★	
4	**To Whom It May Concern**	3:32
5	**Poison & Wine**	3:40
6	**My Father's Father**	3:21
7	**Barton Hollow**	3:26
8	**The Violet Hour**	3:26

Figure 3-8: The Album Playing view shows a list of the songs on the album and a rating for the song that's playing.

Creating Genius playlists

Make sure Genius is turned on in iTunes on your computer (select Store➪Turn On Genius) and then sync your iPhone with iTunes as explained in Book II, Chapter 1. To create a Genius playlist, you select a song and iTunes creates a playlist of 25 songs it thinks go well with the song you selected. To create a Genius playlist, follow these steps:

1. **Tap Playlists from the browse bar.**

2. **Tap Genius Playlist.**

3. **Select the song you want iTunes to use as the basis for the playlist by tapping one of the browse buttons and scrolling through to find the song you want.**

4. **Tap the song you want to be the basis of the playlist.**

   You may see a message that tells you don't have enough songs to make a playlist based on the song you chose.

   The Genius Playlist is created.

5. **Tap the playlist to see a list of songs it contains, as shown in Figure 3-10.**

6. **Tap the first song to begin playback.**

   The playlist plays until you pause the song.

7. **Tap Save to save the playlist; it's given the name of the song you based it on.**

   The name of the playlist is the name of the song you chose at the beginning. It appears at the top of the playlist list and the Genius icon is next to the name.

If you add more songs to your iTunes collection, you can update an existing Genius playlist. Tap the playlist to open it, and then tap the Refresh button. iTunes looks at your content and creates an updated playlist that may include songs you've added since the playlist was created, if any of those new songs meet the criteria of the old playlist.

To delete a Genius playlist, tap the playlist and then tap the Delete button.

Figure 3-9: The Album view in Music.

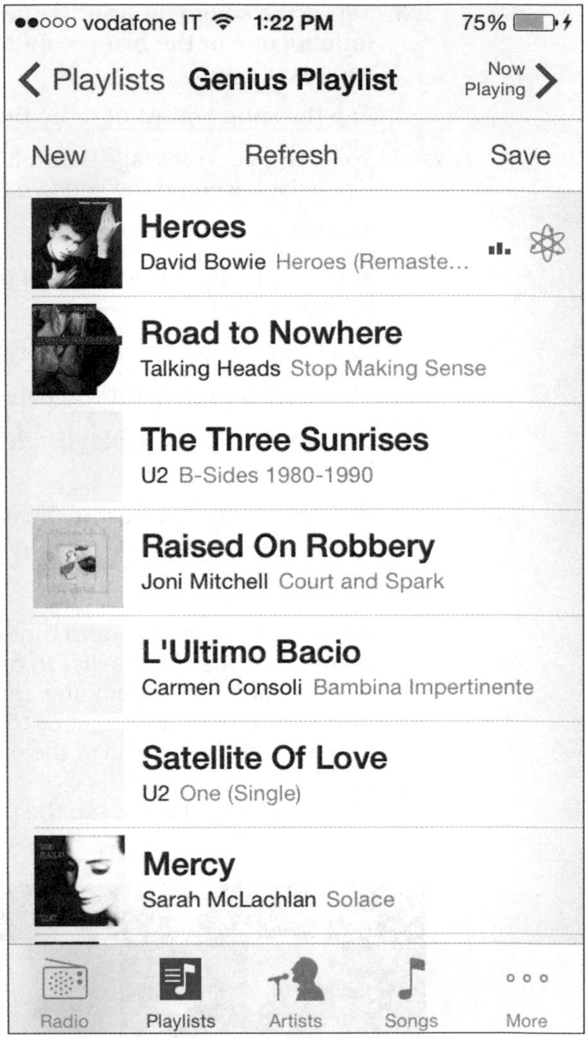

Creating your own playlist

If you already have a playlist in mind, you can create it yourself:

1. **Tap Playlists in the browse bar.**

2. **Tap Add Playlist.**

   A New Playlist box appears as shown in Figure 3-11.

3. **Type a name for your playlist in the field.**

4. **Tap Save.**

   The Songs list opens.

5. **Tap the songs you want in your playlist.**

   You can also go to other views such as artist or album to choose songs.

6. **Tap Done when you're happy with your selections.**

   Your playlist appears on the screen.

7. **Tap the Edit button to do the following, as shown in Figure 3-12:**

●●○○○ vodafone IT 📶 1:22 PM   75% 🔋⚡

❮ Playlists   **Genius Playlist**   Now Playing ❯

New   Refresh   Save

Heroes
David Bowie Heroes (Remaste…

Road to Nowhere
Talking Heads Stop Making Sense

The Three Sunrises
U2 B-Sides 1980-1990

Raised On Robbery
Joni Mitchell Court and Spark

L'Ultimo Bacio
Carmen Consoli Bambina Impertinente

Satellite Of Love
U2 One (Single)

Mercy
Sarah McLachlan Solace

Radio   Playlists   Artists   Songs   More

Figure 3-10: iTunes creates a Genius playlist based on a song you select; the Genius Playlist screen shows the songs in the playlist.

- Touch and drag the reorder buttons up and down to move the songs around in the order you want to play them. You can also let Music randomly reorder the sequence by playing the playlist with the Shuffle button.

- Tap the red and white minus sign next to a song you want to delete and then tap the delete button.

- Tap the plus sign to add more songs. The songs list opens and you select songs to add as in the initial steps.

8. **Tap Done when you finish.**

9. **Tap the first song to begin playing your playlist or tap the Shuffle button to hear the playlist in a random order.**

If you want to change or delete your playlist at a later time, tap the playlist and follow Step 7 in the preceding list to add, delete, or reorder songs. Tap Clear to clear the songs on the playlist and start over with the same title. Tap Delete to eliminate the playlist entirely. You can also swipe across a playlist in the Playlists list and tap the Delete button that appears.

Playlists created on your computer, including Smart Playlists, on your iPhone are synced one to the other the next time you perform a sync if you sync your entire music library or choose to sync selected playlists.

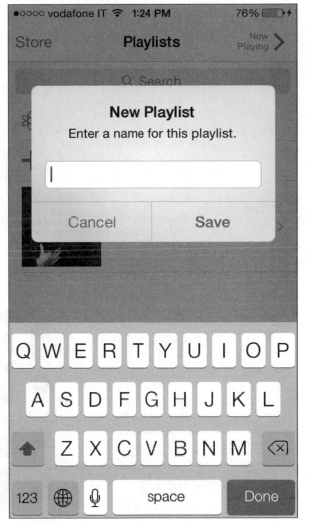

Figure 3-11: Name your playlist when you tap Add Playlist.

Controlling Audio Playback

As with so many things iPhone, there are multiple ways and places to access the same information or controls. The playback controls are no exception. In addition to the playback controls in Music on the Now Playing screen, there are three other ways to control playback: from the multitasking bar, using the headset remote, and with Voice Control.

Using the Playback Controls in the Control Center or Lock Screen

Your iPhone is capable of multi-tasking, so you can listen to music and write an e-mail at the same time. Instead of opening Music and going back and forth to another app, try one of the following:

- ✔ Swipe up from the bottom of any Home or app screen to open the Control Center. Adjust the volume and use the Rewind, Pause/Play, and Fast Forward buttons.

- ✔ Wake your iPhone by pressing the Home button or On/Off/Sleep/Wake button and adjust the playback controls, as shown in Figure 3-13.

Using the headset remote to control playback

You likely listen to music or other media with the headset or EarPods that came with

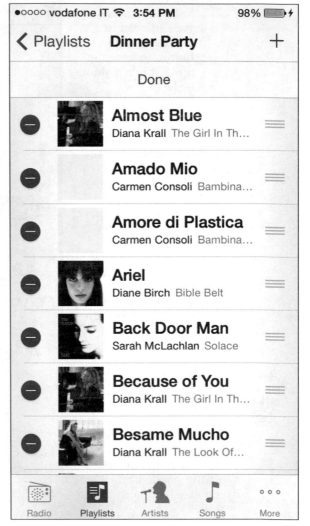

Figure 3-12: You can edit playlists you create.

your iPhone. Both have a microphone and a center button that you press to answer incoming calls and up and down buttons to control the volume of the incoming call. These three buttons control playback when you're listening to audio. Here's how to use them:

- ✔ **Volume:** Press the up or down buttons to increase or lower the volume.

- ✔ **Pause:** Press the center button; press again to resume playing.

✔ **Next song:** Press the center button twice quickly.

✔ **Fast forward:** Press the center button twice quickly and hold.

✔ **Previous song:** Press the center button three times quickly during the first few seconds of a song to go back one song or return to the beginning of the playing song if more than a few seconds have passed.

✔ **Rewind:** Press the center button three times quickly and hold.

If someone calls while you're listening to something, your iPhone rings both in the headset and from iPhone's speaker, unless you have the Silent/Ring button switched to Silent, in which case it just rings in the headset. You have these command options:

Figure 3-13: The Playback Controls on the Lock Screen.

✔ **Answer the call:** Press the center button.

✔ **Decline the call:** Press and hold the center button for a couple seconds; two low beeps indicate you successfully declined the call.

✔ **Hang up:** Press the center button. After you hang up, the music or audio you were listening to resumes playing where you were before the call came in.

If you want to listen to music through a headset that you've paired with your iPhone, you have to adjust the speaker settings in Music. While you're listening to a song, tap the Bluetooth button in the lower right corner. Buttons appear giving you the option to choose which device you want iPod to play through. Tap the button for your headset.

Using Voice Control or Siri to control playback

We think Voice Control and Siri are great, especially when used along with the headset for an almost hands-free command center. Remember to speak slowly and clearly. If you find that Voice Control or Siri misunderstands you, try moving to an area with less ambient noise. If there are still problems, turn your iPhone off, wait a few seconds, and then turn it back on. To control playback with Voice Control or Siri:

1. **Press and hold the Home button until the Voice Control screen appears and you hear a beep or Siri asks how she can help you.**

   If you're wearing the headset, press and hold the center button until you hear the beep, and then speak the commands.

2. **Say one of the following commands:**
   - **"Play" or "Play Music" or "Play Station"**
   - **"Pause" or "Pause Music"**
   - **"Next Song" or "Previous Song"**
   - **"Play album/artist/playlist," and then say the name of the album, artist, or playlist you want to hear**
   - **"Shuffle" to shuffle the playlist or album that's playing**
   - **"Genius" or "Play more like this" or "Play more songs like this" to create a Genius playlist**
   - **Ask "What's playing?," "What song is this?," "Who sings this song?," or "Who is this song by?" to hear information about the song you're listening to**
   - **"Cancel" or "Stop" to pause the song that's playing**

Siri works when you have either a Wi-Fi or cellular data connection. When these are unavailable, you can turn Siri off in Settings and use Voice Control to command the Music app.

You can use Clock's Timer feature to set Music to play for a certain amount of time and you can choose a song as your alarm in Clock's Alarm feature. See Book IV, Chapter 2 to learn how to do both.

Listening to music with AirPlay

AirPlay is Apple's wireless technology that is also integrated into speakers and stereo systems from various companies that include Denon and JBL. You can choose to broadcast music from your iPhone to speakers in different rooms of your house. You can also use AirPlay to stream audio to an AppleTV or to speakers that are connected to an AirPort Express Wi-Fi router or an AirPlay-enabled stereo (such as the Denon AVR-991). Follow these steps to set up AirPlay:

1. **Tap Music on your Home screen.**

2. **Open the song, album, or podcast you want to hear.**

3. **Tap the AirPlay button.**

4. **Choose the speakers you want from the list.**

   If the speakers don't appear on the list of AirPlay devices, check that both your iPhone and speakers are on the same wireless network.

5. **Tap the Play button.**

   The music plays on the speakers you've chosen.

6. **To switch back to play on your iPhone, tap the AirPlay button again and then choose iPhone.**

Customizing Music's Settings

You control a few of your listening options in Settings. These options affect everything in Music, not just one individual song. Tap Settings on the Home screen and then scroll down to tap Music. Refer to Figure 3-14 and consider these options:

- **Shake to Shuffle:** Just shake your iPhone to immediately change the current song.

- **Sound Check:** Often media from different sources plays back at different volume levels. Sound Check

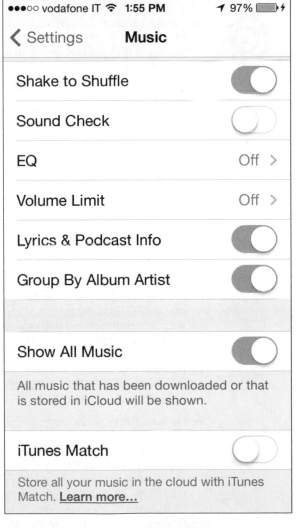

Figure 3-14: The Music settings give you options for your listening pleasure.

corrects so that everything plays at the same volume, saving you from turning the volume up and down with each media change.

✓ **EQ:** Tap to open a list of equalizer settings. Choose one that is best associated with the type of media you listen to most. You may have to try a few different ones to see which you like best.

Music, in general, drains the battery faster than some other common iPhone uses such as making phone calls and texting, or even reading an e-book and EQ drains the battery a bit faster than the usual Music battery consumption.

The Late Night EQ setting lowers the loudest parts of what you're listening to and amplifies the quieter parts so you can listen on speakers and create less disturbance. When you use the headset, this setting improves the sound in areas with a lot of ambient noise, such as an airplane.

✓ **Volume Limit:** Tap to set a limit to how high your headphone volume can reach.

✓ **Lyrics & Podcast Info:** If this setting is on, any lyrics or podcast information available from iTunes is displayed when you tap the album cover or image on the Now Playing screen.

✓ **Group by Album Artist:** By default, this option is on and it groups artists by the information listed under Album Artist instead of information in the Artist field.

✓ **Show All Music:** Songs on your iPhone as well as those in iTunes in the Cloud appear in Music so you know what's available locally and remotely. When off, you only see songs that are stored on your iPhone.

✓ **iTunes Match:** A paid subscription ($24.95/year) where iCloud stores up to 25,000 music tracks along with playlists you have in iTunes on your computer. Even songs in your iTunes library that you didn't purchase through iTunes but that exist in the iTunes store are accessible through iCloud. Songs you have that aren't available in iTunes are uploaded. iCloud then pushes the songs to your iPhone if you turn on this feature. With iTunes Match, Genius Mixes and Genius Playlists on your iPhone are disabled.

✓ **Home Sharing:** Listen to music from your computer on your iPhone, if both are connected to the same network. In iTunes, go to File⇨Home Sharing and sign in with your Apple ID. On your iPhone, type in your Apple ID and password in the Home Sharing section. In Music, tap More in the browse buttons and then tap Shared and tap the name of your computer. (You won't see the Shared option if iTunes isn't open on your computer or if your iPhone is connected to your computer.) Use the Music controls as you would for music on your iPhone. Tap More⇨Shared⇨My iPhone to return to your music collection there.

Playing Audiobooks

Book V
Chapter 3

Listening to Music
and Audio

Music isn't just for listening to music any more than iTunes Store is just for buying tunes. You can download entire books on your iPhone and listen at your leisure. If you stop in the middle, when you open the book again, you pick up listening where you left off.

When a file is larger than 50 MB, you have to connect to a Wi-Fi network or download the file to your computer and then sync.

To play an audiobook, the procedure is the same as for songs:

1. **Tap Music on the Home screen.**

2. **Tap More, and then tap Audiobooks, which only appears if you have downloaded or synced audiobooks to your iPhone or are accessing them through Home Sharing.**

3. **Tap the item you want to listen to.**

   A list of the audiobook chapters appears.

4. **Tap the chapter you want to hear.**

   The audiobook begins playing and you see the Now Playing screen.

5. **The playback controls — Previous/Rewind, Play/Pause, Next/Fast Forward, and the scrubber bar — are the same as for songs. The commands below the scrubber bar are slightly different:**

   - **Repeat:** Functions the same way as for music.

   - **15-second repeat/fast forward:** Tap to replay the last 15 seconds or move ahead 15 seconds.

   - **Playback Speed:** Tap to change the speed — 1X is normal (the button is white), 1/2X plays at half speed, and 2X plays at twice the speed (both are orange).

Listening to Podcasts

In earlier versions of Music (back when it was called iPod), podcasts were part of the scene. Since iOS 6, podcasts have been removed from Music and promoted to having their own app. If, however, you choose not to install the Podcasts app, you can still manage and listen to podcasts in Music, but video podcasts will be available in Videos, and as far as downloading goes, you'll have to download podcasts with iTunes on your computer and then sync them to your iPhone. Make your life simpler: If you haven't downloaded the app yet and podcasts interest you, go to the App Store and download the Podcasts app.

Finding podcasts

If you have podcasts in iTunes and synced them with your iPhone, you find them in the Podcasts app Library and can skip ahead to the next section to learn about the playback controls. If you don't have any podcasts, don't worry, just follow these steps:

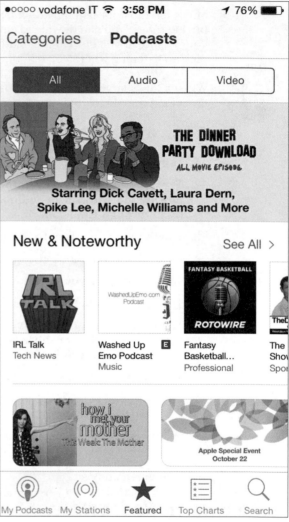

1. **Tap Podcasts on the Home screen, and then tap Featured.**

   The Podcasts Catalog opens, as seen in Figure 3-15. If you've browsed or shopped at the App Store or iTunes Store, it will look familiar to you.

2. **Find a podcast that interests you by tapping one of the following:**

   - **Tabs:** Tap All to see selections for both audio and video podcasts; tap Audio or Video to narrow your choices.

   Figure 3-15: Search for podcasts in the Podcasts app.

   - **Banners:** Tap an ad that interests you when it appears at the top of the screen.

   - **Buttons:** Scroll horizontally through a section, such as New & Noteworthy or tap See All to see a complete list for the section; scroll down to see more advertised podcasts and sections.

   - **Categories:** Tap to open a list of categories and then tap a category to see a list of podcasts in that category.

   - **Browse buttons** across the bottom give you different ways to view the catalog choices: Top Charts shows the top podcasts divided by audio and video, which you can narrow by tapping through the Categories list. Tap Search, and then type a search word or two to find something you like.

3. **Tap a podcast that interests you, and the Info screen opens, as shown in Figure 3-16. You can do the following:**

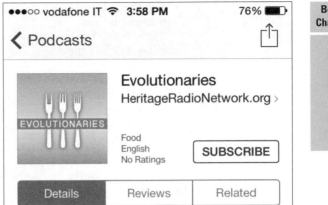

- **Tap Subscribe** to subscribe to the entire podcast series. As new episodes are added, they are downloaded to your iPhone.

- **Tap the download button (the downward pointing arrow)** next to a single episode. Some podcasts download immediately so you can listen to it later; others launch the podcast player. You can immediately listen to it as it streams.

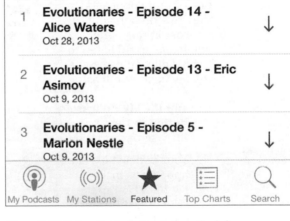

Figure 3-16: Subscribe to podcasts from the Info screen.

If you want to hear other podcasts in the series and make sure you don't miss upcoming episodes, tap the Subscribe button. Most subscriptions and their relative podcasts are free, although some paid programming has been added, and you can listen to downloaded podcasts offline.

- **Tap Reviews** to read reviews and add your own. You can also Like the podcast on Facebook from the Reviews screen.

- **Tap Related** to see other podcasts that are similar.

- **Tap the Share button** (in the upper right) to share a link to the podcast via AirDrop, Mail, Messages, Twitter, or Facebook, or copy the link to another app of your choice.

4. **Tap the back button in the upper left to return to the main Podcasts screen.**

Podcast playback

After you subscribe to one or more podcasts, they're stored in your podcast library, where you manage and listen to them. Follow these steps to play back a podcast:

1. **Tap the My Podcasts button in the browse bar.**

   Your podcast library appears as in Figure 3-17. Tap the Grid or List button to change the view (tap the Status Bar if you don't see them). The number tells you how many unplayed episodes of that series you have.

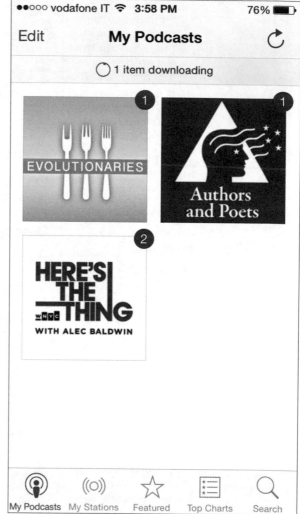

Figure 3-17: Manage podcast subscriptions in your Library.

2. **Tap a series on the grid to see a list of episodes, as shown in Figure 3-18. You can do the following:**

   - Tap the Info button (i) to read a description of the episode.

   - Tap the download button (the cloud with an arrow) to download the episode to your library, you won't see the download button if the episode is already downloaded.

   - The blue dot indicates downloaded episodes that you haven't listened to yet. A half blue dot indicates you begin listening but didn't finish. A speaker means you already heard the episode.

- Tap Add Old Episodes to see a list of previous episodes. Tap to select those you want to listen to and then tap the Add button in the upper right corner. They are added to the list but aren't downloaded until you tap the download button.

- Tap the Share button to share a link to the podcast via AirDrop, Mail, Messages, Facebook, or Twitter, or copy and paste the link in another app.

- Tap the episode to begin listening.

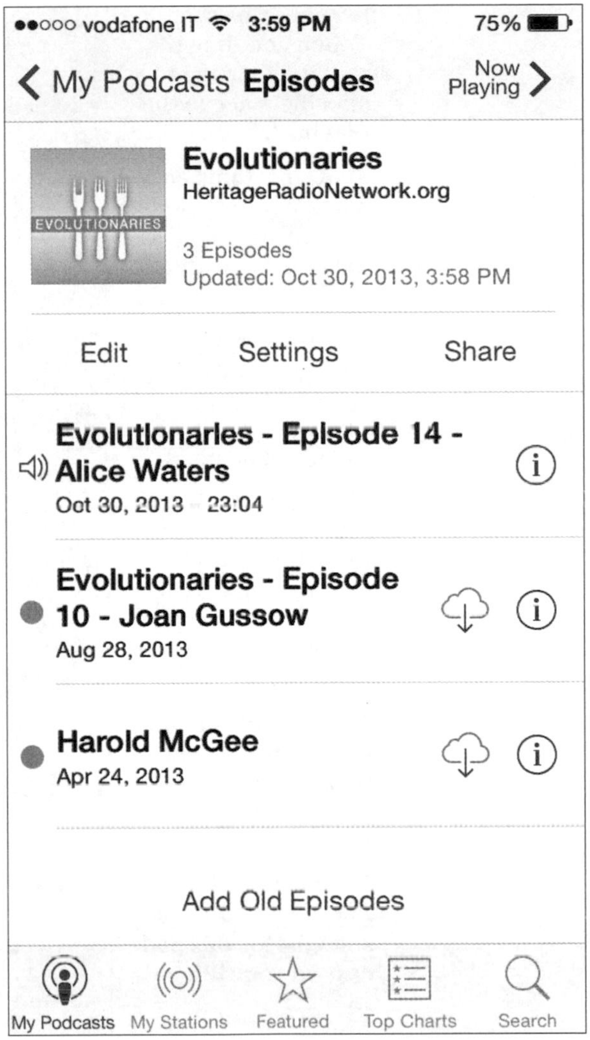

3. **The playback controls appear as shown in Figure 3-19, which shows audio playback controls (video playback controls have similar functions):**

Figure 3-18: See episodes in different states of listening.

Play/pause button: Does just that.

Previous/Rewind: Tap in the first few seconds of the podcast and you go to the previous episode. After that, tap once to return to the beginning; tap and hold to rewind.

Rewind 15 seconds: Goes back 15 seconds.

Go forward 15 seconds: Jumps ahead in the recording by 15 seconds.

Next/Fast Forward: Tap to go to the next episode; tap and hold to fast forward.

Volume slider: Drag left and right to lower or increase the volume.

Scrubber bar: Touch and drag the red line to move to a specific place in the playback.

Share button: Send a link to the episode via AirDrop, Mail, Messages, Twitter, or Facebook.

Playback Speed: Tap to change the speed from half through two times the normal speed.

Sleep Timer: Tap to see a list of choices for setting the podcast to stop playing after a certain time or when the episode ends.

Tap the episode list in the upper right to see a list of other episodes in the series.

4. **Tap the back button to return to the episode list for this podcast on your iPhone.**

5. **Tap Featured, Top Charts, or Search to find more podcasts.**

Figure 3-19: The playback controls appear while you're listening.

If your iPhone is filling up with podcasts and you want to delete some, tap Edit on the opening screen of My Podcasts and then tap the X in the upper left corner to delete a podcast and the contained episodes. To delete episodes singly, open the podcast and swipe across the episode you want to eliminate, and then tap the Delete button.

Podcast stations

Podcast stations group up to four podcasts together. When you subscribe to a podcast, the most recent episode is added to your station in the Most

Recent and/or All Unplayed lists. However, you can also create custom stations, for example, you could create an Arts station, and then subscribe to up to four art-oriented podcasts or even include single episodes you downloaded. First, find and subscribe to podcasts, or download episodes, you want on your station, and then do the following:

1. **Tap My Stations in the browse bar.**

2. **Tap New Station, and type in a name when the New Station dialog opens, and then tap Save.**

   The list of your podcasts appears.

3. **Tap the podcasts you want to include, as shown in Figure 3-20, and then tap Done.**

4. **You see the new station on the My Stations list.**

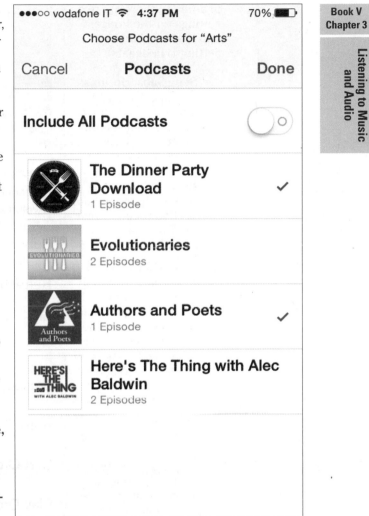

Figure 3-20: Use My Stations to create custom listening "channels."

Tap On-The-Go in the My Stations list and create a custom playlist by adding single episodes you want to listen to.

Podcast Settings

There are settings for individual podcast series and for the Podcasts app. To open settings for a series, tap the My Podcasts tab in the browse bar. Tap the icon of the series, and then tap the Settings button. Here you can manage your subscription settings for specific podcast series, as shown in Figure 3-21.

In addition there are two settings for the Podcast app that you find in Settings⇨Podcasts:

✔ **Sync Subscriptions:** You might want to turn this on if you listen to podcasts on different devices. That way, you'll find the same subscriptions and episodes on your iPhone, iPad, or iPod touch or Mac or Windows computer.

✔ **Subscription Defaults:** If you want to treat all your podcast subscriptions in the same way, rather than change the settings one by one, you can set two defaults that will be applied to all subscriptions:

 • *Refresh Podcasts:* Set the default for how often you want to refresh the episodes of podcasts you subscribe to.

 • *Auto-Downloads:* When this option is set to All or Most Recent,

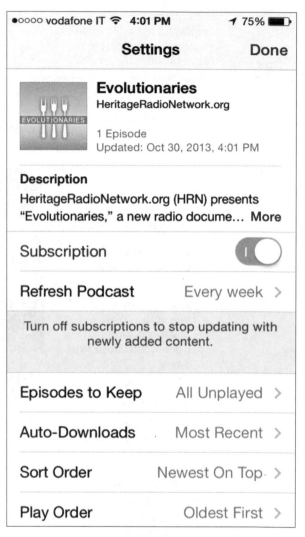

Figure 3-21: Manage subscription settings on a 'cast by 'cast basis.

either all episodes or the most recent episodes will be automatically downloaded when you subscribe to a new podcast.

 • *Episodes to Keep:* Choose how many episodes to keep or choose all or unplayed episodes.

✔ If you do want different settings for some subscriptions, set the defaults first then go in and change the settings for single, specific podcast subscriptions.

✔ **Use Cellular Data:** This setting uses your cellular data service to download episodes to which you have activated automatic download. If you have a limit to your cellular data usage, you might want to leave this in the Off position. In that case, your episodes are automatically downloaded only when you have a Wi-Fi connection.

Chapter 4: Recording, Editing, and Watching Videos

In This Chapter

🖙 **Controlling playback**

🖙 **Recording video with Camera**

🖙 **Slowing down the action**

🖙 **Trimming video in Photos**

🖙 **Editing trailers and movies in iMovie**

🖙 **Sharing your production**

*Y*our iPhone is not only great for watching movies, TV shows, and videos but also for creating your own movies. Whether it's to record an amateur sporting event or produce a full-length film, your iPhone has the capacity to capture, edit, and share videos that are limited only by your imagination.

Apple developed pixels that are 78 micrometers wide and a pixel density of 326 pixels per inch. The Retina display uses in-plane switching (IPS) that offers a wider viewing angle and an 800 to 1 contrast ratio, which means brighter whites and darker blacks. LED backlighting and the ambient light sensor that adjusts the image lets you see it best in the light available. To you, all this means crisp, clear images and type.

In this chapter, we focus on on-screen action: specifically watching videos you download and producing your own digital masterpieces. First, we review getting video onto your iPhone, and then we give details of the video controls of the Videos app, and how to hook up your iPhone to a television so you can watch your videos on a bigger screen. We show you how to capture video with the Camera app and then trim it in Photos or create a full-blown movie, complete with trailer, in iMovie. Aaaannnd. . . action!

Getting and Watching Videos on Your iPhone

We use the term "video" as a generic term to mean a multimedia file, which combines audio with moving images. Video can be a music video, a movie, a television show, a podcast, a home movie, or pretty much anything that you watch, and you can watch most of them on your iPhone. The first thing you have to do is get the video to your iPhone. You have several ways to do that:

- ✔ **Camera app:** Make a video directly on your iPhone, and then watch it in the Photos app on your iPhone. We explain how to do both in this chapter.

- ✔ **iTunes Store/Podcast Catalog/iTunes U:** Download a rented or purchased video from the iTunes Store, a video podcast, or an iTunes U lecture on your iPhone. See Chapter 2 of this minibook for the complete iTunes Store shopping guide. You watch video podcasts in the Podcasts app, which we talk about in Chapter 3 of this minibook.

  You need a Wi-Fi connection to download movies, television shows, and other videos if they're 50MB or larger — small videos can, and will, download over the 3G or 4G/LTE networks.

- ✔ **Streaming:** Watch a video directly from the Internet using Safari or another video app, such as Netflix or Hulu.

- ✔ **Your computer:** Watch video on your iPhone from your computer with Home Sharing or sync the videos on your computer to your iPhone via iTunes as explained in Book II, Chapter 1.

Your iPhone supports H.264 video up to 720 pixels and MPEG-4, part 10 video at 640 by 480 pixels, both at 30 frames per second with stereo audio in .m4v, .mp4, and .mov file formats. Motion JPEG (9M-JPEG) is supported at 1,280X720 pixels with stereo audio in .avi format. Although the popular Adobe Flash format is not supported directly, more website designers are offering Flash streaming for their online videos, so you can see videos that perhaps you couldn't see before.

If you copy a video to your iPhone and it doesn't open automatically, chances are it isn't in one of the supported formats. To see a video's format, open iTunes on your computer and click Movies, TV Shows, Podcasts, or iTunes U from the pop-up menu in the upper left, and then click the video you want information about. Click File ➪ Get Info. Click the Summary tab; the video format is shown next to Kind.

To save the video in an iPhone-readable format, click once on the video in the list in iTunes. Click Advanced➪Create iPod or iPhone Version. The file is saved in the MPEG-4 format with the same name as the original, so you'll want to rename it so that when you sync the file to your iPhone, you sync the one in the correct video format. (To rename the file, click on the name. When it's highlighted, type in a new name or add something like "iP" so you know it's iPhone's version.)

TIP If you have a video that iTunes can't handle, you can try converting the file with a video transcoder utility on your computer such as Handbrake (handbrake.fr/).

Controlling playback

After you have a video on your iPhone or as soon as you begin downloading from the iTunes Store, tap Videos on the Home screen, and then tap the button in the Browse Bar for the type of video you want to watch: Movie, Rentals, or TV Shows although you only see the categories in which you have media. If you have Home Sharing turned on, which we explain in the section Streaming from your computer to your iPhone, you also see a Shared button, as in Figure 4-1. Tap the video you want to watch.

Tap the video you want to watch and an information screen opens. Like the iTunes Store, you can tap the Details tab to see a detailed description about the video or Related to see similar videos. Tapping a related video opens the iTunes Store to information about that item. Tap a TV show and you see a list of episodes you have. The number on the TV show button in the TV Shows screen indicates the number of episodes you have. There's also an option to show the complete season. When you tap that option, episodes you don't have appear on the list and you can purchase them directly by tapping the price button, as shown in Figure 4-2.

Figure 4-1: See the assortment of videos on your iPhone from the Videos app.

Tap the Play button to start the video. Even if it's still downloading you can begin watching. Most video's display in landscape view, the exception being if video was recorded with either camera on iPhone in portrait view.

Initially, you see the playback controls on the screen, which disappear after about six seconds. To open the playback controls, tap the screen; tap the screen again to hide them. Refer to Figure 4-3 for the controls explained here, from top to bottom:

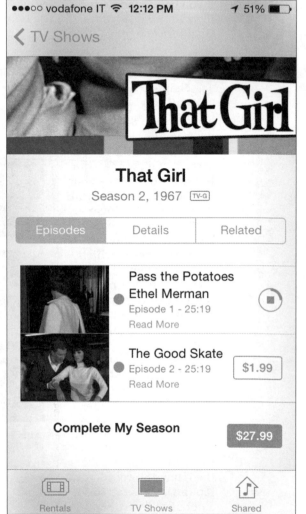

Figure 4-2: Get more details about the video from the information screen.

- ✔ **Done:** Press when you want to stop watching and return to the Videos list. If you stop watching before a video is finished, when you start again, it picks up where you left off. You can also press the Home button to stop watching and return to the Home screen.

- ✔ **Playtime Scrubber Bar:** The time on the left is the time the video has played; the time on the right is the time remaining. Drag the white ball, known as the playhead, right and left on the scrubber bar to move forward and backward in the video. Slide your finger down as you drag the playhead to adjust the speed at which the video moves.

- ✔ **Volume Scrubber Bar:** Drag the white ball on the volume scrubber bar to raise or lower the volume. You can also use the volume buttons on the side of your iPhone.

✔ **Rewind:** Tap and hold to rewind; tap once to return to the beginning of the episode. If you're watching a movie that has chapters, tap twice to go back one chapter.

✔ **Play/Pause:** Tap to pause the video and tap again to resume playback.

✔ **Fast forward:** Tap and hold to fast forward; tap twice to go to the next chapter.

Figure 4-3: The video playback controls.

If you're wearing the EarPods, you can use the volume buttons on the microphone. You can also click twice on the center part to skip to the next chapter, or three times to go back a chapter.

You see a few control buttons only under certain circumstances:

✔ **Fill/Fit:** Tap the Fill/Fit button to toggle between two ways you can view video.

  • **Choose Fit** to see videos in their original aspect ratio, although you will see black vertical or horizontal bands, called *pillarboxing* and *letterboxing*, respectively, depending on the ratio at which the original video was captured.

  • **Choose Fill** to fill the whole iPhone screen but lose some of the edges of the original version.

✔ **Language:** Some movies have subtitle or language options. This button appears when they are available. Tap to see your options.

✔ **Audio Output:** Set the output device you want to use to view your video on another monitor.

Video settings

You have control over a few Video settings. These are your options:

✔ **Start Playing:** Determines where your video picks up when you stop viewing midway through a video. Where Left Off is the default and it's what we refer to in this chapter — stop a video and when you restart, you pick up where you left off. The other choice is to start a video from the beginning when you restart. Tap Start Playing and check From Beginning if you prefer that choice.

✔ **Show All Videos:** Tap to the on position to see both videos that are downloaded to your iPhone and those that are stored in iCloud.

If you want to delete a video from the library on your iPhone, tap the media type in the Browse Bar, tap Edit in the upper right corner, and then tap the X that appears on the video button. Only items that have been downloaded will have the X on them. Items stored on iCloud remain in view if you have Show All Videos turned on in Settings.

✔ **Home Sharing:** Sign in with your Apple ID and password to stream video from iTunes on your computer to your iPhone. See the section "Streaming from your computer to your iPhone" for more information about Home Sharing.

You can turn on closed captioning and SDH (subtitles for the deaf and hard of hearing) in Settings⇨General⇨Accessibility⇨Subtitles & Captioning. When either service is available, you see captions.

Connecting to a monitor or TV

Your iPhone, especially if you have a version with 32 or 64 gigabytes of memory, is a portable video warehouse, and iPhone 5 and later's larger screen and Retina display make watching a pleasure. Nonetheless, watching a documentary about the Himalayas on your iPhone really can't match the thrill of sweeping views that a large-screen monitor or television offers. You can watch the movies and television shows — slide shows of photos, too — that are stored on your iPhone, on your iPhone, or you can connect your iPhone to a television or monitor and enjoy them on a bigger screen.

To attach your iPhone to a television, monitor, or projector, you need one of the following cables:

✔ **Lightning Digital AV Adapter (iPhone 5 or later) or Apple 30-pin Digital AV Adapter (iPhone 4s):** Use this adapter to connect your iPhone to an HDMI cable (sold separately) connected to your HDTV, video projection screen, or other HDMI-compatible device.

✔ **Lightning to VGA Adapter (iPhone 5 or later) or Apple 30-pin to VGA Adapter (iPhone4s or 4):** This adapter, along with a VGA cable (sold separately) connects your iPhone to your VGA TV, projector, or monitor.

✔ **Apple Composite AV Cable (iPhone 4s or earlier):** This connects to your iPhone dock at one end and your television's composite port on the other. Older televisions usually have composite connections.

To play your movie or television show:

1. **Connect the cable to both your iPhone and your television or monitor.**

2. **On your television, select the input device.**

   Refer to the instruction booklet for your television if you don't know how to do this.

3. **Play the video from Videos as you normally would on your iPhone.**

   You see the images on your television.

Playing video with AirPlay

You can stream video and images from the Internet across your iPhone and onto your television if you have an AirPlay-enabled device or Apple TV. To play video wirelessly using AirPlay, follow these steps:

1. **Tap Videos on your Home screen.**

2. **Open the video you want to watch.**

3. **Tap the AirPlay button.**

4. **Choose Apple TV from the list, as shown in Figure 4-4.**

   If Apple TV (or whatever you named your device) doesn't appear on the list of AirPlay devices, check that both your iPhone and Apple TV are on the same wireless network.

Figure 4-4: Stream video from your iPhone to your television monitor with Apple TV.

5. **Tap the Play button.**

   The video plays on your television.

6. **To switch back to play on your iPhone, tap the AirPlay button again and then choose iPhone.**

You can connect to a monitor or use AirPlay to play slideshows and videos from the Photos app by following the same steps.

Streaming from your computer to your iPhone

If there's a video stored on iTunes on your computer that you would like to watch on your iPhone, you can access the video with Home Sharing. You have to have iTunes 10.2 or later and both the computer and your iPhone have to be on the same Wi-Fi network. You also need an Apple ID and password. Follow these instructions:

1. **On your computer, in iTunes, click File⇨Home Sharing⇨Turn On Home Sharing.**

2. **Enter your Apple ID and password, and then click Create Home Share.**

3. **On your iPhone, tap Settings⇨Video.**

4. **In the Home Sharing section, type in the same Apple ID and password.**

   You see Home Sharing only if you have an active Wi-Fi connection.

5. **Open the Videos app from the Home screen and tap Shared in the Browse Bar.**

   The Shared screen opens with two choices: My iPhone and your user name.

6. **Tap your user name.**

7. **A list of the videos stored on your computer appears on your iPhone.**

8. **Tap the video you want to watch and follow the previous instructions for playback control.**

9. **To return to the content on your iPhone, tap Shared and then tap My iPhone.**

Streaming media is when whatever you're watching or listening to is stored somewhere else, as opposed to being stored on your iPhone. The media plays as it comes across the local network or from the Internet and isn't saved or stored on your iPhone.

Shooting Video with Camera

Watching movies and TV shows on your iPhone is fun, but there's nothing like the satisfaction of making your own video and then watching and sharing it with your people you know.

iPhone 4s and later shoots video in high definition, up to 1920X1080 pixels and 30 frames-per-second. This means you can make smooth, clear full-motion videos. Each video can be up to an hour long, although one minute of video takes about 80 MB of memory or close to 5 GB for an hour of video.

To capture video:

1. **Tap Camera on the Home Screen or, if your iPhone is locked, click the Home button and then drag the Camera button up.**

2. **Swipe the screen to the right to highlight Video.**

   On an iPhone 5s, you can swipe another notch to the left of Video to Slo-Mo. This feature actually captures video at a higher frames-per-second speed, which then allows you to play the video at a slower speed. While you're recording, the screen looks the same, and then when you edit the video, you choose the part or parts to play back in slow motion. Choose Slo-Mo before recording; we explain the editing part in the next section.

3. **Point your iPhone at the action you want to capture.**

4. **Tap the Flash button to the On or Auto position if you are in a low-light setting.**

   You have to turn the flash on before you begin recording your video.

5. **Tap the Record button, which is the red dot in place of the shutter button, or press one of the Volume buttons.**

   The Record button becomes a red square in a white circle, whereas the video is recording and a timer appears at the top of the screen (the side if you turn your phone to landscape view), as shown in Figure 4-5.

6. **(Optional.) Tap the shutter button next to the Record button to take a still photo while you're shooting video.**

7. **Tap the Record button or press one of the Volume buttons to stop recording.**

   You can also press the center button on iPhone's earphones to start or stop recording.

8. **A thumbnail of your video's keyframe appears next to the Record button.**

Tap the Switch button if you want to capture video with the FaceTime camera, although there is no flash and the quality is lower.

Viewing and trimming videos

Watching a video that you've recorded is as simple as browsing your photos. Open Photos, and then tap Albums in the Browse Bar. All your videos are kept together in one album. Tap the Videos album to see them.

You also find your videos mixed in with other photos in the Camera Roll album and in Moments in Collections when you tap Photos in the Browse Bar. The video icon and playing time stamped on the thumbnails distinguish videos from photos.

Tap the video you want to watch, and then tap the Play button (the triangle in the middle of the screen and at the bottom center of the screen, where you see the Share and Delete buttons). The Play button becomes a Pause button when the video is playing, but the controls disappear almost immediately to

Figure 4-5: Capture video in the Camera app.

give you a cleaner viewing screen. Tap the screen to see the controls again and tap the Pause button to interrupt playback.

Photos gives you the possibility of trimming from the beginning or end of your video (but not in the middle):

1. **Tap the screen to make the controls visible, as shown in Figure 4-6.**

   A bar across the top of the screen displays the video frame by frame.

2. **Touch and drag the slider on the bar to move through the video in slow motion to identify where you want to trim.**

It's often easier to work in landscape view, even if the video was shot in portrait.

3. **Tap the left end of the bar to trim from the beginning of your video or tap the right end of the bar to trim from the end.**

   The Trim button appears in the upper right corner and the bar is highlighted in yellow, as shown in Figure 4-7.

4. **Drag the end brackets toward the center to trim off the beginning and/or ending of the video.**

5. **Tap the Trim button when you have the bracket positioned where you want.**

   It's a good idea to stop a bit before the actual point where you want to trim.

   You have the option to Trim Original, which overrides the original video, or

Figure 4-6: You can view and edit videos in Photos.

Save as New Clip, which keeps the original and saves the trimmed video as an additional video in Photos and in the Camera Roll and Videos albums.

WARNING!

Video takes up storage space on your iPhone and saving as a new clip means you're storing not one but two videos. Consider moving your video to your computer and keeping only the necessary copies on your iPhone.

6. **Tap Cancel at any time if you want to start over.**

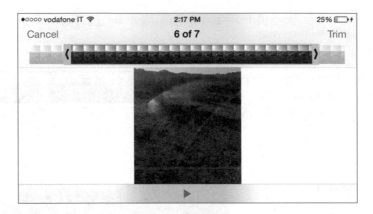

Figure 4-7: Trim removes frames from the beginning and end of your video.

Slowing down the action

If you have an iPhone 5s, you have a Slo-Mo option on the Camera app. You probably don't want to watch the entire recording in slow motion — although you can — but designate a key sequence to play back in slow motion, something that shows a particularly rapid action such as a phenomenal dive from the high board or the sleight of hand during a magic trick. As we mentioned, when you record in Slo-Mo mode, the entire video is captured at a higher 120 frames per second speed and you choose the segment you want to play back slowly by doing the following:

1. **Tap Photos on the Home screen and then tap open the video you recorded in Slo-Mo.**

   You find all videos in the Videos album and slow motion videos are distinguished from other videos (and photos if you look in Moments or Camera Roll) by a circle in the lower left corner of the thumbnail image.

2. **Drag the vertical black bars beneath the frame viewer to set the segment you want to view in slow motion, as shown in Figure 4-8.**

   As you drag the bars, the frame viewer expands so you can better see the part you are selecting.

Directing iMovies

If you purchased a new iPhone after the release of iPhone 5c and 5s, you're eligible to download the iMovie app for free — even if you purchased a 4s. (Previous owners of iPhone can purchase iMovie from the App Store for $9.99.) This pared down version of Apple's iMovie app for Mac lets you create trailers and movies from video captured on your iPhone. You can edit the video and add music, voiceovers, sound effects, still photos, and fades. Here we take you through the steps of creating a project and introduce you to the functions, but we encourage you to have fun trying the different effects and then sharing your production with your friends.

That said, to go a bit easier on your eyes, we recommend using the iOS version of iMovie on an iPad. For the full gamut of editing possibilities, the Mac version of iMovie is a better choice.

Creating a project

Viewing and trimming a video in Photos is fine, but if you want to assemble videos from various sources, add still photos, background music, titles, voiceovers, and special effects, iMovie is a good option — not to mention it's free to download if you recently purchased a new iPhone with iOS 7.

Figure 4-8: Slo-Mo lets you see fast action in slow motion.

Think of iMovie as a timeline illustrated with media. First you insert the still and video images and define the transitions between the parts, and then you overlay titles, voiceover, effects, and background music. Here we go through step by step to create a new iMovie project, although you can pick and choose the type of media and overlays you want:

1. **Tap iMovie on the Home screen.**

2. **Tap the Project button at the top of the screen, and then tap the plus sign (+) to create a new project or trailer.**

3. **Tap Movie.**

   A chooser opens, which displays themes for movies, as shown in Figure 4-9. Tap one, and then tap the Play button to see a preview. Turn your iPhone to the horizontal landscape position to get a better view.

4. **After you decide on a theme, we use Simple for our example, tap Create Movie at the top right of the screen.**

5. **Do one or both of the following to insert video into your movie:**

   1. Tap the Media button (the filmstrip-musical notes combo) to insert existing media. A chooser opens that displays the media on your iPhone — video, photo, audio.

   2. Tap Video in the Browse Bar to see the videos on your iPhone, and then tap the video you want to insert as shown in Figure 4-10.

   3. Tap the Insert arrow to place the video in your movie.

   Or

Figure 4-9: Choose a theme for your movie.

1. Tap the Camera button to record video for your movie.

2. Camera opens and you record video as explained earlier in this chapter.

3. After you tap the Record/Stop button to stop recording, three buttons appear at the bottom of the screen. Tap:

Retake: To substitute the recording you just made with a new one.

Play: To view what you recorded.

Use Video: To place the video you recorded in your movie and return to the iMovie app.

If you don't want to use any recorded video, tap Retake, and then tap Cancel to return to the iMovie app.

New and added video appears on the screen; refer to Figure 4-11.

6. **To add still images, scroll through the videos until the white line is in the position where you want to insert the photo.**

   If you want to insert the image in the middle of a video clip, tap the video clip, and then tap the ellipsis (in the lower right corner). Tap Split. The video is divided and you can insert your still image right where you want it with these steps:

   1. Tap the Media button, and then tap Photos.

   2. Scroll through your albums to find the photo you want to insert.

   3. Tap the Photo.

      You return to the main project screen and your photo is inserted. You see a couple frames of your photo.

Figure 4-10: See all the video stored on your iPhone.

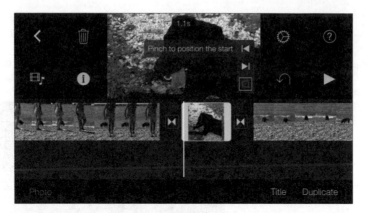

Figure 4-11: Trim or lengthen the time the photo is onscreen.

4. Tap the photo in the timeline once; refer to Figure 4-12 for the next steps.

5. On the image at the top of the screen, tap the Start arrow and then pinch or spread on the image to set the opening shot of your still image.

6. Tap the End arrow, and pinch or spread to set the closing shot of your still image.

7. Drag the yellow grabbers to lengthen or shorten the time the photo is on the screen. The time in seconds is shown at the top. During the length of time the image is on screen, it zooms from the opening shot to the closing shot as you set when you pinched it in Steps 4 and 5.

8. Drag the photo itself around in the upper part of the screen to position it; pinch to zoom.

9. Tap elsewhere to move to edit another part.

When you tap an item to edit it, the appropriate tools appear in the browse bar. When editing in landscape view, tap the "i" button to show and hide the tools (refer to Figure 4-11).

7. **Tap the gear button to open Settings to do the following:**

   • Change the theme to stylize the transitions and titles.

   • Turn on Theme Music to add background music associated with the theme; otherwise, you can add your personal music selection or make a silent film.

   • Choose to fade in and/or out from black at the beginning and end of your movie.

   • Choose whether the speed of the video affects the pitch of any audio, or not.

8. **Transitions are the seconds that occur between clips, and you can set the length of time at 0.5 or 1 second and choose the way one clip flows into the next.**

1. Tap a transition between two clips, and then, in the toolbar at the bottom of the screen, tap the length (0.5 or 1 second), tap a transition style, and tap any choices available in the chosen style:

   None (known as a "jump cut" in video editing jargon): One clip goes directly into the next and the icon is a vertical line. This is the default that appears between two clips whenever you insert media.

   Theme: One clip segues to the next following the colors and style of the selected theme. The icon is a star.

   Cross Dissolve: One clip melts into the next with an overlap between the end of one clip and the beginning of the next. The icon shows two facing arrows.

   Directional: Tap either of the square transitions, as shown in Figure 4-12, to choose the direction that one clip flows into the next and whether the lead in is a thick black line or just an unrolling of the next clip.

   Flash: Choose between a black or white flash between clips.

2. Repeat for each transition.

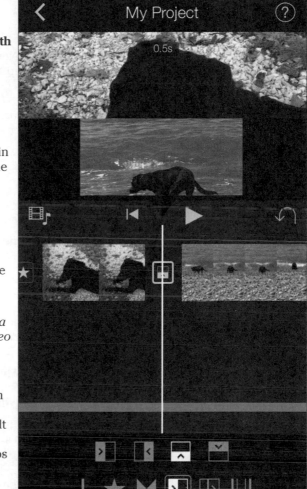

Figure 4-12: Transitions soften the shift from one clip to the next.

9. **Add titles to any of the still images or video clips by tapping the clip, and then**

   1. Tap Title at the bottom of the screen.

   2. Tap one of the title styles — None, Opening, Middle, Closing — to define at what point in the clip the title will appear.

   3. Tap the type style button (T) to choose how your text will appear.

   4. Tap in the text box that appears on the clip in the upper part of the screen. Tap the X in the upper left corner to delete the placeholder text, and then type the title.

   5. Tap Done.

   Clips with titles have a T in the upper left corner.

10. **Add a special sound effect or background music:**

    1. Scroll to position the white line at the point you want to insert the audio effect.

    2. Tap the Media button.

    3. Tap Audio in the Browse Bar.

    4. To choose music or sound effects from iMovie, tap Theme Music or Sound Effects. Submenus open that list music and effects. Tap the play button next to each one to hear a sample.

       To choose music from your Music collection, tap one of the other choices such as Playlists or Songs, to see the list of music in that library. Copyrighted music will be listed as unavailable.

    5. Tap the song or effect that you want to insert, and then tap the insert arrow. It appears on the main screen below the video clips.

    6. Tap once to drag the grabbers and lengthen or shorten the audio.

    7. Use the scrubber bar at the bottom of the screen to adjust the volume, and then tap the elipsis to add other effects such as changing the speed, adding a fade effect, duplicating the audio, or using it as the background audio.

iMovie lowers the volume of background audio when other audio is playing, whether it's added audio or audio that was recorded with the video.

11. **To add a voiceover:**

    1. Scroll to position the white line at the point you want to insert the voiceover.

    2. Tap the Record Audio button.

    3. When you're ready to speak, tap the Record button.

       Three beeps provide a countdown to recording.

4. Say, sing, clap, or whatever you want to record and then tap Stop.

5. Tap one of the buttons on the Recording Finished dialog as shown in Figure 4-13: Cancel, Retake (to try again), Review (to hear your recording), or Accept (to insert the recording in your movie).

6. After you accept your recording, it appears on the main screen below your clips. If it overlaps with other added audio, it will appear below (refer to Figure 4-13); otherwise, it will be on the same line as other added audio.

7. Edit the recording as instructed in Step 9.

12. **A few tips to remember:**

   • While you are creating your movie, tap the Play button to see how it is so far. Playback begins from the white line so scroll the clips left and right to begin from a specific point. Tap the Play button again to stop playback.

Figure 4-13: Add voiceovers while assembling your movie.

   • Tap the Undo button (it looks like a u-turn symbol) to cancel the most recent action you took; tap again to Redo what you undid.

   • Hold and drag any of the parts of your movie to a new position.

13. **Tap the back button to save and close your movie.**

   Tap where you see My Project to open the keyboard. Tap the X to clear the field, type a name for your movie, and then tap Done.

Creating a movie trailer

After you've produced a movie, you might want to create a trailer to tease and entice viewers before they see the final cut. Here's a quick run through of how to make a trailer:

1. **Tap the New Project (+) button, and then tap Trailer.**

2. **Scroll through the styles, and tap the Play button to preview the trailer style.**

   Under the preview, you see the length of the trailer and the number of cast members, if there's more than one.

3. **When you've selected one, tap Create Trailer.**

   The Outline and Storyboard screen opens as seen in Figure 4-14.

4. **Tap in the Outline at the bottom half of the screen and type in the information, such as Movie Name, Studio Name, Director, and so on. There's a pop-up menu for the Studio Logo Style.**

5. **Tap the Storyboard tab.**

   Here you insert media that will be assembled into your trailer, as shown in Figure 4-15.

Figure 4-14: Add your movie credits to the Outline.

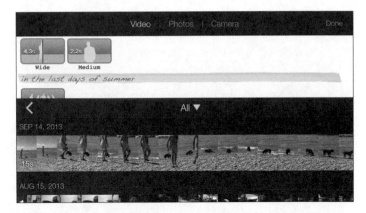

Figure 4-15: Fill the placeholders in the Storyboard to flesh out the trailer.

6. **Tap the placeholder in the storyboard.**

   Buttons for media choices appear at the top of the screen.

7. **Based on the description in the placeholder, tap the media type at the top of the screen.**

   For example, if the placeholder reads "4.3s Wide," you want to tap the Videos button at the top of the screen and select a video that's 4.3 seconds long with a wide angle point of view. Or, tap the Camera button and record 4.3 seconds of wide angle video.

8. **Tap the media you want to use.**

   It's inserted and the next placeholder is at the ready for media to be inserted.

9. **Repeat Steps 7 and 8 until all the placeholders are filled.**

10. **Tap any text fields on the storyboard. Tap Clear (just above the keyboard), and then type something applicable to your movie trailer.**

11. **Repeat Step 10 until you reach the end of the storyboard.**

12. **Tap the Play button on the right to preview your trailer in the editing screen or tap the Full Screen Play (it looks like a playback arrow in a square) to play the entire trailer on your iPhone's screen.**

    Tap the screen to see the playback controls, and tap Done to return to the project.

13. **Tap the back buttons in the upper left corner to return to the Projects chooser.**

Index

B

About the Authors

Joe Hutsko is the author of *Green Gadgets For Dummies, Flip Video For Dummies* (with Drew Davidson), and *Mac All-in-One For Dummies* (with Barbara Boyd). For more than two decades, he has written about computers, gadgets, video games, trends, and high-tech movers and shakers for numerous publications and websites, including the *New York Times, Macworld, PC World, Fortune, Newsweek, Popular Science, TV Guide,* the *Washington Post, Wired,* Gamespot, MSNBC, Engadget, TechCrunch, and Salon. You can find links to Joe's stories on his blog, JOEyGADGET.com.

As a kid, Joe built a shortwave radio, played with electronic project kits, and learned the basics of the BASIC programming language on his first computer, the Commodore Vic 20. In his teens, he picked strawberries to buy his first Apple II computer. Four years after that purchase (in 1984), he wound up working for Apple, where he became the personal technology guru for the company's chairman and CEO. Joe left Apple in 1988 to become a writer and worked on and off for other high-tech companies, including Steve Jobs' one-time NeXT. He authored a number of video game strategy guides, including the bestsellers *Donkey Kong Country Game Secrets: The Unauthorized Edition,* and *Rebel Assault: The Official Insiders Guide.*

Joe's first novel, *The Deal,* was published in 1999, and he recently rereleased a trade paperback edition of it with a new foreword by the author (bit.ly/thedealjoehutsko).

Barbara Boyd is the co-author with Joe of the upcoming fourth edition of *Macs All-in-One For Dummies* and the previous editions of *iPhone All-in-One For Dummies.* She is the author of *AARP Tech To Connect: iPad* and *iCloud For Dummies In A Day,* and co-author of *The Complete Idiot's Guide to Pinterest Marketing.* When not writing about technology, Barbara writes about food, gardens, and travel.

Barbara worked at Apple from 1985 to 1990, beginning as Joe's assistant and the first network administrator for the executive staff. She then took a position as an administrator in the Technical Product Support group. Barbara recalls working with people who went on to become top names in technology — it was an exciting time to be in Silicon Valley and at Apple in particular. That experience instilled a lifelong fascination with technology and Apple products. Her interest and experience led to subsequent jobs in marketing and publishing at IDG (International Data Group) and later for a small San Francisco design firm. In 1998, she left the corporate world to study Italian, write, and teach.

Presently, Barbara stays busy writing, keeping up with technology, growing olives, and beekeeping. (She's a certified honey taster.) Barbara divides her time between city life in Rome, Italy, and country life on an olive farm in Calabria.

Dedication

Joe Hutsko: I dedicate this book to my fabulously thoughtful, kind, caring, smart, creative, beautiful, and amazing co-author — and lifelong friend (and karmic life preserver) — Barbara Boyd.

Barbara Boyd: I dedicate this book to my sweet husband, Ugo de Paula. This book, like others before it, wouldn't have been possible without his loving support.

Authors' Acknowledgments

You see the author's names on the cover, but these books (like any book) are really a collaboration, an effort of a many-membered team. Thanks go to Bob Woerner at Wiley for renewing this title. We've said it before, but we were thrilled to once again work with our superb project editor, Linda Morris, who pulled everything together with a calm demeanor. It's also a pleasure to again work with our favorite technical editor, Dennis R. Cohen; his intelligence, editing skill, and wit do not go unappreciated. Thanks, too, to the anonymous people at Wiley who contributed to this book — not just editorial, but tech support, legal, accounting, and even the person who delivers the mail. We don't know you, but we appreciate the job you do; it takes a lot of worker bees to keep the hive healthy, and each task is important to the whole.

We want to thank our agent, Carole Jelen, for her astute representation and moral support.

Thanks to the folks at Apple who developed such a cool product, and specifically to Keri Walker for her ongoing editorial product support.

Also, a special thanks to the app developers who shared their products and their time — their names are too many to list here, but please take our word for it when we say this book wouldn't have been complete without their support.

Thanks as well to you, dear reader, for buying our book — we had you in mind at every turn of a page.

Joe adds: Special thanks to the awesome team at Philadelphia's Walnut Street Apple Store for their assistance and support with earlier editions of this book.

Barbara adds: Thanks to my sister and tireless cheerleader, Bonnie, for helping out as a virtual assistant. Thanks to Luisa de Paula for a steady stream of iPhone problems that pushed me to learn more than I ever thought I could about iPhone. And as always, extra special thanks to my co-author, Joe for his kind, always-present friendship, which is more important than any writing project could ever be.

Publisher's Acknowledgments

Executive Editor: Bob Woerner

Project Editor: Linda Morris

Copy Editor: Linda Morris

Technical Editor: Dennis Cohen

Editorial Assistant: Annie Sullivan

Sr. Editorial Assistant: Cherie Case

Project Coordinator: Patrick Redmond

Cover Image: © iStockphoto.com/Darren Utt

Math & Science

Algebra I For Dummies,
2nd Edition
978-0-470-55964-2

Anatomy and Physiology
For Dummies,
2nd Edition
978-0-470-92326-9

Astronomy For Dummies,
3rd Edition
978-1-118-37697-3

Biology For Dummies,
2nd Edition
978-0-470-59875-7

Chemistry For Dummies,
2nd Edition
978-1-1180-0730-3

Pre-Algebra Essentials
For Dummies
978-0-470-61838-7

Microsoft Office

Excel 2013 For Dummies
978-1-118-51012-4

Office 2013 All-in-One
For Dummies
978-1-118-51636-2

PowerPoint 2013
For Dummies
978-1-118-50253-2

Word 2013 For Dummies
978-1-118-49123-2

Music

Blues Harmonica
For Dummies
978-1-118-25269-7

Guitar For Dummies,
3rd Edition
978-1-118-11554-1

iPod & iTunes
For Dummies,
10th Edition
978-1-118-50864-0

Programming

Android Application
Development For
Dummies, 2nd Edition
978-1-118-38710-8

iOS 6 Application
Development For Dummies
978-1-118-50880-0

Java For Dummies,
5th Edition
978-0-470-37173-2

Religion & Inspiration

The Bible For Dummies
978-0-7645-5296-0

Buddhism For Dummies,
2nd Edition
978-1-118-02379-2

Catholicism For Dummies,
2nd Edition
978-1-118-07778-8

Self-Help & Relationships

Bipolar Disorder
For Dummies,
2nd Edition
978-1-118-33882-7

Meditation For Dummies,
3rd Edition
978-1-118-29144-3

Seniors

Computers For Seniors
For Dummies,
3rd Edition
978-1-118-11553-4

iPad For Seniors
For Dummies,
5th Edition
978-1-118-49708-1

Social Security
For Dummies
978-1-118-20573-0

Smartphones & Tablets

Android Phones
For Dummies
978-1-118-16952-0

Kindle Fire HD
For Dummies
978-1-118-42223-6

NOOK HD For Dummies,
Portable Edition
978-1-118-39498-4

Surface For Dummies
978-1-118-49634-3

Test Prep

ACT For Dummies,
5th Edition
978-1-118-01259-8

ASVAB For Dummies,
3rd Edition
978-0-470-63760-9

GRE For Dummies,
7th Edition
978-0-470-88921-3

Officer Candidate Tests,
For Dummies
978-0-470-59876-4

Physician's Assistant Exam
For Dummies
978-1-118-11556-5

Series 7 Exam
For Dummies
978-0-470-09932-2

Windows 8

Windows 8 For Dummies
978-1-118-13461-0

Windows 8 For Dummies,
Book + DVD Bundle
978-1-118-27167-4

Windows 8 All-in-One
For Dummies
978-1-118-11920-4

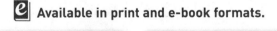 **Available in print and e-book formats.**

Take Dummies with you everywhere you go!

Whether you're excited about e-books, want more from the web, must have your mobile apps, or swept up in social media, Dummies makes everything easier .

Visit Us

Like Us

Follow Us

Watch Us

Join Us

Pin Us

Circle Us

Shop Us

Dummies products make life easier!

- DIY
- Consumer Electronics
- Crafts
- Software
- Cookware
- Hobbies
- Videos
- Music
- Games
- and More!

For more information, go to **Dummies.com®** and search the store by category.

FOR DUMMIES

A Wiley Brand